Defining Canada
History, Identity, and Culture

SENIOR AUTHOR

Nick Brune
Iroquois Ridge High School
Oakville, Ontario

AUTHORS

Mark Bulgutch
Senior Executive Producer
CBC TV News Programming
Toronto, Ontario

Alison Faulknor
Director of Programs
The Dominion Institute
Toronto, Ontario

John Fielding
History and Contemporary Studies
Curriculum Professor, Faculty of Education
Queen's Univerisity

Reg Hawes
Senior Tutor, Ontario Institute for
Studies in Education, University of Toronto

Maryrose O'Neill
Professional Writer, Toronto, Ontario

CONTRIBUTING AUTHORS

Denyse O'Leary
Professional Writer
Toronto, Ontario

Jennifer Burnell
Developmental Editor
Whitby, Ontario

Dick Holland
Pre-Service Instructor, Secondary Education Ontario
Institute for Studies in Education, University of Toronto

Christine Shaine
Principal, Gordon Graydon Memorial
Secondary School, Mississauga, Ontario

CONSULTANTS

Dick Holland
Pre-Service Instructor, Secondary Education, Ontario
Institute for Studies in Education, University of Toronto

Marc Keirstead
Head of Canada and World Studies, Social
Sciences and Humanities, Sacred Heart Secondary School
Aurora, Ontario

Rocky Landon
Teacher, Bayridge Secondary School
Limestone District School Board

Kevin Reed
Teacher, Kingston Collegiate and Vocational
Institute, Limestone District School Board

McGraw-Hill Ryerson

Toronto   Montréal   Boston   Burr Ridge, IL   Dubuque, IA
Madison, WI   New York   San Francisco   St. Louis   Bangkok   Bogotá
Caracas   Kuala Lumpur   Lisbon   London   Madrid   Mexico City
Milan   New Delhi   Santiago   Seoul   Singapore   Sydney   Taipei

McGraw-Hill
Ryerson Limited

A Subsidiary of The **McGraw·Hill** *Companies*

Defining Canada: History, Identity, and Culture

Copyright © 2003, McGraw-Hill Ryerson Limited, a Subsidiary of The McGraw-Hill Companies. All rights reserved. No part of this publication may be reproduced or transmitted in any form or by any means, or stored in a data base or retrieval system without the prior written permission of McGraw-Hill Ryerson Limited, or, in the case of photocopying or other reprographic copying, a licence from CANCOPY (Canadian Copyright Licensing Agency), One Yonge Street, Suite 1900, Toronto, Ontario M5E 1E5.

Any request for photocopying, recording, taping, or information storage and retrieval of any part of this publication shall be directed in writing to CANCOPY.

ISBN: 0-07-091383-8

http://www.mcgrawhill.ca

1 2 3 4 5 6 7 8 9 10   TR1   10 9 8 7 6 5 4 3 2

Printed and bound in Canada

Care has been taken to trace ownership of copyright material contained in this text. The publishers will gladly accept any information that will enable them to rectify any reference or credit in subsequent printings.

National Library of Canada Cataloguing in Publication
Main entry under title:
    Defining Canada: history, identity, and culture / authors, Nick Brune.
Includes bibliographical references and index.
For use in grade 12.

ISBN 0-07-091383-8

    1. Canada. I. Brune, Nick
FC170.D428 2002   971   C2002-901692-4
F1026.D43 2002

PUBLISHER: Patty Pappas
EDITORIAL DIRECTOR: Melanie Myers
SENIOR DEVELOPMENTAL EDITOR: Jennifer Burnell
DEVELOPMENTAL EDITORS: Ellen Munro, Denyse O'Leary
SUPERVISING EDITOR: Cathy Deak
COPYEDITORS: Karen Hunter, Dawn Hunter
PRODUCTION COORDINATOR: Jennifer Wilkie
PERMISSIONS EDITOR: Maria DeCambra
EDITORIAL ASSISTANT: Erin Parton
INTERIOR DESIGN: Dave Murphy/ArtPlus Limited
ELECTRONIC PAGE MAKE-UP: Karen Wolfe/ArtPlus Limited
ILLUSTRATIONS/MAPS: ArtPlus Limited
COVER DESIGNER: Dave Murphy/ArtPlus Limited
COVER IMAGE: Joyce Wieland, *Confedspread*, 1967
            plastic and cloth
            146.2 x 200.4 cm
            National Gallery of Canada, Ottawa
            Purchased, 1968
            Permission to reprint granted by the Estate of Joyce Wieland

COPIES OF THIS BOOK
MAY BE OBTAINED BY
CONTACTING:

McGraw-Hill Ryerson Ltd.

WEB SITE:
http://www.mcgrawhill.ca

E-MAIL:
orders@mcgrawhill.ca

TOLL-FREE FAX:
1-800-463-5885

TOLL-FREE CALL:
1-800-565-5758

OR BY MAILING YOUR
ORDER TO:
McGraw-Hill Ryerson
Order Department,
300 Water Street,
Whitby, Ontario, L1N 9B6.

Please quote the ISBN and
title when placing your order.

Acknowledgements

Being part of the team that created *Defining Canada: History, Identity, and Culture* has reaffirmed some old truths. Truly worthwhile projects are invariably collaborative. Further, it begins, and ends, with people. It truly has been a privilege working with such a highly motivated and talented group of individuals. The writers and contributors brought not just their ideas and words, but their unique perspectives and passions. Thank you to the reviewers and consultants for their insights and guidance. Thank you to the dedicated and professional staff at McGraw-Hill Ryerson, most notably to publisher Patty Pappas for her unflagging belief in this project, and to editor Jennifer Burnell, for her thoroughness, diligence, and unfailing sense of humour. I would be remiss if I did not acknowledge my family, my wife Judy, and children David and Nicole, for their patience and forbearance. Finally, recognition must be accorded to the millions of Canadians who have woven the brilliantly rich tapestry that is Canada with their stories and their lives. We hope that we have been true and told the story as they would have wanted. "While we read history we make history." (George William Curtis)

–Nick Brune

I want to thank my family for their love and encouragement and, of course, my husband, Darryl, for his unfailing patience and support.

–Alison Faulknor

I would like to acknowledge my wife Dianne, children Brendan and Jennifer. Also Kevin Reed and Rocky Landon for their thoughtful advice and sensitivity for my feelings.

–John Fielding

I share my life with two institutions. One is CBC News, and I owe a debt of gratitude to everyone I have worked with there since 1974. It has been a privilege to be with them, telling Canadians about the history being made in their country every day. The other institution is my family. Should anyone ever record my history, let it be known that the happiest parts were with Rhonda, Melissa, and Jessica.

–Mark Bulgutch

For Brothers Bob and Stan, the most loyal of friends; Elaina and Joe, may your qualities and talents meet your hopes; John and Margaret and their inspiration; Jennifer and Patty whose encouragement in this was vital.

–Reg Hawes

Thanks to my parents who helped me understand our past, to my children who are helping me understand our future, and to Patty Pappas and Jennifer Burnell who have been a joy to work with.

–Maryrose O'Neill

We also want to thank all those behind the scenes who worked so hard to ensure the success of this book: Maria DeCambra and Associates who left no stone unturned in the search for photos and permissions; Karen Hunter and Dawn Hunter who worked tirelessly to copyedit and went above and beyond their call of duty; and to Cathy Deak who somehow managed to keep us all on track while dealing with editors, permissions, and the designers.

Finally, the authors and McGraw-Hill Ryerson wish to thank our contributors who helped bring to life the individuals and events that have become an integral part of Canada's culture and identity. To Todd Mercer for his unbelievable enthusiasm in writing so many of the features; to Linda Cornies for writing about the much-missed Peter Gzowski; and to Mike Ford for sharing his experiences about Canadian history in song.

Contents

A Tour of Your Textbook

Cover

Canada's multicultural heritage has often been compared to that of a quilt, where the entirety of the piece cannot be formed without even the smallest of patches. *Defining Canada: History, Identity, and Culture* strives to tell the stories of those who form the pieces of society that make up and define Canada.

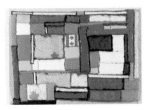

Joyce Wieland, *Confedspread*, 1967

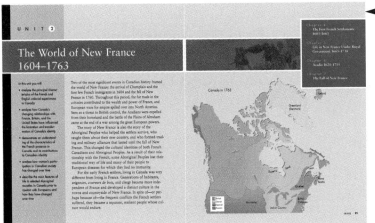

← Unit Opener

- *Curriculum Expectations* Overall curriculum expectations are outlined to help you focus on the main objectives for the unit.
- *Maps* of Canada provide a chronological display of how Canada's political boundaries have changed over time.

Chapter Opener

- *Quotations* from Canadian citizens help frame the content of the chapter
- The chapter *timeline* sequences key events of the chapter.
- *Curriculum Expectations* Specific curriculum expectations are outlined to help you focus on the main objectives for the chapter.

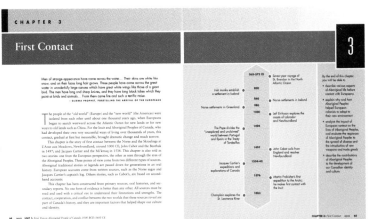

Expression of Culture

Each unit highlights art, literature, or an individual who represents the changing facets of Canada's culture.

Expression of Identity

Each unit highlights poetry, songs, or individuals that reflect the different aspects of the Canadian identity, sometimes focusing on regional identities, or Canada's perception of itself as a nation.

Canadian Leaders

Focuses on the lives and works of women and men who played key roles in the development of Canadian politics, art and letters.

Working With Primary Documents

Allows students hands-on experience with reading, interpreting, and analyzing different types of historical documents. This feature gives students the ability to learn historical research skills from within the textbook.

Web Connection

At least two in every chapter, web connections encourage students to explore topics further using the Internet. McGraw-Hill Ryerson monitors the Web sites and adds new links regularly.

Methods of Historical Inquiry

Appears once in every unit, and takes the student, step by step, through the process of writing a research essay. Each feature ties directly to the unit content and has activities which allow students to practice each step of the research paper.

Chapter Review

Chapter review activities are designed to reinforce the student's learning and development.

- *Knowledge & Understanding* questions help students focus on the essential facts and theories, and relationships of events.
- *Thinking & Inquiry* questions allow students to use critical thinking and inquiry skills.
- *Application* questions allow students to make connections, use technology, and apply or transfer concepts, skills, and procedures in both familiar and new contexts.
- *Communication* questions allow students the chance to use different forms of communication (songs, debates, essays, maps, poetry) to communicate information and ideas.

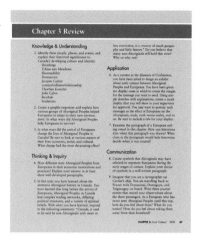

Unit Research Activity

The Unit Research Activity focuses on research and communication of one topic in the unit relating to the changing ideas of Canada's culture and identity, to help reinforce the steps of research, interpretation, and communication.

- *Research* questions help students to get started in various avenues of possible research sites, including interviews, libraries, and the Internet.
- *Interpretation and Analysis* questions encourage students to analyze the evidence they have gathered and to be aware of biases, eliminations, and different historical interpretations.
- *Applying and Communicating Your Skills* questions allow students to communicate the evidence, and their interpretations of that evidence, effectively with the audience.

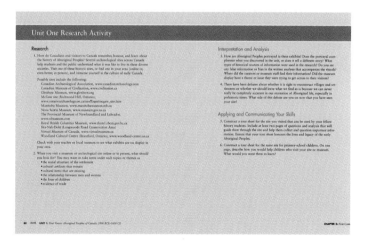

The Evolution of a Canadian National Identity

Just as individuals evolve through defining moments in their lives and the effects of their culture, so too do nations. Your birth, first words, first steps, and first day in school were important events in your life. Your cultural background, family traditions, ideas about what it means to be a citizen, and attitudes to society help define who you are today and what type of person you are likely to become. Nations, which are after all just large groups of individuals, also experience major events that help them define their cultural identity and shape their future.

Millions of people have contributed to Canadian history and culture. Many of these people remain anonymous, unrecorded, and unknown. The actions of more celebrated people have been recorded, though their importance and significance may be debated. The people who have contributed to Canadian identity come from every field of endeavour: from politics, economics, the arts, the military, sports, literature, and business. The celebrated and uncelebrated people of our history are part of our identity and help us understand who we are.

Most of the historical events that shaped Canada happened before you were born. Some happened more recently. A few have occurred within your lifetime. Two of these more recent significant events are the Quebec referendum of 1995 and the death of Pierre Elliot Trudeau in 2000.

The Quebec Question

At issue in the Quebec referendum of October 30, 1995, was whether that province would remain in Canada. The referendum asked the people of Quebec whether they agreed that "Quebec should become sovereign, after having made a formal offer to Canada for a new economic and political partnership...." This was the second time in fifteen years that Quebec had held a referendum. But the path leading up to the referendum began long ago, perhaps as far back as the first meeting between Champlain, his settlers, and the Mi'kmaq people of Atlantic Canada; certainly as far back as the Battle of the Plains of Abraham and the conquest of New France by British forces.

In the 1980 referendum, the vote had been close but clear-cut, about 60 percent against sovereignty-association and 40 percent in favour. But if Canadian history has taught us anything, it has taught us that the forces of separatism are not going to go away. Those separatist forces, led by Quebec Premier Lucien Bouchard, called another referendum in 1995. Perhaps the fear that the 1980 result would be reversed provoked the massive unity rally of more than one hundred thousand people from all over Canada in Montreal on October 27, just three days before the crucial vote. The vote itself was as close as it could be. Of the almost five million eligible voters, 93 percent cast their vote. The margin of victory for the federalist side was razor-thin: 50.6 percent to 49.4 percent. What lessons would Canada take away from this narrow federalist victory? It was certainly a reminder that French–English relations are central to Canadian history. Perhaps one of the most important lessons was that only through the study of history can we analyze and understand how and why Canada and Quebec got to where they did in 1995 and how a unified country might be maintained.

Trudeau Dies

The second recent historical event was Pierre Trudeau's death on September 28, 2000. Many Canadians saw his death as the end of an era. His sixteen years in office had changed many aspects of Canada: its politics, its culture, and its identity. Trudeau had helped redefine the French presence in Canada. His political life started with Trudeaumania, when he achieved the press coverage and crowds of a modern pop star. Repeatedly, Canadians voted Trudeau and his party into office, thereby showing that they approved of his policies.

Some of Trudeau's legislation that changed Canadian political and cultural identity includes:

- The Official Languages Act of 1969, by which French and English became official languages of Canada and all federal institutions were forced to provide services in French and English. By this Act, Trudeau and his political party tried to resolve the French language issue, which had been problematic since the Quebec Act of 1774.
- The proclamation of the War Measures Act in 1970 as a response to the kidnapping of James Cross, the British trade commissioner, and Pierre Laporte, Quebec's labour minister, by the *Front de Liberation du Québec*. Trudeau's decision was not without its opponents, then and years later.
- The patriation of the *Constitution* following the tenth unsuccessful round of federal-provincial negotiations on constitutional issues since 1927.
- The *Charter of Rights and Freedoms*, which was a central component of the Canadian *Constitution* and which the Supreme Court of Canada declared brought to Canadians "a new dimension, a new yardstick of reconciliation between the individual and the community and their respective rights."

Although some of Trudeau's policies raised controversy and dissension, his death seemed to bring the country together. More than fifty thousand Canadians went to Ottawa to pay tribute as his body lay in state on Parliament Hill. Thousands more

It was not just his looks and style, or the fact that he dated film stars that attracted young people to Pierre Trudeau. He spoke to Canada's youth in a way no other politician ever had, and inspired many young people to get involved in the political process.

lined the train route that carried his body from Ottawa to his hometown of Montreal. Trudeau's funeral train was reminiscent of the black-draped train that had carried John A. Macdonald from Ottawa to his hometown in Kingston, Ontario, more than a century earlier. Both men had been charismatic, powerful—and controversial—prime ministers who had left their mark on Canadian history and Canadian identity forever.

The Canadian Cultural Identity

Culture and identity are somewhat difficult to pin down. Culture can be defined as the beliefs, languages, customs, arts, institutions, social relations, and other human endeavours considered together as characteristic of a particular community, people, or nation. Culture is a critical factor in making us human. Each nation has a culture, although some are more clearly defined and articulated than others. Identity is variously defined as "being oneself and not another" or "the set of characteristics by which a thing is recognized or known" or "the set of behavioural or personal traits by which an individual is recognizable as a member of a group."

Just as your individual identity is a product of many elements—your name, appearance, history, beliefs, interests, intelligence, education, age, gender, religion, nationality, and ethnicity—so it is with the identity of groups, such as nations. The world has almost two hundred nations, each different from the others. Despite the rough parallels and similarities, it is the differences that give nations their separate identities.

Canada's identity is the product of many different factors, which you will learn about in the chapters of *Defining Canada: History, Identity, and Culture*—the Aboriginal Peoples who taught the early French and British immigrants how to survive in their new land; the makeup and history of Canadian communities and their conflicts and compromises; the way Canada is perceived by other nations; our international alliances; the ways in which urbanization and industrialization have evolved and influenced our culture and our society; and the factors that have contributed to our diversity and unity, our social programs and policies, and our political structure.

One distinguishing aspect of Canadian identity is the mark left by the successive waves of immigrants who form Canadian communities and define our culture and our regional, provincial, and national identities. Those early United Empire Loyalists, the Irish fleeing the famines in their homeland, the eastern Europeans who settled in the Prairies, the runaway slaves who arrived via the Underground Railway, and the people who are arriving today from countries around the world— these are the people who have formed and will continue to form the Canadian identity.

What Is History?

There are many definitions of history. In his widely read book *What Is History?* E.H. Carr describes history as "a continuous process of interaction between the historian and his facts, an unending dialogue between the present and the past." Others view history as the study of change over time or as the record of significant events and people of the past. Henry Ford was more cynical when he said that "History is more or less bunk." For his part, Napoleon believed that "History is a trick played by the living upon the dead."[1]

However it is defined, history involves studying, observing, and analyzing the significant and recorded events, issues, cultures, and individuals of the past, not for their own sake, but rather to reveal insights into the present and the future. Think about this for a moment. Most of what we are conscious of, as thinking, reflective beings, is the past. Our understanding of the past is the basis on which we make decisions and solve problems in our daily lives. Our personal and our national past provide us with lessons and guidelines that we use to interpret the present and plan for the future. A very practical benefit is gained from studying the lessons of history. We gain

People and events of the 1960s and 70s, made many Canadians begin to think about what being a Canadian meant. Well-known Toronto artist Charles Pachter explored Canada's identity and symbols in his now iconic Queen and Moose images. *Noblesse Oblige* (1979).

greater insight and understanding of present events and the possible future consequences of those events.

In addition, all events, from the expulsion of the Acadians in the mid-eighteenth century to the patriation of the Canadian *Constitution* in 1982, happened within a context. History provides us with an understanding of that context, of the many causes that led to significant events, and of the many effects that flow from them. The passage of the Quebec Act in 1774, Confederation in 1867, and women's attainment of the right to vote in 1918, are all products of many different causes and linked in a chain of causes and effects. The more complex the historical or cultural issue, the more complex are its causes and effects. For proof of this, look no further than to the relationship between French and English in Canada or to Aboriginal Peoples' ongoing struggle for self-government.

Historical Inquiry

Historians wear many hats. At different times, they act as detectives searching out information about the past; as lawyers arguing their case; as teachers educating their readers, listeners, or viewers; as writers communicating their interpretations to others; and as judges who render a verdict on a historical event or figure. But to begin with, historians have to try to be fair, balanced, perceptive, and analytical investigators.

How do historians know what to investigate and research, let alone what to record and what to discard? The historian starts with a question. After having identified a specific problem and having translated it into a fundamental question, the historian then formulates a tentative answer, or hypothesis, to that question. Such hypotheses guide historians in their research and help them decide what evidence should be kept and what should be rejected. The facts collected by the historian will cause him or her to confirm, amend, or reject the original hypothesis.

As they search for their material, historians have to constantly deal with facts. Some facts are more straightforward than others. John A. Macdonald was the first prime minister of Canada. The battle of Vimy Ridge occurred on Easter Monday, April 1917. Dr. Roberta Bondar, neurologist and astronaut, was the first Canadian woman to travel into space. But other so-called facts are more controversial. Did the original inhabitants of North American really arrive using a land bridge across the Bering Strait? Were the Vikings the first Europeans to visit North America? Typically, historians look for evidence or information that is commonly accepted as true. The crucial phrase here is "commonly accepted as true." Not all the information that is presented as factual is actually true. Some information may be exaggeration and distortion; some may be opinion or cliché; some may be interpretation. Distortions, opinions, and interpretations are not facts.

There is also confusion about two broad categories of facts: "facts of the past" and "historical facts." What John A. Macdonald had for breakfast on July 23, 1867, or what you ate for breakfast a year ago on this date, are facts. However, since those facts were judged insignificant, they were not recorded and have been forgotten. They remain facts of the past. What Canadian soldiers had for breakfast before they stormed Vimy Ridge, or what James Cross, the British trade commissioner in Montreal in 1970, had for breakfast on the morning that he was kidnapped by the FLQ are examples of historical facts. Because historians considered these facts important, they were recorded.

Where historians obtain their facts is another important issue. Information is gathered from either primary or secondary sources. Primary sources come from a time that is more or less contemporary with the event being described. For example, Susanna Moodie's *Roughing It in the Bush* (1852), a journal in which she records her experiences as a pioneer in Canada, is a primary source for information about nineteenth-century pioneer experience in Upper Canada. Other primary sources include contemporary letters, speeches, interviews, autobiographies, newspapers, oral histories and stories, government documents, art, and artefacts. A secondary source is written some time after the event that it describes. This textbook, like all textbooks, is a common example of a secondary source. So too are most biographies and encyclopedias. Information available on the Internet is a mixture of primary and secondary information. Among online primary sources are eyewitness accounts of events, written transcriptions of oral histories, and artists' Web sites that display their art. Among the secondary sources are family histories, commentaries on events and cultural artifacts, and academic papers. However, on the Internet it can be difficult to tell how reliable the primary and secondary sources are.

As far as whether primary or secondary sources are more reliable, that will depend on how you assess reliability and on what you are looking for. For example, if you wanted to get the truth about Wilfrid Laurier, would it be more useful to read his autobiography or a biography written a century later? With the autobiography you have a direct, first-hand account. The biographer writing a century later has the advantage of knowing the outcomes and consequences of Laurier's actions. Most historians would probably agree about two things when it comes to sources: (1) always try to obtain your facts from as many different reliable sources as possible, and (2) try to balance primary and secondary source material.

Whatever sources historians use, they must always deal with the issue of bias. Absolutely everyone, including historians, the authors of this text, your teacher, and you, has a bias. Bias is a function of many different components: age, culture, nationality, ethnicity, religion, education, knowledge, intelligence, gender, and experience. For example, to some American historians the conclusion of the American Revolutionary War meant the victory of the forces of freedom, liberty, and independence over the forces of oppression. But to other historians, some of whom are the descendants of the slaves who tried to escape but were returned to their "masters" at the end of the war, the American victory meant the loss of their short-lived dream of freedom and the return of oppression.

Any able historian must ask herself or himself three essential questions:

1. "What happened?" This covers who, what, where, when, why, and how questions and the collection of specific factual detail.
2. "Why did it happen? What were the causes?" The examination of causation lies at the very heart of the historical discipline, because if we are to derive "lessons of history" then we need to have some understanding and appreciation of causes. Many historical debates centre on why something happened.
3. "Why was the event important/significant?" This is perhaps most crucial question. This question is of the highest order, in that it not only analyzes but also synthesizes the evidence that has been gathered.

Historians must organize the evidence they collect in response to these questions, drawing inferences and conclusions from the facts that they have selected and structuring their argument. In establishing any kind of structure, the historian invariably creates some sort of hierarchy. Some facts become more important; some less important. Some facts will be emphasized; some only briefly mentioned. The way in which the historian organizes and presents the facts is intended to support his or her interpretation or thesis. Historians try to persuade their audience as to not only what happened, and why it happened, but also why it was important.

Notes

1. E.H. Carr, *What is History?* (Toronto: Penguin, 1977), p. 30.

First Voices: Aboriginal Peoples of Canada, 1000 BCE–1600 CE

In this unit you will:

- describe the main features of life in selected Aboriginal societies in Canada prior to contact with Europeans and how they have changed over time

Aboriginal people have lived in Canada twenty times longer than people of any other nationality. But, little is known about that long period before the seventeenth century. Aboriginal people have been treated, at various times, as colonized people. Many were forced to live on reserves and all have experienced systematic attacks on their culture and identity by the colonizers: French, British, and Canadian.

Many Canadians have outdated notions of Aboriginal people based on the writings of such prominent anthropologists as Diamond Jenness. He concluded that Aboriginal people were doomed to extinction, either by dying out or by being absorbed into Euro-Canadian culture.[1]

Today, Aboriginal Peoples have the fastest growing population in Canada. They are highly organized, they have articulate leadership, they demand recognition, and they are making progress with both land claims and self-government.

As the Honourable Jim Bourque, privy councillor, elder, and former president of the Métis Association of the Northwest Territories and Yukon, stated to the Royal Commission on Aboriginal Peoples,

> The geese migrate because they have responsibilities to fulfill at different times and in different places. Before they fly they gather together and store up energy. I believe strongly that our people are gathering together now, just like the geese getting ready to fly. I am tremendously optimistic that we will soon take on the responsibilities we were meant to carry in the world at large.[2]

Iceland

Greenland
(Denmark)

Polar Inuit
Greenland
Inuit

Invialuit

Gwich'in

Copper
Inuit

Igloolik
Inuit

Baffin
Land
Inuit

Han

Netsilik
Inuit

Tagish

Tutchone

Dene

Caribou
Inuit

Tlingit

Teslin

Tahltan

Kaska

Tsetsaut

Labrador
Inuit

Tsimshian

Nisga'a

Dene Dháa

Innu
(Naskapi)

Haida
Haisla

Gitksan
Sekani

Beaver

Chipewyan

Beothuk

Bella Bella

Wet'suwet'en

Bella Coola

Chilcotin

Swampy
Cree

Wood
Cree

James
Bay
Cree

Innu
(Montagnais)

Nuu'Chah'Nulth

Sarsi

Mi'kmaq

Comox

Kwagiulth

Wuastukwiuk

Cowichan

Kutenai

Blackfoot
Blood

Plains
Cree

Passamaquoddy

Nitinat

Peigan

Assiniboine

Algonquin

Penobscot

Songish

Gros Ventre

Saulteaux

Ojibwa

Abenaki

Chinook

Flathead

Crow

Sioux

Odawa

Huron

Mahican

Squamish

Nez Perce

Shoshoni

Cheyenne

Menomini

Tobacco

Mohawk

Salish

Sauk Fox

Neutral

Massachuset

Thompson

Winnebago

Potawatomi

Oneida

Lillooet

Lake Okanagan

Illinois

Erie

Cayuga

Onondaga

Miami

Seneca

First Arrivals

Indeed, it is impossible to make sense of the issues that trouble the relationship today without a clear understanding of the past. This is true whether we speak of the nature of Aboriginal self-government in the Canadian Federation, the renewal of treaty relationships, the challenge of revitalizing Aboriginal cultural identities, or the sharing of lands and resources. We simply cannot understand the depth of these issues or make sense of the current debate without a solid grasp of the shared history of Aboriginal and non-Aboriginal people on this continent.

– REPORT OF THE ROYAL COMMISSION ON ABORIGINAL PEOPLES

About 8250 years ago, a Paleolithic hunter was buried by a mudslide near the present day city of Kamloops, British Columbia. His skeleton is the earliest clearly dated human remains found in Canada. Analysis of his bones and the surrounding area by anthropologists and archaeologists indicates that this man lived primarily on land animals rather than on the salmon of the Thompson River. Between eight thousand and three thousand years ago, the area appears to have been occupied by various groups who made microblades—distinctive, small, thin, parallel-sided flakes like miniature razor blades, similar to those used by the people of the Yukon interior. Other microblade sites along the interior rivers indicate that these people were developing and adapting hunting skills and tools based on the salmon resources, but little else is known about them or their way of life.

The First Peoples lived in Canada from about 23 000 BCE to about 1000 CE. Of course, there is much more to this story than presented here. Archaeology provides much of the support, which is why this era is called prehistoric or prehistory. Archaeology, however, is a destructive science; once each site is dug, it is forever destroyed, despite the best efforts to preserve it by photographing, carefully revealing and collecting artifacts, and recording every detail. Aboriginal oral history too has suffered the ravages of time, much of it having been lost over the generations.

From both these sources, this chapter will attempt to narrate the story of the original people of Canada. Because of the scant respurces, this chapter should raise as many questions as it answers.

80 000 to 20 000 BCE — Most recent great ice age

35 000 to 8000 BCE

Migration of Paleolithic hunting peoples across Beringia

13 000 BCE — Glaciers begin to melt and retreat

Bluefish Caves archaeological site reveals evidence of earliest human habitation

10 000 BCE

Glaciers retreat rapidly and corridors open to southern regions of the Americas

6250 BCE — Date of earliest human remains, found in Canada near Kamloops, B.C.

5500 BCE

At L'Anse-Amour, Labrador, one of the earliest mounded burial sites in the world is created

3000 BCE — The end of the Paleolithic Era and beginning of Archaic period, according to archaeological time measurement

2000 BCE

Paleo-Eskimo people arrive in Arctic, bringing with them the bow and arrow

The Serpent Mounds burial sites near Peterborough are created

Clay pottery is in use by the Aboriginal Peoples of Eastern Canada

Old Woman Buffalo Jump used for hunting in western Canada

800 BCE — The Dorset people become the second group of Arctic immigrants

By the end of this chapter, you will be able to

- describe various aspects of Aboriginal life (e.g., economic life, spirituality, relationship with the environment, political organization) before contact with Europeans

- describe the contributions of Aboriginal Peoples to the development of Canadian identity and culture

Origins and Arrival of the First Peoples

They looked over the dry grasslands to the rising sun in the east. The small extended family of Paleolithic hunters[3] had met with another family, and they realized, after sharing stories, that they were related. They agreed they would hunt together for the rest of the season. The relatives told of animal droppings and tracks further to the east. The lure of game drew them to new land in the northeast.

Beringia Glacial Ice Caps, 15 000 Years Ago

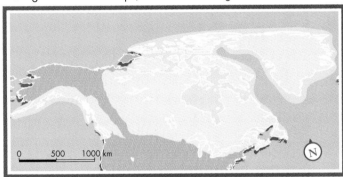

Beringia, 15 000 years ago. Fortunately for the first arrivals, their migration through Beringia acted as a kind of disease filter, letting in humans and animals but keeping out almost all the parasitic diseases that normally preyed on them.[4]

Beringia at Height of Last Glaciation 20 000 Years Ago

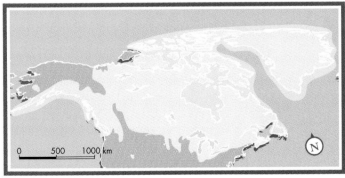

The furs that covered their temporary shelters were bundled together by the women as the men prepared their spears and talked about their strategy for the hunt. Young boys fed the dogs—both were excited about the anticipated hunt. The noise produced by the boys and dogs would help to drive the startled animals into a bog or ravine, where the men would be able to get close enough to launch their spears. The animals, unaccustomed to humans, were slow to react to their presence. It was, however, dangerous. A frightened animal could charge in any direction, and an injury could cost a life. Everyone was on the alert, especially the dogs, for carnivores such as the ferocious Scimitar cat (related to the sabre-toothed cat) and the huge Short-Faced Bear. The bears and cats not only hunted mammoths, but they were also ready to drive off the hunters to scavenge if necessary.

During the time of the last ice age, from about 80 000 years ago to 12 000 years ago, almost all of Canada was covered by a kilometre of glacial ice. With so much water locked in this continental ice mass, the sea levels dropped by 125 metres, creating a plain one thousand kilometres wide in what is now the Bering Sea. It is through this corridor, called Beringia, that Paleolithic hunters pursued large herbivores, such as camels, bison, prehistoric horses, huge ground sloth, and giant beavers to become the first human immigrants to reach North America.

The very gradual migration of these Paleolithic hunters across Beringia to North America is thought to have taken place over thousands and thousands of years, with the oldest archaeological evidence dated about 24 000 thousand years ago. The Blue Fish Caves in the Old Crow Region of northern Yukon, three small caves that overlook a wide river basin, contain what is believed to be the earliest evidence of human occupation: a few chipped stone artifacts dated at 12 000 years old. The artifacts are of a type similar to those of the late Paleolithic era of northeast Asia. They were found in layers of sediment containing the bones of extinct animals, further confirming their age. Although this archaeological site is in caves, which protected the artifacts from the weather, caves were not the favourite dwelling place for early people. Often, caves were considered mysterious, frightening, and, as the home of the bear and Scimitar cat, extremely dangerous. Evidence does show, however, that the Blue Fish Caves were visited repeatedly for short periods by small hunting parties for thousands of years. Paleolithic hunters had developed more comfortable and convenient homes using the furs of the animals they killed. These homes were, for the most part, portable and much easier to heat. Caves, however, could provide temporary shelter for semi-nomadic people.

Exactly when and how the Paleolithic peoples reached North America is still highly speculative. Some archaeologists reject the assumption that humans could have crossed Beringia only when it was fully frozen. The Bering Strait is only ninety kilometres wide today and islands break its width. On a clear day, land is always in sight. Crossing the Strait, either on the winter ice or using an early type of boat, was relatively simple, as the ancestors of the present-day Inuit proved more than one thousand years ago.

Archaeologists also disagree about how Paleolithic hunters migrated further south once they had made the crossing. The traditional view is that there was an ice-free corridor along the eastern slope of the Rocky Mountains, between the Cordilleran glacier over the Rockies and the huge Laurentide glacier covering much of northeastern North America. Although no archaeological discoveries support this theory, most archaeologists concede that a corridor existed. Critics argue that the corridor was extremely inhospitable to human survival: it had a very cold climate, harsh winds, and a landscape of rubble, large lakes, and turbulent melt water rivers.

The Coastal Route Theory

An alternative hypothesis is that a coastal route existed. Moving along the western coast in some form of water craft, fishing, collecting shellfish, and possibly hunting sea mammals, Paleolithic people gradually moved south below the ice fields, where they were able to move inland. Their movement then was east, south, and eventually north as they followed herds of animals and the retreating ice fields. Since the coastal plains were left exposed by the lower sea levels, the travellers had much needed landing areas during their long migration. Unfortunately, this coastline is now submerged, leaving no archaeological evidence to support the coastal route theory.[5]

The two theories, Beringia and coastal, are not necessarily incompatible. It is possible that there were different movements into North America at different times by different people. The arrival of separate populations with different cultures would help to explain the diversity of prehistoric and historic Aboriginal nations. This is especially true of the west coast of Canada, where seventeen languages from five different linguistic stocks were once spoken by Aboriginal Peoples.

A few other highly speculative theories have less support. One suggests a North Atlantic crossing. Most experts, however, agree that crossing three thousand kilometres of ice-choked ocean in some sort of skin-and-wood boat is preposterous. Another theory speculates that a crossing of the North Pacific was possible. Even with the prevailing westerly winds and the North Pacific current, the distance is more than six thousand kilometres, and no evidence exists, anywhere in the world, of a boat capable of making that journey 10 000 to 15 000 years ago. This same argument is used to refute the idea of a South Pacific voyage of more than three thousand kilometres from the Eastern Islands to South America.

DNA and the Migration Theories

The only curious pieces of research that challenge the theory that the Beringia corridor was the only access to the Americas for Aboriginal people are recent DNA studies. Of the five Aboriginal DNA lineages, only one, most commonly detected in Ojibwa (Anishinabe) people, has no known Asian affiliation. It does appear, however, in Europeans. Asian origins are found in the other four lineages that characterize more than 95 percent of Indigenous North Americans. Although this does not prove that Ojibwa have a European ancestry, it does cast doubt on the one origin theory—that all Paleolithic people entered through Beringia—and leaves open the possibility that additional migrations of peoples took place. Clearly, the Beringia crossing theory does have the most supporting evidence, and it is the prevailing view on the origins of Aboriginal Peoples in the Americas.[6]

Paleolithic hunters could not have survived the crossing of the land bridge without:

- control of fire
- tailored clothing
- social organization and cooperation
- a good understanding of the environment, including both animals and plant life
- knowledge of hunting techniques called surrounds and drives, which forced large, heavy animals into bogs, deep snow, or water where they could be approached and killed
- knowledge and skills to process, preserve, and store food
- technology to produce chipped stone spear points for hunting and sharp cutting tools for butchering game.

As winter approached, it was important that the hunters succeed. They needed all the meat and furs they could get to survive. By sharing their hunt, they could pass the winter recounting their successes and telling stories of generations long ago. Winter was also the time for making clothing and preparing tools and weapons. Everyone had their own jobs, including the young people, who would bring the firewood that fuelled the fire for warmth and to keep them safe from the Scimitar cats.

Migration Within the Americas

By 10 000 BCE massive environmental changes had occurred. Changes to the climate affected vegetation, hydrology, erosion and depositional cycles, animal extinctions, and population densities.[7] It was during this time of dramatic changes that descendants of the original Paleolithic hunters worked their way down the Mackenzie Valley and, quite remarkably, within a few thousand years spread to the east coast of Canada and throughout the Americas. Their course was probably south, then gradually east and north, following the retreating ice fields and the game they hunted. Much of what we know about the Paleolithic peoples is based on such famous archaeological sites as the one near Clovis, New Mexico, where large, beautiful, fluted stone tools dated at 9 500 BCE were found.

It was also at Clovis that an interesting technological advance, a weighted throwing device called an *atlatl*, was unearthed. This type of spear thrower appeared for the first time in Canada in southwestern Ontario and later in many archaeological sites across the country. The atlatl part of a spear thrower functioned much like a lacrosse stick. The extension and weighting allowed the spear to be thrown with greater force, a greater distance, and, in the right hands, with more accuracy.[8] These Paleolithic people were very successful hunters of big game. Their success and the changing weather and environmental

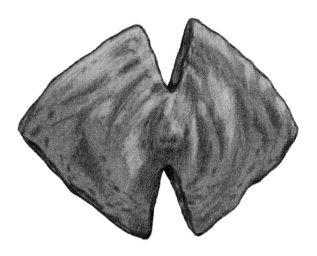

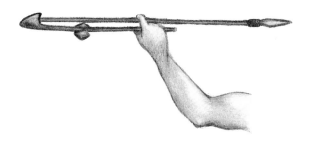

Atlatl weight (enlarged, top) and how the atlatl throwing device was used

conditions led to extinction for 103 mammal species between 12 000 and 10 000 BCE and another 22 species between 10 000 and 8000 BCE.[9]

Aside from what archaeologists and anthropologists can infer from the campsites and the broken stone tools, little is known about the Paleolithic peoples or their descendents, the Archaic people. "Archaic" is a general archaeological term used to describe the hunting and gathering cultures that followed the Paleolithic culture and lasted until the appearance of pottery, which introduced the Woodland period.[10] The Archaic people were the first occupants of Canada. In their search for game, they migrated from the south to the western plains and

east as far as the Atlantic coast. These big game hunters and their families adapted to local conditions and developed their own way of life. By today's standards, their lives were extremely hard. They lived in an unpredictable world where familiar animals disappeared and reappeared for no apparent reason, and an immense lake could slowly disappear as a retreating glacier or the tilting land opened a new outlet to the sea. These Paleolithic people survived, and to some degree prospered, by adapting to the changing climate, landscape, and flora and fauna for more than six thousand years. From these early inhabitants would emerge the distinctive nations of today's First Peoples.

We Were Always Here

There is another interpretation of the origins of the Aboriginal Peoples and that is that they have always been here. Every Canadian Aboriginal nation and people has a creation story that tells of its origins in the land. For Aboriginal people, the oral history or traditional stories told by the elders have more credibility than the theories of archaeologists.

This concept of an Aboriginal origin is expressed in this Mi'kmaq legend: "They came to a wigwam. It was a long wigwam with a door at each end. The man inside the wigwam said, 'I have lived here since the world began. I have my grandmother, she was here when the world was made.'"[11]

Another Mi'kmaq story, recounted by William Asikinack of the Department of Indian Studies at Saskatchewan Indian Federated College, tells of great ice fields, human migrations, and changing seasons. Asikinack believes Aboriginal people were here long before the date that modern science suggests and that they may not have crossed from the Asia through Beringia. It is clear to him that his ancestors lived on the shores of the Atlantic Ocean before the beginning of the last ice age, 80 000 years ago.

Long ago and long ago and long ago and long ago, the People, as a single nation (nin-wa-windwidji-da-ki-wema, we are of the same land), lived along the eastern shores of the great salt water. At that time the People had a protector called Glooscapi. Glooscapi did many things, and brought many things to the People. Glooscapi brought the plant-beings, the various animal-beings, and the swimmers who were placed on the land to help the People survive and live a good life. The people had lived for many generations in this land. Then a strange thing started to happen. The People thought that Glooscapi was the one who had caused this strange thing to happen. Of course the People were right—Glooscapi and Ki-weyd-de-nonk Mmnid-doo (spirit of the North) had got into an argument about who was the stronger spirit. Spirit of the North to show his strength began to make it cold in the land of the People. The thing we call sook-po (snow) began to come to the land. The snow came and did not stop. As the snow got deeper and deeper and ice began to walk on the land, the plant-beings stopped returning for each cycle and the animal-beings left the country. The people finally had to leave too. The People went southward along the edge of the saltwater with Glooscapi following behind to protect them from the Spirit of the North. The People went far to the South and lived there for many generations. Glooscapi, their friend and spiritual protector, made friends with Je-weyd-nonk Mmnid-doo (Spirit of the South). After a time he convinced the Spirit of the South to aid him in an attempt to overpower the Spirit of the North. The three spirits did battle for several generations until finally Glooscapi and the Spirit of the South began to push the Spirit of the North from the original land to the People and back into the northlands. As the battle continued, the spirits found that they could only carry on for a certain amount of time because even spirits become tired. So sometimes the Spirit of the South was the winner and would rein in the land of the People and for almost an equal amount of time the Spirit of the North would reign over the land of the People. When each of these spirits was coming into their time to reign, there were certain

signs that the people learned to understand. When it was the turn of the Spirit of the South to reign, the south wind would bring warmth and the return of the plant-beings. When the Spirit of the North had its turn to rule then the north wind would come and all the plant-beings would go to sleep. Thus it was that the four seasons, spring, summer, fall, and winter, arrived in the original land of the people.[12]

What is fascinating about this story is that the oldest human remains east of the Canadian Rockies were found not on the plains of the west or the Great Lakes–St. Lawrence corridor, but on the coast of Labrador. This story also echoes the geological description of the beginning and end of an ice age. It begins with longer and colder winters, and the slow growth of glaciers, which gradually radiate out from their centres. The swings between warming and extreme cold are dramatic. This seesawing continues for thousands of years, just as this Aboriginal traditional story suggests.

Pointing out the merits of one form of evidence (Aboriginal traditional stories and archaeological evidence) over the other is not the intent in this chapter. Both are recognized and presented here as part of the challenge of knowing the ancestral roots of all Canadians better.

The People of Atlantic Canada: Archaic Period, 6000–1000 BCE

Between 10 000 and 8000 years ago, the world of the Paleolithic people changed dramatically. The massive herds of horses, camels, giant bison, mammoths, and other animals that roamed the tundra and steppes of North America disappeared because of catastrophic changes in the climate and environment. The Paleolithic hunters and their families were forced to change to meet the challenges of their new environment. In pursuit of caribou, they reached the eastern coast of present-day Canada. Along the shores of the Strait of Belle Isle of Labrador, these adventurous peoples encountered

Migration into the Americas, and Archaeological Sites.

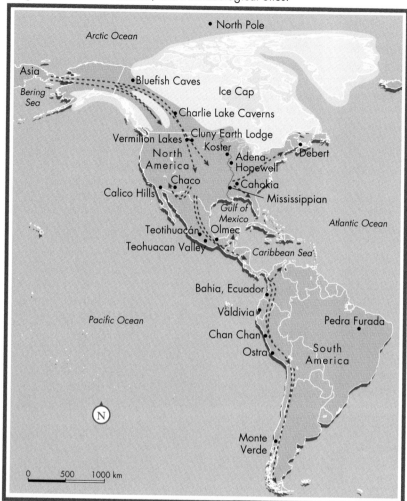

Newfoundland and Labrador to Prince Edward Island and Nova Scotia, the Archaic Peoples developed cultural differences as they adjusted to regional variations in their environment. What they had in common, however, was a reliance on the sea's resources. Their diets included a wide variety of fish, such as the large swordfish, whose bill was an important raw material for tools; sea mammals, including walrus and several species of seals; and an array of sea birds. But the Archaic Peoples did not depend only on the sea for their food; they moved inland during the winter to intercept migrating caribou herds and returned to the seacoast to hunt and fish the rest of the year.

What emerges from the evidence of archaeological sites, however, is a very interesting people with a more complex way of life than the Paleolithic people. Although what these sites revealed can be described, what these people thought and believed can only be hypothesized.

the herds of harp seal that whelp on the spring sea ice. Easily hunted with clubs and spears, this abundant resource led to a relatively stable way of life that lasted for at least six thousand years.[13]

Archaeologists call this new era, with its changed environment, the Archaic period of prehistory. (Prehistory is the period in a culture's development before written historical records.) During this period, from about 6000 to 1000 BCE, the landscape changed from tundra to boreal forests of spruce and pine and later to mixed hardwoods. From

L'Anse-Amour

In 1973, archaeologists James Turk and Robert McGhee began work on a site that included a mysterious pile of rocks, near the village of L'Anse-Amour on the south coast of Labrador. Under a layer of three hundred boulders, in a pit measuring 7 m² and 1.5 m below the surface, they discovered the remains of a young person between eleven and thirteen years of age. McGhee describes their find:

There were several surprises that day. For a start, we suspected from the small size of the skeleton that it had belonged to an adolescent, and not a great tribal chief or priest that we might have expected to be buried with such ceremony. Next there was the unusual position of the body. When people are buried in an extended posture, they are nearly always placed on their backs; this child had been buried in a prone position, face down but with head turned to one side, and a large slab of rock had been placed on the back. In front of the face, a walrus tusk and other grave offerings were scattered around the body. Several spear points chipped from stone or carved from caribou bone were placed above the head, and there were two stone spear points at the left shoulder. Beneath the chest were a decorated bone pendant, an antler harpoon head, and a bird-bone whistle that, when blown, still produces a sound that makes dogs howl. At the left hip were two nodules of graphite covered with red ochre, and a small decorated antler pestle; these objects, probably originally enclosed in a small pouch, may have been a kit for making metallic red paint. Beneath the other hip was a carved, crescent shaped ivory object with a hole drilled into the center, perhaps a toggle for holding the end of a harpoon line. On either side of the body were patches of ash and charcoal, the remains of fires built at the time of burial and covered as the pit was filled with sand.[14]

This amazing discovery, which has been radiocarbon dated at 5500 BCE, is one of the oldest mounded burial sites in the world and allows for a great range of speculation. (Radiocarbon dating is a scientific dating method based on the principle that all living organisms take in the radioactive carbon 14 isotope, which decays at a measurable rate after the organism dies, whether animal or plant. This rate can be measured, and thus it provides a statistical estimate of how long ago the organism died.) Why would a small community of hunters and fishers go to such trouble to excavate a large pit, with only caribou antlers and birchbark baskets as tools, to bury a child with such elaborate ceremony? Even better established, larger farming communities elsewhere in the world had not yet developed this idea. McGhee speculates:

Perhaps the elaborate burial related not to the life of the individual but to the manner of death. Could this have been a young hunter who had been killed by a walrus or bear, an event considered so unlucky that it merited unusual ceremony? Or could this have been a sacrificial victim, who was deeply buried, face down, with a rock on the back and covered with tonnes of sand and boulders, in order to lay a ghost to rest? We can never know. Archaeology tells us only that the ancient Indian inhabitants of Labrador, for whatever reason, once went to much effort to provide an unusual burial for a child. It is, in fact, the oldest burial of this scale and complexity known anywhere on earth.[15]

The L'Anse-Amour site is also unusual because it has survived. Rising sea levels destroyed or submerged most archaeological sites along the Atlantic coast. Any bones not lost to the sea were destroyed by the high acidity of the soil in this region.

These settlers of L'Anse-Amour, who obviously had spiritual beliefs, probably enjoyed music (hence the whistle or flute), had domesticated the dog, and had developed a unique technology in the toggle head spear. Archaeologist James Wright describes the significance of this piece of technology:

[T]o the best of my knowledge the toggling harpoon represents the earliest example of its kind in the world. Unlike harpoons that are fixed into a spear shaft, the toggling harpoon head upon impact detaches from the tip of the spear shaft but remains attached to a hand held line. After penetrating the hide of the sea mammal the line comes under tension and the toggle head "toggles" into a horizontal position under the hide of the seal making it almost impossible to be dislodged from the wound. The toggle handle would be held by the hunter to control the line until the prey weakened and could be drawn into spear or club range.[16]

The Archaic Peoples of the Atlantic later developed local variations of their cultures and distinct regional identities. They became the Innu, Beothuk, Mi'kmaq, Wuastukwiuk, Passamaquoddy, Penobscot, and Abenaki.

First Peoples of the Arctic: 2000 – 0 BCE

Traditional stories of the Inuit tell of a strong but gentle people who once occupied the lands of the Arctic. They were called the Tunit or Dorset:

> According to the Iglulik Inuit, the Tunit once had many villages in their area: They were strong folk, skillful in sea hunting. They hunted the walrus with a long harpoon line and a short one. Their strength was such that when they had harpooned a walrus with the short line, they gave it a jerk that broke the creature's neck.
>
> So strong were these men that a walrus hauled up on the ice was dragged home just like an ordinary seal, by thongs fastened to its body. Their hunting grounds were far away from their houses, and it might happen that they were tired when at last they approached home with a walrus in tow. But when the women came out of their houses, these Tunit were so happy to see them that they forgot their weariness in a moment and with renewed strength dragged the walrus up to the village.
>
> Although the Tunit were a strong people, they were driven from their villages by others who were more numerous and by many people of great ancestors. But they loved their country so much that when they were leaving, one man, out of desperate love for his village, harpooned the rocks and made the stones fly about like bits of ice.[17]

Archaeologists have identified two groups of people who probably migrated across the Bering Sea from Asia to settle in the Canadian Arctic before the present day Inuit arrived, between one thousand to five hundred years ago.

The Paleo-Eskimos

The first Arctic people, the Paleo-Eskimo, arrived about 2000 BCE. They spread very rapidly from Alaska throughout the Arctic, even to northern Ellesmere Island and the north coast of Greenland. These highly mobile people were surprising both for what they had and for what they lacked. Expert producers of small chipped stone projectile points, they introduced the bow and arrow to the Americas. Evidence further suggests that the Paleo-Eskimo brought Asiatic archery with them, and through their contact with Atlantic Archaic people, the bow and arrow spread both south and west to all corners of the new world.

A view of the L'Anse Amour Burial Mound on the south shore of Labrador

Frame of Reference

What Is a Frame of Reference?

Imagine two glasses that have equal amounts of water in them. Some observers would call them half full, while others would say they are half empty. The difference is in the observer. Everyone brings different perspectives to the same fact and therefore interprets that fact differently. This is called our **frame of reference**.

Our frame of reference depends on many factors:

- upbringing
- age
- gender
- religion
- nationality
- culture
- education
- socio-economic status
- prior knowledge
- time period in which we live

In other words, when people observe or read information they do this through the lens of their own experience. Understanding and interpretation are informed or influenced by what people have come to know and value from living in a particular time and place.

Historians select, reject, organize, prioritize, emphasize, and draw conclusions about information based on their frame of reference. Even historians writing in the same time period about the same event have different interpretations based on their knowledge and values, which stem from their upbringing, religion, age, gender, nationality, and socioeconomic status. How do you think cultural background could affect a historian's frame of reference? Think of the Aboriginal versus western understanding of how and when Aboriginal people came to North America.

What Is a Fact?

A fact is an event or occurrence that actually happened. It is a fact that Aboriginal Peoples were in Canada before European discovery and settlement. It is a fact that skeletal remains have been uncovered and analyzed by archaeologists. How and when the Aboriginal people got here and how they lived is based on interpretations of those facts.

Distinguishing Facts from Interpretations

People can be confident that an event or occurrence is a fact when there is general agreement that it actually happened. For example, it is a fact that you are reading this textbook—it is actually happening. When historians agree that an event or situation actually happened, it is a fact. For example, all historians agree that stone tools were used in the Paleolithic Era.

Can Facts Speak for Themselves?

Two people or ten historians can look at an identical event or fact and make radically different interpretations based on their frame of reference. Therefore, **facts can never speak for themselves.** The same fact can be used to support a variety of interpretations, much like our two glasses of water. Historians interpret facts and events very differently based on their frames of reference. It is important to examine a variety of sources to distinguish what is fact and how different historians interpret events and evidence. Then people can develop their own understanding and interpretation of past events.

Questions to Ask to Detect the Author's Frame of Reference

1. Who wrote the piece? What are his or her credentials?
2. What is the author's gender, religion, cultural background, and nationality?
3. When did the author write the piece? Did the author experience the event first-hand?
4. Who is the intended audience? What is the author's purpose for writing the piece?
5. What are the important arguments or interpretations?
6. What evidence or facts does the author use to support the arguments?
7. What sources does the author use for evidence? What are the frames of references of the sources?
8. Does the information and interpretation agree or correspond with other sources?

Practice

For each of the following statements justify why it is a fact or an interpretation. Where it is an interpretation indicate the frame of reference that may have led to that understanding.

Statement	Justification of fact or interpretation	Frame of reference and why it could lead to the interpretation
Palaeolithic people crossed the Bering Strait after the glacial ice receded.	– an interpretation based on geological and man made artefacts.	– Belief that man could not have survived the ice age – therefore came later – cultural belief that carbon dating and geological time frames are reasonably accurate
Palaeolithic hunters developed comfortable and convenient homes using the furs of the animals they slaughtered.		
Fossils, bones, stone, and clay artefacts can tell us what Palaeolithic peoples hunted, and ate.		
Skeletal remains were uncovered in a L'Anse Amour mounded burial site by archaeologists in 1973.		
The abundance of harp seals gave the Archaic people along the shores of the Strait of Belle Isle a relatively stable way of life for at least 6000 years.		
The most dramatic technological innovation for the Archaic people was the introduction of clay pottery.		
It is quite likely, based on the richness of the archaeological finds, that the Aboriginal hunter-gatherers of the Pacific Coast transformed themselves from small-unspecialized groups into larger, more complex societies between 5500 to 1500 years ago.		

What is equally surprising is how these ancient people survived without some of the basic technology now associated with Arctic Peoples. They do not seem to have used any form of boat, and they did not have a float for their harpoons for hunting sea mammals. Although they did possess the toggle head spear previously described, there is no evidence that they had dogs for pulling sleds or hunting. They did not have oil lamps for heating or lighting their tent houses and probably did not build snow houses (igloos), since an open fire could not be used in snow houses. The picture that emerges of the Paleo-Eskimo is of a people who lived in small mobile groups, constantly in search of sufficient food to get them through the next winter.[18]

The Dorset People

The second group to migrate was the Dorset (Tunit) people. These people emerged out of Siberia and Alaska between 800 and 500 BCE and moved eastward, either absorbing or driving away the Paleo-Eskimo. Evidence from the Dorset culture indicates that they lived in larger groups, with much greater numbers and varieties of tools and artifacts. The chipped stone burins of the Paleo-Eskimo were replaced by tools ground to a desired shape. (A burin is a cutting, slotting, and engraving implement of stone used to fashion stone and ivory objects; its most distinctive characteristic is its resharpening procedure, which involves striking off a small flake to create a sharp edge or corner.) Large bone knives were probably used to cut snow blocks for constructing igloos. Rectangular soapstone lamps, used to burn oil from sea mammals, heated and lit their homes. The Dorsets invented ivory sled shoes used to protect the sleds' runners on rough ice or gravel and "ice creepers" made of ivory and tied underneath their boots to prevent slipping on ice. They used dogs for hunting and sledding, and they had developed the kayak. They did not use the bow and arrow.

Their art demonstrates that the Dorsets had a complex worldview, including belief in the supernatural and shamanistic ceremonies. A shaman is a person who acts as a go-between for the physical and spiritual realms and who is said to have special powers. The shaman could use his or her powers for good purposes, such as healing and prophecy, or for evil, such as casting a spell. "Shamanistic" describes the ceremonies involving a shaman calling on the powers of the spirit world. Full-sized masks were carved from driftwood and painted with ochre. Shaman probably wore these in rituals for curing illness, controlling the weather, and ensuring successful hunting. Sets of ivory animal teeth, designed to be held in the mouth, were likely used to transform a shaman into a bear. Wands made of ivory with as many as

An Inuit antler carving

sixty carved faces, human and semi-human, were used perhaps to preserve memories of important events or for religious ceremonies.

The Fate of the Dorsets

What happened to the Dorset people is again a matter of speculation. They were killed, displaced, or absorbed by the Thule People, who are believed to be the forerunners of the modern Inuit. Perhaps the previous story of the Tunit told by the Iglulik or this legend of the Netsilik Inuit is as valid as any theory:

> The Netsilik Inuit tells of their ancestors meeting with the Tunit long ago: The Tunit were strong but easily frightened. We hear nothing of their fighting ability. They used to live by the sea and at the caribou crossing places. They loved to hunt seal and often caught musk oxen and bears as well. It is said they once had land at a caribou crossing around Netsilik Lake (near the modern settlement of Spence Bay). After one of them killed a dog by kicking a harpoon at it, the land was taken away from them. The Tunit fled from their village, crying out to the Inuit: "we hunted the caribou here; now it is your turn."[19]

Review...Reflect...Respond

1. How do the two theories of how Aboriginal Canadians arrived on the continent help to explain the diversity of prehistoric and historic Aboriginal nations?

2. Why do you think that until recently, historians have largely ignored Aboriginal oral traditions, such as the creation myths, in the study of prehistoric Aboriginal history?

3. Are Aboriginal and non-Aboriginal historical methods exclusive of each other? How can a student of Aboriginal history use both types of sources to further their understanding of prehistoric Aboriginal history?

First Peoples of the Great Lakes and St. Lawrence Valley: 8000 BCE–1000 CE

Armed with their spears and spear throwers, the Paleolithic hunters prepared to leave their families in semi-permanent camps on the riverbank of what is present day southwestern Ontario. A three- or four-day walk north along the river led them to the shores of a great lake. (This was Lake Algonquin, the predecessor of most of the Great Lakes, about 10 000 years ago.) In the distance, they saw massive ice fields. Here, the caribou gathered, attracted to the shores of the glacial lake, where cold winds alleviated the annoying mosquitoes and black flies. The hunters built rock cairns (inukshuk) to help them channel the caribou to where they could be more easily killed by spears propelled from their spear throwers. During their foraging, they no doubt encountered the stark,

Southern Ontario, 11 000 years ago

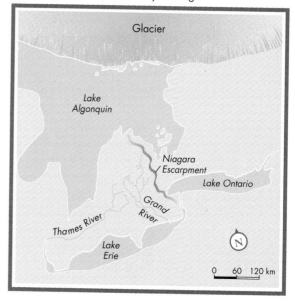

How did these bodies of water change over geological time?

jagged line of limestone cliffs now called the Niagara Escarpment. As they took in this incredible view, they saw a lush green plain where musk oxen and maybe even deer or caribou, which were replacing larger game, grazed. Further south was another immense blue lake. (This was probably Lake Iroquois, the predecessor of Lake Ontario. In this rich land, hunters and their families felt less pressure to move to follow the herds of migrating animals. Now they would stay closer to one area and live off the land that provided them with a diversity of foods and the necessities of life.

The Laurentian Peoples

Archaeologists believe that Paleolithic people inhabited southern Ontario and southwestern Quebec 10 000 years ago, even as sheets of glacial ice were still retreating. Over time, these people developed a wide variety of hunting, fishing, and collecting activities based on the availability and abundance of local resources. By 3000 BCE, the beginning of the Archaic period (3000 BCE to 1000 CE), the people of the Great Lakes and St. Lawrence, often called the Laurentian people, had adapted to environments resembling those of today. They hunted primarily deer, elk, bear, and beaver. Fishing also provided a large part of their diet. Little archaeological evidence remains of wild plant foods such as berries and nuts, although they likely were important seasonal food sources. Laurentian sites, although lacking in the wood, bark, and leather objects that compose the largest part of their cultural artifacts, do contain a variety of chipped and ground stone tools, and implements made of natural or native copper, including projectile points, knives, fishhooks, awls, pendants, and beads. The presence of native copper from northwest of lake Superior and exotic goods such as shell beads from the Atlantic Coast and conch shell pendants from the Gulf of Mexico suggests extensive trade networks and possibly travel. Skull fractures, decapitation, and projectile points found lodged in bones or in the chest cavities of skeletons also tell of violent deaths.[20]

The Shield Archaic Peoples

The more northerly people, called the Shield Archaic people (3000 BCE to 1000 CE) by archaeologists, often had smaller village sites located at narrows of lakes and rivers, where caribou easily made their way across. Fish and caribou, supplemented by bear, beaver, hare, and waterfowl, provided the essentials of life. Settlement sites on islands strongly suggest that the birchbark canoe was already an important, if not essential, part of their way of life. It is logical to assume that they used snowshoes for winter travel.

The most dramatic technological innovation for the Archaic people of this area was the introduction of clay pottery. Archaeological sites in southwestern Ontario reveal an abundance of pottery shards two thousand years ago. It is difficult to say how ceramic vessels changed the lives of these Aboriginal people, but what they do for archaeology is dramatic. Because pottery shards are abundant and virtually indestructible, archaeologists are able to study variations in styles and decoration to isolate cultural groups and periods. Archaeologists also use the introduction of pottery to mark the beginning of the general period that follows the Archaic period, the Woodland period.[21]

The Woodland Peoples

One of the most interesting and important Woodland sites is found near Peterborough, Ontario, on the north shore of Rice Lake. Here, on one of the many drumlin hills left behind by the retreating glaciers, lies a group of nine human-made earth mounds. Eight of the structures are oval, about fifteen metres across and a metre high. The ninth structure resembles a twisting serpent. It is sixty metres long, eight metres wide, and between one metre and two metres high.

Archaeological excavation of the Serpent Mounds near Peterborough, Ontario.

Woodland people probably used this site as a summer camp for thousands of years. Archaeological digs have revealed extensive quantities of shells, suggesting that the residents depended heavily on freshwater mussels. This site is unique for Ontario, and to these people. Its very existence challenges us to understand why this particular group of Woodland people, who buried their dead with exotic grave goods and probably great ceremony, but in single interments for thousands of years, decided about two thousand years ago to mound earth over their dead relatives. The native copper from Lake Superior and seashells from the Gulf of Mexico and Atlantic found in the mounds show that the Woodland people had contact with people from distant places. The closest similar structures are found in Ohio and were built by the Hopewell people or culture. (Hopewell culture is a term archaeologists apply to the people of the Mississippi and Ohio Rivers who developed elaborate burial rituals including the building of mounds.) It is possible that the Woodland people of Rice Lake heard of the magnificent Hopewell burial mounds from traders and were entranced by their stories of powerful burial ceremonies. It is also possible that a party of local men had trav-elled to the Hopewell villages and, having witnessed both the mounds and the religious customs of these wealthy and successful people, decided to emulate them.[22]

"Big Turtle:" The Iroquois Creation Legend

Knowledge of the earliest peoples of the Great Lakes and St. Lawrence is shrouded in mystery, despite the best efforts and evidence produced by archaeologists. Another view of the beginning of the Woodland Peoples is told in this Iroquois creation story. It tells of the close relationship between humans and their environment.

True to Aboriginal oral tradition, this story is timeless but full of meaning as it offers the past to the present. When things are out of balance or not right in the world, "Big Turtle" moves to warn us to change our ways.

Once long ago a Sky Woman fell through a hole in the sky into a wide waste of waters below. Two swans saw her falling and caught her on their backs.

"What shall we do with this Sky Woman?" asked one of the swans.

"We cannot hold her up forever."

"We must call a meeting," said the other.

The water animals came together to decide what to do. Big Turtle said, "If someone will dive down and bring up some earth from below, I will hold the earth on my back. Then we shall have land for this Sky Woman to live on."

So the water animals took turns in diving. First the muskrat tried. When he came up, Big Turtle looked into his mouth but could find no earth. Then the beaver made a dive and came up. He too, had no earth in his mouth. Others tried, but none brought up any earth.

Finally, Little Toad tried. He stayed under water a long time. When at last he came up his mouth was full of earth. The animals spread the earth over Big Turtle's back.

Then a strange thing happened. The amount of earth began to grow until Big Turtle was holding a whole island on his back. The Sky Woman stepped off the swans' backs and started to make it her home.

The island continued to grow until it was as large as all of North America. Sometimes, they say, Big Turtle grows weary and moves his back to shift the island. Then the earth shakes. People cry: "Big Turtle is moving."[23]

Web Connection

www.mcgrawhill.ca/links/definingcanada

Go to the Web site above to learn more about Iroquois language and songs.

First Peoples of the Western Plains: 8000 BCE–1000 CE

As the climate warmed and ice fields retreated from the western lands leaving an expanse of short grass plains, some animals, specifically the bison, rapidly increased in numbers as their competitors for food— the mammoth, horse, and camel—quickly declined and eventually become extinct from this region. The Paleolithic people who had followed and hunted the large migrating mammals onto the plains adapted their technology and culture to a lifestyle centred on hunting the growing herds of bison.

A contributing factor to the Paleolithic hunters' success, and what identifies them as a distinctive people or culture according to archaeologists, was their development of a unique method of chipping stone. This new technology enabled the Plano people to produce thinner and more carefully manufactured spearheads. This change in projectile points was accompanied by a significant change in their weapon system, from a split shaft method of holding the point in place on the spear shaft to a socket hafting. Archaeologists note this change of technology and culture from the Paleolithic era by referring to the new era as that of the Plano culture or people. But the major shift that accompanied the development of new technology was the change from being hunters of a range of big game animals to hunters of buffalo:

It is September and the buffalo have begun to collect into larger herds. The small band, consisting of 46 mostly related men, women and children has followed a small herd of about 200 buffalo for weeks. Often the herd disappears overnight and mysteriously they find it again after a few anxious days. Last night around the fire the older men and women told of the great animals of the past and how their ancestors many, many years ago hunted strange incredible mammals that no longer existed. Now they are dependent on the buffalo and they must keep its spirit alive and know everything about them if they are to survive and prosper. For three days and nights the hunt leaders have not eaten. They fast, meditate, and sing to call the buffalo to them. Sweet grass burns like incense near the sacred buffalo skull. Today they will travel towards the mountains along the paths they followed for many years. They will wait near Head-Smashed-In Buffalo Jump until other people arrive and together they will drive the buffalo over the cliff. This will provide them with all they will need to survive the winter.[24]

A skinning tool made from a caribou leg bone.

Buffalo Jumps

For more than six thousand years, the people of the western plains of Canada hunted buffalo by driving them over cliffs called jumps. Two of the best known are Head-Smashed-In Buffalo Jump, which was declared a World Heritage Site in 1981, and Old Woman Buffalo Jump, both within sight of the Rocky Mountains in present-day Alberta. Archaeological evidence from this latter site revealed masses of buffalo bones extending more than thirty metres along the base of the cliff and more than sixty metres down slope from it. The bone beds are more than four metres deep and include more than one-thousand chipped stone points of lances and arrows, a few heavy stone choppers for breaking bones, stone knives for skinning animals and cutting up meat, and even a single black bead carved from soapstone.[25]

Hunting the buffalo without the use of the jump was extremely dangerous and the results were uncertain at best. Remember, the hunters of the plains began using the horse only in the seventeenth century. Traditional hunting practices required the hunters to use a lance or bow and arrows, to get close enough so that their weapons were effective against these unpredictable beasts that weighed, on average, more than 550 kg and could run at more than sixty kilometres an hour. The hunters, knowing they could not outrun them, would disguise themselves in wolves' skins and slowly stalk the buffalo until they were sufficiently close to throw their spears or shoot their arrows. (It is believed that the bow and arrow was introduced only about two thousand years ago). They took advantage of the animals' poor eyesight, and by keeping downwind, they crawled through the tall dry summer grass to get within striking distance. Long hours of slow creeping might yield one or two buffalo. Winter hunting was easier if a herd was driven into a valley filled with drifted snow. There, hunters on snowshoes could slaughter the floundering animals.

By far the most efficient strategies were the drive and the jump. In early times, hunting groups came together for a buffalo drive along traditional migration routes. They would build a V-shaped corral of brush, branches, and stones. The hunters funnelled the animals into the corral where they were killed with arrows and lances. How long drives were used is not known, but it is known that jumps, such as Head-Smashed-In Buffalo Jump, were used for more than six thousand years. A successful hunt, where hundreds of buffalo were slaughtered, provided large numbers of families not only most of their meat for winter, dried or as pemmican, but also skins for clothing, blankets, and house and floor coverings. Buffalo horns served as spoons, drinking cups, and scrapers. Sinew and hair were made into thread and rope; the large stomach became a water bucket, cooking pot, or pemmican storage bag; and dried buffalo droppings were a good source of fuel, producing little smoke.

Hunting buffalo required a very mobile lifestyle for the Plano people. All their possessions, including their distinctive readily assembled and disassembled tepee homes with their long straight poles and buffalo hide coverings, had to be portable for humans and dogs either to carry on their backs or to drag on a travois as they followed the herds.

Other animals were also hunted and some plants gathered, but without the

Head-Smashed-In Buffalo Jump, in southern Alberta.

buffalo, life for the Plano people of the western plains would have been almost impossible. Despite the large number of buffalo and improved hunting techniques, they were not always successful when the need was greatest. Cold, sickness, and starvation were real. An unlucky band could lose a third of its members over a hard winter.[26]

Oral Traditions of the Western Plains People

This account of the First Peoples of the western plains, based on archaeological evidence, only reveals a small part about how these people lived. What about what they thought and their spiritual life? An example of their traditional oral history that has been passed down through the generations can give us some insight into these aspects. This story about the Origin of Death comes from the Siksika people of the Blackfoot Nation, who live in present-day southern Alberta:

With their dogs pulling travois, Aboriginal people followed the buffalo herds.

> When the world was new, Old Man and Old Woman were walking around.
>
> "Let us decide how things will be," Old Man said.
>
> "That is good," said Old Woman. "How shall we do it?"
>
> "Well," Old Man said, "since it was my idea I think I should have the first say in everything."
>
> "That is good," said Old Woman, "just as long as I have the last say."
>
> So they walked around and looked at things. Then Old Man spoke. "I have been thinking about hunting," he said. "The men will be the hunters. Anytime they want to shoot an animal they will call it and it will come to them."
>
> "I agree men should be the hunters," Old Woman said. "But if the animals come when they are called, life will be too easy for the people. The animals should runaway when they see the people. Then it will be hard for the men to kill them. That way people will be smarter and stronger."
>
> "You have the last say," Old Man agreed. Then they walked around some more.
>
> After a while, Old Man spoke again. "I had been thinking about what people will look like," he said. "They will have eyes on one side of their face and their mouth on the other. Their mouths will go straight up and down. They will have ten fingers on each hand."

An artist's conception of a Buffalo Run.

"I agree that people should have their eyes and their mouth on their faces," Old Woman said. "But their eyes should be at the top of their face and mouth at the bottom and they will be set across. I agree they should have fingers on their hands, but ten on each hand will make them clumsy. They will have five fingers on each."

"You have the last say," Old Man agreed.

Now they were walking by river. "Let us decide about life and death," Old Man said. "I will do it this way. I will throw this buffalo chip into the river. If it floats, when people die they will come back to life after four days and then live forever."

Old Man threw the buffalo chip into the water. It bobbed up and floated." I agree we should decide it this way," Old Woman said. "But I do not think it should be done with a buffalo chip. I will throw this stone into the water instead. If it floats, the people die for four days and then come back to life and live forever. If it sinks, the people will not come back to life after they die."

Old Woman threw the stone into the water. It sank immediately.

"That is the way should be," Old Woman said. "If people live forever, the Earth would be too crowded. There would not be enough food. This way people will feel sorry for each other. There will be sympathy in the world."

Old Man said nothing.

Some time passed. Old Woman had a child. She and Old Man loved the child very much and they were happy. One day, though, the child became sick and died. Then Old Woman went to Old Man.

"Let us have our say again about death," she said.

But Old Man shook his head. "No," he said, "you had the last say."[27]

First Peoples of the Pacific Coast: 8000 BCE–1000 CE

The first settlers of the Pacific coast probably arrived during the end of the last ice age, between 13 000 and 10 000 years ago. These people were different from the Paleolithic people, who, archaeologists theorize, entered North America through a corridor in the Rocky Mountains. One of the theories to explain their differences is that they migrated separately from other Paleolithic people from Asia and made their way along the exposed seabed created during the last ice age on the west coast. With great quantities of water frozen as ice, the water levels of the seas were much lower, creating a corridor west of the mountains along the Pacific Coast.

One form of evidence of fluctuations in sea levels and an ice age is the oral history of the Northwest Coast Peoples. According to Haida tradition, they have inhabited Haidi Gwaii since the end of the last ice age. This makes them one of the oldest traceable populations in the new world.

Many of the Haidi Gwaii stories of the ice age have been recorded. This one was told to a Hudson's Bay Company trader in 1892. It is very specific about glacial events at Honna River on Haida Gwaii:

This is the story of long, long ago told amongst our people, the Hidery, that at Quilh-ca, about three miles west of the village of Illth-cah-geetla, or Skidegate's town, lived a boy whose name was Scannah-gan-nuncus...

...One day, making a further venture than usual, he sailed up the Hunnah, a mountain stream emptying its waters into Skidegate channel, four or five miles west from the place where lived.

Tradition says that the river in those days was three times larger than it was nowadays. At present there is seldom water enough to float a canoe, unless at high water. It is also said that the waters of the sea stood higher on the land than is now the case. Of the rise of the land, evidence is everywhere to be seen; old landmarks show 30 feet.

After pulling upstream, he became tired; so, in order to rest, he pulled ashore and lay down. In those days at the place where he went ashore were large boulders in the bed of the stream, while on both sides of the river were many trees. While resting by the river, he heard a dreadful noise upstream, coming towards him. Looking to see what it was, he was surprised to behold all the stones in the river coming towards him. The movement of the stones frightened him so much that he jumped to his feet and ran into the timber. Here he found he had made a mistake, because all the trees were cracking and groaning, all seemed to say to him, "Go back, go back at once to the river, and run as fast as you can." This he lost no time doing. When again at the river, lead by his curiosity, he went to see what was crushing the stones and breaking the trees. On reaching them, he found that a large body of ice was coming down, pushing everything before it. Seeing this, he got into his canoe and fled toward home.[28]

Kwakiutl Dugout Canoes.

The author of this story is unknown, as is exactly when it happened. It must have been very early in the settlement of the islands as the story has been passed down through many, many generations.

In many other ways, these people of the Pacific coast were different from other Aboriginal Peoples of Canada. They were shorter, had broader faces, and flatter features. They were also linguistically the most diverse, with seventeen languages from five different language groups. This linguistic diversity suggests the possibility that some early people made their way by boat along the coast from Asia as late as four thousand or five thousand years ago.

Archaeology: Piecing Together the Story

Despite the destruction of many of the earliest archaeological sites by the rising sea levels as the great ice fields melted, considerable evidence of stone tools dating back to almost 8000 BCE has been found. "Pebble tools," smooth cobbles or pebbles picked up from the beach or riverbank and bashed to remove a few flakes and create a sharp edge, were recovered in abundance at the lowest levels of the nine-thousand-year-old Milliken site in the lower Frasier Canyon. Although no bones survive to tell us what these Paleolithic settlers ate, the riverside locations of the settlements suggest that fish played a major role. Charred pits of wild cherries, which ripen during the salmon runs of early fall, found at the Milliken site suggest that even during this early period, Northwest Coast Peoples were timing their seasonal movements to coincide with the appearance of salmon.

Other archaeological sites of a slightly later period have produced microblades. It is believed that these were hafted (given handles) as the cutting or piercing edges of composite tools, whose wooden, antler, or bow handles were not preserved. It is quite likely, based on the richness of the archaeological finds, that the Aboriginal hunter-gatherers of the Pacific coast transformed themselves from small, unspecialized groups into larger, more complex societies between 5500 and 1500 years ago. The abundance and reliability of salmon and shellfish allowed their population to grow and their cultures to flourish for thousands of years. Most of the evidence of their prosperity and ingenuity has not survived, because items were fashioned from wood, bark, root, hide, and sinew. Fortunately, some precious evidence of their skills as carvers and weavers of wood fibres did survive in waterlogged sites. Even three thousand or four thousand years ago, the people of the northwest coast were probably beginning to build the solid wood houses, powerful sea canoes, majestic totem poles, and beautiful cedar boxes that demonstrated their mastery of wood construction and carving.

Expression of Identity
WILLIAM RONALD "BILL" REID

Bill Reid was one of Canada's most celebrated and accomplished contemporary artists. Among his major works were the 4.5 tonne cedar sculpture "Raven and the First Humans" in the University of British Columbia's Museum of Anthropology (1980); a bronze killer whale sculpture, "The Chief of the Undersea World" for the Vancouver Aquarium (1984); a canoe commissioned for Expo '86; and "Spirit of Haida Gwaii," which was commissioned for the Canadian Embassy in Washington, D.C., (1991). Reid is credited with the revival of northwest coast Aboriginal arts and particularly Haida Gwaii in the contemporary world.

Reid was the son of a Haida Gwaii mother and a Scottish-American father. His upbringing, however, had little connection to Aboriginal culture, and he spent much of his youth in Alaska and Victoria, British Columbia. For the first ten years of his working life, Bill Reid was a radio announcer for the CBC in Vancouver and Toronto. It was not until he was a teenager and after he met his maternal grandfather, Charles Gladstone, who had trained with the great Haida Gwaii artist Charles Edenshaw, that Reid learned of the artistic traditions of his ancestors.

Awarded many honours for his accomplishments, honorary doctorates from the University of British Columbia, Trent University, the University of Toronto, York University, the University of Victoria, and the University of Western Ontario, the Canada Council's Molson Award in 1976, the Bronfman Award for Excellence in Crafts (1986), the Vancouver Lifetime Achievement Award (1988), the Royal Bank Award (1990) for outstanding Canadian achievement, the National Aboriginal Achievement Award for Lifetime Achievement (1994), the Bill Mason Award (1998) from the Canadian River Heritage Society, the Order of British Columbia, and the Order of Canada, Bill Reid was an eloquent and outspoken proponent of Aboriginal rights in Canada and was especially active in the battle to preserve the national and cultural history of South Moresby in the Queen Charlotte Islands.

In his book *The Road I Followed*, Bill Reid wrote, "It is my hope that the people of today and of tomorrow become aware of the existence of the Northwest Coast and feel enriched by the knowledge they will acquire from this extraordinary testimony of what man can do."

---

1. What does Bill Reid mean when he says, "Haida culture has been wrecked. Their language is gone. Their mythology is gone. The genealogies of the big families are lost. If they're going to find their way back to the world of cultured men, then they have to begin at the beginning" (Bill Reid, quoted in Richard Wright, "The Spirit of Haida Gwaii: La renaissance de l'art haïda," *Enroute*, March 1991, p. 90).

Conclusion

Mystery surrounds our knowledge of the people of prehistoric Canada, but the fact that Aboriginal Peoples have lived here for 10 000 years or more is a certainty. Although differences exist in the type of evidence that Aboriginal people and non-Aboriginal people offer to recreate the past, both are important, and together they enable archaeologists to create a story or paint picture of life in Canada from 10 000 to 2000 years ago. History is always an interpretation of the reconstructed past based on the best available and most reliable sources.

Archaeology provides hard evidence of the physical presence of humans in Canada. Fossils, bones, stone, and clay artifacts reveal what Paleolithic Peoples hunted and ate, the weapons they hunted with, and the utensils they used to prepare their food. Archaeological digs make known their burial practices, and from these, hypotheses about their spiritual beliefs, some aspects of their community life, and their social organization can be made.

Only the traditional stories or oral history, however, can give life to ideas about what these early people thought and what they believed was important. This source reveals the earliest Aboriginal settlers' relationship with nature, their accepted behaviours with one another, and their spiritual world.

Notes

1. Diamond Jenness, *The Indians of Canada* (Toronto: University of Toronto Press, 1932).
2. Government of Canada, *Report of The Royal Commission on Aboriginal Peoples*, 1996.
3. Paleolithic refers to the period of human development when bone and chipped stone tools were used.
4. J.V. Wright, *A History of the Native People of Canada, Volume 1, 10 000–1000 BC* (Ottawa: Canadian Museum of Civilization, 1995), p. 27.
5. Alan D. McMillan, *Native Peoples and Cultures of Canada*, 2nd ed. (Toronto: Douglas & McIntyre, 1995), p. 171.
6. Brian Bethune, "Mystery of the First North Americans," *Maclean's*, March 19, 2001, pp. 24–29.
7. Wright, *A History of the Native People of Canada*, p. 25.
8. Elaine Dewar, *Bones: Discovering the First Americans* (Toronto, Random House Canada, 2001), p. 20.
9. Dewar, p. 19.
10. Wright, *A History of the Native People of Canada*, p. 554
11. Arthur J. Ray, *I Have Lived Here Since the World Began* (Toronto: KeyPorter Books, 1996) p. vii.
12. Dewar, *Bones*, p. 210–212
13. Robert McGhee, *Ancient Canada* (Ottawa: Canadian Museum of Civilization, 1989), p. 50.
14. Ibid., p. 51.
15. Ibid., p. 54
16. Wright, *A History of the Native People of Canada*, p. 84.
17. David Morrison, *Arctic Hunters* (Canadian Museum of Civilization, 1992), p. 62.
18. McGhee, *Ancient Canada*, p. 62.
19. David Morrison, *Arctic Hunters*, p. 63
20. McMillan, *Native Peoples and Cultures of Canada*, p. 56.
21. Ibid., p. 56.
22. McGhee, *Ancient Canada*, p. 83.
23. Told by Marius Barbeau and published in *Connecting Canada*. [full reference to come from author]
24. Michael J. Caduto and Joseph Bruchac, *The Native Stories From Keepers of the Earth* (Saskatoon: Fifth House Publishers, 1989).
25. McGhee, *Ancient Canada*, pp. 73–74.
26. D.F. Symington, *Hunters of the Plains: Assiniboine Indians* (Ginn and Co., 1972), p. 98.
27. Canadian Museum of Civilization Corporation, Civilization.ca Web site, available online at www.civilization.ca/aborig/haida.happole.html
28. Canadian Museum of Civilization Corporation, Civilization.ca Web site, available online at www.civilization.ca/aborig/haida.happole.html

Chapter 1 Review

Knowledge & Understanding

1. Identify these people, places, and events, and explain their historical significance to Canada's developing culture and identity:
   - Beringia theory
   - L'Anse Amour
   - migration theories
   - Dorset people
   - oral tradition
   - Big Turtle

2. Explain the difference between the Beringia theory and the Coastal theory. What type of historical evidence is used to support each theory?

3. Five groups of Aboriginal Peoples are discussed in this chapter: Atlantic, Arctic, Great Lakes and St. Lawrence Valley, Western Plains, and the Pacific Coast. Create a graphic organizer to differentiate and distinguish these Aboriginal groups. Your organizer may include such criteria as time period, lifestyle, spirituality, and political organization.

Thinking & Inquiry

4. Understanding the history of Canada's early Aboriginal Peoples relies largely on the study of archeology. Yet, this method involves the exploration of often sacred areas such as burial sites. Is it reasonable to call archeology a "destructive science"? Why or why not?

5. Explain the significance of the following archeological sites: Kamloops (British Columbia), Blue Fish Caves (Yukon), Clovis (New Mexico), L'Anse Amour (Labrador), and Serpent Mounds (Ontario). What does each site tell us about early Aboriginal Peoples in Canada and North America?

Application

6. In the study of early Aboriginal Peoples in Canada, two types of methodology are involved: Aboriginal (oral tradition), and non-Aboriginal (archaeology, carbon dating, etc.). As a curator for a national museum, you have been asked to research and create a display on Aboriginal Peoples in Canada from 35 000 BCE–1000 CE. What type of historical methodology will you rely on for your research? In a well-written paragraph, give reasons for your choice.

7. If it were possible to interview one person from one of the Aborignal groups discussed, who would you choose? Why? Create ten questions that you would ask this person.

Communication

8. Compare the creation myths in this chapter. What similarities and differences do they contain? In a letter to the editor of the *Canadian Historical Review*, explain why creation myths are essential to the study of early Canadian history.

9. Choose one creation myth from this chapter. Create a series of petroglyphs to help tell the story. Think carefully about what images you will choose to visually tell the story. Once you are finished, give your petroglyphs to a classmate and have him or her interpret the story through your drawings. How similar is their interpretation to the actual creation myth that you based them on?

Aboriginal Peoples of Canada: Early Times to First Contact

I have lived here since the world began.

– MI'KMAQ ORAL TRADITION

Two thousand years ago, Canada was populated by people who spoke more than fifty different languages from twelve different language families. The Mi'kmaq on the Atlantic coast spoke a language and had a culture as different from the Haida on the Pacific coast as Chinese is from English, French, or Somali. The Aboriginal Peoples who lived in Canada before the Europeans arrived were diverse. Two thousand years ago, Aboriginal people were freer to, or simply had to, define their own culture and identity. They created a way of life that enabled them not only to survive, but also to meet their individual and collective needs and desires as human beings.

It is important to realize that Aboriginal nations consist of many individuals, communities, and societies and that one story cannot possibly describe all of them. Nor can one description of a people, at one time in their history, convey the sense of how that society changed over thousands of years. This chapter will provide some sense of the dynamic nature of Canada's Aboriginal people five hundred to two thousand years ago, including the introduction of new technologies such as pottery, the kayak, and the bow and arrow, the use of which took about two thousand years to cross from Labrador to the Rockies. Many changes in hunting techniques, foods and crops, tool making, housing styles, and spiritual ideas resulted from trade and other forms of contact among different Aboriginal groups. Their societies were not static and they should not be seen as stereotypes. As you read this chapter, try to reconstruct the past to understand what life might have been like two thousand years ago, without imposing your values and ideas on those Aboriginal people who lived in Canada before the Europeans arrived.

2

1000 BCE
● Ceramic pottery appears in Iroquoian villages of the Great Lakes and spreads east

Bison reach peak population on the Canadian Prairies

Cultures of the Pacific Coast Peoples begin to expand

The bow and arrow are used on the western plains ●**500 BCE**

Maize (corn) cultivation begins in southern Ontario as the climate warms

The Dorset people migrate into Arctic Canada

800 CE
● The Iroquoian longhouse pattern of settlement is well established

The Inuit (Thule) migrate from Alaska across the Canadian Arctic ●**1000 CE**

The Athapapaskan Peoples migrate to the plateau region of the Rocky Mountains

1350 CE
● Squash and bean cultivation begins in southern Ontario

The creation of the Iroquois League of the Great Peace ●**1451 CE**

1730 CE
● Horses are first used in western Canada by the Plains Peoples

By the end of this chapter, you will be able to

- describe various aspects of Aboriginal life before contact with Europeans

- analyze the impact of European contact on the lives of Aboriginal Peoples and evaluate the responses of Aboriginal Peoples to the spread of disease and the introduction of new weapons and trade goods

- describe the contributions of Aboriginal Peoples to the development of Canadian identity and culture

Iroquoian Peoples

Unsettling rumours stirred the air of the village. Hunters who had travelled east as far as Hochelaga (present-day Montreal) had returned. At Hochelaga, they had heard of strange men who had come to their country—men with hair on their faces, wearing strange clothing and riding large ships pushed by the wind. They saw knives and axes that could be sharpened to a fine edge. These new hatchets of dark black metal would make it much easier to clear the land of trees for the planting of corn. The women could happily use these sharp tools to collect firewood and brushes. The strange men did not stay long before they returned up the great river (St. Lawrence) to Stadacona (present-day Quebec City). The hunters had also seen that many of the Hochelagans were suffering from a sickness that caused them to cough and to spit blood. They had heard that many had died of this disease already.

A second rumour was far less concrete than the first but seemed more threatening. Hunters had returned from the land of many lakes and rivers to the west (present-day Rideau Lake country north of Kingston, Ontario). In this land, traditionally rich with deer, bear, and beaver and a source of fish and fowl, there were signs that Huron hunters had also hunted there. Some of the older women reminded the young hunters of past disputes over the hunting area that had led to a raid and the capture of five women and some children from the cornfields that surrounded their village. The women would again advise the men, in their own way, that the sachems (leaders) should meet with the Iroquoian sachems from the nearby villages to make plans. Maybe they should move further east away from the danger. Besides, they had lived here for more than ten years—the soil was less productive now and the women had to go farther to get firewood. The palisade walls surrounding the village needed repair. The vertical posts on the east had been eroded by heavy rainfall in the spring, and they had lost their hold on the reinforcing liner of bark.

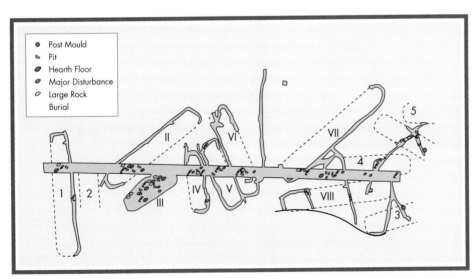

This archaeological site plan of the Roebuck site, showing the floor plans for many longhouses, gives an entirely different picture of the organization of an Iroquoian village than the illustrations created by Europeans do. European illustrations always present the longhouses in a neat, orderly way, as if some central government or town planner had organized the scheme. This arrangement suggests that individual families or clans decided where they wanted their longhouse and built it to suit themselves.

On the banks of the St. Lawrence River, just north of the present-day city of Brockville, Ontario, the Roebuck site of the St. Lawrence Iroquois is a sandy mound that rises about five metres on its south side and less steeply on the other sides. It covers about eight hectares. The site is protected by a black alder swamp on three sides, but it opens to dry, level land on the west. The long oval-shaped sand hill was once crowded with forty longhouses ranging from twenty metres to forty-two metres long. With a population estimated at two thousand, the Roebuck of the St. Lawrence Iroquoians probably displayed a vitality it has not shown since.

What happened to the St. Lawrence Iroquoians? Did epidemic diseases, such as tuberculosis, smallpox, and measles, destroy them? Was crop failure a factor, since the lower St. Lawrence River Valley was a precarious environment for agriculture? Or was it warfare? Perhaps it was a combination of all these factors.

Canada's former chief archaeologist, J.V. Wright, has made a convincing argument that the Huron destroyed the St. Lawrence Iroquoians in warfare. His evidence is the presence of typical St. Lawrence Iroquoian pottery found in late Huron sites and the lack of any pipes. These facts suggest that women and probably children were taken back to Huronia as captives, were adopted into Huron society, and continued to make pots in their traditional fashion. The men were probably killed, explaining the lack of pipes, since making pipes was a man's craft.

The Iroquoian came to Canada at three different times and for three different reasons. The first group, mostly Mohawk and Oneida, came around 1670 because of the missionary efforts of the Jesuits (French Catholic priests) and settled near Montreal at Caughnawaga (Kahnawake) and Oka (Kanesatake). The second and largest wave arrived in Canada after the American Revolutionary war (about 1783). The Mohawk, and to a lesser degree the Seneca, Cayuga, and Onondaga, had fought with the British against the Americans and were forced to flee the newly created United States. They were given land at two locations: on Lake Ontario at the Bay of Quinte, called Tyendinega, and in the Grand River Valley, also known as the Six Nations of the Grand River. The third movement came in the 1840s, because of American forced resettlement programs.

Iroquois Versus Iroquoian

The terms *Iroquoian* and *Iroquois* can be confusing. *Iroquoian* refers to the people who spoke a similar or related language, probably from a common origin. The term *Iroquois* is usually applied only to one specific group of Iroquoian speakers— the members of the League of the Five Nations or Haudenonsaunee (People of the Longhouse). Included in the Iroquoian Peoples of Canada were the St. Lawrence Iroquoians, comprising the Stadaconans, Hochelagans, the people of Roebuck, and all the people from another dozen or more villages along the St. Lawrence River and throughout eastern Ontario. Also included are the Huron (this is the French name for these people who called themselves Wendat, meaning the people who live on a peninsula), Neutral (again a French name applied to these people because they remained neutral in warfare), and the Petun (also called the Tobacco because of their success in growing tobacco). Historian Olive Dickason estimates the total Iroquoian population at more than 60 000, with the Huron accounting for half. The Cherokee, also Iroquoian, are the people from whom the ancestors of the Canadian Iroquoians likely separated about 4000 to 3500 years ago.

All Iroquoians were hunters and farmers (more precisely horticulturalists since they grew crops but did not domesticate animals). They practised slash and burn agriculture, which involved the men clearing the land by stripping the bark from the trees and then burning off the brush and dead timber. Women planted and tended to the crops, which

The Iroquoians and their neighbours at early European contact

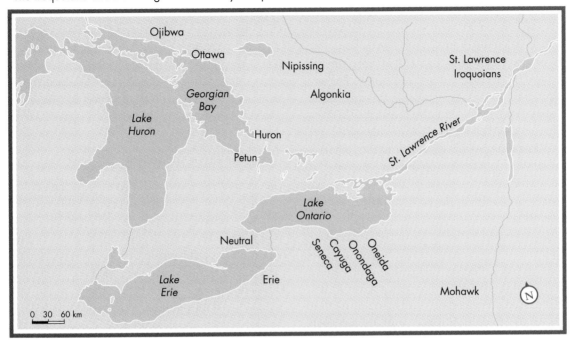

consisted of the "three sisters": corn, beans, and squash. People lived in longhouses clustered in palisaded villages that had 1500 or more inhabitants. Evidence shows that this pattern of settlement was well established in Canada by 800 CE.

Also shared by all Iroquoian Peoples is a similar oral history describing the origin of their most important crop: corn or maize. Here is one version of this popular Iroquoian story called *The Coming of Corn*.

Long ago, an old woman lived happily with her grandson in the shadow of the big mountain. The Grandmother gave him his first bow and arrow and he went out to hunt for game and brought back a small bird.

"Ah," said the Grandmother, "You are going to be a great hunter. We must have a feast." She went out to the small storehouse behind their cabin. She came back with dried corn in her basket and made a fine tasting soup with the small bird and the corn.

Each day Grandson brought back something to add to the corn Grandmother brought from the storage house. One day, though, the boy peeked into the storehouse. It was empty! But that evening, when he returned with game to cook, she went out again and brought back a basket filled with dried corn.

The next day, when he brought back his game, he waited until his Grandmother had gone out for her basket of corn and followed her. He watched her through a crack between the logs and saw a very strange thing. The storehouse was empty, but his grandmother was leaning over the basket. She rubbed her hands along the sides of her body, and dried corn poured out to fill the basket. Now the boy grew afraid. Perhaps she was a witch! He crept back to the house to wait. When his Grandmother returned, though, she saw the look on his face.

"Grandson," she said, "you followed me to the shed you saw what I did there."

"Yes, Grandmother," the boy answered.

The old woman shook her head sadly. "Now that you know my secret I can no longer live with you. Before the sun rises tomorrow I shall be dead. You must do as I tell you, and you will be able to feed yourself and the people when I have gone."

The old woman looking very weary said. "You cannot help now, Grandson. Simply do as I tell you. When I have died, clear away a patch of ground on the south side of our lodge where the sun shines longest and brightest. Drag my body over the ground seven times and then bury me in that earth. Keep the ground clear. If you do as I say, you shall see me again and you will be able to feed the people."

Before the morning came, Grandmother was dead. Grandson cleaned away the space at the south side of the cabin. He dragged his Grandmother's body, and wherever a drop of blood fell a small plant grew. He kept the ground clear around the plants, and as they grew taller it seemed he could hear his Grandmother's voice whispering in the leaves. Time passed and the plants grew very tall, as tall as a person, and the long tassels at the top of each plant reminded the boy of his grandmother's long hair. At last, ears of corn formed on each plant and his Grandmother's promise had come true. Now, though she had gone from the Earth as she had once been, she would be with the people forever as the corn plant, to feed them.[1]

The Great Peace

Before contact with Europeans, the Iroquois—the members of the League of the Five Nations or Haudenonsauncee—lived in a large stretch of territory in northern New York State more than 180 km wide. But their population of about 16 000 was not as great as either the Huron or the Neutral. The Five Nations from east to west were the Mohawk, Oneida, Onondaga, Cayuga, and Seneca. Each nation maintained its own language, villages, and councils. Their confederacy resulted from the continual fighting among the nations. Although there is no agreement as to when the League was formed, traditional oral history links it with the eclipse of the Sun seen in Iroquoia in 1451.[2]

Dekanawidah and Hiawatha meet with Atotarho, the powerful war chief. It is only when they comb the snakes, representing evil, from Atotarho's hair and encourage everyone to throw down their weapons of war that they succeed in creating the Great Peace.

The League of Haudenosaunee is also known as "the Great Peace." The League was founded by Dekanawidah, "Heavenly Messenger," and his disciple, Hiawatha (but this story has no relationship to Longfellow's poem "Hiawatha" written in 1855). The symbol of the Great Peace is the white pine tree with an eagle hovering above it. Dekanawidah is most often called the Peacemaker by Iroquois people, who usually do not refer to him by name.

The Great Peace was governed by a council of fifty chiefs representing the five Iroquois nations. Although each nation was not equally represented, each group had one vote, and decisions had to be unanimous. The Iroquois Confederacy dealt only with external issues. All internal matters were entirely controlled by the individual nations.

In 1713, the original five nations were joined by the Tuscarora to create the League of the Six Nations, a confederacy that still exists today. The Great Peace of the Haudenosaunee has been accepted across North America by all Aboriginal nations.

The Wendat or Huron

Of all the Iroquoian Peoples, the most is known about the Huron or Wendat because the French spent the most time among them. Subsequently, more written records exist that describe them. The Huron was an alliance or confederacy of four nations similar in structure to the Iroquois League of Five Nations. (Some historians believe that there was a fifth Huron nation as well.) The Huron lived in more than twenty villages clustered around the southern end of Georgian Bay, an area of about 2300 km^2. Each village was surrounded by its own cornfields. It was said that in Huronia, "it was easier to get lost in a corn field than in a forest." The village was the granary for the surrounding northern peoples (Algonkians) with whom the Huron traded corn, beans, squash, tobacco, twine for making fish nets, and pottery. In exchange, the Huron received products of the hunt such as meat, hides, and furs, and superior birchbark canoes. Archaeologists have found Huron pottery as far north as James Bay.

The longhouse was the basic unit of Wendat life. Large sheets of cedar, elm, or ash bark were woven between arched poles to form a long structure with a vaulted roof and rounded end. Longhouses ranged from twenty-five metres to forty-five metres long and six metres to ten metres wide. Fire pits located along the central corridor were shared by two families living across from each another. Raised benches that extended along each side of the house were used for sleeping during the summer. In winter, the cold forced the families to sleep on the floor near the fire. Despite openings in the roof above the fire pits, smoke filled the houses and caused serious eye problems. Although the Hurons no doubt enjoyed the warmth and social interactions of their homes, a Jesuit priest described them as "a miniature of Hell." He complained of noise, lack of privacy, smoke, squabbling dogs and children, the smell of rotting fish and urine, and infestations of fleas, flies, and mice.

Huron Society

Who lived in the longhouse was determined by the women. Huron society was matrilocal and matrilineal. Matrilocal housing required that a man move into the household of his wife. This seems to have been the ideal but was not always the rule. Longhouses, however, were occupied mostly by a group of related adult women, their spouses, and their children. Divorce was frequent and simple. It required only that the husband leave the house to reside elsewhere. This was less common once children were involved. Descent was matrilineal, all children belonging to the clan of their mother. Young men could not inherit their fathers' property or position but looked to their mother's brothers. In his old age, a man counted more on his sisters' children than on his own for support.

Iroquoian society was organized into clans; for example, the Huron recognize eight clans: Turtle,

Major central and eastern trade routes, first half of the seventeenth century

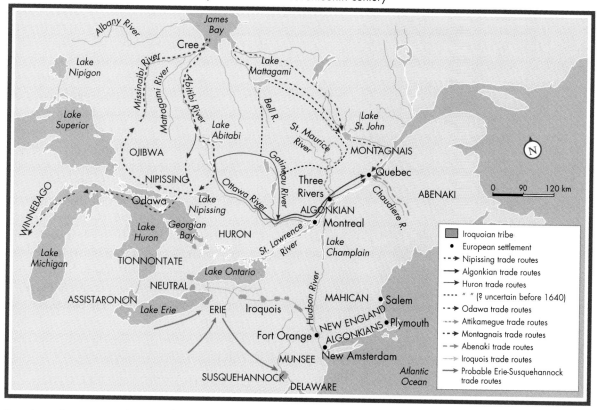

Extensive trade routes existed among Aboriginal groups long before the arrival of Europeans. To what extent do you believe Europeans would have enjoyed the same success in obtaining resources if the these trade routes had not already existed before their arrival?

Wolf, Bear, Beaver, Deer, Hawk, Porcupine, and Snake. Clan members shared longhouses and traced their lineage along the female line. The senior woman in the house was the matriarch (the mother who is the ruler of a family or clan). Several clans usually resided in a village presided over by a council of clan chiefs, peace chiefs (sachems), and wise men.

It might appear from this that politics was male dominated, but in reality, men held their positions based on the ancestry of their mothers. The senior women of the clans also nominated, censured, and even recalled chiefs. Successful warriors, great orators, and men who received recognition could become chiefs, but they could not vote in council or pass their title to their descendants.

Decision making in the council was by consensus, with speeches and persuasion playing major roles. Councils could not force people to obey a decision, but clan and peer pressure usually ensured agreement.

Clans or houses determined who cultivated particular fields and controlled certain trading routes. It was considered a hostile act to travel through someone's land without the head of the clan's permission.

Corn, beans, squash, and pumpkins were the staples of the Huron diet. Corn was dried and pounded into flour in a hollowed-out tree trunk using a long wooden pole. The everyday meal consisted of corn soup (sagamite), with variations created by adding fish, meat, squash, or wild plants, nuts, or

This European illustration depicts Huron women preparing corn. Is this an accurate representation?

berries. Women tended to the crops and the collecting of plants, while the men hunted and fished, with fishing the more important. The consequence of a diet dominated by corn rather than meat was that the Huron, and most Iroquoian Peoples, suffered from a very high rate of tooth decay. Archaeological evidence shows badly worn teeth, numerous cavities, and many missing teeth.

The Demise of the Huron, Neutral, and Petun

Although the French spent less time among the Neutral and the Petun, descriptions of these people and their cultures, along with the substantial archaeological evidence, indicate that they were very similar to the Huron. All three nations, Huron, Neutral, and Petun, were destroyed by a combination of epidemic disease (the 1638–40 smallpox epidemic killed large numbers of Neutral and reduced the Huron population from 30 000 to about 9000) and warfare. In 1648–49, the Iroquois launched a series of devastating attacks on the Huron and Petun that forced them to abandon their villages and flee. Some fled to the Neutral and were either killed or absorbed into that population. The Iroquois adopted many of the women and children to replace their own numbers lost in war. Many Hurons fled west and joined with Algonkian Peoples. These people became known as the Wyandot. A few thousand Huron, with some French Jesuits, retreated in 1650 to Quebec City. Known as the Huron of Lorette, their descendants survive today, although their language is extinct and they are highly acculturated.[3] (Acculturation is the modification of the culture of one group through contact with another group.)

The Algonkian Peoples of the Eastern Woodlands and of the Atlantic

Except for the Iroquoian Peoples living in the Great Lakes area and St. Lawrence River Valley, people who spoke Algonkian languages occupied the area of Canada from the Atlantic Ocean to the Rocky Mountains. The Algonkians are often discussed as two groups: Algonkian Peoples of the Atlantic and Peoples of the northeastern forests and sub-Arctic.

The Mi'kmaq

The most easterly Aboriginal Peoples of Canada (excluding the Beothuk) are the Mi'kmaq, often referred to as the People of the Dawn, the Maliseet, Passamoqoddy, Penobscot, and Abenaki. They shared a common Algonkian language origin and a similar lifestyle that involved a seasonal coastal–inland migration pattern.

Expression of Culture
MI'KMAQ CREATION STORY

In ancient times, the Creator made the first born, the Sun to light the Earth. He also sent a bolt of lightning to create the Earth and from the same bolt he created Kluscap out of the dry earth.

In another bolt of lightning came the animals, vegetation and birds. These life forms gradually gave Kluscap a human form. Kluscap gave thanks to the Creator and honored the six directions: the Sun, the Earth, then the east, south, west and north. The abilities within the human form made up the seventh direction.

Kluscap then asked how he should live. The Creator sent his Grandmother, to guide him in life. Grandmother was created from a rock that was transformed into the body of an old woman through the power of the Sun. Grandmother was an elder whose knowledge and wisdom were embodied in the Mi'kmaq language.

Kluscap then met his nephew, whom Creator had made in his human form from the rolling foam of the ocean that had swept upon the shores and clung to the sweetgrass. Nephew had the understanding of the life and strength of the underwater realms and he brought gifts from the realm to Kluscap, including the ability to see far away.

Finally they met Kluscap's mother, a woman whose power lay in her ability to tell about the cycles of life and the future. She was born from a leaf on a tree, descended from the power and strength of the Sun and made into human form to bring love, wisdom and the colours of the world. She understood how to maintain harmony with the forces of nature.

After living together for a longtime Kluscap told his mother and nephew that he and his Grandmother were leaving to go north. Kluscap told of the Great Council Fire that would send out seven sparks that would land on the ground, each as a man. Then another seven sparks would fly and become seven women. Together they would form seven families and these families would disburse in seven directions and dividing again would become seven different groups.

Like the lightning bolts that created the Earth and Kluscap, the sparks contained many gifts. The sparks gave life to humans and in each human was the prospect of continuity. Like Kluscap, when the people awoke naked and lost, they asked Kluscap how to live. Kluscap taught them their lessons, and that is why he is called "one who is speaking to you" or the Teacher-Creator.[4]

---

1. Describe the close connections to nature that are detailed in this creation story.
2. Why are oral traditions such as this one important to understanding Aboriginal history?

These nations also shared a belief system that appropriately placed the Sun in a prominent role. In the traditional Mi'kmaq creation story, the Great Council Fire, like the Sun itself, gives out sparks that bring life to the human form. The Mi'kmaq believed that all objects possess the spark of life and that every life form should be respected. They taught that all living things have three parts: a form that decays and disappears after death, a spark that travels after death to the land of the souls, and a guardian spirit that aids people during their earth walk.

Politically, Mi'kmaq territory was divided into seven political districts, each governed by a district chief or sagamore. A grand chief presided over the Great Council, which was usually situated on Cape Breton Island. Beneath the district chiefs were local chiefs who headed up a group comprising his extended family bilaterally (meaning family members on both his mother's and father's side), probably some unrelated individuals, and others who allied themselves with the chief.

A district chief not only conferred in council, but also apportioned the hunting territories to families according to family size. Generosity and concern for others were desired qualities in a sagamore. Some chiefs even dressed poorly and gave away their best possessions and furs to their followers as a way to cultivate affection and respect.

A leader could not command his followers to do anything. In the seventeenth century, Father Le Clercq observed

> The most prominent chief is followed by several young warriors and by several hunters, who act as his escort, and who fall in under arms when this ruler wishes particular distinction upon some special occasion. But, in fact, all his power and authority are based only upon the goodwill of those of his nation, who execute his orders just in so far as it pleases them.[5]

Mi'kmaq Society

Everyday work was divided along gender lines. Men spent their time hunting, fishing, participating in war raids, and manufacturing and repairing equipment for these activities. They constructed fish traps and weirs (a fence placed in a stream to catch fish). They made their own bows, arrows, spears, clubs, and all the other wood items, including cradleboards and long-stemmed pipes. They were also responsible for building birchbark canoes and snowshoe frames, although the women corded the snowshoes. Mi'kmaq women transported household goods when moving camp, then set up and maintained the camp. They brought home the kill after the hunt and were responsible for cooking the food and preserving it for winter by smoking or drying it. They also dressed the skins before sewing clothing and moccasins, which they might decorate with porcupine quills. Women collected plants and dug groundnuts for food and medicine. They created household items such as birchbark containers, reed baskets, and woven mats. And, of course, they bore and cared for the children.

At the bottom of Mi'kmaq society were the slaves. It was unusual for a hunting and gathering people to keep slaves, which indicates the relative wealth of the Mi'kmaq people. Slaves were taken during war, though not all captives became slaves. Adult males were usually killed on the field of battle, but sometimes they were allowed to live and taken back to the Mi'kmaq villages. A few were given to women who had lost family members to torture in revenge for their lost ones. Others became assistants to the women around the camp and were forced to do menial chores such as fetching firewood or water. Female and young captives were often adopted into families and treated humanely despite their status as slaves. Slaves who tried to escape and were caught were put to death.[6]

Although the Mi'kmaq were mostly patrilineal, inheriting position and property through the male side of the family, and patrilocal (requiring the wife to take up residence in the husband's home), just as often they were bilateral and bilocal with both sides of the family coming together to live in a common community. This greatly expanded the families and provided more help for fishing, hunting, warfare, and the adoption of orphaned children.

The Mi'kmaq were also different from other Woodland Peoples of the east coast in that they spent more than half the year on the coast and obtained more than 90 percent of their diet from the sea. This early seventeenth-century account by Father Briard, a Jesuit priest, gives us a clear first-hand description of big Mi'kmaq annual cycle:

> In January they have the seal hunting.... In the month of February and until the middle of March, is the great hunt for beavers, otters, bears, (which are very good), and for the caribou.... If the weather is then favorable, they live in great abundance, and are as haughty as Princes and Kings, but if it is against them, they are greatly to be pitied and often die of starvation.... In the middle of March, fish begin to spawn, and to come up from the sea into certain streams, often so abundantly that everything swarms with them.... Among these fish the smelt is the first.... After the smelt comes the herring at the end of April, at the same time bustards [Canada geese],...sturgeon, and salmon, and the great search through the Islets for eggs [of waterfowl].... From the month of May up to the middle of September, they are free from all anxiety about their food; for the cod are upon the coast, and all kinds of fish and shellfish...in the middle of September they withdraw from the sea, beyond the reach of the tide, to the little rivers, where the eels spawn, of which they lay in a supply.... In October and November comes the second hunt for elks [moose] and beavers; and then in December comes a fish called by them ponamo [tomcod], which spawns under the ice.[7]

Not only did the Mi'kmaq have such an intimate knowledge of their environment that they enjoyed a varied and dependable food supply, but also, and equally important, they had developed appropriate technology to exploit the food sources to meet their needs. Their sizable population at the time of contact with Europeans indicates that they prospered. It is estimated that their population could have been as high as 35 000. Tragically, the effect of European diseases, warfare encouraged by competition to trade with the Europeans, and the change to a less healthy diet, including the introduction of alcohol, saw their population reduced to about three thousand people within a few generations of European contact.[8]

Peoples of the Forests and Sub-Arctic

Although known to history by a wide array of names, the Northeastern Woodlands Peoples can be grouped into two language groups, Cree and Ojibwa (Anishinabe). Among the group speaking an Ojibwa dialect are the Saulteaux, Ottawa (Odawa), Nipissing, Mississauga, and Algonkin (Algonquin). Cree dialects are spoken across northern Canada, from Labrador to the Prairies, including by the Montagnais and Naskapi (known collectively as the Innu, which means "person").

Note that Algonkian refers to the language family (the largest in Canada), while Algonkin refers to a specific Aboriginal group, mirroring the use of the names Iroquoian and Iroquois.

It was from the Algonkian Peoples that Europeans learned how to travel in the snow-covered land using the toboggan and snowshoes. Two other contributions of the Woodland Peoples to Canadian culture and identity are maple syrup and sugar.

The eastern woodlands of Canada were rich with both deciduous and coniferous trees and provided a wide range of animals to hunt, including deer, moose, bear, rabbit, beaver, otter, muskrat, fox, wolf, raccoon, skunk, bobcat, and numerous types of birds, geese, and ducks. These animals were hunted with bows and arrows and spears, caught in traps and roundups, or killed in dead falls. Edible fruits, nuts, roots, and wild rice (mostly by the Ojibwa) were harvested. The southern most Woodland Peoples, such as the Odawa, also may have cultivated squash, beans, and corn.

Web Connection

www.mcgrawhill.ca/links/definingcanada
Go to the Web site above to reach the Mi'kmaq online Talking Dictionary and hear the Mi'kmaq language.

This nineteenth-century illustration shows the Ojibwa method of harvesting wild rice (really not a rice but a cereal grass). Their cultivation of wild rice was an early form of farming.

The woodland way of life was based on an annual round of hunting, fishing, and plant collecting. In spring, families returned from their hunting camps and congregated at major fishing sites, where up to two thousand individuals might come together in family groups. Great quantities of fish were netted and speared. Bone fishhooks have been found on Algonkian archaeological sites.

Trade also played an important role in the Algonkian economy. The Jesuit priest Lalemant described their trading patterns this way in 1614:

> They seem to have as many abodes as the year has seasons—in the spring a part of them remain for fishing, where they consider it the best; a part go away to trade with the tribes which gather on the shore of the North or icy sea.... In summer they all gather together...on the border of a large lake that bears their name.... About the middle of autumn, they begin to approach our Hurons, upon whose land they generally spend the winter; but, before reaching them, they catch as many fish as possible, which they dry. This is the ordinary money with which they buy their main stock of corn, although they come supplied with all other goods.... They cultivate a little land near their summer dwellings; but it is more for pleasure, and that they may have fresh food to eat, then for their support.[9]

This highly mobile way of life did not permit many or heavy possessions. Even clay pots were rare, with birch-bark vessels more popular for cooking. Meat and fish were boiled in the bark container with rice or corn and sweetened with berries or maple sugar. Hot stones were taken

The dome house was most common, although the tepee-style home was cooler for the summer, allowing the warm air to rise.

directly from the fire and dropped into the birch–bark vessel until the food was cooked.

Possessions were transported by canoe during the spring, summer, and fall and pulled on a toboggan when snow covered the ground and the waterways froze. Birchbark canoes were ideal: They were tough, lightweight, and easily repaired with spruce or pine gum. In winter, they cached (hid) the canoes, recovering them in the spring.

Housing was easily constructed of readily available resources. The most common house was a dome-shaped structure known by the Algonkian term *wigwam*. Saplings were driven into the ground in a circle then bent over and tied at the top. Sheets of birchbark covered the structure. In winter, moss was added between the layers of birchbark for insulation.

The Cree occupied not only the most-northern areas of the eastern woodlands, but also parts of the sub-Arctic and even the western plains. Although they spoke a single language throughout this large area, they used at least nine major dialects.

Living in an environment that was not bountiful and where winter conditions were very harsh meant that the Cree had to live in small social groups that were constantly on the move. Winter starvation was real and the spectre of the Windigo (a terrifying legendary giant with an insatiable hunger for human flesh) was never far from camp.

The Innu occupied the eastern woodlands and sub-Arctic of present-day Quebec and Labrador. They lived a lifestyle very similar to the Crees', except for Innu who lived near the coast, where seal hunting and eel fishing provided different food sources. The southern-most Innu traded moose hides for corn and tobacco with Iroquoian Peoples.

Today, the Cree and Ojibwa have the largest Aboriginal populations in Canada at 137 680 and

This painting is an example of the now familiar Woodland style originated by Norval Morrisseau, an Ojibwa from the Lake Nipigon area. He was inspired by Algonkian legends and images found in rock paintings and birchbark scrolls. Norval Morrisseau, *The Shaman and his Disciples* (1979).

94 350, respectively.[10] The Mi'kmaq, at 16 965, and Innu, at 10 530, are also among the largest Aboriginal nations in the country. Their languages are also healthy, and despite centuries of contact and pressures to assimilate, their cultures have survived, changing very little.

This photograph of Blackfoot warriors is far more realistic and typical of a plains man after 1730.

Review...Reflect...Respond

1. Who are the Iroquoian Peoples, the Algonkian Peoples of the eastern woodlands, and the peoples of the forests and subartic?

2. What types of social, cultural, or economic similarities do you see among these various Aboriginal groups?

3. The introduction to this chapter states, "Their societies were not static and they should not be seen as sterotypes." What is meant by this statement?

 **Web Connection**

www.mcgrawhill.ca/links/definingcanada

Go to the Web site above to read legends of the Blackfoot and Peigan tribes.

People of the Plains: 1000 BCE–1730 CE

The stereotypical image of the North American Aboriginal is a mounted warrior astride his horse in a full war headdress of eagle feathers. Of course, this is a very unrealistic picture not only because the Plains Peoples were only one minority group of a very diverse Aboriginal population, but also because it represents only a short period in a long history; the first modern horse did not appear on the Canadian Prairies until the 1730s. It then gradually spread in number and use from the south to

the north over the next hundred years. The war headdress, so ubiquitous now as a representation of North American Aboriginal Peoples for tourists, was worn for ceremonial gatherings and only by recognized and influential chiefs.

Life on the Canadian plains centred on a single species of animal—the bison. Archaeologist J.N. McDonald believes that the bison reached their maximum number and range around 1000 BCE.[11] This is also around the same time that Ojibwa and Cree people from the eastern woodlands, and the Sarcee from the north, began to move onto the plains. They were attracted probably by this abundant and more reliable food source. They soon adopted much of what we think of as plains culture: a cycle of mobility based on the migration patterns of the bison herds. The Cree and Ojibwa did, however, keep certain aspects of their woodland culture. Archaeological evidence reveals that unlike the Blackfoot, Blood, Peigan, and Gros Ventre, who also spoke

Algonkian and who are considered to be the earlier inhabitants of the plains, the Ojibwa and Cree made and used pottery. They also fished. It is said that the Blackfoot Peoples did not even consider fish a food.

The Assiniboine and Sioux, who spoke a Siouian language, also moved onto the Canadian Prairies, but this time from the south. Undoubtedly, these movements created pressures on the land and its resources and were a cause of conflict. We do know that the Assiniboine and Sioux were the sworn enemies of all the Peoples of the Blackfoot Confederacy.

The Blackfoot Confederacy or alliance consisted of three tribes: the Siksika or Blackfoot; the Kainai, meaning many chiefs, or Blood; and the Peigan, or Pikuni, meaning "scabby robes." Also allied to this Blackfoot Confederacy were the Sarcee and Gros Ventre. (These latter two separated and became enemies of the Blackfoot in a dispute over stolen horses in 1861.)

As is too often the case, the names that we know Aboriginal groups by are not the names they call themselves, but rather the names recorded by the European explorers who made first contact. Often these names were created by their Aboriginal enemies or by the mistaken ideas or impressions of the non-Aboriginal people. This was the case with the Blackfoot Confederacy. It just happened that one of the early explorers first contacted a Siksika and then applied the name Blackfoot to all the members of that alliance. In fact, the Blood and Peigan were more numerous than the Blackfoot. It is estimated that the total number of Plains Peoples was about 35 000 before significant European contact. The three tribes of the Blackfoot nation composed the largest population at 15 000, while the Sarcee numbered only about 700 people.

Another stereotypical image of the plains nations is of a people continually at war. Even the historian Hugh Dempsey described the Blackfoot, after they acquired the horse, as being in "an

The Plains culture area

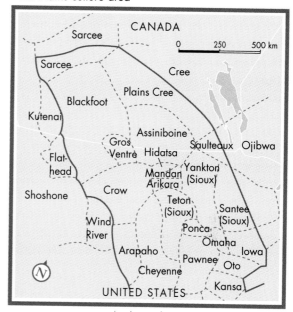

Why would contact with Europeans bring about large-scale warfare among the peoples of the Plains area?

almost continuous state of warfare"[12] in an effort to obtain horses. The Blackfoot launched raiding parties to steal horses from the Crow, Shoshone, and Nez Perce to the south. The Blackfoot were in turn raided by the Cree, Ojibwa, and Assiniboine for their horses and for control of the best hunting grounds.

The reality before and after the introduction of the horse was that raiding parties traditionally involved young men between thirteen and twenty years of age and were carried out as much for the excitement as for the rewards. Older men were generally content to hunt and breed horses. If, however, lives were lost, or a war party fell upon a helpless camp and killed people, or negotiations could not remove trespassers from a favourite hunting site, then more serious warfare involving two- or three-hundred men took place. Larger scale warfare was, however, infrequent before contact with non-Aboriginals.

Food on the Plains

Bison provided the bulk of the calories and many essentials of their way of life for Plains Peoples, but archaeological evidence shows that the they ate a range of animals and vegetation. Pronghorn, white-tail, and mule deer, elk, sheep, mountain goat, beaver, small game, roots, and berries were consumed. The choice and amount, varied depending on the location in which they hunted and the cultural background of the people. Ojibwa and Cree also ate fish. Dried berries, wild parsley, and tubers such as bitterroot were major sources of essential vitamins.

Hunting large game animals, such as bison, presented its own challenges, even if game was plentiful. The problem was how to preserve the meat. Plains Peoples preserved bison by producing pemmican. They made pemmican by drying the bison meat, pounding it into a powder, and then mixing it with rendered fat and bone marrow. It was packed into large bison bladder sacks for transportation and storage. It took two cows or a large bull to produce about forty kilograms of pemmican. A kilogram of pemmican was equal to eight kilograms to twelve kilograms of fresh meat and lasted indefinitely if berries were not added.

Pemmican was the major protein and calorie source after unsuccessful hunts and throughout most of the winter—not only for humans, but also for dogs. Dogs, for thousands of years before the arrival of the horse, were used to transport equipment for these highly mobile Plains Peoples. Even a small tepee required eight to twelve long poles and a minimum of ten hides for the cover and another eight for an interior liner. This alone could weigh

The Many Uses of the Buffalo

Skin (hides): clothing, bags and cases for carrying and storing, horseshoes, knife sheaths, drums, saddles, bridles, bedding, tipi covers, saddlebags

Sinew: threads, strings for hunting bows, games

Hair: plaited into halters, stuffing for saddle pad

Tail: brush to kill flies and mosquitoes

Stomach: cooking pot; water bucket

Hoofs: boiled for glue, rattles

Bladder: food bag

Dung/chips: fuel

Bones: saddle horns, implements for dressing skins, needles, games

Meat: food (heart, liver, kidneys and tongue were also eaten)

Ribs: arrow shafts

Shinbone: knives, fleshing tools for scraping hides

Shoulderblade: digging tool, hammer

Skull: painted and used in religious ceremonies

Bone marrow: fat, fuel for fires

Bone-ends: paint brushes

Hide from neck: warrior shields

Horn: spoons, drinking cups, ladles

Brains: for tanning skins

Teeth: necklaces

Beard: decorating a hunting bow

more than 130 kg. It is estimated that it took twenty to thirty dogs to move a single household, including stored pemmican stocks. Because dogs could only drag this heavy load about fifteen kilometres a day, the migration of Plains Peoples was very slow. Dogs were also a readily available food supply and were occasionally served for ceremonial purposes. Such practices were balanced, however, against the dogs' primary use as a cartage animal.

Reliance on the bison created a regulated settlement pattern for the Plains Peoples. Winter was relatively sedentary as they sought protection from the winds and winter storms in forested river valleys, foothills, and parklands. Here, where the bison also took shelter, men would hunt individually and communally. In spring, the Plains Peoples moved to the valley edges for the sunlight and to be mobile and ready to move with the bison onto the plains. Summer was the most mobile time of the year, as the bison gathered into large herds. The Plains Peoples would also come together during the midsummer for larger-scale hunting at jumps or entrapments (also known as pounds). It was also during the summer months that ceremonial gatherings such as the Sun Dance took place.

Major communal bison drives would occur during late fall, before the shift back to winter quarters.

Generally, people travelled in small, related groups, with bands coming together as tribes or a nation during summer celebrations. The opposite was true during a hard winter, when they would break up into ever smaller family groups to survive.

Housing on the Plains

The tepee, which comes from the Siouian language, *te* for "dwelling" and *pee* for "used for," was an ideal form of housing for the mobile lifestyle of Plains Peoples. Women made and owned the tepees. They also erected them—something an experienced woman could do in a matter of minutes with little assistance.

An early innovation in tepee design, noted by archaeologists and based on telltale rings of stones used to hold down the edges of the tepee covers, was the development of a tilted conical form. With this innovation, the rear slope is steeper than the front. As a result, the floor plan of the tepee is egg-shaped rather than circular. This tilted form permitted the smoke hole to be located beneath the crossing

Artist Paul Kane sketched a Cree buffalo pound near Fort Carleton in 1846, which was the inspiration for this romanticized studio view painted between 1848 and 1853.

The use of the tepee was not universal on the plains and was used mostly in the southwest. The Sarcee, Ojibwa, and Cree kept their traditional wigwam-style home if supplies of wood and bark were available. Notice that all the entrances face east to the rising sun and away from the prevailing westerly winds.

point of the poles, instead of at the centre point, making it possible to vary the size of the hole or close it entirely. A second innovation was the addition of two flaps that flanked the smoke hole and were supported by external poles. By moving these poles, the occupants could regulate the draft to improve ventilation and carry off smoke.

Plains Culture

Spiritual ideas and practices permeated all aspects of daily life. A woman beginning her quillwork said a prayer; an old man waking in the morning sang a prayer of thanks; before eating, a person placed a small morsel of food in the ground for the spirits. Spirits, some good and some bad, inhabited the entire universe. A strangely twisted tree or an unusual rock formation was considered the manifestation of a spiritual power, and a passer-by would leave an offering for good luck. Dreams and visions were also very important. An individual hoping to know his or her future or seeking

personal advantage went to a lonely spot where he or she would fast and pray until a spiritual guardian appeared in a dream (vision quest).

The most significant ceremonial occasion was the Sun Dance, which took place during midsummer when bands and nations congregated at predetermined locations. An individual traditionally arranged the ceremony either as a request for supernatural aid or in response to a vision. Among the Blackfoot and Sarcee, women took the initiative. The Sun Dance took place over eight days, with four days of preliminary ritual and another four days that focused on erecting a sacred dance pole in a sacred lodge. On the final day, several dances took place. The Sun-Gaze Dances symbolized capture, torture, captivity, and escape and the dances often involved self-torture. Dancers frequently enjoyed prestige because of their participation in the Sun-Gaze Dance. The Sun Dance was an emotional experience and an opportunity to renew kinship ties, arrange marriages, and exchange property.

Web Connection

www.mcgrawhill.ca/links/definingcanada

Go to the Web site above to learn more about games of the Plains Cree peoples.

The culture of the Plains Peoples underwent a very dramatic change with the introduction of the horse after 1730. In many ways, horses made them more prosperous as they became more efficient at hunting bison. They also led to more conflict as nations fought over horses and territory. But horses were only a prelude to the greater changes that the arrival of Europeans would bring.

Plateau Peoples: 1000 BCE to European Contact

Between the Rocky Mountains and the Coastal Ranges is a series of extended plateaus and interconnected river valleys with diverse environments, from sagebrush deserts in the south to sub-boreal spruce forests in the north. In this interior lived six principle nations of Aboriginal Peoples from four different language groups.

In the central and southern region where the rivers rush and lakes are plentiful were the Salish-speaking Peoples. They had lived in this land for thousands of years. The Salish included the Lillooet, Thompson, Shuswap (or as they prefer, the Secwepemc), Okanagan, and Lake First Nations. On the northern plateau were four different nations who spoke Athapaskan languages: Chilcotin, Carrier, Tahltan, and Nicola. These Peoples represented a southern expansion into the plateau from the north and were linked in language and culture to their neighbours of the sub-Arctic. Archaeologists now believe that the Athapaskans migrated to the plateau about one thousand years ago. Another distinctive group that lived in the northeast was the Taglish, who spoke the Tlingit language. In the southeast are the Kutenai, the most recent people to occupy the plateau. They were driven westward into the Rocky Mountains around 1750 by the Blackfoot. They are an isolated group that has its own Kutenai language, unrelated to any of the other languages found in Canada. The Kutenai, consequently, do not fit most of the cultural patterns of the people of the plateau. They retained much of their plains culture, including using horses, living in tepee-style houses, and preferring to hunt buffalo rather than to fish for salmon.

Although the Plateau Peoples show a high degree of cultural diversity, they have some major similarities, especially among the largest single language group, the Salish-speaking Peoples, who occupied the headwaters of the major rivers: the Fraser, Columbia, Skeena, and Thompson. Here in the central and southern river valleys, the abundance of salmon was the greatest single influence on their lifestyle. The Salish people developed a migratory pattern to their lives based on the salmon runs and their ability to catch and store salmon for the winter.

The Plateau Culture Area

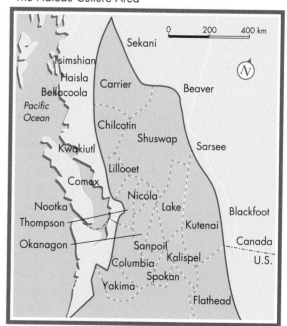

How would the introduction of horses to the Plains Peoples change the way nations interacted with each other?

Pit Houses

One unique characteristic of most plateau people was their relatively permanent winter village, comprising as many as one hundred substantial pit houses and often more than a thousand people. Families from the same band returned year after year to occupy the same houses. Some of the oldest pit houses date back 3500 years and, it is believed that many were used for more than one thousand years.

Ethnologists believe that the prototype for semi-subterranean dwellings of this type originated in northeastern Asia. They contend that it was transferred to North America during migrations across the Bering Strait, after which this type of housing gradually diffused throughout the continent, appearing in the Arctic with the whalebone house of Thule Peoples and on the plateau as the pit house. The pit house is regarded as North America's oldest house type. It was widely used throughout the plateau region until it disappeared in the late nineteenth century. Archaeologist Knute Fladmark describes a rather comfortable life in the winter pit house:

> Imagine entering such a house through the smoke hole, picture the glow of firelight, and feel the warm smoky air; on one side of the central hearth you will see the sleeping area with comfortable beds of pine boughs and furs, and on the other a place of work and play for the women and children, while scattered around the earthen walls are baskets and bags of food and other supplies. On sunny days the people sit outside on the sloping roofs, repairing equipment and chatting with their neighbours, while at night and in times of danger the heavy logs and earth-cover offer warmth and security.[13]

The Plateau Peoples lived primarily on stored foods, supplemented by fresh deer, caribou, and other game from hunting. The Plateau Peoples were known to ice fish during the winter as well. After the comfort and company of winter, families left their pit houses to face the lean times of spring, when resources were at their lowest

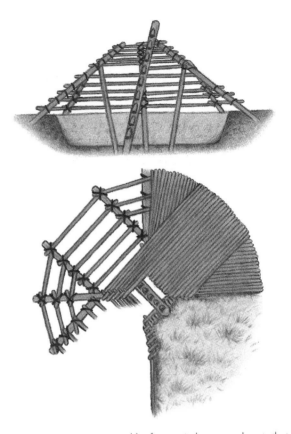

This pit house is supported by four main beams and posts that are placed over a circular pit eight metres to ten metres in diameter. Note the notched log ladder that comes through the smoke hole at the top.

point. At this time of year, any source of food was welcomed. In small family groups, they hunted for large game such as deer, caribou, and bears, as well as small game such as rabbits and beaver. The men fished for suckers and trout, while the women dug for edible roots and bulbs, balsamroot and bitterroot, which were roasted in pit ovens. Plateau Peoples also searched for the fresh green shoots of fireweed and cow parsnips. If they were hard pressed, they could sustain themselves on black lichen that was pressed into cakes and roasted. Even the sugar-rich inner rind of the jack pine could be made edible at this time of year.

Plateau Society

Throughout the spring, summer, and early fall, housing was temporary and simply consisted of a framework of poles covered with mats or bark. Families moved frequently to find sufficient food until the salmon runs began in late summer. Small groups met at favourite sites to work and socialize. Every opportunity was taken to participate in social and ceremonial activities. They visited, played games, told stories. Young men and women met, and marriages took place. These social interactions built family connections and relationships. Archaeologist James Wright argues that the reason for the Plateau Peoples' congregating in winter communities was more because of the complex interplay of social, economic, and technological factors than any single factor like improvements in food storage.[14] Trading also took place as the people of the plateau met people from the west coast and sometimes people from the plains.

Sweating in small lodges heated with hot rocks was a common practice on the Canadian Plateau. People used the sweat lodge to purify themselves before feasts and religious ceremonies. In the larger ceremonial houses, where an influential person or shaman might live, many people would gather to hear stories about the Old One or Coyote, the trickster. The Secwepemc believed that the Old One was all-powerful and had made the world a good place to live. They believed that the Old One sent transformer figures, animal people, to prepare the land for the Secwepemc. The most famous transformer was Coyote. He had a foolish nature but was also cunning and used his magic powers to teach people many lessons. Coyote made the world safe for the Secwepemc by transforming the people-killing monsters. Old One often had to finish Coyote's work, which tended to be incomplete. Eventually Coyote was transformed into the coyote rocks that can still be seen throughout the plateau. The Secwepemc believed that everything in the world had a spirit and a purpose and must be respected.

Secwepemc were known to raid the Chilcotin and the Lillooet for slaves and dried salmon. The reasons for these attacks are the same as they are anywhere in the world: plunder, adventure, revenge, and holding on to land or expanding territory. Although slave taking and even trading for slaves occurred, slaves were eventually absorbed into the community and their children were not considered slaves.

For the most part, peaceful relationships prevailed both for social and for trade purposes. Dried salmon, preserved roots, and berries were common trade items. Rocks, such as nephrite, argillite, and chert, which could be chipped or polished to make knives, scrappers, and points, were also traded for animal skins. Bison robes that originated with the Kutenai and other plains people were a highly sought after trade good.

Not all the Athapaskan-speaking Peoples had access to salmon; for example, the Chilcotin and some Carrier bands did not. Out of necessity, they lived an even more migratory lifestyle, hunting, fishing, digging for roots, and collecting berries throughout the year. They also relied on the Secwepemc and Bella Coola to trade with them for additional food supplies. Some of these more northerly people adopted smaller pit houses (usually for only one family), while others retained more typically sub-Arctic winter houses of logs or poles roofed with bark. Chilcotin women wove beautiful split-root coiled baskets that were traded to the Bella Coola of the west coast for valuable dentalium (spiral-shaped mollusc shells), abalone shells, eulachon oil, and dried salmon. The tubular dentalium shells were commonly worn as nose and ear ornaments, often with tufts of redheaded woodpecker feathers. Archaeologists are confident that the marine shells from the Pacific coast must have passed through the hands of the plateau people to turn up in the hands of plains people.

Late summer and early fall were the most important time of the year for all Aboriginal Peoples of the plateau. Extended families came together along the major rivers to trap and process salmon for the long winter months. Kinship ties were very important, as access to the most productive salmon-fishing stations was controlled by individuals or families. This was especially true for all the Salish-speaking Peoples who lived along the Fraser River. Groups such as the Lillooet kept the best fishing sites open to community members only, while the least productive fishing sites were open to anyone.

The berry grounds, in the case of the Secwepemc, were open to all but were strictly controlled by a hereditary band chief. Harvesting could proceed only when the chief indicated the berries were sufficiently ripe. Special eagle cliffs and most deer fences, used in the hunting of deer, were owned by individuals and were inherited by the closest kin.

To survive the winter, the Plateau Peoples had to catch as many salmon as possible. A favourite fishing technique was to place a large trap at the bottom of the falls so that those salmon that failed to clear the falls dropped back into the trap and could be scooped up with a dip net. All along the rivers the salmon were netted, trapped, and speared. In 1847, artist Paul Kane described a fishery:

> The salmon...continue to arrive in almost incredible numbers for nearly two months; in fact, there is one continuous body of them, more resembling a flock of birds than anything else in their extraordinary leap up the falls.... The chief told me that he had taken as many as 1700 salmon, weighing on an average 30 lbs. each, in the course of one day. Probably the daily average taken in the chief's basket is about 400. The chief distributes the fish thus taken during the season amongst his people, everyone, even to the smallest child, getting an equal share.[15]

Although fishing was primarily a male activity, women were very busy during the salmon runs. Most of a large catch was preserved for later. The fish were cut into filets, roasted, dried, and pounded into a course powder for the making of salmon pemmican. With an ample supply of stored food,

This Chilcotin coiled spruce-root basket has designs with cherry bark and grass.

and weary from their intensive labours, families again congregated at their winter villages to prepare their pit houses for another winter.

European Contact

For the peoples of the plateau, as was the case for all Aboriginal Peoples of Canada, contact with Europeans rapidly changed their lives. Explorers, acting as agents of the trading companies, made the first contact with Canada's Aboriginal people. In the case of the plateau, that person was Alexander Mackenzie, who, in 1793, passed through the interior of what was to become British Columbia. The impact was almost immediate, as noted by Simon Fraser, who, only fifteen years later in 1808, observed that the Salish had acquired copper kettles and one very large gun—but on a more serious note, he saw that several people were already suffering from smallpox.[16]

This illustrates a range of fishing equipment. The small bone splinters sharpened at both ends armed a range of specialized gear including the herring rake, spears, and hooks. Both Plateau and Coastal Peoples used variations on this technology.

It was the Cariboo Gold Rush of 1858 that brought intensive contact and disruption to the Aboriginal Peoples' way of life. The Aboriginal Peoples found that the Europeans no longer needed their services and assistance—they only wanted their land. Particularly devastating was the smallpox epidemic of 1862–63, which killed one third of the Aboriginal population of British Columbia. One group of people, the Nicola, disappeared altogether.[17]

Aboriginal Peoples of the West Coast: 1000 BCE to Contact

The Aboriginal Peoples who lived on Canada's Pacific coast possessed one of the richest natural environments in North America, if not the world. Before contact with Europeans, this rich environment supported the largest concentration of people anywhere in Canada; estimates range from 60 000 to 200 000 people.[18] These West Coast Peoples shared many elements of material culture and

social organization. Established trade networks throughout the coastal region and into the surrounding mountains allowed for an easy exchange of prized materials, manufactured goods, and important food commodities, while intermarriage between groups served to transfer social and ceremonial practices. Despite many shared cultural features, at least seven major groups are evident in six distinct language families in the west coast region: Tlingit, Tsimshian (including Nisga'a and Gitsan), Haida, Nuxalk (Bella Coola), Kwakawa ka'wakw (formerly known as Kwakiutl), Nuu-chah-nuth (Nootka), and Salish.

It was only about 1500 years ago that the Aboriginal cultures of Canada's Pacific coast became identifiable as distinct ethnocultural groups similar to the nations we know today. Archaeologists, using their evidence and working with ethnographers, anthropologists, and historians, have identified three geographic groupings of peoples based on shared cultural features. The Northern group included the Haida, Tlingit, and

The Northwest Coast

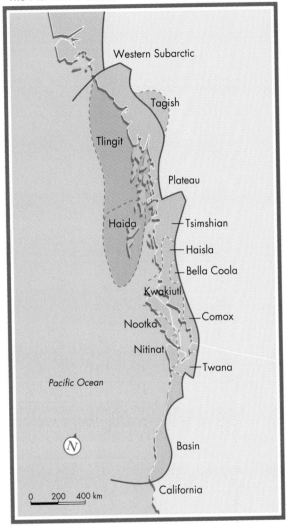

Western Subarctic

Tagish

Tlingit

Plateau

Haida

Tsimshian

Haisla

Bella Coola

Kwakiutl

Comox

Nootka

Nitinat

Twana

Pacific Ocean

Basin

California

N

0   200   400 km

Why would the European concept of "nation" not be applicable to Aboriginal Peoples, such as those on the West Coast?

The Wakahans of the central coastal area included the Bella Coola, Kwakawa ka'wakw (who had three sublanguage groups), and Nuu-chah-nuth (they can also be subdivided into three closely related language groups). All three groups were first identified erroneously with names that they have largely rejected in recent times. In most cases, their languages did not have a word for classifying or identifying a large social group—what we would call a nation. In precontact times, each small community within a larger socially related group had their own name to identify themselves. European explorers, such as James Cook, who thought in terms of nation-states, tried to apply this same concept to the Aboriginal people they met. The name Nootka, for example, is the term Cook, in 1778, applied collectively to all of the Nuu-chah-nuth, which roughly means "all along the mountains." The Wakashans were different from the Northern Peoples in that they inherited through the mother or father's side but most often through the father's side. The Nuu-chah-nuth, who lived on the rugged west coast of Vancouver Island, were the most maritime of all the Pacific Coast Peoples. They often fished the ocean for halibut and hunted whales.

The most southern grouping of Pacific Coast Peoples was the Coast Salish. They spoke six distinct Salishan languages. Although most of the Coast Salish had typical west coast economies based on the sea, one group, the Stalo, lived on the lower Fraser River and did not have access to the sea. The Fraser provided them with an abundance of salmon, eulachon, sturgeon, which could be taken anytime of the year, and waterfowl. The Salish Peoples also differed socially in that they had a more flexible social class system. Although people could not be born into higher status, they did allow for upward mobility for talented individuals. Households were the largest political groups, and even winter villages were only clusters of households without a collective system of governance. There were few slaves in Salish villages.

Tsimshian. Although each people had their own language, they did share a similar lifestyle and achieved the most elaborate material culture and sophisticated art on Canada's west coast. They were also the most feared warriors and slave raiders. They maintained a rigid class system based on inheritance of position and property through the female side of the family (matrilineal).

The Importance of Red Cedar

The wealth of resources from the sea and land gave all the Aboriginal Peoples of the west coast a material culture that included large plank houses, magnificent totem poles, spectacularly colourful masks, ocean-going canoes carved from giant logs, and beautifully crafted watertight wooden boxes. Each group or nation's ability to produce their own unique versions of these items reflected their understanding of the environment and its potential to not only feed, house, and clothe them, but also to permit the development of complex social structures. Archaeologists have dated this blossoming of Pacific coast cultural development at approximately three thousand years ago or 1000 BCE.

The cedar tree dominated the material culture of West Coast Peoples and accordingly had special status in their mythology. Here is a Haida oral account of how the cedar trees were made:

> Tetl, the benefactor of mankind, wanted to create different people for every part of the earth. For this reason he traveled constantly, usually flying as a bird. During one of his flights over the West Coast he discovered several islands just off the mainland and decided to investigate. Here Tetl found rugged coasts hidden behind the spray of huge waves, snow-capped mountains, lush green valleys, and rivers whose ice-cold waters teemed with fish.
>
> The seasons were kind to the land and filled trees with blooms and shrubs with berries. The singing of birds was everywhere. The forests were thick with trees of all kinds. The under growth was heavy with flowers, tall ferns, moss and lichen.
>
> While Tetl feasted on berries dipped in wild honey, he watched salmon jump over rapids and thought that this would be the right place for a special race of people. He created tall, muscular people with deep-red skin and rugged stamina. He gave them the name Haida and they lived peacefully for a long time. It seemed, however, that they found the islands confining and became quarrelsome. Tetl intervened to warn them that they would not have his blessings unless they remained peaceful. Greed, bad thoughts and mean deeds led them soon to forget Tetl's warnings and again they fought each other.
>
> At the height of their fight, darkness came over the islands, and when eventually light returned, all the people had been transformed into huge cedar trees.
>
> Later a new race of people was created. They were of normal size and carried peace in their hearts. As instructed by Tetl, they used cedar trees to build their homes and carve canoes and totem poles. From the bark and the roots they made baskets, mats and clothing. They were very grateful to Tetl for the cedar trees that provided them with many of their daily needs.[19]

Red cedar was paramount to the technology, lifestyle, culture, and art of the Pacific Coast

These Nootka women are wearing woven cedar clothing and carrying open-weave baskets used for collecting shellfish.

Peoples. Cedar was lightweight, strong, and rot resistant. Skilled woodworkers using tools of stone, bone, and shell could also easily shape it. The long, straight grain allowed large planks to be split from cedar logs. Bark and roots of the red cedar provided material for weavers to make beautiful, even watertight, baskets, mats, and clothing. The slender flexible branches of the cedar were also split and twisted to make rope.

Cedar homes were maintained at both summer and winter villages. All of the west coast Aboriginal Peoples built variations of plank houses, with the greatest technical refinement found in the harsher environment of the northern coast, in the Haida and Tsimshian homes. The houses were typically 12 m², smaller and more tightly fitted than those of their neighbours to the south. Built around a framework of massive cedar posts and six main beams, the houses were covered with large planks that could be removed and carried, cantilevered style, by canoe from their summer homes to the more sheltered locations of their winter villages. Another characteristic of Haida and Tsimshian houses was boldly carved house posts and frontal crest columns (totem poles) that incorporated an oval doorway in the gaping mouth of the lowest figure. House frontal columns proclaimed the rank and heritage of the inhabitants. Frontal poles also symbolized position and privileges. Among the Kwakawa ka'wakw, for example, a tall, slender pole topped by a bird figure signified the house of the beach owner. This position belonged only to the chief who had the right to be the first to invite important visitors to a feast. These symbols of rank were extremely important elements of a society where everyone, except for slaves, fit into a precise social order from top to bottom.

Cedar was also the medium of all "totem poles" the best known of the artistic achievements of the west coast woodcarvers. These colourful, beautifully crafted poles, whether freestanding or incorporated into the front of the house, told of the family tree of important people. Powerful chiefs hired reputable artists to carve family crests for all to see. And as wealthy patrons, they commissioned carvers to produce elaborate wooden masks, rattles, and feast dishes for special ceremonies, especially for potlatches.

Another outstanding accomplishment of Pacific coast woodworkers was the ocean-going dugout canoe. Pacific Coast Peoples travelled almost exclusively by water, using dugout canoes of red cedar. Carved figures projecting from the bow and stern not only prevented waves from swamping the craft, but also told who owned the canoe. Canoes varied in size and function from small one- or two-person crafts to vessels sixteen metres long by two metres wide, which could hold forty people and two tonnes of cargo. These sturdy vessels carried Nuu-chah-nuth hunters out into the Pacific in search of whales. For the Salish, the appearance of Haida war canoes on the horizon struck terror into their hearts.

Arguably, the finest example of precision artisanship with wood was the bentwood box. This piece of ingenuity and technology enabled the west coast people to produce containers that served all the roles pottery played for most Aboriginal Peoples of North America. Pacific coast people did not have clay or the ability to make clay pots—they simply did not need them. The bentwood box was formed from a single piece of cedar, cut partly through where the sides and corners were to be and then steamed until the wood could be bent at ninety-degree angles. The fourth side was pegged or sewn with a root cord. A fitted lid completed the box. Most were watertight and could be used as water buckets, for cooking by filling them with water and plunging in hot rocks until the water boiled, or simply for storage of food or other possessions. Some of the most beautifully decorated boxes were used by high-ranking people to store their ceremonial regalia.

This Tsimshian chest has been carved with a beaver design.

The Potlatch

The most important celebration for the West Coast Peoples was the potlatch, which may be derived from the Nuu-chah-nuth word *pachite* meaning "to give." Archaeologist Knute Fladmark wrote this potlatch scenario based on archaeological sites and artifacts, dated from about 3500 to 1500 years ago, and fleshed out from historical records.

From the inlet the village seemed a low buttress of the overhanging mountains, the drifting smoke from its fires mottling the dark green of the forest. The big canoe lifted and surged with the rhythmic strokes of the straining paddlers, while on each side other craft paced them toward the shore. From the village there drifted a resonant beat of wooden drums and the echo of voices chanting a song of welcome as the visitors came into view. In the bow of his burnished black canoe, the red painted serpents coiling along its gunwales, the great chief Niskanna of the island people stood supported by two slaves as he prepared to greet his mainland hosts. In his right hand he held his famous carved killer whale atlatl, inlaid with flashing eyes of abalone shell. To his sweating crew the tall figure in the glistening sea-otter robe signified all the power and wealth of their ancient lineage. How these lowly mainlanders would tremble in his presence!

Inside the great house, orange flames glinted on the finery of the assembled noblemen, as masked spirits danced in and out of the shadows to the eerie wail of flutes and whistles. At the back of the vast plank structure, on a carved and painted throne, sat the body of Quets, the late chief of the town, flanked on either side by members of his household. Around the dead chief's neck hung thick garlands of stone disc-beads; in his ears two precious green stone discs inset with shell shone like the sun and the moon, and at his feet there stood a stone statue of Tias, the salmon chief, in whose face shamans could see the future. One by one Niskanna and the other guests rose and spoke in praise of Quets' greatness, while presenting gifts in honour of his name. But Niskanna's offering outshone all the rest and brought cries of awe from the crowd. Copper was the most rare and valuable of all materials, and the fine copper necklace that he gave so graciously was both a fitting honour to the dead chief and a loud proclamation of Niskanna's sublime wealth. The Islanders were indeed a powerful people!

Tomorrow Quets would be carried from his great house and buried in the style befitting his rank. In all his grandeur, with beads, ear-spools and copper, the old chief would live forever on a far headland overlooking the sea, in a grave heaped high with rocks and earth. Still, all would remember that Niskanna was the greater man.[20]

The potlatch was a ceremony shared by all Pacific Coast Peoples. The chief of one lineage or nation invited outside dignitaries to this memorable celebration, which combined feasting, dancing, singing, storytelling, and gift giving.

Every potlatch culminated with the host chief offering presents to his guests according to rank, and everybody knew their ranks in relationship to their chief. For example, a person ranked fifty-third would receive a more valuable gift than would a person ranked seventy-fourth. All males, except for slaves, inherited their rank. But it was possible to rise or fall in rank depending on events during one's lifetime. Slaves were completely without rights and could be traded, given away at a potlatch, or killed when they were considered useless or simply too old to work.

The more wealth a chief distributed at a pot-latch, the greater was his prestige. Canoes, slaves, carved dishes, bentwood boxes, blankets woven from mountain goat and dog's hair, and eulachon oil were all given away. The chief who impoverished himself through potlatch giving could count on his wealth being returned and even increased at subsequent potlatches he attended as a guest.

Potlatches confirmed the social order. They were called to mourn deaths, bestow names, erase the shame of accidents or ceremonial errors, recognize succession to titles and economic rights, and acknowledge marriages and divorces. The potlatch was a validation feast for important events in the life of a chief. The memory of the event was a record as reliable in Aboriginal oral tradition as a written deed in a registry office is today.

European Contact

When first the Russians then the Spanish arrived off the west coast of Canada in the 1770s, the self-confident Nuu-chah-nuth and Haida were not over-wrought by the presence of the Europeans. They paddled out to meet the Europeans ships, tossing feathers on the water and making other gestures of peace and their desire to trade. In many cases very successful trading relationships were established that brought wealth to both parties. In the early years of contact, the European traders were only interested in making a profit and had no desire to settle the land or change the lifestyle of the Aboriginal people. Those people who did want Aboriginal land and to convert them to Christianity began to arrive in the nineteenth century, along with infectious diseases.

Arctic Peoples: 900 CE–1900 CE

The last group of people to arrive in Canada that most Canadians think of as Aboriginal were the Inuit people of the Arctic. Archaeological records and oral history agree that the present day Inuit began their movement out of northeastern Siberia and Alaska into Canada during an environmentally warm period between 900 and 1200 CE. These people, also identified by archaeologists as the Thule, arrived in Canada around 1000 CE. They did not, however, arrive to an empty land. The Dorset (the term use by archaeologists) or Tunit (the term used by the Inuit), the descendants of an earlier migration out of Alaska and Siberia around 25 00 BCE, occupied the land. There was conflict between the Dorset and Inuit Peoples, and the Dorset subsequently disappeared. The Inuit very successfully migrated and established settlements across the Arctic region of Canada and into Greenland. It was in the northeastern Arctic that the Inuit met, traded with, and sometimes fought with the Norse Viking migrants from Europe.

Historic Inuit Occupations of Arctic Canada

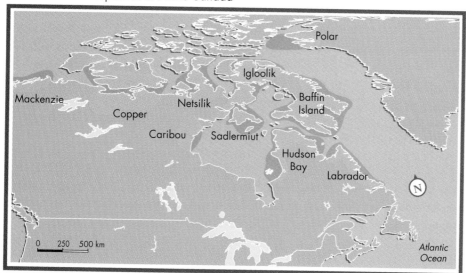

Why and how do the Inuit Peoples of the Arctic differ from other Aboriginal groups in Canada?

The Inuit of the Canadian Arctic are a distinct people, different from other Aboriginal Peoples. They arrived thousands of years later than any other Aboriginal people did. Physically, they are notably Asiatic in appearance. Although there are some regional variations, all Inuit speak one common language, Inuktitut. In each region of this vast frozen land, Inuit settlers adjusted to specific environmental conditions, modifying their traditional hunting practices, technology, and way of life as needed to survive, giving rise to nine regional subcultures.

Inuit Technology

The distinguishing characteristic of Inuit culture, was their way of life, which enabled them to live in the harshest conditions on Earth. Through resourcefulness, inner strength, and a technology more complex than that of any other preindustrial culture, they lived independently and often comfortably on the Arctic tundra, north of the tree line, until non-Inuit contact in the twentieth century changed their lives.

Archaeologists theorize that during the general environmental warming trend between 900 and 1200 CE, the amount of sea ice was reduced, opening up large areas of the Arctic ice for bowhead whales and other large sea mammals. This allowed the Inuit, who were probably experiencing population pressures in Alaska, to range further

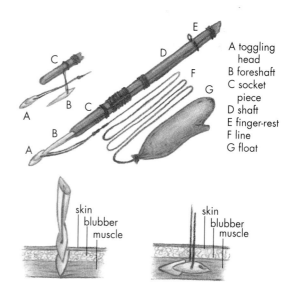

A toggling head
B foreshaft
C socket piece
D shaft
E finger-rest
F line
G float

A Bering Strait Inuit harpoon. Harpoons were used to hunt sea mammals, especially whales, in the open water. The two smaller illustrations (top) show how a harpoon head toggles.

east in their kayaks (a single-person hunting boat completely enclosed except for an opening to admit a hunter) and umiaks (a larger, open, hide-covered boat used for transporting goods and people and hunting whales).

Other new technologies for sea hunting, besides the kayak and umiak, were introduced by the Inuit and contributed to their success. Larger harpoons with floats were used to hunt sea mammals, especially large whales, on the open water. The Inuit also perfected the art of building snow houses (igloos) using special snow knives. The development of soapstone lamps fuelled with seal or whale oil provided low-level heat and light for life in a snow house.

Increasingly important, especially after the end of the warm period, was the technology for winter seal hunting on the Arctic ice. Long bone probes were developed to locate the seals' breathing holes, small stools allowed the hunter to sit for the long wait, plugs prevented loss of precious blood from the seals' wounds, and snow goggles reduced the glare off the ice and prevented snow blindness.

Equally important was the introduction of the dog sled. The Dorset possessed small sleds but did not use dogs to pull them. All Inuit people lived a migratory lifestyle with small family groups wandering widely across the tundra, hunting caribou and fishing throughout the summer and fall. During the winter, they hunted seal on the ice, and when the

A Copper Inuit returns from a seal hunt, with his catch being pulled by a pair of dogs.

In the summer, the Inuit divide into small family groups to hunt caribou and fish in the tundra.

warmer sun of spring began to melt their snow houses, they moved back to the shore where sleds and other winter gear was cached under piles of large rocks to protect them from marauding animals. Dogs were used for more than pulling sleds and sniffing out seal holes during the winter. Throughout the rest of the year they carried possessions, assisted in hunting, and when necessary became a source of food.

Diamond Jenness, who lived with the Copper Inuit in the 1920s, recorded his observations of everyday life.

> July 3rd: Two causes brought about a further division in our little party. The first was the probability of finding caribou farther east, the second the apparent abundance of fish in a certain lake to the North. Accordingly Ikpakhuak and his family went east, while Avranna and his wife, with Kaneyuk, went North. Higilak and Haugak were left to transfer all other things to Lake Kullalluk, some four miles away, while Ikpakhuak and I went hunting. We secured two does and two fawns, an eider duck, a ptarmigan and two lake trout before reaching camp again at 1:00 in the morning. A light south breeze was blowing and the weather was warm and clear, so Higilak left our tent behind at the old camp. During the next three days therefore we slept in the open.

> July 4: Ikpakhuak and I left about noon to hunt, while Higilak and Haugak fished near camp. Early in the afternoon we met Tutsik. He and his family had experienced very little success in their fishing, so we sent him to our camp to have a feast of deer meat. He arranged to join us the following day with his wife and son, as Higilak had caught a large number of fish in the lake beside our camp. Our hunting was again successful; we secured two fine bulls. The skins, head, and legs, with one shoulder blade, we carried back to camp, a distance of about six miles, leaving the remainder for Higilak to bring in later.[21]

Inuit Society

Winter was the hardest time of the year. Darkness and blizzards could make hunting impossible. Dogs were eaten and people went hungry, but no one starved while another ate. Anthropologists, however, have recorded that particularly among the Caribou Inuit, who lived further inland and depended more on the caribou, a bad fall hunting season could lead to abandonment of elderly people and starvation for babies, especially females. For most Inuit, it was during the winter when families came together to live on the ice in communities of 50 to 150 people.

If the seal hunting was good, there was a rich social life in the winter villages. In a specially constructed snow building, which could include a series of connected igloos, members of the community enjoyed each other's company. They played drums, danced, and sang. In some communities, women performed "throat singing" making deep resonant sounds. Popular games involving hand-eye coordination such as "cup and pin" and "cat's cradle" were enjoyed. Most often, however, the Inuit told stories of recent adventures and ancient legends. Some traditional stories helped to explain the spirit world. In a harsh environment where the winds howled for days on end, many stories were violent and tragic. One of the best known was the story of the sea goddess, Sedna. Anthropologist Alan McMillan has summarized this lengthy story:

> Long ago a young woman married a petral or fulmar (a mythical combination of a dog and a bird), which appeared in human form. When her father came in his skin boat to rescue her from the rocky island where the bird had taken her, a great storm came up and threatened to capsize the boat. To lighten the load the young woman was tossed overboard. When she tried to climb back in, the father cut off the joints of her fingers, which fell into sea and became seals. Still she clung to the side of the boat, so her father cut off the rest of her fingers, which became walruses. Still failing to dislodge her, the heartless father cut off her hands, which became whales. The young woman sank to the bottom of the sea, where she lives as the mother and protector of all sea mammals. Sedna demands respect and strict observance of taboos or she will withhold her bounty and the people will starve.[22]

Winter villages were moved every few months as the number of seals declined with successful hunting. Contrary to belief, Inuit did not usually keep a large number of dogs because they could not afford to feed them.

Before winter seal hunting began, an important ceremony to appease the wrath of Sedna for any taboo violations was performed by a shaman, called an *angakok*. A tug-of-war took place between those born in summer and those born in winter, in the belief that if the winter side won, there would be enough food that season. This ceremony sometimes concluded with a short spouse exchange among non-relatives.

The Inuit were also successful in this severely cold environment because of the quality of their clothing. Inuit women worked caribou and seal-skins into soft, warm, water-resistant clothing using five-thousand-year-old patterns from Asia.

Anthropologist Robert McGhee stated, "working with stone knives, bone needles and sinew thread, Inuit women made clothing that is still considered by many Arctic travelers to be finer than any produced by the weaving mills or the chemical factories of the South."[23]

Much of Inuit culture, in the guise of their technology and art, has not only survived the trauma of contact with non-Inuit, but also is used and enjoyed by many Canadians, including the ulu (the semicircular women's knife), kayak, dog sled, parka, mukluk boots, inukshuk, and soapstone carvings. They are now truly part of a redefined, larger Canadian culture and identity.

Conclusion

In the two thousand years before major European contact, Aboriginal nations lived in complex societies that required a sophisticated knowledge of the land and the environment. Their cultures provided outlets for their spiritual and artistic expression. Their family, clan, and group decision making or governance ranged from the very simple, such as that practised by some isolated Innu and Montagnais family groups, to the highly complex—for example, the confederations of the Iroquois Peoples and of the Huron Peoples.

This survey of Canada's Aboriginal Peoples based on archaeological reports, ethnological studies, and oral history provides some knowledge and understanding of the people who inhabited this land two thousand to five hundred years ago. One can begin to imagine the tremendous impact that Europeans had on these well-established peoples when they began to arrive in increasing numbers in the sixteenth century.

Notes

1. Adapted from Joseph Bruchac, Michael J. Caduto, and Joseph Bruchac, *Native Stories From Keepers of the Earth* (Saskatoon: Fifth House Publishers, 1991).
2. Olive Dickason, *Canada's First Nations: A History of Founding Peoples from Earliest Times* (Toronto: McClelland & Stewart Inc., 1992), p. 71.
3. Alan D. McMillan, *Native Peoples and Cultures of Canada* (Vancouver: Douglas & McIntyre Ltd., 1988), pp. 73–74.
4. Adapted from *The Report of the Royal Commission on Aboriginal Peoples*, Volume 1 (Ottawa: The Department of Indian and Northern Affairs, 1996), pp. 48, 49.
5. McMillan, *Native Peoples and Cultures of Canada*, p. 45.
6. R. Bruce Morrison and C. Roderick Wilson, *Native Peoples: The Canadian Experience*, 2nd ed. (Toronto: Oxford University Press, 1986), pp. 355–356.
7. McMillan, *Native Peoples and Cultures of Canada*, pp. 45–46.
8. Dickason, *Canada's First Nations*, p. 111.
9. McMillan, *Native Peoples and Cultures of Canada*, p. 96.
10. *Report of the Royal Commission on Aboriginal Peoples*, p. 18. Based on 1991 estimates.
11. Jerry N. McDonald, *North American Bison: Their Classification and Evolution* (University of California Press: Berkeley, 1981).
12. Hugh Dempsey, *Indian Tribes of Alberta* (Calgary: Glenbow-Alberta Institute, 1986).
13. Knute R. Fladmark, *British Columbia Prehistory* (Ottawa: National Museums of Canada, 1996), p. 43.

14. J.V. Wright, *A History of the Native People of Canada, Volume II, 1000 BCE to 500 CE* (Ottawa: Canadian Museum of Civilization, 1999), p. 851.
15. McMillan, *Native Peoples and Cultures of Canada*, p. 156.
16. Dickason, *Canada's First Nations*, p. 234.
17. Ibid., p. 168.
18. Dickason, *Canada's First Nations*, p. 63.
19. Adapted from Helmut Hirnschall, *The Song of Creation* (Vancouver: Plainsman Publications Ltd., 1979), p. 24.
20. Fladmark, *British Columbia Prehistory*, pp. 66–67.
21. Morrison and Wilson, *Native Peoples: The Canadian Experience*, p. 18.
22. McMillan, *Native Peoples and Cultures of Canada*, p. 257.
23. Robert McGhee, *Ancient Canada* (Ottawa: Canadian Museum of Civilization, 1989).

Chapter 2 Review

Knowledge & Understanding

1. Identify these people, places, and events, and explain their historical significance to Canada's developing culture and identity:
    - Iroquoian/Iroquois
    - League of Five Nations (Haudenonsaunee)
    - matrilineal society
    - pemmican
    - pit houses
    - potlatch
    - kayak
    - the "three sisters"

2. Create a graphic organizer to show the great diversity of various Aboriginal groups. Include Iroquian Peoples, Algonkian Peoples of the eastern woodlands, Aboriginal Peoples of the forests and sub-Arctic, Plains Peoples, Plateau Peoples, Aboriginal Peoples of the west coast, and the Arctic Peoples. Items that you could include in your organizer are location, population, languages, work and economy, political organization (matriarchal or patriarchal), diet, and inventions.

3. What inventions mentioned in this chapter are still very much a part of Canadian life today? How many of these inventions are seens as part of the "sterotypical" Canadian?

Thinking & Inquiry

4. Anthropologist Robin Ridington has argued that before Europeans arrived, Aboriginal Peoples relied on knowledge, not tools, for survival. Write down five pieces of evidence that support or refute this statement. Then in groups of four, conduct a debate with two people supporting this statement, and two people opposing it. After the debate, what is the overall opinion of the group?

5. What stereotypes did you hold about Aboriginal Peoples before reading this chapter? What other stereotypes have you seen in movies, books, or television. How destructive are these stereotypes to our knowledge of Aboriginal history in Canada?

Application

6. Examine the art in this chapter. These are all illustrations by non-Aboriginals. What types of stereotyping do you see in these illustrations? Who do you think was the intended audience for these drawings?

7. List ten questions that you would ask one of the following people about their lifestyle and about contemporary issues of Aboriginal Peoples in Canada:
    - Matriarch of a Huron longhouse
    - Grand Chief of the Mi'kmaqs
    - an Ojibwa hunter
    - a Haida totem pole artist

Communication

8. In 1985, Bruce Trigger wrote *Natives and Newcomers* in which he states, "The study of Native people prior to the arrival of the Europeans is still viewed, not as part of Canadian history, but as the domain of pre-historic archeology." In a well-written paragraph, support or refute Trigger's statement. Use historical facts to support your opinion.

9. On a map of Canada, create a collage of photos, drawings, or symbols that best represent the culture and society of the various Aboriginal groups discussed in this chapter.

First Contact

Men of strange appearance have come across the water.... Their skins are white like snow, and on their faces long hair grows. These people have come across the great water in wonderfully large canoes which have great white wings like those of a giant bird. The men have long and sharp knives, and they have long black tubes which they point at birds and animals.... From them came fire and such a terrific noise.

– OJIBWA PROPHET, FORETELLING THE ARRIVAL OF THE EUROPEANS

The people of the "old world" (Europe) and the "new world" (the Americas) were isolated from each other until about one thousand years ago, when Europeans began to search westward across the Atlantic Ocean for new lands or for new ways to old lands such as China. For the Inuit and Aboriginal Peoples of Canada, who had developed their own very successful ways of living over thousands of years, this contact, gradual at first but inexorable, brought dramatic change and much sorrow.

This chapter is the story of first contact between the Norse and the Skraelings at L'Anse aux Meadows, Newfoundland, around 1000 CE; John Cabot and the Beothuk in 1497; and Jacques Cartier and the Mi'kmaq in 1534. This chapter is also told as two stories: one from the European perspective, the other as seen through the eyes of the Aboriginal Peoples. These points of view come from two different types of sources. Aboriginal traditional stories or legends are passed down for generations in an oral history. European accounts come from written sources, such as the Norse sagas and Jacques Cartier's captain's log. Others stories, such as Cabot's, are based on second-hand accounts.

This chapter has been constructed from primary sources, oral histories, and secondary reports. No one form of evidence is better than any other. All sources must be read and used with a critical eye to understand their limitations and strengths. The contact, cooperation, and conflict between the two worlds that these sources reveal are part of Canada's history, and they are important factors that helped shape our culture and identity.

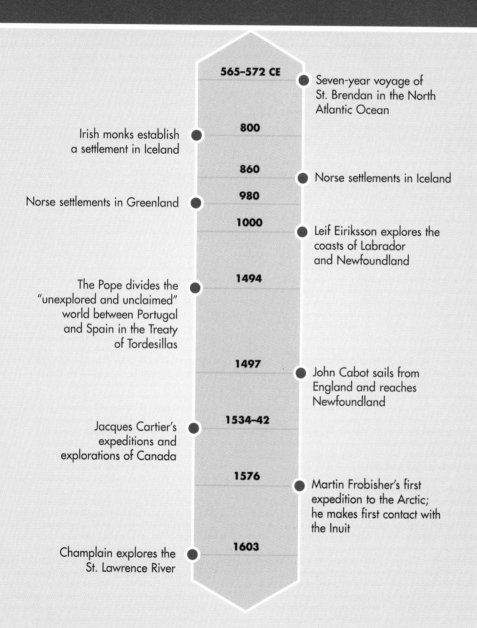

565–572 CE Seven-year voyage of St. Brendan in the North Atlantic Ocean

Irish monks establish a settlement in Iceland **800**

860 Norse settlements in Iceland

Norse settlements in Greenland **980**

1000 Leif Eiriksson explores the coasts of Labrador and Newfoundland

The Pope divides the "unexplored and unclaimed" world between Portugal and Spain in the Treaty of Tordesillas **1494**

1497 John Cabot sails from England and reaches Newfoundland

Jacques Cartier's expeditions and explorations of Canada **1534–42**

1576 Martin Frobisher's first expedition to the Arctic; he makes first contact with the Inuit

Champlain explores the St. Lawrence River **1603**

By the end of this chapter, you will be able to

- describe various aspects of Aboriginal life before contact with Europeans

- explain why and how Aboriginal Peoples helped European colonists to adapt to their new environment

- analyze the impact of European contact on the lives of Aboriginal Peoples, and evaluate the responses of Aboriginal Peoples to the spread of disease and the introduction of new weapons and trade goods

- describe the contributions of Aboriginal Peoples to the development of our Canadian identity and culture

3

The Meaning of Contact

The historian Urs Bitterli defines first meetings as being of three basic types: contacts, collisions, and relationships, none of which exists in a pure form.[1] Each can and often does develop from another. For Bitterli contacts were short encounters, usually peaceful, although ritual displays such as flag or cross plantings were seen as threats. There was always some confusion about and misunderstanding each other's behaviour and culture. Collisions developed in subsequent meetings and included transmission of disease, some sharing and cooperation, frequent taking of hostages or slaves, and an increasing number of misunderstandings, leading to violence. Relationships were characterized by trade, military alliances, evangelism, and imposed controls, leading to colonization.

Contact between Canadian Aboriginal Peoples and non-Aboriginals was not made just once. It occurred many times and in many forms over 900 years, from the first contact with the Norse in 1000 CE, through Cabot and the Beothuk in 1497 and Cartier and the Mi'kmaq in 1534, to the Canadian Arctic Expedition and the isolated bands of Copper and Netsilik Inuit, who had never met a white person, in 1915. At these first meetings, Aboriginal Peoples often thought the Europeans were supernatural beings or ghosts.

The Vikings

The Europeans did not discover Canada or the Americas. It is not possible to discover something that hundreds of thousands of people already knew about. At best, it might be said that the Europeans "rediscovered" the Americas. People had lived in the Americas for more than 10 000 years before Europeans began to venture west to the so-called new world. As for who the first European was to rediscover Canada, the answer is somewhat unclear. Was it St. Brendan, the adventurous Irish monk who, in the six century, wandered the North Atlantic for seven years? Or was

A reconstruction of the settlement at L'Anse aux Meadows, Newfoundland

it Basque, Spanish, or Portuguese fishers? All these are possibilities, but there are no records to substantiate any claims. This history will begin, therefore, with the Vikings, about 1000 CE. Proof of their landing on the shores of North America exists in Norse legends or sagas, a few vague references in other ancient texts, and, most important, in archaeological evidence.

L'Anse aux Meadows

It was 1960 when Norwegian explorer and writer Helge Ingstad and his wife, archaeologist Anne Stine, put to rest all doubts about a Norse settlement when they found the remains of an ancient European colony on the tip of the Great Northern Peninsula of Newfoundland. Near the fishing village of L'Anse aux Meadows, in a grassy meadow facing northward, Ingstad recognized a series of low mounds as the remains of walls built of piled turf. Years of excavations revealed these piles of turf to be eight walled structures, similar to those built by the Norse in Iceland and Greenland. The discovery of three stone hearths and a forge suggested that the settlement was more than a temporary camp. However, the absence of a midden (refuse pit) and any evidence that the houses were rebuilt indicate that the Norse occupation lasted only a few years.

For more than three hundred years, from the eighth through the tenth century, the Norse Vikings travelled, raided, and occupied lands farther and farther from their homelands in Scandinavia. By 860 CE they had occupied Iceland, displacing the Celtic occupants, who left behind religious books and other objects clearly showing their Irish origins. Norse immigrants flocked to Iceland. Within a hundred years, the island had an estimated population of 30 000 people, and all the useful land was taken. It was from these circumstances that Eirik Thorvaldsson, also known as Eirik the Red, began his exploration of Greenland and established a settlement there in 980. It was

from the Greenland settlement that Eirik's son Leif Eiriksson, around 1000 CE, explored and named three parts of Canada: Helluland, a rocky and barren land, which was probably Baffin Island; Markland, a low forested coast, which was probably Labrador; and Vinland, where there was grazing and timber, indicating the greatest potential for settlement.[2] This latter discovery was probably the northern shore of Newfoundland.

According to Norse sagas, Leif Eiriksson's explorations spawned four voyages over the next decade: two by his brothers, one by Thorfinn Karlsefni, and the final one led by his sister Freydis and two Icelandic brothers. It was, however, the third and largest expedition led by Thorfinn Karlsefni that established the settlement at L'Anse aux Meadows. There, his son, Snorri, became the first European child born in the Americas—at least the first for whom there is a record. It was here at the settlement of L'Anse aux Meadows, established about 1008 CE, that the Norse expansion westward across the North Atlantic stopped.

During their three years in Vinland, Karlsefni's people explored the land further and traded for furs with the Skraelings (from the Norse term *Skraelingjar,* which means "small and withered"). The Norse's first meeting was certainly one of contact; it was brief, mostly peaceful, and definitely confusing. The Norse thought of the Skraelings as similar to creatures from their folktales and called them "trolls." In one description they referred to the Skraelings as "small ill favored men with ugly hair on their heads. They had big eyes and were broad in the cheeks."[3]

Web Connection

www.mcgrawhill.ca/links/definingcanada

Go to the Web site above to find out more about L'Anse aux Meadows, a National Historic Site of Canada.

Contact with Aboriginal Peoples

Exactly who the Skraelings were is difficult to say, since the Vikings used this term for all the various peoples they met in North America. On Baffin Island and the coast of Labrador, they were either the Dorsets or the predecessors of the present day Inuit. At L'Anse aux Meadows, they were probably the Beothuk, although the Beothuk were described by other Europeans who met them as anything but "small and withered."

Although there was conflict between the Norse settlers and the Aboriginal Peoples of Newfoundland, recent archaeological evidence suggests that there was considerable trade between the Inuit and the Greenland Norse. Excavations of early Inuit villages have yielded fragments of smelted metal, pieces of woollen cloth, chain mail, and fragments of coopered wooden barrels.[4]

Deterioration of the climate during the fifteenth century, the beginning of the "little ice age" that lasted from about 1450 to 1850, brought increasingly colder weather to the Northern Hemisphere, causing the Norse to abandon their farms and settlements in Greenland. The Inuit, however, did not forget their contact with the Norse. Their oral history kept alive their memories of these Europeans, and when the English explorer Sir Martin Frobisher arrived in 1576, there was no hint of wondering whether the Europeans and their sailing ships were supernatural; the Inuit were ready to trade with them or to defend themselves.

Cabot and Europeans Arrive

First contact between the Norse Vikings and the Dorset or Beothuk, the so-called Skraelings, is shrouded in mystery. Much more is known about John Cabot, who arrived off the coast of Newfoundland about 500 years later, on June 24, 1497. This was the beginning of continuous contact that would go far beyond the brief attempted settlement of L'Anse aux Meadows by the Greenland Norse.

Norse traders used this bronze balance for weighing coins and other small objects. It was found during an archaeological dig in an early Inuit village on Ellesmere Island, 2000 km from the Greenland Norse colonies.

Giovanni Caboto (or John Cabot as he was known in England), an experienced navigator from Italy, was authorized by King Henry VII of England in 1497 to "seek out, discover and find whatever isles, countries, regions or provinces of the heathen and infidels...[that] before this time have been unknown to all Christians."[5] Cabot, like his contemporary Christopher Columbus, who in 1492 sailed to the West Indies, had hoped to find a route to the rich markets of Asia by sailing west. Both of these adventurers and the many who followed were part of what traditional historians called the age of discovery. In this period, from about 1420 to 1620, Europeans sailed all around the world.

Since Cabot's personal writings, if he had any, were lost when his ship sank during his second expedition, the major sources of information about Cabot are the letters of the British spy John Day. Day was present in the court of Henry VII when Cabot told of his exploits during his first expedition to Newfoundland. Day subsequently sold his

Cabot told of codfish so thick in the waters off these "Newe Found Isles" that they could be scooped up in baskets let down from the side of his ship. This news was met with great enthusiasm all over Europe, where Catholics abstained from eating meat for more than 160 days a year. This religious restriction created a great demand for fish and particularly for cod, considered the tastiest and easiest to cook. The result was a steady stream of Basque, Spanish, Portuguese, and English fishers to the Grand Banks, coasts, and shores of Newfoundland.

Cabot's first voyage brought recognition, wealth, and the promise of a second expedition. In a letter written August 23, 1497, to his brothers in Venice, Lorenzo Pasqualigo (a Venetian merchant living in London) not only gives us some interesting details about Cabot, but also gives us a feeling for the times:

This painting of Cabot's ship, the *Matthew*, is based on surviving information about other ships of the period.

report to Spain, Britain's rival in the fifteenth-century race for a passage to China and India.

Although historians have not determined the precise location, Cabot landed somewhere on the northern coast of Newfoundland or Labrador. There, he raised a cross and the banner of England, claiming the territory for Christianity and his patron, the King. Cabot continued his explorations along the coast of Newfoundland and, perhaps, other shores on the North Atlantic coast for a month before returning to his homeport in Bristol, England.

European Penetration of North America

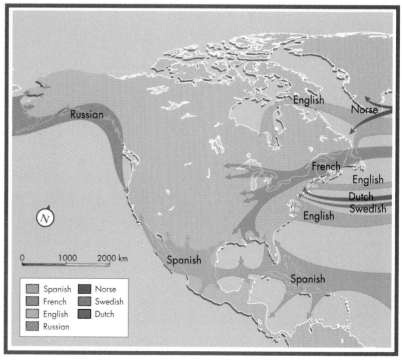

That Venetian of ours who went with a small ship from Bristol to find new lands has come back and says he has discovered mainland 700 leagues away, which is the country of the Grand Khan, and that he coasted it for 300 leagues and landed and did not see any person; but he has brought here to the king certain snares which were spread to take game and a needle for making nets and he found certain notched trees so that by this he judges that there are inhabitants. Being in doubt he returned to his ship; and he has been three months on the voyage; and this is certain. And on the way back he saw two Islands, but was unwilling to land, in order not to lose time as he was in want provisions. The king here is much pleased at this; and he [Cabot] says that the tides are slack and do not run as they do here. The king has promised him for this spring ten armed ships as he [Cabot] desires and has given him all the prisoners to be sent away, that they may go with him, as he has requested; and has given him

money that he may have a good time until then. And he is with his Venetian wife and his sons at Bristol. His name is [John Cabot] and he is called the Great Admiral and vast honour is paid to him and he goes dressed in silk, and these English run after him like mad, and indeed he can enlist as many of them as he pleases, and a number of rogues as well. The discoverer of these things planted on the land which he has found a large cross with a banner of England and one of St. Mark, as he is a Venetian, so that our flag has been hoisted very far a field.[6]

The Beothuk Tragedy

For the Beothuk, Cabot's visit was the beginning of a tragic story. Cabot did not see a single Beothuk person on that first trip, but he knew that

This sixteenth-century painting of the Antwerp market captures the lively atmosphere and great demand for fish in Europe.

Cabot's Route, 1497–1498

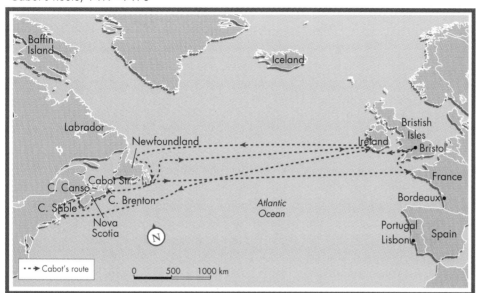

This map shows areas explored by John Cabot from 1497–1498.

the land was already inhabited. When Cabot landed, he followed a trail inland to a clearing with a dead campfire. Here he found a short, carved, and painted stick. Although we do not know what this stick represented, it was evidence that the land was inhabited. Cabot collected fresh water, returned to his ship, the *Matthew*, and sailed away.

Future contact between the Beothuk and Europeans led to many misunderstandings, much violence, and many deaths. It was from the Beothuks' use of red ochre mixed with oil or grease to paint their bodies and hair that the term "red Indian" was coined. The term, unfortunately, was later applied to all North American Aboriginal Peoples. The use of red ochre, although common throughout most of Aboriginal North America, was used most extensively by the Beothuk. Since so little is known about the Beothuk, it is difficult to say whether the red ochre was decorative, religious, or a protective coating against the hordes of biting insects that plagued animals and humans in this environment. The appearance of red ochre on corpses and objects interred with the dead strongly suggests a ceremonial or spiritual association.

Unlike in the Arctic, where whaling provided the Inuit a limited basis for cooperation with Europeans, no common interest developed for the Beothuk. It is known, however, that the Basque whalers established summer shore stations in Red Bay on the Strait of Belle Isle and on Saddle Island on the west coast of Newfoundland. Here, none of the archaeological evidence indicates a conflict between the Beothuk and the Basques. Fragments of red roofing tile imported from Europe and a ten-metre stone wall mark a large area where five large sandstone fireboxes, probably imported from Spain, were used to render the whale blubber into oil. In 1571, a successful whaling voyage could send a thousand barrels of oil back to Spain. Whaling in the Strait of Belle Isle ended by 1600, probably because of intensive hunting, a decline in local whale stocks, and an upsurge in Dutch, French, and English pirating in the North Atlantic. Many Basque whaling ships were commandeered and lost to the Spanish Armada, which was defeated by the English in 1588.

Historians are aware that early attempts at trade between the Europeans and the Beothuk turned to misunderstanding and violence. Conflict escalated with the development of dry fisheries, which meant that European fishers needed shore space for their drying racks. Often, these fishers erected their racks on sites favoured by the Beothuk for their summer fishing. These conflicting needs and claims led to violence. The Europeans, in possession of guns, shot and killed Beothuk people, whereas the Beothuk could only use their spears and bows and arrows. Typical of the attitude of many Europeans is the statement by a French navigator, who described the Beothuk as having "no more God then beasts, and are bad people."[7]

In 1501 the Portuguese entrepreneur Gasper Corte Real, on his second voyage to Newfoundland, captured and enslaved fifty-seven Beothuk men and women. They were described by the Venetian ambassador when he saw them in Lisbon:

> They are of like colours, figure, stature, and respect, and bear the greatest resemblance to the Gypsies.... Clad in the skins of animals,... they may appear mere savages, yet they are gentle, and have a strong sense of shame, and are better made in the legs, arms and shoulders than it is possible to describe...admirably fitted to endure labour, and will probably turn out the best slaves that have been discovered up to this time.[8]

This was certainly not true. Tragically, most of the slaves died of infectious diseases on the voyage to Portugal and the rest soon after landing.

The Beothuk retreated as far into the interior of the island as they could. They only emerged occasionally to attempt to fish and hunt in their traditional locations. Frequently, they were frustrated by the European presence and resorted to raiding and taking any gear left unattended by the intruders. Early in the seventeenth century, a prominent fishing captain, Sir Richard Whitbourne, reported that his operations were hampered, "because the Savages of that country...secretly every year come into Trinity Bay and Harbour, in the night time,

purposely to steale Sailes, Lines, Hatchets, Hooks, Knives, and such like." He wondered whether missionaries would not help to bring them in line with the European concept of civility. The missionaries never came, and little effort was made to develop a working relationship.[9]

The rampant spread of European diseases, particularly tuberculosis, increased fishing, and some settlement made it open season for hunting the Beothuk. Their population, estimated between 500 and 1000 by the seventeenth century, was decimated. By the time Newfoundland was declared a colony in 1824, few Beothuk were left. The last known Beothuk, a young woman named Shawnadithit, died in 1829 of tuberculosis at the age of twenty-nine.

Death by Disease

When Europeans began to arrive in greater numbers in the sixteenth century, Canada's original peoples had already developed regulated patterns of life, with unique technological, social, and cultural adaptations needed for the range of environments and the geography of Canada. With only one exception—the Iroquois Peoples, who combined hunting and gathering with farming—Aboriginal Peoples lived a hunting and gathering lifestyle, with stable food supplies. Their success was based on an intimate knowledge of resources and the best way of exploiting them. Their technology consisted of both knowledge and unique tools. It was through their knowledge of the environment and their ingenuity that Aboriginal Peoples survived and lived as well as they did with comparatively simple technology, considering Canada's northern location and harsh winters.

The estimated population of the Aboriginal Peoples of Canada at first contact with Europeans varies from the widely accepted figure of 500 000 to more than 2 000 000, based on recent demographic studies. Most of the population was thinly scattered because of the land requirements of a hunter-and-

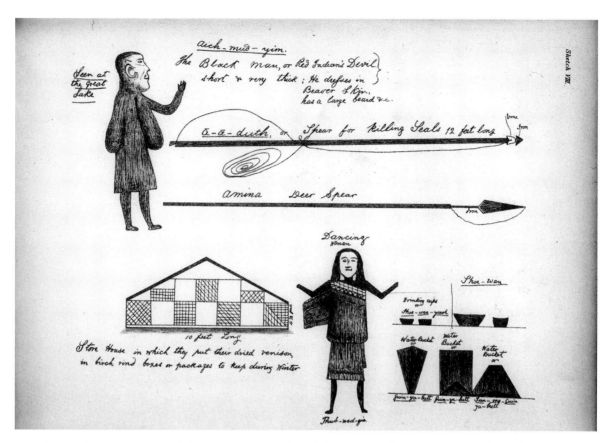

Most of what is known about the Beothuk people was learned through the drawings of and discussions with the last known living Beothuk, Shawnadithit.

gatherer economy. There were two principal population concentrations. One was southern Ontario and the St. Lawrence Valley, where various Iroquoian nations practised farming. Their population was estimated between 100 000 and 150 000. The other population concentration was on the Pacific northwest coast, where about 200 000 people made this area one of the most densely populated nonagricultural regions in the world.[10]

The greatest injury inflicted on the original peoples by Europeans was rarely intended. They brought death with them in the form of smallpox, measles, influenza, diphtheria, typhus, tuberculosis, and mumps. These alien diseases raged through the Aboriginal Peoples, whose immune

systems were defenceless and left them vulnerable. It is now estimated that between 90 percent and 93 percent of the North American Aboriginal population was killed by imported diseases. Disease spread everywhere Europeans made contact. Disease was even carried innocently by Aboriginal people back to their communities. The effect of European sicknesses was devastating. It undermined traditional healers and spiritual leaders. It destroyed, physically and emotionally, families and whole communities.

Death from the Europeans became part of the oral tradition of the Aboriginal Peoples:

Klusap, a Mi'kmaq spirit, warned of this assault: "There will be white people who come and take

Expression of Culture

SHAWNADITHIT

The story of the Beothuk serves as a constant reminder of the devastating effect of the arrival of Europeans to North America. Once a vibrant race of people, by 1829, the entire nation had disappeared. Much of what historians know about the Beothuk comes from a woman named Shawnadithit, who was believed to be the last Beothuk.

By 1824, few Beothuk remained in Newfoundland. William Cormack, a Scottish philanthropist, became increasingly interested in the Beothuk, and he created the Beothuk Institution in St. John's. At its founding, he stated, "the British have trespassed this country and have become a blight and a scourge to a portion of the human race; under their power a defenceless and once independent proud tribe of men have been nearly extirpated from the face of the earth, scarcely causing an enquiring how or why." Cormack made several trips into the interior of Newfoundland, looking for remaining members of the Beothuk. By 1827, he realized that a young girl named Shawnadithit, who was living with a settler family, was the last living Beothuk.

In an attempt to learn all that he could about the Beothuk, Cormack lived with Shawnadithit and tried to teach her English, hoping that she could tell him about the Beothuk way of life. Shawnadithit made a series of sketches that revealed details about food, shelter, tools, chiefs, and Beothuk contact with Europeans. Cormack recorded his impressions of Shawnadithit:

> To this interesting protégé we are indebted for nearly all the information we possess regarding her tribe, the aborigines of Newfoundland. Although she has been five years and upwards among the English, upon her arrival the second time in St. John's she spoke so little English that those only who were accustomed to her gibberish, could understand her. By persevering attention now, however, to instruct her, she acquired confidence and became able to communicate. She evinced extraordinary powers of mind in possessing the sense of gratitude in the highest degree, strong affections for her parents and friends, and was of a most lively disposition.

This learning partnership ended too soon. Shawnadithit had tuberculosis and died in 1829. She was buried in the Church of England cemetery in St. John's, Newfoundland. Tragically, even her remains have disappeared. In 1903, the cemetery was dug up to make way for a road.

Only ten of her sketches remain, with a few notes by Cormack that have also survived—sad reminders of a culture exterminated by European greed, racism, and the desire for power and control.

this forest away from you. But I am going north, to make a place for you where no white person can ever come. No white person shall ever enter here. And this place will be a place where you may not while you are alive. You will only travel there after you die on the Earth World."

In Huron mythology, the direction to escape the whites was west, the direction of death. The world was ruled by twins, Good Brother and Evil Brother, an in an epic battle Good killed Evil, who returned in a dream, saying, "I'm going to the far west. Hereafter all men will go to the west after death." The Nuu'chah'nulth thought the whites were fish that had been transformed into men and had the faces of dog salmon.

The Squamish thought the whites were simply dead. When they saw a Spanish ship for the first time, a Squamish observer noted: "The people did not know what it was. At first they believed that the ship was a floating island with sticks growing on it, and cobwebs were hanged from the sticks.... As they approached this monstrous thing they could see that it was a canoe of tremendous size.... Then as they rested their paddles and looked at this great canoe, they saw a man on board. He was walking on the deck. They thought he was dead—walking; that he was from the spirit world, and that he was carrying his coffin on his back.... You must understand that this man had a big beard, which was something new to the people, and above this great massive black beard his face was white. Now the only pale faces the people that ever seen were on dead men.[11]

Review...Reflect...Respond

1. According to Urs Bitterli, what are the three types of first meetings? What are the differences among them?

2. Why did the devastating effect of disease undermine traditional Aboriginal healers and spiritual leaders?

3. If this era should not be called the "age of discovery," what name would you give it?

Two Conflicting Views of Civilization

When John Cabot sailed from Bristol in 1497, he did so under the authority of the king of England. He, Columbus, and all the other European explorers and adventurers claimed the lands they "discovered" or conquered in the name of their sovereigns, based on the theory of Divine Right of Kings. This was a religious theory of land ownership that developed in the European Middle Ages and was refined during the Crusades.[12] According to this doctrine, the world was the property of the Christian God, who granted stewardship of earthly affairs to the Roman Catholic Pope. Kings received their authority from the Pope in return for fealty (loyalty) and temporal (worldly) support. Heathens and infidels had no place or rights in this scheme and their lands were forfeit to any Christian who could take them by force, guile, or bluff.[13]

This view of the world was not accepted outside Christian Europe and even some Europeans objected to it. This did not prevent the Pope from issuing the Treaty of Tordesillas in 1494, which essentially divided the world (at least all the non-Christian lands) along a mid-Atlantic demarcation line between Spain and Portugal, the two favoured Catholic European countries. This Treaty gave Brazil to Portugal and the rest of Latin America west of the line to Spain.

The next challenging question for the Papacy was whether the newly discovered peoples of the new world were to be considered humans.

In 1537 the Pope issued two proclamations stating that, "Man is of such condition and nature that he can receive the faith of Christ, and whoever has the nature man is fitted to receive the same faith." The New World peoples were proclaimed to be as human as European Christians, could be allowed baptism and converted to Christianity, and could not be enslaved. The papacy was unclear, however, as to whether the heathen nations of the New World had the right to hold land and to prevent Christian occupation of their countries.[14]

An alternative view, that of an Aboriginal Canadian, is presented by Daniel N. Paul in his book *We Were Not The Savages: A Micmac Perspective on the Collision of European and Aboriginal Civilization:*

> Prior to European settlement, the Micmac lived in countries whose culture was based upon two principals: people power and respect for "Mother Earth." A harmonious relationship with nature was considered to be essential for survival.
>
> Micmac societies were well structured, and democratic principals were an established component. For instance, leaders were appointed by the people and served at their pleasure. The citizens of the Micmac "Nation" enjoyed the benefits of living in a relatively peaceful, healthy, and harmonious social environment....
>
> In contrast, up until recent times, European civilizations...were governed by a titled elite who declared themselves to be the ruling class and allowed no interference with what they considered to be their divine right to rule. Average citizens within these autocratically governed domains were routinely denied basic rights and freedoms. They were treated as property and in most cases were held in human bondage from cradle to grave. When disputes arose within these despotic societies, settlements were devised and imposed by the ruling class, with little consideration being given to democratic principles....
>
> These early contacts produced all kinds of imaginative stories about the American native people. In them, the people who inhabited this land were even depicted as non-humans, hairy monsters, or subhumans. Not much consideration was given to the fact that these people were intelligent and civilized human beings.
>
> During this period, the European intelligentsia equated civilization with European conventions; Christianity was its cornerstone. According to this perception, if a land was not Christian it was not civilized.[15]

Paul continues his assessment of the Mi'kmaq people compared with the Europeans:

> The political and territorial relationships of Micmac civilization were well developed, defined, and regulated. Probably after much trial and error, they had developed a society that was functional, colorful, and meaningful, and balanced its tenets of personal freedom with responsibility to the state—a fact totally ignored by the Europeans in their drive for real estate and other assets. The suppression and wanton destruction of these civilizations by European civilizations was in many ways a case of inferior civilizations overcoming superior ones....[16]

Cartier and the First French Intrusion

Contact between Europeans and the Mi'kmaq probably came between 1500 and 1534. Mi'kmaq oral history tells of a young woman who foretold of the event in a dream:

> When there were no people in this country but the Indians...a young woman had a strange dream. She dreamed that a small island came floating in toward the land. On the island were tall trees and living beings. Among them was a man dressed in garments made of rabbit skins. According to the story, the woman followed the custom of consulting the wise men and prophets in the hope of finding out what the dream meant. The elders had no answers, but the next day an extraordinary event explained it. When they got up in the morning, they saw what seemed to be a small island that had drifted near to the land and became fixed there. There were trees on the island, and what seemed to be a number of bears crawling about on the branches. All the Micmac men seized their bows and arrows and spears, and rushed down to the shore to shoot the bears. But they stopped in surprise when they saw that the creatures were not bears but men. And what seemed to be a small island with trees was really a large boat with long poles rising above it. The visitors lowered a strangely built canoe into the water and paddled to shore. A man dressed in white made signs of friendship, by raising his hand toward heaven and he spoke in an unknown language.[17]

Jacques Cartier, an experienced mariner who had already made voyages to both Newfoundland and Brazil, was commissioned by King François I of France to sail to the new world, to find a passage to Asia or at least to find gold. Cartier left St. Malo, France, on April 20, 1534, with two ships and sixty-one men. Cartier landed in Newfoundland twenty days later, prepared to begin his extensive explorations, which would eventually include two more major expeditions.

Cartier was not the European discoverer of the St. Lawrence River. There is enough archaeological evidence, and even a reference in Cartier's writings to meeting French fishers on the shores of the St. Lawrence, for historians to know that there was prior knowledge of the mouth of the great river and of the Gulf of St. Lawrence. Cartier, however, deserves to be recognized as a very competent sailor and an excellent mapmaker and for his detailed records of his meetings with Aboriginal Peoples. He was successful in his first meetings with three different groups of Aboriginal Peoples, as no one was directly injured or died on either side—an impressive achievement in the sixteenth century.[18]

Cartier was very cautious about making contact with the Aboriginal people, and his dominant emotion, as it was for most Europeans of the sixteenth century, was fear. As the French historian Robert Mandrou stated, "Everything combined to produce fear: the natural conditions of life, the precarious nature of the food supply, the inadequacies of the environment, and above all the intellectual climate."[19] Most people were afraid both of the natural world around them and of the supernatural world beyond them. Cartier brought these fears with him, and they infected his relations with the Aboriginal people he met.

Cartier's Logs

After reaching landfall on May 10, 1534, Cartier spent five weeks exploring and charting the coasts of Newfoundland and Labrador. His first impression of the country was, "I'm rather inclined to believe that this is the land God gave to Cain."[20] As he probed further west in search of a pass to Asia and the Orient, he was encouraged by more fertile-looking land and by the abundance of wildlife. On one stop at Iles-aux-Oiseaux,[21] his crew slaughtered more than one thousand birds, many of them great auks, which were hunted to extinction by the mid-nineteenth century.

Cartier's written account provided the first extensive European commentary on the Mi'kmaq and the only detailed descriptions of the St. Lawrence Iroquois. The St. Lawrence Iroquois, a people who were flourishing when Cartier encountered them between 1535 and 1542, had completely vanished from their villages in the St. Lawrence Valley by the time Champlain arrived in 1603.

Cartier recorded his first encounter with Aboriginal people, most likely the Mi'kmaq:

> We likewise made signs to them that we wished them no harm,...and sent two men ashore, to offer them some knives and other iron goods, and a red cap to give to their chief.... They bartered all they had to such extent that all went back naked without anything on them; and they made signs to us that they would return on the morrow with more skins.[22]

During his second encounter, Cartier panicked when forty Mi'kmaq canoes surrounded one of his long boats. Despite the Mi'kmaq signs of joy and indications of their desire to be friends, Cartier ordered his men to shoot two small canons over their heads. The Mi'kmaq paddled away.

Cartier's third meeting at Baie de Gaspé was with a different nation of Aboriginal Peoples, the St. Lawrence Iroquois. After a presentation of gifts and an introduction to their leader, Donnacona, an alliance was formed and celebrated with dancing. This festive atmosphere ended after Cartier erected a ten-metre cross bearing the words "Long Live the King of France." The change in mood was a clear indication that the Iroquois understood Cartier's actions.

Despite some growing distrust, Donnacona was persuaded to leave his two adults sons, Domagaya and Taignoagny, with Cartier in exchange for a promise to return from France with goods to trade. With these two hostages, Cartier returned to France in September 1534. The two Aboriginal captives were an exotic anticlimax to Cartier's first and somewhat unsuccessful voyage of discovery.

Did Donnacona really agree to let Cartier take his two sons back to France or were they kidnapped? It is difficult to say and all historians have to draw from is Cartier's report, which stated that it was an agreement. It is quite likely that the St. Lawrence Iroquois were very eager to trade with Europeans. They probably knew through contact with the Mi'kmaq, or perhaps through direct contact with European fishers, the advantages of using iron utensils. The fact that about three hundred people, including families with women and children, would range this far from their settlements at Stadacona (present-day Quebec City) suggests that they were very aware of the presence of Europeans who were willing to trade.

Domagaya and Taignoagny proved invaluable to Cartier. The young men, within a few months of the return voyage to France, had learned sufficient French to become interpreters and guides for Cartier during his next voyage in 1535. Their descriptions of a great river into the interior of the new world helped Cartier secure the financing to put together a much larger expedition of three ships and 110 men.

Cartier Returns

Cartier's second voyage to Canada is almost the complete story of his relationship with the St. Lawrence Iroquois. It is not known what name the people of this nation called themselves, nor is it known what their perspectives were on Cartier, the French, or events that took place. What is known is that Cartier depended on the St. Lawrence Iroquois to guide him through their lands. He entered their territory at Stadacona or "Canada,"

as Cartier mistakenly named their country, and then proceeded west to explore the St. Lawrence River as far as Hochelaga, a large Iroquois settlement (present-day Montreal).

Web Connection

www.mcgrawhill.ca/links/definingcanada
Go to the Web site above to find out more about how Canada got its name.

The French and the St. Lawrence Iroquois had cultures and worldviews that were dramatically different and as a result were almost mutually incomprehensible. This description of the differences in their political organization, based on the studies of the eminent archaeologist and historian Bruce Trigger, illustrates how far apart their two worlds were.

> Cartier apparently regarded Iroquois society as a very rudimentary version of the European society with which he was familiar: political authority emanated from God, who conferred upon the King of the nation, who in turn conferred lesser amounts upon his noble subjects. The nobles, in turn, defended the nation, maintained order, and ensured that a suitable amount of wealth was transferred from the lower orders to the nobility, royalty and the church. Wealth, status, rank and name were inherited through the male line. The system was based on the individual's recognition of his inherited station and society, submission and obedience to those in higher stations, and a supposed duty to those in lower stations.
>
> The Iroquoian political system, on the other hand, derived its organization and authority from the basic unit of society, the family. Inheritance passed through the female line, and newly married men moved from their childhood homes to live with the families of their brides. The primary unit of Iroquois society was the group of nuclear families headed by a group of sisters, their daughters and nieces, who resided together in a single longhouse or in a certain area of a village, and all of whom were related

The Voyages of Jacques Cartier, 1534–1535

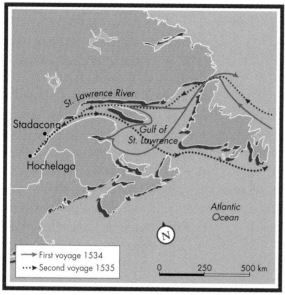

St. Lawrence River

Stadacona

Gulf of
St. Lawrence

Hochelaga

Atlantic
Ocean

N

→ First voyage 1534
•••▶ Second voyage 1535

0   250   500 km

"goods of little value" (a phrase that reoccurs often throughout Cartier's reports); by a combination of bullying threats and stern rebukes; and by the use of violence—including abduction. These methods were the opposite of the Iroquois ideals of politeness and noncoercion in human relations. Cartier also failed to understand Iroquois leadership. He assumed that the spokesperson, chosen strictly because of his special oratorical skills, was a leader who could command people to do what he wanted. (Iroquois chiefs were always male.) Increasingly, misunderstandings led to hostile encounters and a gradual deterioration of relations between the French and the Iroquois.

Cartier's second expedition, guided by Donnacona's two sons, led him further into the Gulf of the St. Lawrence and the St. Lawrence River to the territory called Canada and the settlement of Stadacona. Here, after an apparently joyous reunion with Donnacona, the return of Domagaya and Taignoagny, and some exploring of the immediate area, Cartier determined that he would explore further west. This made the Stadaconians suspicious that Cartier would not honour their agreement to trade exclusively with them and was merely using them as a stepping-stone to reach the wealthier Hochelagans. In an attempt to keep the French in Stadacona, Domagaya and Taignoagny refused to guide and interpret for Cartier.

Regardless, Cartier left and spent the next two weeks exploring the St. Lawrence before reaching Hochelaga. Here, the French were greeted with customary politeness by the Hochelagans. They were led through extensive cornfields to a ceremonial welcome in the central square of the palisade town. They also climbed Mount Royal, where Cartier observed the St. Lawrence and Ottawa rivers flowing out of an unexplored country to the west, rather than from an open Oriental sea.

Cartier's report describes a healthy and prosperous Hochelagan people. He noted that they all lived well and stored quantities of food including

through a single female ancestor. Most Iroquois villages were composed of several of these extended family units. Each extended family elected two leaders (if the St. Lawrence people were like their Iroquois relatives of New York State, the voters were the female members of the family and chief was elected from a noble lineage): a civil chief who dealt with community and religious matters, and a war chief who organized and led the male members of the family in warfare. The affairs of each village were discussed by a council of the civil chiefs; decisions were reached by consensus of this council, and announced by a spokesman who was elected by the chiefs. The affairs of the nation were discussed by a similar council of village headmen.

Iroquoian society was based on the ideals of social equality, decisions by consensus, and the absence of coercion: no individual or organization had the power to force another individual to live by a decision with which he did not agree.[23]

Cartier had little awareness of the complexity of Iroquois society and its leadership. He tried to obtain their cooperation in various ways: by the purchase of goodwill through the distribution of corn, beans, cucumbers, and fruits. He observed: "They have in their houses also large vessels called puncheons, in which they place their fish, such as eels and others, that are smoke[d] during the summer, and on these they live during the winter. They make great store of these as we ourselves saw. All their food is eaten without salt."[24] Cartier recorded seeing fourteen villages on the north shore of the St. Lawrence, of which Hochelaga was the largest, with about fifty longhouses and a population of fifteen hundred people. He stayed only briefly in Hochelaga, both disappointing and insulting his hosts, then returned to Stadacona, where he prepared for the coming winter.

Back at Stadacona, the French hastily constructed a fort, but they suffered a miserable winter and lost twenty-five men to scurvy. They were rescued only when Domagaya showed them how to prepare a drink combining cedar leaves and bark. The Stadaconians also lost more than fifty people to what was probably the first of many European diseases to strike the St. Lawrence Iroquois. Cartier did not report that the French were blamed for the illness and death, but they were probably suspected.

In the spring Cartier again erected a huge cross near his fort at Stadacona. This event attracted the attention of the Stadaconians. Cartier then captured Donnacona, his two sons, three other leaders, and four children who had been living with the French for some time. With ten captives, Cartier

This is an unrealistic drawing by a European artist of an Iroquoian village. The people look like ancient Romans, and the longhouses are in nicely organized rows. Archaeology reveals that longhouses were never so neatly arranged and that villages were enclosed by palisades made of timber and brush, not neat picket fences.

left for France, despite the pleading of grieving relatives who followed in canoes, clutching beaver pelts that they offered as ransom for the hostages. None of the captured St. Lawrence Iroquois people ever saw Canada again; they all perished in France.

Cartier's Final Voyage

Although Cartier's third expedition was the most elaborate, it was the least successful. This failure was probably due to the ill will he created during the first two trips. Cartier left St. Malo, France, on May 23, 1541, with five ships and a complement of gentlemen-adventurers, soldiers, mariners, convicts, and farm animals. On their arrival in Canada, a fort was constructed at Cap Rouge, fifteen kilometres upstream from Stadacona. Cartier probably made this decision because of some well-founded fear of retaliation by the Stadaconians for his failure to bring back any of the kidnapped people, including their leader, Donnacona. Crops were soon planted and two ships with samples of diamonds and gold, which were actually quartz and iron pyrites, were sent back to France before the end of summer.

The winter of 1541–42, however, was a disaster for Cartier. The Iroquois never attacked the fort directly, but they conducted an effective guerrilla war. They killed woodcutters and others who ventured outside the fort. Thirty-five Frenchmen were reported killed. Scurvy, lack of fresh food, and fear took its toll. By the spring Cartier had had enough of Canada and returned to France.

One last effort was made by the French nobleman Jean François de la Roque, Sieur de Roberval, to create a settlement in Canada in 1543, but that too failed miserably after one winter.

France abandoned her attempts to settle Canada for the next half century, until Champlain revived interest again in 1603. The winters in Canada had so far proven too long and cold; the St. Lawrence Iroquois were too numerous and too willing to defend themselves; the St. Lawrence was a disappointment as a waterway to Asia; and the gold,

silver, and diamonds turned out to be worthless rocks. The St. Lawrence, New Found Land, and the rest of the Atlantic coast was left for the various anonymous European fishers and whalers to exploit.

Review...Reflect...Respond

1. What are the two conflicting views of civilization?

2. How did Aboriginals help European colonists and explorers adapt to their environment?

3. How do you think the arrival of Europeans would affect Aboriginal beliefs about the world?

Spreading the News of First Contact

First contact between Aboriginal Peoples and Europeans continued to take place for more than three hundred years after Cartier's last voyage. Each new contact was unique and brought different results—most of which did not favour or benefit Aboriginal Peoples. Aboriginal Peoples often anticipated this first contact. This concluding section presents only a few of the stories of these first meetings as the Europeans moved from east to west across Canada.

Contact with the Ojibwa

Halfway across Canada from where Cabot first saw signs of the Beothuk, and about a century after Cartier's contact with the Mi'kmaq, the Ojibwa met Europeans for the first time. According to Ojibwa oral history, however, the meeting was prophesized in a vision:

It was said: men of strange appearance have come across the water.... Their skins are white like snow, and on their faces long hair grows. These people have come across the great water in wonderfully large canoes, which have great white wings like those of a giant bird. The men have long and sharp knives, and they have long black tubes, which they pointed at birds and animals. The tubes make a smoke that rises in the air just like the smoke from our pipes. From them came fire and such a terrific noise.[25]

Ojibwa legend tells how the people, impatient to meet the strangers, prepared a fleet of canoes and travelled eastward along the Great Lakes and the great river. They finally met the strangers, who possessed axes that could chop down large trees evenly and with ease. They collected wood shavings as evidence of this new technology, as well as brightly coloured cloth, and returned home. Here, their stories created great excitement and pieces of shavings and small pieces of cloth were highly coveted souvenirs. It is even said that other Aboriginal nations of Lake Superior learned about the Europeans through the exchange of these exotic goods and the telling of the Ojibwa experience.

Contact with Peoples of the Pacific Northwest Coast

Three hundred years after the Mi'kmaq encountered Europeans, and two centuries after the Ojibwa, the people of the Pacific northwest coast made contact with the "Moon's People," as they called Europeans. According to Cowichan legend, a despondent chief who climbed a mountain near his village to die first foretold the meeting in a vision. But when he turned to take one last look at the Ocean his vision became real.

> He turned round to take one last look at the Ocean. He saw the moon rising in the distant sky. On the moon-path, a few minutes later, he saw a beautiful big canoe, bigger than any he had ever seen. It had large wings, like a giant sea gull flying. The chief concluded that this had to be the moon's canoe and that the children of the moon must be coming down to

earth. Something unusual is going to happen. Will all of us die, or are our enemies coming to attack us? He rushed back to his village with the news that the moon's people were on their way but was greeted with howls of laughter and scorn. However, the next day the villagers were startled to see a "big canoe" just offshore.[26]

Who were the "Moon's People"? Were they the Russians, who crossed the Bering Strait in 1741 in search of furs? Or were they the Spanish under Captain Juan Perez, who had been sent in 1774 to claim the area for Spain? Or perhaps they were the British under the command of mariner James Cook, who reached the northwest Pacific coast in 1778 in his search for the elusive Northwest Passage?

Cook's crew soon learned that sea otter pelts, which they could trade for goods costing about a schilling a skin, sold in China for ninety pounds each—an astronomical profit of 1800 percent. This news spread rapidly, setting off a scurry among European nations to get to the west coast to exploit the sea otter trade.

Tragically, as everywhere else that the Europeans made contact with Aboriginal Peoples, there were misunderstandings, clashes, the spread of disease, and violence between these two peoples, whose customs and views of the world were so dramatically different. In most cases conflict arose when Aboriginal Peoples refused to accept exploitation or the impositions of the foreign intruders. From the Montagnais in Tadoussac (Quebec) in their dealings with the French under Champlain, to the Nootka in 1792 trading with the English, the Aboriginal Peoples learned quickly to bargain and to be tough minded. They were experienced traders long before the Europeans arrived, and they soon adjusted and learned to keep a sharp lookout for new trading opportunities. Their refusal to be compliant and to do what the Europeans wanted led to deterioration in relations and further misunderstandings.

Expression of Culture
NORTHWEST COAST ART

People migrated to the west coast of Canada from Asia across the Bering Strait about 10 000 years ago. Cut off from the rest of the continent by the Rocky Mountains, these Aboriginal Peoples built permanent villages in the protective inlets and islands along the rocky coastline. Living off the bounty of the sea, rivers, and forests, a complex and technologically advanced culture emerged.

The peoples of the northwest coast used the abundance of materials available to them, particularly the giant cedar, to create an art distinct from any other in the world. Although there is no Aboriginal word for art, skillfully carved and expertly woven and painted objects pervaded everyday life. From a carefully woven matt or basket to a Chilkat blanket, from a painted box to a towering totem pole, art was simply a part of life.

The surplus of food on the northwest coast allowed these groups luxuries other Aboriginal groups across Canada could not afford. Most significantly, the people of the coast lived in permanent villages, enjoyed time for recreation and could accumulate wealth. Men particularly gifted in carving and painting became what would be considered today professional artists. Exempt from male duties such as the hunt, artists apprenticed for years under the guidance of an elder and devoted their life to perfecting their craft.

Art, such as the totem pole or copper crest, allowed this complex coastal society to identify its kin groups. Carved with crest images of animals, humans, and supernatural beings, objects spoke of a family's origin and marked its place in society.

Art also provided the means for the people of the coast to communicate with ancestral spirits or the

creatures of the supernatural world. The Coast Salish of the south practised the Guardian Spirit quest. They performed private rituals to commune with their guiding forces and used objects carved in the likeness of their guardian spirits. The northern neighbour to the Salish, the Southern Kwakiutl, practised a complex system of secret societies during the winter months. They put on theatrical dances and wore elaborate, skillfully carved masks, like the Crooked Beak of Heaven mask used in the ceremony of the Hamatsa or cannibal society.

Most of the northwest coast art we see and enjoy today in museums and galleries around the world was created after contact. Explorers, such as Cook, arrived on the west coast in the mid- to late eighteenth century. Looking for unexplored territory and possible trading partners, these early explorers found a highly populated area and a people with a complex social system and sophisticated technology. Looking for curios to take home, they compiled impressive collections of these strange yet remarkable art objects and described in detail the colourful masks, totem poles, canoes, and other art discovered in every village.

Art historians observe that there was already a sophisticated art tradition thriving on the coast when the first explorers arrived. Highly refined carving techniques and conventions of design suggest that an art tradition had been fostered over hundreds, possibly even thousands of years. It is difficult, however, to trace the artistic and stylistic development of northwest coast prehistoric art, which was created before contact. A culture dependent on wood leaves little evidence behind.

Some prehistoric ceremonial and decorated stone and bone objects have been uncovered in sites along the coast that show evidence of classic northwest coast style. Archaeologists identify on carved objects the repetition of eye forms, ovoid and u-shapes, and the x-ray style indicated by the clear delineation of an animal's ribs. Moreover, primitive versions of commonly used west coast woodworking tools, such as the adze and chisel, have been discovered, suggesting that woodcarving techniques were honed over hundreds of years. Prehistoric wooden artifacts have also been found, such as frontal house poles, house planks, and baskets that provide evidence again of a woodworking tradition.

By 1835, the Hudson's Bay Company had three posts in full operation along the northwest coast. Art production increased and Aboriginal artists began to turn out objects for trade. Trade and travel also brought disease and the Aboriginal population of the west coast rapidly decreased. In the later part of the twentieth century, a new generation of northwest coast artists emerged and revived the artistic tradition of their people. In their totem poles, masks, sculptures, jewellery, and other art objects, these artists bring life to the faces of the animals and supernatural beings celebrated by their ancestors.

Kwakiutl mask

Conclusion

Although there may be some myths and fanciful stories of Europeans reaching North America before the Norse arrived in 1000 CE, there is no solid evidence to support these stories. The story of the Norse at L'Anse aux Meadows and the Skraelings, although interesting, is not significant for its impact on the Aboriginal Peoples of Canada—they did successfully drive the Europeans away. What happened in the fifteenth and sixteenth centuries, with the expeditions of Cabot and Cartier and the many other European explorers and entrepreneurs, did change the lives of Canada's Aboriginal Peoples forever. These explorers led the way for the English and French to claim the Aboriginal land with total disregard for the people who lived there. These so-called discoverers also led the way for more entrepreneurs and settlers from the old world. The process of colonizing Canada had begun.

Notes

1. Urs Bitterli, *Cultures in Conflict: Encounters Between European and Non-European Cultures, 1492–1800,* tr. Ritchie Robertson (London: Polity Press, 1989). First published in German, 1986.
2. The name Vinland was probably an exaggeration of the fertility of the new land, since grapevines do not grow in Newfoundland. The grapes of Eiriksson's accounts were probably wild berries. But the name represents the optimism of this Norse explorer and his desire to encourage settlers to follow his path. There may also be some confusion in interpretation of the word *vin,* which is an Old Norse word for grasslands, not grapes.
3. Olive Dickason, *Canada's First Nations,* first edition (Toronto: McClelland & Stewart, 1992), p. 87.
4. Robert McGhee, *Canada Rediscovered* (Ottawa: Canadian Museum of Civilization), p. 53.
5. Leslie Harris, *Newfoundland and Labrador: A Brief History* (Toronto: JM Dent & Sons, 1968), p. 21.
6. Don Gillmor and Pierre Turgeon, *Canada: A People's History,* Vol. I (Toronto: McClelland & Stewart, 2000), p. 14.
7. Dickason, *Canada's First Nations,* p. 73.
8. Gillmor and Turgeon, *Canada,* p. 14.
9. Dickason, *Canada's First Nations,* p. 96.
10. Ibid., p. 63.
11. Gillmor and Turgeon, *Canada,* pp. 10–11.
12. The Crusades were military expeditions made by European Christians from the eleventh to the thirteenth century. The goal of the Crusades was the retake areas that had been captured by Muslim forces.
13. McGhee, *Canada Rediscovered,* pp. 96–97.
14. Ibid, p. 97.
15. Daniel N. Paul, *We Were Not the Savages: A Micmac Perspective on the Collision of European and Aboriginal Civilization* (Halifax: Nimbus Publishing, 1993), pp. 2–3.

16. Ibid., pp. 2–3.
17. Arthur J. Ray, *I Have Lived Here Since the World Began* (Toronto: Lester Publishing, 1996), pp. 38–40.
18. McGhee, *Canada Rediscovered*, p. 122.
19. Gillmor and Turgeon, *Canada*, p. 21.
20. Ibid., p. 19.
21. Iles-aux-Oiseaux is likely the Island of the Birds in the Faroe Islands, northwest of Scotland and halfway between Iceland and Norway.
22. Gillmor and Turgeon, *Canada*, p. 19.
23. McGhee, *Canada Rediscovered*, pp. 125–26.
24. Dickason, *Canada's First Nations*, p. 100.
25. Ray, *I Have Lived Here*, p. 40.
26. Ibid., p. 41.

Chapter 3 Review

Knowledge & Understanding

1. Identify these people, places, and events, and explain their historical significance to Canada's developing culture and identity:
   - Skraelings
   - L'Anse aux Meadows
   - Shawnadithit
   - Donnacona
   - Jacques Cartier
   - contact/collision/relationship
   - Thorfinn Karsefni
   - John Cabot
   - Beothuk
   - Stadacona

2. Create a graphic organizer and explain how various groups of Aboriginal Peoples helped Europeans to adapt to their new environment. In what ways did Aboriginal Peoples help Europeans to survive?

3. In what ways did the arrival of Europeans change the lives of Aboriginal Peoples in Canada? Be sure to look at various aspects of their lives: economic, social, and cultural. What change had the most devastating effect?

Thinking & Inquiry

4. How different were Aboriginal Peoples from Europeans in their economic motivations and practices? Explain your answer in at least three well-developed paragraphs.

5. In this unit, you have learned about the extensive Aboriginal history in Canada. You have learned that long before the arrival of Europeans, Aboriginal Peoples in Canada had complex trading networks, differing political structures, and a variety of spiritual beliefs. With what you have learned, respond to the following statement: "Canada, it used to be said by non-Aboriginals with more or less conviction, is a country of much geography and little history." Do you believe that many non-Aboriginals still hold this view? Why or why not?

Application

6. As a curator at the Museum of Civilization, you have been asked to design an exhibit about early contact between Aboriginal Peoples and Europeans. You have been given ten display cases in which to create the images for the message you want to send. Using simple sketches with explanations, create a mock display that you will show to your supervisor for approval. You may want to portray such messages as the effect of Europeans on the Aboriginals, trade, myth versus reality, and so on. Be sure to include a title for your display.

7. Examine the pictograph of a European sailing vessel in this chapter. How can historians date when this pictograph was drawn? What clues in the pictograph would help historians decide when it was created?

Communication

8. Create symbols that Aboriginals may have selected to represent Europeans during the early stages of contact. Explain your choice of symbols in a well-written paragraph.

9. Imagine that you are a cartographer on Cartier's ship. You are travelling back to France with Donnacona, Domagaya, and Taignoagny on board. Write three journal entries that record your observations about the three passengers. As a European who has never seen Aboriginal Peoples until this trip, how do you feel about them? What do you notice? How do you feel about taking them away from their homeland?

Research

1. How do Canadians and visitors to Canada remember, honour, and learn about the history of Aboriginal Peoples? Several archaeological sites across Canada help students and the public understand what it was like to live in these diverse societies. Visit one of these historic sites, or find one in your area (online or, even better, in person), and immerse yourself in the culture of early Canada.

    Possible sites include the following:
    Canadian Archaeological Association, www.canadianarchaeology.com
    Canadian Museum of Civilization, www.civilization.ca
    Glenbow Museum, www.glenbow.org
    McGaw site (Richmond Hill, Ontario),
    www.ontarioarchaeology.on.ca/oas/Pages/mcgaw_site.htm
    Manitoba Museum, www.manitobamuseum.mb.ca
    Nova Scotia Museum, www.museum.gov.ns.ca
    The Provincial Museum of Newfoundland and Labrador,
    www.nfmuseum.com
    Royal British Columbia Museum, www.rbcm1.rbcm.gov.bc.ca
    Ska-Nah-Doht (Longwoods Road Conservation Area)
    Virtual Museum of Canada, www.virtualmuseum.ca
    Woodland Cultural Centre (Brantford, Ontario), www.woodland-centre.on.ca

    Check with your teacher or local museum to see what exhibits are on display in your area.

2. When you visit a museum or archeological site online or in person, what should you look for? You may want to take notes under such topics or themes as
    - the social structure of the settlement
    - cultural artifacts that remain
    - cultural items that are missing
    - the relationship between men and women
    - the lives of children
    - evidence of trade

Interpretation and Analysis

3. How are Aboriginal Peoples portrayed in these exhibits? Does the portrayal complement what you discovered in the unit, or does it tell a different story? What types of historical sources of information were used in the research? Do you see any false information or bias in the written analysis that accompanies the visuals? Where did the curators or museum staff find their information? Did the museum display have a theme or issue they were trying to get across to their visitors?

4. There have been debates about whether it is right to reconstruct villages and settlements or whether we should leave what we find as is because we can never really be completely accurate in our recreation of Aboriginal life, especially in prehistoric times. What side of this debate are you on now that you have seen your site?

Applying and Communicating Your Skills

5. Construct a tour sheet for the site you visited that can be used by your fellow history students. Include at least two pages of questions and analysis that will guide them through the site and help them collect and question important information. Ensure that your tour sheet honours the lives and legacy of the early Aboriginal Peoples.

6. Construct a tour sheet for the same site for primary-school children. On one page, describe how you would help children who visit your site or museum. What would you want them to learn?

The World of New France 1604–1763

Two of the most significant events in Canadian history framed the world of New France: the arrival of Champlain and the first few French immigrants in 1604 and the fall of New France in 1760. Throughout this period, the fur trade in the colonies contributed to the wealth and power of France, and European wars for empire spilled over into North America. Seen as a threat to British control, the Acadians were expelled from their homeland and the battle of the Plains of Abraham came at the end of a war among the great European powers.

The story of New France is also the story of the Aboriginal Peoples who helped the settlers survive, who taught them about their new country, and who formed trading and military alliances that lasted until the fall of New France. This changed the cultural identities of both French Canadians and Aboriginal Peoples. As a result of their relationship with the French, some Aboriginal Peoples lost their traditional way of life and many of their people to European diseases for which they had no immunity.

For the early French settlers, living in Canada was very different from living in France. Generations of habitants, seigneurs, *coureurs de bois*, and clergy became more independent of France and developed a distinct culture in the towns and countryside of New France. In spite of—or perhaps because of—the frequent conflicts the French settlers suffered, they became a separate, resilient people whose culture would endure.

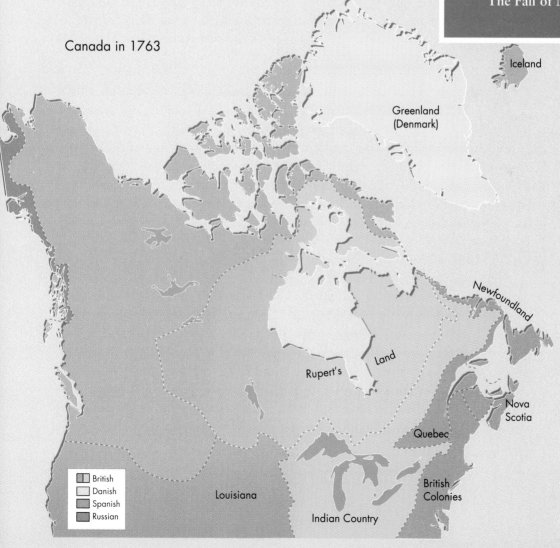

Canada in 1763

Iceland

Greenland
(Denmark)

Newfoundland

Rupert's   Land

Nova
Scotia

Quebec

British
Colonies

Louisiana

Indian Country

British
Danish
Spanish
Russian

The First French Settlements 1603–1663

Ever since the King had the goodness to extend his care to this country...we have seen noteworthy changes in Canada, and we can say that it is no longer the country of horrors...that has been described so unfavourably, but a real New France.

–FATHER FRANÇOIS-JOSEPH LE MERCIER

With the arrival of Pierre du Gua de Monts, Samuel de Champlain, and the first French settlers into the land they called New France, the lives and culture of the Aboriginal Peoples of Canada changed. The new French arrivals—backed by royal, aristocratic, and merchant investors—formed lasting trading and military alliances with the Mi'kmaq Nation in Acadia and with the Montagnais and Huron in Quebec. The Aboriginal Peoples helped the newcomers survive in the dangerous country about which the French knew so little. With the rise of the beaver-hat fashion in Europe, the fur trade became more important than ever. Trading companies brought out settlers and established an economic base that would last—for both Aboriginals and Europeans—until the fall of New France in 1760.

Following Champlain's founding of Quebec, more settlers began to arrive. Some came as seigneurs, some came to farm, some to make their fortune in the fur trade, some to live and trade among the Huron Nation and to fight against the dreaded Iroquois Nation, and some to convert the Aboriginal Peoples to Catholicism. Among those early missionaries were the Jesuits who were determined to live among the Aboriginal Peoples, to learn their language, to study their traditions, and especially to convert them to Catholicism. Among the earliest women to arrive in the colony were Jeanne de Mance, who established the first hospitals, and Marie de l'Incarnation, who founded schools for French and Aboriginal girls.

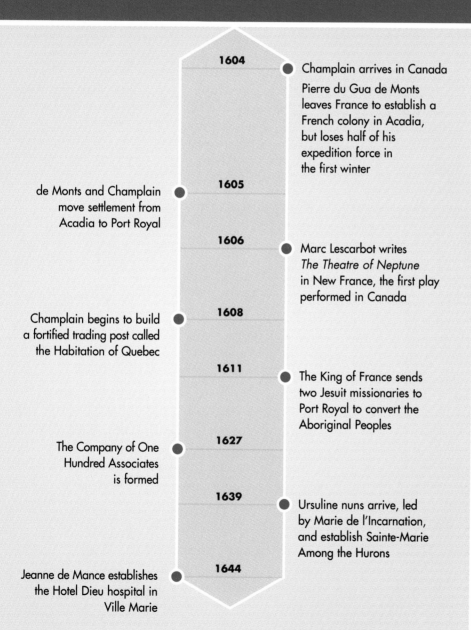

4

1604
Champlain arrives in Canada

Pierre du Gua de Monts leaves France to establish a French colony in Acadia, but loses half of his expedition force in the first winter

de Monts and Champlain move settlement from Acadia to Port Royal
1605

1606
Marc Lescarbot writes *The Theatre of Neptune* in New France, the first play performed in Canada

Champlain begins to build a fortified trading post called the Habitation of Quebec
1608

1611
The King of France sends two Jesuit missionaries to Port Royal to convert the Aboriginal Peoples

The Company of One Hundred Associates is formed
1627

1639
Ursuline nuns arrive, led by Marie de l'Incarnation, and establish Sainte-Marie Among the Hurons

Jeanne de Mance establishes the Hotel Dieu hospital in Ville Marie
1644

By the end of this chapter, you will be able to

- analyze the principal characteristics of the French and English colonial experiences in Canada

- explain why and how Aboriginal Peoples helped European colonists adapt to their new environment

- analyze the impact of European contact on the lives of Aboriginal Peoples and evaluate the responses of Aboriginal Peoples

- compare the colonizing policies of the French and the British in colonial Canada

Champlain and the Beginnings of Settlement in New France

As Canadian historian Christopher Moore says, "Europeans had been crossing the Atlantic since 1000 A.D., and there had been a century of regular visits to Canada before 1608. But it was Champlain who transformed transient contact into a permanent European presence in Canada."[1]

Samuel de Champlain (1567–1635) first arrived in Canada in 1604 and since then he has become a major figure in our Canadian cultural heritage. However, in all his private and published writings, he left little information about his personal life. We know him only through his actions and accomplishments. Champlain was born in the town of Brouage in the southwest of France in 1567 and he started his career as a soldier. He was an experienced and successful seaman who made twenty-three voyages across the Atlantic Ocean. He was an explorer who, before he came to Canada in 1604, had already sailed on a Spanish ship along the coast of South America and on a French expedition that travelled up the St. Lawrence River to the Lachine Rapids. He was a skilled geographer and cartographer whose maps of the east coast of Canada and the St. Lawrence River are still valid today. He was a colonizer at a time when most people were only interested in the wealth they could gain from trade in North America. He was a skilled negotiator who successfully forged alliances with the Mi'kmaq, Maliseet, Montagnais, and Huron peoples. He was a writer and promoter whose books on his experiences in Canada persuaded people in France to invest in future expeditions and eventually to come and settle in Canada.

Champlain's map of 1632 was made with the help of the Aboriginal Peoples who taught him about the geography of the Atlantic coast, the St. Lawrence River, and the Great Lakes region. Champlain drew the map to accompany his *History of New France*, which was published in Paris in 1612.

Those early expeditions from France in the seventeenth century were sponsored by royal, aristocratic, and merchant investors. They were looking primarily for riches by discovering mineral deposits within the country, by finding a sea route to the Orient, or by trading in furs with the Aboriginal Peoples of North America. During those early days, some Europeans had an exaggerated sense of the wealth that could be found in Canada. Sieur de Côbes, writing home to France in 1609, reported that the land held by France "is one of the wealthiest countries of the land of Canada . . . where there are mines of gold and silver in great abundance, which are very rich. And even all along the rivers one sometimes finds . . . little pebbles of fine gold, many precious stones, diamonds and other riches." [2]

This was the impetus for the early expeditions. France was, of course, not alone in looking for wealth in what Europeans called the "New World." European countries had seen Spain grow wealthy and politically powerful because of the gold that the conquistadors had taken from the Incas, Mayans, and Aztecs of South America. The Portuguese and the Dutch were gaining wealth from the products of the East Indies. At the same time, advances in navigation and sailing ships made the voyages safer, surer, and faster than they had been in previous centuries. The sea astrolabe, developed after 1470, allowed greater accuracy in measuring latitudes and following an established route to a destination. The discoveries of Copernicus, Kepler, and Galileo had helped redefine astronomy, a science that was still important to sailors in the seventeenth century. Ship designs had been improved; ships now had rudders and tillers, three masts, square sails, and better rigging than in the past.

But for at least one hundred years, the French had been fishing off the coast of eastern Canada and trading for furs with the Aboriginal Peoples. So, why the change to colonization? The colonies were intended to help establish French interests in North America. There were competitors in this northern region of the continent: English, Spanish, Basque, Dutch, all were trying to establish their rights to territory and claim land—in spite of the Aboriginal Peoples who lived on the land. By 1607, the English had a colony in Jamestown, Virginia, and by 1620, they had other colonies in Massachusetts. They were also trying to establish colonies in Newfoundland and Acadia. By 1626, the Dutch were established in New Amsterdam in what is today New York.

The king of France, Henri IV, sponsored the French expeditions in the hopes that his kingdom could regain some of the glory and wealth that had been lost during the religious and civil wars between Protestants and Catholics in previous decades. There had been wars between the British, the French, and the Spanish in Europe for many years. Henri IV was less interested in conquest than in acquiring wealth to replenish his depleted coffers. In addition, with the defeat of the Spanish Armada by the English fleet in 1588, the seas were safer for the French and English expeditions to the "new" world. Now settlers could be sent out to establish posts for trade with the Aboriginal Peoples and priests could be sent to convert them to Catholicism.

Acadia

In the spring of 1604, Pierre du Gua de Monts set out from Le Havre in France for Acadia intent on establishing a French colony and permanent trading post. De Mont brought with him two Roman Catholic priests, a Protestant minister, artisans and carpenters, masons and stone-cutters, soldiers, vagabonds, several noblemen—and Samuel de Champlain to act as the voyage's geographer and cartographer. [3]

De Monts' mandate from King Henri IV was to establish settlements in New France in exchange for an exclusive right to trade with the Aboriginal Peoples of the regions. Along with his trading

This is Champlain's own drawing of the habitation at Port Royal.

planted gardens on the island and on the nearby mainland.[5]

That winter in Acadia was unusually severe. The first snow fell on October 6 and the snow was still high on the ground late in April. In addition, the ice flows in the river were so thick that the crossing was treacherous. The settlers suffered greatly as they ran out of nourishing food and endured the cold and isolation. Many developed scurvy, a disease caused by lack of vitamin C in the diet which leads to exhaustion and, if not treated, to death. During that first winter, almost half of the expedition died.

In 1605, de Monts and Champlain decided to move their settlement to Port Royal. Having learned from their experience the previous year, the would-be colonizers chose a more sheltered spot along the Bay of Fundy, which they called Port Royal. Now that they knew about the cold, the snow, and the wild winds that accompanied winter on the east coast of Canada, they knew better how to prepare for future winters. As Champlain noted in his diary, "It is impossible to know this country without having wintered here, for in arriving in autumn everything is very pleasant owing to the woods, the fine landscape, and the good fishing for cod and other species which are found. But winter in this country lasts for six months."[6]

This time, they built homes and storehouses that were more suitable for sustaining them over the long cold winter. They also located their habitation close to a forest so that they would have wood to use as building materials and firewood throughout the winter, and they planted wheat and vegetable gardens.

De Monts had to return to France to buy fresh supplies, to persuade his investors to continue

monopoly, he was appointed lieutenant general "of the coasts, lands and confines of Acadia, Canada, and other places in New France".[4] In return he was to establish sixty colonists a year and to convert the Aboriginal Peoples to the Christian faith by supporting Catholic missionaries.

De Monts and Champlain knew that other efforts at colonization in the seventeenth century had failed. In the years prior to 1604, they had both visited the now abandoned settlement at Tadoussac at the mouth of the Saguenay River. So, after Champlain and de Monts negotiated peace and friendship agreements with the resident Mi'kmaq and Maliseet chiefs, they chose Île Ste. Croix at the mouth of the St. Croix River, which is today on the boundary between the U.S. and Canada, as the place to build their settlement. The island was centrally located, had a harbour deep enough for their ships, and could be defended against attack. Also, the members of the French expedition were running out of time before winter. Champlain quickly drew up a plan for the habitation. While some of the group worked on constructing the buildings, others

supporting the new colony, and to fight off the intrigues of other merchants who were trying to break his monopoly so that they too could trade legally in New France. These Atlantic crossings for supplies and financial help from investors and royal patrons were an ongoing feature of early life in New France. The French settlers remained dependent on economic and military support from France for many years. It would be a long time before the French settlers in Canada were able to be self-sufficient. At this time, the funds from France were needed to keep the colonies and the colonists alive.

Port Royal was abandoned in 1607 when de Monts' trading monopoly was revoked. The habitation was left under the care of Membertou, the Mi'kmaq chief. De Monts returned to France, and Champlain set out to head up a new colony on the St. Lawrence River. However, France was not ready to abandon its claims in Acadia. The French government wanted to keep a settlement and trading posts in the region to keep alive its claim to the fishery and the fur trade. By 1609, Jean de Biencourt de Poutrincourt returned to Port Royal as seigneur, was welcomed by Membertou and found the habitation just as it had been left. In 1611, the king sent two Jesuit missionaries with Biencourt to convert the Aboriginal Peoples there. Gradually, settlers started to arrive and maintained themselves by doing some farming, fur trading, and serving the needs of the French fleets who came to fish in the region each year.

Recreation at Port Royal

To help keep up the spirits of the isolated group of men over that first winter at Port Royal, Champlain founded the Order of Good Cheer. As Champlain noted in his *Voyages of 1613*, the Order seemed to contribute to the well-being of the settlers,

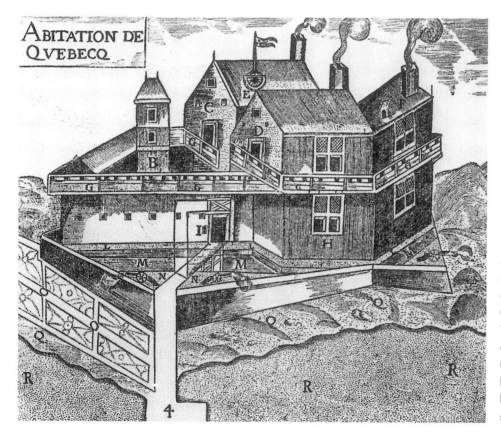

ABITATION DE QVEBECQ

Abitation de Quebecq [sic], drawn by Champlain. The Habitation of Quebec, a trading post built by Champlain and his crew in the summer of 1608.

We spent this winter very pleasantly, and had good fare by means of the Order of Good Cheer which I established, and which everybody found beneficial to his health, and more profitable than all sorts of medicine we might have used. This Order consisted of a chain, which we used to place with certain little ceremonies about the neck of one of our people, commissioning him for that day to go hunting. The next day it was conferred upon another, and so on in order. All vied with each other to see who could do the best, and bring back the finest game. We did not come off badly, nor did the Indians who were with us.[7]

The celebrations were held in the common room of the settlement, on its large wooden tables. Visiting Mi'kmaq often shared in the feast, as well as supplying some of the fresh game. The food—which might include smoked beaver tail and boiled moose nose, otter, bear, rabbit, and sturgeon as well as freshly baked French bread—was cooked over the large kitchen fireplace. And this year the celebrants also had a good supply of Bordeaux wine, unlike the previous winter when the wine

had run out. The feast ended with music, old favourites and new compositions.

Also during this time, Marc Lescarbot, who had arrived at Port Royal from Paris in 1606, wrote the first European play performed in Canada. Lescarbot was a Parisian lawyer who had come to Port Royal with one of his clients, Jean de Biencourt de Poutrincourt, but he was also a published author with books of poetry and biography to his credit. To celebrate the safe arrival of Poutrincourt from one of his voyages to France, Lescarbot wrote *The Theatre of Neptune in New France*, which was staged out of doors. The play, written in verse and performed by both French and Mi'kmaq actors, depicts Neptune coming in a ship across the Port Royal basin to welcome the traveller home and to sing the praises of the colony and of the French king to the accompaniment of trumpets and cannon fire.

After returning to France in 1607, when de Monts' monopoly expired, Lescarbot published histories of the French and Mi'kmaq peoples he had met in Acadia. His *Histoire de la Nouvelle France*

The First Play in Canada, pen and ink reconstruction by C.W. Jeffrey

went through three editions, was translated into French and German, and was influential in fostering French enthusiasm for colonialism and New France that grew throughout the seventeenth century.

Aboriginal Alliances in Acadia

At the time of Champlain's arrival in Port Royal, Membertou was the Chief of the Mi'kmaq peoples of that area and the Grand Chief of the seven Mi'kmaq districts in what is today Nova Scotia. As was customary among the Mi'kmaq, Membertou held his authority because the Mi'kmaq people of that time had decided he was most worthy to do so. By both French accounts and Mi'kmaq oral tradition, he was a strong leader who had convinced his people of his leadership capabilities by his actions, his powers of healing, his ability to foretell the future, and his persuasive speaking ability. Lescarbot, in his history of Acadia, said that had

> under him a number of families whom he rules, not with so much authority as does our King over his subjects, but with sufficient power to harangue, advise, and lead them to war, to render justice to one who has a grievance, and like matters. . .[H]is reputation is far above that of all the other Sagamores of the country.[8]

Membertou and his people received Champlain and his men graciously and offered their assistance. They helped them find food, taught them techniques for surviving in the land, and assisted Champlain in his explorations down the coast of the Atlantic seaboard. The Mi'kmaq people placed great emphasis on hospitality. Giving food and lodging to strangers was a matter of honour among them. As Chrestien Le Clercq, a Roman Catholic priest said, the Mi'kmaq

> make almost no distinction between the home-born and the stranger. They give lodging equally to the French and the Indians who come from a distance, and to both they distribute generously whatever they have obtained in hunting and in the fishery, giving themselves little concern if the strangers remain among them for weeks, months, and even entire years.[9]

What the Europeans saw Aboriginal non-resistance to the their taking over the land was in fact an extension of this hospitality. This Aboriginal policy allowed the French to gain a foothold in the region and was to have unforetold and disastrous repercussions for the Mi'kmaq and other Aboriginal Peoples.

Quebec

Champlain became more and more interested in establishing a lasting colony in New France. He argued successfully to King Louis XIII that such a colony could serve to christianize the Aboriginal Peoples, a powerful argument at that time after the religious wars that had caused such chaos in Europe. There was also the old argument of trade advantage with the Aboriginal Peoples, and there was still the possibility that the St. Lawrence would be the route to the riches of Asia. As the future would tell, Champlain's establishment of the settlement at Quebec would be of major importance in the history of New France for the next 150 years.

Champlain, who had the leadership role in this new colonizing venture, decided on the site of Quebec because it was an advantageous location for trade, it was a beautiful and fertile site, and, with a 98-metre high cliff facing the river, it was defensible in military terms. The site also had the advantage of being uninhabited at the time. The earlier village of Statacona that Cartier had visited was gone, as were the Iroquoian, Donnacona and his people. Champlain was able to make alliances with the Montagnais and Algonkian peoples who used the region for trade with the European ships that came up the St. Lawrence. He had already met the Montagnais Chief Anadabijou at Tadoussac in 1603 and had sealed a pact of friendship with him and his people. This agreement allowed the French to settle on Montagnais territory but did not give the French any title to the Montagnais lands.[10]

In the summer of 1608, Champlain and his crew set about building a fortified trading post, which he called the Habitation of Quebec. Using wood from the nearby forests, the settlers first built a storage site for their supplies and then went on to construct a warehouse and buildings for residences, all with ditches and palisades. They also erected platforms for their cannons, which were positioned to fire into the St. Lawrence.

Their first year was not without peril as Basque and Spanish competitors plotted to kill Champlain and the long cold winter and scurvy again took their toll on the settlement. By the end of the winter of 1609, only eight of the original twenty-eight men survived. With no knowledge of what caused scurvy, they were helpless against the disease. Champlain puzzled that "Scurvy attacks those who take proper care of themselves as well as the most miserable people."[11] Eventually, the French settlers would learn from the Aboriginal Peoples that a tea made from the bark of the white cedar tree could be used during the winter months to keep scurvy at bay.

The English Kirke brothers destroyed Quebec in 1629 and took Champlain back to England as a prisoner. On his return to Quebec in 1632 the settlement had to be completely rebuilt, but Champlain's settlement at Quebec remained the major centre for French colonial power until it was lost finally to the English military in 1760.

Aboriginal Alliances at Quebec

While at Quebec, Champlain sought, and obtained, advantageous fur-trading alliances with the Montagnais, Algonkian, and Huron peoples. The Aboriginal Peoples in this region—like the Mi'kmaq and Maliseet in Acadia—were already accustomed to trading with the Europeans who arrived each summer by ship. The Huron themselves were traders who served as middlemen in a vast trade network. With the Aboriginal hunting peoples, the Huron traded their farm produce for beaver furs. With the Europeans, they traded the beaver furs for

The Battle of Ticonderoga Point, south of Quebec, 1609

European goods, some of which they then traded with the Aboriginal hunters. The extent of this trade network has been proved by archaeological finds in Aboriginal settlements very far removed from the St. Lawrence and Acadian regions.

Champlain's alliances were established, according to Aboriginal custom, by gift distribution and feasting. He cemented these alliances with his allies—the Montagnais represented by Chief Anadabidjou, the Algonkian represented by Chief Yroquet, and the Huron—by helping them attack and defeat the Iroquois in 1609 at the battle of Ticonderoga Point south of Quebec. The conflict between the Iroquois Confederacy and the peoples north of the St. Lawrence and the Great Lakes had been going on for a long time, and would continue into the next century. The powerful Huron and Iroquois Confederacies both wanted control of the fur trade, which was bringing more and more trade goods into their country.

At this battle, the use of European firearms was a deciding factor. Champlain's allies told him how he could identify the three chiefs of the opposing army, and he and one of the other French soldiers in his party killed the chiefs at the outset of the battle. The Iroquois, who had no guns, "lost courage and fled into the woods."[12] This victory temporarily assured peace for trade. Champlain's Aboriginal allies were satisfied, and they believed they had made a good bargain in allowing the French to settle because they gained not only trading advantages but also a military advantage against the powerful Iroquois Confederacy. However, the victory would have far-reaching repercussions. It was not long before the Iroquois were able to acquire guns from the Dutch who had settled at Albany (Fort Orange). They remained the enemies of the Huron and helped cause the destruction of that nation; they also remained enemies of the French right up to and including the last days of the French regime in Canada.

Champlain's Aboriginal allies also helped him explore the region around the St. Lawrence and the

Great Lakes. Not only did he have a mandate from the French king for this exploration, but "discovering" unknown territory remained a passion for Champlain throughout his life. As he said, "The great love I have always had for making discoveries in New France made me more and more eager to travel this country so as to have a perfect knowledge of it."[13] Arriving in Huron lands he discovered a world more sophisticated than he had expected.

> In this stretch of land there are eighteen villages. They have a total of 30 000 souls. Their cabins are covered with the bark of trees, and a space at one end where they keep their corn. In one cabin, there is a place for twelve fires and twenty-four families. The men go out to other nations to trade and to barter what they have for what they lack.[14]

Truchements/Coureurs de Bois

In the early days of the Quebec settlement, Champlain decided to send Frenchmen among the Huron people to explore their lands and to learn their language, their tactics for survival, and their culture. Champlain called them *truchements* and they were the forerunners of the *coureurs de bois* of the 1660s and following years. In later years, their actions would be condemned by King Louis XIV and his colonial administrators who tried to insist—to little effect—that they settle down and engage in farming as they were supposed to be doing. However, in these early days their learning was prized. With the *truchements'* help, the European fur traders' reach would be extended, alliances between French and Aboriginal Peoples would be strengthened, and the colonial administrators would have someone who could translate between French and Huron speakers.

One of the earliest *truchements* was Étienne Brûlé who was only eighteen years old when Champlain allowed him to go to live with the Huron. Brûlé had already proved himself to be a survivor; he was one of only eight original settlers who had survived the winter of 1608. From his Huron hosts, Brûlé learned a great deal that was useful to Champlain and the others at Quebec: he explored their territory with Huron hunters, learned the strategies of forest warfare from their warriors, learned about the laws and language from Huron women, and about the traditions of the people from the elders.[15]

Montreal and Jeanne de Mance

In 1642, a lay Catholic missionary society led by Paul de Chomeday de Maisonneuve arrived in New France. Against opposition from the governor and clergy in Quebec, he and his party set out to establish Ville-Marie at what is today Montreal. The goal for this settlement was to convert the Aboriginal Peoples by having them live among the French and assimilate them into Catholic French society.

Among his party was Jeanne de Mance, one of the first lay women (that is, not a member of a religious order) to settle in New France. Educated by the Ursuline nuns in France, she is thought to have received her nursing training in Langres, helping the wounded in a charity hospital during the Thirty Years War. Arriving in New France, she stopped in Quebec to study the administrative and medical procedures at the Hotel-Dieu hospital and to learn the Huron language. Then she moved on to Ville Marie where, with funding received from the French widow Angélique de Bullion, she opened a hospital in her home and took care of settlers and Aboriginal People. This first hospital was small, with only six beds for men and two for women, and it was surrounded by a defensive stockade. But in spite of the size of her establishment, she was much appreciated by the people of Ville Marie who called here the "Angel of the Colony."

In time, de Mance returned to France to recruit nuns to staff her proposed new and larger hospital and to raise funds for the venture. Through her years in Ville Marie she would return to France a number of times to raise money for both her hospital and for the colony at Ville Marie. Before she could build the new Hotel-Dieu hospital of Ville Marie, she had to do battle with the powerful Bishop Montmorency de Laval of Quebec. He wanted to send nuns from the

Called the "Angel of the Colony," Jeanne de Mance set up the first hospital in Ville-Marie (present day Montreal) in her own home. She would go on to open a Hotel-Dieu hospital in 1644, caring for both French and Aboriginal people for seventeen years.

In 1974, the Government of Canada proclaimed in its National Symbol of Canada Act the "the beaver is a symbol of the sovereignty of Canada." By so doing, it recognized the cultural importance of this familiar rodent as part of the historical identity of Canadians.

Hotel-Dieu hospital in Quebec to staff the new hospital, rather than have it run by de Mance from Ville Marie. But once again, de Mance persisted in her own plan and was finally able to open her Hotel-Dieu hospital in 1644. She went on to administer this hospital for seventeen years and to take care of the French and Aboriginal victims of the Iroquois attacks of the 1640s.

By 1650 the mission at Ville Marie had failed for lack of Aboriginal interest in the enterprise, but Jeanne de Mance's Hotel-Dieu hospital was a success. Although her original building was destroyed by fire in 1696, the Hotel-Dieu hospital was rebuilt and still exists today.

Web Connection

www.mcgrawhill.ca/links/definingcanada
Go the Web site above to find out more about the experiences of the Champlain and the early settlers in Canada.

Review...Reflect...Respond

1. What reasons did Champlain give to convince France to support a colony in New France?

2. How did Champlain transform "transient contact" into a permanent European presence in Canada?

3. How did Champlain and the European presence forever alter warfare between the Aboriginal groups?

The Fur Trade

In Europe, during the late 1500s, a fashion trend began that was to change the map of the world and human history. Hat-makers discovered that the felt material made from beaver skins could be used to make strong, durable hats that could be moulded into many different shapes. And people bought the hats. Well into the 1800s they bought beaver hats in all shapes and sizes. To satisfy the demand, many beaver skins were needed. The source of the best skins was the forests of Northern Canada, from the Aboriginal hunters who trapped them, and the Aboriginal women who prepared the skins for market. Because of hat fashions, ships went out from Europe across the Atlantic, alliances were made and broken, wars were fought, peoples were destroyed or at the least had their culture changed forever, and colonists left Europe to settle in a new land.

The fur trade was very important in the development of Canada, as it was the major economic activity in the early years. If there had not been a market, the fur trade would never have existed. The early investors and sponsors of expeditions and colonizing ventures were banking on commercial success. That's why they participated in the risky ventures.

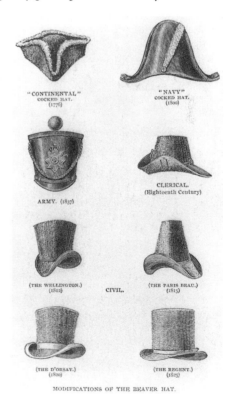

"CONTINENTAL"
COCKED HAT.
(1776)

"NAVY"
COCKED HAT.
(1800)

ARMY. (1837)

CLERICAL.
(Eighteenth Century)

(THE WELLINGTON.)
(1812)

CIVIL.

(THE PARIS BEAU.)
(1815)

(THE D'ORSAY.)
(1820)

(THE REGENT.)
(1825)

MODIFICATIONS OF THE BEAVER HAT.

Fashionable eighteenth-century beaver hats.

The Business of the fur Trade

Date	Ownership and Business Details	Role of Aboriginal Peoples
Pre-1604	There were no monopolies, just open competition among different French merchants as well as Basque and Spanish. The Europeans traded with Aboriginal Peoples from their ships. For the prized beaver pelts, they traded beads mirrors and bells and later needles, knives, kettles, and blankets.	The Montagnais people traded beaver furs with the Europeans at Tadoussac at the mouth of the Saguenay River The Mi'kmaq of Acadia adapted to the fur trade and acted as middlemen between the hunters of the north and the European traders. Both groups of Aboriginal Peoples considered themselves the equals of those they traded with.
1603–1608	Gua de Monts has a monopoly from the king of France that extended from Acadia through the St. Lawrence Valley. The condition for the monopoly was that he establish 60 settlers a year in Acadia and support missionaries among the Mi'kmaq. French merchants purchased shares in the venture.	This monopoly was defied by some French merchants trading illegally, as well as by Dutch and Spanish traders. The Mi'kmaq established a successful fur trading relationship with the French in Acadia based on their sophisticated trading and fur-gathering system with other Aboriginal Peoples They traded furs with Europeans and received European goods in exchange; they traded those European goods with the fur-hunting peoples....
1608	Groups of merchants in France engaged in more or less free trade and paid little attention to colonizing. De Monts and Champlain at Quebec continued with their combination of trade, exploration, and colonizing efforts.	The Montagnais continued to trade with the French. The Hurons begin to take the major role in the fur trade through Quebec.
1612	De Monts, Champlain and their financial partners win a monopoly for trade out of Quebec with French noblemen as investors. They continue to emphasize settlement and exploration, as well as the fur trade.	The Huron traders are the principle source for furs, arriving at Quebec each spring in large flotillas of canoes.

Date	Ownership and Business Details	Role of Aboriginal Peoples
1627	The Company of One Hundred Associates, made up of one hundred French investors, is given a royal charter under the sponsorship of the French Cardinal Richelieu. The Company was given large tracts of property, and had administrative jurisdiction in the colony of Quebec. The Company also agreed to two hundred settlers a year, to maintain the clergy and to pay the soldiers needed for defense against the Iroquois.	The Huron built alliances with the new fur trading company. The Jesuits appear on the scene and the Huron have to accept their presence as a condition for trading with the French; smallpox epidemics in 1634 to 1640

The Aboriginal Peoples were essential to the success of the fur trade. They formed trading partnerships with the French merchants and their representatives, including Champlain and de Monts. The Mi'kmaq in Acadia, and the especially the Hurons in New France, had been trading with other Aboriginal nations for a long time before the Europeans arrived, but now they became the essential middlemen, or, as Arthur Ray called them the "aboriginal trading specialists."[16] They were well-accustomed to trading with Europeans aboard ships. As historian, Olive Dickason, says, "By the second decade of the seventeenth century, as many as 1,000 ships annually are estimated to have been trading and fishing along the North Atlantic coasts and the Gulf of St. Lawrence."[17]

In the early years of the settlement at Quebec, the Huron brought the furs to the merchants as the Europeans did not have the skills, the knowledge, or the alliances to go to the furs. Each spring, flotillas of approximately sixty canoes and two hundred men would come down from Huronia to Quebec. These canoes were between six to eight metres in length, held four or five men, and ninety kilograms of goods. If conditions on the river were good, the Huron traders could travel up to one hundred kilometres a day, in about four weeks the traders could get to Quebec and return home to Huronia. [18] At its height, the Huron were reported to account for 50 percent of the French fur trade.[19] These statistics show that the Huron were skilled not only as traders but also at forming alliances since they had to cross territory of other Aboriginal Peoples on their way from Huronia to Quebec.

The Company of One Hundred Associates (1627)

With so much wealth at stake, there were many people interested in investing in the trade of New France, in spite of the risks. Few investors were interested in settlement. The fur trade was the main focus in the late years of the sixteenth and the early years of the seventeenth centuries. Why go to all the expense and trouble of establishing colonies, when you could just trade with the Aboriginal traders from the deck of your ship? But France was also interested in colonization and religious conversion.

During the early years, a number of different business arrangements were formed around the fur trade. By April 1627, the powerful Cardinal Richelieu helped a group of one hundred French investors gain a royal charter for their company. Richelieu's objective was to establish a French empire in North America for the purpose of trade, settlement, and the conversion of the Aboriginal Peoples to Catholicism. He modelled this company on the successful British East India Company, which was founded in 1600.

The Company of One Hundred Associates was given administrative control over the territory that France claimed, from what is now Florida to the Arctic Circle. Each of the members of the group contributed three thousand livres—about $9 000 in today's money—to the venture. In return, the Company was given full seigneurial ownership of New France and a monopoly over all business in Canada for fifteen years. Over the terms of their contract, the company was supposed to bring out two to three hundred settlers in 1628 and four thousand more Roman Catholics to New France over the next fifteen years and it was to maintain Roman Catholic clergy in the settlement. No Protestant settlers were to be allowed.

The Missionaries

When Catholic missionaries arrived in Acadia and Quebec, they came from an environment of religious conflict and intolerance. After all, it had been less than one hundred years since Martin Luther had started Protestantism by posting his demands for reform on the church door in Wittenburg. It had been even fewer years since Henry VIII had started the Church of England and English people had to pay fealty to the English king rather than to the pope. In France, Huguenot Protestants had been at war with Catholics from 1562 to 1598. This was a time of religious intolerance for the spiritual beliefs of others—only Catholics were allowed to settle in Acadia and Quebec at the beginning of European rule—and of militant commitment to saving the souls of the those who were considered unbelievers. Two of the religious orders that made a large impact on New France were founded during those turbulent times: the Ursuline nuns in 1535 and the Jesuit priests and brothers in 1540.

The Jesuit Mission to the Huron

In 1633, once Quebec was back in French hands after being captured by the British in 1629, the Jesuits were the principle male missionary order in Canada. By this time, these "soldiers of Christ" as they were called, had already had success in converting people in Asia, Africa, and South America. King Louis XIII of France intended to combine the advance of French colonization and trade advantages with the conversion of the Aboriginal Peoples to Catholicism.

Originally the Jesuits had agreed with the Récollet missionaries' plan of moving Catholic Aboriginals to the farming community that had been established at the Sillery reserve just outside Quebec. But the Jesuits soon realized that the Sillery assimilation strategies were not working, and they believed that by living among the Huron people in their own lands, learning their language, and studying their culture, they would have a better chance of converting them to Catholicism. Initially, the Huron were not interested in having the Jesuits live among them; they would rather have had allies who were hunters or soldiers and who carried French guns. Eventually, the Huron gave in after they were convinced that if they didn't accept the Jesuits, they would lose their fur trading advantage with the French.

Father Jean de Brébeuf and three other missionaries arrived in Huronia in 1634 to found the mission of Ste. Marie among the Hurons. The Jesuits decided to focus their conversion efforts on the Huron because they were more numerous than other Aboriginal nations. Also, being farmers as well as traders, the Huron were more settled than some of the other available conversion prospects. The Jesuits intention was to live among the people, learn their ways, and convince them to become Catholics. Eventually, after nine years Brébeuf learned the Huron language and compiled a grammar of the language. The building of the actual mission began in 1639, and when it was finished it contained a chapel, a hospital, stables, and homes for both the French and the Huron converts.

France Bringing the Faith to the Indians — Jesuits preaching to the Huron Indians.

Huron put up with the Jesuits because they believed that otherwise they would have lost their trade advantage with the French.

The epidemics that followed in the wake of the Jesuits arrival led the Huron to believe that the priests had somehow brought the smallpox and influenza that killed so many of their people from 1634 to 1639. In 1641, a Huron woman told Marie de l'Incarnation that her people believed the Jesuits had caused these epidemics. "They came into a village where everyone was doing just fine: as soon as they arrived, everyone died.. . .[I]t is only the places where they never set foot that have been spared death and illness."20 Because they had no natural immunity, the Huron loss of life from these diseases was enormous. The people were outraged, and by the end of 1637 the Jesuit mission was nearly destroyed. There were more clashes between the few Catholic Huron converts and the more numerous Hurons who followed their traditional faith.

As time went on, more Hurons converted to Catholicism, and the converts often came into conflict with those who followed the traditional ways of their people. The Catholic Huron would no longer join in rituals that the majority believed was necessary to maintain the health of individuals and of the nation as a whole. In addition, the Catholic converts were given guns by the Jesuits and the French; the non-Catholic Hurons were not. Eventually, these internal conflicts caused the Huron people to become a house divided against itself.

By September of 1644, the simmering conflict between the Huron and Iroquois people was again open warfare. Now with the advantage of the firearms they had obtained from Dutch traders and recognizing that the Huron ranks had been cut down by the epidemics of the past decade, the Iroquois Confederacy attacked all across New France. The

But what it didn't have was many converts. The Huron people showed little interest in the French God. The practices of the Catholic religion were inimicable to their own beliefs and way of life. They saw no reason why all people should follow one spiritual path, after all, they had their own beliefs and did not try to convert the French. And they also saw that although the Jesuits preached against theft, dishonesty, and drunkenness, there were dishonorable thieves and drunks among the French traders with whom they dealt. Many Hurons also could not understand why the missionaries were so concerned about the power that Huron women had in their society or about the freedom their children enjoyed. Nonetheless, the

Iroquois had more guns at their disposal; only Huron Catholics were allowed to have guns. Throughout the years from 1644 to 1648, the Iroqouis blocked trade routes along the rivers, attacked French settlements, and killed many French and Huron peoples. Then they attacked Huron villages, and finally in 1649, they reached the heart of Huronia destroying the villages of Saint-Joseph II (Teanaostaiaë), La Conception (Ossossanë) and Sainte-Marie. Brébeuf, after dedicating fifteen years to the conversion of the Huron, and Gabriel Lalemant, were captured, tortured, and killed.

It was the end of the Huron Confederacy. Survivors found refuge with other Aboriginal Peoples or fled in small groups. The Jesuits abandoned Ste. Marie, setting fire to the buildings as they left with the remnants of the once powerful Huron people. As one Huron chief said to a Frenchman, "My brother, your eyes cheat you when you look at us; you think you are seeing living beings, whereas we are only the spectres and souls of the departed."[21]

Ursulines

The Ursulines, led by Marie (Guyart) de l'Incarnation of Tours, France, came to Quebec in 1639 to educate French and Aboriginal Catholic girls in the practice of the Catholic faith. The Ursuline convent that she founded in Quebec is the oldest institution of learning for women in North America. Marie de l'Incarnation was accompanied by Madame de la Peltrie, a rich widow from Normandy who provided funding for the venture.

At the request of the Jesuits, she opened her school to the children of the Sillery reserve. The children were expected to board at the Ursuline school so as to be more readily kept under Catholic influence. But this was not very successful. Marie and her teaching sisters were unused to the free ways of Aboriginal children and were quite unprepared when the children ran away, back to their parents.

Although Marie was a visionary who wore an uncomfortable shirt made of knots and thorns to mortify her flesh, she was also a practical businesswoman who had managed her brother-in-law's shipping company in France before entering the Ursuline order. She was skilled in finding—and persuading—wealthy patrons to support her convent in New France. She oversaw the construction of her convents, the original one and a replacement that was built after the first was destroyed by fire. Marie suffered through the trials of the colony, including hunger, deprivation, and the Iroquois attacks in 1661 and 1662. She successfully battled with the Bishop of Quebec, Montmorency de Laval, when he tried to change her order's constitution. And through all of these struggles, she still managed to find food and other supplies for her community.

Marie de l'Incarnation also learned Aboriginal languages and wrote dictionaries, histories, and catechisms in the Algonkian and Iroquoian languages. She wrote letters to her son and others in France—an estimated twelve thousand letters in all—telling her correspondents about the culture and courage, the struggles and achievements, of the people of New France.[22] Throughout her thirty-two years in New France, Marie de l'Incarnation remained what the Dictionary of Canadian Biography calls "a monument of practical and supernatural wisdom, . . .a mystic imbued with a sense of action."[23] Her view of the future for her people was always influenced by this practical realism and by her deep faith and sense of hope for the future of her new country

> There are many poor people here and the reason is that when a family creates a household, it takes two or three years before they have enough to eat, not to mention enough clothing, furniture and a whole range of little things needed for the upkeep of a household; but once these hardships are behind them, they start to feel more comfortable, and if they conduct themselves well, then they become rich over time, as much as a new country like this will allow.[24]

Review...Reflect...Respond

1. Why were Europeans consumed with the belief that Aboriginal Peoples must be converted to Catholicism?

2. How would conversion of Aboriginal Peoples to Catholicism cause divisions within the Aboriginal Peoples themselves? How would attempts to convert Aboriginal Peoples extend into the twentieth century?

3. If there had not been a fashion demand for beaver pelts in Europe, how do you think this would have affected colonization in New France?

The Ursuline nuns, shown here, came to Quebec to educate Catholic and Aboriginal girls.

Notes

1. Christopher Moore, "Colonization and Conflict: New France and its Rivals (1600-1760) *The Illustrated History of Canada*, ed. Craig Brown (Toronto: Key Porter Books, 2000) p.107.
2. Cornelius Jaenen and Cecilia Morgan, *Material Memory: Documents in Pre-Confederation History*, (Toronto: Addison Wesley, 1998). "A Positive Literary Assessment of Canada, 1609", p. 13. NAC, MG 1, J-1, Copie d'une Lettre envoyée de la Nouvelle France ou Canada, par le Sieur de Côbes, Gentilhomme Poicteven, à un sien amy (*Lyon: Léon Savine, 1609), 13 February 1608, ff. 3-4, 12-15. Trans CJJ*
3. Francess G. Halpenny and Jean Hamelin, eds. *Dictionary of Canadian Biography, Pierre du Gua de Monts, Volume 1,* (Toronto: University of Toronto Press, 1966), CD-ROM version.
4. *Can. Bio.*, de Monts.
5. *Can. Bio.*, de Monts.
6. *CSOH*, p. 38.
7. *Champlain, The Voyages*, 1613, from Museum of Civilization Web site <www.civilization.ca/vmnf/vmnfe.asp>
8. Paul, p. 24.
9. Paul, p. 33.
10. Olive Dickason, *Canada's First Nations: A History of Founding Peoples from Earliest Times*, (Toronto: Oxford University Press, 2002) p. 83.
11. Don Gillmor, et al., *Canada: A People's History*, Volume I (Toronto: McClelland & Stewart, 2001) p. 64.
12. Don Gillmor, et al., *Canada: A People's History*, Volume I (Toronto: McClelland & Stewart, 2001) p. 65.
13. Quoted in Moore's article (p. 113) but with no reference to its source.
14. Don Gillmor, et al., *Canada: A People's History*, Volume I (Toronto: McClelland & Stewart, 2001) p. 67.
15. Ibid.
16. Arthur Ray's 1999 introductory essay to Harold Innis's *The Fur Trade in Canada: An Introduction to Canadian Economic History*, (Toronto: University of Toronto Press, 1999), p. xiv.
17. Olive Dickason, *Canada's First Nations: A History of Founding Peoples from Earliest Times*, p. 84.
18. Dickason, *Canada's First Nations: A History of Founding Peoples from Earliest Times*, pp. 103–104.
19. Ibid.
20. Don Gillmor and Pierre Turgeon, *Canada: A People's History*, Volume I, (Toronto: Canadian Broadcasting Corporation, 2000) p. 72.
21. Don Gillmor et al., *Canada: A People's History*, Volume I, p. 74.
22. Alison Prentice et al., *Canadian Women: A History*, Volume I, (Toronto: Harcourt Brace Jananovich, 1998) p. 35.

Chapter 4 Review

Knowledge & Understanding

1. Identify these people, places, and events, and explain their historical significance to Canada's developing culture and identity:
   Mi'kmaqs' idea of hospitality
   religious conversion
   assimilation
   founding of Port Royal
   founding of Quebec
   the battle of Ticonderoga Point
   building of Ste. Marie among the Huron
   Marc Lescarbot
   Membertou
   Jeanne de Mance

2. Think/pair/share the similarities and differences among the Canadian colonial experiences of a) the early French settlers, b) the fur traders and *truchements*, and c) the missionaries. Consider factors such as their economic situation, settlement challenges, adaptation to the environment, and their relationship with the Aboriginal Peoples and colonial administrators.

3. Create an extended concept web to show how the Mi'kmaq, Huron, and other Aboriginal Peoples helped French settlers adapt to life in Acadia and Quebec.

Thinking & Inquiry

4. What effect do you think the economic and colonizing policies of the government of Louis XIII likely had on the future of French rule in Canada? Write a paragraph in which you explain your views on one of these policies and support your opinion with details from information in this chapter.

5. In this chapter, you read Champlain's complaint about Canadian winters. How has this element of the Canadian experience and environment contributed to Canadian culture and identity through the years?

Application

6. Imagine that you have survived the destruction of the mission of Ste. Marie Among the Hurons. You have been taken in by a group of people who are interested in hearing the story of the events leading up to the final battle. In the role of either a Jesuit or a Huron, prepare and present an oral rendition of your story.

7. Page 102 illustrates one way the beaver is used as a symbol of Canadian cultural identity. Select another Canadian symbol and prepare an illustrated timeline to show its development to the present day.

Communication

8. European religious intolerance, ignorance, and disrespect for the spiritual beliefs of others led to injustices against the Aboriginal Peoples of New France. Write an editorial in which you compare such injustices of the past with similar injustices today.

9. Working in small groups, prepare research notes that could be used as the basis for a report on the survival skills that early French settlers learned from the Aboriginal Peoples of Canada. Search for reliable primary and secondary print and online sources that would be helpful in answering your research question. Prepare an annotated list of at least ten sources that could be used in the report.

CHAPTER 5

Life in New France under Royal Government 1663–1738

The ordinary habitants would be insulted to be called peasants. In fact, they are of better stuff, have more wit, more education, than those of France. This comes from their paying no taxes, that they have the right to hunt and fish, and that they live in a sort of independence.

–COLONEL BOUGAINVILLE

With the establishment of Royal Government in 1663, the people of New France gained greater security when French soldiers arrived to defend the sparsely populated colony. The king of France remained the absolute ruler and his appointed administrators ruled the colony. However, citizens did not have the right to vote on the policies that governed so many aspects of their lives and there were no citizenship rights for the African and Aboriginal slaves of the colony. Along the St. Lawrence River, seigneurs held land at the king's discretion for which they paid annual dues for the privilege of farming plots of seigneurial land. But even the early habitants were more independent and self-sufficient than their counterparts in France. As for the Aboriginal Peoples, the French considered them their allies in trade and in war, and hoped someday to assimilate and convert the Aboriginal Peoples to Catholicism.

New France existed to contribute to the wealth and power of France and to supply raw materials for French industries. The fur trade continued to be a mainstay of the colonial economy, and traders expanded into the upper country, especially after the establishment of the Hudson's Bay Company by the English in 1670. Gradually, people came to settle in New France: the *filles de roi* were sent out to marry the men in the colony, members of the Carignan-Salières Regiment also settled, as did many of the *engagés* who came to work as indentured servants before gaining their freedom. In the towns, merchants established trade and built a society around the administrative elite. In the countryside, the habitants, who made up about 80 percent of the population, were governed by the rhythms of the seasons and by the church.

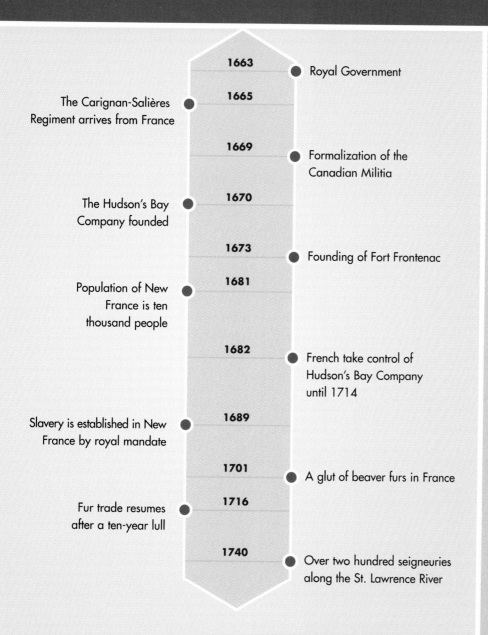

1663 — Royal Government

1665 — The Carignan-Salières Regiment arrives from France

1669 — Formalization of the Canadian Militia

1670 — The Hudson's Bay Company founded

1673 — Founding of Fort Frontenac

1681 — Population of New France is ten thousand people

1682 — French take control of Hudson's Bay Company until 1714

1689 — Slavery is established in New France by royal mandate

1701 — A glut of beaver furs in France

1716 — Fur trade resumes after a ten-year lull

1740 — Over two hundred seigneuries along the St. Lawrence River

By the end of this chapter, you will be able to

- demonstrate an understanding of Canada's role in international affairs prior to Confederation

- demonstrate an understanding of the resistance of French and British settlers to the establishment of European colonial institutions

- demonstrate an understanding of the development of citizenship in Canada

- describe the origins and various incidents of prejudice and discrimination in Canada's history

- analyze how women's participation in Canadian society has changed over time

The Institution of Royal Government

For most people living in the colony of Quebec in the years leading up to 1663, the advent of royal government was welcome if it would also bring relief from the economic and physical threat of the Iroquois. The Iroquois, who had trade alliances with the Dutch and the English, had effectively put a halt to the French fur trade by blocking routes to the interior of the country and by preventing other Aboriginal Peoples from trading with the French.

The settlers and townspeople of New France lived in constant fear of Iroquois raids. The Iroquois, who were masters of guerrilla warfare, did not fight the way Europeans did, arrayed in long lines on the battlefield. Instead, as one Jesuit priest wrote, "They come like foxes in the woods. They attack like lions.

They flee like birds. They could pass before Quebec in broad daylight and nobody would be able to pursue them or recover the captives they had seized."[1] The situation became so bad that settlers no longer cleared their lands. They could not fish or hunt without putting themselves or their families at risk. By 1663, ten percent of the population and a large portion of the settlements' livestock had been killed by the Iroquois. In one of her letters to France, Mother Marie de l'Incarnation summed up the situation: "There are not enough forces in all the land to resist them. If France does not come through for us, we will, in short, either have to leave or die."[2]

During the years prior to 1663, France had not been very interested in going to the expense of sending soldiers to defend its interest in New France. But King Louis XIV, who had just come to the throne at the age of twenty-two, wanted to make New France part of the great empire he intended to build during his reign. It was for reasons of defence that in 1665 he sent out the Carignan-Salières Regiment, which would play such a large part in the expansion of the settlement of New France.

The commercial administrators of The Company of One Hundred Associates had failed to bring in the promised revenues and colonists. In the meantime, the Thirteen Colonies to the south were growing rapidly and were under the colonial control of the English and the Dutch. These colonies posed a threat, especially during a century of frequent wars between the European powers as they fought to expand their empires around the world. There were also trade concerns. New France was seen as potentially a good financial resource and was worth keeping, but it needed efficient administrators, more colonists, and an adequate military defence.

Eighteenth-Century Administrative Structure of New France

- King
  - Minister of Marine and Colonies
  - Versailles
    - Governor-General
      - Local Governors
        - Louisiana ↔ Acadia
        - Île Royale ↔ Quebec*
        - Montréal ↔ Trois-Rivières
    - Sovereign Council
      Members:
      Governor-General
      Intendant
      Bishop
      Councillors or Advisers
      (5 to 12, depending on the period)
    - Intendant
      - Subdelegates of the Intendant
  - Captains of the Militia
  - The People

* The govenor-general was also the govenor of the area of Quebec

Louis XIV of France

The Political Structure in New France

When New France became a royal colony of France under Louis XIV, monarchs still ruled by divine right. They were considered to be at the apex of the earthly human hierarchy and had absolute power over their subjects. In return for their obedience to the king, the French colonies were to have the king's protection. The colonies would bring in needed revenue as well as extend his glory. To help him rule the colony of New France, which then included Acadia, Canada, and the *pays d'en haut*, Louis XIV set up an administrative bureaucracy, with the ultimate legal, military, and financial control was to remain in France. At the head of this bureaucracy was the minister of marine and colonies, Jean-Baptiste Colbert, who never even visited Quebec. The bureaucracy in France established the policies to be put into effect in New France and appointed the

military, administrative, and religious leaders to rule in the colony. These leaders established another bureaucracy, which included lesser officials such as customs officials and surveyors.

Louis XIV may have been an absolute ruler, although the layers of bureaucracy limited his control. He also knew that in order for people to leave France and settle in a foreign environment with a harsh climate, land to be cleared, and a constant threat from hostile Aboriginal Peoples, his rule couldn't be too harsh. At that time in France, there were no major wars or famines to compel people to leave their homeland and the king judged that his subjects in New France would need to have more freedom than those in France. His instructions were "The general spirit of government ought to lean in the direction of gentleness, it being dangerous to employ severity against transplanted peoples, far removed from their prince, and to hazard using an absolute power founded only on their obedience, because having once found a means of resisting they would quickly forget respect and submission."[3]

Jean Talon was the first intendant sent from France after 1663. He had been a military administrator in the provinces of France and was now given responsibility for the civil administration of justice, police, and finances in the colony. His mandate was to bring peace and security to the colony, to expand its resource base, and to grow its population. Rémy de Courcelle, as the colony's first governor, had authority over military matters and external policy. The Sovereign Council, which was established as the highest court in the land, was made up of de Courcelle, Talon, the bishop, and five councillors.

During the early years of royal rule, the king and French court showed considerable enthusiasm for Quebec, but then Louis became distracted by yet more European wars and, as a consequence, Quebec gradually became more independent from France. Initially, principle administrators had come from France, but as time went on, a Canadian administrative class came into power and at least in some cases, appointments were made because of an individual's skill and accomplishments.

Although government policies originated in France, the geographic realities of New France meant that communication between head office and its branch in Quebec could not ensure direct control. Correspondence from the French court regarding policy issues reached Quebec each year once the St. Lawrence River was free of ice. During the summer months, the governor would spend time in Montreal, consulting with post commanders and Aboriginal delegations. Then he would return to Quebec in the autumn and, in consultation with the intendant, bishop, and sovereign council, prepare his report and requests for the officials in France. Before the St. Lawrence froze up over the winter months, these communications would be sent to France. So, the governors in New France often had to take action on their own—they could hardly wait for months to take care of emergency situations.

Jean Talon

Upon his arrival in Quebec, Jean Talon energetically set about housing and supplying the approximately eleven hundred soldiers of the Carignan-Salières Regiment. Then he turned his attention to expanding the settlement in the colony and increasing the agricultural output so that the colony could become self-sufficient and even export its surplus produce to France. From 1665 to 1672, fifteen hundred people arrived in Canada from France, some came as settlers, but a large number arrived as *engagés* or indentured servants. From 1666 to 1673, the census records show that the population of Canada doubled from 3 215 to 7 605 settlers of French descent. During Talon's first

Jean Talon, pictured above, was intendant in New France from 1665 to 1668, and 1670 to 1672.

As controller-general for Louis XIV, Jean-Baptiste Colbert also had control of colonial matters and the powerful French merchant navy.

brief tenure from 1665 to 1668 (he returned in 1670 to 1672), he managed to pursuade the habitant farmers to diversify their agricultural production so that they were even able to export some of their crops to France.[4]

Soon after he became king, Louis XIV appointed Jean-Baptiste Colbert as his controller-general of finances, a position Colbert held until his death in 1683. In 1669, Colbert was also named minister of colonial and maritime affairs, which gave him control over colonial matters. One of Colbert's main goals was to help France gain wealth and power and to that end he put into effect the practice of mercantilism.

Talon also established a number of other industries in the colony. At the beginning of his administration, he had introduced looms into the colony. By 1671 the colony was producing some of its own cloth and its own leather in the tanneries Talon had founded. He was able to boast in his annual report to Colbert that "Nearly a third of the shoes are made from native leathers, and at the present time I have from what is produced in Canada all that I need to clothe myself from head to foot."[5] Colbert had hoped that Talon could establish a shipbuilding industry in the colony. Although shipbuilding was started during Talon's time in office, the industry did not last long after he left. Not only did the colony lack skilled shipwrights, but also because so many of the manufactured components of the ships had to be imported from France, the ships became very expensive to produce. However, Talon did manage to set up a lumber industry.

Talon was also committed to extending France's control in North America and its range for the fur trade. Thanks to his vision, three-quarters of the American continent, to the west and the south, came under French sovereignty within a period of a few years. He also turned his attention to the north, about which little was known at the time but from which came, through trade with the Ottawa peoples, the finest beaver furs.

Citizenship under Royal Government

Citizenship in New France meant something very different from what it means to Canadians today. Individuals did not have the right to vote for the intendant or for the governor of the colony. In the early days only Catholics were allowed to be settlers, and later, once Protestants were allowed into the colony, only Catholics could hold public office and only the Catholic clergy could collect tithes from the habitants. As newspapers were not yet published in New France, there was no free press in the colony. For the most part, the majority of people in New France were "second-class" citizens who had the responsibilities of being loyal subjects of the king of France but without many rights. The fate of the Acadians and the fact that slavery existed demonstrate how little human rights meant in Canada at the time.

By the advent of royal government, the traditional institutions of France were transplanted to New France. The administrators who were appointed by the king, held the authority and were expected to keep order, along with the seigneurs and the military establishment. This élite class ruled the colony. The social teaching of the Catholic Church required of rulers that they be benevolent and paternalistic in their care of people in the lower classes. So as long as the mass of common men and women did what they were told, they would be more or less taken care of by their rulers.

But the old traditions of France changed in the New World. A commoner could rise to the status of a seigneur or military leader or even eventually a bishop of the Catholic Church and the old structure of society changed as people were brought together from different regions of France. Whereas in France, a peasant would likely have grown up in the same village or country region as his or her parents and would be very familiar with the personal and cultural values of their region. But this was not the case in New France, not only did the habitants come from different regions in France, but they also had different experiences when they arrived. A *fille de roi* from Paris might marry a former *engagé* from a French province far distant from the main city. The society that grew out of these new relationships was very different from the society they had left behind in France. The *coureurs de bois* and *voyageurs* who lived among the Aboriginal Peoples were also influenced by Aboriginal traditions of freedom and equality, which were very different from what they saw in French-Canadian society.

The Seigneurial System in New France

The seigneurial system was also imported from France. By 1740, there were over two hundred seigneuries on both sides of the St. Lawrence River. This method of land distribution was based on the feudal system, a hierarchical order with a foundation in noble birth, privilege, and patronage. Seigneurs in New France were given large plots of land which they held at the pleasure of the king, and in the early days they were responsible for recruiting and transporting people from France to clear and settle the land. The habitant was given a section of the seigneur's land and in return was expected to pay annual fees for the land, for having his or her grain ground at the seigneurs' gristmill, and for fishing and hunting rights. Habitants were also expected to work on the seigneur's property for a set number of days a year and to pay tithes to help support the parish priest and maintain the parish church. In 1680 this tithe was set at 1/13 of the habitants' annual crop. However, after numerous complaints from the habitants that this rate was too great a burden, the governor dropped the tithe to 1/26 of their crop.

A View of the Chateau-Richer by Thomas Davies

In France, the seigneurs would have been members of the nobility or the upper echelons of the clergy. But in New France, not all seigneurs were French nobility nor were they much wealthier, in some cases, than their habitants. In order to persuade settlers to leave France and settle in New France, the fees paid to the seigneur were often lower than those in France. If a seigneur could not recruit many settlers, he might not even have enough income to build the gristmill that was part of the contract. Without the mill, or if the land was not cleared quickly enough, a seigneur could lose the rights of the seigneurship. Seigneurs in France did not usually engage in trade as they were members of the nobility and trade occupations were beneath them. But in New France, seigneurs often became involved in the fur trade and other commercial pursuits. This changed their standing in their communities.

Also, unlike the seigneurial system in France, there were few villages in Canada. Even though the isolation of the farms spread out along the shores of the St. Lawrence meant that the farms were more subject to Iroquois attacks, the habitants were not much interested in living in villages. The reasons for this feature of New France are not entirely clear. However, the historian W.J. Eccles speculates that it might have been that the habitants had "unpleasant memories of village life in France, with its constant surveillance by seigneurial, ecclesiastical, and royal authorities, with the attendant extortions, chicanery, and petty tyranny."[6]

Web Connection

www.mcgrawhill.ca/links/definingcanada
Go to the Web site above to learn more about Jean Talon—Canada's first official statistician.

Slavery in New France

According to the Black Cultural Centre for Nova Scotia, historical records show that "slavery was established in Quebec, by the French, through a royal mandate by Louis XIV in 1689." Slaves who had been kidnapped from their African homeland and brought to Quebec were declared to be the property of those who owned them. Although some officials in New France asked that slaves captured in Africa be sent to the colony, in the 1680s, most slaves in New France were Aboriginal Peoples. Before the arrival of the French, some Aboriginal Peoples had also kept slaves and been involved in the slave trade. For example, the Iroquois used prisoners taken in war as labourers in their own lands or traded them among other tribes. The trade and the practice of slavery extended throughout the societies of many of the Aboriginal Peoples in North America.

Royal declarations in 1721, 1742, and 1745, confirmed slavery in New France. In parish records, legal notices, and other official documents of the time, slaves are often listed as part of their owners' additional household effects and property. Slaves from Africa and from among North American Aboriginal nations were often used in New France as domestic servants and

---

Excerpts from the Code Noir

2. All the slaves who are in our said province shall be instructed in the Catholic, Apostolic, and Roman religion and be baptized...

8. We expressly forbid curates [priests] to proceed with the marriage of slaves unless they have obtained the consent of their masters; we also forbid masters to employ any constraints on their slaves to marry against their will.

9. The children born of marriages between slaves remain slaves, and will belong to the masters of the women slaves and not to the masters of their husbands, if the husbands and wives belong to different masters...

12. We forbid slaves to carry any offensive weapons, or large sticks, on penalty of the whip...

13. We also forbid slaves belonging to different masters to gather together during the day or night on pretexts such as a wedding...

14. We forbid slaves to set up stalls at the market...

15. Slaves may not be invested with office or commissions having a public function...

40. We order that slaves be reputed to be moveable property and as such be part of the community of goods...

were owned by French colonial administrators, military officers, and religious communities who used them as a source of unpaid labour.[7] Among those who owned slaves were Marguerite d'Youville, founder of the Grey Nuns, and Bishop Laval, the principal Catholic clergyman of the colony.

Life expectancy for slaves was very short in New France: 17.7 years for Aboriginal slaves and 25.2 for African slaves.[8] A slave's life was bounded by restrictions and the loss of any rights of citizenship.

The Aboriginal Peoples under Royal Rule

As historian Olive Dickason says, "Throughout the history of New France, the French policy towards [Aboriginal Peoples] was consistent: treat them with every consideration, avoid violence . . . and transform them into Frenchmen."[9] Even though the French did not agree with the Aboriginal Peoples' ideas on equality and individual freedom, the French needed to keep the Aboriginal Peoples as allies in the lucrative fur trade and for defence purposes against the Iroquois and the British. So, the French put up with the differences in values, attitudes, and culture between themselves and their Aboriginal allies and trading partners.

This did not mean that the French gave up their goal of assimilating the Aboriginal Peoples, of making them French men and women. They still hoped that the Catholic religion would eventually make them ready to follow the hierarchical structure of French society. The author of an anonymous memo sent from New France in 1663 believed that the "Christian Religion which orders so absolutely submission and obedience to one's superiors" would eventually "soften the wild and libertine humours" of the Aboriginal Peoples of Canada. Once converted they could be attracted "into the colony and the French habitations." Then the French authorities could "reduce them little by little to give up hunting and fishing to

clear the land and render it capable of producing abundantly the things necessary for subsistence, and to consent that their children be raised in public institutions." In a foretaste of the later tragic practice of removing Aboriginal children to church- and state-sponsored residential schools, the writer then says "By these means we will be able to separate them and transplant them, we will imperceptibly take away their children who will be so many hostages, and we will smother all grounds for revolts."[10]

But, in the early days, setting up schools for Aboriginal children didn't work very well. The subjects taught in the French schools didn't make much sense to Aboriginal students, and their parents didn't want their children to leave them to go to boarding schools. The parents simply removed the children, or else the young ones took it on themselves to run back home.

There were also issues about whether the Aboriginal Peoples were to be treated as allies or subjects—along with the colonists of New France—of the French crown. When the French administrators tried to impose French laws, they met with resistance from the Aboriginal Peoples. And, because they needed Aboriginal goodwill so badly, the French had to back off—for the moment. There was not much conflict over land in New France in the early days because the settlement rate was so low, certainly nothing like the conflict over land that was going on in the Thirteen Colonies to the south.

During the early years of royal government, intermarriage between Aboriginal women and French men was a policy of the French. For the Aboriginal Peoples, such marriages cemented trade and military alliances. The French went along with this for the benefits of trade. Champlain had said "Our young men will marry your daughters, and we shall be one people."[11] For the French trader, having an Aboriginal wife had distinctive advantages: she would have the survival skills needed in what was, to the French, a strange land, and she could help in the fur trade by preparing the beaver pelts for market. French policy-makers also believed that this was one way to make the Aboriginal Peoples' French in their culture and to get them to settle down and accept the French hierarchical social, religious, and political systems. Unfortunately for the policy-makers, the acculturation actually seemed to work the other way round, as more French husbands chose to adapt to their Aboriginal wives' culture.

As far as the missionaries were concerned, intermarriage was acceptable so long as the Aboriginal woman was baptized. The missionaries hoped that this would increase the conversion rate to Catholicism. The Jesuits even successfully lobbied for official sanction of the practice by obtaining a fifty livres dowery for Aboriginal as well as French women who married. Few Aboriginal women ever claimed the dowry. On the other hand, there were very few marriages between

A painting called *The Trapper's Bride*. French missionaries felt that it was alright for French men to marry Aboriginal women, as long as the women had been baptized by the church.

French women and Aboriginal men. By the early 1700s, colonial opposition to any marriages between French and Aboriginal Peoples was growing. The French officials realized that, in spite of the intermarriages, their trade alliances were not exclusive as more Aboriginal Peoples traded furs with the English at the Hudson's Bay Company post. Besides, such marriages didn't seem to be helping the French goal of assimilating the Aboriginal Peoples into French society. By 1735 the consent of the governor or commanding officer was required for all marriages between French colonials and Aboriginal women.

Review...Reflect...Respond

1. What steps did Jean Talon take to establish New France and extend its control in North America?

2. Why was there a dilemma over whether to treat Aboriginal Peoples as allies or subjects of New France?

3. How did life under royal government in New France differ from life under royal government in France?

Mercantilism

According to the mercantilist system, the more gold and silver a country had, the wealthier it was. And if a country didn't have mines, then it had to have trade goods that it could use to acquire the necessary gold and silver. Also France wanted to have more exports than imports, and the colonies could be used to achieve that end. New France, and France's other colonies, were supposed to serve as the suppliers of raw materials to France and the buyers of manufactured goods supplied by the mother country.

Mercantilism had an influence on colonization efforts too. If New France had a large population, then it could become self-sufficient agriculturally and would no longer be dependent on France for annual financial support and food supplies. The goal was to have the colony produce more raw materials and buy more finished goods. Mercantilism also had a negative affect on the growth of industry in the colony, often stifling new initiatives. In the early days especially, New France was not to compete with France in the creation of manufactured goods. In June of 1704, Jérôme de Pontchartrain, minister of marine in France, wrote the following directive to the governors of New France:

> His majesty has been very pleased to learn that the growing of hemp has met with the success that we had hoped for. But he must explain that he never intended to allow cloth to be manufactured in Canada so that the settlers might do without that of France. Thus, no weavers will be sent to the colony. The settlers must forward their hemp to France to be sold there either to the state for the servicing of the royal navy, or else to private parties to dispense them from buying this product from foreigners. Generally, they must observe that whatever can compete with the manufactories of France must never be produced in the colonies.[12]

On the other hand, the mercantilist system did provide the colonists in New France with some financial security. By the terms of the agreement, France was to buy all the production of the colonies. When there was a glut of beaver furs in the 1701, France still had to give financial support to the colony in order to keep it running. Merchants living in France also had to make sure that the colony maintained its supplies of trade goods, arms, and ammunition. They had to pay the shipping costs to get the goods across the Atlantic, pay for the insurance, and often bear the loss of ships and cargo due to natural disasters, attacks by pirates, or war.

Fur Trade

Beaver became scarce in the regions bordering the St. Lawrence lowlands by the late seventeenth century and French traders began to go further into the upper country. They began at Fort Frontenac in 1673, going as far west as the country of the Sioux by 1680 in pursuit of new sources of furs and new trading partners. Young men in large numbers went off each year to the upper country to live and trade with the Aboriginal Peoples there. State and church officials were alarmed that such an exodus would not only slow the development of agriculture along the St. Lawrence and the growth of families, but also set a bad example of conduct for the Aboriginal Peoples.

In addition, King Louis XIV became more and more concerned about the *coureurs de bois'* rebellious attitude in leaving the settlements to trade in furs. They were supposed to stay and settle down to be farmers and dutiful subjects. As far as Louis was concerned, there was no excuse for the colonial officials' failure to stop this activity "which is completely opposed to the welfare and the development of the Colony." The king went on to instruct

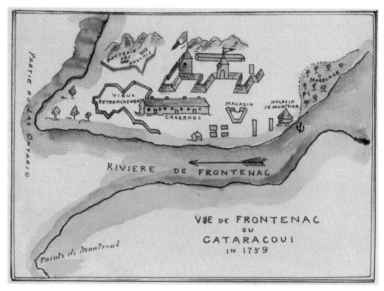

Originally known as Fort Cataracoui, Fort Frontenac (at present day Kingston) was the fortress of the governor of New France, Louis Bouade, Le Comte de Frontenac.

Governor Frontenac in how he was to deal with his rebellious subjects,

> To carry out my orders on this matter you can and you must use the authority which I have granted you to be aware of all the inhabitants who leave their homes for a considerable period of time which serves as proof that they have gone to seek out the Natives in their dwellings in order to carry on trade."

Frontenac was to instruct the sovereign council of the colony to punish the *coureurs de bois* severely, and if that did not work then the governor himself was to have them "made prisoners on your authority and hold them for as long a time as you believe necessary to punish them and serve as an example ...[13]

The custom of trading brandy for furs was one of the most destructive aspects of the French-Aboriginal fur trade. Alcohol was unknown to the Aboriginal Peoples of the time, and they had considerable difficulty adjusting to its effects. The Catholic priests tried repeatedly to stop the use of brandy as a trade good, but to no avail. French monarchs and governors generally deplored the trade, but because it brought in revenue through the fur trade, brandy continued to be used. If it would provide furs, many of the fur-trading companies argued that it was a valid item of barter. The English were also using rum as one of their fur-trading products. No matter that alcohol abuse contributed to violence in Aboriginal communities, to social disorganization, and to the physical deterioration of an originally healthy Aboriginal population.

The English became involved in the fur trade in the upper country. In 1670, a royal charter was granted to the London-based Hudson's Bay Company, which had begun trading operations on the southern shore of the bay, explored by Henry Hudson in 1610. Two French-Canadian traders, Pierre Esprit Radisson and Médard Chouart des Grosseilliers, had brought the wealth of furs in the region to the attention of the London merchants. In 1682, the Hudson's Bay Company built York Fort, as well as several smaller posts where small garrisons of English soldiers were left in charge. The Cree people of the interior, who came with canoes laden with furs, visited these posts each summer. As soon as the ice cleared, the annual supply ships from England arrived.

A small illustration (cartouche) on a map of the inhabited part of *Canada* in 1777. It shows a rather simplified conception of the fur trade, actually a much more complicated business.

Radisson and Grosseilliers exploring Lake Superior. A painting by American artist Frederic Remington depicting famous French-Canadian traders Radisson and Groseilliers exploring beyond Lake Superior.

In response to the English activity on Hudson Bay, French traders built a French trading post on Lake Nipigon and succeeded in diverting more than fifteen hundred Aboriginal traders away from Hudson Bay. In 1682, the French attacked the Hudson's Bay Company posts and held the region's trade until 1714. No matter how hard the French officials tried to control the interior trade, they seldom succeeded. In the upper country, a system of *congés,* or annual official leaves from the governor and intendant at Quebec, was instituted whereby only licenced traders could take up supplies and bring down furs. But despite the *congés,* unlicenced traders, known as *coureurs de bois,* continued to go into the upper country, live among the peoples there, and trade in furs.

After a ten-year lull in the beaver market in Europe, the fur trade resumed its importance in 1716. A new role was assigned to trading post commanders; these officers of the small detachments of marine troops at the scattered military posts in the upper country were given control of the fur trade. Posts were sometimes leased or farmed out, and beginning in 1742, they were even auctioned. Three strategic posts were used to keep out English traders: Frontenac (Kingston), Rouillé (Toronto), and Niagara.

Colonization

One of the major concerns for King Louis XIV, and especially for Intendant Talon in the 1660s, was the relatively low number of people settling in the colony. The earlier plan to have commercial companies, such as the Company of One Hundred Associates, bring settlers to New France in exchange for exclusive trading rights had been a disaster. In 1673, the king and his administrators were intent on sending colonists to New France. Though the king's and Colbert's enthusiasm soon died down, Talon remained committed to the difficult task of growing the colony.

Although it is estimated that over thirty thousand people came from Europe—mainly from France—during the 150 years of French rule, only about a third of that number stayed to settle in New France. Meanwhile, immigration to the Thirteen Colonies meant that the population there was growing much more quickly. By 1740, there were 906 000 people living in the English colonies

The Hudson's Bay Company, now in business for over 330 years, is one of the oldest chartered companies in the world. It too has become an icon of Canadian culture and identity.

versus only forty-three thousand in New France, a ratio of 21 to 1. In a time of frequent wars between France and England and with both countries focused on building empires overseas, this was a worrying discrepancy.

Intendant Talon believed that the king and his minister Colbert were not sufficiently committed to sending settlers to New France. As early as January 5, 1666, Colbert was telling Talon that it would be foolish for the king to "depopulate his realm" to populate New France and besides the country could not yet support them. Colbert also warned Talon to turn his attention to the needs of the colonists already in place rather than worrying about the number of new arrivals. Colbert said,

> that the true means of strengthening this Colony is to make Justice reign there, to establish a sound civil administration, to take good care of the inhabitants, to procure for them peace, repose, and abundance, and to inure them to all sorts of enemies, because all these matters which are the basis and foundation of all colonies being carefully observed, the country will become populated by slow degrees and with the passing of a reasonable period of time it could become quite important . . .[14]

Since the flow of immigration was relatively low and since the goal was to build a thriving colony in New France, Talon and church leaders encouraged the settlers to have large families. The development of the land and territorial expansion of the settlement depended on a high birth rate. Up until 1673, young men who married at twenty years or younger and girls who married at sixteen years or younger each received twenty livres on their wedding day. A yearly pension of three hundred livres was given to families who had ten living children and four hundred livres to families of twelve or more children.

Expression of Culture

Art reveals something of the people who created it, their struggles, their triumphs, and their dreams. The art of the late seventeenth and early eighteenth century of New France speaks to the social climate of the day, to a well-established feudal system in which every individual had a defined role and a life in which the church was central. It is not surprising that virtually all of the art that survived from this early period of New France dealt with religious themes.

In the mid-seventeenth century artists were brought in from France to help decorate churches across New France. Hugues Pommier was the first professional artist living and working in Quebec in the seventeenth century. Originally from France, Pommier arrived in 1664 and became a member of the Quebec Seminary staff. Unfortunately, few works by Pommier survive. Over the years, he has been attributed with painting *Martyre des Pères Jésutes chez les Hurons* (1664, oil on canvas, Hôtel-Dieu, Québec), a copy of a European engraving that depicts the torture of two missionaries by the Iroquois, and two portraits of prominent French nuns, *La Mère Marie-Catherine de Saint-Augustin* (1668, canvas, Hôtel-Dieu, Québec) and *La Mère Marie de l'incarnation* (Monastère des Ursulines, Québec).

We know more today about the artist Frère Luc who came to New France in 1670 to lend his talents to rebuilding and decorating a destroyed monastery in Quebec then we do about Pommier. Frère Luc spent fifteen months on Canadian soil and was responsible for a great number of religious paintings. Most significantly during his stay, Frère Luc drafted the plans for a new chapel, Hôpital-Général, that still stands today, and painted the *Assomption* for the main alter. In the grand style of French Classical Baroque, *Assomption* portrays a rather plump Madonna rising to heaven with the help of two angels. Dramatic and posed, the painting must have seemed spectacular to the local people of Quebec.

Religious paintings were intended to further the mission of the church, teaching habitants and natives important lessons while promoting the Empire. *La France apportant la foi aux Hurons de la Nouvelle-France* (c. 1670, oil on canvas, Monastère de Ursulines, Québec), attributed to Frère Luc, is an excellent example of this type of propaganda. In the centre of the scene stands the female figure of France presenting a religious painting to a young native man. The two stand on the banks of the St. Lawrence, her boat on one side and a row of mission stations on the other. Wrapped in a fleurs-de-lis robe, the native looks up in awe at the regal figure before him who points up to the Holy Family seated in the heavens above.

Not all paintings created in New France were as grand and overtly religious as the paintings of Pommier and Frère Luc. There are many surviving votive paintings from this early period of productivity. These were small and intimate works, commissioned by a family or individual to give thanks for a favour received, to mark a past event, or simply to illustrate ones devotion. Many votives depict an event in which an individual overcame great danger. The presence of a saint in the top portion of the painting demonstrates how the individual was saved by Devine

This productive period of church decoration in the late seventeenth century created the demand for skilled sculptors and wood workers. Since it was more difficult to import large sculpted objects than paintings, trained local craftsman emerged. Instead of stone, church decorators in New France were masters of wood, which was then painted and gilded.

In 1668, Bishop Laval, the first Bishop of Quebec, founded an arts and crafts school in St-Joachim outside of Quebec, hoping that New France would turn out its own trained artists. Jacques Leblond became head of the St-Joachim school shortly after arriving to Canada in 1690. A trained painter, sculptor and architect,

Leblond worked with his students on the decoration of a number of churches, including paintings and sculptures in the Quebec Seminary chapel and the decorations in the chapel of Sainte-Anne de Beaupré. St-Joachim students were also responsible for a number of the votive paintings that are part of an impressive collection at Sainte-Anne de Beaupré.

Jean Guyon was the first Canadian-born Quebec painter. He entered the Petit Séminaire in 1671 and was ordained in 1683. He served for a time as Bishop Laval's secretary and as a cathedral canon. Only a few small watercolour studies are attributed to Guyon along with a painting of the first Canadian to be elected Superior of her convent, *La Mère Jeanne-Françoise Juchéreau dite de Saint-Ignace* (c. 1684, oil on canvas, Hôtel-Dieu, Québec). Guyon travelled to Paris with Bishop Laval to study painting and, sadly, died shortly after his arrival. Canada did not have the opportunity to see the mature career of its first Aboriginal-born artist.

Sculpting and woodworking techniques were passed down through generations of families who settled in New France in the mid-to-late seventeenth century. The Lavasseur brothers, who first arrived in 1651, were among the most famous of these skilled families. Working in the first part of the eighteenth century, their sons Noël and Pierre-Noël were responsible for some of the finest examples of wood working in New France and part of the first generation of Canadian-born artists.

Notre-Dame-des-Victoires. This church has been in Place Royale for more than 300 years, and is one of the oldest churches in New France. The sculpting and woodworking were done by local artisans in the early eighteenth century.

So intent was Talon on increasing the number of people in the colony, that he enacted a law obliging bachelors to marry the young *filles de roi* who arrived from France, under penalty of losing their rights to fish, hunt, or engage in the fur trade. By the end of the 1671, Talon was able to report to Colbert that there had been between six hundred and seven hundred births in the colony over the previous twelve months.[15] On average, women in Canada gave birth to an average of eight or nine children up until 1700, and seven after 1700. The average "completed" family was 5.65 children per couple (compared to 4.5 in France at the time).[16] Infant mortality was high in the colony; one in four children died before they were one year old, but this mortality rate was less than that in France at the time.

Emigrating to New France

Most of the settlers in New France, came from villages in Northern and Western France through the harbours of La Rochelle and Dieppe. Originally it was mostly men who arrived as soldiers, workmen, or servants. Many people, mostly men but also some women, came as *engagés* who had signed contracts with recruiters, seigneurs, shipowners, or merchants.

Filles de Roi

In 1663, most of the inhabitants of New France were men. This, of course, was problematic. The answer to the problem was to have the men marry and the families to produce children. In France, the king and his administrators decided to send young unmarried women, the *filles de roi*, to become wives of these settlers. They were given a dowry of about fifty livres and sent off to find husbands. In New France, Marie de l'Incarnation housed the women at the Ursuline convent and helped them meet the young men of the colony. Marie was pleased with the practical nature of these young women who were, apparently, more interested in

young men, former *engagés* or soldiers from the C Regiment, who already had established their farms. "This is the first thing the girls inform themselves about, and they are wise to do so."[17]

By 1681, the colony had a population of about ten thousand people, and there were not to be many more settlers arriving from France during the rest of the French regime. As the years went by, more and more new French Canadians were born in this country and fewer and fewer arrived from France. As Christopher Moore says, "These ten thousand settlers of 1681 would produce most of the Francophone population of Canada."[18]

The Military

In 1665, King Louis XIV sent out to New France eleven hundred members of the seasoned Carignan-Salières Regiment. The people of Quebec were delighted to receive this military support for the defence of their colony. When they arrived, some of the soldiers were given the task of building forts along the Richelieu River, which was the main invasion route of the Iroquois. As the Marquis de Salières, one of the officers in the endeavour wrote, the soldiers were ill-prepared for the task. He arrived "without so much as a carpenter, or any other workmen to help and very few tools besides. I arrived with 350 men, many of whom were suffering from stomach problems because of heavy rains and the cold. They were badly dressed, barefoot and had no pots in which to cook their lard and make a bit of soup."[19]

The regiment's first military excursion—in the middle of the winter of 1666 and on orders from the new governor, Daniel de Rémy de Courcelle—was a disaster. Against the advice of de Salières, de Courcelle led his soldiers, militiamen, and Aboriginal allies in a futile foray into Iroquois territory. During the weeks that they wandered lost in the forest, four hundred men froze to death. They never found the Iroquois village that they had intended to attack.

The next major military expedition against the Iroquois met with more success. In the fall of 1666, thirteen hundred Carignan-Salières soldiers,

The Sad Departure from Paris of the filles du Roi. Young unmarried women were sent from France to New France to help build the population of the colony.

Canadian militiamen, and Aboriginal allies marched to Iroquois villages around Lake Champlain. They met no Iroquois, but they did burn their villages and destroyed their winter stock of grain. The Iroquois were sufficiently impressed by the power of their French enemies to sign a peace treaty with them.

The officers and soldiers of the Carignan-Salières Regiment were encouraged by King Louis XIV to stay on in Quebec as settlers. The officers were granted seigneuries and the regular soldiers were granted land and money to get them started as farmers. Four hundred members of the Regiment decided to stay and settle in Canada. Not only did this give the colony more settlers, but it also offered the added benefit of having experienced soldiers along the St. Lawrence during the ongoing battles with the Iroquois, the Thirteen Colonies, and the English.

The Canadian Militia

The militia in Canada were an established fighting force before 1663. But after 1669, King Louis XIV formalized it, ordering that all able-bodied males between the ages of sixteen and sixty had to belong. Their main purpose was to defend their colony, their homes, and their families. They were considered to be very effective—and ruthless—fighters who were feared by their enemies. These men knew the Canadian environment well. Some of them had been on fur-trading expeditions into the *pays d'en haut* and they could travel hundreds of kilometres in winter. Because many were hunters, they were also good shots, and they had learned the lessons of guerrilla warfare tactics from their Aboriginal allies and foes. Often, they attacked their enemies at night and burned them in their homes, killing civilians as well as soldiers.

Number of Immigrants to New France by Sex, to 1759			
Period	Men	Women	Total
Pre–1630	15	6	21
1630–39	88	51	139
1640–49	141	86	227
1650–59	403	239	642
1660–69	1075	623	1698
1670–79	429	369	798
1680–89	486	56	542
1690–99	490	32	522
1700–09	283	24	307
1710–19	293	18	311
1720–29	420	14	434
1730–39	483	16	499
1740–49	576	16	592
1750–59	1699	52	1751
Unknown	27	17	44
Total	6908	1619	8527

Source: R. Cole Harris and Geoffrey J. Matthews, *Historical Atlas of Canada, Vol. 1* (Toronto: University of Toronto Press, 1988), plate 45.

By the end of the seventeenth century, each parish along the St. Lawrence had its own militia. Under the control of their militia captain, the men trained for a month or two each year. Their duties extended beyond defence; they also helped with the construction of roads, bridges, and fortifications in their parishes. Although the militia captains did not receive pay, they did have the respect of the members of their society and the benefits of the social prestige that came with that respect.

According to historian René Chartrand, during the time of the French regime, the Canadian militia was the best fighting force on the North American continent [20] excelling at both offensive and defensive actions. In the winter of 1690, when France and England were once more at war and Comte de Frontenac was governor of Quebec, Canadian militiamen successfully attacked the English at Schenectady in what is today northern New York. When the English retaliated by sending a fleet of twenty-four ships from Boston to attack Quebec, the militia won out against the much larger force of their enemy.

Engagés

Another group of eventual settlers in New France arrived as indentured servants. Usually these *engagés*, as they were called, were young men who had signed a contract for three years to work for their master or for those to whom their master rented them out. The recruiter, who might be a seigneur, advanced part of the wages to pay for their Atlantic passage and also agreed to pay for their journey back to France if they decided that they didn't want to settle in New France after their terms were up.

While in service, the *engagé* received room and board and an annual wage as low as seventy-five livres per year. From this small income, living expenses such as food and clothing were deducted. For many *engagés*, the work was very hard as they cleared land and performed other heavy manual labour tasks.

During the years between 1664 and 1671, about one thousand *engagés* arrived in Quebec, with about five hundred staying on to settle in the colony. The other five hundred returned to France, much to the dismay of the Intendant Talon who complained that "This colony will hardly be strengthened by the way people are heading back to France, because as much as you may promote the arrival of fresh people, several people headed back this year, and many more are waiting to head back next year." [21] The king tried to forbid the return of *engagés* to France, but he recognized that he could not settle the country by keeping people in New France by force.

The Society of New France
Women in New France

History books of the past have been, for the most part, the stories of famous men and their accomplishments and failures. The stories of the less-famous people, especially women, and the details about how they lived their lives were often ignored. In *Canadian Women: A History*, Alison Prentice and her fellow historians tell some of these stories and fill in the details of the lives of the women who helped establish Canada and who contributed so much to Canadian culture and identity.

In New France, most men and women were married, except for those belonging to the Catholic religious orders or to the priesthood. In spite of Talon's and the clergy's advocating early marriages, the average age for a first marriage was twenty-two for women and twenty-seven for men. Widows and widowers, especially those with children, usually remarried after the death of a spouse. Death in childbirth was still a very real possibility for women, and colonial statistics from the period show that women of childbearing age had a higher death rate than men of the same age.

The daily life of women in town and in country was filled with work, much of it associated with caring for their children and producing food for their families—the stews, soups, roasts, and bread that were the normal diet of ordinary people in New France. On the farm, women might also help with the butchering, curing, and drying of meat, tend the chickens, milk the cows, churn the butter, grow vegetables and fruit, and preserve them for the winter. Women often kept the family accounts, and in the late summer and autumn, they would help bring in the harvest. During times of their husbands' absence in the militia or in the high country trading for furs, they would run the household and the farm or, in town, the family business establishment.

Within the hierarchical social structure at that time, men were the heads of households and only they could hold political office. However, in a system where no ordinary person had a vote or much influence on government, this was perhaps not as significant for women as it would become in the nineteenth century. Marriage contracts were a common feature of the colony, just as they were in France. In the seventeenth century, 65 percent of all marriages had such contracts, and by the eighteenth century that number had risen to 80 per-

cent. Women were expected to bring a dowry to their marriages, but widows were entitled to receive half of the income generated by their husband's property.

Agathe de Saint-Père, Madame de Repentigny

The story of Agathe de Saint-Père, Madame de Repentigny, represents the women in New France who played major roles in the commercial life of the colony. As a 15-year-old in Montreal, Agathe was left in charge of ten brothers and sisters when her mother died. The youngest child in her care was a newborn baby. In 1685, Agathe married Legardeur de Repentigny and had eight children of her own. And yet even with all of these people to take care of, Agathe still found time to run a business in which she loaned money and bought and sold fur trade licences, contracts, and land.

In keeping with her entrepreneurial spirit, Agathe saw a business opportunity in the shortage of linen and wool in the colony. She decided to experiment with textiles, working first with native fibres such as nettles, bark, cottonweed, and buffalo hair. When one of the ships bringing supplies to the colony sank, Agathe set out to supply an obvious need among the colonists. She ransomed nine kidnapped English weavers from Aboriginal allies of the French. Then she had looms made, brought in apprentices to learn to weave, and turned her own home into a workshop to make linen and other types of cloth.[22]

Agathe also distributed looms to other people in Montreal, and soon there were twenty looms in the town turning out durable and inexpensive cloth. She successfully experimented with different ways of dying cloth and animal hides. Even after the nine English weavers were returned to Boston, her business kept up its rate of production. Louis XIV had been so impressed with her success that he bestowed on her two hundred livres a year in recognition of her achievements.

In 1736, Agathe moved to the Hôpital Géneral of Quebec where one of her daughters, Marie-Joseph de la Visitation, was a nun. It was there that she died at the age of ninety-one.

Townsfolk

The administrative, business, and religious "establishment" of the towns of Quebec, Montreal, and Trois Rivieres was made up of military officers, members of the French aristocracy, the heads of religious orders, and the merchants. The structure of the town of Quebec mirrored the hierarchical nature of its society, as the upper classes lived in the Upper Town and the workers, artisans, and tradesmen lived in the Lower Town. The busy narrow streets of the town were filled with both people and livestock, especially on market days when some of the habitants would be in town to sell their produce.

Ships started to arrive at Quebec from France in the spring. As Margaret Conrad and Alain Finkel report, once the mail from the ships was delivered to the colonists, "dignitaries suitably entertained, supplies placed in storehouses, and the crews rejuvenated in the local taverns, the vessels were loaded for the return journey."[23] As in the countryside, the Church played a part in the social life of the towns. The religious orders of priest and nuns were the main providers of education for the children of New France's towns. On feast days, processions would wend their way through the towns. However, many of the Catholic clergy became concerned about the secularization and what they saw as the lax moral standards of the inhabitants of New France's towns.

Over the years since its founding, Montreal became less a religious island and more of a trading town. Outside the stone wall that protected the town were thriving farms that supplied the townspeople with food. The fur traders and soldiers were at the heart of the town's life, and Aboriginal Peoples set up their communities nearby. While there was a certain degree of intellectual life in the towns, it is noteworthy that no newspapers were printed nor were there any printing presses in New France. The upper classes imported most of their books from France along with many of the finer furnishings for their homes. However, local artisans also produced fine and distinctive pine furniture and other crafts made from local materials.

The hierarchical structure of society was reflected in the incomes received by people working within the colony.

Habitants

In New France, approximately 80 percent of the population were habitants, the farmers who lived within the seigneurial system. The habitant's land was usually 3 arpents at the front by 30 arpents deep (180m by 1 800m) and in the early days many of these farms fronted on the St. Lawrence River.[24]

Although some habitants grew enough food to supply the towns of New France, many others were only able to raise crops to sustain their own families. In years when they were struck by natural catastrophes—such as drought, excessive precipitation, or caterpillar infestations—the habitants might not even have enough to feed their families. In good years, the habitant might have a crop that was plentiful enough so that he could export surplus grain.

The cycle of the seasons dictated the work and lives of the habitants. During the long Canadian winter, they would spend considerable time cutting firewood to keep warm and tending to their animals. To adapt to the harsh cold and snow, they copied and adapted Aboriginal clothing and technologies. The habitants wore fur-lined coats, and made leather mittens and boots from moose hide and lined with beaver fur. To get around in winter, they adapted the Aboriginal Peoples' snowshoes, and they transported their goods across the snow and ice on toboggans.

In the spring, the habitants would repair the fences around their fields and then take their animals to pasture, plough and seed the land, and plant their vegetable gardens. As summer grew to a close, they would collect the hay for the animals and then harvest the cereal crop and take it to the mill for grinding. In the fall, they would store the grain, bring in the animals, store provisions for the winter, and prepare the soil for spring planting. Most habitants produced their own food. The wheat that they grew would provide flour for bread, a staple of the habitant diet. The livestock provided eggs, meat, cream, butter, and cheese. They would also have fruits from their orchards and vegetables from their gardens, most commonly turnips, cabbages, onions, leeks, and beets. In season, they would collect wild blueberries, strawberries, raspberries, currants, blackberries, and plums. Eel, herring, trout, salmon, ducks, geese, partridges, and passenger pigeons could supplement their diets, if they had paid the fee for the privilege of hunting and fishing on the seigneur's estate.

In order for the habitants to survive heavy Canadian winters, they had to adopt and adapt Aboriginal technologies such as snowshoes and toboggans.

The family and the home were very important in New France and children were an important element in the family, a promise for the future as well as a welcome addition for the labour in which the whole family shared. Children usually remained with their parents rather than going off to town to apprentice to a trade, as was often the case in France. Indeed, children were treated differently from children in the old country, and some colonial administrators believed that this was due to the adverse influence of the way that Aboriginal Peoples treated their children. In May 1706, the administrator Jacques Raudot complained that "People in this country love their children madly, imitating in this sense the Savages, and this prevents them from disciplining them and forming their characters."[25]

With few other places to congregate, the home was also the place for socializing; Habitants got together for evenings of card playing or for music and dancing. Some members of the clergy were concerned about the evils of dancing. In 1691, the Bishop of Quebec wrote to parish priest urging them to keep their "parishioners away from popular dances, which are gatherings of iniquity."[26] Nonetheless, the habitants danced, one more fact that convinced the clergy that they were not devout enough and did not have sufficient respect for authority.

Eventually, the habitant of rural Quebec created a society that was very different from that of old France: more self-sufficient, more rebellious, more independent, and strongly attached to their new country. Both the Catholic clergy and the colonial officials worried about the growing independence, but they seemed to be unable to curb it. One colonial administrator realized that he was perhaps fighting a game he could not win. "It is necessary to strengthen more and more the correct subordination which must be present in all discipline, especially among the country people. This aspect of administration has been at all times the most important and the most difficult to implement . . . One dares to observe that the lack of firmness in past administrations has greatly harmed subordination. . ."[27]

A Report On Popular Culture, 1737

The Colony of New France may contain about forty thousand persons, of all ages and both sexes, among whom are found ten thousand men capable of bearing arms.

The Canadians are naturally tall, well proportioned, of a vigorous constitution. As trades are not regulated by guilds, and that at the beginnings of the establishment of the colony workers were scarce, necessity has rendered them industrious generation after generation. The inhabitants of the countryside handle the axe very adroitly; they make most of their tools and equipment for farming themselves, build their houses, their storehouses. A number of of them are also weavers, making canvas, and a cloth *droguet* which they use to clothe themselves and their families.

They love honours and flattery, pride themselves on their bravery, are extremely sensitive to scorn and the least punishment. They are selfish, vindictive, given to drunkenness, make great use of brandy, and are considered untruthful. This image fits a large number of them, especially the people in the rural areas; those in the towns are less depraved. All are religious: there are few villains to be found; they are fickle; have too high an opinion of themselves; all of which impedes them from succeeding as they might in the arts, agriculture and commerce. Add to this the idleness occasioned by the long and rigorous winters. They like hunting, boating, travelling and do not have that crude and rustic air about

them of our peasants in France. They are often quite amenable when they are put on their mettle, and when they are controlled with fairness, but they are naturally lazy. It is necessary to strengthen more and more the correct subordination which must be present in all discipline, especially among the country people. This aspect of administration has been at all times the most important and the most difficult to implement. One of the means to attain thereto is to choose as officers in the rural communities the inhabitants who are the wisest and best able to command, and for the government to pay all requisite attention to maintaining them in their authority. One dares to observe that the lack of firmness in past administrations has greatly harmed subordination. For the past few years crimes have been punished, disorders have been repressed by appropriate punishment. Public order with respect to public roads, cabarets, etc. has been better observed, and in general the inhabitants have been more content than they were before...

For some years now *coureurs de bois* have appeared, principally in the region of Michilimacinac. They have the same life-style as the natives, and not only trade with foreigners but take on ideas from the English that are very pernicious for the colony.

The authorities cannot, for the time being, bring any remedy to this disorder apart from granting amnesty to the *coureurs de bois*, as was done previously. It appears that they will all take

advantage of it but to avoid falling into the same circumstance later on, it is important not to allow any but the voyageurs, on whose faithfulness and good conduct we can count, to go up to the upper country...

All the education which most of the children of officers and gentlemen receive amounts to very little; scarcely can they read and write; they are ignorant of the basic elements of geography and history; it is highly desirable that they be better educated. The teacher of hydrography at Quebec is so busy with his duties as principal of the college, even the functions of a missionary, that he cannot attend as much as is necessary to his work as a teacher.

At Montreal the youth are deprived of all education. The children go to public school which are held at the seminary of St-Sulpice and the Charron Brothers, where they learn only the first elements of grammar. Young people who have no other opportunities can never become useful persons. It is reckoned that if, in each of the towns of Quebec and Montreal, His Majesty would be willing to support a schoolmaster to teach geometry, fortification, geography to the cadets in the troops and that these cadets were made to be hard working at the lessons being taught, that would form persons capable later on of rendering useful service. Canadians generally are intelligent and it is believed that the proposed establishments would enjoy the success hoped for.

National Archives of Canada, MG 1, Series C11A, Vol, 67, "Canada: Details of the Colony," (1737), pp. 40-45, 60-62. Quoted in Cornelius Jaenan and Cecilia Morgan, *Material Memory: Documents in Pre-Confederation History* (Toronto: Addison-Wesley, 1998) pp. 42-43.

1. Although the author of this document is not known, who do you think made these observations about popular culture in New France? What type of biases does the reader need to be aware of when reading this document?

Conclusion

Historian Louise Dechêne summed up the life of the typical early Quebec habitant in these words: "At his death, thirty years after he received the concession, he possesses thirty arpents of arable land, a bit of meadow, a barn, a stable, a slightly more spacious house, a road by the door, neighbours, and a pew in the church. His life has passed in clearing and building."[28]

Notes

1. Don Gillmor et al., *Canada: A People's History*, Volume I (Toronto: McClelland & Stewart, 2001) p. 76.
2. Don Gillmor et al., *Canada: A People's History*, Volume I, p. 77.
3. Ibid. p. 94.
4. Francess G. Halpenny and Jean Hamelin, eds., *Dictionary of Canadian Biography, Talon*, Volume 1, (Toronto: University of Toronto Press, 1966).
5. Francess G. Halpenny and Jean Hamelin, eds., *Dictionary of Canadian Biography, Talon*, Volume 1.
6. W.J Eccles, *France in America*, (New York: Harper and Row, 1972) p. 37
7. See the Black Cultural Centre for Nova Scotia Web site <http://www.bccns.com/>
8. Margaret Conrad, Alvin Finkel, and Cornelius Jaenen, *History of the Canadian Peoples, Volume 1, Beginnings to 1867*, (Toronto: Addison Wesley Longman, 2002) p. 137
9. Olive Dickason, *Canada's First Nations: A History of Founding Peoples from Earliest Times*, (Toronto: Oxford University Press, 2002) p. 141.
10. Cornelius Jaenen and Cecilia Morgan, *Material Memory: Documents in Pre-Confederation History*, (Toronto: Addison Wesley, 1998) "Memorandum on Colonizing New France" p. 15. *NAC, MG 1, Series C11A, Vol. 2, Anonymous memorandum of 1663, pp. 44–49, 53–56. Trans. CJJ*
11. Olive Dickason, *Canada's First Nations: A History of Founding Peoples from Earliest Times*, p. 145.
12. Cornelius Jaenen and Cecilia Morgan, *Material Memory: Documents in Pre-Confederation History*, (Toronto: Addison Wesley, 1998), p. 77. "Mercantilist Directives, 1704-1706: from Pontchartrain to Vaudreuil and Beauharnois, of June 14, 1704." *NAC, MG 1, Series B, Vol. 27, Pontchartrain to Vaudreuil ; Beauharnois, 14 June 1704, fols. 117-118*
13. Cornelius Jaenen and Cecilia Morgan, *Material Memory: Documents in Pre-Confederation History*, (Toronto: Addison Wesley, 1998). "Responsible Control of the Fur Trade (Louis XIV to Frontenac, 29 April 1680," p. 27. Rapport de l'Archiviste de la Province de Québec pour 1926-27 *(Québec, 1927, pp. 113-116. Trans. CJJ*

14. Cornelius Jaenen and Cecilia Morgan, *Material Memory: Documents in Pre-Confederation History,* (Toronto: Addison Wesley, 1998). "Warning Against Colonial Over-Expansion, 1666," pp. 75-76. Rapport de l'Archiviste de la Province de Québec. 1922-1923. *(Quebec: L.-Amable Proulx, 1923), Colbert to Talon, 5 January 1666, p.41*

15. *Dictionary of Canadian Biography*, article on Jean Talon (CD-ROM version).

16. Alison Prentice et al., *Canadian Women: A History* (Toronto: Harcourt Brace & Company, 1996) p. 39.

17. Craig Brown, ed., *The Illustrated History of Canada,* (Toronto: Key Porter Books, 2000) pp. 128-129.

18. Craig Brown, ed., *The Illustrated History of Canada,* pp. 128–129.

19. Don Gillmor et al., *Canada: A People's History,* Volume I. p. 79.

20. Margaret Conrad, Alvin Finkel, and Cornelius Jaenen, *History of the Canadian Peoples, Volume 1, Beginnings to 1867* (Toronto: Addison Wesley Longman, 2002) p. 151.

21. Don Gillmor et al., *Canada: A People's History,* Volume I, pp. 84-85.

22. Alison Prentice et al. *Canadian Women: A History* (Toronto: Harcourt Brace & Company, 1996) p. 40.

23. Margaret Conrad, Alvin Finkel, and Cornelius Jaenen, *History of the Canadian Peoples, Volume 1, Beginnings to 1867,* p.127.

24. "The Habitant in New France," Museum of Civilization Web site <www.civilization.ca/vmnf/umnfe.asp>

25. "The Habitant in New France," Museum of Civilization Web site <www.civilization.ca/vmnf/umnfe.asp>

26. "The Habitant in New France," Museum of Civilization Web site <www.civilization.ca/vmnf/umnfe.asp>

27. Cornelius Jaenen and Cecilia Morgan, *Material Memory: Documents in Pre-Confederation History (*Toronto: Addison Wesley, 1998) "Report on Popular Culture, 1737," p. 42. NAC, MG 1, Series CIIA, Vol. 67, "Canada: Details of the Colony," (1737), pp. 40-45, 60-62.

28. Christopher Moore, "Colonization and Conflict: New France and its Rivals (1600–1760) *The Illustrated History of Canada,* Craig Brown ed., p. 131.

Chapter 5 Review

Knowledge & Understanding

1. Identify these people, places, and events, and explain their historical significance to Canada's developing culture and identity:

   divine right of kings
   citizenship
   seigneurial system
   mercantilism
   Louis XIV
   Jean Talon
   fille de roi
   Carignan-Salières regiment
   institution of Royal Government
   royal mandate instituting slavery

2. Create a chart outlining the policies of the French government in New France following the institution of Royal Government in the colony. For each policy, state what the French government hoped to achieve and how the policy was changed by the reality of life in New France.

Thinking & Inquiry

3. Administrators in New France originally sanctioned marriages between French men and Aboriginal women but not between French women and Aboriginal men. In small groups, discuss the reasons for this situation. Report the results of your discussion to the rest of your class.

4. The Canadian Constitution Act of 1982 states that "Every individual is equal before and under the law and has the right to the equal protection and equal benefit of the law without discrimination and, in particular, without discrimination based on race, national or ethnic origin, colour, religion, sex, age or mental or physical disability." Create a chart in which you compare this statement with the protection given to citizens in New France.

Communication

5. Working in a small group, research, plan, outline, script, and storyboard a short documentary on the life of a male or female town-dweller or habitant living in New France. Consider how your subject's culture and identity has been shaped by the environment; by the need to earn a livelihood; and by relationships with the Aboriginal Peoples, the Church, the local community; and the French administrators of the colony.

6. In role as an Aboriginal leader, prepare a speech designed to warn your people against the dangers to them of the fur trade. Select the kind of evidence that is likely to convince your audience that your interpretation of the situation is correct.

Application

7. In spite of the relatively benign attitude of the French towards the Aboriginal Peoples of New France, there is still evidence of bias in their relationship. First conduct research using a variety of information sources that present different perspectives on this issue. Watch for bias and lack of substantiation in statements. Write an essay in which you state your opinion and offer support for your viewpoint.

CHAPTER 6

Acadia 1621–1755

Whereupon the Council advised and it is accordingly determined that [the French Acadians] shall be removed out of the Country, as soon as possible.... And for this purpose, orders are given for a sufficient number of Transports to be sent up the Bays with all particular dispatch for taking them on board; by whom you will receive particular Instructions as to the manner of their being disposed of, the places of their destination and every other thing necessary for that purpose.

– CORNELIUS JAENEN AND CECILIA MORGAN, "CONFIDENTIAL RESOLUTION ON THE EXPULSION OF THE ACADIANS, 1755"

Along the eastern seaboard, in what is today Nova Scotia and New Brunswick, the small French colony of Acadia took firm root, despite its turbulent beginnings. The colony changed hands between France and England fourteen times before the Treaty of Utrecht in 1713 gave the English permanent control over most of the region. The great fortresses of Louisbourg and Halifax that were built by France and England after the Treaty kept the animosity alive between the two powers. Even when the European colonial powers were not at war, internal feuding over rights to the fur trade and the choicest land meant insecurity for the resilient Acadians.

Through all the turmoil, the Acadians built their dikes along the Bay of Fundy, tended their farms, fished for cod, and maintained their close family ties and their loyalty to the Catholic church. They formed lasting trade and military alliances with the Mi'kmaq and other Aboriginal Peoples of the region. After 1713, the Acadians and Aboriginal Peoples refused to sign an unconditional oath of allegiance to the English king. By 1749, the Mi'kmaq nation had declared war on the English. By 1755, the English had decided that the French colonists were too great a threat, and the Acadians—who had lived in the region for generations—were expelled from their homeland.

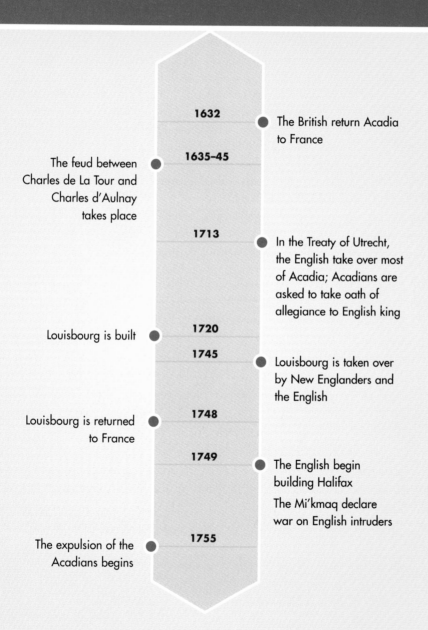

	1632	The British return Acadia to France
The feud between Charles de La Tour and Charles d'Aulnay takes place	**1635–45**	
	1713	In the Treaty of Utrecht, the English take over most of Acadia; Acadians are asked to take oath of allegiance to English king
Louisbourg is built	**1720**	
	1745	Louisbourg is taken over by New Englanders and the English
Louisbourg is returned to France	**1748**	
	1749	The English begin building Halifax The Mi'kmaq declare war on English intruders
The expulsion of the Acadians begins	**1755**	

By the end of this chapter, you will be able to

- analyze the principal characteristics of the French and English colonial experiences in Canada

- analyze the impact of European contact on the lives of Aboriginal Peoples, and evaluate the responses of Aboriginal Peoples

- analyze how Canada's changing relationships with France, Britain, and the United States have influenced the formation and transformation of Canada's identity

- demonstrate an understanding of the resistance of French and British settlers to the establishment of European colonial institutions

- demonstrate an understanding of the characteristics of the French presence in Canada and its contributions to Canadian identity

- describe the origins and various incidents of prejudice and discrimination in Canada's history

Turbulent History

Acadia was a turbulent place in the seventeenth and eighteenth centuries. In the early seventeenth century, powerful French families fought over access to the fur trade and for territorial rights. Throughout Acadia's almost 150-year history, there were frequent attacks—and sometimes occupations—by one of the feuding French families or by the Dutch, English, Virginians, or New Englanders.

Part of the reason for the disorder was that Acadia was on the sea and could be attacked by ship, making it easier for various powers to attack and take control of the colony. Another reason was that, as historian W.J. Eccles said, Acadia was France's "neglected colony."[1] Even though Acadia was located in a strategically important position for the defence of the French colonies in Canada, and even though the cod-fishing trade of the region was very important in economic terms, France was not as interested in Acadia as it was in its colonies in the West Indies and Quebec. To King Louis XIV and his minister of marine, Jean-Baptiste Colbert, Acadia was a marginal colony. France seemed to want to keep possession of the land so that the English could not have it, but they did not want to finance sending settlers to colonize Acadia or finance the military support to defend it.

Because of such neglect, the people of Acadia grew more independent from France and more interdependent with their Mi'kmaq and Maliseet allies. After the start of royal government in 1663, very few settlers were sent to Acadia, and the population was estimated at fewer than one thousand. These Acadians were mostly of French descent, with a few Scottish, Irish, and Basque sprinkled throughout the colony. With few newcomers arriving from outside the region, France's influence became increasingly weak. During the 1660s, when other French colonies were being institutionalized and run by relatively efficient colonial bureaucracies, Acadia was not. For the most part, the Acadians held their lands directly from the Crown, rather than from seigneurs. Unlike in Quebec, Acadia had no militia districts organized for colonial defence; even the missions were not organized into parishes, with resident priests supported by tithes.

Nova Scotia in the Eighteenth Century

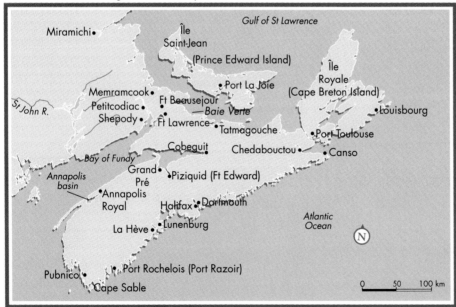

As the years passed the French Acadians, in their relative isolation, became a distinctive and resilient people, whose culture and identity would stand up even to the extreme effects of expulsion from their homeland.

Internal Conflict

Much of Acadia's turmoil began in 1635 as the result of the feud between Charles de Saint-Étienne de La Tour and Charles de Menou d'Aulnay. La Tour had been among the earliest settlers in Port Royal when he arrived with his father, Claude, and Charles Biencourt de Saint-Just. When De Monts and Champlain left Acadia in 1607, the two boys (Biencourt was nineteen and La Tour was fifteen) stayed behind, living with the Mi'kmaq and trying to find a way to make their fortunes. Eventually, Biencourt settled at Port Royal and La Tour at the mouth of the Penobscot River. Both men brought settlers over from France and struggled for control of the lucrative fur trade.

When Biencourt died in 1624, he was only thirty-two years old. His successor was Isaac de Razilly, a nephew of the powerful Cardinal Richelieu. For the few years before his early death in 1635, de Razilly and La Tour worked out compromises for control of territory and trade. But when Charles d'Aulnay, who also had Richelieu's backing, took over from de Razilly, he began a feud with the La Tours.

La Tour and his father were quite willing to form alliances with the English or with the New Englanders when it served their purpose. During one period when England occupied the colony, La Tour was even granted the rights to part of Acadia— along with Thomas Temple and William Alexander, the Scottish poet who led an abortive attempt at a Scottish settlement in Port Royal.

By the terms of their contracts with the French government, d'Aulnay and La Tour were supposed to share the profits of the fur trade, each of them controlling the trade in their own part of Acadia. This did not stop the fighting between them. Between 1635 and 1645, the colony suffered through what amounted to a civil war between the two houses. Finally, d'Aulnay gained control of Fort La Tour when La Tour was away, taking the Fort from La Tour's wife, Françoise-Marie de La Tour. She died, three weeks after the fort was taken, and La Tour fled to Quebec. When d'Aulnay drowned in 1650, La Tour came back to Acadia and married d'Aulnay's widow, Jeanne. He was governor of Acadia for one year, until it fell to the British again. La Tour was sent to England as a prisoner, but he returned to his beloved Acadia as a fur trader. In 1656, he retired with Jeanne to Fort La Tour, where he died in 1666.

Madame de la Tour pleading for the lives of her men, with d'Aulnay. The men were hanged.

The wives of La Tour and d'Aulnay were involved in the family battles and intrigues. They proved themselves quite capable of running their family's affairs with courage and skill. Françoise-Marie went to France several times to obtain support and supplies for her family and its forts and to fight in court to defend her husband against charges of plotting with the English against d'Aulnay. She was unsuccessful in her husband's defence in court, but she was able to defend their property, at least for a time. When d'Aulnay's men attacked Fort La Tour in 1645 while her husband was away, Françoise-Marie took command of her men and held off the larger d'Aulnay force for five days. Before she finally surrendered, she extracted a promise from d'Aulnay that the lives of her men would be spared. The promise was broken, and she was forced to watch—with a rope around her own neck—as they were hanged. While still a captive of d'Aulnay's, Françoise-Marie died of unknown causes.

Jeanne Motin d'Aulnay worked for her family's success during the feud, administering the family properties and business while her husband was off battling with La Tour and his forces. When d'Aulnay died, Jeanne sent a force against a new contender, Nicholas Denys, whom she clapped in irons and imprisoned. In 1653, Jeanne and Charles La Tour married, ending the decades-old feud between their families.

The Outside Threats

Champlain had been concerned about whether the long shoreline of Acadia could be defended, and history proved his concern to be well founded. Between 1627 and 1763, Acadia was passed back and forth between owners fourteen times. Acadia was also beset by attacks from the Dutch, the English, and New England's colonial militias.

Acadians' relationship with the New Englanders remained ambivalent throughout the colony's history. The Acadians even referred to the New Englanders as *nos amis l'ennemi*—our friends, the enemy. Even

Conflict Timeline	
1627–1632	Acadia occupied by England and New England
1632	Acadia returned to France by the Treaty of Saint-Germain-en-Laye
1654	Sedgewick captures Port Royal for England/New England
1667–1670	Treaty of Breda returns Acadia to France and French administrators return
1673	Dutch pirates attack and destroy trading posts at Pentagouet and Jemseq on the St. John River
1690	William Phipps of Boston captures and occupies Port Royal for England/New England
1697	Treaty of Ryswick returns Acadia to France
1710	English soldiers capture Port Royal during War of Spanish Succession; Port Royal is renamed Annapolis Royal and now remains under English control
1713	most of Acadia is ceded to England permanently by the Treaty of Utrecht
1739–1740	War of Austrian Succession with battles at Canso
1745	Louisbourg falls to the English and New Englanders
1748	Treaty of Aix-la-Chapelle returns Louisbourg to French
1749	the English build Halifax; Mi'kmaq declare war on English
1752	Treaty 239 between English and Mi'kmaqs
1755	beginning of the Seven Years' War
1755	beginning of expulsion of the Acadians
1758	Louisbourg falls to England/New England and is destroyed
1761	Peace treaty between English and Mi'kmaq, Wuastukwiuk, and Abenaki of Acadia
1763	Treaty of Paris. Cape Breton becomes a British possession

though most Acadians were French, and France and England were often at war, the Acadians continued to trade with the English who had settled in New England. Despite the fact that the Acadians suffered attacks and occupations by the New Englanders, the two peoples needed each other. The Acadians were isolated from France and found it more expedient to trade with New England, which was closer than Quebec.

By the Treaty of Utrecht in 1713, France gave up its rights to Acadia and to the territories of Hudson Bay and Newfoundland, to which it had laid claim. In the Atlantic region, France retained Ile Royale (Cape Breton), Ile Saint-Jean (Prince Edward Island), and its fishing rights off Newfoundland. The estimated five thousand Acadians then living in what became peninsular Nova Scotia became British subjects. England had gained control of Nova Scotia. However, the boundaries had not been clearly defined, which led to more disputes. Did Nova Scotia mean only the Nova Scotia peninsula? Or did it also include the area north of the Bay of Fundy?

In 1717, the English appointed Colonel Richard Philipps as governor of Placentia and Nova Scotia, but he spent little time there. The English were not interested in settling many people in the region. There was still too much turmoil, and there was always the danger of hostilities erupting again with either the French Acadians or their Mi'kmaq, Maliseet, and Abenaki allies. The colony had changed hands so many times that it was not extraordinary to think that it would do so again. For the Acadians, life went on much the same as it had before. Most of the administration of the colony was done from London. True, there were now British fishing fleets off Canso and the eastern coast of Newfoundland. But for the most part, there were no major changes in the structure of the colony, and life continued much as it had when the colony was under French control.

In 1713, the Acadians were told by British military administrators that they had a choice to make in the next year. They could leave the colony, with whatever goods they could carry, or they could stay, keep their lands and their property, and have the right to practise their Catholic religion freely. Their priests would now come from Quebec rather than France. The downside was that they would have to swear an oath of allegiance to the British king. Most Acadians chose to stay. After all, they were accustomed to having their colony change hands, and some Acadians probably believed that the English takeover was temporary.

That oath of allegiance remained an unresolved issue between the English, the Acadians, and the Aboriginal Peoples of the region. In spite of the long-standing neglect they had suffered by France, most Acadians did not want to have to take arms against their mother country. Besides,

Anglo-French Land Claims in North America, 1713

the Acadians at Grand Pré and Beaubassin argued that the boundaries of their regions of Acadia were still in dispute between England and France. How were they to know whether they were actually English or French subjects? The allegiance issue would one day have tragic repercussions, but for four decades the French Acadians managed to avoid taking an unconditional oath.

Without taking that oath, what was the citizenship of Acadians? Were they or were they not subjects of Great Britain and citizens of this new English North American colony? By the Treaty of Utrecht, those Acadians "who [were] willing to remain here, and to be subjects of the Kingdom of Great Britain" were to be allowed to practise their religion, but were they also to be granted the rights of British subjects? If they would not accept the responsibilities inherent in the oath of allegiance to the English monarch, then how could they have the rights of citizenship? By Article 14 of the Treaty between England and France, Queen Anne of England stipulated that her administrators in Acadia were to "permit such of [the French settlers] as have any lands or tenements in the places under our Government in Acadia and Newfoundland...and are willing to continue our subjects, to retain and enjoy their said lands and tenements without molestation, as fully and freely as our other subjects do."[2] Although this article allowed the Acadians to remain, it did not resolve the issue of their citizenship or their responsibilities and rights.

The English were quite willing to have the Acadians remain for the moment. Without them, the English soldiers would be without food and other supplies that were bought from Acadian farmers, fishers, and merchants. Besides, if the Acadians left and went to Cape Breton as the French there were urging them to do, the French would gain a valuable asset: people who knew the country well, who would fight for what had long since become their homeland, who were highly skilled in the use of canoes and snowshoes, and who were allies of the feared Mi'kmaq nation. As

Colonel Vetch reported to his superiors, one hundred Acadians "who were born upon that continent, and are perfectly known in the woods; can march upon snow shoes; and understand the use of Birch Canoes...are of more value and service than five times their number of raw men, newly come from Europe." Vetch feared that those facts combined with their skill in the fishery and as farmers would make of Cape Breton "the most powerful colony the French have in America."[3]

Louisbourg

The French settlers who did leave Placentia, Newfoundland, by the terms of the Treaty of Utrecht, were moved to Ile Royale, now named Cape Breton by the English. By 1720, the French had begun to build a fort and naval base on the island, which was one of their few remaining possessions in Acadia. They named the fortress Louisbourg after their king, and it gave the French a base from which they could provide protection for French fishing fleets and trading ships, defend the colony in Quebec, and attack the English colonies along the Atlantic seaboard. Although officials in France tried to convince some of the Acadians now under English rule to move to Louisbourg (and about five hundred people did move), the majority of Acadians stayed in their villages and on their farms.

Most of the population of Louisbourg, therefore, came from France. Military officers and men made up a good portion of the population. The Recollet priests and the Hospitalier and Notre Dame nuns came to tend to their flocks. Louisbourg also had German and Swiss soldiers and some settlers from the British Isles. Some of the European fishers and sailors who stayed in the town for the winter also settled there.

Louisbourg became a thriving town and a major centre for French trade in North America and for the export of fish and fish oil. As historians Margaret Conrad and Alvin Finkel report, "the wharves in Louisbourg harbour were awash with

The Fortress of Louisbourg circa 1774

manufactured goods, fishing supplies, and food-stuffs from France: molasses, sugar, and rum from the West Indies; foodstuffs and building supplies illegally shipped from New England, and foodstuffs and forest products from Canada."[4] The fishing industry contributed to the growth and economic health of Louisbourg. If the fishing was poor in any season, then the merchants and their employees in Louisbourg suffered, and if it was good, they prospered. Not only did the fishing industry draw trading ships to the area, but it also supplied jobs for sailors and people who worked in the ware-houses that stored the fish and trade goods.

Louisbourg, however, was a thorn in the side of the English colonials in the Thirteen Colonies. In 1745, New Englanders made plans to attack the supposedly impregnable fortress. Governor William Shirley of Massachusetts organized a volunteer militia force of 4300 from Massachusetts, Connecticut, and New Hampshire. With the sup-port of a British naval squadron, they surrounded the fortress and bombarded it for seven weeks, until the French surrendered. The large French squadron that was sent out from France to retake Louisbourg was caught in a terrible hurricane, its commander died suddenly of apoplexy, and the crew became ill with infectious diseases. Louisbourg remained under English control. When the French and English once again signed a treaty—the Treaty of Aix-la-Chappelle—in 1748, Louisbourg was returned to France. The New Englanders were shocked at England's lack of forethought in failing to consider the strategic importance of this French fortress on their northern flank. But England wanted to regain its possessions in the Netherlands and its trading station of Madras in India, and handing over Louisbourg was part of the empire-building bargain.

The Aboriginal Peoples in Acadia

The Mi'kmaq and Maliseet (also called Wuastu-kwiuk) who lived in the region they called Megumaage had complex and well-developed social structures. They were skilled traders as well as sailors, fishers, and hunters of walrus, seals, and even small whales. During the seventeenth century, Mi'kmaq sailors learned to handle the French shal-lops with ease, and by the eighteenth century, they could handily sail the schooners that they took from the English.

The Mi'kmaq and the Maliseet remained allies of the Acadians throughout the years after Champlain's arrival. They traded furs with the Acadians and received various French goods in return, shared the tasks of hunting and fishing and even the Catholic faith with the Acadians, taught them the skills they needed for survival, and built kinship ties through intermarriage. Without the

This is a view of the Fortress of Louisbourg as it appears today.

support of French troops in a turbulent colony that was so open to attack from the sea, the Acadians depended on their Aboriginal allies' military support and skills in guerrilla tactics.

Although the Mi'kmaq and Maliseet had not lost much of their land to the French, through their close contact with Europeans, they had lost many of their old ways of life. By the 1660s, some of the animals that had formed part of the Aboriginal diet and whose hides had been used for clothing were becoming harder to find. Because of the over-hunting for the fur trade, moose, elk, and other fur-bearing animals were becoming scarce. The Mi'kmaq had to buy European clothing, which also meant that the women were no longer using and passing on to their daughters their traditional

Mi'kmaq male

Mi'kmaq female

These drawings of a Mi'kmaq man ("homme Acadien") and a Mi'kmaq woman ("femme Acadienne") are by print artists St. Saveur and Labrosse, and dated 1796.

clothes-making skills. Because of the loss of resources, the Mi'kmaq people moved closer to the Acadian settlements and began to eat their foods rather than their own. Traditional hunting techniques also fell into disuse, as the Aboriginal Peoples became more dependent on European guns and ammunition. Like the Aboriginal Peoples of other regions of North America, the Mi'kmaq were susceptible to European diseases and epidemics. It is estimated that by the late seventeenth century, only two thousand to three thousand Mi'kmaq people lived in Acadia; in the late sixteenth century, between 10 000 and 15 000 Mi'kmaq had called the land home.

Consequences of 1713

Throughout the many French–English conflicts of the seventeenth and eighteenth centuries, the Mi'kmaq remained allies of the French rather than the British for several reasons. Not only were there trade benefits and kinship ties, both of which were valuable to the Mi'kmaq, but also they remembered the earlier English slave raids along the Atlantic coast. Thus, they were on the wrong side of the war that led up to the Peace of Utrecht. The fact that many Mi'kmaq were Catholics was yet another aggravation to their Protestant rulers.

The Peace—and treaties—of Utrecht in 1713 was a major event for the Mi'kmaq and Maliseet, as well as for the French. No consideration was given to the rights of the Aboriginals by either the French or the English in the treaty negotiations and documents. Although these treaties were very important to the British and French in their empire –building, and although the signatories included England, France, Austria, the Netherlands, Prussia, Portugal, Nice, Sicily, Naples, Milan, and Savoy, the Aboriginal Peoples of Acadia were not even mentioned.

For the previous century and a half, few disputes over land had arisen between the Aboriginal Peoples and the French in Acadia, but France considered that the lands of Acadia were hers by the right of "discovery." There was also a general European view that the Christian peoples of Europe had a greater claim to sovereignty than non-Christian peoples. If they became Christian, the Aboriginal Peoples also became subjects of the ruling colonial power. Of course, as far as the Mi'kmaq and Maliseet were concerned, the French were allies whom they allowed to live in their territory because land could not belong to one or another group. The land was there to be shared by all the people who lived on it. Because the French had so few colonists in Acadia at the time and because they needed the Aboriginals for trade and military alliances, they did not quarrel over the issue of land.

When the English took over Acadia in 1713, they did not consider compensating the Mi'kmaq, Maliseet, and Abenaki Peoples for their land. In the English view, the Aboriginals and their lands had been conquered by the French before them and then had been, in turn, conquered by the English in their war with the French. Indeed, the English believed that the issue was irrelevant. Because the Mi'kmaq and Maliseet had not been organized into permanent states on specific plots of land, they held no sovereign rights to the land.

The English demanded that the Mi'kmaq and Maliseet take an oath of allegiance to the English king, but this seemed an absurd request to the Aboriginal Peoples. They had made no such oath to the French king; they had not been his subjects, nor were they now subjects of the English king. They were a sovereign people.

The Aboriginal Peoples of the region soon realized their plight, especially after the English started to build a fortified naval base at Halifax in Mi'kmaq territory in 1749 and brought out three thousand British and German settlers to colonize the area. The Mi'kmaq fought on sea and on land to reclaim their home; they knew that the Abenaki peoples were being forced from their land throughout the Thirteen Colonies by English settlers moving inland from the Atlantic coast. The Ohio Land

Company had been founded in the same year that construction had begun on the fortifications at Halifax. This company, made up of Virginians and English investors, was promoting settlement in Abenaki and other Aboriginal Peoples' territories in what is now part of the United States.

The Mi'kmaq attacked fishers at Canso, raided two ships at Chignecto, burned a sawmill near Halifax, and then captured a detachment of eighteen British soldiers. The English military governor, Cornwallis, threatened to bring in troops to search out the Mi'kmaq, and his council proposed a bounty of ten guineas for every Aboriginal prisoner or Aboriginal scalp. In September 1749, the Mi'kmaq, aided by French missionaries sympathetic to their cause, issued a formal declaration of war on the British intruders. That declaration contained the following words:

> The place where you stand, where you build houses, where you build a fort, where you wish as it were to enthrone yourself, this land of which you now wish to make yourselves absolute masters, this same land belongs to me. I have grown up on it like the grass, and it is the very place of by birth and my residence. It is my land, me a native. Yes, I swear, God gave it to me to be my country forever....
>
> Show me where I, a native, will lodge? You chase me away, and where do you want me to take refuge? You have seized nearly all this land in all its vastness. All that is left to me is Kchibouktouk [Chebouctou]. You begrudge me even this bit....Your settlement at Port Royal does not trouble me because as you see for a long time I leave you in peace there. But at the present time you force me to speak out because of the considerable theft you inflict upon me.[5]

The wars between the English and New Englanders on the one side, and the Aboriginal Peoples and their French allies at Louisbourg on the other, were ferocious. The Aboriginal Peoples were fighting to reclaim their homeland, and the English were fighting for territory and absolute control. Each side committed atrocities against the other. On October 19, 1744, William Shirley, governor of Massachusetts, issued a "Proclamation for encouragement of volunteers to prosecute war"[6] against the Mi'kmaq and Maliseet peoples of Nova Scotia. In this document, Shirley declared that the General Assembly of Massachusetts had voted that "there be granted to be paid out of the Public Treasury to any Company, Party, or person singly of His Majesty's Subjects...[who] go out and kill a male Indian of twelve years or upwards...and produce his scalp in evidence of his death, the sum of one hundred pounds in bills of credit of this Province of New England."[7] For captive males, the sum of one hundred and five pounds would be paid. The reward for killing women was fifty pounds and the same for children under twelve. Captive women and children would earn their captors fifty-five pounds each.

Web Connection

www.mcgrawhill.ca/links/definingcanada

Go to the Web site above to see the Mi'kmaq Portraits Collection.

Anglo-Aboriginal Peace Treaties

After 1713, the British signed treaties with the Mi'kmaq, Abenaki, and Maliseet peoples in the region: the Treaty of Portsmouth, the Treaty of Boston, and Treaty 239 (also called Mascarene's Treaty). These treaties of "peace and friendship" were used to end hostilities between the English and their Aboriginal "subjects" and to assure the Aboriginal Peoples of "free liberty for Hunting, Fishing, Fowling, and all other their Lawful Liberties & Privileges."[8]

The following excerpt is from the Treaty of 1725, which was signed at Boston and is a representative example of the tone and language generally used by the English in their treaties with the Aboriginal Peoples.

We, the said Delegates for and in behalf of the several Tribes abovesaid, Do promise and

Engage that at all times forever from and after the date of these Presents, We and They will Erase and forbear all Acts of Hostility, Injuries, and Discords towards all the Subjects of the Crown of Great Britain and not offer the least hurt, violence of molestation to them, or to any of them in their Persons or Estates, but will, henceforward, hold and maintain a firm and constant Amity and Friendship with the English, and will never Confederate or Combine with any Nation to their Prejudice.[9]

The treaty goes on to say that "we" (meaning the Aboriginal Peoples who would sign the treaty) agreed that the Crown of Great Britain and King George's heirs and successors were the "rightful owners and lawful proprietors" of the region, that the Aboriginal Peoples would be subject to British law, and that they would not interfere with future settlement of their lands—although the treaties called them British lands.

The language of the treaties was a major source of difficulty for the Aboriginal Peoples. Not only were the treaties in English, but they also were written in a dense, convoluted legal language that made them difficult for even native English speakers to understand. The treaties were translated for and read to the Aboriginal Peoples by interpreters who sometimes missed the point and sometimes deliberately misrepresented the content. For some English words, there simply was no Mi'kmaq or Maliseet equivalent. For example, the whole concept of "exclusive land ownership" was foreign to their thinking.

In addition, getting the signatures of all parties was a problem because the Mi'kmaq and Maliseet did not have any supreme chief who could sign for all. Some bands might allow a chief to sign for the band, but even that had to be after consensus was reached.

Building a Society: The People of Acadia

Despite the conflicts going on around them and the sometimes precarious state of their existence, the Acadians managed to build a stable society centred on their families, their church, and their work as farmers, fishers, merchants, and artisans. Many Acadians were

Pen and ink drawing of a Mi'kmaq encampment (1791) by Hibbert Newton Binney (1766–1842)

related by marriage or blood ties, because there were so few of them in the early years of the settlement. They had learned to depend on each other and on their Aboriginal allies. Oftentimes, they lived their lives within the same small communities into which they had been born. The children with whom they played in their early years grew into the elders of the community with whom they would share celebrations and the bereavements of their final years. By the time of their expulsion, the Acadians had been in the region for almost 150 years. They had become an established people, with their own culture and deep ties to their homeland.

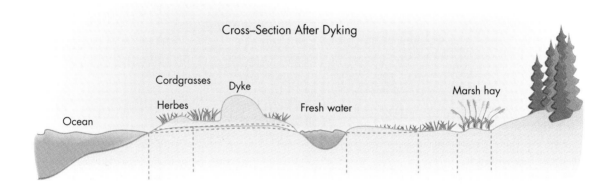

Cross–Section After Dyking

Cordgrasses
Dyke
Herbes
Fresh water
Marsh hay
Ocean

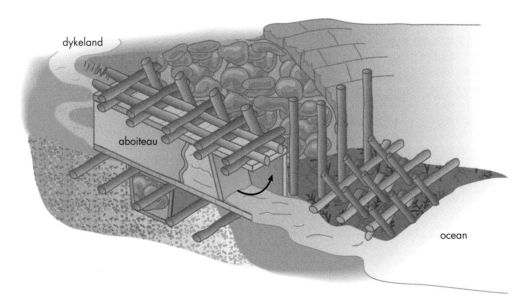

dykeland
aboiteau
ocean

The dyking systems in early Acadia: top, a cross-section after dyking and bottom, an aboiteau.

Farming

One of the most distinctive features of farming in early Acadia was the construction of dikes to enclose land reclaimed from the sea. Many of the French people who settled the marshlands that bordered the Bay of Fundy and the Minas Basin had come from regions in southwestern France, where dikes were used to keep out the sea. These settlers knew that such reclaimed land could be very fertile for growing crops. Each day the potentially valuable marshland was flooded by salt water, it could not be used for farming. However, much of the rest of the land in the area was either rocky or filled with dense forests. So, the settlers chose to build not only the dikes around the land they wanted to reclaim from the sea, but also one-way sluice gates, called *aboiteaux,* that would open and shut automatically and would drain fresh water off the reclaimed lands. These gates, which were constructed as tunnels inside the dikes, were so skillfully engineered that they also kept the salt sea-water from flowing back in and flooding the land.

The sediment-rich reclaimed land could not be used without patience and a lot of hard work. First, the dikes themselves had to be built of wooden stakes and piled up sod, soil, and rocks. Some of these dikes were two metres high to keep out the waters of the Bay of Fundy, which has the highest tides in the world. Usually, several families would work together and build a network of dikes to surround their land. Back in the seventeenth and eighteenth centuries, cooperation was essential in this type of venture, and the families would work together to repair breaches in the dikes caused by normal erosion or by severe weather. Such team efforts helped to foster a strong sense of community among the Acadian farmers.

For the first couple of years after a field had been drained, the salt in the soil meant that the land could only be used to grow hay or as pasture for livestock. But once rainwater had washed much of the salt out of the land, the soil was good for growing a wide variety of crops. Even today, the soil of this region is among the richest in North America.

Repairing a dyke

The Acadians choice of farmland had another benefit. Unlike other regions in North America, the marshlands were not used by the Aboriginal Peoples of the area. Any conflict that might have arisen over clearing a forest did not arise in Acadia.

Housing

French historian Rameau de Saint-Pere described the Acadian homes as being made of "squared logs or of heavy beams planted in the soil with the interstices sealed with moss or clay."[10] The chimneys were built using poles and hardened clay, and the roof was covered with rushes, bark, or sometimes sod. Because there was lots of wood available in the nearby forests, the houses could be built relatively easily, which was just as well since when the English attacked the region, they often destroyed the homes. Saint-Pere further describes how the Acadians responded to these attacks: "the settlers fled to the woods without worrying about what was left behind."[11] They would take along their livestock and whatever household belongings they could carry. All the Acadians knew "the trails to safe retreats in the heavily wooded valleys only a gunshot away but impenetrable to everyone save themselves and their friends, the [Mi'kmaq] of the interior."[12]

Fishing

As historian Christopher Moore states, during the time of French rule in Canada, "[t]he cod fishery... was France's great economic interest in North America, more valuable than the fur trade, source of an important foodstuff, great employer of ships and men."[13] The fish trade was of vital importance to both France and New France, and its return on investment was four times more valuable than the fur trade. At first the fishers came ashore only long enough to dry the cod, but eventually some of them and their families started to winter in Acadia. It was because of the fishing trade that both France and England established small colonies on Newfoundland: the English in the areas of Trinity Bay, Conception Bay, and St. John's and the French on the south shore, where a few hundred people settled.

This painting depicts early eighteenth-century Acadian farmers cutting saltmarsh hay.

A View of a Stage & also of ÿ manner of Fishing for, Curing & Drying Cod at NEW FOUND LAND.
A. The Habit of ÿ Fishermen. B. The Line. C. The manner of Fishing. D. The Dressers of ÿ Fish. E. The Trough into which they throw ÿ Cod when Dressed. F. Salt Boxes. G. The manner of Carrying ÿ Cod. H. The Cleansing ÿ Cod. I. A Press to extract ÿ Oyl from ÿ Cods Livers. R. Casks to receive ÿ Water & Blood that comes from ÿ Livers. L. Another Cask to receive the Oyl. M. The manner of Drying ÿ Cod.

A drawing of a cod curing and drying operation in Atlantic Canada, early eighteenth century

Every year in the Acadian region in late winter or early spring, fishers came out from France to catch cod for the markets of France. The fishers who came out were migrant workers whose income depended on their daily and seasonal catch. Many returned to France in the fall of the year, but some stayed to settle and continue to fish year-round. Others stayed and became merchants, traders, innkeepers, and providers in one way or another for the lucrative cod trade.

In his article on Charles Renaut, a fisherman off the coast of Scatary near Île Royale, Moore describes a typical day fishing in the region. The boats in which these men fished were called shallops, were about nine metres long, and were equipped with sails and oars:

Before the dawn departure, someone had gone out to tend bait nets near the harbour. Now the shallop's bait barrels were packed with fresh herring or mackerel. Stashed near by were long, multi-hooked lines, a heap of weights, and a grapnal. A chart and a compass, spare clothing, bread, a keg of spruce beer or watered wine—all the sundry supplies of a day's work—were stowed beneath the bows.[14]

The fishers had to be highly skilled sailors; their lives depended on it. No matter the weather and sea conditions, they had to set sail, and they had to be able to find the cod. Once they arrived at their fishing location, they would anchor or drift while they baited and dropped their multi-hooked lines, then they hauled in the fish, dropped them on the bottom of the shallop, and rebaited and dropped the lines again. In any season of the year, a mistake or a sudden change in the weather could mean death. In winter, the sea spray turned to ice that covered the men and their fishing gear and left them bitterly cold in their open boats. Once they were finished for the day, they would bring their catch back to shore, where the fish would be dried or salted and cod-liver oil would be extracted. The fish would then be stored until it could be taken back to French markets.

Catholic Church

The Catholic Church remained an important focal point for the Acadians and the Mi'kmaq. From the earliest days of the French presence in Acadia, the Mi'kmaq people had accepted Catholicism and remained committed to the religion through the years. The Church was the centre of the Acadian community, where people met for Mass on Sundays and feast days and stayed afterward to talk and share the news of the week.

Acadians came to their churches for baptisms, marriages, funerals, and feast-day celebrations. They also came in times of war, attack, and struggle. The church was a gathering place for people of a common faith. Rameau de Saint-Père, who visited the area in 1860, drew on accounts written by one of the early parish priests of the colony, Ignace de Senlis, to describe the Sunday scene. Farmers and Mi'kmaq families would arrive in canoes or on horseback and mingle together on the church grounds. "After the service, the colonists relaxed on the *champs commune,* discussing crops, hunting, progress of clearing the land,...a thousand and one topics about their private lives and gossiping the way it is done in all French countries."[15]

One popular church-related annual celebration in Acadia was that of *Mi-Carême,* which means "the middle of Lent." By a long-standing tradition that started in France in the middle ages, this holiday was held on twentieth day, or third Thursday, of the Lenten season. It was intended to relieve the self-denial, penitence, and fasting of the Church season that led up to Easter. For *Mi-Carême,* Acadians would disguise themselves with hand-crafted masks—some of which were works of art—and costumes and go to visit friends and neighbours. Their hosts were challenged to identify the disguised guests. The evening would be spent in feasting, music, and dancing.

Web Connection

www.mcgrawhill.ca/links/definingcanada
Go to the Web site above to find out more about the celebration of *Mi-Carême.*

Review...Reflect...Respond

1. Why did the Acadians refuse to swear an oath of allegiance?

2. What were the consequences of the Peace of Utrecht in 1713 for Acadians and the Aboriginal Peoples in Acadia?

3. What was it about Acadian life that gave Acadians such a distinct and strong cultural identity?

Expulsion of the Acadians

After 1713, when France was defeated in Acadia for the last time, the English left the Acadians alone, largely out of fear of the superior numbers and the strength of the Acadians and their Mi'kmaq allies. The 1720s and 1730s were relatively peaceful years in the region, and the Acadians were able to maintain their neutrality.

The English, however, could not convince the Acadians to take the oath of allegiance to the English king. For decades, the Acadians had insisted that though they would not take up arms against England, neither could they take an oath that might force them to fight against French forces or that might jeopardize their Catholic religion. Assurances that, as Catholics, they could not be part of the English army or navy did not persuade the Acadians. Veiled threats didn't move them. Finally, in 1730, the Acadians agreed to sign an amended oath of allegiance. The official version of the oath read, "I promise and swear by my Faith as a Christian that I will be entirely faithful and will truly obey His Majesty King George II, whom I acknowledge as the sovereign lord of Acadia or Nova Scotia, so help me God."[16] In the margin, next to the French translation, there was an amendment stating that the Acadians were exempt from fighting alongside the English against the French. Whether the colonial powers in England knew of this amendment remains in question.

By 1749 the English had founded Halifax, and more than 2500 English settlers and English troops were brought in to take over what was still Mi'kmaq territory. Although they were harassed by raids as the Mi'kmaq people tried to retake their land, the English remained and Halifax was built. The Acadians continued to try to maintain neutrality in the struggles between the empires of France and England and in the battles in Acadia between the English and the Aboriginal Peoples. As far as the English were concerned, the fact that some Acadians and their Mi'kmaq allies did, at times, join in defence of French forts along the Nova Scotia border proved their disloyalty. Furthermore, French ships continued to harass the English off the Atlantic coasts.

The English became convinced that the Acadians would never be loyal subjects of the English king, and the Acadian population kept growing. As the years passed, the Acadians increasingly became a force to be reckoned with in the eyes of the English colonial administrators. The last straw for the English came in July 1755, when the Acadians refused to sign a new oath of allegiance, this time without the condition of not taking up arms against the French.

Exile

At Halifax, on July 28, 1755, Charles Lawrence, the acting governor of Nova Scotia, and his English council decided that England could no longer put up with the Acadians' refusal to take the unconditional oath of allegiance to the English king. Ignoring any considerations of the French-Acadians' property or citizenship rights, the governing English council proclaimed their resolution:

Whereupon the Council advised and it is accordingly determined that [the French Acadians] shall be removed out of the Country, as soon as possible.... And for this purpose, orders are given for a sufficient number of Transports to be sent up the Bays with all particular dispatch for taking them on board; by whom you will receive particular Instructions as to the manner of their being disposed of, the places of their destination and every other thing necessary for that purpose."[17]

This is an artist's portrayal of John Winslow announcing the expulsion of the Acadians at a Church meeting in Grande Pré.

Expression of Culture
EVANGELINE

"Evangeline" was written by the American poet, Henry Wadsworth Longfellow, and published in Boston in 1847. His epic narrative poem tells the story of a young Acadian woman whose father died on the shore the night before the Acadians were exiled from their homeland. We pick up the tale as the Acadians wait on ships or on the beach to be transported. It is late at night. The English have started to burn their homes, and the exiles watch hopelessly while the night sky fills with flames.

Suddenly rose from the south a light, as in
    autumn the blood-red
Moon climbs the crystal walls of heaven, and o'er
    the horizon
Titan-like stretches its hundred hands upon
    mountain and meadow,
Seizing the rocks and the rivers, and piling huge
    shadows together.
Broader and ever broader it gleamed on the roofs
    of the village,
Gleamed on the sky and the sea, and the ships
    that lay in the roadstead.
Columns of shining smoke uprose, and flashes of
    flame were
Thrust through their folds and withdrawn, like
    the quivering hands of a martyr.
Then as the wind seized the gleeds and the burn-
    ing thatch, and, uplifting,
Whirled them aloft through the air, at once from
    a hundred housetops
Started the sheeted smoke with flashes of flame
    intermingled.

These things beheld in dismay the crowd on the
    shore and on shipboard.
Speechless at first they stood, then cried aloud in
    their anguish,
"We shall behold no more our homes in the vil-
    lage of Grand-Pre!"
Loud on a sudden the cocks began to crow in the
    farmyards,
Thinking the day had dawned; and anon the
    lowing of cattle

Came on the evening breeze, by the barking of
    dogs interrupted.
Then rose a sound of dread, such as startles the
    sleeping encampments
Far in the western prairies or forests that skirt the
    Nebraska,
When the wild horses affrighted sweep by with
    the speed of the whirlwind,
Or the loud bellowing herds of buffaloes rush to
    the river.
Such was the sound that arose on the night, as
    the herds and the horses
Broke through their folds and fences, and madly
    rushed o'er the meadows.

[Following the death of Evangeline's father]
"Let us bury him here by the sea. When a
    happier season
Brings us again to our homes from the unknown
    land of our exile,
Then shall his sacred dust be piously laid in the
    churchyard."
Such were the words of the priest. And there in
    haste by the seaside,
Having the glare of the burning village for funeral
    torches,
But without bell or book, they buried the farmer
    of Grand-Pre.
And as the voice of the priest repeated the service
    of sorrow,
Lo! with a mournful sound, like the voice of a
    vast congregation,
Solemnly answered the sea, and mingled its roar
    with the dirges.
'T was the returning tide, that afar from the
    waste of the ocean,
With the first dawn of the day, came heaving and
    hurrying landward.
Then recommenced once more the stir and noise
    of embarking;
And with the ebb of that tide the ships sailed out
    of the harbor,
Leaving behind them the dead on the shore, and
    the village in ruins.

The council members kept their decision secret to prevent the Acadians from trying to escape with their livestock and other belongings. By the expulsion order, all the Acadians' possessions were "forfeited to the Crown" and "applied towards a Reimbursement of Expense the Government will be at in Transporting them out of the Country." The Acadians were to finance their own expulsion! The council planned to call the heads of families together on some pretext and then keep them as prisoners until the ships arrived that would take them into exile. To prevent the prisoners' wives and children from removing any of their possessions, the English would steal their shallops and canoes and would post soldiers on the roads to prevent their leaving. When they were sent into exile, the Acadians were not to be allowed to "carry away the least thing" except their money and the household furnishings that they could carry.

On September 5, 1755, at three in the afternoon, 418 Acadian men assembled at the church in Grand Pré. Before making them "the King's prisoners,"

Joshua Winslow, a native of Massachusetts and commissary general of the British forces in Nova Scotia, read to the assembled Acadians the king's "final resolution" as to what to do with them. In a reference to the decades-long Acadian refusal to sign the oath of allegiance to the English monarch, Winslow said that the English king had shown them more indulgence than he had shown any other subjects in all his lands. And then he read the order of expulsion: "That your lands and tenements, cattle of all kinds and livestock of all sorts are forfeited to the Crown" and by his majesty's orders "the whole French inhabitants of these districts be removed."[18]

Winslow picks up the story again in his report of the actual deportation at Grand Pré. The inhabitants, he wrote, "sadly and with great sorrow, abandoned their homes. The women, in great distress, carried their newborn or their youngest children in their arms. Others pulled carts with their household effects and crippled parents. It was a scene of confusion, despair, and desolation."[19]

A Cajun celebration in Louisiana.

An artist's conception of the Expulsion of Acadians—why were the Acadians sent into exile?

During 1755, approximately 7000 out of an estimated 10 000 Acadians were sent into exile. By 1763, 10 000 Acadians had been deported from their homeland. Fewer than one thousand French Acadians remained in Nova Scotia. Many of the exiles died of typhoid, smallpox, and yellow fever on their journey. Some of the ships transporting them sank with the loss of all on board. Some arrived safely in the Thirteen Colonies, where they were not particularly welcome, not only because they were poor refugees, but also because they were Roman Catholics in a Protestant country. The deportations continued until a year after the signing of the Treaty of Paris in 1763. Groups of Acadians were shipped in "human cargo" boats to American colonies from Massachusetts to the Carolinas, to the Poitou region of France, and even to English seaports.

Their forced removal, their later incarceration in refugee camps, and the ravages of disease greatly depleted their number, but most held tenaciously to their Acadian identity. Of the approximately 10 000 who were deported, about 2000 managed to escape to Canada, and several hundred trekked overland from the southern coastal colonies to the lower Mississippi and Louisiana. The Acadians in the south became known as "Cajuns," and they continue to form a sizable portion of Louisiana's population.

Web Connection

www.mcgrawhill.ca/links/definingcanada

Go to the Web site above to find out more about the expulsion of the Acadians.

Conclusion

Once the Acadians were gone, the English administrators lost no time in bringing in settlers from Britain and New England to take over the fertile farmlands that the Acadians had worked so hard to wrest from the Bay of Fundy shoreline.

As for the Mi'kmaq people, who were now bereft of their Acadian allies and kinfolk, historian Olive Dickason sums up their situation this way: "This once assertive, far-ranging people on sea and land now had to take what they could get, and that was not very much; in fact, the process was in reverse, as lands were taken from them as settlers began streaming into the homelands they had fought so hard to protect."[20]

<table>
<tr><td>

Review...Reflect...Respond

1. Is there a close connection between present-day Acadians in Canada and Cajuns in the United States? Why or why not?

2. Was there any proof that the Acadians posed a threat to English interests in the country?

3. If you had been a citizen of Acadia, would you have sworn an oath of allegiance to England if it meant keeping your home and land? Why or why not?

</td></tr>
</table>

Notes

1. W.J. Eccles, *France in America,* rev. ed. (Fitzhenry and Whiteside, 1990), p. 68.
2. As quoted by Jim Bradshaw in "Remembering our Acadian Heritage," a supplement to the Lafayette *Daily Advertiser* of September 29, 1994. Available online at <www.acadian-cajun.com/acartic25.htm>
3. Cornelius Jaenen and Cecilia Morgan, "Colonel Vetch's Report on the Conquered People," *Material Memory: Documents in Pre-Confederation History* (Public Archives of Nova Scotia, MS documents, Vol. V. Vetch to Lords of Trade, November 24, 1714).
4. Conrad and Finkel, *History of the Canadian Peoples, Beginnings to 1867,* Vol. 2 (Toronto: Copp Clark, 1998) p. 120.
5. Cornelius Jaenen and Cecilia Morgan, "A Mi'kmaq Declaration of War, 1749," *Material Memory: Documents in Pre-Confederation History* (Archives de Séminaire de Quebec, Lettres P. No.66, abbé Maillard to abbé Du aru, 18 October 1749. Trans. CJJ).
6. Daniel N. Paul, *We Were Not the Savages* (Nimbus Publishing, 1993), p. 100.
7. Ibid.
8. Frederic Kidder, "The Abenaki Indians, Their Treaties of 1713 and 1717," *Collections of the Maine Historical Society,* 1st ser., 6 [1859], pp. 250–253.
9. Paul, *We Were Not Savages,* p. 79.
10. Rameau Saint-Pere, as quoted by Jim Bradshaw in "Remembering our Acadian Heritage," a supplement to the Lafayette *Daily Advertiser* of September 29, 1994. Available online at <http://www.acadian-cajun.com/acartic25.htm>
11. Ibid.
12. Ibid.
13. Carol Wilton (ed.), "Charles Renaut's Letter," in *Change and Continuity: A Reader on Pre-Confederation Canada* (Toronto: McGraw-Hill Ryerson, 1992), p. 81.
14. Ibid., p. 83.

15. From Bradshaw, "Remembering."

16. Don Gillmor and Pierre Turgeon, *Canada: A People's History,* Volume I (Toronto: McClelland & Stewart, 2000), P. 104.

17. Cornelius Jaenen and Cecilia Morgan, "Confidential Resolution on the Expulsion of the Acadians, 1755," *Material Memory: Documents in Pre-Confederation History* (Toronto: Addison Wesley, 1998), p. 68. NAC, MG18, Series 1, Robert Monckton Papers, p. 81

18. Cornelius Jaenen and Cecilia Morgan, "Summons at Grand Pré, 5 September 1755," *Material Memory: Documents in Pre-Confederation History* (Toronto: Addison Wesley, 1998), p. 69. Winslow's Journal, September 5, 1755. Report of the Public Archives of Canada for 1905 (Ottawa: King's Printer, 1906–1909), Vol. II, pp. 19–29. Text modernized.

19. From Jim Bradshaw, "Remembering our Acadian Heritage," a supplement to the Lafayette *Daily Advertiser* of September 29, 1994. Available online at <http://www.acadian-cajun.com/acartic25.htm>

20. Olive Dickason, *Canada's First Nations: History of Founding Peoples from Earliest Times* (Toronto: McClelland & Stewart, 1992), p. 137.

Chapter 6 Review

Knowledge & Understanding

1. Identify these people, places, and events, and explain their historical significance to Canada's developing culture and identity:
   - oath of allegiance
   - *nos amis l'ennemi*
   - Charles La Tour
   - Françoise-Marie de La Tour
   - William Shirley
   - Charles Lawrence
   - Treaty of Utrecht
   - the building of Louisbourg
   - the building of Halifax
   - Acadian expulsion

2. Write a paragraph summarizing the ways in which the Treaty of Utrecht of 1713 violated the human rights of the Aboriginal Peoples of Acadia.

Thinking & Inquiry

3. Investigate the Web sites of current Mi'kmaq and Acadian organizations. What purpose do these Web sites serve? Who is the intended audience? What are the highlighted features of the sites? In your opinion, why are these features considered important?

4. Historian W. J. Eccles said, "Had even a fraction of the energy, manpower, and money subsequently devoted in vain attempts to regain Acadia been employed in its defense, France would not have had to surrender it in the first place." Discuss the reasons that France lost Acadia and the consequences of that loss for the future of Canada.

Communication

5. Imagine that you have the opportunity to investigate first-hand how the expulsion of the Acadians came about. Prepare five questions that you would ask in an interview with an Acadian farmer who refused to take the oath of allegiance and with a British administrator in the colony. Focus your questions on issues of citizenship rights. Then prepare responses to those questions from the perspective of your interviewees.

6. Create a flow chart to demonstrate how relationships between colonial administrators and the Aboriginal Peoples of Acadia changed following the Treaty of Utrecht of 1713.

Application

7. In your role as an Acadian, write a fictional story that demonstrates how isolation from France, receiving few settlers from outside the colony, and being alert for the almost constant attacks helped form your distinctive culture and identity. Develop your setting, plot, characters, and dialogue with a focus on Acadian culture and identity.

8. Prepare a list of research questions that you could use to write a comparison essay in which you investigate the similarities and differences between the colonial experience of French settlers in Quebec and in Acadia. Research and evaluate possible sources, and then draw up a thesis and outline for your essay.

CHAPTER 7

The Fall of New France

The real tragedy, the greatest wound inflicted upon us, what that an entire continent slipped out of French hands in the eighteenth century. Ever since, we have been orphans who have only survived by withdrawing into our shell, increasingly concerned about our future as we emerge from it into the outside world. the separation from our mother country was the most traumatic aspect of our infancy as a people.

– LÉON DION, POLITICAL SCIENTIST

The fall of New France, which brought about lasting social, economic, and political changes, was a very significant event for Canadian history, culture, and identity. The conquest of New France by Britain was one of the concluding events of the European empire-builders' Seven Years' War. During this time, there was also animosity between the settlers in the Thirteen Colonies and the French Canadians and their Aboriginal allies. The war took a large toll on the people of Quebec. The men went to war and some never came home; the women took over the farms and businesses; the people were plagued by food shortages throughout the war years; and their homeland became a battle zone. To many Aboriginal Peoples, the war was a fight for survival; they knew that the advance of British settlements would mean the loss of their lands.

The governor of Quebec and the French general clashed over battle strategies, but the early battles between the French Canadians and the British usually resulted in victories for the French. With the fall of Louisbourg, though, the tide began to turn as New France's military and supply positions weakened. In the siege of Quebec and the battle of the Plains of Abraham, the British defeated the French. French Canadians and the Aboriginal Peoples of Canada came under British rule.

Following the Conquest, the British administrators in Quebec—facing the threat of the discontented Thirteen Colonies to the south and the need to govern a conquered people—decided that leniency would be the best policy. The Aboriginal Peoples, who had lost their bargaining power between French and English and who were losing their lands to settlers, tried and failed to rid their lands of the British. The Royal Proclamation of 1763 tried to address the question of land ownership, but unresolved issues from that document still haunt relations between Canadian governments and the Aboriginal Peoples of Canada.

1757

William Pitt becomes Prime Minister of Britain and begins to concentrate British forces on defeating France in North America

1758

British forces attack Montcalm at Fort Carillon, but are defeated

Louisbourg falls to British forces

1759

General James Wolfe sets out from London to New France with orders to conquer Quebec

British forces take Quebec; Wolfe and Montcalm are among the casualties

1760

Governor Vaudreuil signs the Articles of Capitulation and surrenders all of New France to Britain

1763

The Treaty of Paris ends the Seven Years' War, and New France becomes the British colony of Quebec

1764

Some Acadians return to the Atlantic colonies

1765

Pontiac signs peace treaty with the English, and tries to enforce that the surrender of French forts did not mean that Aboriginal territory had been surrendered

By the end of this chapter, you will be able to

- analyze the principal characteristics of the French and English colonial experiences in Canada

- analyze the impact of European contact on the lives of Aboriginal Peoples, and evaluate the responses of Aboriginal Peoples

- analyze how Canada's changing relationships with France, Britain, and the United States have influenced the formation and transformation of Canada's identity

- describe the role of selected significant events and legislation in the development of the current Canadian political system

- demonstrate an understanding of Canada's role in international affairs prior to Confederation

- assess whether British colonial policies were directed towards the creation of a homogeneous society in Canada

The Beginning of the End: The Seven Years' War

During the Seven Years' War (1756–63) the great empires of Europe struggled to maintain colonial territory, economic wealth, and power on the European continent and in lands far removed from Europe. Involving the largest armies and navies in human history up until that time, the war was fought on all the seas of the world and aligned France and Austria against Britain and Prussia. Quebec was only one of many colonial possessions at stake and to the rulers of France and England, Canada and the colonies in other lands were only pawns in a much larger game. But to the French Canadians and to many of the Aboriginal Peoples of North America, the Seven Years' War was a struggle for survival.

In the decades before the war, France's empire had flourished, both in Europe and in colonies as far away as India. Once war was declared, France's attention was focused on winning the war in Europe. But when William Pitt became British prime minister in 1757, he began to concentrate British forces on defeating France in North America. If France was gaining ground in Europe the British would focus their attention on winning the war in North America. Britain already controlled the Thirteen Colonies, the land under the Hudson's Bay charter, which was almost a third of the territory that makes up Canada today, and most of Acadia from which it had expelled the Acadians in the years following 1755. Now Pitt sent one-quarter of the British navy, two hundred ships, and at least twenty-three thousand troops to conquer New France.

France in America, 1663–1755

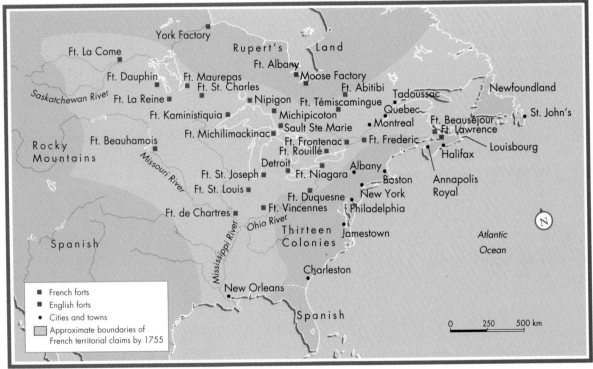

French Expansion and The Thirteen Colonies

New France's expansion into the Ohio and Mississippi valleys had started back in the mid-seventeenth century with Intendant Talon. The goal had been—and remained—to protect and extend French interests in the fur trade and to cement alliances with the Aboriginal Peoples living in the vast territories north, west, and south of Quebec. By 1755 the French held the Mississippi Valley all the way to the Gulf of Mexico. But while they claimed the land, they had only a few widely scattered French trading posts and forts to back up their claim.

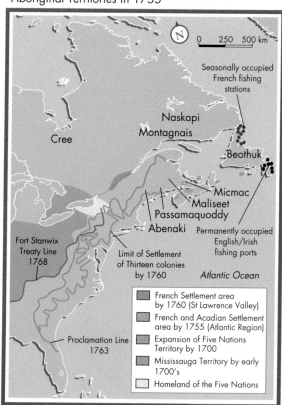

Aboriginal Territories in 1755

In the Ohio Valley, French colonial governors had built forts along the Ohio River and its tributaries. Roland-Michel Barrin de La Galissonière, commandant-general of New France from 1747 to 1749, extended the fortifications, trying to ensure French control over the region and to keep the Thirteen Colonies contained.

In the meantime, a group comprised of wealthy Virginians and English investors had formed the Ohio Land company to promote settlement on 500 000 acres of Aboriginal lands over which the French claimed sovereignty. The Ohio Land Company established trade relations with some of the Aboriginal Peoples in the region and built its own fortified posts in the hope that settlers would feel secure enough to move into the newly acquired territory.

During the years between 1747 and the outbreak of the Seven Years' War, there were battles in the Ohio valley between the French, French Canadians, and their Aboriginal allies on the one side and the British, the militia of the Thirteen Colonies, and their Aboriginal allies on the other side. Discontent with British rule may have been growing in the Thirteen Colonies, but the colonial militia fought alongside the British against the French. The Ohio valley became a killing ground as the two sides fought for territory. Oftentimes the victims were the settlers, and their scalps were taken to prove the kill.

The Aboriginal Position

While there were still some Aboriginal groups who remained allies of the French and some who became allies of the British, other Aboriginal Peoples of the Ohio region believed that neither the French nor the English would protect their land for them. As one Delaware chief told a British emissary: "We have great reason to believe you intend to drive us away and settle the country, or else why do you come to fight in the Land that God has given us . . . Why don't you and the French fight in the Old Country, and on the Sea? Why do you come to fight on our Land? This makes everybody believe you want to take our land from us by force and settle it."[1]

Nonetheless, many Aboriginal Peoples continued to prefer alliances with the French rather than the English in the Thirteen Colonies as the French treated them with more respect. Knowing that their Aboriginal allies were essential to their survival, the French continued to treat them as independent peoples with whom alliances were the appropriate action. In return, their Aboriginal allies gained advantages in trade and also in the power over other Aboriginal nations. In addition, the French Canadians, with only 43 000 people as opposed to the 906 000 in the Thirteen Colonies, did not try to settle in Aboriginal lands.

As one Iroquois explained to the French when he sought refuge in a French mission in 1754, there was a distinction between the French and English peoples who lived in Aboriginal territories:

> Brethren, are you ignorant of the difference between Our Father [the French king] and the English? Go see the forts our Father has erected, and you will see that the land beneath his walls is still hunting ground, having fixed himself in those places we frequent, only to supply our wants; whilst the English, on the contrary, no sooner get possession of a country than the game is forced to leave it; the trees fall down before them, the earth becomes bare, and we find among them hardly wherewithal to shelter us when the night falls.[2]

Montcalm and Vaudreuil

The governor of Quebec, Pierre de Rigaud de Vaudreuil, and the French General Louis-Joseph, the Marquis de Montcalm, clashed over how to wage battles and defend the colony of Quebec. Vaudreuil, a native French Canadian, knew the country and believed that his strategies would keep Quebec from being conquered by the British. He wanted to strengthen the Canadian militia with thirty-six hundred French regular troops, co-ordinate large numbers of Aboriginal war parties with the French force, and launch a series of surprise guerrilla raids at various points along the wide American frontier.

Montcalm thought these strategies would not be effective, and they were contrary to the European tradition of war. He complained that "It is no longer the time when a few scalps, or the burning of a few houses is any advantage or even an object. Petty

A portrait of Pierre de Rigaud de Vaudreuil de Cavagnial on the left, and the Marquis de Montcalm, on the right.

means, petty ideas, petty councils about details are now dangerous and a waste of time."[3] Montcalm wanted to concentrate French troops along the inner defences of the St. Lawrence and Richelieu rivers, and he wanted the Canadian militia incorporated into the regular army, where they would be subject to traditional military discipline. He also wanted to fight decisive battles with armies arrayed against each other in a field of war. Vaudreuil insisted that the outer defence lines had to be strengthened and that the guerrilla warfare had to be kept up in the Ohio valley.

Vaudreuil knew and valued his Aboriginal allies, but Montcalm had only contempt for the Aboriginal allies and for the French-Canadian militia. Vaudreuil reported to the minister of marine in France that Montcalm "goes as far as to strike the Canadians. I had urgently recommended to see that the land officers treat them well, but how could he keep them in order, if he cannot restrain his own vivacity?" To Vaudreuil, Montcalm set the worst possible example for unity among the French and Canadian soldiers.

Montcalm's aide-de-camp, Antoine de Bougainville, had greater respect for the abilities of their Aboriginal allies. He admired their skills, especially when it came to tracking down the enemy.

> They see in the tracks the number that have passed, whether they are Indians or Europeans, if the tracks are fresh or old, if they are of healthy or of sick people, dragging feet or hurrying ones, marks of sticks used as supports. It is rarely that they are deceived or mistaken. They follow their prey for one hundred, two hundred, six hundred leagues with a constancy and a sureness which never loses courage or leads them astray.[4]

The Battles

Before the Seven Years' War was officially declared, the French achieved a number of victories against the British. They defeated British troops at Fort Duquesne, and stopped attacks at Fort Niagara and in the Lake Champlain area. In the early days of the war, both Montcalm and Vaudreuil achieved more

victories. Montcalm and his troops attacked Oswego on the south shore of Lake Ontario to prevent the British from entering the Great Lakes. In the Lake Champlain area, the French captured Fort William Henry. There were heavier losses among the British and the militia of the Thirteen Colonies than among the French-Canadians and their allies. The fighting was bloody, with scalps being taken on both sides. Governor Vaudreuil told his superiors in 1756 that one of his officers had been "occupied more than eight days merely in receiving scalps."

Montcalm and Vaudreuil continued to quarrel over how the battles should be fought. Finally, Montcalm requested to be recalled to France, but instead, he was placed in supreme command of all French forces in North America. Future battles would be fought according to Montcalm's rather than Vaudreuil's strategies. As Vaudreuil observed, "Now war is established here on the European basis . . . . It is no longer a matter of making a raid, but of conquering or being conquered. What a revolution! What a change." Montcalm would meet the British invaders in the same manner as they attacked—by following European tactics and conventions.

For a while the French held their own. In July of 1758, a British force of fifteen thousand soldiers, the largest army amassed in North America to that time, attacked Montcalm and the French at Fort Carillon. Montcalm, with only thirty-six hundred soldiers, kept the British at bay, though with a heavy loss of life. But Jeffrey Amherst had laid siege to Louisbourg, and the tide began to turn against the French.

The Fall of Louisbourg

The British determined that they had to capture Louisbourg, the remaining and powerful French fort in the Atlantic region. The fortified town had become a thorn in the side of the British. It served as a base for the French navy, protected the entrance to the St. Lawrence River, and offered a refuge for French pirates who captured ships belonging to New Englanders.

Using Historical Sources

Historians use a variety of sources to try to understand the different perspectives that individuals and groups have on historic events, situations, and issues. If historians want to be objective, they need to explore as many perspectives as possible. They also need to be aware that both primary and secondary sources may be based on political, economic, and social values that reflect the time frame in which the author is writing.

What are Primary Sources?

Primary sources are direct or firsthand accounts written or created by people who actually experienced the event or the situation. Examples of primary sources include journals, logs, letters, government documents, manuscripts, speeches, statistics, newspaper articles, and artwork. These sources provide the historian with a variety of frames of reference. Examples of primary sources on the subject of the September 11, 2001 attack on the World Trade Centre would include newspaper articles, television and video accounts, President Bush's speeches, photographs, and email messages from people who were there. Examples of primary sources on the subject of the Fall of New France might include Montcalm and Wolfe's letters, diaries and official reports, as well as Aboriginal Peoples' oral histories.

Primary sources provide information that
- reveals the perspective of participants in an event or situation
- reflects the culture, attitudes, language and style of a past time
- often reflects the speaker's personal involvement in the event
- helps readers, viewers, or listeners understand beliefs and values at the time of the event

What are Secondary Sources?

Secondary sources are accounts of an event written or created by people who are explaining an historic event or situation after it has happened. Examples of secondary sources include textbooks, articles, manuscripts, history books and art. Secondary sources provide a retrospective or hindsight view of an event. Examples of secondary sources on Canada's role in World War II could include books and articles written on the causes and effects of the war, biographies of participants, documentary films, and speeches made at Remembrance Day ceremonies. To be objective, historians who write secondary sources material need to use a variety of primary and secondary sources with different viewpoints.

Secondary sources provide information that
- presents a perspective based on distance in time from the event
- presents the event in a larger context which includes the consequences of the event
- may be more readily available and easily accessed than primary sources
- are often compiled from a number of different sources

Why is it Important to understand historical sources?

Whether you are reading primary or secondary sources, it is important that you try to understand exactly what the author is saying, both explicitly and implicitly. Historical sources can sometimes be challenging, especially if they were written in the past where the use of language, values and references are different from what people use today. When you read, you understand based on your own lifetime experience. To read or view material from the past critically, you need to place the source in its historical and cultural context and recognize the differences between the values of the past and those of contemporary society. The following strategies will help you to read critically.

Strategies to use before you read

- Think about what you already know about the period, event, or topic.
- Determine who wrote the document: Is it a primary or secondary source? When was it written? Do you know anything about the political, economic or social values at that time? What was the writer's intended purpose and who was the intended audience?
- Scan the text and look for unfamiliar vocabulary. Guess the meaning based on the context of the word in the sentence. Make note of these words; the meaning may become apparent as you read or you may need assistance with these terms later.

Strategies to use while you read
- Note the main ideas in the document.
- Note points related to or supporting the main idea.
- Write questions that arise as you read; for example, "Why was this information used to support the main idea?"
- Use post-it notes or written notes to highlight points that you think are interesting or questionable or that challenge your beliefs or values.

Strategies to use after you read

- Write down the point of view and/or main idea expressed by the writer.
- List the points, data, information, evidence, bias, logic, and reasoning that the author uses to support his/her point of view.
- Think about those points of view that were not included or considered by the author.
- Think about who the author's intended audience might be or might have been.
- Generate questions to help you clarify and extend what you have just read. For example, What don't I know? What vocabulary or terms do I still not understand? What other information do I need? What questions might my teacher ask about the information I just read?

Practice

List the primary and secondary sources used in this chapter. Review the sections of the chapter where those sources were referenced. Select one of the sources for further study. Use the before, during, and after reading strategies recommended above to help you understand and appreciate the source. Then discuss in a small group why you think these particular primary and secondary sources were chosen for this chapter.

In 1758, the British sent thirty-nine ships, more than twelve thousand troops and almost one thousand mounted guns to attack Louisbourg. The British commander, General Jeffery Amherst, laid siege to the fort and began the bombardment. The governor of Louisbourg, Augustin de Drucour, reported the situation: "It seems that the British intention is not just to breach the walls but rather to kill everyone and burn the town." His wife, Marie-Anne Drucour, tried to keep up French morale by going each morning to fire three cannons at the British. The soldiers who manned the guns gave her the nickname, "La Bombardière."[5]

Augustin de Drucour knew that his people and his town could not hold out forever. Food supplies were getting dangerously low, and the hospital had been destroyed. But he also knew that if he could keep the British at Louisbourg until the middle of summer, they wouldn't be able to get to Quebec that year because of the threat of the ice that formed in the St. Lawrence River. Once the ice started to form, any ship in the river would be trapped until the following spring.

On July 26, 1758, Drucour finally surrendered to Amherst. The people of Louisbourg were deported to France. William Pitt had a direct influence on the destruction that followed. The British prime minister ordered that Louisbourg be "totally demolished, and razed, and all the materials so thoroughly destroyed, as that no use may, hereafter, be ever made of them."[6]

Web Connection

www.mcgrawhill.ca/links/definingcanada
To learn more about the fall of Louisbourg go to the web site above.

The Effect of the War on the People of Quebec

For the people of Quebec, the human cost of the war was high. The colony again became a society at arms. Habitant women took over the running and even defence of farms as the men left to serve in the militia. Some would never return. Farms were

This painting is entitled *A View of Louisbourg from the Lighthouse, 1758*, that is, after it was beseiged by British forces.

neglected without enough people to work them, and to make matters worse there were crop failures during the war years. In the towns, it was a similar story as the men left and their wives took over the running of the business. Farms and homes were destroyed by the British as a tactic of war.

The intendant at the time, François Bigot, was not impressed with living in Quebec; he wanted to be back in the more sophisticated society of France. However, while he was in Quebec, he made a fortune from contracts to provide supplies for the French military. Like many colonial officials of his time, he was corrupt by today's standards of ethical behaviour in public office. Bigot and his associates of the *Grande Societé* in Quebec indulged in the excesses of the casino, the ballroom, and the banquet hall while the ordinary people of Quebec faced rationing and privation.

Nonetheless, Bigot and his associates did manage to have food and equipment shipped from France to Quebec at a time when costs were growing at a

Compilation of Quebec's Colonial Revenue and Expenditures

Year	Income (in livres)	Expenditures (in livres)
1713	442 348	445 455
1715	548 246	548 243
1720	381 499	381 499
1725	393 577	393 594
1730	496 253	494 217
1735	485 852	520 484
1740	417 968	503 766
1745	500 038	1 337 722
1750	904 722	2 774 715

During the years before the Seven Years' War, the cost to France of protecting and running Quebec rose at an alarming rate. What effect might these costs have had on France's determination to save the colony?

tremendous rate. But there was never quite enough food as refugees, soldiers, and allies moved into the walled city. Food shortages became so severe that in April 1759 rations were cut to a few ounces of bread per day. The price of food—even horsemeat—rose dramatically and some people were reduced to eating grass. And, into this misery, came a smallpox epidemic.

The Conquest

In early 1759, General James Wolfe started out from London under instructions from King George II and William Pitt to conquer Quebec. Wolfe brought with him twenty-nine ships: warships that had at least two gun decks and were heavily enough armed that they could take a position in the line of battle, twenty-two frigates (warships capable of high speeds), eighty transport ships, and fifty-five smaller ships. In total, the ships carried fifteen thousand soldiers, two thousand cannons, and forty thousand cannonballs. Among those on board were surgeons, Protestant ministers, children and their parents, and livestock. When the fleet arrived in the St. Lawrence River, it stretched for 150 kilometres and had a population greater than that of Quebec.[7]

The Siege of Quebec City

The bombardment of the town of Quebec began on July 12, 1759 and lasted for nine weeks. Night after night British cannon and the fires that followed the cannon shots destroyed homes, warehouses, churches, convents, and streets in Quebec. Sister Marie de la Visitation and the other nursing sisters at the Hôpital Géneral on the outskirts of the town witnessed these events at close hand. The nuns were caring for the soldiers who had arrived from France suffering from a "malignant fever." They were also caring for injured British soldiers who had been captured by the French. Sister Marie de la Visitation recalled the siege, "During one night,

A view of the ruined Place Royale in Quebec City, after the British conquest of New France.

upwards of fifty of the best houses in the Lower Town were destroyed. The vaults containing merchandise and many precious articles did not escape the effects of the artillery. During this dreadful conflagration, we could offer nothing but our tears and prayers at the foot of the altar at such moments as could be snatched from the necessary attention to the wounded."[8]

In an effort to force the Canadians to surrender, General Wolfe had ordered that the habitants' farms and livestock be destroyed for 150 miles along the St. Lawrence. Sister Marie de la Visitation wrote, "famine, at all times inseparable from war, threatened to reduce us to the last extremity; upwards of six hundred persons in our building and vicinity, partaking of our small means of subsistence, supplied from the government stores, which were likely soon to be short of what was required for the troops."[9]

As General Montcalm had told his superiors in France, he was not optimistic about the French chances for winning the battle for Quebec. To him, the loss of one more French colonial outpost was not all that significant. For his part, General Wolfe was suffering from the late stages of tuberculosis. In his last letter to his mother before his death, he told her that he had decided to leave the military after his tour of duty in North America.

September 13, 1759

Just before midnight on September 12, 1759, British troops began to launch small boats from their ships in the St. Lawrence alongside the citadel of Quebec. By 2:30 a.m., the soldiers, their guns, one small cannon, and ammunition were underway. When they reached the shore at Anse au Foulon a few kilometres from the town, the men climbed a steep 50-metre-high cliff and moved silently through the night towards the abandoned cornfield where General Wolfe hoped to engage his enemy. By 5:00 a.m., Wolfe's army was in place, on the Plains of Abraham.

As Rear-Admiral Charles Holmes, who was third in command of the British forces, reported to his superiors in London, Wolfe had decided the

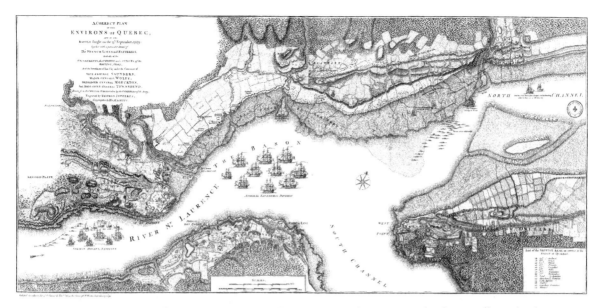

A Correct plan of the environs of Quebec, and the battle fought on September 13, 1759, by Thomas Jeffreys, dated 1762.

day before to launch the stealthy attack. He wanted to try one more time to engage the enemy before his ships would be forced out of the St. Lawrence River by winter ice. Most of Wolfe's officers disagreed with his plan, thinking that it was far too risky. Success was highly unlikely. But Wolfe was in command, and so just before dawn on September 13, the British waited on the Plains of Abraham. The French did not even know they were there. The morning mist, the overgrown condition of the terrain, and a hill between the town and the field obscured the view, even from the high walls of Quebec.

Montcalm and most of the French troops were at Beauport where he and his men had watched all night for an expected British attack. When he heard that the British were outside the walls of Quebec, Montcalm quick-marched his troops back to the town. They arrived exhausted from the journey and from a night with little sleep.

On the British side of the battlefield were soldiers of Irish, Scottish, and English descent, as well as militia from the Thirteen Colonies. On the French side were soldiers from France who were fighting yet another colonial battle and who had no particular interest in the land for which they were fighting. French-Canadian militia from Quebec, Acadians who had escaped the expulsion, and Iroquoian and Algonkian allies accompanied the French solders. Among the ranks of the French-Canadian militia were descendants of families who had been in Canada for 150 years. These men and boys—some were no older than twelve—were fighting to save their homeland.

At 8:00 a.m. the British fired their small field cannon. The French troops—whose soldiers and militia had never trained together—attacked in three ragged columns. As Maurès de Malartic, a participant in the battle reported, the left column of the French force was too far in the rear and the centre column too far in front. "The Canadians who formed the second rank and the soldiers of the third fired without orders and, according to custom, they threw themselves on the ground to reload." The French soldiers misunderstood their action, thinking they had been cut down. At this point, the first line of the British force, which according to one witness was a mile long, fired on the French. Then the feared Fraser Highlanders charged. Joseph Trahan, an Acadian survivor of the battle, remembered "the Scotch Highlanders flying wildly after us with streaming plaids, bonnets and large swords—like so many infuriated demons—over the brow of the hill."[10] Though Canadian and Aboriginal snipers tried to cut down the Scots and the other British soldiers from the woods, the battle was lost; the surviving French and Canadians retreated back into the ruins of Quebec.

Sister Marie de la Visitation and her fellow nuns witnessed the carnage from the windows of the Hôpital Géneral: "We were in the midst of the dead and the dying, who were brought in to us by hundreds, many of them our close connexions; it was necessary to smother our griefs and exert ourselves to relieve them. Loaded with the inmates of three convents, and all the inhabitants of the neighbouring suburbs, which the approach of the enemy caused to fly in this direction, you may judge of our terror and confusion. . ."[11]

Before the day was over, French reinforcements led by Governor Vaudreuil and Colonel Louis-Antoine de Bougainville had arrived. But it was too late. Quebec was lost, and although Montreal did not fall until the following spring, French rule in Canada was over. The battle ended less than three hours after it started and left 220 French and Canadian militia dead and more than 400 wounded. The British casualties were sixty-seven British dead and almost six hundred wounded.[12] Among the British wounded were General James Murray and Brigadier General Guy Carlton who would become the first two governors of the new British colony of Quebec. Wolfe was killed in the battle, and Montcalm died the next day from his wounds.

On September 18, Admiral Holmes reported to London that "We have at last brought to a happy conclusion the great Service we were sent upon; and the Capital of all Canada acknowledges the superior Bravery & Success of his Majesty's Arms."[13] To Sister Marie de la Visitation, the view was very different: "Alas! Dear Mothers, it was a great misfortune for us that France could not send, in the spring, some vessels with provisions and munitions; we should still be under her dominion. She has lost a vast country and a faithful people, sincerely attached to their sovereign; a loss we must greatly deplore, on account of our religion, and the difference of the laws to which we must submit. . ."[14]

The Capitulation of Montreal

With three separate British forces converging on Montreal and with many of their Aboriginal allies already having signed peace treaties with the British,

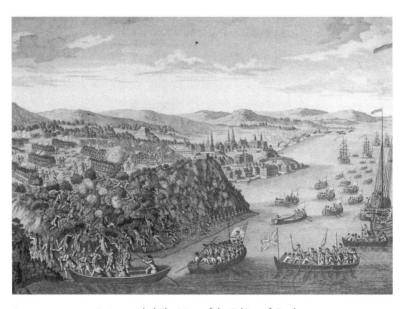

A contemporary painting entitled *The View of the Taking of Quebec*.

Governor Vaudreuil decided that the war for the French colony had been lost. There was nothing to be gained from further bloodshed and loss of life. On September 8, 1760, Vaudreuil signed the Articles of Capitulation and surrendered the whole of New France to General Amherst.

By these Articles of Capitulation, Amherst took possession of the town of Montreal in the name of the British Crown. Members of the French-Canadian militia were allowed to evacuate the town, and any other French possession in Canada, and to return to their habitations, "without being molested on any pretense whatever, on account of their having carried arms" against the English. The governor and other French colonial administrators and senior military personnel were to be carried "by the straitest passage to the first seaport in France." Catholic nuns who chose to remain in the former French colony were to be exempt from lodging any military and received a guarantee that they would not be molested in any way by the British. The French-Canadian clergy and seigneurs were to continue to have their rights and privileges.

Also in the Articles of Capitulation were two points that would have long-term significance for French Canadians in Quebec and the Aboriginal Peoples of Canada:

> Article XXVII: The free exercise of the Catholic, Apostolic, and Roman Religion, shall subsist entire, in such manner that all the states and the people of the Towns and countries, places and distant posts, shall continue to assemble in the churches, and to frequent the sacraments as heretofore, without being molested in any manner, either directly or indirectly.

> Article XL: The savages or Indian allies of his most Christian Majesty, shall be maintained in the lands they inhabit, if they chuse to remain there; they shall not be molested on any pretense whatsoever, for having carried arms . . .

Those who were slaves in French territories at the time of the Capitulation did not fare as well as the French Canadians and Aboriginal Peoples. Article 47 stated that "The negroes and panis of both sexes shall remain, in their quality of slaves, in the possession of the French and Canadians to whom they belong . . ."[15]

The Death of General Wolfe by Benjamin West, NGC, 8007

Many artists were inspired to paint the deaths of the two heroes of the Battle of the Plains of Abraham. On the left is a version of the *Death of Montcalm*, and on the right, the most famous portrayal of the *Death of Wolfe*, by artist Benjamin West, who painted the scene in 1770, several years after the fact.

The Consequences of Conquest

The Treaty of Paris, which ended the Seven Years' War, was signed on February 10, 1763, by representatives of England, France, Spain, Portugal, the Netherlands, and Prussia. There were no representatives of the Aboriginal Peoples of North America present at the signing. By the treaty, various territories in Europe shifted from the control of one country to another. In addition, the European rulers and their delegates settled the fate of colonial and Aboriginal Peoples in Canada, in many West Indian islands, in Senegal and other African colonies, and in India, Malabar, Sumatra, Bengal, and Majorca. In Canada, the French king renounced "all pretensions which he [had] heretofore formed or might have formed to Nova Scotia or Acadia in all its parts" and he ceded to the king of England "in full right, Canada, with all its dependencies, as well as the island of Cape Breton, and all the other islands and coasts in the gulph and river of St. Lawrence." The French were left with the islands of St. Pierre and Miquelon "to serve as a shelter to the French fisherman" but the islands could not be fortified nor could there be any more than fifty soldiers stationed there.[16]

At the bargaining table in Paris, France had decided that the sugar-rich island of Guadeloupe in the West Indies was more valuable in economic terms than was Canada. France also managed to retain fishing rights off the coast of Newfoundland, perhaps hoping to regain New France in the years to come. In the Thirteen Colonies, there was talk of rebellion against British rule. Also, there was word that the Aboriginal Peoples whose lands were being taken from them along the Ohio valley and in the Great Lakes basin were on the verge of "taking up the hatchet" against the settlers.

With the signing of the treaty by the European powers, New France became the British colony of Quebec. Military rule ended and James Murray became the first governor of the colony. Quebec was to be ruled as a British crown colony, separate from the Thirteen British Colonies to the south. In some ways, life continued as before for the French Canadians, but in other ways life changed. After the defeat, the members of the Canadian colonial militia had taken their oath of allegiance to the British sovereign and returned to their farms and towns. French Canadians would keep their religion and its institutions, including the seigneurial land-holding system. Some British military officers bought up seigneuries from departing military commanders, French government officials, and members of the French nobility. The fur trade remained intact, but French Canadians now served as guides and traders, rather than having controlling interest in the trade.

Life in Quebec under Murray and Carlton

Both of the early British governors of the colony of Quebec—first General James Murray and then his replacement Brigadier General Guy Carlton—tended to be fairly lenient toward the conquered people. They had to be concerned about the expense of running a large military establishment and they were also very aware of the discontent in the Thirteen Colonies and feared the possibility of French and/or Aboriginal uprisings. Murray and Carlton recognized that their relatively small British army was surrounded by seventy thousand French-speaking, Roman Catholic Canadiens who had a well-established culture and identity in Canada.

Governors Murray and Carlton also knew the value of the Catholic Church in keeping the French Canadians under control and in offering social assistance where necessary. Most of the French-Canadian clergy counselled their people to submit to British rule, knowing that if they didn't offer this advice they might be removed from their positions and replaced with more obedient ministers. The British governors recognized that the Catholic Church and the seigneuries also represented an aristocratic and hierarchical ideal at a time when the Thirteen Colonies were growing in their republican demands for more power.

Among the French-Canadian merchants who chose to stay in Quebec, there was hardship. Mercantilism was still the main force governing colonial economic policy. But now the mercantile power was England not France. And all of the trading alliances that the French-Canadian merchants had forged with members of the French court and merchants were no longer of any use. The few British merchants who set up shop in Quebec tended to get the best contracts and made the biggest profits. In Montreal, the British merchants also took over much of the fur trade.

The French Canadians knew about the expulsion of the Acadians and they feared the same fate. However, as Murray and then Carlton believed, they had a better chance for stability with the French Canadians than with the rebellious inhabitants of the Thirteen Colonies. Indeed, Murray told the Board of Trade in London in 1764 that the French Canadians were "the bravest and best race upon the face of the globe."[17] He went on to argue, as Carlton would argue later regarding the terms of the Quebec Act of 1774, that if only the people were "indulged with a few privileges which the laws of England deny to Roman Catholics at home," they would soon "become the most faithful and most useful set of men in this American empire."

Because of their religion, French Canadians were not allowed to vote or hold public office. In the beginning of British rule, only Protestants could be lawyers, judges, or jurors. Eventually, French-Canadian Catholics were allowed to become lawyers and to serve on juries, but they still found the British civil law code foreign to their culture and their society. Eventually, Carlton appointed twelve Canadian seigneurs to his council, so the French Canadians had at least some representation even if it wasn't an elected one.

Meanwhile, in Atlantic Canada, some of the expelled French Acadians started to return to the region. In Nova Scotia, they found their fertile, diked farmlands taken over by New Englanders. Many of them went on to what is today New Brunswick, while others started homesteads along the Gulf of St. Lawrence, Cape Breton, and St. Pierre and Miquelon. Between the years of 1764 and 1800, the Acadian population in the British Atlantic colonies increased from a low of sixteen hundred to eight thousand. Acadia became once again a flourishing French community in Canada.

Aboriginal Peoples and the Conquest

As the historian Olive Dickason says, while the defeat of France was a "bitter blow" to French Canadians, it was a disaster for the Aboriginal nations of Quebec, of the east coast, of the Great Lakes region, and of the northwest. These peoples lost their bargaining position between the French and the English; they lost the gift distributions upon which they had come to depend, and settlers encroached farther and farther into their lands.

During the century and a half that the French and the English had been battling for control of North America, the Aboriginal Peoples could form alliances or remain neutral as it best suited their interests. They could play one colonial power against the other. But with the British in control, they lost their strategic position.

The Aboriginal Peoples had not ceded their lands to the European powers. As Ojibwa chief Minwewheh told the English: "Although you have

This is an artist's depiction of life for French Canadians living under British military rule after the conquest of Quebec.

Pontiac, the War Chief

Pontiac, an Ottawa (Odawa) war chief, had fought as an ally of the French at Montreal. As other war chiefs had done before him, Pontiac had earned his status and his right to lead war parties by past victories in battle. After the British conquest, he had tried to build trading alliances with the British, but without success. He saw his people suffering from scarcity as the gift distributions lessened and as they received less and less in trade for their furs. The Confederacy of the Seven Fires (or Seven Nations) held councils to consider what to do about their desperate situation. At these meetings of leaders from branches of the Iroquoian, Mohawk, Algonkian, Abenaki, Nippissing, Onondagas, Oneida, and Odawa nations, Pontiac emerged as a leader and a spokesman for the confederacy.

British perspectives on Pontiac varied. Major Robert Rogers, stationed at Fort Detroit during these years, said that Pontiac had "great strength of judgement and a thirst after knowledge."[19] Another British officer wrote of how much he was "Ador'd by all the Nations herabouts" and praised him for his integrity and humanity. Other reports were less complimentary, saying that Pontiac was "proud, vindictive, warlike, and very easily offended."[20]

Pontiac wanted the Aboriginal Peoples to rid themselves of their dependence on European goods and to return to their traditional way of life.

> Why do you suffer the white men to dwell among you? . . . Why do you not clothe yourselves in skins, as your ancestors did, and use the bows and arrows, and the stone-pointed lances, which they used? . . . You have bought guns, knives, kettles, and blankets, from the white men, until you can no longer do without them; and what is worse, you have drunk the poison firewater, which turns you into fools. Fling all these things away . . . as for the English . . . you must lift the hatchet against them.[21]

Pontiac succeeded in convincing the members of the Confederacy to make war against the English, to drive them out, and to send them back to their homeland. On May 5, 1763, he told the Grand

conquered the French, you have not conquered us. We are not your slaves. These lakes, these woods, and mountains were left us by our ancestors. They are our inheritance, and we will part with them to none."[18] To British Commander-in-Chief Jeffrey Amherst, however, there was no question of Aboriginal Peoples having rights to the lands that the British and French had fought so hard to conquer.

As for gift distributions, Amherst saw no need to continue the practice that he considered little better than bribery. He did not agree with the Aboriginal Peoples' view that the gifts were "the agreed-upon price" for allowing the French and the English to live on Aboriginal land. And, with the loss of guns, ammunitions, and trade goods that they had been receiving for generations, Aboriginal Peoples were in dire straits.

In the regions to the west of the Thirteen Colonies, instead of settlers being removed from the land as had been promised, they continued to move into Aboriginal territory. No matter what the British assurances to the Aboriginal Peoples, land speculators—including George Washington and Benjamin Franklin—were not going to be prevented from taking over Aboriginal lands and selling it in parcels to those who wanted to move west into what was still known as Indian territory.

Two European portrayals of Chief Pontiac: One as he meets his council and the other with him wielding a war hatchet in battle against the British in 1763. What do these pictures reveal about European attitudes toward this Aboriginal leader?

Council of the Huron, Odawa, and Potawatomi peoples of his futile attempts to obtain supplies from the English, and of how the English commander only laughed at the death of his people. "If I ask anything for our sick, he refuses with the reply that

he has no use for us." Pontiac concluded that the English were seeking the ruin of all Aboriginal Peoples.[22] Together, the assembled chiefs drew up a war plan to rid their homelands of the British.

During the summer of 1763, a war belt and hatchet were circulated among the Aboriginal Peoples of the Ohio, Great Lakes, and Northwest regions. Any French who remained in the regions encouraged the Aboriginals in their discontent. British traders were attacked, forts were taken, settlers were killed, and their homes and farms destroyed. Although Pontiac's attack and seige on Fort Detroit was unsuccessful, nonetheless between May 16 and June 20, 1763, the Seven Nations Confederacy took nine British forts and were in control in the regions north and west of the Thirteen Colonies. The British only retained control of Fort Detroit, Fort Niagara, and Fort Pitt.

Amherst was outraged and determined to use any method—even biological warfare—to exterminate his enemy. Pontiac had warned his people about the danger of European diseases, "I warn you, that if you allow the English among you, you are dead, maladies, smallpox, and their poison will destroy you totally."[23] Amherst's plan was to spread smallpox among the Aboriginal People by giving them blankets used by those who were infected with the disease. Colonel Henry Bouquet, one of his officers, put Amherst's plan into effect. Bouquet had an infected blanket cut into small pieces and placed in small tin boxes. The boxes, which the British claimed contained medicine, were given to a delegation at Fort Pitt with instructions that they were not to be opened until the members of the delegation were back among their own people (see primary source feature in this chapter).[24]

Pontiac signed a peace treaty with the English in 1765 in which he again stated that the French surrender to the British of their forts did not mean that the Aboriginal lands had been surrendered. Pontiac was present and spoke at the final ratification of agreements in Fort Ontario in 1766. But his influence dwindled. As the British failed to rid Aboriginal lands of settlers and as the peoples' sufferings increased, he was expelled from his tribe. On April 20, 1769, he was murdered by Illinois tribesmen said to have been bribed by an English trader.

The Royal Proclamation, October 7, 1763

> Whereas We have taken into Our Royal Consideration the extensive and valuable Acquisitions in America, secured to our Crown by the late Definitive Treaty of Peace, . . .and being desirous that all Our loving Subjects, as well of our Kingdom as of our Colonies in America, may avail themselves with all convenient Speed, of the great Benefits and Advantages which must accrue therefrom to their Commerce, Manufactures, and Navigation, We have thought fit, with the Advice of our Privy Council. to issue this our Royal Proclamation . . ."[25]

The Royal Proclamation of October 7, 1763 set the boundaries and governmental policies of the colony of Quebec, along with those of East Florida, West Florida, and Grenada. The ultimate authority in the colonies would be the governors who were appointed by the English monarch, his or her council, and the British parliament and House of Lords. While the colonial governors were directed to work with elected representatives of the people, the appointed council had seniority over any elected assembly. The monarch, English government, and appointed governors were to have the power to "make, constitute, and ordain Laws, Statutes, and Ordinances for the Public Peace, Welfare, and good Government of our . . . colonies."

The governors also had the power to settle land, which now belonged, by right of conquest, to the English king. British military offers and common soldiers were to be given land grants to encourage them to settle in Quebec. The proclamation laid out the details of these grants:

- To every Person having the Rank of a Field Officer–5000 Acres
- To every Captain–3000 Acres.
- To every Subaltern or Staff Officer–2000 Acres

North America, 1763

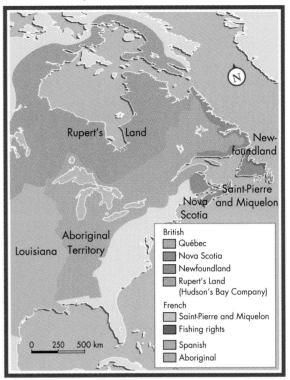

British
- ■ Québec
- ■ Nova Scotia
- ■ Newfoundland
- ■ Rupert's Land (Hudson's Bay Company)

French
- ■ Saint-Pierre and Miquelon
- ■ Fishing rights
- ■ Spanish
- ■ Aboriginal

- To every Non-Commission Officer–200 Acres
- To every Private Man–50 Acres

Following the conflicts over Aboriginal lands during the summer of 1763, the proclamation was designed largely to counteract the fears of the Aboriginal Peoples over the loss of their lands. Although they had ultimately lost those battles, the Aboriginal Peoples had shown that they were a distinct threat to British power in North America. By drawing the boundary line west of the Appalachians, British authorities hoped to be able to continue established French alliances and keep the peace. The upper country was to be a vast Aboriginal reserve and all settlers were ordered to leave. Ownership of this land could only go to the English crown. No private individuals or land companies could hold claim to land in the region.

Royal Proclamation of 1763: Aboriginal Provisions

And whereas it is just and reasonable, and essential to our Interest, and the Security of our Colonies, that the several Nations or Tribes of Indians with whom We are connected, and who live under our Protection, should not be molested or disturbed in the Possession of such Parts of Our Dominions and Territories as, not having been ceded to or purchased by Us, are reserved to them, or any of them, as their Hunting Grounds — We do therefore, with the Advice of our Privy Council, declare it to be our Royal Will and Pleasure, that no Governor or Commander in Chief in any of our Colonies of Quebec, East Florida. or West Florida, do presume, upon any Pretence whatever, to grant Warrants of Survey, or pass any Patents for Lands beyond the Bounds of their respective Governments. as described in their Commissions: as also that no Governor or Commander in Chief in any of our other Colonies or Plantations in America do presume for the present, and until our further Pleasure be known, to grant Warrants of Survey, or pass Patents for any Lands beyond the Heads or Sources of any of the Rivers which fall into the Atlantic Ocean from the West and North West, or upon any Lands whatever, which, not having been ceded to or purchased by Us as aforesaid, are reserved to the said Indians, or any of them.

And We do further declare it to be Our Royal Will and Pleasure, for the present as aforesaid, to reserve under our Sovereignty, Protection, and Dominion, for the use of the said Indians, all the Lands and Territories not included within the Limits of Our said Three new Governments, or within the Limits of the Territory granted to the Hudson's Bay Company, as also all the Lands and Territories lying to the Westward of the Sources of the Rivers which fall into the Sea from the West and North West as aforesaid.

And We do hereby strictly forbid, on Pain of our Displeasure, all our loving Subjects from making any Purchases or Settlements whatever, or taking Possession of any of the Lands above reserved, without our especial leave and Licence for that Purpose first obtained.

And We do further strictly enjoin and require all Persons whatever who have either wilfully or inadvertently seated themselves upon any Lands within the Countries above described. or upon any other Lands which, not having been ceded to or purchased by Us, are still reserved to the said Indians as aforesaid, forthwith to remove themselves from such Settlements.

And whereas great Frauds and Abuses have been committed in purchasing Lands of the Indians, to the great Prejudice of our Interests. and to the great Dissatisfaction of the said Indians: In order, therefore, to prevent such Irregularities for the future, and to the end that the Indians may be convinced of our Justice and determined Resolution to remove all reasonable Cause of Discontent, We do, with the Advice of our Privy Council strictly enjoin and require, that no private Person do presume to make any purchase from the said Indians of any Lands reserved to the said Indians, within those parts of our Colonies where We have thought proper to allow Settlement: but that, if at any Time any of the Said Indians should be inclined to dispose of the said Lands, the same shall be Purchased only for Us, in our Name, at some public Meeting or Assembly of the said Indians, to be held for that Purpose by the Governor or Commander in Chief of our Colony respectively within which they shall lie: and in case they shall lie within the limits of any Proprietary Government, they shall be purchased only for the Use and in the name of such Proprietaries, conformable to such Directions and Instructions as We or they shall think proper to give for that Purpose: And we do, by the Advice of our Privy Council, declare and enjoin, that the Trade with the said Indians shall be free and open to all our Subjects whatever, provided that every Person who may incline to Trade with the said Indians do take out a Licence for carrying on such Trade from the Governor or Commander in Chief of any of our Colonies respectively where such Person shall reside, and also give Security to observe such Regulations as We shall at any Time think fit, by ourselves or by our Commissaries to be appointed for this Purpose, to direct and appoint for the Benefit of the said Trade...

Given at our Court at St. James's the 7th Day of October 1763, in the Third Year of our Reign.

GOD SAVE THE KING

In the Thirteen Colonies, the proclamation was viewed as an attempt to hold back expansion westward. But, for the Aboriginal Peoples, it was recognition of their right to a share in the lands of North America. The Ohio valley, over which the French and the British had fought before and during the Seven Years War, was designated as part of the "Indian reserve" and would remain so until the Treaty of Paris of 1783, which ended the American War of Independence.

The Royal Proclamation and the Royal Commission

The 1996 Report on the Royal Commission on Aboriginal Peoples, *People to People, Nation to Nation*, speaks of the need to examine the past to "reveal a cache of secrets" that have been long ignored in traditional histories of Canada. As Violet Soosay of the Montana First Nation community said during the hearings related to the Commission, "History has not been written yet from the Indian point of view." And the writers of the report explain that all Canadians need to examine their history carefully, "for its ghosts haunt us still."[26]

According to the 1996 report, the Royal Proclamation of 1763 was a defining document in the relationship between Aboriginal and non-Aboriginal people in North America. The proclamation outlined the rules that were to govern British dealings with Aboriginal People, "especially in relation to the key question of land." The Aboriginal Peoples of North America were not to be "molested or disturbed" on their lands.

King George II and his privy council had realized that it was "essential" to British interests and to the security of British colonies in North America that the Aboriginal Peoples "not be molested or disturbed in the Possession of such Parts of Our Dominions and Territories as, not having been ceded to or purchased by Us, are reserved to them." Therefore no governor had the right to grant lands to settlers or land speculators within the territories reserved for the Aboriginal Peoples unless those lands were ceded or sold to the crown. In addition, the Proclamation declared that anyone who had either "willfully or inadvertently" settled on the lands reserved for the Aboriginal Peoples were "forthwith to remove themselves from such settlements."[27] Trade between the British colonials and Aboriginal Peoples was to continue so long as colonial traders obtained licences from the governor or commander-in-chief of the colonies and so long as they adhered to the regulations.

Review...Reflect...Respond

1. How did the Conquest change life in New France?

2. Why is the Royal Proclamation a defining moment in the relationship between Aboriginal Peoples and non-Aboriginals in North America?

3. As an Acadian who had been expelled, would you have chosen to return to your homeland or stay in the United States? Explain your decision.

Conclusion

As the 1996 Royal Commission Report says, the Royal Proclamation of 1763 "portrays Indian nations as autonomous political entities, living under the protection of the Crown but retaining their own internal political authority." However, while the Proclamation seemed to give Aboriginal Peoples rights over their land, it also set the stage for future settlement on land claimed by the Crown. The 1996 Commission report goes on to say that the document "walks a fine line between safeguarding the rights of Aboriginal Peoples and establishing a process to permit British settlement."

Notes

1. Margaret Conrad, Alvin Finkel, and Cornelius Jaenen, *History of the Canadian Peoples, Volume 1, Beginnings to 1867,* (Toronto: Addison Wesley Longman, 2002) p. 153.
2. Conrad, Finkel, and Jaenen, *History of the Canadian Peoples,* Volume 1, p. 146 taken from W.J. Eccles, *The Canadian Frontier, 1534-1760* (New York: Holt, Rinehart and Winston, 1969) p.158.
3. Don Gillmor et al., *Canada: A People's History,* Volume 1, (Toronto: McClelland & Stewart, 2001) p. 112.
4. Gillmor et al., *Canada: A People's History,* Volume 1, p.112.
5. Gillmor et al., *Canada: A People's History,* Volume 1, p. 115.
6. Gillmor et al., *Canada: A People's History,* Volume 1, p. 116.
7. Gillmor et al., *Canada: A People's History,* Volume 1, p. 117.
8. Thomas Thorner ed., *"A Few Acres of Snow": Documents in Canadian History, 1577–1867,* (Peterborough: Broadview Press, 1997) p. 132.
9. Thorner, *"A Few Acres of Snow:" Documents in Canadian History, 1577–1867* p. 132.
10. Gillmor et al., *Canada: A People's History,* Volume 1, p. 130.
11. Thorner, *A Few Acres of Snow:" Documents in Canadian History, 1577–1867* p. 134.
12. Gillmor et al., *Canada: A People's History,* Volume 1, p. 130.
13. *Letter from the Plains of Abraham,* University of Waterloo Special Collections, Web site <www.lib.uwaterloo.ca/discipline/SpecColl/archives/holmes/holmes.html>.
14. Thorner, *A Few Acres of Snow:" Documents in Canadian History, 1577–1867* p. 136
15. Cornelius Jaenen *and Cecilia Morgan, Material Memory: Documents in Pre-Confederation History* (Toronto: Addison Wesley, 1998), pp. 111-113.
16. *Treaty of Paris, 1763,* the Avalon Project at Yale Law School, Web site <www.yale.edu/lawweb/avalon/paris763.htm>.
17. Conrad, Finkel, and Jaenen , *History of the Canadian Peoples,* Volume 1, p. 166.
18. Olive Dickason, *Canada's First Nations: A History of Founding Peoples from Earliest Times,* (Toronto: Oxford University Press, 2002) p.157
19. Dickason, *Canada's First Nations: A History of Founding Peoples from Earliest Times* p. 158.
20. Dickason, *Canada's First Nations: A History of Founding Peoples from Earliest Times* p. 158.
21. Conrad, Finkel, and Jaenen, *History of the Canadian Peoples,* Volume 1, p. 143.
22. Gillmor et al., *Canada: A People's History,* Volume 1, p. 137.
23. Dickason, *Canada's First Nations: A History of Founding Peoples from Earliest Times,* p. 158.
24. Conrad, Finkel, and Jaenen, *History of the Canadian Peoples, Volume 1,* p. 138.
25. The Royal Proclamation of October, 7, 1763, Solon Law Archives Web site, <www.solon.org/Constitutions/Canada/English/PreConfederation/rp-1763.html>
26. Highlights from the Report of the Royal Commission on Aboriginal Peoples, *People to People, Nation to Nation,* published 1996. Web site <www.ainc-inac.gc.ca/ch/rcap/rpt/index_e.html>.
27. *Royal Proclamation of 1763* The Solon Law Archives Web site

Chapter 7 Review

Knowledge & Understanding

1. Identify six of the following people, concepts, and events and explain their historical significance to Canadian history and the development of its culture and identity.
    - battle strategies
    - empire
    - territorial expansion
    - military alliances
    - William Pitt
    - James Wolfe
    - the Seven Years War
    - the siege of Louisbourg
    - the Conquest
    - the Royal Proclamation of 1763

2. Create an annotated timeline of the events that affected the destiny of the Aboriginal Peoples of Canada from the beginning to the end of the French regime. In the notations on your timeline, briefly explain the significance of those events.

Thinking & Inquiry

3. Compare the policies that the British put into place in Acadia following their takeover of that French colony with the policies that they enacted in Quebec following the Conquest. What were the policies in each instance? What were the causes for the policies? What were the effects of the policies on the French Canadians?

4. Chart the chronology and investigate the relationship between Pontiac's unsuccessful uprising and the contents of the Royal Proclamation of 1763. In your opinion, how much of an influence did Pontiac and his people have on the Proclamation?

Application

5. Imagine that you are a French-Canadian citizen of Quebec following the Conquest. Write two journal entries, the first of which is dated September 14 immediately after the French defeat at the Plains of Abraham, expressing your fears for your people and your cultural identity. Your second journal entry should be written on September 14, 1760, with your colony now under James Murray's administration. In this second entry, relate your actual experience to your earlier fears.

Communication

6. In June 1759, General James Wolfe sent a manifesto to the people of Quebec suggesting that they could not win against the British forces and that they would be better off to surrender at once.

    In this great dilemma, let the wisdom of the people of Canada shew itself; Britain stretches out a powerful yet merciful hand, faithful to her engagements, and ready to secure her in her most valuable rights and possessions; France, unable to support Canada, deserts her cause at this important crisis, and, during the whole war has assisted her with troops who have been maintained only by making the natives [Canadians] feel all the weight of grievous and lawless oppression.

    You and your follow French Canadians have read this manifesto and have met to debate the possibility of surrender. Take one side or the other in this issue and present an argument that is intended to convince those who oppose your stand. Should you fight? Do you have any chance of victory? What are likely to be the consequences if you fight and win? Or fight and lose?

Unit Two Research Activity

Research

1. The *coureurs de bois are* in many ways symbolic of New France and have added a unique flair to the image of Canada. Men such as Étienne Brûlé and Pierre Esprit Radisson are popular figures on interest for students of history at all ages. Writers such as Joseph-Charles Taché and Léo-Paul Desrosiers wrote novels centred around the life of the coureurs-des-bois. Research the reality behind the image and discover who it was that became voyageurs (as they eventually became known).

Interpretation and Analysis

2. How symbolic were the *coureurs de bois* of New France? Did they represent positive aspects of society, negative aspects of society, or both?

3. How has the meaning of *coureurs des bois* changed over the years? What did it represent in the beginning? What did it change in to? What image does it create in the minds of today's Canadian citizens?

4. How have the lives and legends of the *coureur de bois* shaped Canadian identity? Does the spirit of their adventures live on in any way today?

Applying and Communicating Your Skills

5. Write a short biography (three pages) of a *coureur de bois*. This will come largely from your imagination. but be as accurate and as reasonable as possible as you summarize his or her life. Pay attention to details of their life from birth to death, but concentrate mostly on their time as a voyageur.

6. Create a visual that shows how the image of the *coureur des bois* fits in with the Canadian identity. Is it an image that Canadians still associate with and try to replicate today? Make sure the observer will understand the ideas you are trying to get across.

English Colonial Culture

In this unit you will:

- describe the main features of life in selected Aboriginal societies in Canada prior to contact with Europeans and how they have changed over time

- analyze the principal characteristics of the French and English colonial experiences in Canada

- analyze how Canada's changing relationships with France, Britain, and the United States have influenced the formation and transformation of Canada's identity

- describe Canada's transformation from a rural, agricultural nation to an urban, industrial nation

- describe and evaluate the nature of the Canadian political system and the groups and individuals who contributed to its development

During the century between the conquest of New France and the birth of Confederation, immigrants continued to arrive in the British colonies of North America. They came mainly from the British Isles and from the United States, fleeing civil unrest, oppression, famine, poverty, and slavery. They arrived hoping to find a better life, and they contributed their cultural identities to the society of their new land. Meanwhile, the Aboriginal Peoples, who were not considered in the various treaties between France, Britain, and the United States, lost ground. More Aboriginal land was taken by settlers, more of their people died in epidemics, and their way of life was changed forever as a result of their trade and military alliances.

Although the Quebec Act of 1774 had ensured the survival of French-Canadian culture, initially it gave the French-Canadian people little control over governmental policies that affected their lives. But through the years, colonial society evolved. Towns and cities became commercial as well as administrative centres, rudimentary social support systems were established, education of children became a public concern, and a distinct literary culture took root. Colonists' attitudes towards government also evolved. After a long struggle, responsible government was in place and politicians in the colonies met and worked out the details of a confederated union. In 1867, with the passing of the British North America Act, Canada became a nation.

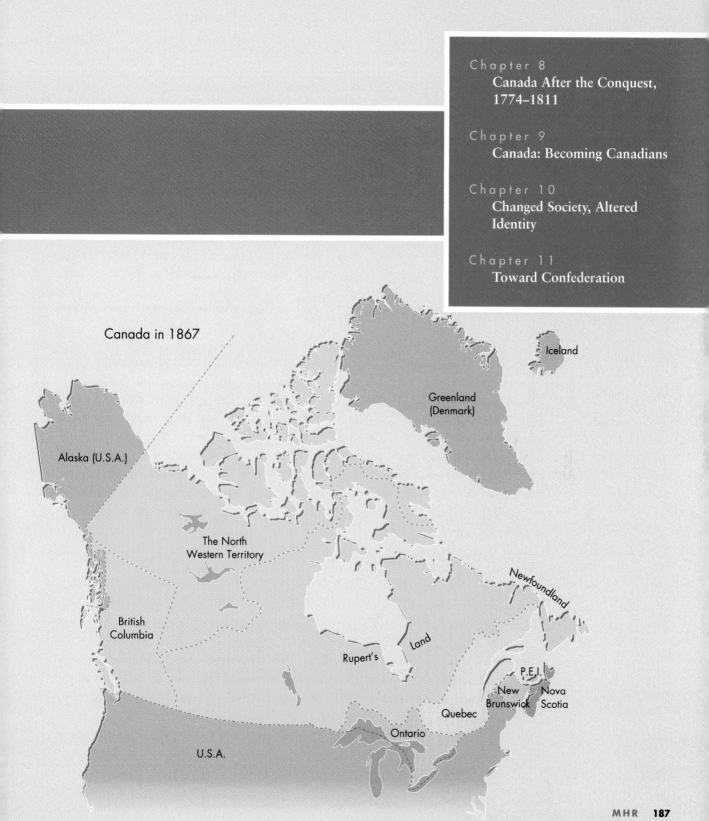

Canada in 1867

Iceland

Greenland
(Denmark)

Alaska (U.S.A.)

The North
Western Territory

Newfoundland

British
Columbia

Rupert's   Land

P.E.I.

New   Nova
Brunswick   Scotia

Quebec

Ontario

U.S.A.

Canada After the Conquest, 1774–1811

It has been the opinion of very many able lawyers, that the best way to establish the happiness of the inhabitants is to give them their own laws, as far as relates to their own possessions.

–BRITISH PRIME MINISTER LORD NORTH

In the years following the conquest, British administrators in Quebec remained cautious in their treatment of French Canadians, especially in light of the growing discontent in the Thirteen Colonies. The Quebec Act confirmed that French Canadians would retain their language, religion, and hierarchical structure of society. However, they would not have an elected legislature, nor would they have representative government. To the outrage of settlers in the Thirteen Colonies, the Quebec Act also limited their takeover of more western Aboriginal territory. The American Revolution tore apart the society in the Thirteen Colonies with neighbour fighting against neighbour, revolutionary against British loyalist. When Quebec was attacked, most French Canadians remained neutral as the two groups of Englishmen fought for control. Many Aboriginal Peoples found it impossible to remain neutral; leaders such as Joseph Brant knew that they would lose more land if the revolution succeeded

After the Revolution, thousands of refugees fled north to the remaining British colonies; they were soldiers, farmers, city-dwellers, merchants, artisans, assemblymen, slaves, and Aboriginal Peoples. In settling the refugees, the British governors faced great challenges. Land-owning practices were reformed in order to find land for the new arrivals. In Atlantic Canada, land grants were cancelled and land was redistributed; land west of Quebec was taken from the Aboriginal Peoples for the new settlers. By the Constitutional Act of 1791, Upper and Lower Canada were formed with elected assemblies, which had little real power. There were also inequities in the treatment of the black Loyalists in Nova Scotia and of Aboriginal Peoples throughout the British colonies.

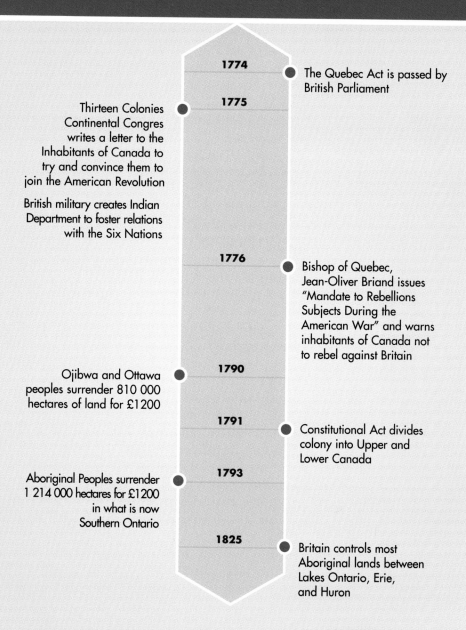

1774

The Quebec Act is passed by British Parliament

1775

Thirteen Colonies Continental Congres writes a letter to the Inhabitants of Canada to try and convince them to join the American Revolution

British military creates Indian Department to foster relations with the Six Nations

1776

Bishop of Quebec, Jean-Oliver Briand issues "Mandate to Rebellions Subjects During the American War" and warns inhabitants of Canada not to rebel against Britain

1790

Ojibwa and Ottawa peoples surrender 810 000 hectares of land for £1200

1791

Constitutional Act divides colony into Upper and Lower Canada

1793

Aboriginal Peoples surrender 1 214 000 hectares for £1200 in what is now Southern Ontario

1825

Britain controls most Aboriginal lands between Lakes Ontario, Erie, and Huron

By the end of this chapter, you will be able to

- analyze the impact of European contact on the lives of Aboriginal Peoples and evaluate the responses of Aboriginal Peoples

- compare the colonizing policies of the French and the British in colonial Canada

- describe significant waves of immigration and settlement patterns, and how they helped shape Canadian identity and culture

- analyze how conflicts and compromises between Canada and the United States have helped to shape Canadian identity

- demonstrate an understanding of the development of citizenship in Canada

- describe the role of selected significant events and legislation in the development of the current Canadian political system

Quebec under British Rule

Guy Carleton, Governor of Quebec

Sir Guy Carleton, an Irish army officer and the 1st Baron of Dorchester, became lieutenant governor of Quebec in 1766 and governor in 1768. In his early years as governor, he was very concerned about the security of the colony. Worried that the growing discontent in the Thirteen Colonies might spread to Quebec, he also faced the threat that France might try to reclaim its territory, and a possible revolt by the French-Canadian majority. Only 1627 British troops and 500 British immigrants lived in Quebec compared to 69 275 conquered French and 7400 Aboriginal People.

Carleton realized that his best chance for success was to win over the French Canadians and to inspire them "with a cordial Attachment and zeal for the King's Government." By using the established French-Canadian seigneurs and clergy as

A Portrait of Sir Guy Carleton, lieutenant governor of Quebec, 1766

go-betweens, he hoped to achieve his goal of peacefully governing the people of Quebec. He believed that by keeping the seigneurial order in place, he could maintain a hierarchical system of government and society. As historian J.M. Bumstead said, "Carleton was a firm believer in a landed aristocracy, the subordination of a tenant class, and the close connection between Church and State."[1]

To ensure that children were taught the proper respect for hierarchical principles, Carleton encouraged and helped the Catholic orders that educated the young in Quebec: the Sulpician and Jesuit priests and the Congregation of Notre-Dame nuns. To give the colony a firm economic base, he promoted production of agricultural products, encouraged establishment of Canadian manufacturing, and recommended that French Canadians be hired as guides and interpreters for the fur trade. As early as 1764, Carleton argued that French civil law in regards to property and civil rights should be brought back into force in Quebec, though he advocated keeping English criminal law.

Carleton did not believe that the English form of representational government, which gave the vote to male property owners only, would work in the colony. By British law, no Catholic in Quebec could vote or hold public office, leaving only Protestant male property owners as possible elected "representatives" and Carleton feared that if such a system were to be put into place it would "give a strong Bias to Republican Principles" in Quebec. In this regard, he opposed his own English Board of Trade, which declared in 1769 that it was "necessary in the present State of Quebec, that a complete Legislature should be established."[2]

This situation in Quebec was quite different from that in the Atlantic colonies. On October 2, 1758, the first elected legislative assembly in Canada had been convened in Halifax, Nova Scotia. Prince Edward Island gained an elected assembly in 1773, and New Brunswick in 1784, when it was created as a colony separate from Nova Scotia. But even in the Atlantic region, the

Colonial lands claimed by 1774

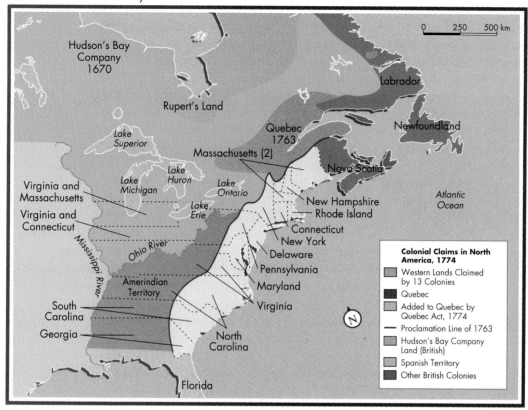

Map legend: **Colonial Claims in North America, 1774**
- Western Lands Claimed by 13 Colonies
- Quebec
- Added to Quebec by Quebec Act, 1774
- Proclamation Line of 1763
- Hudson's Bay Company Land (British)
- Spanish Territory
- Other British Colonies

real power of government remained in the hands of the executive council and the colonial governors. The majority of Canadians had little say in how they were governed. Any law that the elected assembly tried to enact could be blocked by the council or by the governor or by the British government. It wasn't until 1848 that Nova Scotia had an elected, responsible government, and again it was the first Canadian colony to have done so.

The Quebec Act

The Quebec Act of 1774 was passed by the British Parliament with no representatives of French Canada or Canadian Aboriginal Peoples involved in the process. The Act was specific to Quebec and did not change British colonial policies in English-speaking Nova Scotia or the Thirteen Colonies, as the situation in Quebec—with its large French-speaking and Catholic population—was judged to be unique in North America.

In 1774 there were few English settlers arriving in Quebec and the population remained overwhelmingly French Canadian. Because of this situation, the British government agreed with Carleton that it was politically wise to re-establish French civil law. As British Prime Minister Lord North said, "It has been the opinion of very many able lawyers, that the best way to establish the happiness of the inhabitants is to give them their own laws, as far as relates to their own possessions."[3] British criminal law was to remain in effect in all matters having to do with public law and order and offences for which the punishment might be a fine, imprisonment, or even death.

After their victory over France in the Seven Years War, the British laid claim to vast tracts of land on which the Aboriginal Peoples of North America had lived for centuries. The British had little knowledge of the peoples, the culture, or the land over which they now held power and did not realize the geographic boundaries of each Aboriginal group. Eventually they signed treaties that left ambiguities for later legislators to try to resolve, with many of these treaty issues remaining problematic to this day. The British were not even sure of the boundaries they were establishing, as some of the language of the Act shows. For example, although the boundaries of Quebec were extended as far as the Ohio River valley, neither the British, the French, nor the colonists knew exactly where those boundaries were.

> But in case the said Bank of the said Lake shall not be found to be so intersected, then following the said Bank until it shall arrive at that Point of the said Bank which shall be nearest to the North-western Angle of the said Province of Pennsylvania, and thence by a right Line, to the said North-western Angle of the said Province; and thence along the Western Boundary of the said Province, until it strike the River Ohio . . .[4]

The Quebec Act also confirmed that Catholics in the colony could "have, hold, and enjoy, the free Exercise" of their religion, though this right would always be "subject to the King's Supremacy." The Catholic clergy were to regain "the right to hold, receive, and enjoy, their accustomed Dues and Rights" and could again demand tithes from Catholics in the colony. The British believed that if they could win the support of the religious leaders in Quebec, they would be more likely to keep French Canadians from joining the rebellious subjects of the Thirteen Colonies to the south. But this provision of the Act also gave the Catholic Church the political and economic power that it would use in the next century to acquire even greater status and influence that it had had under the French regime.

The British kept tight control over the government at Quebec. As the Act states, the British had decided, in agreement with Carleton, that it was "at present inexpedient to call an Assembly" similar to those that existed in Nova Scotia and the Thirteen Colonies. The British government and its representative, the colonial governor, would have the ultimate say in all decisions. His Majesty, his Heirs and Successors, "by Warrant under his or their Signet or Sign Manual, and with the Advice of the Privy Council," would select who would rule Quebec. Compared to the full rights of citizenship, as we would consider them today, the citizens of Quebec possessed few rights under either the Quebec Act or the French colonial system.

One significant change in the Quebec Act from the Royal Proclamation of 1763 was that the Aboriginal Peoples were no longer mentioned within the Act. Although they were still allowed to live on their lands, their territorial rights were not declared. This would have severe consequences for the Aboriginal nations of Canada in the years to come.

Web Connection

www.mcgrawhill.ca/links/definingcanada

Go to the Web site above to read the text of the Quebec Act of 1774.

Reactions in the Thirteen Colonies

Britain's decision not to give Quebec an elected assembly, even an assembly with limited powers such as those that existed in Nova Scotia and the Thirteen Colonies at the time, raised suspicions among the English colonists that their assemblies could also be revoked. By passing the Quebec Act, Britain reminded people in the older, established North American colonies that their elected assemblies were a privilege, not a right. People who had become accustomed to having input into their own political affairs could, at the whim of their colonial rulers, come under the complete rule of the British governor and his appointed council.

The importance of elected assemblies, and the growing independence of those assemblies, were

A satirical picture titled *Bostonians Paying the Excise Man.*
What has happened to the taxman?

without representation." In the "Declaration and Resolves" of the First Continental Congress of 1774, the writers made it clear that in their eyes:

> The foundation of English liberty, and of all free government, is a right in the people to participate in their legislative council, and as the English colonists are not represented, and from their local and other circumstances cannot properly be represented, in the British Parliament, they are entitled to a free and exclusive power of legislation in their several provincial legislatures, where their right of representation can alone be preserved.[5]

The "representation" was by no means universal since only free, male, Protestant landowners had a right to vote in the elected assemblies: no women, no slaves, no Aboriginal Peoples, no Jews, and no Catholics were allowed to vote or hold public office.

The suspicions of the colonists in the Thirteen Colonies were further confirmed by those sections of the Quebec Act that annexed land west of the Ohio valley and around the Great Lakes to Quebec, thereby creating a large Aboriginal reserve in the region. The colonists already felt that the Royal Proclamation of 1763 hemmed them in and kept them from lands in which they believed they had a right to settle. Now, not only were those lands placed under the rule of the governor of Quebec, but the Catholic Church was confirmed in its situation of power in the colony. The British were granting privileges to the Roman Catholic Church at a time when the practice of the Catholic faith in England, Ireland, and Scotland still carried severe penalties. In the opinion of the July 1775 Continental Congress, the terms of the Quebec Act demonstrated "a despotism dangerous to our very existence."[6]

The Empire and Trade in the North American Colonies

During the years following the Royal Proclamation of 1763 and the Quebec Act of 1774, mercantilism remained the main economic principle for Britain in its relationship with all its colonies in North

significant causes of the American Revolution. Over the previous century and a half, Britain had left the Thirteen Colonies alone, for the most part, to sort out their own internal affairs. This neglect had led the colonists to believe that indeed they did have the right to govern themselves without interference from Britain.

The resistance to British rule intensified when Britain tried to impose a series of taxes to help defray the debt they had acquired during the Seven Years War and the costs of keeping a standing army of ten thousand soldiers in the forts of the West, which at this time was the land west of the Ohio Valley taking in the western United States and Canada. The colonists rejected the measures on the basis that there should be "no taxation

America. As it had been during the years of the French Empire, the key to economic health for the mother country was a favourable balance of foreign trade. When Britain's exports were greater than its imports, its reserves of gold and its percentage of the world's wealth increased. The colonies in North America were to provide the sugar, tobacco, timber, and furs from which British manufacturers would make products and help maintain a positive balance of trade. Britain would tax and sell manufactured goods back to the colonials at a profit. In the days of the British Empire, the colonies existed for the economic benefit of Britain, to increase its wealth and prestige. There was to be no competition from the colonies in achieving that purpose.

In the beginning, the mercantilist system had suited the colonists well enough. It had helped the development of the colonies and had contributed to a higher standard of living for many people than they could have had in any other country at that time. But, by the late 1700s, the Thirteen Colonies were ready to chart their own economic future.

The American Revolution

French-Canadian Neutrality during the American Revolution

While the Quebec Act won the support of the Catholic hierarchy and some of the seigneurs in Quebec, it was less successful in winning over the habitants, many of whom resented the reintroduction of tithes, taxes, duties, and controls. The Act seemed to reinforce the economic power of both church and seigneurs. Some of the British merchants in Quebec were angry that Britain had refused them a colonial elected assembly and that there were concessions to French law and the Catholic Church. However, the merchants and the habitants' frustrations with the Act did not pose a serious threat to British authority in the colony. During the revolutionary war, the policies of the Thirteen Colonies tended to alienate what little support the revolutionaries had within Quebec.

The upper classes and the church in Quebec remained firm in their loyalty to Britain. Not only had British policy protected their interests by the Quebec Act, but the whole social outlook and culture of the seigneurs and the Catholic hierarchy was one of co-operation with constituted authority. But the opposing sides in the larger struggle used whatever media and means they had in order to try to gain the loyalty of the ordinary citizens of Quebec.

French Canadians were subjected to the propaganda of the Thirteen Colonies' Continental Congress, which tried to convince them to join the revolution. In a Letter to the Inhabitants of Canada of May 29, 1775, the members of the Congress called the Canadians "fellow-sufferers" of the "fetters of slavery" imposed by British rule.[7]

> By the introduction of your present form of government, or rather present form of tyranny, you and your wives and your children are made slaves. You have nothing that you can call your own, and all the fruits of your labour and industry may be taken from you, whenever an avaritious governor and a rapacious council may incline to demand them.

The letter went on to remind French Canadians that even the enjoyment of their religion depended "on a legislature in which you have no share, and over which you have no control." Perhaps the next king or queen of England would not be as lenient as George III, and "should a wicked or a careless king concur with a wicked ministry in extracting the treasure and strength of your country, it is impossible to conceive to what variety and to what extremes of wretchedness you may…be reduced." But French Canadians remained suspicious of the promises of friendship and civil rights.

However, Jean-Olivier Briand, the Bishop of Quebec, in his "Mandate to Rebellious Subjects During the American War, 1776," warned his people that if they rebelled against British rule and joined the American revolutionaries, they would suffer the most "rigourous punishment."[8] He asked them to consider whether "an empire as powerful as the British Empire, whose navy can resist the united navies of Europe, will be denied, and that it will not accomplish the task which it has set itself?" He called on them to defend their country and their British king with all the strength they possessed.

The bishop also pointed out that as a conquered people the French Canadians had received unaccustomed concessions from the British and declared that they "should have praised and thanked Providence" for their good fortune and been bound by duty and gratitude "to the person, the authority, and the glory of your Sovereign."[9] He also scolded them for resistance to paying their seigneurial dues and tithes to the Catholic Church. When the British "promised you exemption from seignorial dues," the bishop said, "you loved this injustice." And when the British "promised that you would pay no more tithes,...you were not moved with horror at such sacrilegious ingratitude towards the God without whose blessing your fields would remain infertile and your labour would be fruitless."[10] As a last resort, for those who betrayed their lawful king, he imposed the threats of excommunication and damnation.

Yet while most Canadians were attached to their church, their loyalty was never blind, and few French Catholics fought on the side of the British. Most Canadians maintained their neutrality. Even when General Richard Montgomery was on the verge of capturing the last holdout of Quebec City on the last day of 1775, the habitants refused to take up arms against the invaders. They stayed on their farms, prepared to trade with both British and American soldiers and to deal with the winning side. Most farmers were more interested in staying alive and preserving their families, homes, and livelihoods than in going to war on behalf of either of two groups of warring Englishmen. Several seigneurs tried to raise militia among their tenants, but had little success.

Quebec Attacked Again

By 1775, battles between American militia and British troops had taken place on what was soon to become American soil. The Continental Congress decided it that it was time to attack Quebec to rid them of that threat and possibly to gain allies among the French Canadians who had so recently been conquered by the British. In the summer, one arm of the militia started up Lake Champlain and along the Richelieu River. In late September, another group started up through Maine and advanced towards the St. Lawrence River.

When Carleton got word of the advancing armies, he was concerned about how ill-prepared the colony was to defend itself. As he reported to his superiors in Britain, he had "not six hundred Rank and File fit for Duty upon the whole Extent of this great River, not an armed Vessel, no Place of Strength." As for the military force in the colony, it was weak "and broke to pieces." Military discipline had been lost, and "the Minds of the People poisoned by the same Hypocrisy and Lies practised with so much Success" in the Thirteen Colonies to the south.[11] Even Bishop Briand's directions could not shake the neutrality of the French Canadians, and he realized to his shock and dismay how little control the Catholic hierarchy had over the average habitant. However, Colonel Allan Maclean, a Canadian army officer of Scottish descent, was able to gather together two battalions of Scottish Highlanders from New York and Nova Scotia who fought to defend British Canada.

In spite of the military weaknesses of the Quebec forces, the Americans were unable to take Quebec City or Montreal. Their leaders, General Richard Montgomery and Benedict Arnold, tried to keep discipline and order among their militia who came from different colonies and had different loyalties. But as the weeks passed and smallpox, the harsh weather of late fall and early winter, and scarce supplies took their toll, more and more of the Americans returned home. By the time the Americans arrived at Quebec, Colonel Maclean had convinced some French Canadians to join his defensive force, telling them that their fate under the Americans would be much worse than it was under the British. When the Americans attacked on New Year's Eve, the combined British forces and French Canadians managed to hold their city successfully against the Americans. By May of 1776, British reinforcements arrived up the St. Lawrence, and this show of force convinced the Americans that the conquest of Canada was not worth the effort it would take to accomplish.

Patriots/Rebels and Loyalists/Tories

In the Thirteen Colonies, the American Revolution meant civil war. One side was loyal to Britain, calling themselves "loyalists" and their opponents "rebels." The other side wanted to rid themselves of Britain's restrictive policies and taxes and called themselves "patriots" and their opponents "tories." The two sides had very different political goals and were developing different cultural identities. Often, opponents lived in the same region or even on adjoining farms, holding opposing allegiances and fighting for their respective sides. There was disorder in the society at every level, not because of the threat of outside conquest, as had been the case in Quebec ten years earlier, but because of the struggle within their own country.

People whose families were firmly established in the cities and rural areas of the colonies suddenly found their property, their families, and their own lives threatened. Some loyalists tried to wait out the storm quietly; some were sent into exile; many lost their property and were harassed by patriot neighbours; some fought with the British against the rebels; others were put in prisons such as the infamous Simsbury Mines. They were the descendants of Scots, English, Irish, and Germans who had come to the colonies to build a better life for themselves, but they were content, more or less, to remain under British colonial rule and have the benefits of British trade. Among the warring parties on both sides

were slaves. According to historian Christopher Moore, "By 1770, forty per cent of Virginians were slaves." George Washington, who was to become the first president of the U.S. after the revolution, was from Virginia and owned hundreds of slaves.[12]

Over time, the people in the Thirteen Colonies became more independent of British colonial rule. Although there were colonial governors and administrators, the peoples' assemblies in the Thirteen Colonies had more power than the French colonials had had in Quebec under French rule. But in Britain, William Pitt was elected prime minister and his attitude was to bring the colonists under control: "They must obey and we must prescribe."[13]

British Aboriginal Allies

During the American Revolution, the Mohawk, Onondaga, Cayuga, and Seneca Peoples of the Six Nations Iroquois Alliance fought alongside the British because they believed it was their only hope of retaining any claim to their territory in the Ohio Valley and the Great Lakes regions. These people were fighting for survival, the battlefields were their homelands, and the casualties were often their families.

The British had made some gains in fostering alliances with the Six Nations. In 1755, they had established an Indian Department as a branch of the British military. The officials of the department, who were called "superintendents," had responsibility for maintaining good relations with the Aboriginal Peoples to ensure that they would be allies of the British in times of war and would not rise up against the British. The first superintendent to the Iroquois Six Nations was Sir William Johnson. Living in the Mohawk Valley which would eventually become part of the United States, Johnson married Mary Brant, the sister of the Iroquois leader Joseph Brant about whom you will read more later in this chapter.

Mary Brant or Konwatsi'tsiaiénni, was a powerful leader of her people and one of the most important Aboriginal women of her day. Her role as matron of the society of Six Nations women gave her a greater status among her people than her younger brother Joseph and she was consulted by her people on all matters of importance. Mary Brant influenced the decision of the Six Nations to ally themselves with the British during the American Revolutionary war.[14]

The Iroquois alliance with the British and the ferocity of their attacks so enraged the American general, George Washington, that he ordered "the total destruction and devastation of their settlements and the capture of as many prisoners, of every age and sex, as possible." Washington sent soldiers to "lay waste all the settlements around, with instructions to do it in the most effectual manner, that the country not be merely overrun but destroyed."[15] Within two months after issuing the order, it was done. Even the villages of the Oneida and Tuscarora, who had remained neutral in the war, were destroyed.

At the signing of the Treaty of Versailles and the Treaty of Paris, which ended the war between the British and the Americans, once again the Aboriginal Peoples were not considered or even mentioned in official documents. The lands west of the Ohio Valley and south of the Great Lakes were ceded to the United States with no protections offered to the Aboriginal People whose lands they were. Now, with the determined push westward in the United States, the Aboriginal Peoples had no chance to regain their land. Although the British did not immediately abandon their western posts, this was at best a temporary measure, since they had promised to do so by the terms of the British-American Jay Treaty of 1794.

Joseph Brant

Joseph Brant was a Mohawk chief who had been educated in English and had served with the British in the Seven Years' War. William Johnson was responsible for sending Joseph Brant to Moor's Indian and Charity School in Connecticut. After he had become fluent in English, Brant acted as an

Joseph Brant (Thayendanegea) by George Romney, NGC, 8005

This is a famous painting of the distinguished Aboriginal leader Joseph Brant, done by artist George Romney and preserved in the National Gallery of Canada.

interpreter between the Indian Department of the British military and his people, he also translated religious documents into the Mohawk language.[16]

Brant knew that the Aboriginal Peoples of North America would lose their lands if the Americans succeeded in breaking away from Britain. Brant's Mohawk name, Thayendanegea ("He Who Places Two Bets") gives some idea of how successfully he managed to bridge the two worlds in which he lived. Once he had visited London and received King George III's approval for his plan, Brant rallied warriors from the Mohawk, Onondaga, Cayuga, and Seneca Peoples to fight with him against the Americans as allies of the British, and he and his warriors effectively terrorized the revolutionaries. After such loyalty, Brant felt betrayed when the Six Nations Peoples were not even mentioned in the Treaty of Paris of 1783.

[Given] what friendship we had shown to the English, and being conscious of the active part . . . we have taken in their favour in every dispute they have had with their enemies, we were struck with astonishment at hearing we were forgot in the treaty. . . We could not believe it possible such firm friends and allies could be so neglected by a nation remarkable for its honour and glory whom we had served with so much zeal and fidelity.[17]

Though he tried to rally Aboriginal Peoples to join together in defence of their homelands, he was unable to unite them into a force strong enough to regain Aboriginal lands.

Although the Six Nations had been severely weakened by the war, Britain was still afraid that Brant and his people might turn on them to regain their territory. So, the British arranged for their relocation to the 275 000 hectares of Crown land that they had acquired from the Mississauga Peoples in territory north of Lake Erie along either side of the Grand River. Brant and eighteen hundred of his followers settled there in 1784. By 1828, only one third of the original land remained in the hands of the Six Nations, the rest having been lost to errors in the original land grants, encroaching settlers, and land sales and leases.

Review...Reflect...Respond

1. What was the purpose of the Quebec Act of 1774?

2. Why did French Canadians remain neutral during the American Revolution?

3. Explain how the American Revolution and the peace treaties that ended the war changed the lives of Aboriginal peoples.

The United Empire Loyalists

The forty to fifty thousand United Empire Loyalists who came to Canada were a wide-ranging group. Some were British soldiers and colonial militia who had fought with Britain against the American revolutionaries. Others were civilians who had joined the royal British regiments when they were expelled from their hometowns or regions because they wouldn't join the rebels. There were city dwellers and farmers, successful merchants, newspaper owners, blacksmiths, silversmiths, and shop owners. Entire families came; sometimes the families were made up only of women and children, without husbands and fathers who had been killed in the American war. They were all refugees, people who had become embroiled in the conflict and who fled or were exiled from their homeland.

Some of the Loyalists had been leaders in their communities, members of the elected assemblies, who had firm ideas of their rights as citizens under British colonial rule. Although they had rejected revolution, some of the new arrivals held republican ideas and believed that they should have a chance to be represented in their government. These ideas would have an effect on how white, male, property-owning Loyalists viewed their rights as citizens in Canada.

Loyalists in Atlantic Canada

During the 1760s, land speculation had run rampant in the Atlantic colonies, and land grants were given to those land promoters who had power and connections at the English court. By the time the loyalists were on their way north, much of Nova Scotia had been given away, including land along the St. John River in what is now New Brunswick. This presented a major problem for the British authorities and for Governor John Parr. The loyalists had been promised land of their own and would have little interest in serving as tenants. Somehow land had to be found on which to settle the new refugees.

Parr, with the support of the British government, managed to have the land grants cancelled in Nova Scotia. This was an extraordinary event at a time when society was structured along hierarchical lines and when a person's court connections had such power in decision making. However, because those who held the land had not fulfilled their obligation to settle the land, by the principle of *escheat*, the property was turned over to Britain and its representative. The British Crown reclaimed title to 1.1 hectares in Nova Scotia and so had land available for the incoming refugees from New York. Male heads of households would receive 40.47 hectares of land plus an extra 20 hectares for each member of the household. Retiring senior British military officers received additional acres.

In the island of St. John, which later became Prince Edward Island, the situation was especially problematic. The island had been divided into sixty-seven lots of 8094 hectares and turned over to British soldiers and court favourites, the major-ity of whom were absentee landlords. The landowners of St. John Island had managed to have their island established as a separate colony, so when the policy of escheat took place in Nova Scotia it didn't take effect on St. John Island. Loyalists who could have their own land were not interested in coming and establishing themselves as tenants on someone else's land. So, the colony remained relatively unsettled during this time.

Even with the land problem on its way to being resolved, Parr still had a formidable task. He and his administrators had to survey and portion out the land, organize and distribute food, tools, and other supplies to the refugees when they arrived. The British government would continue to support the new settlers for several years while they cleared the land, built their homes, planted crops, and moved towards becoming self-sufficient. Even so, the settlers faced a grim situation as they established themselves along the St. John River and the shores of the Bay of Fundy in what would become

Part of the Town of Shelburne in Nova Scotia, with the Barracks Opposite, a water-colour painted by William Booth in 1789.

Encampment of the Loyalists at Johnstown, a New Settlement on the Banks of the St. Laurence [sic] in Canada, painted in 1784 by James Peachey

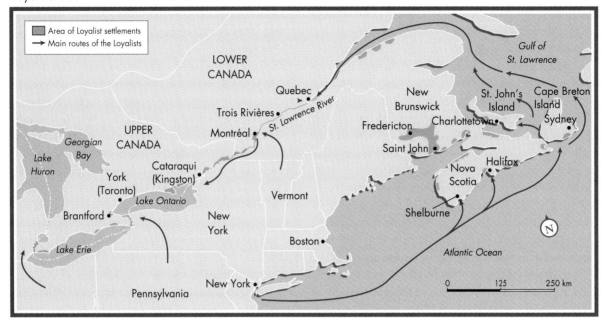

Routes into Quebec, Upper Canada and Atlantic regions, and Settlements of Loyalists before 1800

New Brunswick. Their first winter was an especially harsh one, and many died of disease and exposure in their tents and in the holds of ships.

The Black Loyalists in Nova Scotia

The writers of the American Declaration of Independence and the patriots who demanded freedom for themselves seem not to have noticed the irony in their being, in many cases, slave owners. Though slavery was prohibited in Britain by this time, it was still in effect in the Thirteen Colonies and the economies and wealth of many of the southern plantations depended on slave labour.

Many slaves, including those owned by George Washington, sought refuge among the British. Estimates say that as many as on 100 000 African Americans may have fled from their owners during this time.[18] Many were recaptured, and their punishment for escaping was severe. David George, who was born of African slaves in Virginia and who later became a powerful Baptist minister in

Nova Scotia, related what happened to his brother when he was caught. "After he had received 500 lashes, they washed his back with salt water, and whipped it in, as well as rubbed it in with a rag; and then directly sent him to work in pulling off the suckers of tobacco."[19]

At the end of the war, when George Washington met with Guy Carleton to negotiate the articles of peace between the United States and Britain, one of the first things on Washington's agenda was his concern that the British should remove any slaves who were the "property" of American citizens. As J.M. Bumstead reports, "every Wednesday between May 30 and August 7, 1783—from 10 a.m. to 2 p.m. —blacks who already held certificates as refugees were liable to be challenged at board meetings at New York City's Fraunces Tavern."[20] As a result of these meetings, many African Americans were returned to their slave-owners. Eventually, approximately three thousand free black Loyalists made their way to Nova Scotia. But among the white Loyalist refugees fleeing the Thirteen Colonies were former plantation owners who still owned the slaves they brought with them.

Although they had been promised farms by the British, very few black Loyalists ever received them. Some were given small plots of land, but the intention was that they would serve as poorly paid labourers for the white Loyalists now settling in places like Shelburne, Nova Scotia. About fifteen hundred of these former slaves built a town called Birchtown a few miles outside of Shelburne. There they built homes and established Baptist, Methodist, and Anglican churches. Within the society, these churches served as educational and charitable, as well as religious, centres for the black community.

The black people of the Thirteen Colonies had gone over to the British side because they wanted freedom and equality, but the racial bigotry and ill-treatment continued in Nova Scotia. They suffered famine and conditions that were little better than those they had left in the southern states of America. In Shelburne in 1784, with home building for settlers slowing down, disbanded British soldiers rioted and threw the former slaves out of town because they worked for lower wages than the soldiers wanted. There was a clear inequality between legal penalties handed out to white and black settlers. In Shelburne during this time, one black woman was given two hundred lashes for stealing less than a shilling.[21] Because of such conditions, when a British anti-slavery society announced that it was building a colony in Sierra Leone on the west coast of Africa, at least twelve hundred black Loyalists chose to leave Nova Scotia. They founded the colony of Freetown in Sierra Leone where they hoped to own their own land and escape the inhumane treatment they had experienced in Canada.

Web Connection

www.mcgrawhill.ca/links/definingcanada
To find out more about black Loyalists in Canada, go the above Web site.

Loyalists in Quebec

In Quebec, Frederick Haldimand was governor when approximately ten thousand Loyalists began to arrive during and after the American Revolution. Like John Parr in Nova Scotia, he faced an enormous challenge in accommodating these refugees. At first he built temporary refugee camps for them, to give them shelter and to keep them and their ideas of liberty and representative government away from the habitants. The refugees had to be supplied with food, guns, tools, seeds, clothing, and land on which to settle along the St. Lawrence west of Montreal and in the Niagara region of Lake Ontario.

Land was a problem for Haldimand, as it had been for Parr, but Haldimand's solution was somewhat different. This land had to be provided for the Loyalists; it was part of the price to be paid for their loyalty during the American Revolution. And since the British government forbade anyone but a representative of the crown to purchase land from Aboriginal Peoples, Haldimand entered into formal treaties with various Aboriginal Peoples in the region. According to historian Olive Dickason, by the land and friendship treaty of 1781, the Mississauga People surrendered a six-kilometre-wide strip along the west-bank of the Niagara River to the British in exchange for three hundred suits of clothing. In the years to come, the representatives of the British continued to take over Aboriginal land. By 1825, they had control of almost the entire peninsula between Lakes Ontario, Erie, and Huron.[22]

Once Haldimand had acquired the land, he had it surveyed, and allowed prospective settlers to chose lots for their land. Among the settlers in what would soon become Upper Canada were members of regiments of disbanded British military and their families. Some of these groups stayed together, as others had in Nova Scotia, and kept the military structure to create their civilian society. Many of the refugees had been farmers in the pioneer regions of northern New York, New England, and Pennsylvania. They were accustomed to establishing homes and farms on land that had been forest. Nonetheless, settling the land in the region was difficult, back-breaking, and lonely work. As historian Desmond Morton says, the task of clearing the land was formidable. "Huge first-growth trees resisted the puny axes and saws of the settlers as they struggled to clear fields or even to break through the overhanging gloom to the sun." The loneliness and the danger on land surrounded by dense forest could be severe. "Women faced the terror of childbirth without even a neighbour to help. A single careless blow with an axe could cripple a man or leave him to die in the stench and agony of gangrene."[23]

But the land was rich and many of the Loyalists were industrious. Before many years had passed there was a thriving trade along the Great Lakes. Those who had land and successful farms, who were educated, and who were well connected with the British governors and administrators became the leaders of the society. By 1791, the colony was well established with the beginnings of a powerful base in industry and trade, as well as agriculture.

The Constitutional Act of 1791

From the beginning, the Loyalists had expressed their discontent with the conditions of the Quebec Act. They wanted an elected assembly, and they wanted their own separate colony. If the English settlers and the French Canadians were to remain in the same colony and have only one assembly, as William Grenville, the British colonial secretary said, there would probably be "dissensions and animosities." Grenville and other British politicians came to believe that "the natural remedy… would be the separation of the province into two districts."[24]

So, it was decided that to divide the colony into two parts, one part English-speaking and the other part French-speaking. Though each would have an elected assembly, the real power would remain with the appointed governor of each colony and his appointed legislative council. Once the dividing line was established, and one-seventh of all crown lands set aside for the maintenance of a Protestant clergy, Upper and Lower Canada came into being following the Constitutional Act of 1791.

Once again an Act deciding the fate of the peoples of Canada originated in England, which needed to be passed by the British parliament before it could become law in Canada. And, once again, no representatives of the Aboriginal Peoples were consulted on the passage of an Act concerning their lands. The French would keep their civil law, their language in the courts, the seigneurial system, and the Catholic Church.

John Graves Simcoe was appointed the first lieutenant governor of Upper Canada. He had served as an infantry officer with the British during the American Revolution and then as a British member of parliament. His dream for Upper Canada was that he would make it a model of England and by so doing would encourage settlers to come from the United States. He believed that many Americans would eventually grow tired of the democratic culture in the United States, and would be persuaded to come to his colony if it embodied "British Customs, Manners and Principles in the most trivial as well as serious matters."[25]

From his home base of Newark, which is today Niagara-on-the-Lake, Simcoe drew up plans for extensive constitutional, religious, and educational development in the colony. He knew that the long-term hope for Upper Canada's future would have to rest on sound economic growth, and he believed that such growth would be more likely to happen if a small select group of large land owners, who were also members of his government, were in control. With a society structured along traditional hierarchical lines and the "wise Principle…of blending civil and military Advantages," he hoped to set up educational systems for the landed gentry, a well-established Anglican church, an infrastructure of roads and a structured society that would attract settlers to the region. Even though some of his plans met with little success, he was determined that Upper Canada would someday become the enviable colony that he envisioned.

Eventually, under orders from the British colonial secretary, Simcoe did assign free land to the settlers who wanted to come to the province. However, he also firmly established the system of giving away large tracts of land to the Protestant church and absentee landlords who had little interest in developing the colony.

Conclusion

Aboriginal Loss of Land

By the terms of the peace between Britain and the United States, all the lands west of the Ohio River and south of the Great Lakes became American territory. During the late 1700s and 1800s, thousands and thousands of American settlers moved westward until they had taken over almost all of the Aboriginal territory that makes up today's United States.

In Canada, the British acquired land for settlement through a policy of signing land treaties with Aboriginal nations. Where once treaties had been for purposes of trade and peace, they were now land transfers to provide the land first for the Loyalists of the 1780s and then for the great wave of immigration from Europe during the 1800s. There were still unresolved issues over whether a chief could speak for all of his people and over ill-defined boundaries. Language barriers were still a major hurdle that were often ignored by the British; some translators were not dependable and others were dishonest. Some land agreements were not recorded or were lost.

The Six Nations Reserve, the land on which Joseph Brant and other Aboriginal refugees from the United States settled along the Grand River, had been transferred to the British from the Mississauga nation. Three million acres, known as the Haldimand Grant, were "sold" for the value of £1180 in trade goods.[26]

Brant realized that the old way of life was no longer possible for Aboriginal People, and he believed that the only way of sustaining them and himself was

Land Granted to Aboriginal Loyalists

to sell off or to lease land to the settlers. The people of the Six Nations reserve eventually sold 154 385 hectares of their reserve lands to settlers, though they were often not paid in full or at all. Other Aboriginal nations also ceded their lands to Britain. In 1790 the Ojibwa and Ottawa people gave up 809 400 hectares in the Thames River region of Southern Ontario for £1200 and 1 214 100 hectares in 1793 for the same amount.[27] Throughout the 1800s, the land on which the Aboriginal Peoples had once lived freely continued to be taken over, bit by bit, by encroaching European settlement.

Review...Reflect...Respond

1. How did settlement of the Loyalists change Canada?

2. What would be the long-term affects of the Constitutional Act of 1791 on Canadian culture?

3. During this time, did Canada differ from the United States in its treatment of blacks and Aboriginal Peoples? Explain your answer.

Notes

1. J.M. Bumsted, *The Peoples of Canada: A Pre-Confederation History* (Toronto: Oxford University Press, 1992), p. 145.
2. Francess G. Halpenny and Jean Hamelin, eds., *Dictionary of Canadian Biography, Sir Guy Carleton*, Volume 1 (Toronto: University of Toronto Press, 1966), CD-ROM version.
3. Bumsted, *The Peoples of Canada: A Pre-Confederation History*, p. 146.
4. *The Quebec Act of 1774*, The Solon Law Archives, <www.solon.org.Constitutions/Canada/English/Preconfederation/qu-1774.html>
5. Paul Bennett et al., *Canada, A North American Nation* (Toronto: McGraw-Hill Ryerson, 1995), p. 164.
6. *The Declaration of Taking Up Arms, July 6, 1775*, The Avalon Project, Yale University, <www.yale.edu/lawweb/Avalon/Contcong/05-29-75.html>
7. *Letter to the Inhabitants of Canada, May 29, 1775*, The Avalon Project, Yale University, <www.yale.edu/lawweb/Avalon/Contcong/05-29-75.html>
8. Thomas Thorner, ed., *A Few Acres of Snow: Documents in Canadian History, 1577–1867* (Peterborough: Broadview Press, 1997), p.146.
9. Thorner, *A Few Acres of Snow: Documents in Canadian History, 1577–1867*, p.146.
10. Ibid., p. 148.
11. Bumsted, *The Peoples of Canada: A Pre-Confederation History*, p. 149.
12. Christopher Moore, *The Loyalists: Revolution, Exile, Settlement.* (Toronto: Macmillan of Canada, 1984), p. 15.
13. Moore, *The Loyalists: Revolution, Exile, Settlement*, p. 35.
14. Alison Prentice et al., *Canadian Women: A History* (Toronto: Harcourt Brace Javanovich, 1988), p. 99
15. Gillmor et al., *Canada: A People's History*, Volume 1 (Toronto: McClelland & Stewart, 2001), p. 156.
16. James H. Marsh, ed., *The Canadian Encyclopedia* (Toronto: McClelland & Stewart, 2000), p. 293.
17. Gillmor et al., As quoted in *Canada: A People's History*, Volume 1, p. 156.
18. Moore, *The Loyalists: Revolution, Exile, Settlement*, p. 102.
19. Gillmor et al., *Canada: A People's History*, Volume 1, pp. 157–158.
20. Bumsted, *The Peoples of Canada: A Pre-Confederation History*, p. 165.
21. Gillmor et al., *Canada: A People's History*, Volume 1, p. 159.
22. Olive Dickason, *Canada's First Nations: A History of Founding Peoples from Earliest Times* (Toronto: Oxford University Press, 2002), p. 165.
23. Desmond Morton, *A Short History of Canada* (Toronto: McClelland and Stewart, 1997), p. 39.
24. Gillmor et al., *Canada: A People's History*, Volume 1, p. 160.
25. Halpenny and Hamelin, eds., Dictionary of Canadian Biography, John Graves Simcoe, CD-ROM version.
26. Dickason, *Canada's First Nations: A History of Founding Peoples from Earliest Times.* p. 164.
27. Ibid., p.165.

Chapter 8 Review

Knowledge & Understanding

1. Identify six of the following people, concepts, and events and explain their historical significance to Canadian history and the development of its culture and identity.

   representative government
   land grants
   absentee landlords
   Guy Carleton
   United Empire Loyalists
   Governor John Parr
   Joseph Brant
   The Québec Act (1774)
   Constitutional Act (1791)
   Exodus of black Loyalists from Nova Scotia

2. Explain the difference between an elected assembly and representative government as viewed by the rebels in the Thirteen Colonies.

Thinking & Inquiry

3. In this chapter, there are a number of instances of language being used as a propaganda tool, either to offer benefits or to threaten penalties to a group of people. Review these quotations and analyse the rhetorical language and the style that the speakers use to achieve their goals. Then hold an open class forum in which you compare the propaganda styles and goals of the past with those used today.

4. Compare the social, economic, and political dimensions of the lives of French Canadians before and after the proclamation of the Québec act. How were their lives the same and how were they different?

Communication

5. Write a personal essay in which you give your opinion on how the present and future attitudes and sense of identity of the United Empire Loyalists would likely have been affected by living through what amounted to a civil war in the Thirteen Colonies and by their forced territorial relocation.

Application

6. In this chapter, you were introduced to Molly Brant who was described as a powerful leader of her people and one of the most important Aboriginal women of her day. Research the role of female leaders in past and present Aboriginal political organizations. Use primary and secondary resources, including online materials, to prepare a research report on this subject. Use an accepted form of academic documentation to credit your sources.

Canada: Becoming Canadians

We have planted the Standard of Liberty in Canada, for the attainment of the following objects: ...An end forever to the wearisome prayers, supplications, and mockeries attendant upon our connection with the lordlings of the Colonial Office, Downing Street, London.

–WILLIAM LYON MACKENZIE

The War of 1812 was yet another conflict between the British colonies and the United States. One of the main causes of the renewed hostilities was the American determination to take over more western territory from the Aboriginal Peoples. American politicians expected an easy victory in the war, especially in sparsely populated Upper Canada, but the American invasion failed.

This was also a time of conflict within the British colonies. Reformers in the elected assemblies gained popular support in their fight against the political and commercial power held by the oligopolies. The reformers demanded that more power be given to the elected assemblies; they wanted responsible government. However, the governors' councils continued to halt reform by vetoing changes recommended by the assemblies. In Upper Canada, William Lyon Mackenzie led the attack. In Lower Canada, where a small English-speaking minority controlled the fate of the much larger French-speaking majority, Louis Joseph Papineau and his reformers fought to save French-Canadian culture. The drive for reform led to short-lived and ineffective rebellions in both Upper and Lower Canada.

In the vast North-West region, the Aboriginal Peoples continued to form trading alliances with the fur-trading companies: the Hudson's Bay Company and the North West Company. The companies sent out adventurers who—led by Aboriginal guides—explored and mapped the territory. The western Métis People, descended from Aboriginal mothers and either British or French fathers, hunted the buffalo and eventually settled in the Red River region, though their rights to the territory were ignored by the English settlers who moved into the area.

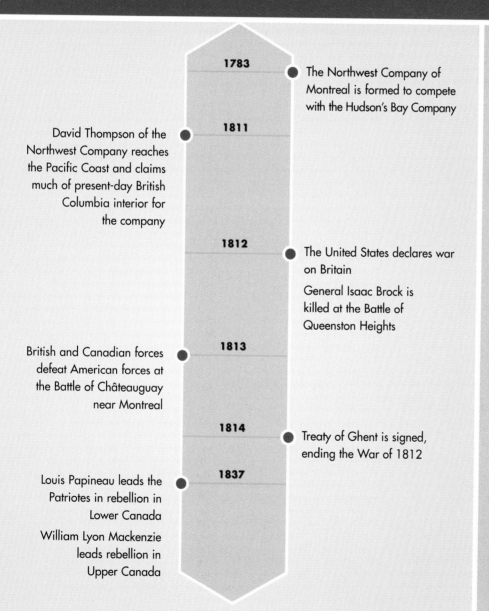

9

1783 — The Northwest Company of Montreal is formed to compete with the Hudson's Bay Company

1811 — David Thompson of the Northwest Company reaches the Pacific Coast and claims much of present-day British Columbia interior for the company

1812 — The United States declares war on Britain

General Isaac Brock is killed at the Battle of Queenston Heights

1813 — British and Canadian forces defeat American forces at the Battle of Châteauguay near Montreal

1814 — Treaty of Ghent is signed, ending the War of 1812

1837 — Louis Papineau leads the Patriotes in rebellion in Lower Canada

William Lyon Mackenzie leads rebellion in Upper Canada

By the end of this chapter, you will be able to

- describe the contributions of Aboriginal Peoples to the development of Canadian identity and culture

- demonstrate an understanding of colonial history as it contributed to the concept of Canada as the product of "two founding nations"

- describe significant sectarian divisions within colonial society and how they shaped the political and cultural issues of the period

- demonstrate an understanding of the resistance of French and British settlers to the establishment of European colonial institutions

- analyze how conflicts and compromises between Canada and the United States have helped to shape Canadian identity

- demonstrate an understanding of the development of citizenship in Canada

- analyze why and how the people of Quebec have acted to preserve their political identity

1812: Canadian-American Conflict

The Causes of the War

Less than thirty years after the American Revolution, Britain and Canada were again at war with the U.S., as unresolved issues continued to strain relations between the two countries. Neither the British nor the Americans had fulfilled all of the terms of the 1783 Treaty of Versailles, signed at the end of the American Revolution. The British had agreed to vacate the western forts in what was now U.S. territory, however, they were still in command of those forts. Stating that they were defending Loyalists' rights, the British wanted to remain in the west until the Americans compensated the Loyalists for property taken from them during the revolution. By the terms of the Treaty of Versailles, each American state was responsible for paying its own compensation to the Loyalists, but most just ignored Loyalist claims, as they did the American federal government's repeated requests that they pay the compensation.

The British also delayed giving up the western forts because they hoped to create an Aboriginal buffer zone between Canada and the U.S. They hoped that the buffer would protect Canadians from the U.S. and prevent reprisals from the Aboriginal Peoples over Britain's failure to consider them in the Treaty of Versailles. But the Americans believed this was all a ruse, convinced that the British and Canadians were deliberately preventing them from opening up the west for settlement. However, the British did surrender these western fur-trading posts in 1794. The Americans also blamed the British and Canadians when Tecumseh, the great Shawnee chief, and the Aboriginal Peoples in the American midwest fought to try to keep their lands from the hordes of settlers moving into Aboriginal territory. The Americans remained very suspicious of any alliance between the Aboriginal Peoples and the Canadians.

The Americans also accused the British of kidnapping American citizens. By 1803, the British were fighting a war against Napoleon, and they augmented their forces—especially the navy—by "pressing into service" any able-bodied civilian or seaman they could get their hands on. In those days, a sailor's life was very difficult with low pay, long and dangerous voyages, and often, brutal discipline from naval officers. Some British sailors had deserted into New York and other American ports and onto American ships, and the British claimed that they were only capturing these deserters. However, when the British went after the deserters, they sometimes—accidentally or intentionally—pressed American citizens into service as well.

A group of aggressive American nationalists, the War Hawks, wanted war with Canada in order to acquire more land and to avenge national honour over issues from the previous war. One of these Hawks, Richard Johnson, the congressman from Kentucky, declared, "I shall never die contented until I see [Britain's] territories incorporated with the United States."[1] Some Americans, including Thomas Jefferson, mistakenly believed that the conquest of Canada would be "a mere matter of marching." They also believed that once the British were ousted, Canada would be part of the U.S., and the Americans would be free to take over Aboriginal lands.

The War in Canada

When the United States declared war on Britain on June 18, 1812, it was still in its infancy and was not well prepared, militarily, to take on the task. Nonetheless, American military officers believed that they would be able to defeat the British and that Canadians would be quite willing to help them do so. The Americans decided to attack Upper Canada first as it was sparsely populated and not very well defended. Once they took Upper Canada, the Americans hoped their Aboriginal enemies would be cut off from their source of military supplies.

Upper Canada

Major-General Isaac Brock was military commander of British forces and of the Canadian militia. He was well aware of the warlike attitude of the Americans towards the British and the Canadians. "Every American newspaper teems with violent and hostile resolutions against England," he wrote, "and associations are forming in every town for the . . . purpose of attacking these provinces."[2]

Many of the people of Canada, as Brock well knew, were not much interested in joining the militia. And yet, to Brock the situation was critical; Canada could be defeated. Even the demographics were against a successful defence of the colonies. Canada at the time had only 500 000 people while the U.S. had seven million and it was difficult to rouse the populace to defend itself. In Upper Canada, many of the recent immigrants from the U.S. were still adjusting to life in their new country. Survival, in what was for many, a hostile wilderness was their first concern. Most of the new Canadians were occupied clearing their land, building their homes, and establishing themselves on the farms that would become the main source of livelihood of Upper Canadians for years to come. And there were others among the recent immigrants from the U.S. who sympathized with the Americans' goal and joined the fight against the British.

In 1812, Brock put his forces into play first by surprising and capturing the American garrison at Michilimackinac, near the head of Lake Huron. Even though the victory was not terribly important in and of itself, it was significant because it convinced the Aboriginal Peoples of the region that by allying themselves with the British they might be able to win back some of their lands that were being taken over by the Americans. In mid-August, Brock and his ally Tecumseh, succeeded in taking Fort Detroit with no loss of life on either side. This second victory convinced at least some Canadians that the fight against the Americans

could be won, and there was greater interest in joining the militia to defend Canada. All in all, throughout the years of the war, about eleven thousand Upper Canadians joined the militia.

In October, the Americans attacked Queenston Heights on the Niagara River but with a rather disorganized and uncommitted militia army. Many of the American soldiers were not especially committed to the war, some believed that they had no right to attack Canada and some deserted when they had the opportunity to do so. Others refused to cross the Niagara River into Canadian territory because they had not been recruited to fight on foreign soil. Even their commander, Major John Lovett, deplored the war, saying that "History, while recording our folly, will dress her pages in mourning, ... for the sponge of time can never wipe this blot from the American name ..."[3]

The British, the Canadians, and Tecumseh's warriors won this bloody battle, however, General Brock was killed, picked off by a rifle shot in the early stages of the fight. The Canadian victory at Queenston Heights showed the Americans—who lost thirteen hundred men to the Canadians one hundred—that Upper Canada could not be conquered easily. Nor would the invaders necessarily be welcomed as liberators.

The Battle of Queenston Heights. British, Canadian, and Aboriginal Warriors defeated the United States in 1812.

Although Brock had not lived to see the end of the battle, he and the battle for Queenston Heights became part of the mythology of Upper Canada. Brock became an heroic figure for those who preached maintaining the British hierarchical social structure for Canada and who hated anything that sounded in the least like American republicanism. As historians Margaret Conrad and Alvin Finkel stated, a cult developed around Isaac Brock, who was "presented as the very embodiment of the manly virtues to which loyal colonial males aspired."[4]

Then, after an unsuccesful campaign in Lower Canada, the Americans returned to Upper Canada in 1814 to try once more to take that colony. They burned the town of Niagara and the parliament buildings in York (Toronto). The British and Canadians then launched an attack on the American capital of Washington and burned the capital buildings in retaliation for the burning of York.

Throughout the night of July 25, 1814, the two sides fought again in the Niagara region at Lundy's Lane, one of the bloodiest battles of the war. The night was so dark that sometimes the Canadians and the Americans could not even tell who was an enemy and who was an ally. By morning, the generals of both the British and American armies had been seriously wounded. There were about 640 British and Canadian and about 740 American casualties. The cost had been high, but neither side was a clear victor in the battle.

Web Connection

www.mcgrawhill.ca/links/definingcanada
Go to the above Web site to read more about the importance of the Battle of Queenston Heights to Canadian history.

Lower Canada

In Lower Canada, the Bishop of Quebec, Joseph-Octave Plessis, preached to the French Canadians a stern message of support for the British and a horror of the republican ideas of the Americans. Those "godless" ideas were too much like the cries of the French revolutionaries who had so recently declared that they would turn France from a Catholic into an atheistic country. France had gone through its own revolution just a few years before and the atheism of the new order horrified the Catholic hierarchy in Canada. Whether the bishop's message influenced the French Canadians or not, the Americans met with little success in their battles for Lower Canada.

At the Châteauguay River, Charles-Michel de Salaberry was in command. He had been born in Beauport, Quebec, but had served in the British army in Ireland and the West Indies, and had fought in the Napoleonic Wars, only returning to Canada in 1810. Salaberry with his company of sixteen hundred *voltigeurs*, French-Canadian light infantry, successfully defeated a larger force of Americans in 1813 at the battle of Châteauguay near Montreal. Other companies of Quebec French-Canadian militia defended the borders at Lacolle River, Odelltown, and Four Corners. When the French Canadians were again successful in the battle for Chrysler's Farm, 150 kilometres from Montreal, the Americans decided to give up trying to take Lower Canada.

Tecumseh

Tecumseh, like Joseph Brant before him, tried to unite the Aboriginal Peoples—the Delaware, Wyandot, Kickapoo, Seneca, and Potawatomi—to prevent the American takeover of their lands in the Ohio valley. Tecumseh was a respected ally of Isaac Brock; Brock said of him, "A more ... gallant Warrior does not I believe exist."[5]

Once the British had promised to help the Aboriginal Peoples regain their lands in the Ohio valley, Tecumseh travelled from village to village trying to convince his people to ally themselves with the British and the Canadians. He well knew that the loss of Aboriginal lands was inevitable unless they could defeat the land-hungry Americans.

TECUMSEH
Imaginary portrait, from "Tecumseh, a Drama,"
by Charles Mair

Tecumseh, Chief of the Shawnee—"A more gallant warrior does not I believe exist."

As he told all who would listen "At first they only asked for land sufficient for a wigwam, now, nothing will satisfy them but the whole of our hunting ground from the rising to the setting sun."[6]

Tecumseh was a brilliant military strategist and was a contributing factor in the Canadians being able to defend their land against the Americans. At the battle for Fort Detroit, for example, he paraded his warriors in front of the fort three times to give the Americans the impression that his force was larger than it actually was. General Brock, who was present, also used subterfuge, dressing his militia in red coats so that the Americans would think they were dealing with professional British troops. Not only did Tecumseh's friends, like Brock, respect him but

also so did his enemies. William Harrison, who had acquired land title to large areas of what is now Indiana, Wisconsin, Missouri, and Illinois and who wanted the Aboriginal Peoples out of the territory, said of Tecumseh that he was "one of those uncommon geniuses which spring up occasionally to produce revolutions."[7]

Tecumseh was killed when he and his warriors stayed to fight the Americans after the British-led retreat from the battle near Moraviantown (present day Thamesville). Tecumseh had been thoroughly disgusted with what he saw as the cowardice of the British commander, General Henry Proctor, who retreated as soon as the Americans attacked. Tecumseh and his five hundred warriors faced the American force of three thousand alone. Tecumseh died, still fighting for his people and his cause. Proctor was later court-martialled for his actions on that day.

With Tecumseh died his dream of an Aboriginal Confederacy with sufficient strength to rid their land of the invaders. With the end of the War of 1812, there was no stopping the American expansion west. The real losers of the war of 1812 were the Aboriginal Peoples.

The End of the War

By 1814 both sides were tired and at a stalemate. On December 24, 1814, the Treaty of Ghent was signed to end the war. Once the War of 1812 was over, the British authorities in Canada strengthened the defences of the colonies and encouraged immigration and economic development, while at the same time pursuing a policy of peace and expanded trade with the Americans.

The War of 1812 has been commonly portrayed as the "seedtime" of British Canadian nationalism, especially in Upper Canada. The war gave the young colony of Upper Canada its own folklore, which held that its Loyalist population turned back the American threat almost single-handedly in the face of treasonable behaviour by non-Loyalist settlers and the indifference or incompetence of British authorities. This Loyalist myth unified and helped to legitimize the authority of the small Loyalist elite. However, some historians have pointed out that not only were some of the Upper Canadian leaders undeserving of their reputation but that most of the general population refused to volunteer for active service.

Nevertheless, the men who had led Upper Canada during the war believed they should continue to lead it afterward. Known as the "Family Compact," they would use the myth of their loyalty as a powerful political weapon in the years to come, opposing land reform and increased power for elected assemblies on principle. Their bonds with Britain—and their suspicions of anything that seemed American republicanism—were strengthened as a result of the war.

Rebellions and Reform in Upper and Lower Canada
Oligopolies

The years between 1812 and 1850 were a time of economic growth in Canada. Wheat and lumber became the staples of the St. Lawrence colonial economy; the Montreal-based fur trade pushed farther and farther into the northwest regions; Nova Scotia and New Brunswick became centres of trade with the U.S. More immigrants were arriving from Britain and the United States, settling especially in Upper Canada. Nonetheless, it was during this time that popular movements to reform the government sprang up, especially in Upper and Lower Canada and in Nova Scotia.

Excerpts from William Lyon Mackenzie's "Proclamation to the People of Upper Canada"

We have planted the Standard of Liberty in Canada, for the attainment of the following objects:

Civil and Religious Liberty, in its fullest extent, that in all laws made, or to be made, every person to be bound alike....

The Abolition of Hereditary Honors, of the laws of Entail and Primogeniture, and of hosts of pensioners who devour our substance.

A Legislature, composed of a Senate and Assembly chosen by the people.

An Executive, to be composed of a Governor and other officers elected by the public voice.

A Free Trial by Jury—Sheriffs chosen by you, and not to hold office, as now, at the pleasure of our tyrants. The freedom of the press. Alas for it, now! The free presses in the Canadas are trampled down by the hand of arbitrary power.

The Vote by Ballot—free and peaceful township elections.

Ample funds to be reserved from the vast natural resources of our country to secure the blessings of education to every citizen.

An end forever to the wearisome prayers, supplications, and mockeries attendant upon our connection with the lordlings of the Colonial Office, Downing Street, London. [8]

William Lyon Mackenzie

The political system then in place throughout the colonies of Canada gave the real power to the British governor and to his executive and legislative councils who were appointed for life. Colonial governors might come and go, but the councils remained. These men—many of whom had arrived as Loyalist refugees after the American Revolution—formed an oligarchy. Not only did they make up the governor's councils, but they also held the highest bureaucratic and judicial positions. They were well-connected men of property with commercial interests to defend.

Known as the Family Compact in Upper Canada and the Chateau Clique in Quebec, they held a stranglehold over the commercial and political life of their colonies. As the oligarchy members made all governmental appointments, they were able to control the legal, religious, and educational systems in the colonies. Using their political power, they put policies in place that were favourable to themselves and their interests rather than to the majority of citizens in the colonies. They could—and did—spend public monies on canals that would further their business interests rather than on the roads that the settlers needed.

Reform in Upper Canada

Historian David Mills states that the Family Compact members of Upper Canada drew upon Loyalist beliefs that the ideal society would be "strengthened by its imperial connection and hostile to the U.S. It idealized British institutions such as a balanced constitution, a hierarchical society and an established church."[9] The Family Compact ignored the growing demands from reformers for increased power to be granted to the elected assembly, for land reforms, and for secularization of clergy reserves.

In Upper Canada, the oligarchy controlled the clergy land reserves, keeping new immigrants as tenants on the land and keeping the Anglican Church in its dominant position. The appointed council members, along with the governor, could veto any recommendation made by the elected assembly, which had little real power.

This system was obviously unfair and gradually the reform movement in both Upper and Lower Canada attracted popular support. But even when the reformers won majorities in the elected assemblies, they could not get their bills past the Family Compact and the Chateau Clique. The assemblies could not get the funding they needed to improve roads in the colonies because such funding was vetoed by those in power. They could not establish an adequate school system without revenues and they could not get the revenues unless they could sell off some of the clergy reserves.

Land distribution and ownership emerged as the earliest reform issue in Upper Canada. More and more people were arriving in Upper Canada from England, Ireland, and Scotland. But the land agents and individual settlers who tried to obtain crown land from the Family Compact members found their efforts in vain if the land was of interest to the more powerful group. At that time, one-seventh of the land in the colony was crown land and the established church—the Church of England—controlled another one-seventh of land in Upper Canada.

Although the land was designated clergy reserve, only the Anglican Church had control of it. Indeed, only the Anglican clergy could solemnize marriages and burials. When, in 1824, reformers in the elected assembly tried to pass a bill that would have allowed Methodist clergy to also perform these rites, the bill was vetoed by the executive council. Since religious leaders, as so often in those days, controlled education it too was under the control of the Church of England. However as the Methodist movement acquired more converts in the colony, those converts added their voices to the call for reform.

Rebellion in Upper Canada

The problems of the 1820s and 1830s remained as colonial governments were removed from the concerns of the majority of their citizens and appointed councils and the elected assemblies still battled. In Upper Canada the reformers won majorities in the 1824 and 1828 elections, but they were not able to achieve the political changes that they wanted. In 1828, William Lyon Mackenzie, the publisher of the *Colonial Advocate* newspaper assumed the leadership of the radical wing of the reform movement. Mackenzie's provocative editorials angered the power elite of the colony. When a mob of their sympathizers raided his office and dumped his presses into Toronto Harbour in 1828, Mackenzie gained a popular reputation as a champion of the common people.

During the 1830s, the reformers made little headway. Mackenzie's call for an elected legislative council and a responsible executive council so enraged the governor, Sir John Colborne, that he branded Mackenzie a traitor. Mackenzie also alienated the more moderate members of the reform movement. So much so that Reverend Egerton Ryerson and other reformers broke with the more radical wing of the party. In spite of the divisions, the reformers managed to capture a majority in the assembly in 1834. After facing more blocks from the executive councils, Mackenzie and a committee of other reformers wrote a report documenting abuses of government power and recommending political reform. Mackenzie began to advocate an American-style democracy in which the legislative councils as well as the assembly would be elected by the people.

The situation deteriorated further after Sir Francis Bond Head became lieutenant governor in 1836. In Bond Head's opinion, he didn't need either the elected assembly or the appointed councils and went ahead and made several political appointments without any consultation. The council resigned and the assembly voted non-confidence and refused to grant funds. Bond Head called an election, and although he and the conservatives won, there were strong suspicions about the tactics used.

After this election defeat, Mackenzie and his faction became more radical and began to consider rebellion for which Mackenzie argued in his new journal, *The Constitution*. The economic depression of 1837 heightened the sense of frustration among the people as farm exports dropped and prices fell. Bond Head's refusal to allow the Bank of Upper Canada to suspend payments on loans made conditions worse. When Mackenzie and his party heard about a rebellion in Lower Canada, Mackenzie gave the signal to take up arms.

The rebellion itself though was poorly led, disorganized, and short-lived. Mackenzie's plan was to overrun the York (Toronto) city hall, seize the arms stored there, and overthrow the government. On December 7, 1837, a motley collection of a few hundred armed rebels marched from Montgomery's tavern in the north end of the city and was quickly dispersed by Colonel James Fitzgibbon and his force of one thousand volunteers. Mackenzie fled to the U.S. and the Tories believed that they had squashed a republican conspiracy. They executed two men and sent almost one hundred others into exile to Van Diemen's Land (Tasmania).

Reform in Lower Canada

In Lower Canada, the conflict went even deeper than it did in Upper Canada. Added to the French-Canadian reformers drive for a government that was responsible to the elected assembly, were the racial divisions within the society. The Parti Patriote, as the reformers were called, wanted to ensure the cultural survival of the French-Canadian majority by providing them with real political power. The reformers wanted to institute a responsible system of government allowing the majority of French Canadians a more active say in their own lives and ensuring that their culture and their language would be preserved.

However, the small English-speaking minority —the Chateau Clique—dominated the governor's councils and held much greater control over governing the colony than did the larger, more rural French-speaking majority. The Clique, made up mainly of English merchants, not only exercised both political and commercial control but it also received all of the government contracts and Crown land grants. Between 1795 and 1840 almost 7 million hectares of land in the Eastern Townships of Quebec were granted to mainly English land speculators. Even though few habitants, as the farmers of Quebec were known, could afford to buy land and establish themselves on their own farms, they joined the reformers in their outrage at the practice of granting the land of their ancestors to the English-speaking real-estate speculators.[10]

The Patriotes wanted to keep their traditional Roman Catholic society intact and as a seigneur, Louis Papineau, the reform movement's leader represented the land-holding tradition of old Quebec. But he also represented the new, emerging French-Canadian intellectual elite. Papineau was one of a number of French-Canadian lawyers, journalists, doctors, priests, and administrators who were refused appointments to the governors' executive councils, and so didn't have any real political power. Papineau was first elected to the Lower Canadian assembly in 1808 when he was only twenty-six. He later became speaker of the assembly and held that position from 1815 until 1837.

Papineau knew that he would be more likely to force changes in the government if the elected assembly could control the spending of public monies. When, in 1818, then governor Sir John Sherbrooke found that he didn't have enough money to meet his government's expenses and pay his appointees, he asked the assembly to vote him the extra money he needed. The assembly did so. But the following year, the assembly refused a similar request unless it was given control over government expenses. The new governor, Lord Dalhousie, refused the demand out of fear that once the assembly had control over the finances, it would also control the governing of the colony. The battle over who should control the colony's finances continued to rage over the next decade.

Rebellion in Lower Canada

The revolt in Lower Canada grew out of this intense political struggle for control over colonial affairs. As speaker of the elected assembly for more than twenty years, Papineau spoke for many of the people of Quebec. When during an election riot in 1832, three French Canadians were killed

Rebellion in Lower Canada: The Burning of the Parliament Building, Montreal, attributed to Joseph Légaré (1795–1855)

by British troops, resentment against the English governor and his Chateau Clique became even more intense. After the 1834 elections, which Papineau and his party won yet again, he successfully passed the 92 Resolutions which criticized the oligarchic system of government in the colony and demanded that colonial revenues be controlled by the elected assembly, that the executive council be responsible to the assembly, and that the assembly elect the council.[11] Those who had been elected by the people should have control of Quebec. In 1837, the government in Britain rejected all of the Parti Patriote's demands.

That same year the assembly refused, yet again, to vote money for the use of the governor and his council. The governor, Lord Gosford, dissolved the assembly and appealed directly to the voters. Even though Papineau and his reformers won this election in a landslide, the governor refused to allow them to assemble. At the same time, the radicals among the reformers gained more support as the people of Lower Canada went through an agricultural crisis when overfarming exhausted the soil on many habitant farms. Farmers were reduced to a subsistence level and were unable to buy products made in the towns and cities. Unemployment became widespread during 1837.

On November 7 of that year, extremists on both the English and the French sides clashed in Montreal. The governor was afraid that Papineau was intent on firing up the habitants to rebel, and tried to have him arrested. But when the British arrived at St. Denis to arrest Papineau, they were beaten back by an armed body of Patriotes. However, the larger forces of trained British troops had little difficulty defeating the Patriotes at St. Charles on the Richelieu River. Before the rebellion was over St. Denis had been destroyed and at St. Eustache, fifty-eight Patriotes were killed and their homes burned. The British declared martial law in the colony and the rebel leaders, including Papineau, fled to the United States.

Review...Reflect...Respond

1. Did the War of 1812 help solidify a Canadian identity? If so, how?

2. How did the causes of the rebellions of 1837 differ between Lower Canada and Upper Canada?

3. To what degree do you believe the rebellions helped to change the course of how governments were formed in Canada?

Canada's North West

The movement of Europeans into the vast northern and western regions of Canada began with the seventeenth-century French fur traders who were in search of high-quality beaver pelts. The traders were followed by English officials of the Hudson's Bay Company who had, for the most part, the same financial interest. Then came the missionaries, the soldiers, and the government officials to convert, rule, and organize the Aboriginal Peoples of the regions, whose ancestors had lived on the land for thousands of years. Guides from among these Aboriginal Peoples helped the adventurers, most of them Hudson's Bay Company employees, explore further and further west until they reached the Pacific Ocean. By the mid-nineteenth century, forts and trading posts had been extended all the way to Fort Vancouver, which was established in 1825.

The land that lay north and west of Upper and Lower Canada—today the Prairie provinces, British Columbia, Nunavut, and the Yukon and Northwest Territories—was as largely unknown to most Canadians living in the east of the country. Those who did venture into the territory from the seventeenth to the early nineteenth centuries relied heavily on the Aboriginal Peoples of the region as guides, hunters, trappers, teachers of survival tactics and technologies, and suppliers of the all-

Encampment along Lake Huron Isle, by Canadian artist Paul Kane shows his vision of life for Aboriginal Peoples in the Canadian Northwest. Why is this called a romanticized view?

important pemmican, the food that was necessary for survival in these regions. The settlers didn't come until later, once at least preliminary governmental institutions were in place.

This was quite a different story from the movement west in the United States, where land companies owned by private individuals laid claim to huge tracts of Aboriginal lands and where pioneers trekked looking for land on which to settle. The difference between the settlement processes in Canada and the U.S. had a profound impact on the future development of both nations.

The Fur Trading Companies

The Hudson's Bay Company, the "Company of Adventurers," had been established in 1670, by royal charter from the English King Charles II.

Almost every year, for 249 years, supply ships would come in the spring from England and would return home, before the onset of winter ice, with a cargo of furs. Peter C. Newman, in his book *Empire of the Bay,* tells how the English ships would anchor seven miles offshore from the York Factory company post at a place called Five Fathom Hole. Then, "sloops sent out from (York) Factory ferried ashore cargoes of guns, brandy, textiles, knives, axes and other trade goods. The vacated holds were then filled with bundles of furs brought to York Factory from the trading posts strung out over the (7 million square kilometres) of the Company's empire." From faraway northern and western posts and through the breadth of the interconnected Canadian river systems Aboriginal Peoples would bring their furs, in the early decades by canoe, and later by York boats.[12]

As you can see by the map in Figure 9-5, the area controlled by the Hudson's Bay Company was vast to begin with and only became larger after the English defeated the French at Quebec. Eventually the company even controlled parts of British Columbia from which it joined American companies trading with China, sending sea otter pelts in exchange for silks, porcelain, and spices, which were taken back to England.

The North West Company was formed in 1783 in Montreal to compete with the Hudson's Bay Company for the lucrative fur trade. However, in contrast with the HBC, the North West Company sent "wintering partners" to live in their company's trading posts and to trade for furs directly with the Aboriginal Peoples. As the French traders and voyageurs had done before them, the English partners of the North West Company went to their Aboriginal suppliers to get the pick of the best furs to send to the European markets. The company hired French Canadians who were experienced in trading and trapping, and who knew the languages and the cultural traditions of the Aboriginal Peoples who were the actual trappers, processors, and suppliers of the furs.

The Adventurers

In response to the growing threat of the North West Company and the growing scarcity of good beaver pelts, the Hudson's Bay Company tried to diversify by sending some of its employees into the interior of Canada—the upper halves of the provinces and into the Northwest Territories—to search for minerals. As early as 1770, Samual Hearne set out with his Dene guide, Matonabbee, for the Coppermine River following a route that had been mapped out in advance by Matonabbee. When they finally reached their destination, after a long and difficult journey and after encounters with the Copper Indians, Hearne found little to justify their trip: "This mine, if it deserve that appellation is no more than an entire jumble of rocks and gravel."[13] After four hours searching for copper, they found only one piece of any size. And with that, they turned around and returned home.

In later years, Hearne wrote and published a book about his travels, *A Journey from the Prince of Wales Fort in Hudson Bay to the Northern Ocean* which was quite successful and was translated into French, German, and Dutch. Such combined travel-adventure books not only had a wide audience during the eighteenth and nineteenth centuries, but they also inspired later adventurers to explore Canada's northern and western territories. Alexander Mackenzie, who travelled to the Arctic Ocean with the help of his Aboriginal guides, published his book, *Voyages from Montreal* which was also popular during the time. The journals of David Thompson, the British-born fur trader and mapmaker who explored and mapped much of the northwest, which became so respected in later years, remained unpublished at his death.

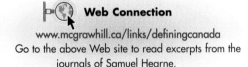

Web Connection

www.mcgrawhill.ca/links/definingcanada

Go to the above Web site to read excerpts from the journals of Samuel Hearne.

David Thompson

When Hearne returned to the Bay after his voyage to the Coppermine River, he was assigned to Fort Churchill where he encountered David Thompson, another Hudson's Bay Company employee. Thompson seems to have been endowed with deep-rooted scientific curiosity and aptitude; he became a great geographer, a mapmaker of much of the Canadian west, and a keen observer of life around him. According to historian John S. Nicks, Thompson's maps which were "based primarily on his own explorations and observations, were the first to provide a comprehensive view of the vast western territories that became part of Canada in 1870."[14]

On his first journey into the interior of the continent, Thompson marvelled at the sight of the Rocky Mountains, "like shining white clouds on the horizon" with "immense masses of snow" that seemed an impassable barrier, "even to the eagle."[15] He absorbed all that he could about the country and the traditions of its people, spending hours listening to a Peigan elder telling the history of his people. He also learned about practical astronomy from Philip Turnor, the Hudson's Bay Company's chief surveyor. With this knowledge, he spent the next twenty years measuring latitude and longitude of places that had never before been so measured.

Eventually, Thompson joined the North West Company which sent him out to map their trading posts and to try to find a route to the Pacific Ocean so that the company could trade with the coastal peoples and establish trade with China. In 1811, he reached the Pacific coast and claimed much of what is now the interior of British Columbia for the North West Company. As he said of his accomplishments,

> Thus I have fully completed the survey of this part of North America from sea to sea, and by almost innumerable astronomical Observations have determined the positions of the Mountains, Lakes and Rivers and other remarkable places of the northern part of this Continent; the Maps all have been drawn, and laid down in geographical position, being now the work of twenty-seven years.[16]

In his later years, Thompson perfected his maps and wrote the story of his exploration, which, though it wasn't published during his lifetime, is considered by many historians to have been his greatest achievement.

The Aboriginal Peoples and the Fur-Trading Companies

While the Hudson's Bay Company and the North West Company were in competition for their furs and hides, the Aboriginal Peoples of the Northwest often received a better price than they had before the founding of the North West Company. However, with all of the competition for furs, the stocks were becoming depleted. The Aboriginal Peoples were also giving up their traditional ways of life and becoming more dependent on European goods. In addition to the scarcity of animals, they faced disease epidemics and the danger of starvation. Hunters had to work harder and to travel farther to trap the animals upon which their lives and the lives of their families depended. They became caught in a vicious circle as they became more dependent on the fur-trading companies just at the time when the over-exploitation of fur-bearing animals made them harder to catch.

Originally, the Blackfoot Peoples of southern Alberta had little interest in travelling to Hudson's Bay to trade their buffalo hides. These independent people provided well for themselves through hunting the buffalo. But when both the Hudson's Bay Company and the North West Company built posts on the edge of their country, the Blackfoot began to trade first fox and wolf skins and then pemmican for the traders at the posts. Eventually the Blackfoot too experienced cultural change with increased trade and the arrival of the missionaries.

Once the Hudson's Bay and the North West companies joined together in 1821 under the name of the Hudson's Bay Company, it resulted in a monopoly and the number of goods exchanged for beaver pelts were reduced. The monopoly caused the same kind of hardships as the eastern Aboriginal Peoples had suffered after the English conquest of French Canada. In addition, Sir George Simpson, governor-in-chief of all Hudson's Bay Company territories in North America from 1826 to 1860, decided that it was time to rule with a firmer hand. He declared that the Aboriginal Peoples' "immediate wants" had been fully supplied and that "the scenes of extravagance" were at an end. The Aboriginal Peoples were now to be dependent on their rulers: "I have made it my study to examine the nature and character of the Indians and however repugnant it may be to our feelings, I am convinced they must be ruled with a rod of iron, to bring, and keep them in a proper state of subordination, and the most certain way to effect this is by letting them feel their dependence upon us."[17]

Expression of Culture

PAUL KANE – "A ROMANTIC VISION"

Paul Kane is a romantic figure in Canadian history. His is a story of adventure, travel and discovery, an arduous journey across the country, and an artistic mission to capture a culture on canvas.

Born in Ireland in 1810, Paul Kane moved as a young boy with his family to the town of York (present day Toronto) in 1819. Little is known of his childhood, early career or studies, but he was apprenticed at a young age and made a modest name for himself in York as a decorative painter. While still a young man, he moved to the growing town of Cobourg, Ontario, and started a career as a portrait painter, an occupation that he continued in Detroit, Saint Louis, Mobile and New Orleans.

It was not until 1841, at the age of twenty-one, that Kane saved enough money to set sail for Europe and, like scores of artists before him, studied and copied the works of the masters. For Kane, however, it was not the art he saw in Italy and France that affected him most, but rather an exhibition of paintings in England that would alter the direction of his career entirely. The exhibition featured the work of then well-known American painter George Catlin who had made a name for himself for his travels, paintings and writings on North American Aboriginals. Kane was struck by Catlin's work and observations of Aboriginal culture and was inspired to return home and paint the portraits of Canadian Indians himself.

Paul Kane left for his first sketching trip on June 17, 1845. He traveled as far as Sault St. Marie and Manitoulin Island, spending the majority of his time among the Ojibwa. It was his intent to "sketch pictures of the principal chiefs, and their original costumes, to illustrate their manners and customs, and to represent the scenery of an almost unknown country."

On May 9, 1846, Paul Kane set out on his second and most famous journey with the support of Sir

Portrait of Paul Kane

George Simpson, the Governor of the Hudson's Bay Company. Over the next two years, he sketched in every post of the Company, reaching as far as Fort Victoria. By canoe and on foot, he endured a long, often demanding journey across difficult terrain in the company of the men of the Hudson's Bay Company. In each village, Kane sought out the chief and most prominent individuals and invited them to sit for portraits. While many of his hosts were quite willing and excited about having their likeness reproduced on canvas, others resisted his invitations because of a common Aboriginal belief that a portrait or image would become a 'second self' and bring bad luck.

Paul Kane returned to Toronto in 1848, with an impressive collection of more than 500 sketches of the countryside, buffalo, and Aboriginal peoples.

Expression of Culture

That same year, an exhibition of his sketches in oil and watercolour was held in the Toronto City Hall. His work received favourable reviews. In 1850, he was commissioned by the legislature to complete twelve paintings from his sketches and then, later, he was commissioned by the Honourable George W. Allan to create a series of 100 canvases for the sum of $20,000.

In studying both Kane's original watercolour and oil sketches and his final painted canvases, one notices the marked difference in style of the two mediums. His sketches are fresh, direct and colourful, while his paintings are staged and subdued. Often, Kane made revisions from sketch to painting, adding and omitting details to heighten the scene. His style pleased his wealthy, English patrons, who still favoured the picturesque, traditional English landscape. In *Indian Encampment on Lake Huron*, we see a peaceful scene of village life. People go about their daily chores, canoes, paddles and tents are perfectly propped and scattered, and the camp is nestled gently in a setting of lush, green woods.

In 1859, Kane published his journals under the title *Wanderings of an Artist among the Indians of North America*. In it he records his travels with great detail and enthusiasm, recalling legends and stories told to him first-hand by his hosts, describing in detail the Aboriginal customs and villages, and recounting the more exciting events of his journey. He describes objectively the injustices he sees taking place in Aboriginal villages, such as their use of alcohol and the apparent poverty. In both his writings and his paintings, Kane plays the role of historian and sometimes storyteller, making historical notes and regaling the reader with colourful adventures.

Paul Kane occupies a significant place in the history of Canadian art, despite his tendency to romantic sentimentality. In his day, Kane received impressive commissions from both the Canadian government and his patrons, was the first Upper Canadian artist to gain wide recognition, and was granted one of the first solo exhibitions in Canada.

The Métis

Intermarriage between Aboriginal women and fur-trading European men and soldiers had begun in the seventeenth century. As you know from Chapter 4, intermarriages were quite common, well accepted, and even at times encouraged by both colonial administrators and the clergy as they thought that such unions would promote trade alliances with the Aboriginal Peoples. In the early days, the clergy had also hoped that these unions would bring more converts to the Catholic faith and would help serve their goals of assimilating Aboriginal Peoples into French society.

Some of the children of these families did join the French Canadians in Quebec; others joined the Aboriginal Peoples of their mothers. But there was another group of mixed-blood people—the Métis—who identified with other people of similar background and culture and who saw themselves as a distinct nation. Before the English took over Canada, there were already Métis groups in the upper Great Lakes region and in today's Prairie provinces.

Originally, the Métis were nomadic people who followed the buffalo that was their main source of food. But as time passed and the buffalo became scarce they had begun to settle down to an agricultural life. By the mid-1800s, there were about ten thousand Métis people in the Red River area of what is today Winnipeg, Manitoba. However, because the Métis held no paper title to their land, they were regarded by the British as having even fewer rights to the land than the Aboriginal Peoples had.

There were two groups of Métis, the first were those who were descended from French and Aboriginal parents. The second had ancestors of Aboriginal and English or Scottish origin. Even though the Hudson's Bay Company forbade marriages or liaisons between their traders and Aboriginal women, nonetheless there were also Métis people who were descended from Hudson's Bay workers and traders. But, whatever European ties might have once existed, the Métis saw themselves as a separate nation and they did not become absorbed into either the Aboriginal nations or European communities. The French-speaking Métis developed their own language, Michif, which blended elements of French and of the Cree languages. The English-speaking Métis developed Bungi, a combination of Scots and Cree languages. Among their achievements was the development of the Red River carts, which had wheels that could withstand the Prairie mud and which could be removed when necessary to turn the cart into a boat.[18]

In the nineteenth century, English-speaking Métis men often worked as labourers at the trading posts and the French-speaking Métis men worked as guides, boatmen, and providers of pemmican for voyageurs, exploring parties, and in bad years even for the settlers. Pemmican was a very important staple food to the voyageurs and traders working for the Hudson's Bay and North West companies. The word "pemmican" comes from a Cree term meaning "he who makes grease." The product was made from buffalo meat, which had been cut into strips, dried in the sun, and then pounded into a pulp. To this was added boiling buffalo fat and wild berries which helped prevent scurvy. The mixture was carried in a bag made from buffalo hide. An average *voyageur* would receive a pound and a half each day that could be eaten raw, made into a soup, or covered with flour and fried.[19]

Web Connection

www.mcgrawhill.ca/links/definingcanada
Go to the above Web site to see Canadian World Heritage Sites and find out how Parks Canada is helping preserve Canada's heritage for future generations.

The Red River Colony

Lord Selkirk, a Scottish landowner, who brought dispossessed Scots and Irish to settle in the area, established the Red River Colony. Selkirk had already established similar settlements in Prince Edward Island and in Upper Canada. He believed that the government should help settlers establish themselves in new regions; the settlers should not be abandoned once they arrived. He also saw a great potential in Canada's vast wealth of land: "There are still in Canada millions of acres of fertile land at the disposal of the Government; there is a great surplus of population at home, who might be employed to cultivate those lands."[20]

What he failed to acknowledge, however, was that there were already Métis settlements in the Red River region. Neither Selkirk nor the Hudson's Bay Company official consulted the Métis about the proposal to settle their land. After all, according to the Hudson's Bay Company charter, the land "belonged" to the company, which granted over 300 000 square kilometres to Selkirk in what is today Manitoba, North Dakota, and Minnesota.[21]

The first thirty-five settlers suffered from scurvy the first winter just as the early French had at Port Royal and at Quebec. When their first crops failed, the settlers survived on pemmican that they obtained from the Métis people. Pemmican became a source of conflict between the British and the Métis. The first governor of the small colony pro-claimed that the Métis could no longer export pemmican to the rival North West Company traders nor could the Métis run the buffalo without permission. The next governor, Robert Semple, also forbade the sale of pemmican out of the colony. Relations between the British settlers and the Métis continued to deteriorate. In March 1816, Semple and some of his colonists attacked a group of Métis and Semple was killed, but this didn't stop the settlement of the Red River colony. More British settlers arrived after the merger of the Hudson's Bay Company and the North West Company when a large number of employees were let go.

Review...Reflect...Respond

1. To what extent did the exploration for beaver belts help settle different areas in Canada?

2. Why did the Métis become a distinct nation and did not join together with other Aboriginal groups?

3. How did the merger of the Hudson's Bay Company and the North West Company affect Aboriginal Peoples?

Notes

1. Don Gillmor et al., *Canada: A People's History, Volume 1* (Toronto: McClelland & Stewart, 2000), p. 165.
2. Gillmor et al., *Canada: A People's History, Volume 1*, p. 164.
3. Gillmor et al., *Canada: A People's History, Volume 1*, p. 167.
4. Margaret Conrad, Alvin Finkel, and Cornelius Jaenen, *History of the Canadian Peoples, Volume 1, Beginnings to 1867* (Toronto: Addison Wesley Longman, 2002), p. 277.
5. James H. Marsh, ed., *The Canadian Encyclopedia* (Toronto: McClelland & Stewart, 2000), CD-ROM version.
6. Gillmor et al., *Canada: A People's History, Volume 1*, p. 169.
7. Gillmor et al., *Canada: A People's History, Volume 1*, p. 170.

8. *Proclamation to the People of Upper Canada*, World of Education Library Web site
9. Marsh, *The Canadian Encyclopedia*, p. 816.
10. Conrad, Finkel, and Jaenen, *History of the Canadian Peoples, Volume 1*, pp. 278–279.
11. Marsh, *The Canadian Encyclopedia*, p. 1755.
12. Peter C. Newman, *Empire of the Bay* (Viking Studio/Madison Press Book, 1989), p. 9.
13. Gillmor et al., *Canada: A People's History, Volume 1*, p. 193.
14. Marsh, *The Canadian Encyclopedia*, p. 2345.
15. Gillmor et al., *Canada: A People's History, Volume 1*, p. 198.
16. Gillmor et al., *Canada: A People's History, Volume 1*, p. 201.
17. Gillmor et al., *Canada: A People's History, Volume 1*, p. 311.
18. Conrad, Finkel, and Jaenen, *History of the Canadian Peoples, Volume 1, Beginnings to 1867*, p. 306.
19. Newman, *Empire of the Bay*, p.121.
20. J.M. Bumsted, *The Peoples of Canada: A Pre-Confederation History* (Toronto: Oxford University Press, 1992), p. 185.
21. Bumsted, *The Peoples of Canada: A Pre-Confederation History*, p. 184.
22. *Head-Smashed-In Buffalo Jump Provincial Historic Site*, Parks Canada Web site

Chapter 9 Review

Knowledge & Understanding

1. Identify six of the following people, concepts, and events and explain their historical significance to Canadian history and the development of its culture and identity.

   buffer zone
   Aboriginal Confederacy
   Family Compact
   Isaac Brock
   Tecumseh
   David Thompson
   War of 1812
   Battle of Queenston Heights
   rebellion in Upper Canada
   rebellion in Lower Canada

2. Explain what oligopoly means and how the term may be applied to the political system in place in Upper and Lower Canada in the early 1800s.

3. Why did issues around the control of government expenditures become so important in the reform movement and in the rebellion in Lower Canada?

Thinking & Inquiry

4. Create a chart or graphic organizer in which you compare the reasons for the Hudson's Bay Company's success as a fur-trading company with the reasons for the failure of the Company of 100 Associates in early 17th century New France. Before you begin this activity, work together as a class to decide on the criteria that should be used for the comparison.

5. Think/pair/share the impact that competition had on the Aboriginal Peoples who traded in furs. The early competition was between the French and English in the east; the later competition was between the Hudson's Bay Company and North West Company in the west. What happened to the Aboriginal People when they had to deal with a monopoly: the English colonial government in the east and the Hudson's Bay Company in the west?

Communication

6. What was different about the causes and effects of the rebellions in Upper and Lower Canada as compared with the causes and effects of the American Revolution? In small groups, discuss these differences. Consider issues of population, culture, views on government, structure of society, and economic situation. Reach a consensus opinion within your group and report that opinion to the rest of the class.

7. Research one of the journeys of either Samual Hearne, Matonabee, or David Thompson. Create a map to show the journey and accompany the map with at least two paragraphs in which you describe the difficulties and achievements of the journey.

Application

8. Write an expository essay in which you explain how the conflicts that resulted in reform movements and rebellions in Upper and Lower Canada helped shape Canadian culture and identity. Develop a clear thesis argument for your essay and then substantiate that thesis with supporting evidence.

CHAPTER 10

Changed Society, Altered Identity

Nothing hardly but an ox-cart can travel along the roads, and even that with difficulty, occupying two days to perform the journey; and the worst of the matter is, that there are times when the most necessary articles of provisions are not to be procured at any price. You see, then, that a settler in the bush requires to hold himself pretty independent, not only of the luxuries and delicacies of the table, but not unfrequently even of the very necessaries.

–CATHARINE PARR TRAILL, 1832

During the nineteenth century, the society of the North American British colonies changed as hundreds of thousands of immigrants brought their culture and traditions to their new land. As the new settlers arrived at the island Grosse-Île, epidemics took thousands of lives as a result of the miserable conditions suffered by the Irish immigrants in the holds of the lumber ships in which they had crossed the Atlantic. Other immigrants—escaping slaves from the Thirteen Colonies—made their way along the clandestine routes of the Underground Railroad. In the towns and rural communities, society remained hierarchical in the early years. Women were believed by some to inhabit a "separate sphere" from that of the men, though this was often far from the reality of daily life.

Throughout the colonies, many new arrivals settled in the towns and cities, which became centres of commerce and eventually of industrialization. Class distinctions remained a prominent feature of the landscape. In the cities, the upper classes lived in relative wealth, while the lower classes lived in poverty and worked at unstable, low-paying, seasonal jobs in the shipyards and on the railroads and canals. Both social aid and education were in the hands of the churches in the early part of the century. But eventually education became a public concern with the goal that all children should be educated. Canadian literary productions in both French and English were written and published.

The Aboriginal Peoples lost more of their independence and their land as their territory became Crown Land and the Indian Affairs Department took greater control. Their numbers continued to decrease through epidemics, and settlers continued to encroach on their land.

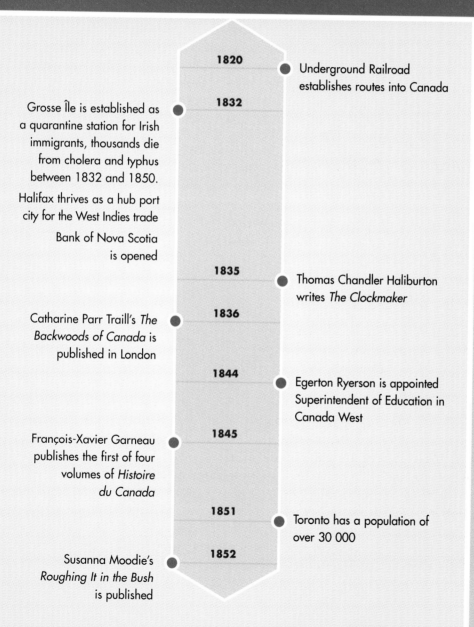

1820

Underground Railroad establishes routes into Canada

1832

Grosse Île is established as a quarantine station for Irish immigrants, thousands die from cholera and typhus between 1832 and 1850.

Halifax thrives as a hub port city for the West Indies trade

Bank of Nova Scotia is opened

1835

Thomas Chandler Haliburton writes *The Clockmaker*

1836

Catharine Parr Traill's *The Backwoods of Canada* is published in London

1844

Egerton Ryerson is appointed Superintendent of Education in Canada West

1845

François-Xavier Garneau publishes the first of four volumes of *Histoire du Canada*

1851

Toronto has a population of over 30 000

1852

Susanna Moodie's *Roughing It in the Bush* is published

By the end of this chapter, you will be able to

- describe significant waves of immigration and settlement patterns, and how they helped shape Canadian identity and culture.

- analyze how obstacles that made it difficult for immigrants to participate fully in Canadian society have been challenged and reduced over time

- analyze how Canada and Canadians have been portrayed by a representative sample of writers, visual artists, musicians, and composers

- describe the strategies that French Canada has used to preserve francophone culture

- demonstrate an understanding of the history, development, and extent of Canada's social programs

- analyze the contributions of women to the Canadian identity

The People of Canada

Demographics

It was difficult to classify the demographics of Canada early in the nineteenth century. Today during the Canadian census, households receive their questionnaires through the mail and Statistics Canada has an organized system and the technology for tabulating the data. The early census in the Canadian colonies was a disorderly affair. Some records were poorly kept and the census was taken at different times in different colonies—and even in different regions of the colonies. Some people lived on isolated farms where the roads were poor and communication between places almost nonexistent. New immigrants arrived in one centre, swelling the ranks of that locale for a time, and then moved on to Upper Canada or to the United States. For example, in 1831 fifty thousand immigrants from Britain landed in Quebec, but there are no records of where they eventually settled.

Structure of Canadian Society

Colonial society in the early- to mid-1800s, was structured along hierarchical lines and modelled after the structure of society in Britain. In the upper class of Canadian society were the governor and his appointed executive and legislative councils and those to whom he granted favours of prize jobs, contracts, and land grants. Even in Lower Canada, with its large French-Canadian population, the men in the upper reaches of society and their families were English Protestants. Close to the top of the hierarchy were the higher ranking military officers in the colony and the successful merchants, doctors, lawyers, clergymen, members of the elected colonial assemblies, and educators in the schools for the upper classes. Many of these people lived in the capital cities of each colony: York, Montreal, Halifax and St. John's.

Landowning was still a source of power and status. In Lower Canada the majority of seigneurs were no longer French-Canadian Catholics but

Bush Farm Near Chatham, c. 1838 by Philip James Bainbrigge

rather English Protestants who had come from England or the United States. In all the colonies, there were also retired military officers on half-pay who tried to establish landed estates with tenant farmers.

The next rung of the social ladder was made up of the ordinary farmers in the countryside, some of who had managed to become financially well-off, but most barely managed to sustain themselves and their often, large families. In Newfoundland and Prince Edward Island, farmers were still likely to be tenants on land held by absentee landlords, but in some areas of Upper and Lower Canada small farmers owned their land or were in the process of buying it. In the towns and villages there were the families of skilled artisans, blacksmiths, writers for local newspapers, clergymen, and small shopkeepers.

At the bottom of the social hierarchy were the poor: the newly arrived immigrants, the landless, and those who worked when they could find jobs as road or canal builders, casual labourers, servants in the upper-class houses, or increasingly as the century went on, in the factories of the new industrial age. During the winter months these casual workers were not likely to be employed. Yet they had to pay more for their food and the wood to heat their homes in comparison with farmers. Most impoverished farmers could at least keep warm because of the vast supplies of timber on their uncleared lands, but this was not the case in the cities.

The Separate World of Women

By the nineteenth century, an idea was growing among the middle and upper classes, mainly those living in the towns and cities, that there was a clear demarcation line between the worlds of men and women. They were designed by God and by nature to inhabit separate worlds. As historians Alison Prentice and her colleagues write, on the one side was "the personal, domestic world of women and the family, where it was assumed that traditional female work would and should continue to go on." But now, on the other side of the divide, was "a newly developing public world, from which wives and children were most appropriately excluded."[1]

Many clergymen supported this idealized view. A woman's only place was in the home where, according to one commentator of the period, she was destined "by Providence" to create "a cloister wherein one may seek calm and joyful repose from the busy, heartless world."[2]

This may have been one vision of a woman's place, but the lives of many women who were trying to establish themselves on farms in the Canadian colonies were not so different from those of the earlier habitant women of Quebec under French rule. Many of the labour-intensive tasks were similar, and without women's labour no farm could have succeeded in the early days.

As W. H. Graham writes, "farm women were responsible for the child-rearing, meal preparation, and laundry of the household." But in addition "They grew their own hops to make their own rising [yeast] to make their own bread. They saved ashes to make their own lye to boil with collected fat to make their own soap. They made their own candles. They spun wool, they made clothes, cutting up old garments for patterns."[3] They also milked the cows, churned the butter, made the cheese, and tended the poultry. They helped butcher the animals that would be used for the family's food, and prepared sausages and smoked hams. In the springtime, they would work into the night keeping fires going under cauldrons in which the maple syrup was being distilled. In the summer, they tended the vegetable garden and preserved berries, pickles, and fruits, and made tea and coffee substitutes from dandelion roots and sumach leaves. At any time of year, they also dyed wool and knitted clothing to ward off the bitterly cold Canadian winters.

Immigration

During the nineteenth century, there was a great wave of immigration to the British colonies in Canada from the British Isles, especially after the end of the War of 1812. Between 1790 and 1845, 750 000 immigrants came to Canada from Britain, with almost half coming from Ireland. The British immigrants came because of the dire economic conditions in their homelands; there were fewer jobs where they could earn their living. For example, by the late 1700s and early 1800s, the industrial revolution in the textile industry in England was well underway. Inventions such as the flying shuttle and the spinning jenny—and the later introduction of steam and the power loom—meant that spinners and weavers were thrown out of work. By 1800 the number of workers needed to turn wool into yarn had been reduced by four-fifths. And by 1840 the labour cost of making the best woollen cloth had fallen by at least half.[4] In the Scottish highlands, the large landholders discovered that wool from sheep was a more valuable commodity than tenant farmers. Some of the farmers who lost their lands to sheep grazing and industrialization, in a process known as the clearances, left their Scottish homeland and came to Canada. British politicians had also begun to advocate sending the poor from the British Isles to Canada.

Among the early Irish immigrants, some came because of poverty and others because the British wanted to get rid of Irish troublemakers who continued to rebel against British rule in Ireland. Indeed, the governor of Lower Canada said that the British scheme for assisting Irish settlers who wanted to come to Canada had "no other end than relieving the South of Ireland of a burden which [was] thrown upon the industrious classes of this young country."[5] The Irish came by the thousands both before and after the great famines in Ireland. Over 300 000 Irish came to Canada between the years of 1845 and 1850.

Some British immigrants received assistance from the British government to settle in Canada; such was the case for the decommissioned officers and soldiers of the Napoleonic wars. Other immigrants came to work as tenants on land owned by large landowners like Colonel Thomas Talbot who had control of hundreds of thousands of acres of land in Upper Canada. Some land companies brought settlers over from Britain for a fee, and other companies had nothing to do with transporting the settlers but sold them land once they arrived. Some immigrants arranged for their own passage but arrived in Canada with no real destination. The poorest immigrants arrived in the holds of timber ships. Shipowners who had ships returning empty from Britain after delivering timber recruited immigrants to defray at least some of the costs of the return voyage. The people travelling in the holds of these ships were so undernourished and the conditions on board ship were so terrible that many developed cholera, a deadly and contagious disease.

The Canadians who were already established held different views about what should be done with the immigrants once they arrived. Some believed that they should be given land of their own to farm and should be encouraged to become independent. Robert Baldwin Sullivan, an Upper Canada lawyer, believed that trying to establish the kind of landholding class system that existed in Britain would only "produce a greater inequality of condition" which could never work to society's benefit in Canada.[6] Others, like William Allen, first president of the Bank of Canada, believed that immigrants should not be given land because they were needed to serve as labourers for the wealthy and to grow the economy in the colony. In Allen's view and the view of other conservative land holders, wages were already too high because there were not enough labourers. Acquiring cheap labour was the most important ingredient for the future health of the colony: "the main cause of the scarcity of hired labor in a new Country is the

Cheapness of Land, and it seems to follow, as an irresistible conclusion, that the *Free gift of Lands*, must increase that scarcity a hundredfold."[7]

Grosse-Île and Cholera Epidemics

As historian, Pádaic Ó Laighin says, for the Irish immigrants coming to Canada, Grosse-Île became an island of death during the years from 1832 to 1847.[8] In the second decade of the nineteenth century, a disease called *cholera morbus* spread from India, through Russia, and then across Europe to the seaports of Ireland. Lord Aylmer, who was governor-in-chief of Lower Canada in 1832, and the Lower Canadian House of Assembly established a quarantine station under military control on Grosse-Île. All ships arriving from British ports were to anchor off Grosse-Île to be inspected for disease before they went on to Quebec.

The first serious outbreak of cholera occurred with the arrival of the first ship early in June 1832. On the voyage from Dublin, forty-two people had died, but in spite of this fact, the ship was cleared for entry to the port of Quebec. At first the local English-language newspaper, *The Quebec Mercury*, attributed the deaths to "some unknown disease," but by June 9 the same paper announced that there was cholera in the city. Before a month was out, cases of cholera had been reported in Montreal, Cornwall, Brockville, Kingston, Cobourg, York, and Bytown (Ottawa). The quarantine system at Grosse-Île broke down completely when during June alone thirty thousand immigrants arrived from Ireland. Ships were allowed to proceed without health clearances. As a consequence, during 1832, more that forty-five hundred people in Lower Canada died of cholera, 1885 people in Montreal alone, another fifteen hundred people died in Upper Canada, including eight hundred in the city of York. The total number of Irish immigrants who died at Grosse-Île during 1832 is not known.

But a greater tragedy was to follow fifteen years later when thousands of Irish fled what is known in Ireland as "the great famine." On February 19, 1847, the medical superintendent of the Grosse-Île station told the Legislative Assembly of the Province of Canada (Upper and Lower Canada had been united in 1841 by the Union Act) that he feared "a greater amount of sickness and mortality" during the coming shipping season. Across the Atlantic, one hundred thousand Irish immigrants were waiting to undertake the dangerous crossing for the chance of a better life in North America. On May 17, 1847, the first of the "coffin ships," the *Syria*, arrived. Nine people had died on the voyage, many others were weak and malnourished, and eighty-four were placed

The inscription at the base of this monument to the memory of the Irish immigrants who died on Grosse-Île reads, "Children of the Gael died in their thousands on this island having fled from the laws of the foreign tyrant and an artificial famine in the years 1847–48. God's loyal blessing upon them. Let this monument be a token to their name and honour from the Gaels of America. God save Ireland!"

in the hospital on Grosse-Île. By May 21, of the *Syria's* passengers, 202 were ill, and more ships were arriving.

By May 24, twenty-four more ships had arrived. By May 28, there were thirty-six immigrant ships at anchor near Grosse-Île with 12 450 passengers being detained on board under deplorable conditions. Sometimes the dead lay in bunks alongside those who were ill. By early June there were forty immigrant ships extending down the St. Lawrence River for two miles.

On Grosse-Île, the doctors, nurses, and administrators were overwhelmed. There was insufficient food, housing, hospitals, medical care, and clothing. The workers on the island pitched tents when the hospital was filled, and in spite of the risk some immigrants were still kept in quarantine on board ship. By June 4, 1847, the medical commissioners estimated that 25 398 passengers had arrived at quarantine, 1097 had died of cholera at sea, 900 had died at Grosse-Île, 1150 were sick in hospital, and 1550 were sick on board ships.

The number of Irish immigrants who died at Grosse Île is still disputed by historians; it may have been twenty thousand or thirty thousand or more. In the early days of the epidemic, officials tried to keep records but eventually every waking hour had to be spent to help the living. Today at Grosse-Île National Park, there are some separate graves, but many other cholera victims lie in unmarked graves on the island.

Web Connection

www.mcgrawhill.ca/links/definingcanada
Go the Web site above to find out more about the National Historic Site of Grosse Île.

The Underground Railroad

The road to freedom for more than thirty thousand African American slaves was named the Underground Railroad. Originally started by the Quakers of Pennsylvania in the early nineteenth century, the railroad was as much an idea as a physical fact. There were no stations, track, cars, engines, or rolling stock. The Underground Railroad was a secret operation carried out by thousands of courageous people who were linked by their hatred of slavery and their love of freedom. Harriet Tubman, known as "the Black Moses," led more than two thousand slaves to freedom, resulting in an unheard-of bounty of $40000 being placed on her head by the American authorities.

In order to deceive the bounty hunters, runaway slaves and those who helped them used a long series of safe havens along the route north into Upper Canada. An intricate system was developed where routes zigzagged, changed direction, and sometimes doubled-back to throw the hunters off the track.

The cities of Windsor, Ontario, and Detroit, Michigan, commissioned sculptor Ed Dwight to create this International Monument to the Underground Railroad, which was unveiled in the autumn of 2001.

Canadian Leaders

MARY ANN SHADD

Teacher, writer, editor, publisher, abolitionist, suffragette, integrationist, lawyer, and activist—these are just some of the words that describe Mary Ann Shadd. A tireless advocate of equal rights, Shadd displayed an unwavering commitment to integration between black and white races in Canada.

Although her ancestors were slaves, Shadd grew up free in Wilmington, Delaware, where her father's shoemaking store was part of the Underground Railroad that helped escaped slaves flee to Canada. Since it was against the law to educate black people in Delaware, Mary Ann's parents sent her, at the age of ten, to a Quaker boarding school in Pennsylvania. Six years later, she returned to Wilmington to open a private school for black children

In 1850 passage of the United States Fugitive Slave Act gave full legal support for the capture of slaves anywhere in America. Shadd joined the emigrationist movement in 1851 and with her brother Isaac, moved to Canada, settling in Windsor, and then in Chatham, Ontario. While in Windsor, she fought for integrated education, battling both black and white segregationists to found Canada's first racially integrated school in an abandoned army building.

Shadd also made significant contributions as a writer and publisher. To discourage runaway slaves from fleeing to Canada, many lies were spread by southern slave-owners about former slaves starving in Canada or being eaten by cannibals. Shadd attempted to kept black people in the United States informed about the true conditions in Canada through a forty-four page pamphlet she wrote, entitled *Notes of Canada West*.

From these early writing efforts Shadd recognized the need for a newspaper for blacks, particularly fugitive slaves. She established a weekly newspaper, *The Provincial Freeman* in 1853 to discuss aspects of black life in Canada. In addition, Shadd wanted to spread her views in both the United States and Canada to "acquaint the white citizens with the noble deeds and heroism of the coloured American," and thereby justify the claim for "equal and exact justice." By creating *The Provincial Freeman*, Shadd became the first black woman in North America to found and edit a newspaper.

Some of Shadd's strongest opponents were Canadian black segregationists led by Henry Bibb, an escaped slave. Bibb saw black immigrants as fugitives in exile from America, while Shadd viewed them as new Canadians with no home left in America. Bibb published a newspaper called the *Voice of the Fugitive* in which he frequently attacked Shadd's character and desire for assimilation.

Shadd believed that separate churches, schools, and communities would ultimately undermine the struggle for freedom. Through her editorials, she challenged not only Bibbs' views on segregation, but also the prevailing emigration views of abolitionists in Toronto. So influential was her opinion that an international debate about emigration followed.

Shadd would eventually abandon her belief in emigration, but maintained her strong advocacy for integration. When the Emancipation Proclamation was declared in the United States in 1863, she returned to America and was appointed army recruiting officer to enlist black volunteers in Indiana to fight during the Civil War. After the war, Shadd moved to Washington, D.C. to enroll in Howard University Law School. She became the second black woman in the United States to earn a law degree in 1883 and began practicing law at the age of 60.

The legacy of Mary Ann Shadd's work in education, publishing, and law are a testament to her refusal to accept the socially-imposed limits based on colour, and, or, gender.

MRS. MARY ANN SHADD CARY

By the 1820s, the Underground Railroad had established definite routes into Upper Canada. Runaway slaves were passed through a network of stations throughout Ohio, Michigan, New York, and Pennsylvania. Buffalo, Rochester, Cincinnati, and Detroit were major crossing points. Hiding in cellars, swamps, and on steamers, and travelling mostly at night made for a very difficult and dangerous journey. Not only the physical realities—little food or water, few if any possessions, long and dangerous marches—but the emotional terror of being stalked and the psychological pain of leaving loved ones behind made it a nightmare experience. But the goal was freedom, and so the dangers were accepted. Once in Upper Canada, many of the former slaves settled on the shores of Lake Erie, in Windsor, Amherstburg, and Sandwich, and also in Chatham, St. Catharines, Hamilton, Brantford, Oakville, and Toronto.

Living in Nineteenth-Century Canada

Towns and Cities

The establishment and growth of the early towns of the French regime—Quebec, Montreal, Trois Rivieres—was based largely on colonial, military, and trade needs. These and later towns like Halifax in Nova Scotia and St. John in New Brunswick were administrative centres for the colonial governors and their staff. They also served as entrepôts for the mercantile system, commercial centres that had access to the sea for the export of colonial resource goods to France first and then to England and the import of manufactured goods from the mother country back to the colonies.[9]

By the early 1800s, the towns took on greater importance for the commerce of the different Canadian colonies where they served as centres for their regions. As the population in the Canadian towns grew and they became cities, more artisans set up workshops in the urban settings and shopkeepers opened stores. In 1837, one Toronto inhabitant reported the progress for consumers: "Two years ago we bought our books at the same shop where we bought our shoes, our spades, our sugar and salt pork! Now we have two good booksellers' shops, and at one of these a circulating library of two or three hundred volumes of common novels."[10]

By mid-century, new transportation technologies—the railroad and the steam ship—and increased industrialization and new factories changed the face of Canadian cities and encouraged their growth. Streets and homes started to

Toronto Harbour ca. 1873

spread out rather than being built along the lines of the earlier surveyors or military planner's grids. However, most cities did not have sidewalks, sewers, water supplies, or lighting on sidewalks. Some water and sewer systems were in place but they were expensive and few and far between.

By 1851, fifteen percent of both Upper and Lower Canadians (or Canada East and Canada West as they were known after 1840) lived in towns or cities of one thousand people or more. In Upper Canada, five cities had one-half of the total urban population of the colony: Toronto (which had been called York until 1834), Kingston, and Bytown (Ottawa), Hamilton, and London. Toronto, which was the centre of a thriving agricultural district, grew from 2235 people in 1828, to 12 571 in 1838, to 30 000 in 1851. In Lower Canada, two cities—Montreal and Quebec—with a much longer history than their Upper Canada counterparts, accounted for three-quarters of the total urban population.

Montreal was the largest city in Canada at the time, having absorbed English, Irish, and Scottish immigrants, especially since the end of the War of 1812. By 1840, the majority of people living in Montreal were English-speaking.[11] Montreal was still a mercantile city, thriving on trade with Britain. Wheat from both Upper Canada and the U.S. was shipped from Montreal to Britain. During the early decades of the century, Quebec City developed a thriving squared-timber industry, sending timber out of its port to England on the ships that would return with cargoes of British immigrants. Between 1812 and 1834, the number of ships anchoring at Quebec city increased from 362 to 1213.[12]

In the Atlantic colonies, towns also grew into cities. By the mid-1800s, Halifax, Nova Scotia, which began as a garrison town with a fine natural harbour, was a thriving port city that served as a centre of trade for the West Indies. The wealthy merchants opened banks—the Bank of Nova Scotia opened in 1832—and ruled business in the city. Samuel Cunard started a steamboat ferry service between Halifax and Dartmouth in 1836 and went on to build the Cunard Line, a transatlantic steamship service that is still one of the great shipping lines of the world. St. John was the largest city in New Brunswick and also the largest shipbuilding port in the Atlantic region. Approximately half of its ships were sold to Britain and the merchants of St. John bought the remainder.

Urban Class Divisions

In both Upper and Lower Canada, the difference in the style and structure of urban homes reflected the wide gap between rich and poor. The substantial brick homes of the wealthy were set apart from the wooden shanties of the poor, which were drafty, ill-heated, unsanitary, and dirty. In Montreal, the division between rich and poor was strengthened by the division along religious and language lines. The Protestant-English upper class lived in large homes with their own newspapers, clubs, and Anglican

City of Halifax, 1835 painted by William Eager.

and Presbyterian churches, well insulated from the French middle and lower classes.

Many of the poor in the colonial cities worked at unstable, low-paying jobs. Wages were so low that workers were not able to save enough to better their condition. And the arrival of new immigrants willing to accept even lower wages meant that the owners of businesses were able to keep workers' wages very low. Fire was a constant danger for those who lived in the crowded wooden shanties that blazed like kindling once a fire got started. Fires in both Montreal and Quebec in the 1840s and 1850s led to a great loss of life. Inadequate food, clothing, and housing also contributed to a high mortality rate. At the inquest into the death of a young girl in Montreal during the severe winter of 1816–17, a witness reported the conditions he found:

The hovel in which the deceased had lived, with her mother, and two sisters, is not fit for a stable. It is open in many parts of the roof and on all sides. There is no other floor than the bare earth. It is a mere wooden stall: it has no window nor any chimney. In the middle is a shallow hole made in the earth, in which there are marks of a fire having been made; and the smoke escaped through the open parts of the roof and sides.[13]

The witness concluded his testimony by saying that, in the dead cold of a Montreal winter, there was no fire in the shallow hole on the day that the girl's body had been found.

Religion and Voluntary Societies

To British colonial officials in the early 1800s, the establishment of a strong Anglican Church in Upper Canada and the Atlantic colonies was essential to ensure political and social stability and to avoid the republican ideas that had brought about the

A painting of a typical Upper Canada rural landscape in the mid-nineteenth century, by Thomas Burrowes.

American Revolution. In Quebec, Catholicism remained the religion of the majority of French Canadians. In the Atlantic region, the Anglican Church did not gain much headway against the Catholic and Evangelical religions (Baptist and Methodist). In Upper Canada, where the Anglican Church was stronger, its ties to the Family Compact meant that it had to spend considerable time and effort defending its privileged status. In addition, both established settlers and new immigrants belonged to a variety of Christian sects: Presbyterians, Quakers, Mennonites, Roman Catholics, and Evangelicals.

Methodism, called the "enthusiastic religion" by some people, stressed the importance of the individual's experience of religious faith. Each person needed to feel a sense of his or her own sin as acutely as possible and needed to struggle to renounce it, experiencing in the process a conversion to salvation. Methodists and Baptists sent out itinerant ministers to travel through an assigned area, preaching and holding services as they went. In a time when people lived in small and scattered settlements, this was an effective method of spreading the faith. The camp meetings and revivals, where people would gather in a secluded area for a few days and listen to forceful sermons on repentance and salvation, helped remind settlers of the role of religion in their lives. The meetings also served as social gatherings and helped establish a sense of community among people widely dispersed throughout a region.

The Evangelical movement was strong in both the Atlantic region and Upper Canada, and its principles would have consequences for the culture and sense of identity of the Canadian people. Because evangelical Christians emphasized each person's individual responsibility, freedom, and his or her personal communication with God, some government officials thought the itinerant preachers were dangerous. Not only did they lack formal education but they also were able to appeal to people's emotions. John Strachan, the Anglican bishop of Upper Canada, believed that Methodism in particular threatened the established political and social order because its supporters were likely to believe in political dissent and even in republican ideas.

Social Welfare

Throughout the Canadian colonies, churches were often the base from which voluntary and benevolent societies operated. These charitable organizations helped to alleviate the severe needs of the poor and the victims of disasters, sponsoring social institutions such as orphanages, hospitals, and shelters for the homeless or destitute. However, they also tried to convince those whom they helped to convert their lives to the principles of their benefactors' religion. These institutions were, according to historians Margaret Conrad and Alvin Finkel, "financed by the more affluent church members and often administered by the women of the church, for whom charitable acts were among the few public roles considered appropriate."[14]

One of the strongest movements associated with the Protestant Church in Canada at this time was the Temperance movement, which started in the late 1820s. Temperance believers advocated the reform of society through the abolition of alcohol. They preached the evil effects of drink on workers who spent their earnings on drink rather than on their families. The movement also published newspapers to further their cause. Indeed, by the 1840s, many religious denominations had their own newspapers that were as widely read as were the political papers.

Along with the religious organizations, there were agricultural societies formed for mutual help among farmers, worker's groups who tried to gain higher wages and safer conditions for their members, immigrant societies made up of people from a specific country or even region of the country, and patriotic societies. In Upper Canada, John Strachan helped form the Loyal and Patriotic Society of Upper Canada at York in 1812. The initial purpose of the society was to provide warm clothing for the militia who were defending Upper Canada's borders against the Americans. The Society's directors would go on to form the nucleus of the Family Compact during the following quarter century. As far as Strachan was concerned, the war had shown the dangers in reform and republican ideas and the need for Upper Canadians to stand as an "immaculate beacon of God's truth in North America."

Education

In the early years of the nineteenth century, education in the Atlantic colonies was largely in the hands of the different Protestant and Catholic Churches, as it was in Quebec. In all the colonies, there were private schools for the wealthy upper classes. In some locales, older children would teach the younger ones, in other places Sunday School was the main educational forum. Most people in the Atlantic colonies and Quebec did not want a public system, fearing that it would interfere with the elements of culture and religion that were taught in local school. During the years between 1838 and 1855, six universities were founded in the Atlantic colonies—Prince of Wales and St. Dunstan's in Prince Edward Island; Mount Allison in New Brunswick; St. Francis Xavier, Acadia University, and St. Mary's in Nova Scotia—and they were all connected to religious denominations.

In Upper Canada, John Strachan, who went on to become the first president of King's College (that later became the University of Toronto), believed that education had three aims: 1) to form character with sound moral and religious principles, 2) to instill religious conviction, and 3) to develop a deep affection for the British Monarchy. The religious and moral formation aspect of education was so prevailing that *An English Spelling Book with Reading Lessons*, one of the first spelling books printed in the colony in the 1840s, opened with the following first lesson: "All sin. I sin. You sin. Sin is bad. Do not sin at all. Sin is not hid. God can see it. Go not in the way of sin. The way of sin is a bad way."[15]

As the century progressed, more Upper Canadians became convinced that schools should be controlled by government rather than by parents in the home or by religious institutions. In 1844, Egerton Ryerson was appointed the superintendent of education in Canada West. Ryerson was a Methodist minister, one of the elected assemblymen who opposed the Anglican Church's dominance of clergy reserves in Upper Canada. Largely through Ryerson's effort, elementary schools, paid for through taxes, were established throughout the colony and eventually became compulsory for all children between the ages of five and sixteen. Ryerson probably did more than anyone else to ensure public education in Canada.

Although enrollment numbers in Upper Canada's public schools increased from 158 159 in 1851 to 423 033 in 1871, the numbers are rather deceiving.[16] In fact, many children in both rural and urban areas did not attend school regularly even though they were on the roles of the schools and school boards. According to one school superintendent of the time, "Irregularity of attendance is the bane and curse of the public schools; it is a log and chain upon the progress of instruction for it blasts and withers the noblest purposes of the best of teachers."[17]

There were many reasons for this irregularity. While it is true that some parents were not convinced that their children needed a school education—or at least not the one that was part of the curriculum in those days—this was also a time when there were no social security safety nets. If parents were out of work or if the family had to move to another place to find work, then the children did not attend school. Families could not always afford to send their children to school in difficult economic times. In rural areas, children were often needed to help on the farms, especially if the family was new to the country and still establishing its farm. In the cities, some children were employed in the factories, though in Canada—unlike England—these numbers were not high. Crop failures and economic depressions, such as the one that occurred in 1851, also contributed to school absenteeism as children tried to contribute to sustaining the family, as did disease and epidemics of cholera, diphtheria, scarlet fever, and smallpox.

Movement of Aboriginal Peoples

During the 1830s, the British parliament instituted investigations into the situation among Aboriginal Peoples throughout the British Empire. The British recognized that the numbers of Aboriginal People were decreasing rapidly. They also believed that Aboriginal Peoples should either be removed to isolated reserves or should be assimilated into the growing British culture in the Canadian colonies. In the words of Charles Grant, the colonial secretary from 1835 to 1839, the goal was "to protect and cherish this helpless Race . . . [and] raise them in the Scale of Humanity."[18]

The Crown Lands Protection Act, which was passed in 1839, declared that all Aboriginal lands were to be Crown land. While this law was supposed to protect the Aboriginals from unscrupulous land agents, it also meant that the British Crown now effectively owned all Aboriginal lands in Canada.[19] Beyond the passing of the Act, little was done about the plight of Aboriginal Peoples in Canada. The superintendent-general of Indian Affairs acted for the Crown and for the Aboriginal Peoples, a situation that led to conflicts of interest. In addition, each colony had its own policy for dealing with Aborignals. While in the Atlantic colonies the policy led to isolation, in Upper and Lower Canada the goal was more assimilation.

In Newfoundland, the last Boethuk had died in 1829, and the few remaining Mi'kmaq people on the island were not accorded status. In New Brunswick, there were fewer than one thousand Mi'kmaq, Wuastukawiuk, and Abenaki left living on a small plot of land along the Miramichi River. In Prince Edward Island, with all land divided among sixty-six absentee landlords, no land was set aside for Aboriginal Peoples.

In Nova Scotia, in 1838, there were only 1 425 Mi'kmaq left, and their numbers continued to decline on the poor land that had been "reserved" for them by the colonial government.[20] Settlers even tried to encroach on these lands. Mi'kmaq hunting grounds, including the land on which Halifax was situated and growing, had been taken from them. In 1841, Peminuit Paul, a Mi'kmaq chief, tried an appeal directly to Queen Victoria, echoing words spoken many times by the Aboriginal Peoples of North America over the previous one hundred years.

> I cannot cross the great Lake to talk to you for my Canoe is too small, and I am old and weak. I cannot look upon you for my eyes do not see that far. You cannot hear my voice across the Great Waters. I therefore send this Wampum and Paper talk to tell the Queen I am in trouble. My people are in trouble . . . No Hunting Grounds–no Beaver–no Otter . . . poor for ever . . . All these Woods once ours. Our Fathers possessed them all . . . White man has taken all that was ours . . . Let us not perish.[21]

For the most part, colonial authorities ignored Aboriginal pleas.

In Upper and Lower Canada, the estimated Aboriginal population living near settled areas was

---

Review...Reflect...Respond

1. How did new ideas about women among middle and upper class urban residents change the lives of women everywhere in Canada? Why did these ideas originate in urban areas?

2. How would immigrant voyages to Canada, such as those of the Irish, change the definition of what it meant to be a Canadian in the nineteenth century? How much is the immigrant experience a part of the Canadian identity today?

3. Did the Bagot Commission help or further harm Aboriginal Peoples in Upper and Lower Canada?

eighteen thousand. The Indian Affairs superintendent wanted to establish reserves to "civilize" the Aboriginal Peoples of the region using the sale of Aboriginal lands to finance what were to be model farms and villages. The recommendation of the Bagot Commission of 1842–44 was the establishment of a central control for all the colonies and recognition that the Aboriginal Peoples had a claim to land in Canada. Reserves were to be established with clear boundaries, and the people were to be taught the agricultural methods of the whites and encouraged to hold individual rights to parcels of land rather than holding land communally as a people.

Workers and Culture in Canadian Colonies

Working in Upper Canada

In Upper Canada, many people worked as farmers during the early- to mid-1800s. With the growing market for wheat in Britain, the grain quickly became the main crop and many farmers were able to sell their surpluses to merchants for export. According to historian, J.M. Bumsted, "In 1840—admittedly a very good year—the St. Lawrence mercantile system exported, mainly to the United Kingdom, over 1.7 million bushels of wheat and flour."[22] Many of the larger cities and towns, such as Brantford and London, served as export ports as well as suppliers for their region.

For workers in the cities and towns of Upper Canada, the nineteenth century was a time of transition, from pre-industrial to semi-industrial. For example, in Hamilton, where the population grew tenfold from fourteen hundred in 1833 to fourteen thousand in 1851, workers were employed in the ironworks, the Gurney stoveworks, and carriage factories.[23] Men could find seasonal work as labourers in canal construction in both Upper and Lower Canada. Though the work was dangerous and the pay low, many of the new immigrants had no option but to take whatever work they could get. The

workers sometimes went on strike for better wages and conditions, but these strikes were quickly put down by colonial administrators who called in the troops to support the employers against the workers.

In both the cities and the rural areas of Upper Canada, work was often transient. Factories employed workers for as long as needed. If there was a slowdown in the economy or if the factory owners hit a bad stretch, then workers were let go. According to historian, Ian E. Davey, large numbers of people in both the rural and the urban areas were on the move during the eighteenth century. Labourers might work by the day or the week and then be out of work again. Farmers would work in logging camps for the winter months. Canal, railroad, and road construction workers worked their way through the countryside; skilled workers moved on when there was no more work to be found in a particular city or town. At other times, whole families would move on in hopes of finding work or a better life in a new part of Canada or the United States.

Literary Culture in Upper Canada

During this time, the colonial literary culture of Upper Canada was still heavily influenced by British culture. There were not many homegrown productions; most books came from England and the northern American states. Newspapers were plentiful throughout the colony and had a wide audience for the political and regional concerns, as well as for the fiction, serialized novels, and poetry that made up their content. Newspapers became the vehicles for spreading popular culture as well as opposing political views.

John Richardson, an Upper Canadian who had fought in the War of 1812 alongside Tecumseh, wrote and published *Wacousta*, a romanticized and rather bloody fiction based on the siege of Detroit and the capture of Michilimackinac in 1763 when Pontiac and his warriors were fighting against British domination. Richardson's book was published in London and Edinburgh in 1832 and eventually in

Montreal in 1868. Richardson was never able to earn a living by his novel writing though and continued to serve in the military at various times and worked as a journalist for both English and Canadian newspapers as well as trying his hand in politics and publishing.

The Strickland sisters, Susanna Moodie and Catharine Parr Traill were published writers in England before they came to Upper Canada in 1832 and settled on farms. Their father had died in 1818 and they and their sisters earned their living by writing. Catharine Parr Traill's, *The Backwoods of Canada*, was published in London in 1836. In eighteen letters from Canada to her family and friends in England, the author describes her natural surroundings in precise detail and offers suggestions on how other pioneer women could survive living in the "backwoods."

Before she left England, Susanna Moodie was involved in the anti-slavery movement in London where she wrote books against slavery. Moodie and her husband first homesteaded near Cobourg and then in the backwoods north of Peterborough, where she lived for five years and raised five children. Her sister and her family lived nearby. Moodie's *Roughing It in the Bush* is an autobiographical account of her life as a pioneer and of the people whom she encountered. She also published poetry, novels, and short stories in the literary magazine the *Literary Garland*, which was published in Montreal.[24]

Web Connection

www.mcgrawhill.ca/links/definingcanada

Go to the Web site above to read Catharine Parr Traill's letters about arriving in Canada.

Lower Canada

During the first half of the nineteenth century, the farmers of Lower Canada suffered through an agricultural crisis. The seigneurial system was still in place, and farmers worked plots that were generally smaller than those in Upper Canada. The emphasis on growing wheat for export had weakened land that had been overfarmed for the previous two hundred years by the habitants had been in the region. In addition, the acreage belonging to each family unit had shrunk as farms were subdivided to give land to the sons to start their own homes, families, and farms. By the 1830s, Lower Canadian farmers could not produce enough wheat to feed the colony's growing population. The combination of crop failures, poor prices for wheat and other produce, and the need to pay seigneurial dues out of harvested crops contributed to the agricultural crisis. In addition, the prospects of gaining seasonal work in the fur trade as *voyageurs* had eroded after 1790, when furs became less important to the Canadian colonial economies than wheat and timber.

In Montreal and Quebec, workers lived in conditions similar to those of their counterparts in Toronto or Hamilton. French Canadians and newly arrived immigrants worked in the timber and ship-building industries and on the bridges, canals, and railways that were now being constructed to link Montreal with the United States and Upper Canada. But their work was seasonal and dangerous; they lived in crowded quarters and received poor pay. By the 1830s and 1840s, workers were beginning to form organizations for mutual support. Tailors, shoemakers, bakers, carpenters, printers, mechanics, firefighters, painters, stonecutters, and milkmen all had their own associations.[25] There was also a growing middle class of French-speaking professionals—lawyers, notaries, journalists, and clerks—in the cities. These men had been trained in the classical seminaries established by the French-Canadian Catholic bishops to train priests after the French Revolution. Even though allegiance to the church was not always strong among these professionals during the first half of the century, the commitment to French history, language, and culture was growing throughout the colony.

Literary Culture in Lower Canada

In Lower Canada, the French Canadians were fighting for the survival of their culture.

The masthead of *Le Canadien*, a French-language newspaper started in 1806, read "Our religion, our language, and our laws." The paper and its editors, Pierre Bédard and François Blanchet, denounced the British rule of Lower Canada and aroused nationalist feelings among French Canadians. As time went on the journalists helped polarize the gap between English and French-Canadian interests and aspirations as they advocated the right of the elected assembly to decide public policy for the colony. The French writer Alexis de Tocqueville said of *Le Canadien* "Anything which can inflame popular passions great and small against the English is raised in this paper."[26] Sir James Henry Craig, the governor of Lower Canada in 1809–10 tried to halt the newspaper's publication as he considered it a threat to British authority in the colony. For a time, he even imprisoned Bédard and Blanchet in an effort to stop their attacks.

François-Xavier Garneau also believed in French nationalism. He is viewed among many Quebecers as French Canada's first national historian. He went to school in Quebec City where he trained as a notary but also had a lifelong interest in French-Canadian politics and history. When Lord Durham, in his report of the causes of the rebellions in Upper and Lower Canada, claimed that the French Canadians were a people without a history or a literature, Garneau decided to write his history of the French in North America. He would prove that his people did indeed have a long history. Garneau's history is considered by many to be the beginning of literature in French Canada. He called his work, *Histoire du Canada*, and published it in four volumes between 1845 and 1852. He wrote about the history of French Canadians as a struggle for survival against the untamed wilderness and Aboriginal Peoples in the early days, then against the early settlers of the Thirteen Colonies, against the British conquerors, and then against the English-speaking inhabitants of Lower Canada. His work was very influential and helped inspire a sense of national pride in French Canadians.[27]

The French nationalist theme and appreciation for French-Canadian ancestors also appeared in Lower Canadian poetry written by Octave Crémazie, Antoine Gérin-Lajoie, and Philippe Aubert de Gaspé. Crémazie's *Le Canada* was written in 1859 and reflects the growing sense of a unique and honoured French-Canadian culture and identity within the British colonies of Canada:

Greetings, O Heaven of my fatherland!
Greetings, O noble St Lawrence!
In my softened soul you name
Flows as an intoxicating perfume.
O Canada, you son of France,
Who covered you with her blessings
You, our love, our hope,
Who will ever forget you?[28]

Behind Bonsecours Market, Montreal by William Raphael, NGC, 6673.

Bonsecours Market, Montreal in the early nineteenth century, as painted by William Raphael.

Review...Reflect...Respond

1. How did the rise in industrialism lead to a more transient work culture for both urban and rural workers in Canada?

2. Are newspapers still the vehicles for spreading popular culture today as they were in the nineteenth century?

3. Why is François-Xavier Garneau viewed by many as Quebec's first national historian?

Working in the Atlantic Colonies

In the Atlantic region, people earned their living in the industries that predominated in each colony: timber production and ship-building in New Brunswick; fishing in Newfoundland; farming for internal use and for export to the Atlantic region in Prince Edward Island; and farming, fishing, ship-building, and the import and export trade in Nova Scotia.

The closeness to both timber supplies and open water were contributing factors to the development of shipbuilding as an important industry throughout the Atlantic colonies. The region became a major producer of ocean-going vessels that were sold in Britain, in the Canadian colonies, and in the United States. Between 1815 and 1860, more than 2 million tonnes of shipping was built in the region. Saint John, New Brunswick, had twenty-five shipyards. [29] A newspaper commentator said, in 1848 that "Whatever Saint John is, it must be admitted that shipbuilding and the timber trade have made it." [30] And there were many more shipyards throughout the colony. For the men who built the ships, as for their counterparts in Lower Canada, the work was seasonal and could be dangerous, especially when the onset of frost in autumn made the timber slippery. As in the other colonies of Canada, workers in the Atlantic region received no compensation for injuries suffered on the job.

In Newfoundland, during the early years of the nineteenth century, fewer fishing ships came from Britain to catch cod. As a consequence the dried-cod industry's growth was dramatic and became based in Newfoundland. In 1754, Newfoundland fishers produced 212 616 of the 437 316 quintals (a weight of 100 pounds) of the cod harvested off the island. By 1816, their share of the total was 739 977 out of 819 200. [31]

The wave of immigration from Britain during the first half of the nineteenth century made a difference in the industrial and cultural landscape the Atlantic colonies, especially of Nova Scotia. Between 1785 and 1849, approximately forty thousand Catholic and Protestant Scots arrived to settle mainly in Nova Scotia. Many became involved in the import-export trade of the colony and in timber and shipbuilding. The Irish also settled in the region. By 1850, they made up one-half of the population of Saint John and Fredericton in New Brunswick and the city of St. John's in Newfoundland. The Catholic Irish, separated from the more powerful Protestant merchant class by language, religion, and tradition, often worked as labourers in the ship-building and timber trades, as farmers, or as domestic servants.

Literary Culture in the Atlantic Colonies

One of the most important figures in the development of the Atlantic region's literary culture was Joseph Howe of Halifax, Nova Scotia, who followed his father into the family printing business in 1818. By the time he was twenty-four, Howe was publishing his own newspaper, *The NovaScotian*, which became the leading newspaper in the colony. As did many other colonial newspapers, *The NovaScotian* carried international news, reports on local politics, mercantile advertising, poetry, essays, and serialized fiction. [32] Joseph Howe was also a political reformer who successfully defended himself against a case of libel brought by government officials whom his paper

François-Xavier Garneau's *Histoire du Canada*

In 1845, François-Xavier Garneau published the first volume of his *Histoire du Canada* in Quebec. His work became the most important history book for a century in Quebec and fostered French Canadians' pride in themselves as a people. In his introduction, Garneau says that history has become by his time "a rigorously analytic science." Not only are the facts of history told, but the causes of those facts are investigated "with precision and discernment." He goes on to praise the presence of the common people in history books of his time, whereas before the stories were all about the great chiefs and their actions. Then he goes on to speak of the French people in Canada.

In a young colony, each forward step is full of import for the future. We should grossly mistake, if we regarded the early pioneer, with hatchet in hand, leveling the trees in his way in the Laurentian valley, as mere woodman, toiling only to satisfy the daily wants of his body. The work he was then engaged in, humble as it might seem, drew after it results far more vast and infinitely more durable than the contemporary feats of arms stricken in his own country, the report of which rang through Europe. The history of the discovery and foundation of French Canada has general interests as great as the recorded origin of any other colonial empire on this continent. The boldness of a Cartier, the first who set up a tent at the mountain foot of Hochelaga, amidst unknown tribes of wild men, inhabitants of a region well nigh 300 leagues inland; the perseverance of a Champlain, contending, not merely with material obstacles but also with the apathy which denied him means to overcome them, yet succeeding at last in founding a colony yet to become an empire; the sufferings of its first inhabitants, and their sanguinary wars with the famous Iroquois tribes, confederated against them; the exploration of nearly the whole interior of North America, from Hudson's Bay to the Mexican Gulf on one traversing line, from Acadia to the Rocky Mountains on another; the military expeditions of Canadians in the North, in Newfoundland, towards Virginia, and into Louisiana; the foundation, by seculars or missionaries, of the earliest European settlements in Michigan, Wisconsin, Louisiana, and eastern Texas: here is surely a striking amount of operations of import high enough to arrest our attention and win the admiration of our posterity. Their recorded incidents attending these impart to our early history a variety, a richness of coloring, constantly affecting the imagination and interesting the mind of those who read it....

When we contemplate the history of Canada as a whole, from the time of Champlain till our own day, we first remark its two great divisions - the period of French supremacy, and that of British domination. The annals of the former are replete with the incidents of wars against the savages and the people of the conterminous British colonies, since become the United States; the other portion is signalized by parliamentary antagonism of the colonists to all infractions of their nationality and designs against their religion. The difference of the arms defensively used during these two periods, shows the Canadian nation under two very distinct aspects; but it is the second epoch which, naturally enough, may most interest the existing generation. There is something at once noble and touching in the spectacle of a people defending the nationality of their ancestors; that sacred heritage which no race, how degraded soever, has every yet repudiated. Never did cause of a loftier character or more holy nature inspire a heart rightly place, or better merit the sympathies of all generous minds.

1. As *Histoire du Canada* was written in 1845, to what document might Garneau have written this in response?
2. What does Garneau mean when he writes, " The difference of the arms defensively used during these two periods, shows the Canadian nation under two very distinct aspects..."?

The Royal William, built in the shipyards of Lower Canada, was the first ship to travel from North America to England using only steam power. She left Pictou, Nova Scotia, on August 17, 1833, and ushered in the era of trans-Atlantic steamships.

had strongly criticized. According to Howe, his aim throughout his publishing and political careers was to elevate his fellow Nova Scotians to "something more ennobling, exacting and inspiring, calculated to enlarge the borders of their intelligence, and increase the extent and area of their prosperity"[33]

Thomas McCulloch, the author of *Letters of Mephibosheth Stepsure*, was a Presbyterian minister who was born in Scotland and who came to Nova Scotia in 1803. He became principal of the highly respected Pictou Academy in 1809 and the first president of Dalhousie College in 1818. McCulloch's *Letters* was first printed in serial form in the newspaper *The Acadian Reformer* and was reprinted in book form as *The Stepsure Letters* in 1862. In his fiction, McCulloch presented a humourous and satirical commentary on the characters and interests of the colony.

McCulloch's writings influenced Thomas Chandler Haliburton who wrote *The Clockmaker, or the Sayings and Doings of Samual Slick of Slickville*. Haliburton was a member of the elected assembly for Nova Scotia, a lawyer, a judge, and a businessman, as well as the author of many books. From 1823 to 1860, he wrote books and articles on provincial history, political pamphlets, and fiction.[34] Haliburton's *Clockmaker* was first published in twenty-two installments in Joseph Howe's *NovaScotian* during 1835. Howe was also the book publisher for the first, second, (1838) and third (1840) installments of the *Sam Slick* stories. In the series, Sam Slick is a Yankee peddler who tricks Nova Scotians into buying his goods; the stories are told using local dialects of the time and short incidents to point out moral lessons for the people of the colony. Haliburton's books were very popular during their day—going through eighty editions during the nineteenth century—and Haliburton was the first Canadian writer to gain an international reputation. Indeed, even today Windsor, Nova Scotia, still has a Sam Slick Society which celebrates Sam Slick Days each August.

Conclusion

By the mid-nineteenth century, the people of the Atlantic colonies—as well as those of Upper and Lower Canada—were forming a clearer idea of who they were. British North Americans were gaining a distinctive culture and identity and a sense of their own independence. Their politics, economies, and society were becoming less English, Irish, Scottish, German, and Welsh. They were Nova Scotians now, or Eastern and Western Canadians, New Brunswickers, Prince Edward Islanders, or Newfoundlanders. In 1850, they did not know it yet, but the people living in the northern half of North America were also well along the path to becoming Canadians.

Notes

1. Alison Prentice et al., *Canadian Women: A History*, (Toronto: Harcourt Brace Javanovich, 1989) p. 72.
2. Prentice et al., p. 157.
3. W.H. Graham, *The Tiger of Canada West* (Toronto: Clarke, Irwin, 1962), pp. 92–93.
4. Professor Gerhard Rempel, Western New England College, "The Industrial Revolution."
5. J.M. Bumsted, *The Peoples of Canada: A Pre-Confederation History* (Toronto: Oxford University Press, 1992) p. 190.
6. Ibid., p. 197
7. Ibid., p. 197
8. Pádaic Ó Laighin, "Grosse-Ile: The Holocaust Revisited," in *The Untold Story: The Irish in Canada*, Volume 1, eds. Robert O'Driscoll and Lorna Reynolds, pp. 75-95.
9. James H. Marsh, ed., *The Canadian Encyclopedia*, (Toronto: McClelland & Stewart, 2000) p. 2431
10. Bumsted, *The Peoples of Canada: A Pre-Confederation History*. p. 217.
11. Margaret Conrad and Alvin Finkel, *History of the Canadian Peoples*, Volume 1, (Toronto: AddisonWesley, 1998) pp. 256, 262.
12. Don Gillmor et al., *Canada: A People's History*, Volume 1, (Toronto: McClelland & Stewart, 2001) p. 248 .
13. Conrad and Finkel, *History of the Canadian Peoples*, Volume 1, p. 264.
14. Conrad and Finkel, p. 235.
15. Bumsted, *The Peoples of Canada: A Pre-Confederation History*. p. 263.
16. "Education in Colonial British North America," by Ian E. Davey, in J.M. Bumsted's *Interpreting Canada's Past*, Volume 1, 2nd edition, p. 462.
17. As quoted in Davey, p. 466.
18. Olive Dickason, *Canada's First Nations: A History of Founding Peoples from Earliest Times*, (Toronto: Oxford University Press, 2002) p. 203.
19. Dickason, *Canada's First Nations*. p. 225.
20. Dickason, *Canada's First Nations*. pp. 206-208.
21. Bumsted, *The Peoples of Canada: A Pre-Confederation History*. p. 229.
22. Ibid., p. 209.
23. Conrad and Finkel, *History of the Canadian Peoples*, Volume 1, p. 257.
24. *Canadian Encyclopedia* CD-ROM, Susanna Moodie entry.
25. Conrad and Finkel, *History of the Canadian Peoples*, Volume 1, p. 263
26. *Craig Brown, ed., The Illustrated History of Canada*, (Toronto: Key Porter Books, 2000). p. 210
27. *The Canadian Encyclopedia*, CD-ROM version, entry for François-Xavier Garneau.
28. *Conrad and Finkel, History of the Canadian Peoples, Volume 1*, p. 388.
29. Conrad and Finkel, *History of the Canadian Peoples*, Volume 1, p. 223.
30. Bumsted, *The Peoples of Canada: A Pre-Confederation History*, p. 213.
31. Conrad and Finkel, *History of the Canadian Peoples*, Volume 1, p. 221.
32. Bumsted, *The Peoples of Canada: A Pre-Confederation History*, p. 231.
33. *The Canadian Encyclopedia*, p. 1110.
34. *The Canadian Encyclopedia*, pp. 1033–1034.

Chapter 10 Review

Knowledge & Understanding

1. Identify six of the following concepts and explain their significance to Canadian history and the development of Canadian culture and identity.

   census
   immigration
   epidemic
   Underground Railroad
   Methodism
   temperance movement
   social welfare
   social class divisions

2. Explain the meaning of the term "separate sphere." Write two paragraphs in which you summarize the ideal implied in the term and the reality of women's lives in mid-nineteenth century Canada.

3. Describe the causes and influences that lay behind reforms to the education system in Upper Canada during the nineteenth century.

Thinking & Inquiry

4. Research at Statistics Canada to find census data for the beginning, the middle, and the end of the 20th century. Create a comparison chart, beginning with the date 1845 and including data for each of the provinces and territories of Canada. Then create a bar graph to visually represent the data in your chart. Write an extended caption for your bar graph in which you explain how the changes that have taken place have been affected by immigration and urbanization.

5. Create a chart listing the different groups of immigrants who came to Canada during the nineteenth century. For each group, explain their reasons for leaving their homelands (push and pull factors), explain why they settled where they did, and describe how each group has left its mark on Canadian culture.

Communication

6. Write a letter to the editor in role as one of the medical personnel on Grosse Île during the epidemic. The newspaper you are writing to is published in Upper Canada.

7. There were a number of Canadian books and newspapers mentioned in this chapter. Investigate and write a media report on one of these publications. Your report should focus on how the book or periodical presents the popular culture and way of life of Canadians of the time in which it was written. You should also comment on how useful the publication would be as a research resource for someone studying Canadian history, culture, and identity. Consider bias and stereotyping as you evaluate the publication.

Application

8. Imagine that you have the opportunity to interview four members of Canadian society in the mid-19th century: a political reformer, an urban worker, an education reformer, and a female settler. Write five questions that you might ask each of these people about the social conditions in which they live. Then respond to each question from the perspective of the interviewee.

9. Find a monument commemorating an historic event in your city, town or region. Research the person or event being commemorated and write a narrative that answers the questions Who? What? Where? When? Why? and How? Also comment on the ways this monument contributes to your region's culture and identity.

CHAPTER 11

Toward Confederation

The one thing needed for Canada is to rub down all sharp angles and to remove those asperities which divide our people on questions of origin and religion. I look to the future of my adopted country with hope though not without anxiety.

–D'ARCY MCGEE

Lord Durham's report on the causes of the Upper and Lower Canadian rebellions recommended the union of Upper and Lower Canada into one legislature and the institution of responsible government. In 1838, the British government accepted the first of his recommendations but rejected the second. With the repeal of the Corn Laws that had protected Canadian exports through preferential tariffs, the British North American colonies became more independent from Britain and started to look to the United States for economic alliances. Throughout the colonies, politicians, promoters, and investors advocated expansion of railroads, which employed thousands of workers. In the minds of many, the railroads would benefit both society and the economy.

The union of Upper and Lower Canada into one elected assembly brought further conflicts between French and English, conservative and reform Canadians. Coalitions between politicians in Canada East and West—first between Robert Baldwin and Louis Hippolyte LaFontaine and later between George-Étienne Cartier and John A. Macdonald—allowed some calm in the tumultuous assemblies of those years. However, the elected assembly had little real power until 1848 when the first colonial responsible government became a reality in Nova Scotia.

Throughout the British North American colonies, ideas of political reform continued to flourish. By the end of the Charlottetown Conference of 1864, there was general agreement that a federal union could benefit all the colonies. The politicians worked the details of the constitution for the new union at the Quebec Conference later the same year. Although it took some time to get the politicians and the people of the colonies to agree by 1867 Queen Victoria signed the British North America Act into law. Canada had become a nation.

11

1839 — Lord Durham issues report to British government on the state of affairs in Upper and Lower Canada

Act of Union unites Upper and Lower Canada — **1841**

1846 — Britain repeals the Corn Laws, ending preferential treatment for Canadian wheat and grains

Baldwin and LaFontaine form the first responsible government in the combined colony — **1848**

1852 — The Grand Trunk Railway is incorporated and completed five years later

Charlottetown Conference discusses the possibility of uniting Nova Scotia, New Brunswick, Prince Edward Island, and Newfoundland — **1864**

Quebec Conference produces 72 resolutions, the basis of the British North America Act

1867 — Queen Victoria signs the British North America Act into law on March 29

By the end of this chapter, you will be able to

- demonstrate an understanding of colonial history as it contributed to the concept of Canada as the product of "two founding nations"

- demonstrate an understanding of the causes and implications of Canadian regional differences

- analyze why and how the people of Quebec have acted to preserve their political identity

- describe the role of significant Quebec-based political figures in the development of the French presence in Canada

- demonstrate an understanding of the principles of the Canadian political system

- describe the role of selected significant events and legislation in the development of the current Canadian political system

Lord Durham's Report

In May of 1838 the British sent John George Lambton, the earl of Durham, into the turmoil that had led to the rebellions in Upper and Lower Canada. As governor general and high commissioner of British North America, Durham had two assignments: to govern Canada and to set up an inquiry into the causes of the rebellions. Durham immediately appointed five members of his own staff to assist him rather than any of the members of the executive councils or leaders of either the English or French parties in Upper and Lower Canada.

Durham's first challenge was what to do with the more than 150 prisoners from the Lower Canada rebellion. By obtaining confessions from nine of the prisoners, whom he exiled to Bermuda, he pardoned the other 141 on Queen Victoria's coronation day. However, Durham did not have the authority to do either, nor to permanently exile Louis Papineau and several others of his party. When the British government disallowed his exile orders, Durham felt that he had to resign and return to England. He had been in Canada only five months.

John George Lambton, Lord Durham, Governor General of British North America, 1838–1840.

Nonetheless, Durham's report, which he presented to the British government in 1839, carried weight and had an impact on the future of Canada. He offered an incisive analysis of the causes of the unrest, and he proposed major reforms in the political and constitutional structure of the Canadian colonies. He identified two fundamental sources of the discontent in Upper and Lower Canada. The first was the friction between the appointed legislative councils and the elected legislative assemblies. He felt that it was the Family Compact that was blocking the economic and social development of Upper Canada. The second source of the problem, was the "two nations warring in the bosom of a single state" in Lower Canada and, the backward nature, in Durham's view, of the French Canadians whom he called "a people with no literature and no history." French Canadians were, understandably, outraged at Durham's description of them.[1]

Durham made a number of recommendations that started a chain of events that would lead, eventually, to the Charlottetown and Quebec Conferences and ultimately, to Canadian Confederation. He proposed that Upper and Lower Canada be united in a common assembly. He hoped that this union would cause French Canadians to become assimilated into the English Canadian majority. And in 1841 Upper Canada became Canada West and Lower Canada became Canada East. Durham also recommended that a form of responsible government, based on the British cabinet system, be instituted. He believed that the politicians who were elected by the voters—rather than the governor who was appointed by the British government—should make domestic policy in the colonies. The governor's executive council should be selected from, or at least approved by, the party that held the majority in the elected assembly. This proposal was rejected by the British government, which was afraid that responsible government would weaken the power and control of the British empire. Responsible government was not put in place until 1847. The first responsible party governments were elected to power in 1848 in Nova Scotia and then in the united Canadas.

Excerpts from Lord Durham's Report, 1839

With both Upper and Lower Canada in a state of turmoil, in 1838 Britain sent Lord Durham to investigate the grievances held by the citizens in each of the colonies. Durham's mandate was to determine the cause of the discontent and submit a report to the Imperial Parliament in London. Despite the government's resistance to adopt many of the proposals advocated by Lord Durham, the ideas put forth in his A Report on the Affairs of British North America influenced much of the political reforms taking place in the Canadas during the 1840s.

...From the peculiar circumstances in which I was placed, I was enabled to make such effectual observations as convinced me, that there had existed in the constitution of the province, in the balance of political powers, in the spirit and practice of administration in every department of the government, defects that were quite sufficient to account for a great degree of mismanagement and dissatisfaction.

... I expected to find a contest between a government and a people: I found two nations warring in the bosom of a single state: I found a struggle, not of principles, but of races; and I perceived that it would be idle to attempt any amelioration of laws or institutions, until we could first succeed in terminating the deadly animosity that now separates the inhabitants of Lower Canada into the hostile divisions of French and English.

... It will be acknowledged by every one who has observed the progress of Anglo-Saxon colonization in America, that sooner or later the English race was sure to predominate even numerically in Lower Canada, as they predominate already by their superior knowledge, energy, enterprise, and wealth. The error, therefore, to which the present contest must be attributed, is the vain endeavour to preserve a French Canadian nationality in the midst of Anglo-American colonies and states.

... The fatal feud of origin which is the cause of the most extensive mischief, would be aggravated at the present moment by any change which should give the majority more power than they have hitherto possessed. A plan by which it is proposed to ensure the tranquil government of Lower Canada, must include in itself the means of putting an end to the agitation of national disputes in the legislature, by settling, at once and for ever, the national character of the province. I entertain no doubts as to the national character which must be given to Lower Canada; it must be that of the British Empire; that of the majority of the population of British America; that of the great race which must, in the lapse of no long period of time, be predominant over the whole North American continent. Without effecting the change so rapidly or so roughly as to shock the feelings and trample on the welfare of the existing generation, it must henceforth be the first and steady purpose of the British government to establish an English population, with English laws and language, in this province, and to trust to none but a decidedly English legislature...

The utter want of municipal institutions giving the people any control over their local affairs, may indeed be considered as one of the main causes of the failure of representative government, and of the bad administration of the country. If the wise example of those countries in which a free representative government has alone worked well, had been in all respects followed in Lower Canada, care would have been taken that, at the same time that a parliamentary system based on a very extended suffrage, was introduced into the country, the people should have been entrusted with a complete control over their own local affairs, and been trained for taking their part in the management of that local business which was most interesting and most intelligible to them. But the inhabitants of Lower Canada were unhappily initiated into self-government at exactly the wrong end, and those who were not trusted with the management of a parish, were enabled, by their votes, to influence the destinies of a State....

Two kinds of union have been proposed. federal and legislative. By the first, the separate legislature of each province would be preserved in its present form, and retain almost all its present attributes of internal legislation; the federal legislature exercising no power, save in those matters of general concern, which may have been expressly ceded to it by the constituent provinces. A legislative union would imply a complete incorporation of the provinces included in it under one legislature, exercising universal and sole legislative authority over all of them, in exactly the same manner as the Parliament legislates alone for the whole of the British Isles.

Free Trade and Reciprocity

In 1840, Britain did away with its preferential trading system for British colonies. This meant the end of mercantilism as the primary focus in the economic relationship between Britain and her colonies. The British were moving more heavily into industrialization—40 percent of Britons were employed in mining and manufacturing by 1841—and they needed raw materials from many countries to satisfy the demand for manufactured goods. In 1846, Britain repealed the Corn Laws, which had been in effect since 1791. These laws had set customs duties on wheat and other grains imported into Britain and had given preferential treatment—a lower import duty—to imports from Canada and other British colonies. For Britain, the repeal was preliminary to establishing freer trade, especially with the United States.

Canadian farmers felt the repeal of the Corn Laws sharply because they had come to depend on Britain as a market for their wheat and other grains. The economies of both Canada East (Lower Canada) and Canada West (Upper Canada) depended on these wheat exports to Britain. As the *Quebec Gazette* editorialized,

> Our great ground of complaint is that the British Acts of Parliament created the [empirical] trade, caused capital to be invested in the trade, trusting to these acts, which by the uncertain character they now assume may ruin thousands. We never asked for protection; it was given on the grounds of national policy.[2]

In 1847, Canadian wheat exports were 628 000 bushels; by 1848, after the repeal of the Corn Laws, they fell to 238 000 bushels. In 1847, Canada had exported 651 000 barrels of flour to Britain; in 1848, only 383 000 barrels were exported.[3]

The repeal of the Corn Laws had other consequences for Canada. As the economic considerations that had been so important to Britain in establishing its empire became less critical, Britain decided that Canadians should have more say in their own affairs.

Canadians started to think in terms of a continental rather than a colonial trade system. The construction of canals, the development of the Great Lakes shipping, and the great enthusiasm for railroad construction all seemed to make trade with the United States a viable alternative to colonial trade with Britain.

With the possibility of greater trade with the United States, some Canadians in Canada East and West argued for reciprocity: a cooperative agreement granting trade privileges or freer trade between the United States and Canada. The idea of reciprocity was also popular in the Atlantic colonies. New Brunswickers looked forward to trading more timber and to opening a larger market for their ships if prices could be reduced as a result of lower tariff duties in the United States. Nova Scotians and Prince Edward Islanders thought reciprocity would provide them with new markets for their agricultural products. In 1854, Canada and the United States did sign a Reciprocity Treaty, which lasted until 1866. However, the freer trade was limited to relatively few products, and these were mainly raw materials such as grain, fish, and coal.

The Reciprocity Treaty did change the way that Canadians viewed themselves. Canadians began to realize that they were not necessarily confined to the British mercantile system to survive and to grow. Canadians also began to realize that they could manufacture their own products. As industrialization increased in Canada, they could also find markets for their products within the colonies (with all of the additional immigrants who arrived during the 1850s) as well as exporting them outside the country.

Railways

In the mid-nineteenth century, some people believed that the railroad would not only change agriculture and markets as more produce flowed to growing urban centres, but that it would also help open up new settlement opportunities in today's Prairie provinces. However, railroads were very expensive

A photograph of the opening of the Wellington, Grey & Bruce Railway at Fergus Ontario, 1870

two cities. The contract for the line between Toronto and Sarnia went to a Canadian engineer, Casimir Gzowski, who had emigrated to the colony from Poland. While the Montreal to Toronto line ran into massive cost overruns, Gzowski's portion kept within its budget. During the Grand Trunk's construction as many as fourteen thousand workers and two thousand horses worked on the project in Canada West alone. The Grand Trunk also rented and acquired track from smaller railway companies. At the time of Confederation in 1867, the Grand Trunk was the largest railway system in the world, with 2055 km of track.[5]

The Philosophy of Railroads

In 1850, Thomas Coltrin Keefer, a civil engineer, wrote a pamphlet titled *The Philosophy of Railroads*, which praised the benefits that would come to Canadian

to build and corruption was rampant among the politicians and the railroad promoters and investors. Most politicians and business leaders saw nothing wrong in a member of the elected assembly being an officer in a railroad company that received loans from the politician's party in the government. During the years between 1852 and 1867, railway speculators in Canada, Nova Scotia, and New Brunswick invested over $100 million in Canadian railways. The most expensive and ambitious of these projects was the Grand Trunk Railway, which nearly bankrupt the colony of the United Canadas.[4]

The Grand Trunk, which linked Montreal and Toronto, was incorporated in 1852 and completed in 1857. Much of the financing for the railway was raised in England and an English company, Peto, Brassey, Jackson, and Betts was hired to build the track between the

On June 29, 1864, one of the worst train wrecks in Canadian history took place at the Beloeil Bridge in Canada East. Ninety-nine people died when a Grand Trunk railway worker missed the signal that the drawbridge was open and the train plunged into the river below. Among the dead were ninety-seven immigrants and two railway employees.

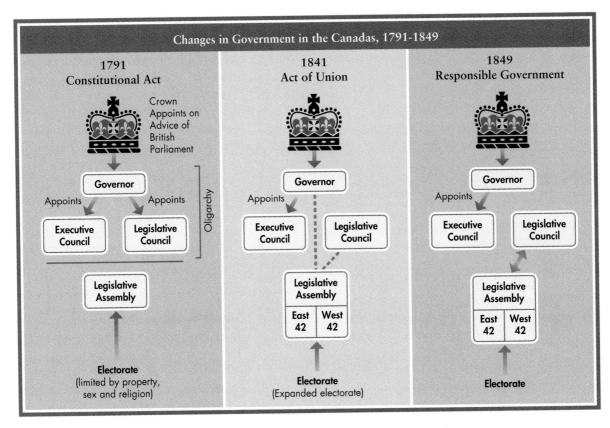

Changes in Government in the Canadas, 1791-1849

1791
Constitutional Act

Crown
Appoints on
Advice of
British
Parliament

Governor

Appoints   Appoints

Executive   Legislative
Council   Council

Oligarchy

Legislative
Assembly

Electorate
(limited by property,
sex and religion)

1841
Act of Union

Governor

Appoints

Executive   Legislative
Council   Council

Legislative
Assembly

| East | West |
| 42 | 42 |

Electorate
(Expanded electorate)

1849
Responsible Government

Governor

Appoints

Executive   Legislative
Council   Council

Legislative
Assembly

| East | West |
| 42 | 42 |

Electorate

Changes in the Government of the Canadas, 1791-1849 — What are the key changes over time?

society and its economy once railroads were built. Keefer's pamphlet gained wide acceptance among railway investors and promoters. Keefer had earlier worked on the expansion of the Welland Canal, and, as a highly respected hydraulic engineer, he went on to establish public water systems—with pumping stations and water pipes—for Montreal, Hamilton, and Ottawa.

Keefer argued that speed, economy, regularity, safety, and convenience were the advantages that would follow the expansion of railroads in Canada. Speed was becoming more important in the transport of goods, and the costs of transporting goods by rail were decreasing as compared with travelling overland by horse-drawn carts or travelling by water through the canal systems. Keefer explained,

Compared with all other land communications, [the railroad's] freighting capabilities may be inferred from the consideration that a horse usually draws from fifteen to thirty hundred weight on a good turnpike of macadamised road (exclusive of vehicle), four to six tons on a plate rail tram road, and fifteen to twenty tons on an edge rail including the wagons; . . .it is needless to enlarge upon its power when travelled by iron horse, with which hunger and thirst are but metaphorical terms, which knows no disease or fatigue, and to which a thousand miles is but the beginning of a journey, and a thousand tons but an ordinary burthen.[6]

Keefer went on to argue that certain goods could only be carried to distant markets by rail:

fresh meats, cattle, pigs, and poultry. Once a railway was in place, the transportation system would become a "public benefactor" to farmers and merchants and indeed to all the people living in the region.

As proof of the superior regularity and dependability of rail transport over canal transport, Keefer noted that railways had been selected to carry the mail and went on to say that "in the winter season" this mode of transportation had "no competitors." As proof of the safety of railway travel, he compared the railway with steamship travel and found that the "explosion, fire, collision, or wrecking" were much more frequent occurrences on the boats than on the trains. As for convenience, he argued that unlike the restrictions of water transportation, which depended on navigable rivers, canals, and lakes, railroads "clamber over mountains and penetrate the most remote corners of the land." Furthermore, there is no "limit to the number of its auxiliary branches, which can be multiplied and extended" until these extensions "give the required facilities to every wharf and every warehouse—to the solitary mill or factory, or to the most neglected districts as an outlet to otherwise worthless products."[7]

Politics in the Canadian Colonies

The British North American reform movements early in the nineteenth century may have led to rebellions in Upper and Lower Canada, but most people in the colonies wanted neither rebellion nor the republican form of government of the United States. The reform movements of the 1820s, 1830s, and 1840s were generally quite conservative in spirit with most reformers wanting to reform the colonial system and preserve the older traditions that were being threatened by economic and social conditions. In Lower Canada, especially, the reformers were intent on preserving and protecting the traditions, religion, and language that formed French-Canadian culture.

The Union of Canada East and Canada West

In 1841, acting on the recommendations of Lord Durham two years earlier, the British government united Upper and Lower Canada with the Act of Union. What had been two colonies became Canada, now designated Canada East and Canada West. There would be just one governor, one elected assembly, and one language—English—in the legislature of the colony. French and English, Protestants and Catholics would have to learn to compromise and work together.

Neither the citizens of Canada East nor those of Canada West much liked the union. Because there were more French- than English-Canadians in 1841, Britain had decided that each of the Canadas would have equal representation in the elected assembly. This was supposed to allay the people of Canada West's fear of domination by the French Catholics; however, that fear remained a divisive factor throughout the time the two colonies were united. French Canadians suspected—with justification—that the intention of the union was to assimilate them and erode their French culture. In the assembly, now held in Montreal, French Canadians banded together and often voted in a block. With this united front they were often able to defeat the policies of Canada West, which was beset by political divisions and parties with different agendas.

LaFontaine was one of the few reform political leaders left in Canada East after the failed rebellion of Lower Canada in the 1830s. Neither LaFontaine nor his French-Canadian colleagues had any interest in being assimilated into English culture and identity, and they decided that they had to work with the English reformers in Canada West if they wanted to retain their French culture. When LaFontaine and his fellow French Canadians were prevented from voting in 1841 by a mob of English conservatives, LaFontaine withdrew his name from the running to avoid bloodshed.

THE HON. ROBERT BALDWIN.

Sir Louis-Hippolyte La Fontaine

Robert Baldwin and Louis-Hippolyte LaFontaine

Also in 1841, executive council member from Canada West, Robert Baldwin, was soon pushed to resign his position when the governor refused to grant responsible government to the colony. He then convinced his father, who was the member for North York and also a firm believer in responsible government, to resign his seat and allow LaFontaine to run for election in his place. LaFontaine won the by-election and was returned to the legislature of the united Canadas. In the next election, Robert Baldwin ran in Rimouski in Canada East where he was elected by the largely French-Canadian electorate. Robert Baldwin then sent a letter to Louis Hippolyte LaFontaine suggesting that the two men form a coalition to govern the new colony of the united Canadas. The Baldwin-LaFontaine coalitions of 1842 to 1843 and 1848 to 1851 continued to fight against the oligarchies and the appointed executive council and for responsible government. As historians Margaret Conrad and Alvin Finkel report, several governors were unwilling to grant the assembly this power. Lord Sydenham (governor from 1840 to 1841, Sir Charles Bagot (1841–43),

and Sir Charles Metcalfe (1843–46) "attempted, in varying degrees, to retain the former powers" of earlier lieutenant governors and their Family Compact and Chateau Clique members. Finally in 1848 when the British government was changing its colonial and mercantile policies, Lord Elgin, the new lieutenant governor, called on La Fontaine and Baldwin to form a ministry that would be the new executive council to the governor.

In 1848, with a large reform majority, Baldwin and LaFontaine formed the first responsible government in the combined colony. From this time on, the executive council, now called the cabinet, would need the support of the majority in the elected legislature in any of its decisions. The members of the old oligarchy in both Canada West and Canada East reacted with fury to the onset of responsible government. If they could not be guaranteed a privileged place in the executive councils of the governors, their powerbase would be destroyed. When in 1849, LaFontaine sponsored a bill that would compensate people in Canada East for losses incurred in the rebellions in Lower Canada, the conservatives were further enraged. They demanded that the governor, Lord Elgin, refuse to sign the Rebellion Losses Bill. Even though Elgin personally disagreed with the bill, he signed it into law, saying that the bill had been passed by the duly elected Canadian legislature and he had no right to veto it, a riot broke out in which the parliament buildings in Montreal were burned.

The Macdonald-Cartier Coalition

By the 1860s the Civil War had broken out in the United States and Canada was once again threatened with invasion from the south. The Americans believed that Britain was siding with the southern Confederate states against the northern states. And some Americans were talking, yet again, of annexation of the Canadian colonies to the United States. There was widespread fear of invasion, both in Canada East and West as well as in the Atlantic colonies.

George-Étienne Cartier was an urbane, sophisticated French-Canadian lawyer who was equally comfortable in French or in English, and with merchants, politicians, and clergymen. In his youth

Cartier had been a member of the Parti Patriote and had been a rebel, but he had fled to the United States early on. After swearing allegiance to the British Crown, he had been allowed to return to Montreal. Once in Montreal he ran for office in the elected assembly and won his first election in 1848, as he would win the elections in his riding for years to come. Once in office Cartier worked to advance his city and French Canada, redrafting property laws and the civil code and working to ensure primary schools for both Protestants and Catholics. While holding public office, Cartier saw no conflict of interest in remaining the lawyer for the Grand Trunk Railway.

John A. Macdonald arrived in Canada from Glasgow, Scotland, as a young boy. He too became a lawyer and lived in Kingston, Ontario, with his wife and infant son. When first his child and then his wife died, Macdonald withdrew from society for a time. After a period of deep mourning, he rejoined the game of politics, which he so thoroughly enjoyed and which he played with such skill for the rest of his life. Macdonald clearly had a

Georges Étienne Cartier

Sir John A. Macdonald

genius for politics and a brilliant legal mind. Even his enemies acknowledged his persuasive skill. Joseph Rymal, a Liberal rival, said of him "Good or bad, able or unable, weak or strong, he wraps them around his finger as you would a thread."[8]

The coalition which Cartier and Macdonald established during the 1850s was based on their solid understanding of what they had to do to remain in control of the tumultuous elected assembly of the united Canadas. They also agreed that the future of the railways was interwoven with the future of Canada. They both dreamed of a transcontinental railway that would someday reach from sea to sea. Their coalition had its share of disagreement, many of which were caused by George Brown, Macdonald's political rival in Canada West and the publisher of *The Globe* newspaper. Brown, who also was born in Scotland, started *The Globe* in 1844 and his newspaper eventually became the most important newspaper in the Canadas.

Brown was both anti-French and anti-Catholic, and he insisted that "nunnery and monkery" should not be imposed on Canada West. In his newspaper, he railed against interference of the French-Catholic clergy in political affairs, calling it "papal aggression," proclaiming that there would be "no permanent peace in Canada until every vestige of church domination is swept away."[9] However, Brown also knew how difficult it was to govern the united Canadas as the conflicts between East and West were ongoing. As Francis Hincks, inspector general in the Baldwin-LaFontaine government of 1848–51, said "The truth was that the people occupying Upper and Lower Canada were not homogeneous; but they differed in feelings, language, laws, religion and institutions, and therefore the union must be considered as between two distinct peoples, each returning an equal number of representatives."[10]

Cartier and Macdonald both opposed Brown, but he had a powerful vehicle in his widely read newspaper, which gave him a chance to expound on his political views. When the 1861 census showed that, thanks to the large influx of immigrants during the 1850s, Canada West had a larger population than Canada East, Brown began to advocate that representation in the legislature should be according to population. "Rep by Pop," a slogan he created, became a rallying cry among other people in Canada West who agreed with Brown's views.

However, Cartier, Macdonald, and Brown were all reformers at heart, and they believed that there had to be a better way to structure Canada East and West. In 1862, there was a stalemate between Brown supporters on the one side and Cartier-Macdonald supporters on the other. In four years, there were four failed governments in a row. The two Canadas were half Catholic, half Protestant, one-third French and two-thirds English and were clearly ungovernable. After 1862, Brown began to talk seriously about the benefits of uniting all of the British North American colonies. Brown had been to London and had heard the British politicians speaking in ways that led him to believe that Britain might let the British North American

Population of British North America, 1851-1871			
	1851	1861	1871
Ontario	952 004	1 396 091	1 620 851
Quebec	890 261	1 111 566	1 191 516
Nova Scotia	276 854	330 857	387 800
New Brunswick	193 800	252 047	285 594
Prince Edward Island	62 678*	80 857	94 021
Newfoundland†	—	122 638	158 958
British Columbia	55 000	51 524	36 247**
Manitoba	—	—	25 228
Northwest Territories	—	—	48 000

* Figure is from 1848
† Figures are from 1857 and 1874
** This figure probably understates the Native population of the province by about 15 000

Source: "Series A 2-14. Population on Canada by province, census dates, 1851 to 1976" in *Historical Statistics of Canada*, 2nd ed., ed. F.H. Leacy (Ottawa: Minister of Supply and Services, 1983) and James Hiller, "Confederation Defeated: The Newfoundland Election of 1869" in *Newfoundland in the Nineteenth and Twentieth Centuries: Essays in Interpretation*, ed. James Hiller and Peter Neary (Toronto: University of Toronto Press, 1980

The Population of British North America

colonies form their own nation. Brown, Macdonald, and Cartier formed a coalition to work towards that end. They thought that they might even be able to convince the Atlantic colonies to join in the union, and someday, other provinces in Rupert's Land and British Columbia might also join.

D'Arcy McGee also understood that there would have to be coalitions and compromises. McGee was a former Young Ireland rebel who escaped from Ireland with a price on his head and who after a sojourn in New York, moved to Montreal where he was elected to the assembly in Montreal in 1857. In McGee's words, "The one thing needed for Canada is to rub down all sharp angles and to remove those asperities which divide our people on questions of origin and religion. I look to the future of my adopted country with hope though not without anxiety."[11]

The Atlantic Colonies

In the Atlantic colonies, political reform came about without the degree of strife that accompanied the process in Canada East and Canada West. Although there was sometimes strife in the region, it never reached the volatility or the dimension that it reached in the united province of Canada. The oligarchies were not as entrenched, nor did politicians use loyalty to the crown and the stigma of republicanism as political weapons to keep reformers in line.

Nova Scotia

In Nova Scotia, both conservatives and reformers claimed loyalist ancestry and close ties to Britain. For the most part, they had no wish to take on the republican ideas of the Americans. Joseph Howe, who remained a powerful voice in the Atlantic region for decades, argued strongly—in his newspaper, *The NovaScotian*—FOR RESPONSIBLE GOVERNMENT *and* for firm ties with Britain. In 1836, he was elected to government where he announced his position, "The idea of republicanism, of independence, of severance from the mother country, never crosses my mind . . . I wish to live and die a British subject."[12]

Nonetheless, Howe continued to battle against the colonial elite who had been appointed by a succession of British lieutenant governors and to work for reform and the abolition of the power held by the executive council and their appointees. Howe argued that the people of Nova Scotia should have the same rights as the people of Britain. He agreed with Lord Durham's report on this issue and sent many letters to the colonial secretary in London arguing his case for responsible government. By 1847, the colonial office decided that the governor of Nova Scotia should indeed choose his executive council from members of the ruling party in the assembly. And early in 1848, the elected assembly in Nova Scotia became the first responsible government in the British Empire. Howe was delighted and crowed that Nova Scotians would be proud to be a model for the rest of the British North American colonies, "showing them how representative institutions may be worked to ensure internal tranquillity and advancement in subordination to the paramount interest and authority of the empire."[13]

Howe opposed Confederation. Nova Scotia was the most populous and prosperous colony among the four Atlantic colonies and it had strong ties to Britain. What could Nova Scotians possibly gain from such a union, especially one controlled by Canada East and Canada West? Howe presented his opposition to Confederation in a series of letters called "The Botheration Letters" that were printed in *The NovaScotian*. In one letter, Howe wrote about the loss of identity Nova Scotians would feel if the colony were to join Confederation: "Take a Nova Scotian to Ottawa, away above the tide-water, freeze him up for five months, where he cannot view the Atlantic, smell the salt water, or see the sail of a ship, and the man will pine and die."[14] These letters helped to turn public support behind Howe. As historians R. Douglas Francis, Richard Jones, and Donald Smith wrote in *Origins: Canadian History to Confederation*, "In Howe's opinion, the province looked eastward to the Atlantic Ocean and Britain, rather than westward to the continent and the Canadas."[15]

Analyzing Information

Analyzing information that you hear or read uses a combination of many skills. To effectively use these skills you need to be able to interpret and analyse sources.

Finding and summarizing the main idea and supporting evidence

The main ideas form the backbone, the element that holds the various parts and pieces of the written or verbal information together. Identifying the main ideas and restating them in your own words will help you understand the content and structure of a reading selection or oral presentation.

Identifying the strengths and weaknesses of the supporting evidence

Examining the strengths and weaknesses of the supporting evidence helps you clearly understand the author's argument and eventually to test his/her reasoning or judgment. You need to check the accuracy of facts, examples, statistics and supporting points used by the author as well as their relevancy to the main idea. As well, you must look carefully for omission of facts, examples or statistics that may support a different interpretation.

Evaluating the logic of an argument.

All writers make assertions that they want you to accept. As a critical reader or listener, you should not accept any argument or thesis at face value but recognize that it must be carefully evaluated. An argument or thesis consists of a claim and a support. The claim declares an idea, opinion, judgment or point of view. The support includes evidence (facts, examples statistics, sources) and reasoning (assumptions, beliefs, values). When you evaluate the logic of an argument or thesis you need to be concerned with the process of reasoning as well as the accuracy of the evidence.

Making connections

Many of the historians and authors that you read explore the same issues but approach them in different ways. Comparing and contrasting evidence, assumptions and processes of reasoning can help you to understand the issues in a larger context and test the accuracy of evidence.

Practicing our analysis

Read the following excerpt from Michel Brunet *French Canada and the Early Decades of British Rule, 1760-1791*.

Emigration and the Decapitation of Society

[French] Canadians of the upper class, who refused to submit to the [British] victors, emigrated. The most powerful business men understood that their enterprises would not prosper within the British commercial system. The majority was drawn from honourable families who did not wish to suffer the humiliation of foreign occupation and who wanted to keep all of the advantages which the French empire provided: royal pensions, access to public office, business relations, official protection, contracts with the government and so on. It has been calculated that at least two thousand Canadians left their native land during the ten years which followed the surrender of Montreal. Can one speak about the loss of social leadership? What became of the former leaders who remained in Canada? Their fall, which was inevitable in a vanquished colony where a new body of administrators and executives of British origin was being assembled, is the most striking phenomenon of the first generation after the conquest.

Those who could legitimately regard themselves as leaders of the Canadian community, discovered not without astonishment, that they had no public rights in their own country. The Test Act barred them, as Catholics from careers in administration, whether as councillors or mere justices of the peace.[1]

Michel Brunet, *French Canada and the Early Decades of British Rule*, 1769–1791. (Ottawa: Canadian Historical Association, 1981).

An analysis chart such as the one below will help you prepare to write an analytical report on a document or presentation.

Main Idea or Argument	Supporting Evidence	Strengths & Weaknesses of Evidence	Logic of The Argument	Connections
The British conquest of New France "decapitated" or destroyed French Canadian society	– over two thousand Canadians emigrated – the majority of the emigrants were businessmen and social leaders – the Test Act prevented Catholics from involvement in politics	– strong evidence for why certain Canadians returned to France – questions without answers were weak evidence – impact of the clergy on Canadian society was not addressed	– reasoning behind the evidence is that French society was controlled by business and political leaders	– the loss of the upper strata and leadership in Canadian society left room for the British and Catholic clergy to dominate

Complete an Analysis Chart for the following quotation from Desmond Morton, *A Short History of Canada*.

In September 1760, with Quebec in British hands and Montreal surrounded, the surviving French troops burned their standards, boarded ships, and went home. So did most of the merchants and leaders of the colony. The remaining Canadiens, abandoned in the hands of their enemies, would retain an enduring suspicion of remote imperial strategies and their bloody consequences.

It had taken a century and a half to create New France but now the French were finished with it. To the French Ministry of Marine, the colony had represented huge costs, small returns, and no advantage that fishing concessions off Newfoundland could not match. Voltaire's blunt dismissal of Canada as "several acres of snow" became the official consensus. The British seemed hardly more interested. His Majesty's new Province of Quebec would be made as hospitable to British settlers as the imposition of English law and an elected assembly reserved for Protestants could make it. Narrow boundaries for the new colony cut off the fur-trading hinterland, but incoming British merchants would presumably find other ways to become rich. The conquered Canadiens would undoubtedly accept the blessings of the new regime and become English-speaking, if not necessarily Anglican.[2]

Desmond Morton, *A Short History of Canada*, 3rd revised edition. (Toronto: McClelland & Stewart Inc., 1997), p. 31.

Main Idea or Argument	Supporting Evidence	Strengths & Weaknesses of Evidence	Logic of The Argument	Connections

Web Connection

www.mcgrawhill.ca/links/definingcanada

Go to the above Web site to read an excerpt from one of Joseph Howe's Botheration letters.

But with the adoption of freer trade with Britain and that country's desire to give more power to the colonial assemblies to govern themselves, Howe was out of step with British wishes. Then in November 1861, Americans from the northern states boarded the British ship, the *Trent*, in neutral waters and captured two Confederate officials who were on their way to Europe. The English were outraged and threatened war and sent troops to reinforce the border between the United States and the Atlantic colonies. Although the incident was settled peaceably, there were some in New Brunswick and Nova Scotia, including Joseph Howe, who realized just how vulnerable the Atlantic region was to an American attack and takeover. The combined force of pressure from the British colonial office and of the threat of American aggression eventually persuaded many Nova Scotians that union might be a good deal for them after all. However, Joseph Howe remained an opponent of Confederation.

New Brunswick

In New Brunswick, as in Nova Scotia, there was controversy over the governor and his executive council's control and misuse of revenue from crown lands, particularly timber rights. In 1837, the Colonial Office in London proposed a compromise between the governor and his appointees on the one side and the reformers in the elected assembly on the other. The revenues from the crown lands and timber rights would come under the elected assembly's control, and the assembly would agree to guarantee the salaries of the governor's appointees. Reluctantly, the elected members of the assembly agreed, and control of the crown lands revenue passed to them. The fact that the Colonial Secretary also instructed the governor to choose executive councillors who had the confidence of the assembly also eased tensions.

Through the 1840s and 1850s, for the most part, the path to responsible government progressed quietly in New Brunswick. By the 1860s, the question of an Intercolonial Railway became an issue to both proponents and opponents of union with the rest of the British North American colonies, with some powerful forces arguing for a railway link to the United States rather than to the Canadas.

But then the threat of Fenian raiders caused many New Brunswickers to look more favourably on Confederation. The Fenians were a secret society of Irish Americans who believed that by attacking the British in Canada they could end British rule in Ireland. By the mid-1860s, the Fenians, many of them soldiers who had fought for the north in the American Civil War, threatened to invade Canada. In April of 1866, a small number of Fenians actually landed in New Brunswick and many colonists saw that their best defence lay within a confederated nation. As the Catholic bishop of Arichat on Cape Breton wrote to then Premier Charles Tupper on April 12, 1866 "Altho' no admirer of Confederation on the basis of the Quebec Scheme, yet owing to the present great emergency and the necessities of the times, the union of the Colonies, upon a new basis, we receive with pleasure."[16] Throughout British North America, Fenian raids helped turn the tide towards Confederation.

Prince Edward Island

In Prince Edward Island, the absentee landlord/tenant farmer issue dominated politics in the decades leading up to Confederation. By 1831, elections were being fought over the issue, which became associated with reform principles and the fight for responsible government. William Cooper, who had once been a land agent for one of the absentee landlords, ran on a platform of "our country's freedom and farmers' rights."[17] In 1838,

Cooper's party won the election. He travelled to London to argue the tenant farmer's case to the colonial secretary, but the secretary refused to even meet with him.

By May 1864, the frustrated tenant farmers on the Island had formed the Tenant League, which urged farmers not to pay rent to the agents of the absentee landlords. Throughout the island, tenants not only refused to pay rent but also often met the agents of the landlords with hornblower lookouts. When an agent arrived to either collect rent or to evict non-paying tenants, the lookout would sound the alarm, a crowd would gather, and the agents would be forced to retreat. Some of the politicians on the island had taken up the cause of the Tenant League; others believed that non-payment of rents was doomed to fail and that only constitutional methods would help them win the battle against the powerful British landholders. At the Charlottetown Conference, the Prince Edward Island politicians hoped to gain support for their tenant-farmers' cause and to get a promise of financial support to help them buy out the absentee landlords. However, they never did receive that support and this was the major reason why Prince Edward Island did not join Confederation until 1873.

Newfoundland

Newfoundland's history during the time leading up to Confederation was rather different from that of the other three Atlantic colonies. Although the population of Newfoundland increased during the nineteenth century, most of the Irish and English immigrants came to work in the fishing industry. There was little farming or industry on the Island at the time. The fishers who came from specific coastal communities in England and Ireland tended to stay together in the outposts and small towns of their new home. As for politics, Newfoundland did not even have a resident governor until 1825.

But, as more towns were established and more immigrants arrived, Newfoundlanders began to resent their status as a mere fishing station and petitioned the British government for representative and responsible government. In 1832, Newfoundland was granted the right to hold elections for a representative government, and the first election took place in 1834. By that time, there were strong tensions between the region's Catholics and Protestants, fishers and merchants, rural inhabitants in the outports and urban dwellers in St. John's, and Liberal and Conservative party members.[18] Because of the degree of conflict, Newfoundland did not get responsible government, nor did it become a full British North American colony until 1855. As it was such a new colony, though one of the oldest settled regions of North America, Newfoundland's people and politicians were not much interested in Confederation in 1864.

Review...Reflect...Respond

1. What was the importance of Lord Durham's report to changing the future of Canadian government?

2. What impact would the repeal of the Corn Laws have on the Canadian economy?

3. Why would "Rep by Pop" become a rallying cry of Canada West? What implications for future relations between Canada East and Canada West would this have?

Confederation

Charlottetown Conference

The Charlottetown Conference of 1864 really came about because Arthur Gordon, the lieutenant governor of Nova Scotia, wanted the governors of the Atlantic colonies and their appointed executive councils to discuss the possibility of a union of Nova Scotia, New Brunswick, Prince Edward Island, and

The Fathers of Confederation at the Charlottetown Conference

Newfoundland. In such a union, Gordon saw himself as playing a leading role as the governor of the largest of the colonies. Charles Tupper, the conservative premier of Nova Scotia was invited as part of the executive council, but he insisted that he and the other Atlantic premiers bring along the leaders of the opposition as well. This was a clever political move on Tupper's part. Having the opposition leaders involved in the discussion meant that they could not complain to the electorate that they could have done a better job if only they had participated. This was an especially astute manoeuvre since there was not much popular support in Nova Scotia for Atlantic union at that time. The presence of opposition parties at the conference would prevent them from using the union as a political issue. From New Brunswick came Leonard Tilley, the reform premier, and from Prince Edward Island, the host colony, came Colonel John Hamilton Gray, the conservative premier of P.E.I. Newfoundland refused even to send any delegates.

The Canadians (from Canada East and Canada West) also attended the conference. The fifteen representatives from Nova Scotia, New Brunswick, and Prince Edward Island decided to hear what the Canadians had to say before discussing the possible union of the Atlantic colonies. The leading members of the Canadian delegation were well rehearsed and they knew what they wanted. Cartier hoped the Atlantic colonies would join the union and offer some sort of balance for the size, weight, and population of Canada West; Brown wanted something to end the political stalemate that was impeding the progress of Canada West; Macdonald knew the reality of the threat that the American Civil War brought to the colonies and hoped they would be better able to defend themselves if they were united.

The three men impressed their Atlantic hosts with their strong arguments for a British North American union. Macdonald and Cartier both talked persuasively about the benefits that all the colonies would gain. Alexander Galt, minister of finance in the Macdonald-Cartier coalition government, explained the financial arrangements of the proposed Confederation, whereby the central government would assume the debts of the provinces that joined as well as some of their revenue-raising powers, and also pay the provinces an annual per capita subsidy. George Brown outlined the two fundamental problems of federalism. The first concerned the structure and composition of the legislature, comprised of the House of Commons and the Senate, and the second involved the crucial division of powers between the central and provincial governments. In addition, among many of the delegates the dream of a railway from sea to sea was beginning to be a symbol of the country that would be formed by uniting the colonies.

By the end of the summer conference, though the details had in no way been worked out, there was a general agreement that the principle of a federal union was a possibility that could benefit all the colonies.

The Quebec Conference

In October of 1864, thirty-three delegates, now including two from Newfoundland, arrived in Quebec City to flesh out the details of the new federation. Many of the delegates arrived by train, and almost all had extensive business interests in banking, timber, land, or railways. Representatives of the railway companies also came to the conference with the hope that a political union of the British North American colonies would mean an opportunity for them to extend or build railways that would unite the new country by rail. A new sense of urgency was felt because of the St. Albans raid, which had occurred only nine days before the start of the conference. A group of Confederate agents had robbed banks in St. Albans in Vermont and had fled across the border to Canada. They had been arrested but had been freed on a legal technicality. The outraged northern Americans were again threatening war against Canada. To the

At the Quebec
Conference, 1864

delegates gathered in Quebec—some of whom had been children during the invasions of the war of 1812—the threat of American invasion was very real.

Using George Brown's ideas of federation that he had outlined at Charlottetown as a basis, the politicians began the difficult task of creating a constitution for the new nation. On some issues, there was easy agreement, while on others there was profound disagreement. All of the delegates agreed that ties with Britain would be kept and that "the well-understood principles of the British constitution" would be adhered to as much as possible. There was also agreement about the fact that this would be a federation, meaning that there would be more than one level of government. There would be a national government that would address the needs of all the regions, and there would also be local or provincial governments that would look after regional concerns. There was also agreement that the central government would be made up of a House of Commons and a Senate.

However, there was disagreement about how power would be shared between the two levels of government. The question of representation, both in the commons and the senate, and the financial terms of Confederation took much time to resolve. The same could be said of the question of federal appointments. For the Prince Edward Island delegates there was bitter disappointment when they realized that there would be no help in their plan to buy out the absentee landlords and provide land for the tenant farmers of their colony. The delegates from Nova Scotia and New Brunswick had misgivings that they would be swallowed up by the larger Canadian colony.

The men who were delegates at the Charlottetown and Quebec Conferences were not in the least interested in revolution. They believed in material progress and rejected political values based on issues of the social contract. They wanted to deal with the more practical concerns of expansion and enterprise, not matters of the inalienable rights of man—or woman, or Aboriginal Peoples, or minorities like the Irish and the Acadians. Not surprisingly, they fashioned through a series of compromises, a government that would meet and, they hope, expand their interests. The resolutions, taken as a whole, are conservative.

Challenges to Confederation

The delegates at Quebec did not legally represent their respective colonies. After working out the details for their new government and new nation, a number of the delegates rashly suggested that they might submit their draft constitution to the electorate for approval. In the end, only New Brunswick did so; the united Canadas and Nova Scotia followed a British suggestion that they seek ratification for the proposed union from their provincial legislatures. This course would involve the delegates in a difficult and acrimonious battle that would delay the establishment of the new federal union for almost three years.

Six months after the Quebec Conference, Confederation was at a standstill. Only one colony—Canada—clearly supported it, and even then, French Canadians were divided. The only colony that had allowed its electorate to vote on the proposal—New Brunswick—rejected it. In fact, every one of the Atlantic colonies was either in opposition or indifferent to Confederation.

Britain strongly approved of the union scheme, convened a conference to expedite it, and quickly passed the necessary legislation to implement it. The American cancellation of the Reciprocity Treaty in 1866 left New Brunswick without a viable alternative to Confederation and in open defiance of Britain's wishes. The real or exaggerated threat of Fenian raids further led to New Brunswick's reversal in the June 1866 election. On the last day of June, the new assembly voted in favour of Confederation. A similar change of heart took place in Nova Scotia as its assembly approved Confederation. But on Prince Edward Island, the lack of a resolution of the absentee landlord issue prevented approval to join.

The Delegates in London

By November 1866, the Confederation delegates from Eastern and Western Canada, Nova Scotia, and New Brunswick were in London to discuss final details and to present their constitution, the British North America Act, to the British government for approval. The united colonies would be called Canada, which as historian J.M. Bumsted says, "openly announc[ed] the importance of Canada in the united governments." Joseph Howe, opposing Confederation up to the last minute, was there as well to argue against passage of the bill. But once it was passed, Howe accepted it, although with reluctance, "We must submit of course, because we cannot fight the British Government, but if the Queen's troops were to withdraw I would die upon the Frontier rather than submit to such an outrage. . . .Our first duty will be to punish the rascals here who have betrayed and sold us. If then convinced that the Canadians are disposed to act fairly, we may try the experiment."[19]

Queen Victoria signed the British North America Act into law on March 29, 1867 and declared that the date of proclamation would be July 1 of that year. John A. Macdonald would be Canada's first prime minister and the Dominion of Canada would be proclaimed in the new Parliament Buildings in Ottawa, which Queen Victoria had chosen to be Canada's capital.

The Government after Confederation

Confederation, the most dramatic change in Canadian history since 1760, had conservative aims and was instituted in a conservative manner. There was no break with the idea of British parliamentary supremacy. The tradition of the rule of law would be maintained. So would be the principle of responsible government, with the executive—the cabinet—being held accountable to the elected assembly. The ties with Britain would be maintained and the British monarchy would remain as a source of authority and stability.

However, the Canadian government that was created with Confederation was the product of political, regional, and cultural compromises. It combined aspects of both the British and American systems, and it tried to address the needs of both French and English cultures and several different regional identities. The new system was dynamic enough to solve the immediate problems facing the new Canadians and to provide for the future

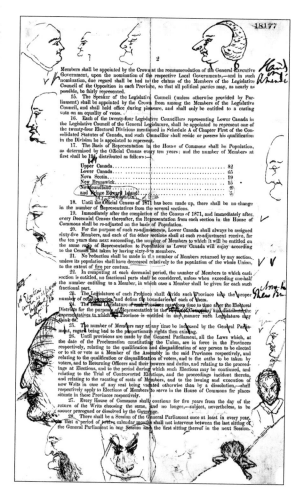

A draft of the BNA, the British North America Act – John A. Macdonald's art work.

growth and development of the country. It had to allow for the expression of the wishes of the majority; but it also had to protect the wishes of the minority.

The union was to be based on the power of a federal government. Otherwise Cartier and Quebec for sure, and probably also Nova Scotia and New Brunswick, would not have joined. Cartier especially was concerned about the future of French-Canadian culture and identity if English Canada gained greater control through larger provincial powers. So, the central government would address national concerns, while provincial governments would take care of local matters.

Pointing to the American Civil War and its roots in the principle of states' rights, Macdonald had argued that the American started their republic "at the wrong end." Because they had "declared by their Constitution that each state was a sovereignty in itself, and that all the powers incident to a sovereignty belonged to each state, except those powers which, by the Constitution, were conferred upon the General Government and Congress" they were doomed to civil war. Macdonald went on,

> Here we have adopted a different system. We have strengthened the General Government. We have given the General Legislature all the great subjects of legislation. We have conferred on them, not only specifically and in detail, all the powers which are incident to sovereignty, but we have expressly declared that all subjects of general interest not distinctly and exclusively conferred upon the local governments and local legislatures, shall be conferred upon the General Government and Legislature.[20]

The clear intention of the Fathers of Confederation was to have the federal central government as the dominant body. The federal government would have thirty-seven distinct powers as opposed to the fifteen for the provinces, and would have the responsibility for the "peace, order, and good government" of the new country. To add economic strength to its political power, only the central government would have the right to levy both direct and indirect taxes. Finally, the central government was given the right to disallow any provincial law that it considered in contravention of a federal statute.

The provinces would have control over property and civil rights, as well as language and religion. This was what Cartier believed was necessary for the survival of French-Canadian cultural traditions. The Nova Scotians and New Brunswickers also saw this as a shield against their being swallowed up by the larger provinces of Ontario and Quebec. The majority might rule but the rights of at least some minorities were to be protected. The Aboriginal Peoples were not mentioned in the documents, nor were they represented at either the Charlottetown or the Quebec conferences. There were no "Mothers of Confederation;" women were not yet persons under the law.

Web Connection

www.mcgrawhill.ca/links/definingcanada
Go to the Web site above to read the text of the British North America Act and compare it to the Constitution Act of 1982.

Review...Reflect...Respond

1. What arguments did the Canadians (Canada West and Canada East) use to try to convince the Atlantic colonies to join the union at the Charlottetown Conference?

2. What did Macdonald mean when he stated that the Americans had "started their republic at the wrong end"? How did this view change how the new government of Canada was formed?

3. Who was left out of all the Confederation discussions? What impact would this have?

Conclusion

D'Arcy McGee, who was to be killed by an assassin less than a year after Confederation, warned the newly confederated country, that it would remain intact only so long as respect was given to all of its peoples:

So long as we respect in Canada the rights of minorities, told either by tongue or creed, we are safe. For so long it will be possible for us to be united. But when we cease to respect these rights, we will be in the full tide towards that madness which the ancients considered the gods sent to those whom they wished to destroy.[21]

Notes

1. As quoted in *The Canadian Encyclopedia*, "Durham Report," p. 797.
2. J.M. Bumsted, *The Peoples of Canada: A Pre-Confederation History* (Toronto: Oxford University Press, 1992), p. 207.
3. Bumsted, *The Peoples of Canada: A Pre-Confederation History* p. 284.
4. Margaret Conrad and Alvin Finkel, *History of the Canadian Peoples: Beginnings to 1867* (Toronto: AddisonWesley, 1998), p. 370.
5. *The Canadian Encyclopedia*, "The Grand Trunk Railway," p. 1001.
6. Carol Wilton, ed.,"Philosophy of Railroads" in *Change and Continuity: A Reader on Pre-Confederation Canada*, (Toronto: McGraw-Hill Ryerson Ltd., 1992) pp. 348–350.
7. Wilton,"Philosophy of Railroads" in *Change and Continuity: A Reader on Pre-Confederation Canada*, p. 350.
8. Don Gillmor et al., *Canada: A People's History* (Toronto: McClelland & Stewart Inc., 2001) p. 259.
9. Christopher Moore, *1867: How the Fathers Made a Deal*, (Toronto: McClelland & Stewart, Inc., 1997) p. 13.
10. Moore, *1867: How the Fathers Made a Deal*, p. 15.
11. Quoted in video, *Canada: A People's History, Volume 8*, "The Great Enterprise."
12. Quoted in *Canada: A North American Nation*, p. 244.
13. Quoted in video *Canada: A People's History*, Volume 8, "The Great Enterprise."
14. R. Douglas Francis, Richard Jones, Donald B. Smith, *Origins: Canadian History to Confederation* (Toronto: Holt, Rinehart, and Winston, 1988) p. 387.
15. Ibid., p. 387.
16. Bumsted, *The Peoples of Canada: A Pre-Confederation History*, p. 334.
17. Conrad and Finkel, *History of the Canadian Peoples, Volume 1*, p. 229.
18. Ibid., p. 229.
19. Bumsted, *The Peoples of Canada: A Pre-Confederation History*, p. 337
20. "Speech of John A. Macdonald, *Parliamentary Debates*, 1865.
21. Gillmor et al., *Canada: A People's History*, Volume 1, p. 278.

Chapter 11 Review

Knowledge & Understanding

1. Identify six of the following people, concepts, and events and explain their significance to Canadian history and the development of Canadian culture and identity.

   Thomas Coltrin Keefer   responsible government

   John A. MacDonald   railway construction

   George Brown   American Civil War

   George-Étienne Cartier   Charlottetown Conference

   free trade   Quebec Conference

2. Lord Durham's report had long-term significance for the future of Canada. What were the main proposals in his report? What was the British government's reaction to those proposals?

Thinking & Inquiry

3. Create an extensive mind map in which you show the factors that contributed to the growing independence of Canadians during the late 18th 19th centuries.

4. Canadian historian, Desmond Morton, comments on the relationship between French and English Canadians:

   Before and long after Confederation, sensible Canadians have understood that peace, order, and good government in their country have depended on the reasonable long-run harmony of French and English. That notion was not embodied in the British North America Act; it was left for ensuing generations to rediscover or neglect at their peril.

   In small groups, discuss this quotation. How did the Confederation conferences deal with French-English question? Since Confederation, how have peace, order and good government been affected by French-English issues? Contribute your group's conclusions to a full-class discussion.

Communication

5. During the 1840s and 1850s, technologies for producing photographs were improved. What did the new technology mean for historians? Are photographs more objective than paintings? Consider these questions, and prepare an illustrated report on photographs as a reliable or unreliable historical resource.

6. Imagine that you have been contracted to write a newspaper article—either for Joseph Howe's The Nova Scotian or for a London newspaper of the day—about the results of the Quebec Conference of 1864. You will have the opportunity to interview any three of the politicians who participated in the conference. Prepare a list of five interview questions for each politician and compose likely responses each one would give. Then draft, edit, revise, and publish your article.

Application

7. In an 1865 parliamentary debate, John A. MacDonald made the following statement: "I am strongly of the belief that we have, in a great measure, avoided in this system which we propose for the adoption of the people of Canada, the defects which time and events have shown to exist in the American Constitution." Prepare arguments for or against MacDonald's statement. Debate this question in an open class forum.

Unit Three Research Activity

Research

John Ralston Saul, a Canadian writer and social scientist, asserts that Canada should make March 11 a national holiday because of its importance in Canada's political development of democracy and the creation of responsible government.

1. Research the significance of March 11, 1848 and the events that surrounded it.

Interpretation and Analysis

2. John Ralston Saul states that "1848 was the moment when the very legitimacy of our society was switched from the colonial elites to the citizens." What does he mean by this?

3. Was this date a significant step forward in the creation of democracy in Canada?

4. Is democracy a part of Canadian identity?
   Is there a distinct Canadian democracy?

Applying and Communicating Your Skills

5. Write a formal proposal to the Heritage Minister of the Canadian Cabinet (with copies to go the Prime Minister and your local Member of Parliament) for the creation of this date as a national holiday. Set up a three-page proposal with the following headings:
   Title
   Summary
   Rationale
   Details
   Timeline
   Sources

Consolidating Culture and Identity, 1876–1918

The half-century following Confederation was a time of immense change for Canada and its emerging identity. In 1867, the country had fewer than four million people scattered in four provinces. There was concern whether this bold experiment in nationhood would be successful. More factors appeared to pull the new nation apart rather than bind it together.

But early Canadians—the famous and the anonymous— persevered in the face of challenges. Immense tracts of land were acquired, five new provinces were added, a transcontinental railway was built, a national police force created, industries and cities appeared, immigrants streamed in and an early sense of Canadianism began slowly to develop.

Progress, however, came not without its costs. Aboriginal populations were moved and marginalized, immigrant groups faced discrimination and prejudice, political scandal surfaced, labour unrest became evident, and cities developed sections of squalor.

The real end of the nineteenth century and the start of the twentieth century occurred with World War I. It redrew the map of Europe and ended the romantic concept of war. At the same time, the war also had a significant impact on Canada. Gaining a sterling reputation on the battlefields allowed Canada to sign the Versailles Peace Treaty independently. The war also changed the role of women in the political and economic life of Canada.

Chapter 12
Confederation Postscript

Chapter 13
Changing Times: Economics, Industrialism, and Urbanism

Chapter 14
Striving for Accommodation: Laurier's "Sunny Ways"

Chapter 15
The Great War: A Nation Emerges

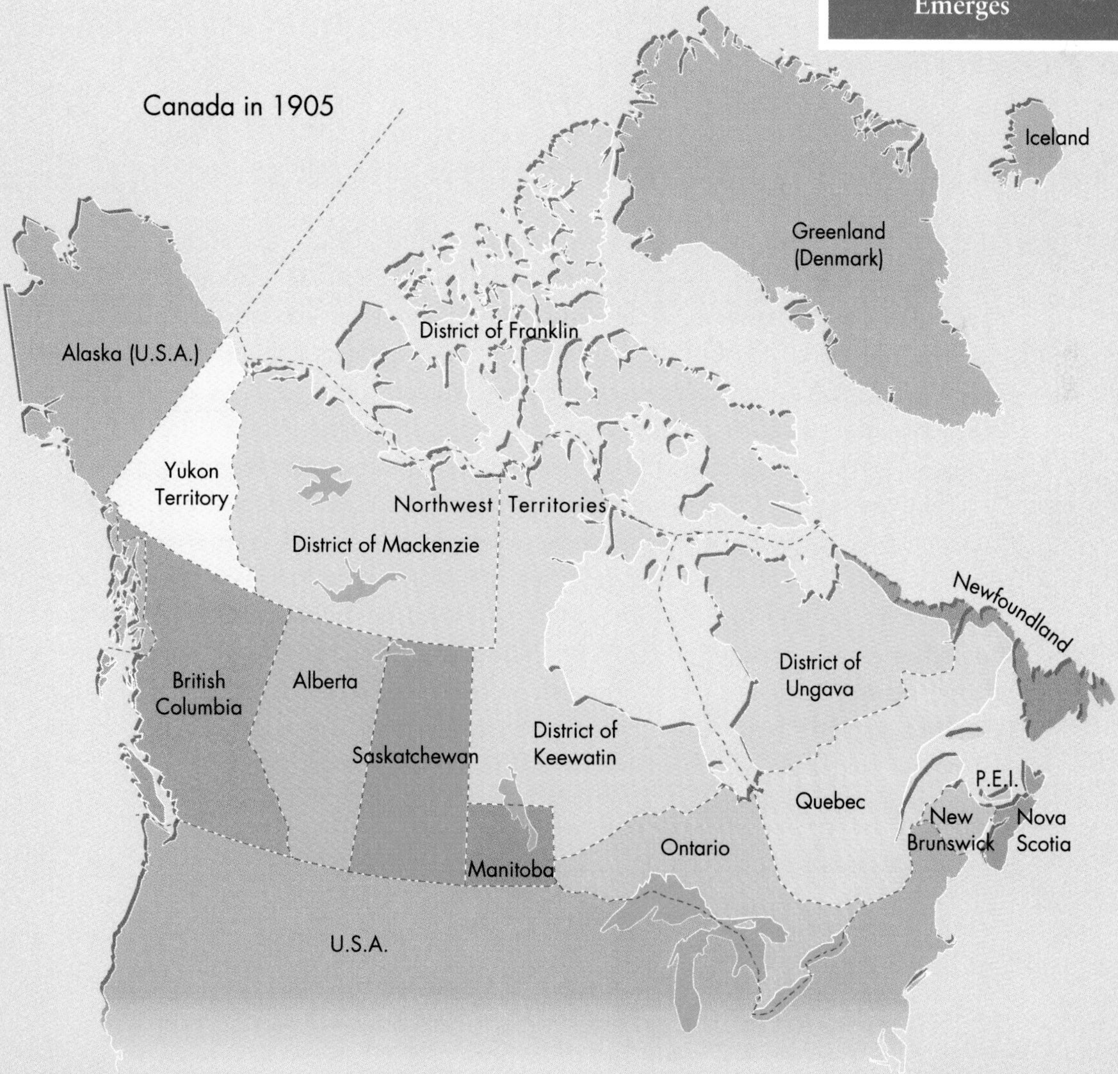

Canada in 1905
Iceland
Greenland (Denmark)
Alaska (U.S.A.)
District of Franklin
Yukon Territory
Northwest Territories
District of Mackenzie
Newfoundland
District of Ungava
British Columbia
Alberta
Saskatchewan
District of Keewatin
P.E.I.
Quebec
New Brunswick
Nova Scotia
Ontario
Manitoba
U.S.A.

Confederation Postscript

Let us see what these Canadians desire to do. They are not...a very harmonious or homogeneous community.... A more unpromising nucleus of a new nation could hardly be found on the face of the Earth.

–JOSEPH HOWE

After the bells had stopped ringing, the guns roaring, and the fireworks exploding in celebration of July 1, the serious business of building a new country had to be undertaken. Barely three and a half million people were scattered over a wide expanse of land, from the western shores of Lake Superior to the eastern tip of Cape Breton Island. However, more factors divided, rather than united, the tiny population. Politics, religion, geography, and language were but four of the divisive elements that worked against the formation of a unifying national identity.

In the coming decades, this tiny population would expand so that Canada would stretch *a mari usque mare a usque mare* (from sea to sea to sea). As the inhabited land area would be increased by more than seven times, so too would the population.

The postscript to Confederation was perhaps as vital to the forming of an early Canadian identity as was the actual achievement of July 1 itself. Events such as the Rupert's Land Act, the Red River Rebellion, the North-West Rebellion, the addition of Manitoba, British Columbia, Prince Edward Island, Saskatchewan, and Alberta to Confederation, the creation of the Royal North-West Mounted Police, and the completion of the Canadian Pacific Railway, were all crucial in changing the nation. However, some of these events that were deemed victories for Canada, came at the expense of the people who inhabited the country.

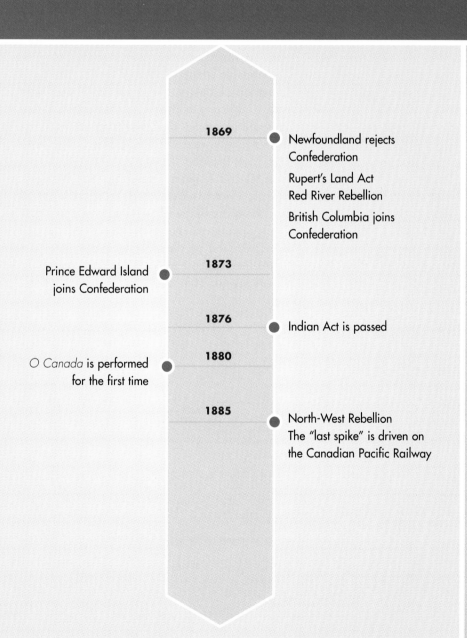

12

	1869	Newfoundland rejects Confederation
		Rupert's Land Act
		Red River Rebellion
		British Columbia joins Confederation
Prince Edward Island joins Confederation	**1873**	
	1876	Indian Act is passed
O Canada is performed for the first time	**1880**	
	1885	North-West Rebellion
		The "last spike" is driven on the Canadian Pacific Railway

By the end of this chapter, you will be able to

- demonstrate an understanding of the resistance of the Métis to the establishment of European colonial institutions

- analyze how obstacles made it difficult for immigrants to participate fully in Canadian society

- explain how and why citizenship rights have been denied at particular times to certain ethnocultural minorities

- describe the character and development over time of francophone communities outside Quebec

- analyze how Canadian governments and leaders have used symbols and supported organizations to promote Canadian culture

To Join or Not to Join

The Canadian government soon realized that not only had the work of building a nation just begun, it also had to fight to keep the provinces that had already joined Confederation from repealing their decision. Anti-confederate emotions ran high in many colonies, but economic troubles and the constant threat of annexation by the United States forced many colonies to reconsider. Determined to expand the boundaries of Canada, Macdonald and his successors would see their dream of a nation come true, but at the cost of wounds that even today, remain unhealed.

Clashing Identities: Nova Scotia Objects

One of the first orders of business for the new Dominion was to deal with the desire of Nova Scotia to leave Confederation. Two of the other Atlantic colonies, Prince Edward Island and Newfoundland had already rejected joining Confederation, and in the initial election in New Brunswick in 1865, Sir Samuel Tilley's pro-Confederation party had been voted out of office.

The Maritime colonies were distant, remote, and isolated and they felt that they had been dragged into Confederation to address the needs of central Canada. They also feared losing their distinctive identity that was founded on British roots, Maritime surroundings, and sense of independence.

With a population of little more than 600 000, Maritimers felt that they would be constantly outvoted in the House of Commons in Ottawa. They felt that the policies and programs that would protect and perpetuate their culture and identity, such as railways, economic assistance to deal with the loss of their shipbuilding monopoly, and linkage with New England, would be rejected. There were far more votes in Quebec and Ontario, so they feared that the Canadian Parliament would simply ignore them. Easterners felt that their tax money would be used for projects, such as opening up the Northwest, which had little relevance or benefit for them. There was a lingering suspicion in the minds of many Maritimers that, socially and politically, they were being used as a convenient tool to help resolve the interminable French-English dispute and as a means of ending political deadlock.

Economically, 1867 was a time of unease in the Atlantic colonies as the age of "wind, water, and wood" had been replaced by one of steam and steel. Their monopoly in the production of wooden ships was fast disappearing and it was questionable if they could successfully make the transition. Industry and trade with the United States stagnated at the end of the American Civil War and it was felt that the promised federal tariffs would kill what was left of their lucrative trade with New England. The old idea of combining the four Maritime colonies was offered as the answer to their problems. It had been the original idea for the convening of the Charlottetown Conference at the beginning of September 1864.

The mood on the morning after July 1, 1867 in Halifax and other Nova Scotian communities was skeptical. They distrusted the other colonies,

By the 1870s, Halifax was the leading commercial centre of the Maritimes. Despite this, Halifax still could not compete with the factories and large port facilities of Montreal. How would this affect regional differences in Canada?

disliked the financial terms of union, and had an abundance of local pride. They had agreed to join Confederation in return for an annual per capita subsidy of 80 cents. Now they were wondering if they had sold themselves for too little. Joseph Howe, the journalist behind the "Confederation—Botheration" letters, became the champion of the movement to remove Nova Scotia from Confederation. Howe rose in the first session of the Canadian Parliament and declared, "I do not believe that the people of Nova Scotia will ever be satisfied to submit to an act which has been forced upon them by such unjust and unjustifiable means....The people of my province were tricked into this scheme."[1] Under the banner of the Nova Scotia Party, he promised to protect the cherished identity of his beloved province. In the first federal election, held only two and a half months after the

Anti-confederate Joseph Howe believed that Nova Scotia should keep closer ties to Britain rather than unite with Ottawa. His "Botheration Letters," which were published in the *Morning Chronicle* swayed many Nova Scotians away from Confederation. Why did Macdonald go to great lengths to ensure that Nova Scotia remained in Confederation? What might have happened if Howe had succeeded in releasing Nova Scotia from its union with Canada?

celebrations of July 1, his party captured eighteen of the nineteen federal seats. Provincially, his party did equally as well winning thirty-six of thirty-eight seats. A separatist party controlled both levels of government and it was clear that the people of Nova Scotia wanted out of Confederation.

Howe felt it was time to argue his case for the separation of Nova Scotia from Confederation before the British government. In June 1868, he travelled to London, only to be rebuffed. Undeterred, Howe tried a second time, only to hear the curt reply from the colonial secretary, the Duke of Buckingham, "Repeal is not even a matter of discussion." Some rabid anti-Confederationists in Canada suggested annexation to the United States, but Howe dismissed this option even more quickly with the argument that Maritime identity would have even less chance of survival under the Americans than it did with the Canadians. Howe even desperately considered open rebellion but realized its futility and abandoned the idea.

Although the repeal movement had stalled, Macdonald realized that something had to be done and that Howe was the key. He journeyed to Halifax in July 1868, while a repeal convention was taking place, and presented his terms to the Nova Scotian. Macdonald held out an "olive branch" by increasing the annual subsidies by more than thirty percent over the next ten years. In truth, the adjustment simply provided revised financial terms similar to what had already been given to New Brunswick. In addition, Macdonald offered Howe a federal cabinet portfolio. And with these new conditions, Macdonald kept Nova Scotia in Confederation.

Newfoundland Holds Strong

The 1869 election in Newfoundland was basically a referendum on Confederation. A slight upswing in the economy, coupled with forceful and fanciful propaganda—including rumours that Newfoundland children would be used as ammunition in Canadian cannons—turned the majority of voters against Confederation. The anti-Confederationists, led by Charles Fox Bennett, won two-thirds of the seats and defeated Premier Frederick Carter. As the anti-Confederation song from 1864 had declared, they were not willing to sell their birthright for a few Canadian dollars. The people of Newfoundland had overwhelmingly rejected Confederation again—a rejection that would last for eighty years.

Prince Edward Island Enters Reluctantly

Just like Newfoundland and Nova Scotia, the people of the tiny island colony of Prince Edward Island were grappling with the same issue of protecting a fragile identity and distinctive lifestyle in the face of great change. The first residents of the island, the Mi'kmaq, called P. E. I. "Epekwitk" or "resting or cradled on the waves." The English pronunciation became "Abegweit." The French named it Île Saint-Jean, while the British called it St. John's Island. Finally, in 1799, it was renamed Prince Edward Island in honour of Edward, Duke of Kent and the father of Queen Victoria. The population was small in number, but they were fiercely proud. They were a tiny island colony, unconnected with the mainland, determined to preserve their unspoiled splendour.

The island colony had rejected Confederation back in 1864, even though their premier, John Gray, had been elected chairman of the Charlottetown Conference. The points of opposition were the same ones as the other Maritime provinces, but perhaps they were intensified given P. E. I.'s tiny population and the fact that there was no physical connection with the rest of Canada. But now as Prince Edward Island entered the 1870s, Confederation with Canada was reconsidered as its economy suffered the impact of a global depression, which was worsened by the islanders' attempt to build their own railway. Costs greatly exceeded estimates, resulting in the provincial debt mushrooming from $250 000 in 1863 to $4 million dollars a decade later.

The problem was worsened by the high number of absentee landlords, which led to a diminishing of the available tax base. In 1767, the island was divided into sixty-six townships and given out to British investors in a lottery. Although the landowners had been required to settle on their properties within ten years, few did. Their absence led directly to economic stagnation. The option of increasing taxes was not viable as the people who actually resided on the island could not bear an increase.

Under such economic troubles, greater numbers of islanders began to look favourably on joining Confederation. Macdonald agreed that Ottawa would assume the island's debt, pay $800 000 to buy

Prince Edward Island declined joining Confederation in 1867, but due to large debts, Charlottetown was forced to come back to the bargaining table in 1873. Since union with Canada was more out of financial need than a desire to be a part of a nation from "sea to sea," how did this affect the Islanders' sense of nationalism in the years to come?

out the absentee landowners, offer a generous subsidy, and ensure continuous communications between the island and the mainland (by federal ferry service).[2] After a near unanimous vote—only one island MLA, Cornelius Howatt voted against the Canadian offer—on July 1, 1873, the seventh anniversary of Confederation, Prince Edward Island joined as the seventh province.

Looking West

Westward expansion had long been of concern and interest, especially to those living in Canada West where it was widely believed that the best available farmland had already been claimed. A decade before Confederation, the Canada West government sponsored the 1857–58 Hind expedition to map the prime agrarian areas in the prairies and to site the optimal route for future roads and railway lines.

For decades there existed a major concern that if Canadians did not establish a physical presence in the west, it would not be long before the Americans did. Macdonald was clear to point out the American threat: "[The Americans] are resolved to do all they can, short of war, to get possession of our western territory, and we must take immediate and vigorous steps to counteract them."[3] The 1858 Gold Rush along the Fraser River brought in thousands of Americans seeking their fortune. Most came up empty-handed but many of the influx remained and settled in British Columbia. The American Civil War (1861–65) briefly relieved the fear of an American annexation of the prairies. As the Union and Confederacy fought one another in hundreds of battles, they had no time or energy to entertain notions of a land-grab to the north. However, once the war ended, Americans could once more look northward. Canadians were anxiously aware of the powerful American philosophy of Manifest Destiny (the belief that the United States was intended by God to eventually cover all of North America). That idea was shockingly reinforced when in 1867,

American Secretary of State William Seward negotiated the purchase of Alaska from the Russians for $7.2 million. It raised fears of American encirclement and spurred the new Canadian government into action. The colony of British Columbia was now squeezed between American territories. Seward was confident of what the future held as he complimented Canadian colonists on their hard work, "You are building excellent states to be hereafter admitted into the American Union."[4] Perhaps equally disturbing was the American government dispatching of a consul to the Red River area in the hopes of acquiring that territory.

Rupert's Land Act

For almost two centuries the Hudson's Bay Company had conducted a highly profitable fur trade in the huge area called Rupert's Land, which consisted of all the land that drained into Hudson Bay. An 1863 Company reorganization saw its focus shift from fur trading to land sales and control of communication. As a result, it was willing to entertain offers for Rupert's Land. The B.N.A. Act had explicitly stated that the new Dominion would stretch *a mari usque ad mare* and had provided conditions by which the western lands would become part of Canada.

The Rupert's Land Act was the largest real estate deal in history, but it was a new government in Britain in 1869 that dictated the final terms of transfer. The Hudson's Bay Company insisted on retaining substantial portions of arable land and the British agreed. In return for acquiring the huge tract of land, the Canadian government paid £300 000 (approximately $1.5 million dollars) to compensate Hudson's Bay Company shareholders, granted the Company thousands of hectares of land around its trading posts, and finally, gave the Company one-twentieth of all land in the territory. The official date of transfer for the newly acquired land was December 1, 1869 making Canada six times its original size.

The acquisition of Rupert's Land increased the size of Canada by almost six times. The Government of Canada made a deal with the Hudson's Bay Company. What major interest was left out of the negotiations? What long-term effect would this have?

Canada in 1870

Map labels: Alaska (U.S.A.), Greenland (Denmark), Yukon Territory, Atlantic Ocean, The North-West Territories, British Columbia, Newfoundland, Pacific Ocean, Manitoba, Ontario, Quebec, P.E.I., Nova Scotia, New Brunswick, UNITED STATES OF AMERICA, 0 250 500 km

Manitoba: "The Postage Stamp" Province

In annexing the North-West from the Hudson's Bay Company in 1869, no consideration, provision, or mention was made of the area's twelve thousand inhabitants, most of whom were of Métis background. In the 1800s, the Métis population had increased substantially. Thirty years earlier, in 1840, there were approximately four thousand Métis who represented half the population of the colony. Now, in 1869, they comprised about ten thousand of the area's total population. The term "Métis" came from the Old French language meaning "mixed." More than eighty percent of the region's population were descendants of colonial fur traders and the Aboriginal women they married. Most Métis (48 percent) were French-speaking Catholics although a sizeable number (34 percent) were English-speaking Protestants, which added diversity to the community. Almost all Métis spoke Cree, and many spoke a distinct dialect that combined Cree and French.

They had their own customs, beliefs, and rituals. Originally nomadic and dependent on the annual buffalo hunts, the Métis had begun to settle and engage in agriculture. Still, the annual buffalo hunt defined them and was the centre of their cultural life.

The Métis had settled on the land owned by Hudson's Bay, and had cleared it, and farmed it. Or they had led a transient existence as buffalo-hunters. But now they feared that the land transfer would threaten their land claims as well as their unique culture, as the Métis, according to Aboriginal practice, had no legal paper title to their land. Now, the new owner, the Canadian government, was playing a very different role than had the HBC. The government dispatched surveyors to divide up the land into townships and sections ahead of the anticipated influx of white settlers from Ontario. This act infuriated the Métis because it disregarded not only their ownership of the land, but also their traditional long, narrow, rectangular strip pattern of land holding based on the seigneurial system of New France and it threatened their very way of life. Add to that volatile mix the fact that 1868 had been an economic and social disaster due to a widespread crop failure and a terrible buffalo hunt, all the ingredients for an uprising were at hand.

The Red River Rebellion

The final requirement for a rebellion was a leader. He emerged in the person of Louis Riel. Born in St. Boniface, the 24-year-old, from a French, Irish, and Aboriginal background, belonged to one of the more prominent local families. Louis Riel was educated and literate as well as a zealous defender of the Métis way of life. Elected secretary of the Red River council, he moved swiftly to put his faith into action. On October 11, 1869, stepping astride a surveyor's chain on the property of Andre Nault, he indignantly shouted, "You shall go no further." Joined by a small band of unarmed Métis, Riel delivered an unmistakable message. The Canadians were trespassers and had no right to be there.

A second act of defiance occurred on November 2, when another band of Métis, led by

Ambroise Lepine, travelled just south of the border outside of Pembina and stopped the newly appointed Lieutenant-Governor, William McDougall, from entering. The newly formed National Committee of the Métis was emphatic in forcing the issue. Signed "Louis Riel, Secretary," they issued the following message: "The National Committee of the Métis orders William MacDougall not to enter the Territory of the North West without special permission of the above-mentioned committee." The Métis used the rationale that the Canadian authority had no jurisdiction in the North-West.

After seizing Fort Garry (present-day Winnipeg) in a bloodless coup and establishing a Provisional Government, Riel, now the president, issued a "Declaration of the People of Rupert's Land and the North-West" and a Métis List of Rights. He hoped that they would become the basis for negotiations with the Canadian government on Manitoba's entry into Confederation. Macdonald was willing to negotiate and sent Bishop Tache, the spiritual leader of the Catholics in Red River and Donald A. Smith, head of the HBC, to Fort Garry to explore the possibilities of a compromise. The bargaining was intense but Riel got Smith, a seasoned negotiator, to agree to a Convention of Forty, a new representative assembly. The peace, however, was shattered in February 1870, when six-hundred Canadian settlers, organized under the Canadian Party and led by John Schultz, launched an unsuccessful attack on Fort Garry to try and free their colleagues who had been captured by Riel's forces in the December 7 raid on Schultz's guard

Louis Riel and members of the Red River Council, circa 1869–70 — all the ingredients for a rebellion were at hand.

house. Forty-eight prisoners, including Thomas Scott, had been taken prisoner by Riel and his men. To Riel, who had shown restraint up to that point and was planning to release the remaining prisoners, this attack was intolerable. He viewed it as open and violent defiance. He recognized that he could only maintain his authority by making an example of the conspirators, and Thomas Scott, an Ontario Orangemen, was chosen. An all-Métis jury found him guilty of insubordination and sentenced him to be executed.

Donald Smith, sent by Macdonald as emissary, pleaded unsuccessfully with Riel for mercy. Scott was put before a Métis firing squad and executed. His last words echoed through the land. "This is horrible! This is cold-blooded murder!" English-Protestant Ontario was outraged, and demanded retaliation against Riel. Canada became divided. While French Canada saw Riel as a brother locked in a similar struggle to preserve a threatened culture, English Canada viewed him as a traitor. In their eyes, Riel had defied the legally constituted authority of the Canadian government.

Negotiations opened between Riel's Provisional government and Macdonald's government in Ottawa. Three delegates, most notably Father Noel-Joseph Ritchot, worked tirelessly to meet the wishes of the colonists. On May 12, 1870, the final agreement was reached, and Canada's fifth province, Manitoba, was officially born on July 15. In accepting most of the terms of Riel's List of Rights, the Manitoba Act created the new land as an officially bilingual, bicultural, and bi-educational province. The new province was also given a name of Aboriginal nature that derived from "manitou" meaning Great Spirit. Ironically, Riel was twice elected as one of the four MPs allocated to the "postage stamp" province, but was both times denied his seat in the House of Commons as his requests for amnesty were denied by Macdonald.

The joys of the Métis victory, however, were short-lived. To appease the outraged Canadians, Macdonald ordered federal troops, under the command of Colonel Garnet Wolseley, out to Red River. Macdonald sent the military troops to Red River to both discourage American attempts of taking over Canadian territory, and to control any further uprising from the Métis. The military expedition terrorized the Métis, forcing Riel to flee to the United States.

Within a few years, the Métis underwent disastrous changes to their population and their homeland. The buffalo—the main staple of their diet—were disappearing, the fur trade was declining and could no longer offer the Métis a reliable source of income, the building of the railroad through their land, a rapid influence of aggressive

Expedition to the Red River in 1870 under Sir Garnet Wolseley, Advance Guard Crossing a Portage by Frances Ann Hopkins. This painting shows government troops on the Kaministiquia River, as they travel west to stop the Red River Rebellion. Do you believe that Ottawa was justified in sending out troops?

settlers, and the implementation of police, government, and laws from Ottawa that did not allow for their own cultural traditions to survive.

As they watched European settlers receive immediate grants and deeds for land, the Métis were forced to wait for their land grants from the government. For many Métis, the only thing left to do was to move further west to land (now Saskatchewan) that still had buffalo and where they could control their own lives and people once again. But even that control would not last for long.

The North-West Rebellion

By the mid-1880s there were about twenty thousand Aboriginal Peoples in the North-West. Their population had been sharply reduced by starvation and disease. In 1876, Ottawa passed the Indian Act, which legislated Aboriginals to second-class citizenship and gave the federal government wide legislative control over Aboriginals living on reserves. Many of the discriminatory terms of the Act, such as loss of status if an Aboriginal voted or if an Aboriginal woman married a non-Aboriginal, remained well into the twentieth century. Because of the influx of Ontario farmers and the departure of Métis, by 1885 only seven percent of Manitoba's population was Métis. Struggling to preserve their culture and identity, they had migrated to Saskatchewan around Qu'Appelle, Batoche, and Duck Lake.

Many Aboriginal Peoples had already been displaced onto reservations through a series of treaties. The Canadian government wanted to open up the prairies to agriculture, settlement, and the railway. South of the border, the Americans were fighting a costly series of battles against the Plains Indians. Learning from that experience, the financially strapped Canadian government set out to acquire the land west of Manitoba before the railway and settlers arrived. The first of seven numbered treaties, signed between 1871 and 1877, gave Canada the land through which the railway would pass. (There would be eleven treaties in all, the last one signed in 1921.)

Normally, the signed treaties involved the exchange of land for a lump sum payment, plus annual payments, along with government assurances of schools, services, and other resources. Other items, such as emergency relief and needed supplies, were usually negotiated verbally, but were often never fulfilled by the government. Ottawa was ruthless in negotiating the treaties. It would normally conclude treaties with those Aboriginals in the most dire conditions. Louis Riel claimed that the Aboriginals were "...being bartered away like common cattle."

While Aboriginal Peoples initially resisted signing the treaties, starvation, loss of land and control of their communities forced them to agree to the unfair and discriminatory treaties. As the buffalo herds disappeared, Aboriginals faced an increasingly bleak future. Poundmaker (Pitikwahanapiwiyin), headman of one of the River Band Peoples and a Cree chief, only signed Treaty No. 6 in August 1876 after the government amended it to include a "famine provision." Big Bear (Mistahimaskwa), chief of the Prairie River People and also a leader of the Cree, refused to sign that same Treaty and held out until 1882. But starvation and destitution of his people forced him to reconsider and the winter of 1883-84 was particularly severe. Big Bear and Poundmaker unsuccessfully tried to unite their nations to press Ottawa for better conditions, but the government was slow to give them a response to their requests. Many Cree began to call for more militant action. The Métis, too, were in despair as they saw their culture and people again threatened. They turned to the one person whom they knew Ottawa would listen to—their old leader, Louis Riel.

Web Connnection

www.mcgrawhill.ca/links/definingcanada

Go to the Web site above to find out more information about the treaties.

Riel had drifted to Montana, married and settled down to the life of a teacher. He had suffered from mental illness during his exile, but he could not ignore the call of his people. After travelling northward across the border in December 1884, Riel sent a "Bill of Rights" to Ottawa demanding settlement of Métis and white settlers' grievances. However, his petition was ignored by government authorities. In March, Riel, his military adjutant, Gabriel Dumont and a band of Métis took ammunition and provisions from a store in Batoche. Days later, Riel sent an ultimatum to NWMP Superintendent Crozier demanding that he surrender Fort Carlton, otherwise it would be taken in an armed attack. After Crozier refused, Dumont attacked and defeated a contingent from the Fort at Duck Lake. Macdonald, intent on crushing this second Rebellion, dispatched a force under Major-General Middleton. Because of the newly built railway, the troops arrived within days and marched on the Métis stronghold of Batoche. Outnumbered three-to-one, the Métis were forced to surrender on May 12 after four days of fighting.

While Dumont slipped away, Riel surrendered to General Middleton on May 15. Although Riel was an American citizen, he was formally charged with high treason on July 6. His trial began in Regina on July 28 before an all-white, male, Protestant jury. Riel vehemently refused his lawyers' advice of an insanity plea and in fact made a passionately eloquent statement in his own defence.

> The North-West is my mother. She is the mother country of my nation....God cannot create a tribe without locating it. We are not birds. We have to walk on the ground....The North-West Council is a sham legislature and not representative government at all....British civilization has defined such government as irresponsible, and by all the science which has been shown here yesterday, you are compelled to admit if there is no responsibility, it is insane. The federal government....besides doing nothing to satisfy the people of this great land, it has even hardly been able to answer once or give a single response.[5]

The jury found him guilty of high treason, but recommended mercy. The judge, Hugh Richardson, ignored their recommendations and sentenced Riel to be executed. A final appeal rested with the prime minister. Ignoring petitions and pleas, Macdonald, eyeing the electoral ramifications of his decision, said, "He shall hang, though every dog in Quebec bark in his favour." Riel's execution on November 16 was to have a lasting impact on Canadian history.

The Capture of Batoche by D. Campbell. How can historians use contemporary paintings like this when researching events such as the capture of Batoche?

Because the Métis were largely French-speaking Roman Catholics, English-Protestant Canadians viewed Riel as a traitor and a murderer of their fellow protestant Thomas Scott. He had, in their eyes, illegally taken up arms against the legally constituted authority and had murdered English Canadians. Riel had been exiled for his earlier transgressions, but he had returned and repeated his actions. His execution, from the English perspective, was warranted and justified.

To French-speaking Roman Catholics, Riel was a defender of Catholic and francophone rights in Canada. He was a martyred victim of the heavy-handed power of an English majority. He had legitimately struggled for the very same thing that monopolized much of their attention—cultural preservation and survival—and his execution unleashed a wave of French-Canadian nationalism that saw Riel as a hero. Less than a week following the execution, in a massive rally on the Champ de Mare in Montreal, Quebec Liberal leader Honoré Mercier and the future Liberal Prime Minister Wilfrid Laurier, adamantly attacked Macdonald's decision. Quebec's large Roman Catholic population would sever its ties with Macdonald's Conservatives and find a voice in Mercier's Parti National at the provincial level, and Laurier's fifteen year reign as prime minister. As powerful as Riel had been in life, it would be nothing compared to his influence after his death. In many ways, Louis Riel became the lightening-rod for "the two solitudes" within the Canadian persona. Riel's legacy is still contested today.

A RIEL UGLY POSITION.

A Riel Ugly Position by Canadian cartoonist J.W. Bengough. How does Bengough capture the dilemma in determining the fate of Louis Riel faced by Sir John A. Macdonald? What elements does Bengough use to make his point?

In his own defence Riel said, "The federal government...besides doing nothing to satisfy the people of this great land, it has even hardly been able to answer once or give a single response." Do you believe this sentiment is felt by Aboriginal leaders in Canada today?

Sir John A. Macdonald and his Indian Policy

The following is an excerpt from John A. Macdonald's speech to the House of Commons on June 2, 1886, in which he responds to his government's policy on Aboriginal Peoples:

It is the policy, and it will be the policy of the Government so long as I have anything to do with this Department, to see that the Indians go on their reserves and work there, and the Government will then fulfil the treaty obligations and even more. By strictly carrying out that policy it has been in a degree successful. The Indians are going on their reserves, and this year the accounts are much more favourable as to the number of Indians on the reserves, the quantity of land broken and the quantity of roots and grain put in. The Indian will allow himself to run almost to death's door rather than move from the place where he is. It was only because with Christian feelings we could not see them starve that they were given quarter rations. That is the policy of the Government, and it is the correct policy. The committee must remember that the Government are under no obligations to furnish food to the Indians. He has got his hand and his head; he has the capacity for work if he chooses. The white immigrant goes there and he must "root hog or die"; he must work or starve.

...

Why, Sir, before the buffalo disappeared, we gave no food to the Indians. Hon. Gentlemen opposite, when they were in power, did not give food to the Indians. There were treaty obligations; a certain number of cattle and implements; a certain amount of seed grain and so on, were all given under treaty obligations, and that was all required to be given and all that was given until the sudden disappearance of the buffalo. Canada, or the Canadian Government, or the Canadian people, was under no obligation to feed these Indians, but as Christian men they could not allow them to starve; they supplied them with food; and every vote we asked for the purpose of feeding these Indians was opposed by hon. Gentlemen on the other side, and especially by the hon. Member for Bothwell, who said we were pauperizing the Indians, and that they should work as well as the white men.

...

Although the Indian will keep himself in a starving condition, there has been the greatest tenderness on the part of Parliament to put money at the disposal of the Government, and there has been a careful and judicious disposition of the vote to the Indian, without letting him feel that he had enough for himself and his family without working. The great trouble is to get the Indians to work, for they can work and they are now working. But if they are told by pseudo-philanthropists, by men who are led more by their hearts than by their heads, that they are suffering, that it is the duty of the Government not to allow them to starve, then they will never work...

1. How does Sir John A. Macdonald describe the "Indian problem"?
2. Who is the intended audience of Sir John A. Macdonald's speech?
3. How does the audience affect what evidence a historian can use from this document? Name two other sources that you would try to find in order to understand a balanced view of this issue.

The Entrance of British Columbia

British Columbia became Canada's sixth province on July 20, 1871. Originally the smallest British North American colony, with a scattered population of ten thousand people, the gold rush of the 1850s had brought an influx of people to the area sending the colony's population to over thirty thousand. Many of those people were American and ties of geography, trade, and commerce resulted in a strong southern pull within British Columbia. In the 1860s, the gold rush ended, leaving the colony over $1 million in debt, as it had borrowed heavily from British banks during the previous boom times to build roads and provide other services. The diminishing population could not support this debt as half of colonial revenues went to discharge the interest payments alone and something clearly had to be done.

One option, supported by a dwindling number of merchants, was to accept annexation to the United States. Prominent Americans such as William Seward, former secretary of state for Presidents Abraham Lincoln and Andrew Johnson, and Massachusetts Senator, Charles Sumner, welcomed such a prospect with open arms. A legislative petition requesting annexation to the United States was sent from Victoria to U.S. President Ulysses S. Grant. However, the very "Britishness" of the colony, coupled with a multitude of other obstacles, made annexation unlikely.

However the alternative of union with Canada was also fraught with problems, such as the communication and transportation barriers imposed by the Rockies and the prairies. Many also believed that the Canadian market was simply too small to ensure the economic prosperity of British Columbia. The current government, led by the governor Frederick Seymour, was not in favour of such a union. They were, after all, *British* Columbia, a proud colony of the Empire. Joining up with the upstart Canadians would simply not do given the strong British strain and character of the colony.

Seymour died in late 1869 and his replacement, Anthony Musgrave, worked tirelessly to bring British Columbia into Confederation as he felt that joining Canada offered the best prospects for British Columbia. However, the man who turned the tide and who is regarded as "the father of B.C." called himself Amor de Cosmos ("lover of the world"), but his real name was William Smith. He had been a journalist in his native Nova Scotia as well as a photographer in California during the 1849 gold rush. Founding the *British Colonist* newspaper, Smith was able to rally a number of other newspapers round the cause of union with Canada. He also organized his followers into the appropriately named Canadian Party to lobby for entrance into Confederation. The final barrier to B.C.'s union with Canada was removed when the Canadian government acquired Rupert's Land.

In the spring of 1870 a motion to join Canada received unanimous approval in the B.C. Legislative Assembly. A three-man delegation set off to Ottawa to negotiate the terms. Macdonald, wanting to see his country truly be "from sea to sea" scarcely drove a hard bargain. The B.C. delegates received virtually everything they asked for and more. Ottawa assumed all provincial debts as well as providing a rich annual subsidy. British Columbia retained control over most of the public lands within its borders. Asking merely for a wagon road to be built through the mountains so there would be some physical connection between themselves and the rest of the country, the delegates were shocked when they were offered a transcontinental railway. Macdonald committed Ottawa to start the incredible operation within two years and complete it within ten from the date of union. The remaining opposition to union disappeared and British Columbia became Canada's sixth colony.

Symbols and Signs of the New Canada

Even at this early point in its history, Canada was developing some of the symbols of nationhood. These new national symbols developed and evolved within the context of what already existed and was accepted. This process of national building was markedly different from the American experience that witnessed British symbols and values being rejected. Nevertheless, they provided an early common reference point for Canada's first citizens. By the mid-1870s, just fewer than five and half million people were scattered across a huge landmass from Victoria to Halifax. Some viewed themselves as transplanted Europeans, mostly British or French. And a few, even at this very early stage, were beginning to think of themselves as a distinctive people.

Parliament Hill

Perhaps one of the earliest symbols of identity in this period was the Parliament Buildings in Ottawa. After Queen Victoria had decided on the compromise of Ottawa (Bytown) as the colonial capital in 1857 rather than the more established Toronto, Kingston, Montreal, or Quebec City, construction of the elaborate and impressive buildings began. Farther from the border, her surprise choice of Ottawa appeared much safer from the potentially threatening Americans. On September 1, 1860, the Prince of Wales laid the cornerstone for the buildings that would dwarf all other structures in the city of fifteen thousand. It would take until 1866 for the three Blocks, Centre, East, and West, to be built. The 92.2 metre Peace Tower and the impressive Library would be added in later years. Lavishly appointed with its own various symbolic details designed within its careful construction, Parliament Hill would be an enduring symbol for all Canadians.

The North-West Mounted Police

As changes in the west created upheaval among the inhabitants, lawlessness on the prairies became an increasing problem. The area west of the newly created Manitoba, one quarter the size of the entire continent, was home to less than fifty thousand people. Food, particularly buffalo meat, was becoming increasingly scarce. As Métis hunters pushed further west, they infringed on the territory of the Cree, who in turn, were forced onto the hunting grounds of the Blackfoot Confederacy. An intense war raged between the two in 1869, with hundreds dying. The troubles compounded as a smallpox epidemic killed hundreds more in the early 1870s. The final straw may have been the

The Parliament Buildings in Ottawa. Today, only the library at the rear remains from the original buildings. Fire destroyed the rest in 1914, and Parliament was rebuilt with the addition of the Peace Tower in 1919.

influx of ruthless American traders who offered whisky in return for buffalo. The environment among the people of the prairies became turbulent. It had already exploded with the Red River Rebellion and new uprisings were on the horizon.

Macdonald and the federal government were responsible for keeping the peace and maintaining law and order in the west. The Lieutenant-Governor of Manitoba, Alexander Morris, warned Macdonald of the urgent need for a police force in the new Canadian West, but the law creating such a force was stuck in Parliament. However, when news of the Cypress Hill massacre reached Ottawa in 1873, the politicians were spurred into action. On May 31, 1873, about a dozen drunken American "wolfers"—hunters who poisoned buffalo carcasses and then harvested the fur from the wolves that fed off of them—attacked a defenceless band of Assiniboine Indians. Incorrectly believing that the natives had stolen a horse from them, the "wolfers" murdered twenty Assiniboine, including the elderly and children. In a horrific display of brutal lawlessness, one elderly tribesman was clubbed to death and his severed head tied on to a pole. Canadians

demanded action, as they feared the lawlessness was an open invitation for American annexation. The formation of the North-West Mounted Police was the government's solution. Modelled on a police force in Ireland, they were to be the quasi-military arm of the Canadian government on the prairies. In the planning stages, the force was originally to be called the North-West Mounted Rifles. However, when the United States objected, claiming the name was too aggressive, Macdonald simply crossed out "Rifles" and substituted "Police."

Their mandate was extensive: end the illegal whisky trade, patrol the border, end smuggling, gain the respect and confidence of the Aboriginal Peoples, and maintain law and order. On July 8, 1874, a contingent of three hundred officers and men, equipment, and six months of provisions left Manitoba on the famous "Great March" west under the command of George Arthur French. It was to be a sixteen hundred kilometre trek from Ontario out west during which they had to endure the elements and starvation. After three months and only 430 kilometre, French decided to break his procession in two. The healthiest went to Fort

The Royal Canadian Mounted Police (shown above) was initiated in an attempt to help Ottawa control its new western lands and peoples. Why has the Mountie become a Canadian symbol popularized in print, television and movies?

Whoop-Up country close to the American border, while the other journeyed north to Fort Edmonton. Almost another three months of hunger, insects, mud, and cold had to be endured before the latter reached its destination.

After the westward journey, the Mounties began performing their duties with efficiency and consideration. They restored law and order, ended smuggling, and performed a number of vital services (delivering mail, relief, and health care) for the indigenous population.

As exemplary as the reputation of the NWMP was, it could not disguise the fact the Canadian government's treatment of Aboriginal Peoples was racist. The new Canadian nationality that the government was trying to forge did not encourage differences. This was nowhere more evident, despite the NWMP's efforts, than in the treatment of Aboriginals on the prairies. The series of numbered treaties in the 1870s and 1880s were signed whereby Aboriginal claims to huge tracts of land were exchanged for reserves of much less attractive land. It was the NWMP that was entrusted with enforcing the unfair treaties. It was a clash of cultures, and values. Just as Aboriginals were being shunted off their land, so too their culture was being sacrificed. The early Canadian sense of nationhood did not put a premium on tolerance. Rather, it attempted to silence dissent and eliminate diversity.

Even Aboriginal traditions were seen as a threat to Canada's colonization of the west, and as a barrier to assimilating the Aboriginals into a Canadian society based on European culture. Sam Steele, superintendent of the NWMP, attended a Sun Dance ceremony, and wrote to the government, "Old warriors take this occasion of relating their experience of former days counting their scalps and giving the number of horses they were successful in stealing. This has a pernicious effect on the young men; it makes them unsettled and anxious to emulate the deeds of their forefathers."[6]

Annual ceremonies like the Sun Dance and the oral history that was passed down from generation to generation were vital to the survival of the Aboriginal culture. Yet the survival of their culture was exactly what the Canadian government did not want. In 1885, an amendment was added to the Indian Act that placed restrictions on what the ceremonies could include and how long they could be. And it was the NWMP that was given the responsibility of enforcing these restrictions.

In an attempt to "civilize" Aboriginal Peoples, the Canadian government banned many Aboriginal rituals, such as the Sun Dance (shown above) and the potlatch. They believed that the continuation of such practices would only encourage Aboriginal resistance to Christianity.

O Canada!

A musical symbol of early Canadian identity appeared in 1880. After an adventuresome life that included fighting and being wounded in the American Civil War and musical performances in the United States, South America, Mexico, and the West Indies, Calixa Lavallee wrote the score for what would become O *Canada*. In 1880, he received a request to set to music a patriotic poem written in French by Adolphe-Basile Routhier. It was a rousing success at its initial performance on the Plains of Abraham for the 1880 St. Jean Baptiste celebrations. It would be exactly one hundred years, less fourteen days, when on July 1, 1980, the composition, with Lavallee's music, French lyrics by Judge Adolphe Routhier, and English lyrics by Robert Stanley Weir, was officially proclaimed the Canadian national anthem. Interestingly, Weir, another Quebec judge, penned the English lyrics thirty years after Routhier had written the French version, but the English version is not a direct translation of the original French.

The Canadian Pacific Railway

Gerald Freisen's recent *Citizens and Nation: An Essay on History, Communication, and Identity* argues that much of the Canadian identity is to be found in successive changes in communication which altered ordinary citizens' perception of time and space. It was not that the country got smaller, it was more that the means of interacting were taken to a new level. Canadians would develop their own unique identity through ingenuity and hard work. Through invention and application, Canadians enabled themselves to convey their own histories, concerns, and visions and in the process developed a common heritage. In the immediate post-Confederation era, the Canadian Pacific Railway radically altered the perception of time and space for the inhabitants of the infant country.[7]

Much has been written about the incredible struggle to construct the CPR. The problems were legion, beginning with obtaining the requisite financing and charting the optimal route. Having originally awarded the contract to Sir Hugh Allan and his American partners in 1873, the project languished amid internal squabbling and insufficient funds. Finally, in February 1881, the Canadian government agreed to a new Montreal Syndicate, again headed by Allan, to complete the project. The terms were indeed generous. The CPR received $25 million, 10 million hectares of land, a

Chinese immigrants were used for some of the most gruelling and dangerous work on the Canadian Pacific Railway. It is said that three Chinese men died for every kilometre of track that was laid. How might this change our view of the railway that many have called the "national dream"?

tax exemption on railway stations, grounds, and buildings, all existing railways that had already been built as part of the transcontinental system (estimated to be worth $30 million), and a guarantee that no other line could be built south of the CPR for twenty years.[8] Sir Sandford Fleming's survey crew took ten years to survey the optimal route, eventually finding passes that have gone down in Canadian folklore—Kicking Horse, Roger's, and Eagle. The actual construction, supervised by William Van Horne, an American of wide talents, was a marvel of engineering and physical determination.

The Railroad At Any Cost

The physical challenges were immense: the muskeg and granite of the Canadian Shield, the immense distance of the prairies, the blasting in the mountains of British Columbia. Andrew Onderdonk, the contractor in charge, turned to Chinese labourers to fill the vacant jobs. Not only did Onderdonk pay Chinese labourers less than half of what white workers made, he also assigned them the most dangerous work. Close to seven hundred Chinese labourers lost their lives while building the CPR. In fact, it is said that three Chinese men died for every kilometre of track. It would seem incomprehensible that on November 7, 1885, at Craigellachie in the B.C. interior, after Donald Smith drove in "the last spike," Van Horne concluded with "All I can say is that the work has been well done in every way."[9]

It is difficult to fathom the impact that the transcontinental railway had on Canada, both as a symbol and as a physical reality. It has been argued that it made the country. It was the "bands of steel" that gave definition to a scattered and distant people. It created a nation east-to-west through the natural north-to-south direction of Canada's geography. It was the transportation crux on which the National Policy would grow. Immigrants were initially brought westward from eastern ports. Their produce, from the "western breadbasket," would ultimately be shipped back eastward along those same tracks. Finally, the manufactured products of eastern industries were then conveyed to that guaranteed domestic market that Macdonald had envisioned. It created a host of western towns, such as Regina and Calgary that sprang up along the railway line. Other western centres, such as Winnipeg and Vancouver, experienced significant growth because of the railway. It allowed Ottawa to quickly dispatch troops west to the South Saskatchewan River area and quickly end the North-West Rebellion of 1885. The transcontinental railway put to rest the nagging fears of an American takeover of the western lands.

Prior to the completion of the CPR, the nation was little more than an idea in the minds of people like Macdonald and Cartier and Brown. Now, the tracks of the railway would bind the country together and give substance to what had been largely the abstract notion of Canada. Symbolically as well, the transcontinental railway became an abiding metaphor for the country and its people. They had overcome derision and disbelief when the idea was first voiced, struggled against overwhelming odds, persevered over many years, and ultimately, tamed the rugged land. Perhaps no more fitting symbol of the Canadian identity exists than "the national dream." It is interesting to note that by the time the CPR was completed, Van Horne renounced his American citizenship and became a Canadian. "Building the railway," he claimed, "would have made a Canadian out of the German Emperor."

Web Connection

www.mcgrawhill.ca/links/definingcanada

Go to the Web site above to find out more about Chinese immigrants and their work on the Canadian Pacific Railroad.

Review...Reflect...Respond

1. Are the Canadian symbols discussed in this chapter still considered symbols of Canada today? Why or why not?

2. Can you think of other symbols that reflected the new country that were not included in this chapter? Give reasons for your choice.

3. Were the symbols discussed in this chapter truly representative of all the different groups of people who were present in Canada at this time? Whom did they represent? Whom did they exclude?

Conclusion

As Macdonald set out to create a country *a mari usque mare a usque mare*, colonies that were as different from each other in their people as their geographies were lassoed by the rope of Confederation. It would seem that the new provinces were held together only by the name of the country to which they now belonged. Even as the young country became bound together by the "bands of steel" of the railway, its tracks had been laid on land that had been traded away in a series of treaties that pushed Aboriginals onto reserves.

Yet, despite Howe's statement that "...a more unpromising nucleus of a new nation could hardly be found on the face of the earth," the young country somehow managed to stay together. Small symbols started to emerge that even began to be recognized across the land as "Canadian." But the desire to create one identity would face the enormous task of taking on the strength of the regional personalities.

Notes

1. Joseph Howe, Speech to the House of Commons (November 8, 1867).
2. R. Douglas Francis et al *Destinies: Canadian History Since Confederation, Third Edition* (Toronto: Harcourt Brace, 1996), p. 39.
3. Conrad and Finkel, Volume II pp. 38-40.
4. Ibid
5. Louis Riel, Address to the Jury (August 1, 1885).
6. Arthur J. Ray, *I Have Lived Here Since the World Began* (Toronto: Key Porter Books, 1996), p. 230.
7. Gerald Freisen, "Citizens and Nation: An Essay on History, Communication, and Identity" (Toronto: University of Toronto Press, 2000).
8. J.M. Bumstead, *The Peoples History of Canada: A Post-Confederation History* (Toronto: Oxford University Press, 1992), pp. 50–51.
9. Francis et al, p. 56.

Chapter 12 Review

Knowledge & Understanding

1. Identify these people, places, and events and explain their historical significance to Canadian history and the development of its culture and identity:
   - The North-West Rebellion
   - Alexander Morris
   - Joseph Howe
   - Métis
   - Bill of Rights

2. Create a graphic organizer that lists the factors that divided Canada and the factors that united Canada in the wake of Confederation. Be sure to provide a brief explanation of the impact of each factor.

3. Draw an extensive mind map indicating the many short and long term results of western settlement. Be sure to think of the effects on Aboriginal peoples, nature, and the rest of Canada.

Thinking & Inquiry

4. Louis Riel has been called a hero, a martyr, a madman, a criminal, and a visionary. The moving of his statue from the Manitoba legislature in the early 1990s, more than a century after his death, caused a major controversy. In a well-written paragraph, explain what you believe is the most accurate label with which Louis Riel should be remembered.

5. Several symbols of Canadian identity were discussed in this chapter. Which do you believe has had the most enduring significance to Canada? Explain your answer with supporting arguments.

Application

6. You are a journalist interviewing Louis Riel the night before his execution. Make a list of ten questions that you would ask him. How might your list of questions be different if you worked for either a French or an English language newspaper?

7. Look again at the painting "The Capture of Batoche" in this chapter. Could you use this painting as an accurate source of information about the Battle of Batoche? Why or why not?

Communication

8. The Canadian government has decided to issue an apology to Chinese Canadians who suffered inhumane treatment during the construction of the Canadian Pacific Railway, and they have asked you to write the apology that will be read in a public ceremony. Write a three hundred word speech that would address the contributions of Chinese labourers and a public apology for their treatment.

9. As a follower of Joseph Howe's anti-Confederation forces in Nova Scotia, you plan on organizing a protest outside the building where Sir John A. Macdonald has come to meet with Howe to convince him to allow Nova Scotia to stay in Confederation. Design an anti-Confederation poster that advertises the protest and also shows why Nova Scotians should leave Confederation.

Changing Times: Economics, Industrialism, and Urbanism

It is we who plowed the prairies; built the cities where they trade;
–INTERNATIONAL WORKERS OF THE WORLD LABOUR SONG

Beginning slowly in the mid-nineteenth century, the Industrial Revolution soon gained momentum and initiated a host of permanent political, social, and economic changes. This new industrialism and the resulting urbanism, fostered a complete and profound transformation of Canadian culture and society. Gone were the days of a rural, pioneer, agrarian society, as production shifted from small family farms and business to large factories. The lure of factory jobs was a beacon for both rural inhabitants and new immigrants, and cities grew at an astounding rate, changing Canada into a modern industrial state with both positive and negative consequences. Canada's traditional economy, based on the export of staple products such as fish, fur, timber, and wheat, grew much more diversified when Sir John A. Macdonald implemented his National Policy.

The National Policy was Sir John A. Macdonald's response to the claim of Canadian manufacturers that they could not compete against Americans. It would also help to alleviate the effects of the global depression, which had begun in 1873. This worldwide depression reduced the world market for Canadian wheat and other staples and also discouraged immigration. The three interconnected components of the Policy—protective tariffs, completion of the Canadian Pacific Railway, and settlement of the west—would address both of these issues. The tariffs would protect fledgling Canadian industries by allowing them to become established, and in the process provide thousands of jobs. The transcontinental railway would be the lifeline for transporting goods between central Canada and the West. It would also open the door for immigrants who would settle the West and make Canada a "western breadbasket." Although enacted in 1879, the effects of the National Policy became obvious once the CPR was completed in 1885 and the global downturn ended by the mid-1890s. Many new industries were established, tens of thousands of jobs were created, a few fortunes were made, and the relationship between government and business was firmly cemented. Trade with the United States soared, rising more than 50 percent between 1878 and 1896.

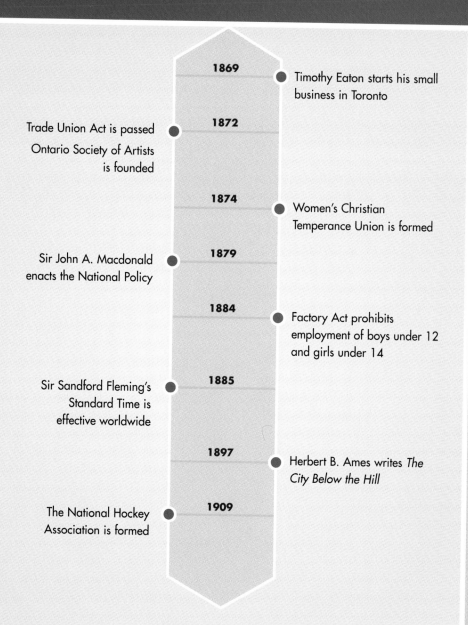

13

1869 — Timothy Eaton starts his small business in Toronto

Trade Union Act is passed
Ontario Society of Artists is founded — 1872

1874 — Women's Christian Temperance Union is formed

Sir John A. Macdonald enacts the National Policy — 1879

1884 — Factory Act prohibits employment of boys under 12 and girls under 14

Sir Sandford Fleming's Standard Time is effective worldwide — 1885

1897 — Herbert B. Ames writes *The City Below the Hill*

The National Hockey Association is formed — 1909

By the end of this chapter, you will be able to

- describe the evolution of industrialization and urbanization in Canada

- assess the effects of industrialization on the regions and peoples of Canada

- assess the origins and results of Macdonald's national policy

- evaluate the economic and cultural contributions of Canadian cities

- analyze how changes in transportation and communication technology have influenced Canadian society and identity

- analyze the evolution of the labour movement in Canada

- assess the extent to which education has been used in Canada as an instrument for shaping regional, provincial, and national identities

A "National" Policy?

The benefits of the National Policy were very unevenly distributed. Central Canada, the industrial heartland of the nation, prospered but many alleged that it did so at the expense of eastern and western Canada. The Maritimes suffered a severe economic downturn. Having relied on the lucrative trade of staple products to both the United States and Britain, they could not make an easy transition when those markets disappeared. There were further difficulties in making the shift from the prosperous days of "wind, water, and wood." Maritime prosperity had depended on wooden sailing ships and the end of Maritime shipping and shipbuilding was signalled with the advent of the ocean-going steamships. By 1868 these accounted for more than a third of the tonnage in St. Lawrence ports. The Maritimes' distance from the political and economic centre of Canada, the small population, and the shortage of capital all assigned them to a less prosperous economic status.

The western region did not fare any better. They too were on the periphery of the country with a small population and little political clout. Initially, they suffered because the western settlement envisioned by Macdonald never materialized during his lifetime. In 1891, the year of his death, the population of the West had only grown to about a quarter of a million. Land in the American west was still available on more favourable terms and appeared to be a more attractive destination for prospective immigrants than the largely deserted Canadian prairie. The post-Civil War years saw an unprecedented economic boom in the United States. The American "Guilded Age" witnessed a tremendous industrial expansion that was a magnet for both immigrants and capital. Although over 1.5 million immigrants did come to Canada during the decade of the 1880s, the country's overall population rose very modestly, as there was a net migration of almost two million out of Canada to the United States between 1871 and 1891.

With the return of world prosperity by the mid-1890s and the belief that the American frontier had closed up, immigration to Canada grew substantially and the prairies became more populated. However, western farmers had to contend with the high freight rates of the CPR in order to send their grain to the central Canadian markets. Finally, in 1898 after a decade of arguing and complaining about the rates, the Crowsnest Pass Agreement reduced them. The CPR was granted a $3.3 million subsidy to build a railway over the Crowsnest pass in the BC interior. In return, the CPR agreed to reduce freight rates (rates on fruit and produce were cut by 33 percent, on coal oil 20 percent, 10 percent off manufactured goods important for

What was this political cartoonist saying about the National Policy?

farmers, and off grain and flour 3 cents per hundred weight). The agreement once again pointed out the high degree of government involvement in the economy.

Western farmers were also concerned with the tariff stipulations of the National Policy. The very tariffs that benefited and enriched Ontario and Quebec manufacturers, put western farmers in a double bind. They had to "buy expensive and sell cheap." The finished products they were purchasing were protected by tariffs. That lessened competition, which in turn raised the price. On the other side of the ledger, the grain they were producing was not protected by tariffs and therefore faced considerable competition, which lowered the price. Tariffs, freight rates, and little political influence were the pillars upon which western alienation was founded.

From Water to Steel

As new products were churned out in central Canada, the system needed to transport these goods to the other regions of Canada had to be faster and better. The first transportation links had been the waterways that acted as the arteries of trade. Pre-dating the Industrial Revolution was the canal-building era when in rapid succession, those water highways were joined with the construction of canals such as the Lachine (1823), Welland (1829), and the Rideau (1834). The trip upstream from Montreal to Kingston was reduced to a mere nineteen hours, compared to the seven-day trip by road. However, even in its heyday, canals were insufficient, unreliable, and inefficient—particularly with winter freeze-ups—to meet the demands of the coming industrial age.

The reorientation of Canadian trade and economic policies caused by the British repeal of the Corn Laws in 1846 and the American abolition of reciprocity in 1866, necessitated a transportation revolution. Canals may have been adequate in the earlier days of a protected market, but if a domestic market was going to be created and enlarged, transportation had to be improved and expanded. Thus, a railway boom followed quickly after the canal-construction era. In 1850, there were only one hundred twenty kilometres of railway track in all of British North America. By 1865, more than thirty three hundred kilometres were being fully utilized. The Great Western (Windsor to Hamilton), the Buffalo ; Lake Huron (Goderich to Buffalo), the Northern (Toronto to Barrie), and the Grand Trunk (Sarnia to Halifax) were four of the more significant pre-Confederation tracks that were laid across the country. In conjunction with the CPR, as well as long extensions to existing lines, the four railways established an effective internal arterial system.

Railways were the symbol of industrialism. The wood-burning steam engines were fast, modern, efficient, and dependable. They were the vital link between the emerging producers and their markets. Farm produce could be transported more cheaply to cities and ports, and manufactured products were now whisked from city to countryside. Everything was carried on the new "iron horses"—people, necessities, and luxuries. The new railways provided tens of thousands of jobs in their construction, in their service and maintenance, and in their many spin-off industries. Scores of metal-making foundries sprang up in central Canada in the 1850s to meet the seemingly unending needs of the railways. The railways also helped to build a symbiotic relationship between government and business. Many of the lines would never have been built had it not been for the generous government subsidies that their owners received. Even short lines cost substantial sums, well beyond the means of private enterprise. Initially British investors were the principal source of capital for railway projects. Gradually, the federal government began to take on more of a role as the prime source of investment capital and Canadian entrepreneurs increasingly looked to Ottawa for financial support. Both before and after Confederation, ranking politicians such as Georges Cartier, Francis Hincks, Allan McNab, and Alexander Galt, were all major stockholders of railway companies. Complex, lucrative, and interlocking interests drew together the federal government and the Hudson's Bay Company, the banks, leading insurance companies, and major railway and construction interests.

Although the railways were responsible for much economic progress railway construction also involved the exploitation of minorities and labourers desperate for work. But it was not just the actual labourers who built the railways who were exploited. Aboriginal Peoples lost their land, culture, and way of life and in order to make way for the railway line, many settlers lost the land that they had spent years clearing. Finally, once the railways were completed, farmers faced the monopolistic power of the CPR and its high freight rates.

Aside from its dramatic economic and political impact, the new railroads had a major social impact as well. Travel times were reduced and communities were brought closer together. Winter's tight grip was loosened and the isolation of the outlying regions diminished. During the last half of the nineteenth century, as trains chugged across the land, they brought irreversible economic, social, and political change to the lives of many Canadians.

The Captains of Industry

Central Canada continued to grow in wealth and power, as did certain individuals, the so-called captains of industry, who established incredible personal fortunes. The Conservative Party was "Canada's political party" of the nineteenth century, being in power for all but eight of the thirty-three years. A key reason for its success came from the close relationship it forged with business tycoons. For example, Macdonald once referred to Sir Hugh Allan's CPR syndicate as the "sleeping partner" of the Conservative government. Between Macdonald's return to office in 1878 and his death in 1891, the CPR syndicate and its supporters poured more than $1 million into the party's election coffers.

Other entrepreneurs emerged in different fields. Jean-Baptiste Rolland, a Montreal bookseller, came to be a dominant player in the pulp and paper industry. George Stephen, like many of his colleagues who came to Canada at a young age, he parlayed his insights into careers as a bank president, financier, and railroad builder. Frederic Nicholls, president of Canadian General Electric, was typical of the new breed of "self-made men" in that he was one of those new daring entrepreneurs who created his own wealth. Senator George Albertus Fox, as president of Canada Life, the Bank of Commerce, Central Canada Savings and Loan and six lesser companies, as well as the founder of Dominion Securities, controlled over $50 million by 1900, a staggering sum at that time. Fortunes were made in virtually every field—steel, railways, banks, insurance, liquor, mining, and retailing. These men, by combining entrepreneurial talent and timing, became some of the captains of industry who dominated Canadian business during the last quarter of the nineteenth century.

Perhaps most representative of this new capitalist spirit was Timothy Eaton. Born in 1834 in Ireland, he emigrated to British North America at the age of 20 along with his two older brothers. They established a general store in St. Mary's, in southwestern Ontario and revolutionized retailing in Canada with three innovative ideas. First, Eaton insisted on cash only sales, eliminating the system of bartering and haggling. Second, "Satisfaction Guaranteed, or Money Refunded" became the credo of the new organization. Third, realizing that there was a lucrative, untapped rural market that could not come to his store, Eaton had the store go to them. His mail order business, founded upon the legendary Eaton's Catalogue, completed his retailing revolution.

After recognizing that St. Mary's could not contain his entrepreneurial ambition, he started a small dry goods business in Toronto in 1869. Fourteen years later, spurred by competition from

The Eaton's Catalogue for 1903-04. What was this cover trying to tell potential Eaton's customers? Would this approach work today?

rival department stores such as Simpson's, he opened a much larger store with four floors, two elevators, and electric lighting—the department store was born. When Timothy Eaton died in 1907, he left behind an immense commercial empire with two large stores in Toronto and Winnipeg, a thriving catalogue branch, and nine thousand employees.

Changing Times

The coming of the railway not only limited the influence of canals, it also demanded a new standard system of time. In the early days of train travel the common practice was to move your watch one minute ahead for every twelve miles (twenty kilometres) travelled in a westerly direction. Thus, noon in Kingston (12:00 p.m.) was twelve minutes later than noon in Montreal (12:12 p.m.) and thirteen minutes before noon in Toronto (11:47 a.m.).

Such a system became impractical and unworkable once people began travelling hundreds of kilometres a day by train. Designing railway schedules became an incredibly complicated task. Something had to be done, and Sir Sandford Fleming, the Scottish-born chief engineer of the CPR construction, devised a solution earning him the name "the Father of Standard Time".

Fleming's idea was simple, practical, and solved the problem. He believed that time had to be global rather than local. Thus, he divided the Earth into twenty-four equal time zones. Each time zone would have a uniform time and there would be a one-hour time difference between contiguous zones. He first introduced his concept in 1879 in Toronto at the Canadian Institute for the Advancement of Scientific Knowledge. It was met with skepticism and fierce opposition from governments and scientists alike. They argued that it was difficult and impractical. However, he persevered and eventually obtained official approval at the International Prime Meridian Conference in Washington, D.C. Standard Time came into effect world-wide on January 1, 1885, although Canada had adopted the idea in 1883 largely at the urging of railway and business owners. For his "timely" invention, Fleming was knighted in 1897 at Queen Victoria's Diamond Jubilee.

How did Sir Sandford Fleming change the way people around the world think about time?

Organizing and Classifying

We organize and classify information in a variety of ways for a range of purposes. Organizing information or data helps us to better understand the overall structure, the parts of the whole, and the context.

Organizing

Writers organize their material according to their purpose and their audience. Some organization methods work better for some subjects than for others. When you are researching written materials, it can be helpful to understand which organizational principle a writer is using. Once you are familiar with the possible methods of organization, you will be able to use them to structure your own communications. For example, when you are writing your essay or preparing your oral presentation, you can select the organizational method that will best serve your purpose. Some of these methods of organization are

- Chronological: events arranged in the order in which they occurred in time
- Spatial: an object (or a process) described according to the physical arrangement of its parts
- Order of importance: events or situations arranged in either increasing or decreasing order of importance
- Comparison: the similarities and differences of subjects (or events) according to a focused, appropriate, and useful basis of comparison
- Narrative: an account of an action, an event, or a sequence of events that take place over time
- Exposition: objective explanation of how something is done or how it has happened

Classifying

When you classify, you organize your information into categories and subcategories. For example, if you were to start with the category "Canadian Citizenship and Heritage," you might use the subcatgories "Canadian

citizenship," "French-Canadian identity," "Culture and identity," and "Human rights in a just society." These subcategories would allow you either to categorize the research information you are collecting or to organize the information you are going to use in the plan of your essay or presentation. You could even use classification, which is an effective way to deal with a complex subject, as the main principle of organization in the outline for your written or oral communication.

Whether you are using classification to organize your research or to create an outline for your essay, a tree diagram can be a helpful tool.

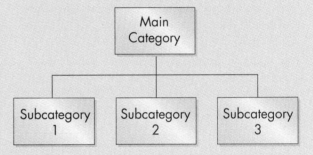

Using notes to help you organize and classify

Taking notes from a variety of different research sources can be challenging. One effective and efficient way to record your research notes is to enter the information into a database.

An alternative, equally effective way to organize your research is to use cue cards. By putting main points on cards, you can easily arrange your information in the proper order for your presentation, seminar, or essay. When you are finished you research, you can review your thesis statement and the organizational plan you have developed to see if you need to add, delete, or revise any of your cue cards.

Include the page number necessary for proper documentation.

Only the title is necessary. Other details are contained in the bibliography.

Source: The Missing of the Somme   **Section of essay:** D

Page: 111–114

Main point (s):

– what the Vimy Ridge monument looks like (different parts of it)

– quote from the sculptor (Walter Allward) who built the

monument describing the symbolism (The grieving woman

represents Canada, a young nation mourning her dead...)

– comparison of Lloyd George a speech in 1914 with

Allwards comments in 1936

This section is filled in when research is complete and the essay outline is developed. This allows for the easy organization of ideas under subheadings.

Each card should contain information about only one topic.

Practice

Practice your organizing and classifying skills by selecting one major section of this chapter and preparing a tree diagram to classify the elements of its structure. Then prepare note cards on the organizational methods that the author has used in the section. Present your findings to a small group of fellow students.

A Radical Shift in Production

Beginning shortly before Confederation and gaining rapid momentum after, a new system of production radically altered the Canadian economic environment. The Industrial Revolution brought about a fundamental reorganization of the nature of work. Formerly, production had been a small-scale activity, usually centred in the family home set within a rural environment, and most products were made by hand. But the advent of machines changed where and how people worked. By mid-century, business owners were gathering large groups of workers together in one location. Here, their work could be closely monitored, disciplined intensified, and production made more efficient. As production became centralized, it also grew more regimented and specialized. In addition, it produced new products at lower prices because of the benefits of the economies of scale. It brought thousands of jobs to men and women. The emergence of the factory system, with its immense economic and social impacts, was to transform the entire economic and social scene.

Whereas before 1850, the overwhelming majority of Canadians earned their livelihood from fish, fur, timber, and wheat, in the latter half of the century, industry, manufacturing, trade, and commerce would become key. Wealth prior to Confederation had resulted from the export of staples. By the 1870s, the Canadian economy was becoming much more diversified. Staples, and their export, were certainly still important. But now, Canada was becoming a manufacturing nation. It was Canadians who were turning their wheat into flour, their timber into various finished wood products, and their minerals into metal. They were producing many of the goods that they formerly had imported. Because manufactured products sold for more than raw materials, Canada was developing a more favourable balance of trade. Infusions of European capital indicated that Canada had become an attractive investment opportunity. Everything appeared to be going along smoothly until 1873 when an international depression began.

The Ugly Side of Industrialization

Timothy Eaton honestly believed that he was an abnormality among his peers. He felt that he was a true friend of the working person. He argued

Toronto Rolling Mills (1864) by William Armstrong. This was the largest iron mill in Canada and made railway equipment and rails for various railway companies including the Grand Trunk.

that his business, unlike those of mining, factory, and textile workers, engaged in fair labour practices. He closed his stores at 8 p.m., two hours before his competition. He even inaugurated Saturday afternoon off in July and August. The painful reality was that life for the hundreds of thousands of working people was much grimmer than the picture painted by Eaton.

Making the adjustment to urban factory life was difficult for the majority of workers who came from Canadian or European farms. Socially and psychologically, industrial methods of production forced a very different relationship between worker and employer, and between worker and his or her work. The landmark "Report of the Royal Commission on Labour and Capital," published in 1889, uncovered widespread abuses within the industrial system. The Commission rightly located the responsibility with the owners. Because owners wanted to, according to the Commission's Report, "acquire vast fortunes in the shortest interval of time," they demanded "a very large percentage of work with the smallest possible outlay of wages."[1] The ready labour pool allowed employers to exact long hours for low wages under unhealthy working conditions.

The Plight of Farmers

If the situation of the urban working person was bleak, that of farmers was scarcely much brighter. The traditional family farm was changing. The mechanization of agriculture came well before Confederation. For example, the horse-drawn McCormick reaper for harvesting grain was already in use in the 1830s. Mowers and hay rakes were similarly mechanized. The first steam threshing machine, used for separating grain from the stalk, appeared in Woodbridge, Ontario in 1877. It could process more grain in one day than the average farmer could in a year. The first mechanical hay mowers appeared in the 1880s, enabling a man to cut ten acres a day as opposed to a tiny fraction of an acre. Gasoline-powered tractors followed by threshers and other equipment completely altered the agrarian landscape. Such equipment required huge outlays of cash and thus the mechanization of agriculture occurred gradually. But as it did, it radically altered the farming environment. In short, the new technology enabled a farmer in 1900 to produce a bushel of wheat in less than one-hundredth of the time it might have taken his father in 1870.

The mechanized threshing machine could process more grain in one day than a man could do in a year.

The new machines were not limited to wheat farming. The cream-separator, designed in 1900, revolutionized the dairy industry. The perfecting and popularizing of canning as a means of food preservation was another important advance. So too were refrigerated railway cars. Perhaps the single greatest technological improvement in the quality of rural life was Bell's telephone. It helped end countryside isolation. Again, as with farm machinery, phones were not quickly or easily installed in rural Canada, and even until fairly recently, many rural western settlements shared phone lines.

Then, as now, the farming life was a tough one. Whereas today only about five percent of current Canadians derive their income from farming, in the latter part of the nineteenth century more than half of Canadians did. Farmers were prisoners of the uncertainties of weather and crop prices. Even when crops were good, it meant that everyone enjoyed the same bounty producing an abundant supply, thereby lowering the price received. When a plague of grasshoppers or locust or a natural disaster such as a drought or hailstones hit, many families were wiped out. Most, having borrowed from banks for seed and machinery could not repay even the interest on their loans from the low prices they obtained for their crops. Farm foreclosures were rampant and the exodus to the city began. While allowing millions of hectares of land to come under cultivation and making agriculture more efficient, mechanization further impoverished the agrarian community.

Web Connection

www.mcgrawhill.ca/links/definingcanada
To find out more about agriculture in late nineteenth century Canada, go to the above Web site.

The Rise of Labour

Workers' attempts to improve their appalling conditions were consistently frustrated by the 1833 British Combination Act. The Act deemed any collaborative action on the part of workers to discuss an improvement of their working conditions a "conspiracy." However, the landmark Trade Union Act was passed in 1872 legalizing unions and eliminating the threat of future arrest for peaceful strikers. Banding together in an attempt to improve working conditions could no longer be regarded as an illegal conspiracy. But the prime minister's support of the emerging labour movement was lukewarm at best. He may well have passed the Act more to embarrass his old political rival, George Brown, who as the owner of *The Globe* was facing the Toronto printers' strike.[2]

The first unions were small, local organizations centred in skilled trades. These craft unions attempted to improve the working lives and to reduce the impact of technological unemployment for groups such as printers, cigar makers, bakers, and shoemakers. They faced fierce and sometimes violent opposition from employers and government. Even after the passage of the Trade Union Act, union organizers faced considerable intimidation, blacklisting, harassment, and arrest, particularly when they attempted to unionize semi-skilled and unskilled workers.

Gradually, assemblies grew larger and stronger, however, the union movement was side-tracked by the depression that began in 1873. The Canadian Labour Union (CLU), formed in that same year as a political arm of the labour movement, was comprised of thirty-one craft unions. Despite its name, all unions came from Ontario, but they could not fight against the devastating round of wage cuts and firings that came in the wake of the economic downturn. Its own internal squabblings, largely centred on the issue of immigration, led to its demise before the end of the decade. Immigration would cause conflict in the labour movement for a long time to come as union organizers were concerned that a large pool of immigrant labour would depress wages and take jobs away from non-immigrants.

The Knights of Labour

In the 1880s, the American-based Knights of Labor (KOL) utilized a new organizing tactic. Rather than solely targeting skilled craft workers, the KOL wanted to organize skilled and unskilled workers into one big union. They managed to make significant inroads in major industrial cities such as Toronto and Hamilton, as well as in smaller communities. They claimed over twenty thousand members in almost a hundred locations. A wave of strikes in the last half of the 1880s was met by stiff opposition from owners, government, and even the public. Such strikes were seen by many as anarchist-driven and were said to incite class conflict. Authorities branded organizers as outside agitators who wanted more than to simply improve the working conditions of their members. They wanted to topple the government and incite

The Knights of Labour, seen here parading through the streets of Hamilton, Ontario in 1885, were members of an industrial union who sought better working conditions for both skilled and unskilled workers.

a workers' classless society, according to the Establishment. Outside of Ontario, the KOL's success was mixed. Significant support was gained in major Quebec industrial cities, but it had difficulty making progress in rural French-Canadian communities against the added opposition of the Catholic Church, which would remain staunchly anti-labour well into the middle of the twentieth century. Out west, the KOL made headway in the larger railway towns of Winnipeg and Calgary, but found little support elsewhere. In Eastern Canada, the KOL was not much of a factor because most of the region's mine, dock, and shop workers rallied behind the Provincial Workingman's Association. Founded originally in 1879 near the Springhill Mining Company in Nova Scotia, the PWA, under the leadership of Robert Drummond, made admirable progress by increasing its membership and winning improvements in working conditions.

Craft workers responded to the challenge of the KOL by forming the Trades and Labour Congress in 1886. They believed, however, that by including unskilled workers the strength of any organizing attempt would be weakened and they insisted any larger, umbrella structure had to exclude unskilled workers. That central division between skilled and unskilled workers would slow any future organizing efforts for decades to come. Even by the turn of the century, fewer than ten percent of industrial workers were organized. In the process, hundreds of thousands of workers would be left prisoner to the arbitrary whims of employers.

The International Workers of the World

Common labourers, especially navvies—men who worked in construction camps—often faced the worst conditions and received little help from unions such as the KOL. Navvies were usually fed, housed, and paid in the cheapest way possible while living and working in labour camps. In 1928, Edmund W. Bradwin wrote *The Bunkhouse Man: A Study of Work and Pay in the Camps of Canada*

Called "bunkhouse men" these workers were part of a mobile labour force that moved from job to low paying job in the logging, harvesting and mining industries. These men were working in northern Ontario for the Transcontinental Railway.

western Canada and northern Ontario. "Wobbly" songs became popular among the camp workers.

Solidarity Forever

*When the Union's inspiration through
    the worker's blood shall run,*
*There can be no power greater any-
    where beneath the sun.*
*Yet what force on earth is weaker than
    the feeble strength of one?*
But the Union makes us strong.

Chorus:
Solidarity forever!
Solidarity forever!
Solidarity forever!
For the Union makes us strong.

*Is there aught we hold in common with
    the greedy parasite*
*Who would lash us into serfdom and
    would crush us with his might?*
*Is there anything left for us but to
    organize and fight?*
For the Union makes us strong.

*It is we who plowed the prairies; built
    the cities where they trade;*
*Dug the mines and built the work-
    shops; endless miles of railroad laid.*
*Now we stand outcasts and starving,
    'mid the wonders we have made;*
But the Union makes us strong.

1903–1914. In his book, Bradwin wrote about the housing conditions of the camp labourers, "The whole surroundings were fitter for the stabling of cattle than the abode of men at a whiff therefrom a well-reared pig would grunt disapproval."[3]

Another organization from the United States, the International Workers of the World (IWW), came north to try and organize the labourers. The "Wobblies" as they became known, rejected traditional unions and focused on using the strike as the bargaining tool to better the inhumane conditions of the workers. While the IWW did not find a large audience in Canada, they did have a strong following of railway construction workers from

*All the world that's owned by idle drones, is ours
    and ours alone.*
*We have laid the wide foundations; built it skyward
    stone by stone*
It is ours, not to slave in, but to master and to own,
While the Union makes us strong.

*They have taken untold millions that they never
    toiled to earn.*
*But without our brain and muscle not a single
    wheel can turn.*
*We can break their haughty power; gain our free-
    dom when we learn*
That the Union makes us strong.

*In our hands is placed a power greater than their
    hoarded gold;*
*Greater than the might of armies, magnified a
    thousand-fold.*

We can bring to birth the new world from the ashes
of the old,
For the Union makes us strong.[4]

Web Connection

www.mcgrawhill.ca/links/definingcanada
To hear Solidarity Forever and other Wobbly Songs,
go to the Web site above.

Despite the difficulties and opposition, gains for many workers were achieved. Unions were legalized and the 1884 Factory Act prohibited employment to boys under twelve and girls under fourteen, although it was poorly enforced. Labour Day was made a statutory holiday in 1894 to recognize the essential contribution of all working people. A separate Department of Labour within the federal government was created in 1900. However, as previously mentioned, the one event that may have advanced the labour movement the most was the 1889 "Report of the Royal Commission on the Relations of Labour and Capital." The report was a harsh condemnation of the abuses of the industrial system and the need for government to improve it: "Your Commissioners think that young persons should not be required to work during the night at any time. Further, it is believed that the regular employment in mills, factories, and mines of children less than fourteen years of age should strictly be forbidden."[5]

The Labour Movement on the Farm

Like their urban cousins, farmers saw organizing and banding together as the solution to their economic plight. The Dominion Grange, an offshoot of the 1.5 million-member American National Grange, grew rapidly in rural Ontario and Manitoba. The Grange championed cooperative action among farmers whereby they would own and operate their economic concerns. The rationale was that this would reduce the powerful agricultural middlemen and promote their own well

being. In Ontario, Grangers set up a variety of companies—trust, fire insurance, and wholesale supply—while out west, they established storage and farmers' elevators. The cooperative movement also enabled farmers to reduce their overhead by creating a mechanism by which expensive machinery could be widely shared among many farmers. Like its urban counterpart, the Knights of Labour, the Grange disappeared by the late-1880s. As the internal divisions within the movement appeared, they lost the support of the vital agrarian newspapers and had their membership and policies co-opted by mainstream political parties.

Out of the Grange's demise, grew the Patrons of Industry. Beginning in Sarnia in 1889, it grew rapidly claiming a hundred thousand members in two thousand clubs by 1894 in Ontario alone. It achieved similar success in Quebec and Manitoba. Much more political—and less conservative—than its forerunner, the Patrons lobbied for lower freight rates, land distribution reform, reduced tariffs, and an end to railway monopolies. In Ontario, the Patrons became a political party, capturing seventeen of Ontario legislative's seats, and threatening Oliver Mowat's Liberal administration as well as the traditional two-party system. The Patrons, however, went into decline after an attempted alliance between farm and labour fell apart. Had such an alliance proven viable, some of the abuses of industrial capitalism in Canada may have been alleviated much earlier.

The earlier Dominion Grange, building on the tremendous success of the American movement, had lobbied government for reforms but had expired by the middle of the 1880s. The Patrons followed in their wake and although they had more success, they too succumbed to internal bickering and division. However, the groundwork had been laid for Canadian-style populism.

Populism did much to improve the lives of Canadian farmers. The flood of immigrants, mechanization, and international competition were altering life in rural Canada and learning from the labouring cousins, farmers recognized that the key to improving their lot lay in organizing. Populist was an umbrella term that covered different ethnic, regional, and political groups. What they had in common was an abiding desire to better the lot of farmers. They feared that industrialism might leave them behind in its wake. And if not left behind, they felt sure that they would be disadvantaged. The solution was to organize, lobby governments, and publicize their views.

Success was achieved on a number of fronts. The Crowsnest Pass Agreement achieved some reduction in the dreaded freight rates. Banks became slightly more accommodating to farmers' needs and interests. Significantly, the co-operative movement helped to make farmers less dependent, by allowing them to establish their own retail stores, storage facilities, and trust companies and by giving them a hard-won sense of independence. But it would take until after World War I before the rural reform movement became politically viable. The creation of the Progressive Party, a rural western farm organization, was so successful that it enjoyed the distinction of being the first third-party to form the federal official opposition.

Review...Reflect...Respond

1. Why were the benefits of the National Policy unevenly distributed?

2. Did the railway have more of an impact on Canada's economy, or its society? Explain?

3. How did the emergence of the factory change Canadian culture?

The Coming of Urbanism

In 1871 one in six Canadians lived in a town or city and by 1900, that number was one in three. In 1881, Canada had a population of 4.325 million of whom 3.349 million, or more than 77 percent, lived in rural areas. Forty years later, less than 55 percent of Canada's 8.8 million people lived in the countryside. And almost 20 percent lived in cities of over a hundred thousand. Montreal had more than tripled in size from 115 000 in 1871 to over 380 000 in 1901. So did Toronto, going from a population of 59 000 to just under 210 000. But as rapidly as cities in the Maritimes, Quebec, and Ontario grew, they were eclipsed by the phenomenal growth of western cities. Winnipeg's growth was astonishing, going from under 250 in 1871 to over 42 000 thirty years later.

The big attraction of the cities was the jobs in the newly built and expanded factories. However, cities offered other attractions and advantages. There were far more schools concentrated in cities than scattered across the countryside. General stores, the forerunner of department stores, offered a wide variety of goods. A range of services and amenities—tailors, innkeepers, cobblers, newspapers, libraries, lawyers, and many others—were conveniently located within city boundaries. Cities spoke of convenience, efficiency, and progress, the very watchwords of industrialism.

A number of other factors contributed to urban growth. One of the most critical was transportation, and in the 1800s that meant railways. Particularly in western Canada, the competition to attract main- or branch-lines was intense. Becoming a railway stop meant the ability to attract businesses and people. Growing communities used any means to attract the railways: bribes, subsidies, advertising, or even parades. By the early twentieth century, however, as the car began to replace the railways, roads became the prize. To be located on a provincial highway was akin to having formerly been on the main-line railway junction.

Land speculation was also a major factor in the rise of cities. More of a western phenomenon, artificially created land booms appeared in almost all growing towns. Land speculation, normally originating with businesses, became a mania that no one could avoid. Prices soared, but then inevitably plummeted. But while it was underway, it was a natural magnet.

Another factor was simply the immigrant "reception line." Often immigrants would arrive in cities fully intent on going out west. However, that dream was shattered because of their penniless state so thousands remained where they were. In turn, they would be the "reception" or hosts for relatives and friends from their former countries.

A final factor, along with all the other amenities afforded by cities, was the process of suburbanization. Although commonly associated with the twentieth century, in truth suburbanization was born in the late 1800s. Suburban growth was the product of three factors: the flight by prospering professional and business classes from the squalor of the central core; the rising cost of both land and taxes in the downtown areas; and finally, the advent of first public transit and then the private automobile freed the middle and upper classes from having to reside close to their places of work.

Urban Poverty

As attractive as late nineteenth century cities may have been for some, for the great majority they were places of filth and squalor. The most serious problem—and the root of a host of other difficulties—was poverty. The number of people living in poverty tripled from mid-century. Although statistics are less than accurate, existing evidence indicates that up to half of all urban working class lived below, or at, the "poverty line." There was no such thing as zoning by-laws so development was haphazard at best and dangerous at worst. Development was totally unplanned and often resulted in the strangest neighbourhoods. Within a few blocks, one might find a factory, a business, a church, a cemetery, a school, several stores, as well as assorted types of housing. Land prices rose sharply, especially in downtown core areas effectively making most urban dwellers renters and boarders. Larger cities built street railways to open up surrounding suburbs for housing. The horse

Streetcar workers in Halifax, in the 1890s. As in other Canadian cities, horse-drawn streetcars were being replaced by electric streetcars.

trolley and later the electric trolley completely changed urban transit. Stores, businesses, and housing followed the transit lines radiating out from the centre of the city. In many cities, notably Montreal, Toronto, and Winnipeg, the rail lines sectioned off the city into identifiable residential neighbourhoods, rich and poor (hence the expression "the wrong side of the tracks"). As the largest cities developed middle-class suburbs, one's place of residence came to be increasingly defined by income and ethnic origin.

Urban problems were rampant and made living conditions highly unattractive for all but the wealthiest. That tiny minority, hidden away in their multistoried brick houses staffed by servants, fronted with manicured lawns, could remain blissfully ignorant of the appalling conditions around them. The fashionable "Golden Mile" on Montreal's central Sherbrooke Street was home to forty millionaires, while in Toronto, Jarvis Street and Sherbourne Street were the favoured locations. In many cities, most of the land was owned by ten percent of its citizens.

Cities dramatically revealed the tremendous disparity between the few very rich and the many

A view of downtown slum housing in 1913 Toronto. Living conditions for the poor and working class were deplorable—little or no heat, no light, no indoor toilets and no way out for most families.

very poor. Cities such as Montreal, Toronto, and Winnipeg had large sections of slums. The majority of urban dwellers owned neither house nor land. With high demand and limited supply, tenant rents were excessive. Home ownership, in a remote suburb, was a dream that only the very thrifty skilled worker could entertain. Dilapidated tenements competed with shabby rooming houses for space. Families of six and more were crammed together in a single room. Heating was inadequate and there was no running water. Garbage and sewage collected outside the front door.

Crime was rampant with pickpockets, petty thieves, and professional criminals. Policing was in its infancy and largely ineffective. The same could be said for early fire departments, which continued their volunteer tradition. Ambulance service was practically non-existent. Toronto's first municipally owned ambulance service began in 1883 with one two-horse unit operated by the Department of Public Heath.

Public health and sanitation was primitive. As urban centres expanded, it rapidly became apparent that water supply and sewage disposal systems were inadequate. Toronto only began chlorinating its water in 1910 and it was only in the following year that it prohibited the dumping of raw sewage in Toronto Bay, within metres of the city's water intake. The few health inspectors frequently found many water samples infected. If the water was bad, the air was arguably worse. Chimneys belched out sickening smoke and refuse-lined alleys and streets were much more than an eyesore. As a result, typhoid, typhus, diphtheria, smallpox, and other diseases commonly broke out in turn-of-the century cities. Working in damp, cold factories and living in crowded, unclean dwellings, made urban citizens especially susceptible to epidemics that killed thousands. In Montreal, tuberculosis was the biggest killer. Montreal's death rate from TB reached its height in 1895 at almost 25 per thousand. Winnipeg's, which had fallen to 11.4 per thousand in 1896, more than doubled to 23.2 per thousand by 1906 in the wake of the immigrant influx into the city's north end. (By comparison the present-day national average death rate is 7.3 per thousand.) Cities were breeding grounds for disease and the most at risk were infants. Between impure milk, the prevalence of garbage and sewage, and inadequate medical care, infant mortality rates were extremely high. In 1900, one in three babies in Montreal died before its first birthday.

Grinding poverty, tedious work, poor diet, and inadequate housing meant a bleak existence for most urban dwellers. Municipal officials recognized that the public would not shoulder higher taxes in order to provide sewage, running water, and electricity in the poorer sections of cities, so they simply went without. Toronto did not install sewers in its centre core until the 1920s. City fathers found it more palatable to build parks, libraries, and hospitals as well as improve public transportation—something that would ostensibly benefit everyone.

The ills of urban industrialism were producing a diminished quality of life—and a reduced life expectancy—for the majority of city dwellers. Eking a pitiful existence was the lot for the bulk of late nineteenth-century urban residents. Urban crime, poverty, housing, disease, prostitution, and poor sanitation all set the stage for zealous social critics and reformers.

The Reform Movement: Progressives, Populists, and Suffragists

Turn-of-the-century Canada was in a state of flux. Change was heaped upon change and no one was quite certain if the emerging product was an improvement for everyone. Whenever substantial social and economic change is experienced, there are always winners and losers. The greater the amount of change, the more likely it is that there will be increasing numbers who do not see success. The necessity for improvement in the quality of life of city dwellers began to be the focus of zealous social

critics and reformers. Humanitarian, Social Gospel, religious, professional, and corporate reformers began to fight to improve urban conditions.

Humanitarian Reform

Originating out of the crusading Christian and temperance movements, the humanitarian reform movement arose to address many of turn-of-the-century problems. Religious missions were established in many areas of urban blight. Providing food, shelter, and comfort to the dispossessed, they were a small voice of altruistic reform. William Howland, founder of the Toronto Mission in 1884 and later a mayor of the city, was one of the best examples of this philanthropic effort.

After a phenomenally successful business career in his twenties, Howland had something of a religious awakening and began working with the poor and indigent of Toronto. He also targeted liquor as a problem worsening the lives of the urban poor. In a population of 104 000, Toronto had over eight hundred licensed and unlicensed saloons.

The Social Gospel

The Social Gospel movement, originating in the Methodist Church and then spreading to other Christian denominations, attempted to attack the contemporary and social ills with a more organized passion. Protestant reformers espoused that it was every Christian's duty to help improve the lives of those less fortunate. They believed not just in the moral duty of uplifting their fellow man, but that in improving the ills of society, they would finally achieve the moral vision of perfection. People were fed and clothed but as well their spiritual needs were answered. The establishment of Toronto's Fred Victor Mission in 1894, followed in rapid succession by several other settlement houses, ultimately led to the formation of the Social Service Council of Canada. One of the most famous of their ranks was

James S. Woodsworth who, having observed the squalor endured by immigrants in the north end of his native Winnipeg, worked tirelessly to eradicate it. His social humanitarianism would ultimately find its home in the 1932 Regina Manifesto, the founding document of the Co-operative Commonwealth Federation, which he would lead with passion and conviction.

Canadian "Muckrakers"

Taking their cue from well-publicized American "muckrakers" (Teddy Roosevelt applied the label to writers who exposed evil and corruption) such as Jabob Riis (*How the Other Half Lives*), Lincoln Steffens (*The Shame of the City*), and Upton Sinclair (*The Jungle*), Canadian reformers attempted to expose and attack the same urban ills. A few wealthy philanthropists emerged to try and improve living conditions in the cities. One such reformer was Herbert B. Ames, who in 1897 wrote *The City Below the Hill*, an expose of Montreal's poverty-stricken area. Ames observed two sections in Montreal, the "city above the hill" where "...tall handsome houses, stately churches and well-built schools..." with clean streets, yards, and good plumbing and sanitation systems housed the middle and upper class, and "the city below the hill," where poor families lived together in dilapidated tenement houses where plumbing was non-existent and nearby factories polluted the air. Ames concluded by writing "The sanitary conditions of 'the city below the hill' is a disgrace to any nineteenth century city in this or any other continent."[6] Ames estimated that a family needed five dollars a week just to subsist, but he found over 888 families in the "city below the hill" who earned far less than that. He believed that irregularity of work was one of the main causes of poverty:

> Think of it, of fifteen hundred families...six hundred do not know what it is to have a regular income and steady work....With most of the wage-earners of these families the programme for the year is as follows: work upon the wharves in summer and odd jobs of any sort during the five long winter months. When spring arrives, overdue rent and debt at the corner grocery have so mortgaged the coming summer's earnings that saving becomes impossible. This irregularity of work is doubtless the main cause of poverty, for the prolonged idleness unfits many a man for steady work even when he at length succeeds in getting it. Once irregular, always irregular is apt to be true, and irregularity, demoralization, and poverty is the order of descent.[7]

While it must be remembered that Ames had the luxury of writing about the poor while enjoying a wealthy lifestyle, his attempts to expose the horrific conditions of the poor urban dwellers were significant to the reform movement.

Montreal's Night Mayor on his Ghostly Rounds (Dedicated to the Board of Health). In this cover to the Canadian Illustrated News in 1875, Death is shown riding through the streets. Who are the ghosts in the background?

Although reformers disagreed about priorities and strategies, there was a consensus that meaningful change would only come about with government reform. Boards of health, sanitation departments, building codes, and health inspectors appeared. Corrupt politicians were removed. Newly built parks, schools, museums, and hospitals all improved the quality of life. Much of this was accomplished through electing municipal reformers who then altered the priorities and programs of their city councils.

Women and Reform

Women were a major part of the reform movement sweeping Canada at the turn-of-the-century just as they were in the urban and rural labour force. It was often women who bore the brunt of the inequities of the labour system, but it was also women who were at the forefront of the work done by charitable organizations. By the turn of the century, middle-class women concentrated their reform efforts on four fronts: temperance, child welfare, public health, and obtaining the right to vote.

With their hard lives, it was perhaps not altogether surprising that working men would sometimes turn to find solace in the bottle. In doing so, they depleted their already inadequate financial resources. All around them, women saw the evils of "the demon rum." It took the food out of the mouths of children, broke up families, and destroyed moral character. The answer was the temperance movement. With zeal in the rightness of their cause, the Women's Christian Temperance Union (WCTU) was founded in 1874 by Letitia Youmans. Less than twenty years later, the WCTU had over nine thousand members nation-wide.

The Right to Vote

Being consistently rebuffed by governments in their demand for prohibition, women quickly realized that accessing the levers of political power was the key. They had to win the right to vote and the suffragette movement was born. Social conditions and society reform would never happen, women argued, if decisions were left completely in men's hands. They only had to point to history to find ample evidence in that assertion. Simple justice demanded equality and equality clearly included the right to vote. They would not listen to arguments that it was "unladylike" or that they would simply duplicate their husbands' votes. Inspired by their more radical British and American sisters, suffragette societies were created across the country. Women like British Columbia's Helena Gutteridge, Ontario's Flora Denison and Dr. Augusta Stowe-Gullen, and Manitoba's Nellie McClung and Dr. Mary Crawford fought ceaselessly and bravely to get the right to vote for women.

They campaigned more modestly than suffragettes elsewhere, preferring petitions, plays, and mock parliaments to parades and demonstrations. Beginning with the three prairie provinces in 1916, women were granted (the exception being Quebec, which waited until 1940) the right to vote in provincial elections and in 1919, the first Canadian woman took her seat in the House of Commons.

One of the more popular women's movement songs came from American working class women, who marched in a 1912 strike under the banner "Bread and Roses." It is a song about equal pay, for equal work, but the desire to still have consideration as women,

As we go marching, marching, in the beauty of the day,
A million darkened kitchens, a thousand mill lofts gray
Are touched with all the radiance that a sudden sun discloses,
For the people hear us singing: Bread and Roses! Bread and Roses!
As we go marching, marching, we battle too for men,
For they are women's children and we mother them again.
Our lives shall not be sweated from birth until life closes;

Hearts starve as well as bodies; give us bread, but give us roses.
As we go marching, marching, unnumbered women dead
Go crying through our singing their ancient call for bread.
Small art and love and beauty their drudging spirits knew.
Yes, it is bread we fight for, but we fight for roses too.
As we go marching, marching, we bring the greater days,
The rising of the women means the rising of the race.
No more the drudge and idler, ten that toil where one reposes,
But a sharing of life's glories: Bread and roses, bread and roses.[8] But a sharing of life's glories: Bread and roses, bread and roses.[8]

Cultural Life on the Rise

While industrialism and urbanism brought many problems in their wake, unquestionably they also helped add to Canada's cultural life. With their large numbers of people and concentrations of wealth, cities produced a rich and varied cultural life. They helped consolidate intellectual and artistic activity as witnessed by the explosion in the number of newspapers. There were but sixty-five newspapers in all of British North America in 1840. Forty years later there were over 450 newspapers, with fifty-six of them being dailies. Rarely neutral in their reporting, nineteenth century newspapers regularly praised their friends and chastized their enemies, usually in very forceful language. Because most literate people—and their numbers were rising quickly due to educational advances—read the papers, their influence was far-reaching.

The relatively new vehicle of education did much to encourage Canadian values and identity. By the 1870s, school had become part of the daily routine of most children. An 1871 Ontario law compelled all children between the ages of seven and twelve to attend school at least four months out of the year. Egerton Ryerson, serving as chief superintendent of education from 1844 to 1876, moved his province towards the principles of full state support and universality, at increasingly higher grade levels. Ontario's lead was widely copied as by 1905, all provinces except Quebec had

Students in the classroom of a school in Vulcan, Alberta circa 1900

mandated free education. However, education was directed mainly towards younger children. The requirements of either factory or farm work meant only about half of teens over fourteen attended high school. As early as 1868, a Canadian National Series of Readers was introduced to Ontario school children and offered a national focus. Added to the traditional curriculum of "the three R's," (reading, writing, 'rithmetic) were domestic science, military drill, physical education, history, woodworking, music, and art.

While education was viewed as a tool to raise the morality and knowledge among children, it was also seen as a way to "Canadianize" immigrants. In 1897, Empire Day was established to celebrate Queen Victoria's sixtieth year as the Queen of England. In Ontario, the Department of Education sent out a memorandum of instructions on how schools should celebrate the day: "The aim of the teacher in all of his references to Canada and the [British] Empire should be, to make Canadian patriotism intelligent, comprehensive, and strong."[9] Education for students, no matter what their heritage, was seen as a method by which all young people would be taught to be, speak, and act like Canadians and celebrate the glory of the British Empire.

Web Connection

www.mcgrawhill.ca/links/definingcanada

To see more works of Canadian artists in the 1800s, go to the Web site above.

Literature

Canadian writing and poetry, largely imitative of European styles prior to Confederation, began to develop its own distinctive style. Susanna Moodie's 1852 *Roughing It in the Bush* was a ground-breaking depiction of the trials of mid-nineteenth century pioneer life. Her nineteen years of struggle and toil started optimistically as she noted in her introduction.

> In 1830, the great tide of emigration flowed westward. Canada became the great land-mark for the rich in hope and poor in purse. Public newspapers and private letters teemed with the unheard-of advantages to be derived from a settlement in this highly favoured region. Its salubrious climate, its fertile soil, commercial advantages, great water privileges, its proximity to the mother country, and last, not least, its almost total exemption from taxation...[are great attractions].[10]

Another female author, Emily Pauline Johnson, daughter of a Mohawk chief and an English mother, celebrated Canadian life and landscape as well as conveyed the richness of Aboriginal life and traditions, "My aim, my joy, my pride is to sing the glories of my own people." Maritimer Thomas Haliburton's creation of Sam Slick still survives today. Haliburton coined such phrases as "the early bird gets the worm," "it's raining cats and dogs," "you can't get blood out of a stone," and "six of one and half a dozen of another." Bliss Carman, Isabella Valarey Crawford, and Archibald Lampman helped create the emerging indigenous literary tradition. Carman, along with his cousin Charles G.D. Roberts, have subsequently been referred to as the "Confederation poets" writing about the physical beauty of the natural landscape with sensitivity and insight. Most of their contemporaries similarly focused on the majesty of the land and tried to fit into the romantic genre of the Victorian Age with fairly stock characters and predictable plots. Several writers banded together and founded "Canada First," although they were unabashedly racist in their scorn for Aboriginals, French, and immigrants. Although the movement did help begin to forge an early sense of Canadian nationalism, its scope was narrow and barely reflected the true make-up of Canadian society.

The Visual Arts

It was painters who took the lead in promoting a nascent sense of Canadian identity. The Ontario Society of Artists, founded in 1872, set professional standards and publicized the work of Canadian painters. In 1880, with the assistance of Governor General Lord Lorne, the Society played a major role in the formation of the Royal Academy of Arts as well as the National Gallery. In that same year of 1880, the Canadian Society of Graphic Art was also established. Two years later, in 1882, the Royal Society of Canada was founded to promote research and learning in the arts and sciences. Like the Royal Academy of Art, the Royal Society, headquartered

Cathedral and Street, Montreal, Winter 1906 by James Wilson Morrice.

Indian Woman and Child (c.1886), by Canadian artist Robert Harris. How has Harris pictured this Aboriginal mother and child?

in Ottawa, saw its mission as the raising of the cultural and intellectual bar on a national scale. Provincialism and parochialism were to be shunned; nationalism and culture were to be embraced.

Many of the premiere works of the period were still based on natural landscape themes. Lucius O'Brien, the first president of the Royal Academy, painted *Sunrise on the Saguenay* (1880). Homer Watson painted a number of landscape masterpieces, including *The Pioneer Mill* (1880) and *Before the Storm* (1887). Horatio Walker painted idealized interpretations of Quebec rural life in such works as *Oxen Drinking* (1899) and *Ploughing—The First Gleam* (1900). As increasing numbers of Canadian artists gained confidence by studying in Paris, they began tackling the human form. Charlottetown's Robert Harris's *A Meeting of the School Trustees* (1885) was one of the earliest. Paul Peel was the first Canadian artist to paint nudes in such works as *A Venetian Bather* (1889) and *After the Bath* (1890). James Morrice of Montreal, inspired by the American painter James Whistler and French artist Henri Matisse, painted foreign scenes in bold colours.

Music

Musical life was similarly raised through both individual achievements and organized efforts. Most notable of the former was Calixa Lavallee, best known today for having composed the music for *O Canada* and Emma Albani (nee Lajeunesse) who became a world renowned opera singer. Bands and choirs were formed in most communities. They provided both a musical and a social outlet. Some of the more notable groups were Montreal's Oratorio Society and Mendelssohn Choir, Vancouver Island's Aboriginal Band, and the Royal Engineers in Vancouver. The turn of the century saw many cities build one and two thousand seat opera houses, such as Toronto's Royal Alexandra (1906) and Winnipeg's Walker Theatre (1907). Those theatres were fully utilized by touring companies, local amateurs, and international stars such as Sarah Bernhardt in the 1880s and Charlie Chaplin after the turn of the century. Domestic theatre, both writing and performing was slowly beginning to establish itself. But it faced the twin obstacles of religious disapproval and foreign competition from the theatre centres of London and New York.

Sports

Another component of culture—sports—also grew in popularity in the latter years of the nineteenth century. Most, with the notable exception of lacrosse and hockey, were imported. The decades before and after the turn of the century were the peak of amateur athletics. Lacrosse originated as an Aboriginal game called "baggataway" which was played by entire villages by both men and women. William George, a Montreal dentist, promoted the game to such an extent that by Confederation there were 80 lacrosse clubs across the country. For the next two decades, lacrosse enjoyed spectacular growth as a spectator sport. Snowshoeing clubs provided winter diversion for the nation's elite. Baseball, originally centred in Upper Canada/Ontario, became a major summer sport throughout Canada at the amateur, semi-pro, and professional levels. Requiring little in the way of equipment, it was enjoyed, both as a spectator and participant sport, by all levels of society. Football, growing largely out of universities, became a fall passion. Hockey, like baseball, developed largely as a rural participant sport. Gradually, once it developed more formal structure, organization, and rules, it would come to be recognized, along with the original lacrosse, as Canada's "national sport."

A baseball game between the University of Toronto and McGill University teams, around the turn of the century.

Expression of Culture

LACROSSE: CANADA'S OTHER NATIONAL SPORT

Lacrosse is one of many contributions of Aboriginal culture to modern Canadian society. It is also one of the rare instances in which an element of Aboriginal culture was originally accepted and embraced by Canadian society.

Lacrosse originated among the Algonkian tribes of the St. Lawrence Valley, and it is believed the game dates back to the 1400s. For this reason, lacrosse is often described as the oldest organized sport in North America. The Native name for the game was *baggattaway*, derived from the Ojibwa word for ball. In 1636 Jean de Brébeuf, a Jesuit missionary among the Huron people, mentioned the game in his diary. Brébeuf called it "la crosse," because the sticks used by the Aboriginal players resembled the cross of the Bishop.

Viewed as a gift from their Creator, the game held great religious significance for its Aboriginal players. In addition to serving as a form of recreation, lacrosse was used to settle tribal disputes and train young warriors. And, since wagers were frequently made on matches, lacrosse could raise or lower a tribe's economic fortunes.

One of the most famous lacrosse games was played in 1842 between the Montreal Lacrosse Club and the Caughnawaga. It was the first match between Aboriginal and non-Aboriginal people to take place since 1763, when an Ojibwa tribe staged a lacrosse game to gain entry to Fort Michilimackinac, and once inside massacred English soldiers and captured the fort.

One of the most influential figures in the development of lacrosse in Canada was a Montreal dentist, Dr. George Beers, now known as "the father of lacrosse." A strong Canadian nationalist, Beers saw lacrosse as a way of encouraging fitness and bravery among men of the new nation. An effective promoter, Beers fostered the idea that lacrosse was Canada's national game, largely through his 1867 motto, "Our Country–Our Game".

Among Beers' other contributions to the game were establishing lacrosse's first code of rules, replacing the hair-stuffed deer-skin ball with a hard rubber ball, and designing a stick suited for catching and accurately throwing the ball. And in 1867, Beers organized the Kingston conference where the National Lacrosse Association of Canada was formed as the sport's national governing body. The popularity of lacrosse grew in the late nineteenth century. By the end of 1867 there were eighty clubs across Canada, and by 1893 every province in Canada had clubs playing lacrosse.

In 1901 Governor General Lord Minto presented the Minto Cup for the senior amateur Canadian championships. The trophy eventually became emblematic of the professional championship. In 1910, Sir Donald Mann, an architect for the Canadian Northern Railway, donated the gold Mann Cup for the Canadian amateur title. During the 1930s lacrosse had to compete with other sports such as baseball for fan support, and the Canadian Amateur Lacrosse Association adopted box lacrosse as its official game.

In 1994, Bill C-212 was introduced in Parliament to officially declare hockey Canada's national sport. Supporters of lacrosse, who wanted to recognize the traditional and cultural significance of the sport, mounted opposition. Soon a true Canadian compromise was struck. On May 12, 1994, Canada's National Sport Act became law, reading: "To recognize Hockey as Canada's National Winter Sport and Lacrosse as Canada's National Summer Sport".

The first hockey league appeared in Montreal in 1885. Five years later, the Ontario Hockey Association was born, followed in rapid succession by leagues in Winnipeg, Halifax, and many other locations. With the donation of the Stanley Cup by Governor General Lord Stanley (representing national amateur hockey supremacy) and the introduction of artificial ice in 1895, hockey began to take off. The most divisive issue was the status of professional athletes. Small towns believed that paying players, such as Fred "Cyclone" Taylor, the highest paid athlete of his day, was the only way they could compete with the larger urban centres.

The first professional league, the National Hockey Association (NHA), appeared in 1909. Consisting originally of Montreal, Haileybury, Renfrew, and Cobalt, they enticed the best players with big salaries eliminating the smaller venues. In an effort to save money, teams were reduced from seven to six players. The Pacific Coast Hockey League was founded by the Patrick brothers, Frank and Lester, in 1911. Using a ploy that would be widely repeated in the future, in order to gain credibility, they lured Taylor west for the unheard of sum of $22,200 for fourteen games. The Patricks also built arenas in Vancouver and Victoria. Finally, the two leagues agreed to meet for a championship in the 1913–14 season. Three years later, in 1917, the NHA became the National Hockey League (NHL) and targeted larger Canadian urban centres. It was not too long before expansion into the United States would change the face of hockey.

Many, from Ken Dryden to Roy MacGregor have seen hockey as the enduring Canadian metaphor. If that is the case, arguably at no time was it more valid than turn-of-the-century Canada. The rough, rural amateur gave way to the skilled, urban professional. The city displaced the town and village. The arena replaced the outdoor ponds. And finally, as many would contend "love of the game" gave way to the "big bucks."

A turn of the century amateur hockey game in Montreal.

Conclusion

In the fifty years following Confederation, every aspect of Canadian society changed. Macdonald's National Policy fuelled the fire of industrialization that in turn rapidly changed the urban centres and brought both positive and negative effects. Workers and farmers who had long been exploited began to find a voice of solidarity in unions, and social reformers began to take on the task of trying to solve the problems of urban poverty. And amidst all this change, Canadians began to express their own reflections and visions of their society through art, literature, music, and sports. Although they were probably not aware of the full impact of their actions, these Canadians were beginning to verbally and visually paint a picture of what it was like to live in Canada, and to be a Canadian.

Notes

1. *Report of the Royal Commission on the Relations of Labour and Capital* (1889).

2. The printers were part of the Nine Hour Movement, which was attempting to win approval for a nine-hour a day, fifty-four hour work week. The nine-hour movement came to Canada after achieving success in Britain in 1872. James Ryan, a Hamilton machinist for the Great Western, was the driving force behind the movement. The Toronto printers joined 1500 Hamilton workers to petition both their employers and government. Plans for Canada's first co-ordinated strike fell apart, and Brown took the offensive. He invoked the Combination Act, which branded the strike as an illegal conspiracy. Brown had two dozen printers arrested, including strike leader Daniel O'Donoghue. Shortly after 10 000 people rallied at Queen's Park, Macdonald passed the Trade Union Act that legalized unions in Canada.

3. Edmund W. Bradwin, *The Bunkhouse Man: A Study of Work and Pay in the Camps of Canada, 1903-1914,* (New York: Columbia University, 1928).

4. "Solidarity Forever" lyrics can be found at the Canadian Museum of Civilization web site at http://www.civilization.ca/hist/labour/labv17e.html.

5. *Report of the Royal Commission on the Relations of Labour and Capital* (1889).

6. Herbert Ames, *The City Below the Hill,* quoted in Conrad and Finkel, Volume II, p. 118-20

7. Ibid.

8. "Bread and Roses" lyrics can be found at the following web site: http://www.fortunecity.com/tinpan/parton/2/breadrose.html.

9. Garfield Newman et al. *Canada: A Nation Unfolding, Second Edition* (Whitby: McGraw-Hill Ryerson Limited, 2000) pp. 52-54, 59

10. Susanna Moodie, *Roughing It In the Bush* (London: Richard Bentley, 1852).

Chapter 13 Review

Knowledge & Understanding

1. Identify the following terms, people, and events and explain their historical significance to Canada's developing culture and identity:
    - National Policy
    - Sir Sandford Fleming
    - Social Gospel
    - Royal Commission of Labour and Capital
    - Urbanism
    - The Dominion Grange

2. What were the origins of Sir John A. Macdonald's National Policy? What was it designed to do?

3. How did industrialization affect Prairie farmers between 1870–1915? Create a graphic organizer to show the benefits and costs of industrialization on the Prairies.

Thinking & Inquiry

4. Contemporary and historical critics of the National Policy contend that it was the antithesis of a truly "national" policy. Are they correct in their description? Write a clearly articulated thesis statement and develop three arguments to support your thesis. Be sure each argument is its own paragraph and is supported with historical evidence.

Application

5. Critically examine the cartoon "Montreal's Night Mayor on his Ghostly Rounds" in this chapter. This cartoon was dedicated to the Board of Health in Montreal. If you had been the president of the Board of Health, how would you have responded to this cartoon? Write a 300-word editorial outlining what action the Board plans to take.

6. You are a commissioner on the Royal Commission on the Relations of Labour and Capital, and have been asked to draw up two lists of questions: one for the industry, manufacturing, or mine owner, and one for the worker. Create ten questions for each list. Be sure to keep in mind what information you want to find out before creating the questions.

Communication

7. The cultural, economic, and political life of the city was often very different from the country. Imagine two sisters in 1890, one living outside of Winnipeg, Manitoba, and the other living in Toronto, Ontario. Write two letters, one from each sister to the other sister, that reflect the thoughts and feelings of the life around them.

8. Songs such as the "wobbly" song in this chapter were a popular way of generating enthusiasm among movements or groups such as unions. Take a popular song from the radio and compose new lyrics based around one of the following scenarios:
    1. You are a 24-year-old woman who has joined the Social Gospel movement and is trying to raise awareness of urban poverty and the moral duty of others to help.
    2. You are a 20-year-old miner is a non-unionized mine, where working conditions are deplorable.

Striving for Accommodation: Laurier's "Sunny Ways"

If there is anything to which I have given my political life, it is to try to promote unity, harmony, and amity between the diverse elements of this country. I shall not deviate a line from the policy that I have traced out for myself.

–SIR WILFRID LAURIER

The first French-Canadian prime minister, Sir Wilfrid Laurier, was in power from 1896 to 1911 and during this fifteen-year period, sometimes referred to as the Golden Years, Canada and its identity were changed considerably. This time period was marked by economic growth, particularly after a quarter of a century of depression, and the issues of industrialism, immigration, the CPR, the return of prosperity, imperialism, and universal education all had an impact on the lives of ordinary people. Coming to power at the age of fifty-four, Laurier appeared to be the ideal leader to guide the nation through these confident years. He was knowledgeable, an able orator, fluently bilingual, highly intelligent, and perhaps most importantly, fair-minded. Through all the changes at the turn of the century, Laurier continued the process of nation building adopting what he referred to as "the sunny ways" approach. Directed primarily at finding a compromise between the French and English in Canada, this approach became the theme of his administration. And that spirit of compromise would become an enduring hallmark of the Canadian identity.

The country grew in both size and economic strength during the first decade of the twentieth century. While ties to Britain were being loosened, the influence of the United States was growing stronger. A tremendous wave of immigration was changing anglo-conformity and the "two nations" concept. As nationalists challenged imperialists, Canadians were slowly becoming more autonomous, and through the further development of the arts and culture, the Canadian identity was cautiously becoming more confident and distinctive.

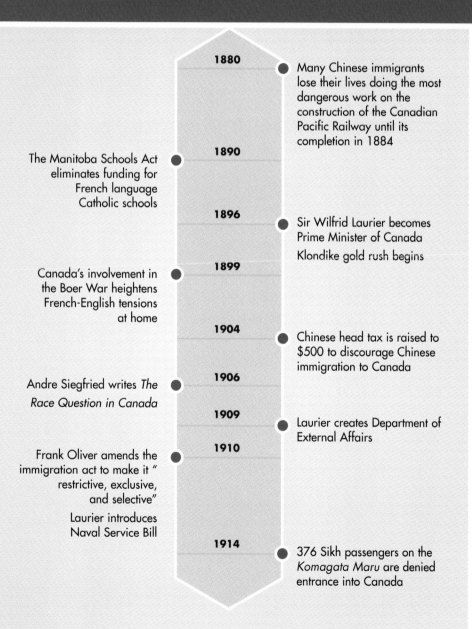

1880
Many Chinese immigrants lose their lives doing the most dangerous work on the construction of the Canadian Pacific Railway until its completion in 1884

1890
The Manitoba Schools Act eliminates funding for French language Catholic schools

1896
Sir Wilfrid Laurier becomes Prime Minister of Canada
Klondike gold rush begins

1899
Canada's involvement in the Boer War heightens French-English tensions at home

1904
Chinese head tax is raised to $500 to discourage Chinese immigration to Canada

1906
Andre Siegfried writes *The Race Question in Canada*

1909
Laurier creates Department of External Affairs

1910
Frank Oliver amends the immigration act to make it " restrictive, exclusive, and selective"
Laurier introduces Naval Service Bill

1914
376 Sikh passengers on the *Komagata Maru* are denied entrance into Canada

By the end of this chapter, you will be able to

• analyze factors that led to revisions of Canada's immigration policies

• describe the types of immigrants the Canadian government sought to attract at the end of the nineteenth century and the strategies immigration officials used to attract them

• describe the significant steps in Canada's changing role within the British Empire and Commonwealth

• describe the character and development over time of francophone communities outside Quebec

• analyze how conflicts and compromises between Canada and the United States have helped to shape Canadian identity

The Immigration Boom

The immigrants that arrived between 1896 and 1914 had a lasting and important impact on Canadian history, identity, and culture. They would cause the creation of two new provinces, Saskatchewan and Alberta, and irrevocably change the face and identity of their new homeland. Turning the prairies into a domestic market, as well as a breadbasket, they would swell the population so that by 1920 Canada's population had almost doubled to 10.4 million. Over time, the arrival of new immigrants would force Canadians to acknowledge, if not embrace, a more multicultural vision of their nation. At first, however, the new arrivals faced prejudice, discrimination, and rejection.

The world-wide depression had earlier restricted Canada's immigration, and the population increased by less than 25 percent between 1881 and 1891. Canada experienced a net outflow of immigration in the 1880s to the United States. Between 1890 and 1910, however, Canada's population increased by almost two thirds. In the first twenty years of the new century, Canada's population went from 5.4 million to 10.4 million.

The arrival of immigrants had many consequences in western Canada. In the quarter century after 1891, Manitoba's population sky-rocketed from 152 000 to 554 000. British Columbia's rose even more sharply from 98 000 to 456 000. In 1891, there were fewer than 100 000 people living in the area between Canada's fifth and sixth provinces, Manitoba and British Columbia, respectively, but by 1916 there were over one million.

The Manitoba Schools Issue

After Manitoba's entry into Confederation in 1870, its population had enjoyed the benefits of a dual educational system for both French-speaking Roman Catholics and English-speaking Protestants. Constitutionally guaranteed by both the Manitoba Act and the British North America Act, it had experienced some modifications in the early 1870s, but continued without any public opposition. However, the demographics of the province had dramatically changed by 1890. The influx to Manitoba of English-speaking

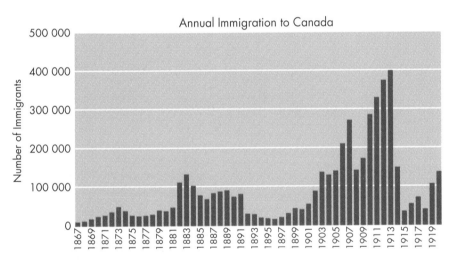

Annual Immigration to Canada

1. What year had the highest number of immigrants? Can you suggest reasons for the high rate in that year?

2. What year had the lowest number of immigrants? Can you suggest reasons for the low rate in that year?

3. There was a world-wide depression from about 1873 to 1896. What general conclusion can you make about the relationship between immigration and the economy? Can you suggest reasons for that relationship?

4. What happens to the rate of immigration in 1914? Explain why this occurred. Can you predict what immigration rates will be like for the period of World War I, 1913 to 1918? Explain your answer

Protestants, mainly from Ontario, and the exodus of Métis and Aboriginals westward meant that the new majority no longer felt the need for such a dual system in education.

In 1890 the Manitoba Schools Act eliminated funding for French-language Catholic schools in the province and made English the only official language of instruction. At the same time, it also abolished the use of French in government services. The aim of the Manitoba Schools Act was to reduce educational costs, but many saw the Act as a means of assimilating an increasingly diverse population. Manitoba's French Catholic population, 7 percent of the province's population by 1891, appealed to Ottawa to repeal the Act. The issue was a political landmine, and Macdonald procrastinated until his death in 1891. Four successive Conservative prime ministers, Sir John Abbott, Sir John Thompson, Sir Mackenzie Bowell, and Sir Charles Tupper, were unable, despite their efforts, to resolve the issue.

In 1896 the problem fell to Laurier to devise a solution and although he may have sided with the French Catholics of Manitoba, he had learned to proceed cautiously. In the aftermath of Riel's execution, Laurier had declared, "I myself would have shouldered a musket to fight against the neglect of governments....[However] [W]e are attempting to unite the different conflicting elements which we have into a nation...."[1]

This stance had won Laurier the 1896 federal election whose central issue was the Manitoba Schools Act. Searching for a mutual concession from both sides that would form the basis of a lasting resolution, Laurier and Manitoba Premier Thomas Greenaway worked out the compromise. While the province would not be compelled to finance Catholic separate schools, it did have to provide thirty minutes of religious instructions at the end of each school day. In addition, where numbers warranted, French-language teachers and resources would be provided. Founded upon compromise, the resolution of the Manitoba Schools issue was to be the model for future debates. Before long the same issue resurfaced in both Ontario (Regulation 17 in 1912) and in New Brunswick. Again funding for French language instruction was eliminated and the minority could only find solace in a negotiated compromise.

The Manitoba Schools crisis of the 1890s foreshadowed the growing divide between French and English Canadians. Language is central to identity and culture and therefore groups will struggle to preserve and retain their languages. Sometimes that struggle becomes a losing proposition when faced with a population that relegates a group to minority status. The Manitoba Schools controversy also brought to light the issue of minority rights. At the most profound and practical level, how does a democratic country, like Canada, treat its minorities? Since the hallmark of democracy is majority rule, what happens to the rights of minorities? The Manitoba Schools dispute revealed that minority rights must be recognized and respected and perhaps the best way to accomplish that is through compromise.

The Klondike Gold Rush

For nineteenth-century prospectors, gold had an appeal bordering on madness. At the first sign of gold, thousands of men would abandon their families and trek across the continent and sometimes the oceans in search of fortune. It inspired courage, wildness, ingenuity, and adventure. Gold rushes were amazingly short-lived; they burst on the scene bringing fabulous wealth for a lucky few and despair and failure for the vast majority. Boom towns became ghost towns, virtually overnight. That pattern had already occurred in 1858 on the Fraser River and in 1860 in the Cariboo. But it would be the biggest strike in the Klondike in 1896 that would become legendary.

After three prospectors discovered gold in Rabbit Creek, near the Yukon River, over forty thousand people streamed into the region. The

Klondike lay in the heart of the Yukon's ice and snow-capped mountains and the odds were decidedly against the gold-seekers. They had to endure frigid temperatures, vast distances, heavy supplies, unforgiving snow and ice, dangerous rivers, and treacherous mountain passes such as the famed Chilkoot. They also had to find the gold, lay their claim, and protect it from other fortune-seekers.

The search for riches in the rugged environment inspired many stories, songs, and poems. Robert Service (1874–1958) became known for his poetry about the Klondike. In "The Spell of the Yukon," Service writes about how the lure of gold consumed many men and women:

> I wanted the gold, and I sought it
>   I scrabbled and mucked like a slave.
> Was it famine or scurvy — I fought it;
>   I hurled my youth into a grave.
> I wanted the gold, and I got it —
>   Came out with a fortune last fall, —
> Yet somehow life's not what I thought it,
> And somehow the gold isn't all.
>
> You come to get rich (damned good reason);
>   You feel like an exile at first;

Gold-seekers in the Klondike, Yukon, 1886.

> You hate it like hell for a season,
>   And then you are worse than the worst.
> It grips you like some kinds of sinning;
>   It twists you from foe to a friend;
> It seems it's been since the beginning;
>   It seems it will be to the end.
>
> The winter! The brightness that blinds you,
>   The white land locked tight as a drum,
> The cold fear that follows and finds you,
>   The silence that bludgeons you dumb.
> The snows that are older than history,
>   The woods where the weird shadows slant;
> The stillness, the moonlight, the mystery,
>   I've bade 'em good-by — but I can't.
>
> There's gold, and it's haunting and haunting;
>   It's luring me on as of old;
> Yet it isn't the gold that I'm wanting
>   So much as just finding the gold.
> It's the great, big, broad land 'way up yonder,
>   It's the forests where silence has lease;
> It's the beauty that thrills me with wonder,
>   It's the stillness that fills me with peace.[2]

In less than three years, Dawson City mushroomed from a small fur-trading post to a wild, frontier town of twenty-five thousand. It was unrestrained and untamed and gold-crazed miners frequented the many dance halls, saloons, and provision stores. At the end of one of the two trails into the gold fields was the port town of Skagway. Run by a notorious crook named Soapy Smith who cheated miners on the way to the gold fields, it was known as "the roughest place in the world." The North-West Mounted Police struggled to maintain some degree of law and order and to protect the population from its own craziness. The legendary Mountie Sam Steele claimed that the NWMP had inspected every single boat—some thirty thousand in all—that had gone down the dangerous Yukon River and prevented those with the flimsiest from trying their luck. However, given the pervading spirit of lawlessness, the Force's efforts, were largely futile.

Dawson City's bust was as abrupt as its boom. As finds became increasingly more infrequent and news of another gold strike across the

Dawson City during the Klondike goldrush, ca.1899

mountains was heard, the exodus was on. Saloons and hotels were empty, hospitals and sawmills unnecessary, and dance halls and streets quiet. As the people departed, so too did Dawson City's fame. It returned to a quiet town of a few hundred people.

ing season and therefore production could be expanded into more northerly prairie areas. In 1900 the value of Canada wheat exports (nicknamed "prairie gold") was $6 million and by 1915 that figured had risen to $45 million.

The Opening of the Canadian West

The Wheat Boom

As the global depression lifted, a wheat boom began. Prices rose as Europe's growing urban industrial population created a huge market for Canadian foodstuffs. At the same time, technology was reducing the cost of shipping farm produce both overland and over the water. Farm machinery, such as mechanical threshers and tractors, was making production far more efficient. A Canadian government scientist, Charles Saunders, invented a new strain of wheat called Marquis. It required a shorter grow-

Canada, The Granary of the World, a 1903 government pamphlet encouraging immigration to the Prairies

Attracting Immigrants

At the turn of the century, Clifford Sifton, Laurier's Minister of the Interior recognized that the time was ripe to attract permanent European settlers and he launched a massive advertising campaign to promote Canada. Using the phrase "The Last Best West," Sifton and his department spent over $1 million in Britain, continental Europe, and the United States using pamphlets, hundreds of speeches, newspaper articles, and tours to sell the virtues of the Canadian prairies. Sifton also paid lucrative bonuses to steamship agents to direct suitable settlers to Canada. However, perhaps the greatest incentive for prospective immigrants was the free land offered to homesteaders. In return for building a homestead and clearing the land, the federal government offered 160 acres (one-quarter section) of

Web Connection

www.mcgrawhill.ca/links/definingcanada
Go to the Web site above to see how the Canadian government used posters to attract immigrants to the Canadian west.

free land. To many struggling peasant farmers, that was a bounty beyond their wildest dreams.

They also left their homes and countries to escape over-crowding, religious persecution, economic difficulties (unemployment, high taxation, or inability to obtain their own land), or the growing political and military unrest in Europe. These "push factors" convinced over 2.5 million people to endure a difficult trans-Atlantic voyage in order to come to Canada between 1896 and 1914. Almost half of that total migrated on to the prairies. In addition to the "push factors", Canada attracted immigrants with its "pull factors", such as free land, new opportunities, religious tolerance, and political freedom.

Arrival and Reaction

The unprecedented growth had a major positive impact on the national economy. While the immigrants became the producers of valuable wheat exports, they also acted as an essential domestic market for Central Canada manufacturers, and proved the CPR's worth.

The rapid settlement also raised the demand for provincial status. The three jurisdictions, Alberta, Saskatchewan, and Assiniboia, were in fact, territories of Canada. More power, representation, and money would accompany any grant of provincial status. However, views differed on the geographical boundaries of that province. Some wanted one large prairie province, others wanted two or more provinces, and a few wanted some of the prairie land to be absorbed into Manitoba. But all agreed that they urgently wanted to be citizens of a province, not a colony.

This pamphlet addressed to potential immigrants is advertising free farms in Western Canada.

At the time, there were no specific requirements for provincial status. In 1904, both federal parties agreed in principle to the grant of provincial autonomy. After the Laurier Liberals were returned in the election of 1905 with a bigger majority than they had captured in 1900, they were eager to move ahead. They decided to create two provinces, named Alberta and Saskatchewan, to run from the American border to the 60th parallel of latitude. Generous financial terms were offered. The two new provinces were given constitutions similar to Ontario's, except for one term that permitted the federal government to retain control over natural resources.

Although thousands of immigrants were diverted from farming and stayed in the east, augmenting the labour force in factories, mines, and railway camps, most found their way out west. Prairie farmers faced many daunting challenges. Initially, they had to build a homestead and clear the land. The cement-like soil, baked by the sun and trampled by buffalo herds for centuries, had to be turned to get it ready for seeding. In May, after the earth had been sufficiently loosened, seeds were sown. The wheat was then harvested in the fall, with threshing taking place in late September and early October. Finally, the wheat had to be hauled to market before the roads became impassable. Farmers had to acquire and learn to use many different tools and implements. There were inevitable financial problems, usually involving the banks and the CPR. Homesteaders had to endure isolation, homelessness, lack of medical care, and a harsh climate. They also had to face a less than welcoming reception from their hosts.

Sifton had anxiously sought out experienced farmers, but many had no such background and those that did, found that much of their experience was not useful in their new environment. The first set of immigrants from Britain and western Europe did not adjust well to the prairies. Realizing this, Sifton then sought out the "stalwart peasants in sheepskin coats."[3]

Sifton may have articulated an "open door" immigration policy but in reality, by labelling some as "desirable" (British, European, and American), he implicitly was rejecting many others. For most Anglo-Canadians, the influx of immigrants was unsettling at best and threatening at worst. They perceived the new arrivals, particularly those from central and eastern Europe as strange and even dangerous. From their clothes to their food, from their language to their customs, many were simply too different. Stephen Leacock, a turn-of-the century Ontario writer and humourist, for example, called them "unfit material from which to build the commonwealth of the future."[4] To Anglo-Canadians the solution was assimilation.

Emigrants on an Atlantic oceanliner bound for Canada in 1913

An immigrant family boards an oxen wagon to travel from the railway station to their homestead in Saskatchewan.

Asian immigration was also an issue, but mostly in British Columbia. At the turn of the century, eleven percent of British Columbia's population was made up of people of Chinese, Japanese, and East-Indian extraction. Fifteen thousand Chinese laboured, between 1880 and 1884, on the building of the CPR, and often on the most dangerous jobs such as placing nitro-glycerine and lighting dynamite. Immediately after completing the transcontinental railway, the Canadian government, responding to pressure, passed a Chinese head tax of $50 in order to discourage further immigration. In 1901, it was doubled and then three years later, the entry tax for Chinese immigrants was raised to $500, the equivalent of a year's wages. Despite this "head tax," Chinese immigration continued to increase, reaching a record of seventy-five hundred in 1913. Thereafter, the "head tax" had its desired effect as Chinese immigration to Canada virtually ceased in the post-World War I period. Similarly, Japanese immigration, largely through the questionable efforts of the B.C.-based Nippon Supply Company, also rose. In 1905, Japanese immigrants numbered only four hundred, while by 1909, the figure had increased to twelve thousand.

Many in British Columbia worried that the Asian immigrants would create a loss of jobs, diminish wages, and create a lowered the moral tone. The Asiatic Exclusion League in Vancouver was so popular that it was able to assemble thirty thousand people for an anti-immigration rally in 1908. The meeting degenerated into a riot as the crowd ransacked Japanese and Chinese homes and businesses. Although Laurier apologized for the incident, at the same time, he negotiated a tacit agreement with Japan to limit annual immigration to Canada to four hundred. In the future, many other incidents of racial prejudice would be directed against the Japanese community: Japanese-Canadian internment during World War II and their exclusion from voting or certain professions, such as teaching and the civil service, into the 1950s.

Immigration and the Canadian Identity

The disquieting conflicts between new immigrants and the established Canadian population were forcing many to examine the new emerging national identity and "The Canadian Question" was debated long and loud. In 1906, a young Frenchmen, Andre Siegfried, analyzed politics and ethnicity in his widely read *The Race Question in Canada*. He argued that "[t]he English Canadians consider themselves the sole masters of Canada; they were not its first occupants admittedly, but it is theirs, they maintain by right of conquest. They experience, therefore, a feeling of indignation at the sight of the defeated race persisting in their development instead of fusing or being submerged."[5]

Most English Canadians had little doubt in their minds about the inherent superiority of their culture and therefore the need to assimilate all others, including French Canadians. They tolerated the French as they were of European background but they still perceived them as somewhat backward, largely due to the confining influence of the Catholic Church. The Church, in their view, kept French Canada submissive and largely rural and agrarian. The Roman Catholic focus on the hereafter and piety, conflicted with the more commercial and acquisitive notions of the Protestant work ethic.

How immigrants could be absorbed into the Canadian mainstream was a question that perplexed politicians, writers, and reformers. A tiny handful advocated a "melting-pot" approach including Ralph Connor, a former missionary and best-selling author, in his book *The Foreigner* (1909). *The Foreigner* opens: "In western Canada there is seen to-day that most fascinating of all human phenomena, the making of a nation. Out of breeds diverse in traditions, in ideals, in speech, and in manner of life...one people is being made. The blood strains of great races will mingle in the blood of a race greater than the greatest of them

all." Even though the radical notion of concession and conciliation towards immigrants was advanced, it was softened by counselling the new arrivals to conform to the values and practices of the host Anglo-Canadian culture. Even the social democrat, J.S. Woodsworth said the multitude of immigrant problems—"[I]gnorance of the language, high rents, low standards of living, incompetency, (sic), drunkenness, and other evils" left few other options.[6]

The seventy-five hundred pacifist Doukhobors from Russia and the 170 000 Ukrainian peasants who came to the west between 1896 and 1914 were the two main groups singled out for resentment and attack on the Prairies. The former's refusal to swear an oath of allegiance and the latter's grinding poverty and perceived insularity, made them easy targets for bigoted newspapers and politicians. Such groups were simply too different, in appearance, beliefs, and customs, to attain easy acceptance.

Frank Oliver was Sifton's successor and in 1910, he amended the Immigration Act to make it, in his words, "restrictive, exclusive, and selective." Section 37 left little doubt. While requiring every immigrant to have a minimum sum of money, the actual amount could "vary according to the race." So while business and industry championed Sifton's alleged "open door" immigration policy, that door was beginning to close by World War I.

The *Komagata Maru*

Oliver's "restrictive, exclusive, and selective" immigration policy became evident during the summer of 1914. *The Komagata Maru* was a Japanese freighter that had been rented by an Indian businessman to carry

Doukhobor women pulling a plough, in the Yorkton area of Saskatchewan in 1902

376 men from the Punjab, mainly Sikhs, who wanted to immigrate to Canada. Canadian exclusionist policies towards East Indians stipulated that they could only come to Canada by continuous passage from India, something that was impossible as no steamships offered direct service between these two countries. East Indians were also required to have $200 on their person when arriving in Canada. When the *Komagata Maru* arrived in Vancouver in May 1914, most of the passengers were detained on board for two months during the summer heat, while immigration officials decided on their status. Finally, the Canadian government ordered the Navy cruiser *Rainbow* to escort the *Komagata Maru* out of Canadian waters or blow up the ship if it did not leave Canada. Forced back to Calcutta, it was a crushing blow, not only for the passengers, but for the Indian-Canadian population as well. Discouraged by the treatment that the *Komagata Maru* passengers received, many Indian Canadians chose to move back to India.

Web Connection

www.mcgrawhill.ca/links/definingcanada
Go to the Web site above to see more historical photographs of The *Komagata Maru*.

Review...Reflect...Respond

1. How did the Manitoba Schools issue highlight the issue of minority rights in Canada?

2. How does the image of the Klondike fortune-seeker fit in with the image of the Canadian identity?

3. What facts in Canadian immigration history during this time period prove that Canada was an exclusionist country?

Passengers from India aboard the *Komagata Maru* waiting for immigration clearance from authorities in Vancouver, in 1914

Canada's Emergence on the World Stage

Early in Canada's existence, Britain largely controlled its foreign policy. One of the earliest foreign policy issues occurred in 1884 when Britain found itself in difficulty in the Egyptian Sudan. Sir John A. Macdonald, although his 1891 election slogan "A British subject I was born; a British subject I will die" implied immediate assistance to Britain, but he sought a much more moderate role. He asked, "Why should we waste our men and money in this wretched business?"[7]

Ultimately however, Macdonald believed it wise to accede to the British request. He dispatched a contingent of 367 civilians, mostly French Canadians but also including some Aboriginals, to assist the distressed British Army in Khartoum.

The Canadian imperialists in the late nineteenth century, led by such luminaries as Stephen Leacock, Charles G.D. Roberts, and George Denison leapt to the defence of Britain. They felt Canada should be immediately compliant to Britain's request. In their minds, the British way was innately superior to all others and it was therefore Canada's duty to help.

Anti-imperialists, led by Goldwin Smith, took a very different tact. In his *Canada and the Canadian Question* (1891) he saw no commonality of interests with an Empire that included "an Asiatic dominion extending over two hundred and fifty million Hindoos (sic) [or] a group of West Indian Islands full of emancipated negro slaves."[8] In an earlier book,

The Political Destiny of Canada (1878) Smith predicted four forces that would diminish British influence in Canada. Those forces were "distance, divergence of interests, divergence of political character, and the attraction of the great mass of English-speaking people which adjoins us on this continent." While many anti-imperialists failed to share Smith's continentalist approach, they did challenge British power in Canada. Many championed a genuine domestic national consciousness, free of restraining ties to the Empire. Lawyer John S. Ewart, rising to prominence in his vigorous defence of Manitoba's Catholic minority during the Schools question, advocated not a complete separation from Britain, but an evolutionary development of Canadian institutions, practices, and customs. Henri Bourassa, Joseph Papineau's grandson, was a fiery Quebec politician who wanted a fully bicultural nationalism. He believed that "[t]he only possible basis for the solution to our national problems is one of mutual respect for our racial characters and exclusive devotion to our common land....My native land is all of Canada, a federation of separate races and autonomous provinces...."[9]

The Boer War

The issue of imperialism in Canada reached a climax with the start of the Boer War in South Africa in 1899. The Boers (Dutch settlers) in two South African republics, the Transvaal and the Orange Free State, had declared war on Britain. Britain wanted a commitment from Canada and other colonies for regular and systematic military and naval support. The request for Canadian troops to be sent to South Africa to help the British deeply divided the French and English, and the nationalists and imperialists in Canada. Many English, especially in Ontario, saw it as their duty as part of the Empire to answer the call. Britain, they argued had assisted Canada on numerous occasions and now Canada had an obligation to reciprocate. French Canadians and nationalists, led by Henri Bourassa,

THE GREAT CONTINGENT JUGGLER, OR TRYING TO PLEASE EVERYONE.

The Great Contingent Juggler, or Trying to Please Everyone. This political cartoon is aimed at Prime Minister Wilfrid Laurier's leadership on whether or how Canada will contribute to the British forces in South Africa fighting the Boer War.

Canadian troops at a field hospital during the Boer War in South Africa, 1900. Why did some Canadians object to this involvement in a British war?

Naval Service Crisis

In 1909 a naval arms race between Britain and Germany reached fever pitch. Britain feared that Germany might overtake its centuries-old naval supremacy. Ships, especially the Dreadnoughts, were the favoured weapons. Britain re-doubled its commitment, financial and manpower, to the Royal Navy and at the same time asked members of the Empire for immediate assistance to help alleviate the high costs of building the Dreadnought battleships.

Once more Laurier was in the same imperialist–nationalist tug-of-war. Imperialists wanted Canada to immediately contribute funds to the building of the Dreadnought. Nationalists believed that any contribution toward Britain's navy would lead to greater Canadian involvement in Britain's conflicts. In January 1910, Laurier introduced his Naval Service Bill, which he designed to find compromise between the two opposing sides. The bill called for the establishment of a small Canadian Navy and a naval college. While the bill specifically rejected the notion of regular financial contributions to the Empire, it did provide that in the event of war, any Canadian armed force, could, with the consent of Parliament, be placed at the disposal of Britain. As with the Boer War, Laurier had satisfied neither side. While Robert Borden and the Conservatives denounced the creation of a "tinpot navy," as a failure of Canada's support to the British Empire, Bourassa and the nationalists chided Laurier for caving in to imperial demands.

saw it as a foreign war that had nothing to do with Canada. They felt that they had too many domestic problems to spare the money or men to help rescue Britain from its imperial adventures.

The fierce debate hinged on the question of whether or not there should be conscription to obtain the necessary contingent to be sent to South Africa. Laurier recognized that invoking conscription would alienate French Canadians, but he also knew that if Canada did not provide military assistance, it would alienate the imperialists. Eventually, he found that elusive middle ground of compromise. There would be no conscription, but the Canadian government would look after the training, equipping, and transporting of a volunteer force of one thousand soldiers. In the end, about seven thousand Canadian soldiers, doctors, nurses, and drivers served in South Africa. Laurier's compromise was not hailed as an ideal solution by either side. English Canadians criticized it as grossly inadequate support for Britain, and French Canadians condemned it because Canadian troops had been sent at all. Although Laurier's "sunny way" failed to please either side, his compromise helped to cool the tension, at least for the time being.

Growing Ties and Tensions with the United States

Canada had experienced an earlier foray into the intricate world of international diplomacy that had served to point out its need for autonomy. As Canada began to move away from Britain, it became increasingly involved with the United States in a series of contentious issues.

Canadian Leaders
MARTHA BLACK

Martha Black was very much a woman of her times, her words displaying traditional, late nineteenth-century attitudes and values about the place of women in society. Yet, in her actions, she was a gender trailblazer, becoming the second woman elected to Parliament. Throughout her life, she displayed independence, a spirit of adventure, a profound love of the Canadian North, and dedication to serving the Yukon people.

Born into all the advantages of a wealthy Chicago family in 1866, she was fascinated by the Canadian North from an early age. In 1898, with her husband William Purdy, she abandoned Chicago society to join the Klondike Gold Rush. In Seattle, Purdy decided he was not up to an arduous journey and decided to go to Hawaii. Undeterred, Martha chose to continue on with the Yukon journey, which required travelling 92 kilometres on foot over the Rocky Mountains through Chilkoot Pass. Granted, Martha's party was able to walk across the Chilkoot unimpeded by tons of gear, since they paid a packer $900 to have it all delivered to Lake Bennett.

Still, it was a grueling trek. Martha Black's own writing vividly describes the trip and reveals details about the life and attitudes of women during that time,

Martha Black (1866–1957)

I cursed my hot, high buckram collar, my tight heavily boned corsets, my long corduroy skirt, my full bloomers, which I had to hitch up with every step...

Only 10 feet more! Oh, God, what a relief! Then my foot slips! I lose my balance. I fall only a few feet into a crevice in the rocks. The sharp edge of one cuts through my boot and I feel the flesh of my leg throbbing with pain. I can bear it no longer, and I sit down and do what every woman does in time of stress. I weep....

Adding to the difficulty of the journey was the fact that Martha was pregnant with her youngest child by William Purdy. After arriving in Dawson City, she supported her three sons by forming a gold-mining partnership and later a successful sawmill business.

In the course of her business dealings she needed a lawyer, and George Black came highly recommended. Gradually a relationship blossomed, and in 1904 she married Black. Although a woman of independent means and strong spirit, Martha Black's attitudes about a woman's place in a marriage may seem surprisingly backward to a modern reader:

I am a firm believer in the principle that married couples, from the beginning, should be in complete harmony in religion, in country, and in politics. So immediately after my marriage, without compunction, I became an Anglican, an Imperialist, and a Conservative.

She was completely supportive of her husband's developing political career. In 1912, George was appointed Commissioner of the Yukon and she served as the First Lady of the Yukon. Both she and George were extremely popular, maintaining an open door policy at Government House to all Yukoners. Said Martha, "this beautiful 'house of the people' should be open to all who wished to come, irrespective of social position."

In 1916, George resigned as commissioner to join Canada's World War I effort. Martha was permitted to travel to Europe on the troop ship, the only woman among three thousand, five hundred men. There she nurtured wounded Canadians, later receiving the Order of the British Empire for her war service.

Back in Canada, George was elected Member of Parliament for the Yukon in 1921, retaining the seat until 1935, when he was forced to resign due to ill health. At the age of sixty-nine, Martha ran in his place, becoming only the second woman ever elected to Canada's Parliament (the first had been Agnes McPhail). Martha served as the Yukon Territory MP until 1940, during which time she focused on such issues as public health, pensions for the blind, and nature conservation.

By 1940 George was well enough to successfully run for election and held the seat until 1949.

Martha Black's contributions were by no means limited to politics; she was a naturalist, artistic botanist, and a writer. In 1917, Martha was made a Fellow of the Royal Geographic Society for a series of nearly four hundred lectures on the Yukon that she presented in Great Britain, and for her work on Yukon flora. She published the book *Yukon Wild Flowers* IN 1936, but she is perhaps best remembered for her autobiography, *My Seventy Years*, which chronicles her evolution from a fashionable wife, to a mining pioneer, to a politician.

Martha Black, "Mother" of the Yukon, possessed qualities appreciated by Yukoners: spirit and style. She and her husband were the first "real Yukoners" to hold high public office in the Territory. In 1950, when the Yukon capital moved from Dawson to Whitehorse, she and George relocated there too, where they lived until Martha's death in 1957 at the age of 91. Black Street in Whitehorse commemorates the Blacks' accomplishments, as do two mountain peaks in the Yukon, named in their honour.

Alaska Boundary Dispute

The most serious tension occurred in 1903 with the Alaska Boundary dispute. At issue, particularly after the Klondike gold rush, was the location of the international boundary between Canada and Alaska, stretching one thousand kilometres down the coast of Yukon and British Columbia. Exactly where the line was drawn would determine how the Lynn Canal was divided and who would own the valuable port town of Skagway.

American President Theodore (Teddy) Roosevelt, recognizing that Britain wanted to maintain good relations between their two countries, took the offensive. It was decided that resolution would be sought through a six-man joint commission. Three "judges" on the panel would be American, two Canadian, and one, Lord Alverstone, would be British. Given the fact that the American judges were anything but neutral—they had all in fact come out publicly in favour of the American position—the result was a largely a foregone conclusion: four to two for the U.S. claim. Lord Alverstone, not wanting to antagonize Roosevelt, voted with the U.S. secretary of war and two American senators.

Many Canadians were outraged that their national interests had been sacrificed by Britain. Accordingly, Laurier began steps to slowly get control of Canadian foreign policy out of British hands. The 1909 creation of a separate Department of

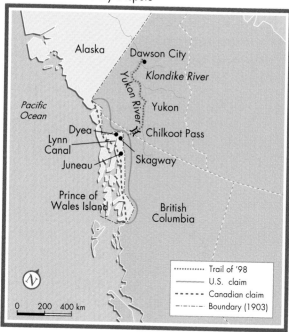

The Alaska Boundary Dispute

External Affairs was a major move towards Canadian autonomy. Also, recognizing that maintaining good relations with their southern neighbour was important, Laurier joined with the United States in the creation of the International Joint Commission, again in 1909. Its mandate was to serve as a permanent means of resolving Canadian-American border disputes.

Before the 1911 general election, the windows of the offices of the *Toronto Star* and *Toronto News* newspapers echoed the arguments for and against reciprocity in trade with the United States.

Reciprocity

The evolving Canadian identity came into sharper focus in the federal election of 1911. The nation had undergone some profound changes—industrialism, urbanism, immigration, and imperialism. And now, after fifteen years of supporting Macdonald's protective tariffs, the Laurier Liberals wanted to abandon them in favour of reciprocity with the United States. Although the tariff had produced well over $100 million of direct American investment, the Liberals believed even more investment, jobs, and prosperity would come if the tariff wall were to be eliminated. The 1911 election was largely a referendum on free trade. Critics denounced the intended move claiming that it would ultimately end the British connection and lead inexorably to American annexation.

Borden and the Conservatives, under the banner of "Canadianism or Continentalism," won a resounding victory taking 134 of 221 seats. In Quebec, Bourassa argued decisively that the Laurier naval policy would commit Canada in advance to future British wars. Laurier himself captured the essence of the dilemma. "I am branded in Quebec as a traitor to the French, and in Ontario as a traitor to the English....In Quebec I am attacked as an imperialist and in Ontario as an anti-imperialist. I am neither. I am a Canadian."[10] So for the first time since Riel's execution, Quebec had aligned itself with the Conservatives to oust the Liberals from power. Nationalists revelled in the defeat of free trade. But that would be short-lived. The National Policy had already enabled the creation of over four hundred American branch plants, the beginnings of massive direct foreign investment, and an incipient branch plant economy. Already sixty percent of Canadian imports originated from south of the border. All these trends, branch plants, investment, and trade, would increase sharply in the future. A number of significant trends—waning British influence, strengthening of the American connection, increasing cultural diversity, and French-English conflict—would all intensify with the advent of the Great War.

Review...Reflect...Respond

1. What events during the period marked Canada's attempts in trying to carve out its own role on the world stage?

2. If you could travel back in time to 1900 in Canada, would you be an imperialist supporter, or an anti-imperialist? Why?

3. Was Laurier's position of compromise a help or a hindrance to Canada's unity and to Canada's image in international affairs?

Notes

1. R. Douglas Francis, Richard Jones, and Donald B. Smith, *Destinies: Canadian History Since Confederation, 3rd Edition* (Toronto: Harcourt Brace, 1996) p. 85.
2. Robert Service, "The Spell of the Yukon" in *The Best of Robert Service* (Whitby: McGraw-Hill Ryerson Limited, 2001), p. 1-3.
3. Alvin Finkel and Margaret Conrad, *History of the Canadian Peoples, Volume II* (Toronto: Addison Wesley, 1998) p. 102.
4. Stephen Leacock, "Beating Back to Prosperity" in the *Imperial Oil Review*, 1931.
5. J.M. Bumsted, *The Peoples of Canada: A Post-Confederation History* (Toronto: Oxford University Press, 1992) p. 158.
6. Ibid., p. 93.
7. Ibid., p. 150.
8. Ibid., p. 152.
9. Denis Moneire, *Ideologies in Quebec: Historical Development* (Toronto: University of Toronto Press, 1981), p. 189-90.
10. Francis, *Destinies*, p. 114.

Chapter 14 Review

Knowledge & Understanding

1. Identify these people, places, and events and explain their historical significance to Canada's developing culture and identity:
   - Manitoba Schools Act
   - Laurier's "sunny ways"
   - Clifford Sifton
   - Frank Oliver
   - *Komagata Maru*
   - Chinese head tax
   - Reciprocity
   - Alaska Boundary Dispute
   - Boer War
   - Naval Service Bill

2. Create a graphic organizer of push and pull immigration factors to Canada at the turn of the twentieth century.

3. How did Canadas international presence change during this period? What major incidents forced Canada to declare its own role on the world stage?

Thinking & Inquiry

4. While Lauriers art of compromise is often seen as a crucial element for keeping Canada united, he was also referred to as "Waffly Wilfy" by his critics. Describe and explain how the concept of compromise is a part of the Canadian identity. Does it allow Canada to stay together and play "middle ground" roles, or does it make "fence-sitting" part of the Canadian identity?

5. How did turn-of-the-century immigration to Canada impact on the emerging sense of Canadian identity and culture? Write a well-written paragraph for your answer and be sure to use historical evidence to support your opinion.

Application

6. Critically analyze the immigration pamphlet in this chapter. What images are used to attract potential immigrants? How truthful are these images to what the immigrant would find in reality. What images might be used now to attract immigrants to Canada?

7. As mentioned in this chapter, in 1909, Ralph Connor wrote *The Foreigner* in which he writes, "In western Canada there is seen today that most fascinating of all human phenomenon, the making of a nation. Out of breeds diverse in traditions, in ideals, in speech, and in manner of life...one people is being made. The blood strains of great races will mingle in the blood of a race greater than the greatest of them all." What does this quote say about turn-of-the-century views towards immigrants and their diverse cultures? How does this differ from our views of multiculturalism today?

Communication

8. Draw a political cartoon depicting Laurier's handling of one of the following situations: the Manitoba Schools Act, the Naval Service Bill, or Canada's role in the Boer War.

9. Write a short story depicting a dialogue between two immigration officials—one believing that immigration is a threat to Canadian unity, and the other believing that immigration is the key to Canada's future success.

The Great War: A Nation Emerges

We have them on the run. That means we have to do it over again in another twenty-five years.

–GENERAL ANDREW MCNAUGHTON

During his time in office, Wilfrid Laurier had tried to clearly define Canada's relationship with Britain. Although highly criticized, Laurier's "tin pot navy" and newly established Department of External Defence were symbolic steps that signalled to Britain that Canada should be taken seriously as an independent nation in international affairs. Sir Robert Borden and the Conservatives won the election of 1911, but Borden continued in the same vein, trying to establish Canada's growing autonomy.

When war broke out in Europe in 1914, Borden's leadership abilities, Canada's resilience as a country, and the character of the Canadian people were put to the test. It was an opportunity for the young country to claim a place on the world stage.

Canadians in the early 1900s never imagined that the rivalries and disputes in Europe would have any effect on their daily lives. They watched the events in Europe unfold, but many felt removed from the conflict. Increasing unemployment and an economic depression, the threat of crop failure, and an oncoming drought preoccupied most Canadians.

Many countries had enjoyed tremendous industrial growth, but as nations became more powerful, rivalries grew, and squabbles over land and resources mounted. Britain and Germany were at the centre of the hostilities in Europe. The British Empire controlled 25 percent of the Earth's land mass and owned the world's largest naval fleet. Germany, still a young country, boasted a large army and a thriving economy, and possessed an insatiable appetite for expansion. To challenge the British Empire, Germany took to building its own great navy and set its sights on acquiring colonies controlled by Britain and France.

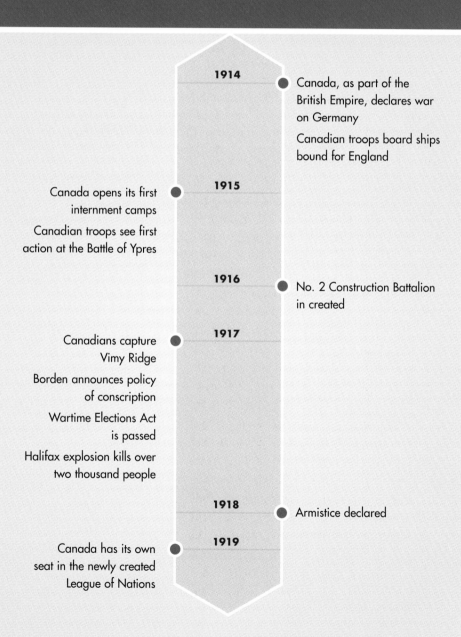

15

1914
Canada, as part of the British Empire, declares war on Germany

Canadian troops board ships bound for England

1915
Canada opens its first internment camps

Canadian troops see first action at the Battle of Ypres

1916
No. 2 Construction Battalion in created

1917
Canadians capture Vimy Ridge

Borden announces policy of conscription

Wartime Elections Act is passed

Halifax explosion kills over two thousand people

1918
Armistice declared

1919
Canada has its own seat in the newly created League of Nations

By the end of this chapter, you will be able to

- demonstrate an understanding of how Canada's participation in significant international conflicts changed the way the country was perceived by the international community

- describe the ways in which the world wars altered Canadians' self-image

- analyze how obstacles that made it difficult for immigrants to participate fully in Canadian society have been challenged and reduced over time

- analyze how and why citizenship rights have been denied at particular times to certain ethnocultural minorities

- analyze why and how the people of Quebec have acted to preserve their political identity

The Global Stage

Canada was not the only nation pulled into the rivalry between Britain and Germany. France's resentment of the successful British Empire was only outweighed by its bitterness over the loss of the border provinces of Alsace and Lorraine to Germany in the Franco-Prussian War in 1870. Italy had recently become an independent nation and, like Germany, was eager to expand. Austria-Hungary, on the other hand, was preoccupied by an impending civil war as the Czechs and Slavs desired to break away from Austro-Hungarian domination and it looked to Germany as its natural ally. Russia, a massive empire that suffered from a weak military and poor economy, saw itself as protectors of the Slavic states.

By the end of the first decade of the twentieth century, Russia, England, and France had formed an alliance, the Triple Entente, promising to come to each other's defence if either country was attacked. Germany, Italy, and Austria-Hungary responded by forming their own pact named the Triple Alliance.

On June 28, 1914, the Archduke Franz Ferdinand of Austria-Hungary visited the capital of Bosnia, Sarajevo, which had been taken over by Austria-Hungary in an earlier conflict.

On that day, a Serbian member of a radical nationalist group, called the Black Hand, assassinated the Archduke and his wife, Duchess Sophia.

The assassination forced Austria-Hungary to make a series of harsh demands from Serbia. Although most of the demands were met, Austria-Hungary still declared war on Serbia. Russia came

Europe and the Alliance Systems, 1914 (Prior to World War I)

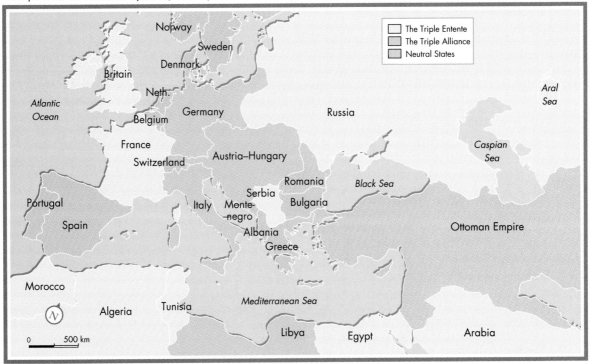

Europe and the Alliance System before World War I: much of Europe was divided into two camps: the Triple Alliance and the Triple Entente.

to Serbia's defence and the system of alliances began to unfold. On August 1, Germany declared war on Russia and then, on August 3, France. On August 4, German troops invaded neutral Belgium on their way to invade France. Outraged by Germany's clear disregard for Belgium's neutrality, Britain gave Germany an ultimatum to retreat by midnight; when Germany ignored their request, Britain declared war on Germany. As part of the British Empire, Canada was immediately involved.

Back by the Holidays

Although Canada was involved in the war, what it would contribute to the war effort was up to the Canadian government. On August 1, Prime Minister Borden offered Britain a force of twenty-five thousand men should it declare war. The offer was accepted on August 6. In a special session of the Dominion Parliament, in August 1914, Borden declared, "In the awful dawn of the greatest war the world has ever known...all are agreed; we stand shoulder to shoulder with Britain and the other British dominions in this quarrel."[1]

The opposition eagerly backed Borden. Sir Wilfrid Laurier conceded that the appropriate response for a nation of the Commonwealth should be "Ready, Aye, Ready". Even Henri Bourassa, a French-Canadian spokesperson and anti-Imperialist, was in support of Canada's involvement, reasoning that the war could unite the country. In the streets, Canadians responded with an outpouring of enthusiasm and support.[2]

Borden's Minister of Militia, Sam Hughes was given the task of assembling and training twenty-five thousand volunteers. Pre-war Canada supported an army of just over three thousand men and when war broke out Canada's small military was unprepared for the scope of what lay ahead.

Unexpectedly, by September, over thirty thousand men volunteered to enlist in the army. The majority of the volunteers were recent British immigrants who wanted to support the "Mother Country". Mark Tanner, a pilot originally from Montreal commented

> In those days the British Empire was the great fact of life to most young people. We were brought up in the believe that the sun never set on the British Empire...We were all taught in school by maps showing the far-flung British Empire marked in red... You could look at these maps, and you'd see Canada, Australia, New Zealand, India, other parts of Asia, and large sections of Africa, all in red, showing the magnitude and the power of the British Empire.[3]

Not all men enlisted in 1914 to serve for Britain. Some men volunteered to escape the unemployment line, to fight against the growing militarism of Germany and Austria-Hungary, or simply to seek adventure.[4]

Hughes was praised for preparing over thirty thousand Canadian civilians to be soldiers and organizing the troops so quickly and efficiently at

Valcartier camp was set up by Minister of Militia Sam Hughes to train and organize Canadian troops.

the new Valcartier training camp near Quebec City. On October 3, 1914, the first contingent of Canadian troops left their families behind and set sail for Britain. Canadians envisioned a short, heroic war, and everyone was confident that the troops would be "home by Christmas."

Strategy and Training

The first Canadian contingent arrived in England on October 14, 1914. Any romantic notions of the war were put on hold on Salisbury Plain, where the Canadians spent their first four months waiting for battle. It rained 89 of the 123 days. The men spent a good deal of their time bored and discouraged.

In February 1915, the first Canadian Division was sent to France and trained by veteran British officers. It was immediately apparent that the Canadians were unprepared. Sam Hughes was responsible for the Canadian troops having been outfitted with defective equipment. The mass-produced boots literally dissolved in the wet terrain of England and France. The MacAdam shovel, a device that served as a shield when firing, proved cumbersome and collapsed when digging ditches. But it was the Ross rifle that was Hughes' most costly mistake.

The Ross rifle had been used by the Canadians in the Boer War and Sir Charles Ross, a British inventor, had offered to build a plant in Canada, signing a contract to produce thousands of rifles. Early designs were problematic and, even before the war Canadians were encouraged by the British to adopt the Lee Enfield rifle to maintain the cohesion of British and Dominion armies. Hughes ignored public pressure, however, and sent his men to England and onto the battlefields of France with the Ross rifle. It jammed in rapid fire and only worked effectively with Canadian manufactured ammunition, which was in short supply at the front: many Canadians died attempting to use their Ross rifles in battle.[5] Hughes' actions were criticized and caused Borden great political difficulties. His erratic behaviour, stubbornness, and tendency to play favourites in selecting officers, resulted in a disorganized and ill-prepared army.[6]

The Ross rifle controversy was part of Hughes' continuing struggle against British officials during the Great War. He was determined to maintain the identity of his troops, and arming them with Canadian manufactured weapons was symbolic of this greater effort. The Ross rifle was an embarrassment for the Canadian government.

Canadian Troops in training on Salisbury Plain, winter 1914–1915. It rained 89 days of the 123 days.

When the Canadians had arrived in Europe in 1915, no great gains had been made on the Western Front by either side. Modern artillery, like the machine gun, forced soldiers to dig into the earth and create barriers or "trenches" to defend themselves. In the first year of war, the Western Front was literally carved out by an intricate web of trenches. The British had moved to Flanders in Belgium in early October and were defending the Ypres Salient, where the British line ran frighteningly close to the Germans. Following their training, the Canadians took over a portion of this line between the village of Aubers and the town of Amenitières.

Canadian Expeditionary Force

The Canadian Expeditionary Force (C.E.F) was first made up of the thirty thousand men who had trained at Valcartier and sailed for England in October of 1914. A second division arriving in England in the spring of 1915, became the 1st Canadian Division and eventually, a third and fourth division were formed. Overseas, the C.E.F. was under the direction of British officials. British General Alderson, who had led the Canadians in the Boer War, was put in charge of the Canadian Corps. The Canadians arrived overseas generally unprepared for the discipline, environment, and training. Unfortunately, the lack of organization of the Canadian troops and their faulty equipment earned them a bad reputation.

Leading the Canadian Troops

As the war waged on, imperialistic fervour waned for many Canadians, and Sam Hughes was the first to become disillusioned. He was quick to blame failures and the casualties of early battles on General Alderson. General Haig, head of the British forces, eventually replaced Alderson with Sir Julian Byng, who had made a name for himself in the Boer War and was a favourite among the troops.

Prime Minister Borden also became increasingly preoccupied with gaining control over the Canadian troops overseas. In 1916, he created the Ministry of Overseas Military Forces. Tired of mediating complaints about Sam Hughes, Borden chose George

The Western Front

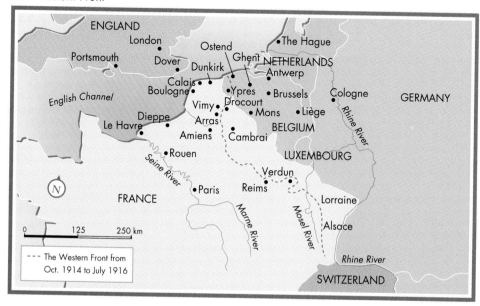

The Western Front, 1914–1916

Perley, Acting High Commissioner in Britain, to be his Minister of Overseas Militia. By November of that same year, the infuriated Hughes resigned.

A White Man's War: Who were in the C.E.F.?

In the beginning, not all Canadians were welcome to volunteer for the C.E.F. Black Canadians were able to enlist only if a local regiment would accept them. Eventually, they were granted the privilege of forming a non-fighting unit. In 1916, a black Canadian battalion was created under white leadership. The Nova Scotia No. 2 Construction Battalion worked in lumber mills providing wood for trenches and railways, and they also defused land mines. As the war progressed, a number of soldiers from the No. 2 Construction Battalion were transferred to other units to serve on the front line. Racism, however, did not disappear overseas and black Canadians were segregated, even in hospitals and were separated from fellow white officers, even when watching entertainment. Despite the enormous hurdles thrown in front of them by fellow Canadians, black soldiers achieved much success while fighting for Canada and the British Empire. William White became a chaplain of the construction battalion and the first black Canadian officer. James Grant from St. Catherines, Ontario, originally with the construction battalion, went on to serve in a combat unit and won a Military Cross. Roy Fells of Yarmouth, Nova Scotia, earned the Military Medal while serving with the 25th Battalion from Nova Scotia.[7]

Aboriginal Peoples in the Great War

The government did not expect that Aboriginal Canadians would join the war effort and, in the beginning, adopted a policy to discourage them from enlisting. The government argued that the enemy forces would stereotype Aboriginal soldiers as "savage" and treat them cruelly if captured. Unfounded statements like this only tried to mask

Saskatchewan Indians, members of the File Hills Colony, departing Regina for service during World War I.

the prevalent racist attitudes of the time. As casualties in the war mounted, however, the government abandoned this policy in 1915 and, over the course of the war, approximately four thousand Aboriginal Canadians volunteered for service.

The Iroquois Six Nations of Grand River, south of Brantford, Ontario, had the largest enlistment with over three hundred men. In 1919, the Prince of Wales visited the Six Nations reserve and presented the soldiers with a plaque, recognizing their war service. Many Aboriginal Canadians won medals for their bravery. Francis Pegahmagabow, an Ontario Ojibwa who was a sniper and scout, became the most decorated Aboriginal Canadian soldier.[8]

Women in the War Effort

Canadian women were sent overseas as nurses, ambulance drivers, and staff officers. Two thousand women worked as nursing sisters during the Great War, another six thousand worked in the civil service. Margaret MacDonald was made Matron-in-Chief of the Canadian nursing sisters and, on November 4, 1914, she was granted the rank of Major. MacDonald was the first woman in the British Empire to be given this rank.

Two thousand Canadian women went overseas as nursing sisters. They put their lives in jeopardy serving in Casualty Clearing Stations and hospital ships. These nurses are voting while serving in France, 1917.

Nursing sisters, like male doctors, witnessed the devastation of war on a regular basis, and put their lives at risk, working in casualty clearing stations close to the front lines and on hospital ships.

They served on the Western Front in England and France and as far away as the Mediterranean and Africa. Forty-six nursing sisters gave their lives during the Great War. Fifteen of these nurses died at sea, when a German submarine attacked and sunk the hospital ship, *Llandovery Castle*.

Canadians in a New Kind of War

Before the Canadians arrived on the Western Front it had been carved out by an intricate trench system. Trenches were organized into forward, support and reserve functions. The day-to-day living conditions of the trenches were abominable. Donald Fraser, a private from Calgary, Alberta, remembers, "The dug-outs were small, damp and cold and overrun with rats. It is needless to add once a fighting soldier leaves England he practically sleeps in his clothes till he gets back there again."[9] In Northern France and Belgium, the Canadians stood knee-deep in water and often suffered an affliction known as "trench foot". Soldier Gregory Clark, of the 4th Canadian Mounted Rifles (who later went on to become a leading journalist in Canada) wrote about live in the trenches:

The Western Front was carved out in a series of trenches. Like all who served in the trenches, Canadian soldiers stood knee-deep in water and mud, slept and ate little, and shared their space with rats, lice and disease.

They speak of trenches. Trenches is too romantic a name. These were ditches, common ordinary ditches. As time went by they became filthy. We had no garbage disposal, no sewage disposal. You would dig a little trench off the main trench, dig a deep hole and that was your latrine...it was in that sort of setting men lived as if it were the way men should live, year after year....There was nothing in it except rats, by the countless millions. Wherever you went, in the daylight, at night, the whole place squeaking and squealing with these huge and monstrous rats....That added that last mad feature.

As troops dug into the earth on the Western Front and protected their trenches, it became more and more difficult for either side to make an advance. Few could make it across the vast expense of land, the "no man's land" of shell-torn ground and barbed wire, between the front-line trenches. Those who tried met a barrage of machine gun fire. A stalemate followed for almost three years.

The Allies were desperate for a weapon that could break through the barbed wire and protect the troops in the long trek across "no man's land". Britain was experimenting with a new armored

vehicle that ran on treads. Referred to as the "tank", the new vehicle failed in its early trials as the engine faltered and left men stranded on the battlefield. However, as war waged on, modifications were made and communication strategies between the vehicles and the troops improved. In November 1917, during the Battle of Cambrai, 380 tanks were successfully deployed, crossing trenches quickly and throwing the enemy off guard. By the end of the Great War the tank effectively replaced the horse.

War in the Air

Airplanes were still new at the outbreak of the Great War. The Royal Flying Corps had only been established in Britain since 1912. Planes were used mostly to carry supplies and observe enemy positions. Eventually, airmen were supplied with machine guns to shoot at enemy planes; they also dropped darts and grenades over the battlefield. Prime Minster Borden and Sam Hughes were skeptical of the benefits of aircraft and would not support a Canadian Air Force. Only one plane crossed with the Canadian contingent. Those Canadians who did join the Air

Tanks replaced horses at the front and helped the Allies cross the dreaded no man's land. These soldiers are shown at the Somme in 1916.

Most Canadians fought with the British Royal Air Force during the Great War. A Canadian Flying Corps was not created until 1917

Force, fought with the British and, in the early years of the war, were not supported financially by the Canadian government. It was not until 1917 that the Royal Flying Corps opened schools in Canada. By April 1918, over twenty thousand Canadians belonged to the Royal Air Force. An independent Canadian Force was created in the last months of the war.

Canadian Heroes in the Air

Of the twenty-seven flying aces in the Royal Air Force, eleven of them were Canadian. With seventy-two victories to his name, Billy Bishop from Owen Sound, Ontario was the top scoring Canadian Ace of the Great War. Known as the "Lone Hawk," Bishop was also the first Canadian Airman to win the Victoria Cross. Raymond Collishaw from Vancouver won over sixty victories and Fighter Pilot, William Barker, born in Dauphin, Manitoba, was credited with fifty-three aerial victories. Barker is remembered most for a monumental battle in October of 1918, where he took on some sixty German aircraft alone. Barker won a Victoria Cross for this epic feat and during his career as a fighter pilot, he was also awarded a Military Cross, two bars to his Military Cross, a Distinguished Service Order, and a bar to his Distinguished Service Order, making him Canada's most decorated war hero. Canadian pilot Roy Brown is credited with shooting down the "Red Baron," Germany's most famous World War I flying ace. During the war, stories of heroes such as Billy Bishop, Raymond Collishaw, William Barker, and Roy Brown made it back to Canada, and they became legends to Canadians on the home front.

War at Sea

Before the war, Canada possessed only two naval ships, the *Rainbow* and *Niobe*, and a small service of three hundred men for its navy. No naval ship-building was undertaken until 1917. During the war, 1471 men enrolled in the Royal Naval Canadian Naval Reserve and 7360 joined the Royal Naval Volunteer Reserve. The RCN performed minesweeping operations and patrolled the Atlantic and the West Coast.

One of Canada's most significant contributions to the Great War was in providing convoys to protect cargo ships in their long trip over the Atlantic. In a convoy, a number of military vessels would accompany the cargo ships, and locate German U-Boat periscopes. Most of the convoys were organized in Halifax Harbour preventing the German navy from dominating the sea and allowing Allied supplies to reach Britain.

However, during the war, the German submarine, called a U-Boat, (for the German word *Unterseebooten* for "undersea boat"), became an increasing threat to the Allies. The U-Boat could attack without warning and sank British ships on the Atlantic at an alarming rate. Within the first year of World War I, German U-Boats sank over two hundred British supply ships. On May 7, 1915, a German U-Boat sank a British luxury passenger ship, the *Lusitania*, killing over 1000 innocent civilians, 128 of whom were American. The sinking of the *Lusitania* was a catalyst for the Americans to join the war in 1917.

Early Battles for Canada

When Canadian soldiers arrived in England in 1914, they were poorly equipped and had been hastily trained. On Salisbury Plain, they received nine more months of training. But little of this would prepare them for the horrors of war they were about to face.

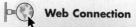

Web Connection

www.mcgrawhill.ca/links/definingcanada

Go to the Web site above to hear interviews with World War I Canadian veterans.

The Second Battle of Ypres

In the first week of April 1915, Canadian troops moved to the Allied line at the city of Ypres in Belgium. On April 22, the Germans unleashed a secret weapon on French troops and a strange green haze crept across the battlefield. A gap was created in the Allied line as men choked, dropped dead, or fled from the caustic chlorine gas. The 1st Canadian Division was sent in to fill the gap in the Allied line that evening.

On April 24, the Canadians received their baptism of fire. Breathing through mud or urine-soaked handkerchiefs, choking on chlorine gas and hampered by jammed rifles, they held on to their position until reinforcements arrived. In forty-eight hours, the Canadian Division suffered 6035 casualties, yet they still managed to hold their ground. Despite a lack of coherent guidance and their basic inexperience, the Canadian soldiers demonstrated remarkable endurance at Ypres. Praise flooded in from all over the world as news of their gallant efforts reached home. In their first major engagement, the Canadians earned themselves a reputation as a formidable force.

Battle of the Somme

Early in 1916, the Allies decided that the only way to break the stalemate was to plan a full-scale offensive across "no man's land." In the West, the area near the Somme River was selected for the attack. On July 1, 100 000 men climbed out of their trenches and advanced on the enemy in broad daylight. Fifty-seven thousand, five hundred soldiers from Britain and Newfoundland were lost, wounded or missing in one day.

Canadians were spared the early battles of the Somme, but a separate Newfoundland force, the 1st Newfoundland Regiment, made up of 790 men, was almost completely annihilated at the village of Beaumont Hamel on that first day of the Battle of the Somme. At 7:20 a.m. a mine went off under the enemy's front trenches and alerted them of the oncoming Allied troops. The Newfoundlanders had to cross 230 metres of treacherous ground before even reaching the front lineóa line they never reached. As soldier Ken Goodyear from the Royal Newfoundland Regiment wrote:

> We went four abreast, sixty men all in line, down through the gaps that we cut in the

The battle of the Somme began in July 1916, and by the time the fighting ended five months later, some 1.25 million men had been killed. The British forces had advanced less than twelve kilometres.

barbed wire and you see the thing is, the Germans had their machine guns trained exactly on those gaps. Those gaps were marked with white tape and rock. We were just sitting ducks, nothing more or less....

Another soldier from the same regiment described the horrific losses that morning:

A lot of our men were killed before they got to the front line, and the gaps in the wire were full of our dead...I'll never forget the looks on them kids' faces...they were kids fresh from home and to see the dead and dying around there everywhere and blood and the noise of shells...it was awful introduction to warfare.

In August the 1st Division of the Canadian Corps moved to the Somme where it took over a section of the front line. The 2nd and 3rd Divisions followed in the fall. Again and again, the three Canadian divisions launched attacks along a series of German entrenchments, holding on until the 4th Division arrived on November 11. They succeeded in taking two coveted German defences, "Regina Trench" and "Desire Trench". In general, the Somme was considered a travesty, a battle where little was gained and too much sacrificed. The Allies suffered over 600 000 casualties, and gained only six miles of land. Canada alone suffered 24 029 casualties. In 1925, Beaumont-Hamel Memorial Park opened in France with a monument of a bronze caribou with the emblem of the Royal Newfoundland Regiment at the highest point. Today, July 1 still holds a double meaning for Newfoundlanders, as a day of celebration of Canada Day and also a day of mourning for the hundreds of soldiers who never came home.

Enemy Aliens at Home

Many Canadians at home perceived the enemy to be in their own backyard. The government introduced the War Measures Act in 1914, giving the federal government authorization to suppress the rights of those considered "enemy aliens," people who had emigrated from nations now considered the enemy and who had not yet gained their Canadian citizenship. The Act was created by Borden's Conservatives in part to protect Canada from the war in Europe, but also to placate an increasingly suspicious and anxious Canadian public.

During the Great War, thousands of immigrants from the Austro-Hungarian empire who had once been encouraged to settle the west, now found themselves considered the enemy in their new homeland. Harsh measures were taken against Canadians of Ukrainian, German, Polish, Austrian, Czech, and Slovac decent. Newspapers were censored and banned, churches and businesses closed and many individuals lost their jobs. Riots ensued in areas with large German populations, such as Calgary, Alberta and Berlin, Ontario. Fears grew so

Ukrainian-Canadians entering an internment camp. Many worked in remote areas in the western provinces.

intense that the citizens of Berlin voted to change the small German community's name to "Kitchener," after Lord Kitchener, the British Secretary of War.

After October 14th, 1914, enemy aliens were forced to register with the Canadian government, report firearms. Those considered most dangerous, namely Ukrainians and Germans, were taken from their homes and sent to internment camps. During the Great War, over eight thousand "enemy aliens" were interned, including five thousand Ukrainians. Over eighty thousand Ukrainians were forced to register with police, and carry identification papers with them at all times. Interned Canadians were forced into labour, clearing roads and forests in national parks such as Banff, Jasper, and Mount Revelstoke, and working in logging camps and mines across Canada. Internment of "enemy aliens" continued for two years after the war.

Web Connection

www.mcgrawhill.ca/links/definingcanada

Go to the Web site above to learn more about the internment of Ukrainians in Canada during World War I.

Pacifists

Canadian war-supporters were not just suspicious of enemy aliens, they also began to question the loyalties of Canadian pacifists: those who opposed war on moral or religious grounds. Religious groups, such as Mennonites and Hutterites, who objected to the war on both religious and moral grounds, were exempt from military service under the terms of their immigration. While these groups faced ridicule and harassment, conscientious objectors who were not part of these groups, and still refused military involvement faced possible imprisonment. By the end of the war, there were still thirty-four men imprisoned for their nonviolent beliefs. A letter from a prison warden in Lethbridge, Alberta to the Deputy Minister in the Department of Justice on July 6, 1918, shows the lack of tolerance many people had for conscientious objectors:

> The Military Authorities at Calgary have sentenced eleven men to this Institution to serve Two Years less one day in each case, because as Conscientious Objectors they refused to obey some Military commands.

> Now, what I want to know is, what is the attitude of your Department towards these men, and what treatment do you expect us to give them here? Do you desire us to pay attention to their various "conscientious whims"[6] For example, do you wish to accede to the request of the Seventh Day Adventist that he not be required to work on Saturday.

Canadian WWI recruitment poster. Who did not fight?.

Win the War and Lose Canada

The following article appeared in the *Quebec Daily Telegraph*, 1917.

We are opposed to further enlistments for the war in Europe, whether by conscription or otherwise, for the following reasons: (1) Canada has already made a military display, in men and money, proportionately superior to that of any nation engaged in the war; (2) any further weakening of the man-power of the country would seriously handicap agricultural production and other essential industries; (3) an increase in the war budget of Canada spells national bankruptcy; (4) it threatens the economic life of the nation and, eventually, its political independence; (5) conscription means national disunion and strife, and would thereby hurt the cause of the Allies to a much greater extent than the addition of a few thousand soldiers to their fighting forces could bring them help and comfort....

Conscription is sure to bring serious troubles in the labour circles. Indiscriminate enlistment has already disorganized labour conditions. Rightly or wrongly, labour leaders apprehend that conscription is sought for not so much for military purposes as with the object of controlling wages and work. The enforcement of conscription will certainly be resisted by the organized labour in Canada.

There is also in Canada a large foreign enlistment to which conscription is distasteful to the extreme. Most of these foreigners were invited to come. The government paid premiums to secure them. They [such as Mennonites] were assured that Canada was free from military service. They have therefore against conscription a case much stronger than that of the so called "hyphenated" Americans [such as Hutterites who migrated to Canada in 1917–18 to escape the U.S. draft.]

The situation and sentiments of the French Canadians, who form between one-third and one-fourth of the population of Canada, have also to be reckoned with. Such silly things have appeared about them in some of the English-Canadian papers, and occasionally in the American press, that elementary truths have to be recalled....

Without any previous declaration of war, Canada has thrown herself into the conflict as a mere satellite of Great Britain. She was not forced to do so, either by constitution of previous understandings. On the contrary, a well-defined agreement with Great Britain made it clear that, in case of war, Canada had no other duty to perform than that of defending her own territory, if attacked....

In spite of all the statements to the contrary, the French-Canadians are loyal to Great Britain and friendly to France; but they do not acknowledge to either country what, in every land, is considered as the most exclusive national duty: the obligation to bear arms and to fight.

So that in the eyes of all French-Canadians, the adoption of conscription would not only result in an economic collapse of the country: it would also shake their faith in the honour and truthfulness of their public men.

Finally, the economic readjustment of the country is sure to bring dispute between the rural provinces of the West and the industrial provinces of the East....

In short, apart from the menace to the economic equilibrium of the country, the inevitable outcome of conscription and of any overstrained effort for the war in Europe is three-fold: (1) labour troubles and class hatred; (2) racial strife; (3) a deep cleavage between East and West....

Opposition to conscription and war-madness in Canada is not anti-patriotic; it is essentially patriotic and clear-sighted.

-Henri Bourassa

---

1. Do you agree with Henri Bourassa's last sentence? Why or why not?
2. How wide-spread do you believe Henri Bourassa's anti-conscription views were among Canadians? What points of view are missing from Bourassa's argument?
3. By confronting government actions like conscription, how did Henri Bourassa help develop French consciousness in Canada?

Do you wish us to continue this course or shall we begin to accede to the conscientious whims of these apparent pro-German prisoners.

I am sorry these men are being sent here. I think they should be sent to the Front and made to take their share in the defence of our Country or as an alternative sent to the Detention Camps and herded with kindred spirits there.

I wish you would order their removal from this Jail if possible, and stop any more of this Kind from coming to a respectable jail."[10]

The War Time Canadian Economy

At first, the war had hurt the troubled economy. As men left to become soldiers the unemployment rate grew and the debt-ridden railway systems became a national disgrace.

By 1915, military spending matched the entire government expenditure of 1913. In November 1915, the British Ministry of Munitions created an Imperial Munitions Board (IMB) in Canada. Run by a prominent Toronto businessman, Joseph Flavelle, the IMB turned out shells, ships, explosives and planes that were sent overseas. By 1917, the Munitions Board was the largest business in Canada, employing 150 000 workers.

By 1917, Britain could no longer afford Canadian goods, and the IMB turned to the United States as business partners, since they had recently joined the war.[11] However, this new business relationship made Canada increasingly dependent on America for supplies.

In 1915, Thomas White turned to the Canadian public to financially support the war effort. The government introduced Victory Bonds and asked for $50 million. The loans would be repaid after the war. By 1917, the victory loan campaign had brought in $100 million. Victory Bonds covered more than 80 percent of war costs, but generated a large national debt. At first, the Minister of Finance, Thomas White, opposed increasing taxes; however, the Wartime Business Profits Tax was introduced in 1916 and a temporary income tax was introduced in 1917.

Review...Reflect...Respond

1. How would racism in the Canadian Expeditionary Force affect how many Canadians would view and support the war effort?

2. Why do incidents such as the internment of thousands of enemy aliens during World War I change the way we view Canada and its history? Are events such as this usually hidden from general discussions about Canada's past?

3. Why is it said that a new Canadian identity was forged on the battlefields of Europe?

Canadian Women on the Home Front

The Canadian War effort at home was fuelled by volunteers and the wives and family members left behind. In the early years, the government established a Patriotic Fund, as it had in the Boer War, and money was collected to support families whose husbands and fathers were overseas. The Military Hospital Commission cared for the sick and wounded. Churches and women's groups, such as The Daughters of the Empire, the Red Cross, and the Dorcas Club, rallied to support husbands, family and friends. Women sewed pajamas and socks and sent care packages to troops overseas. Aboriginal women, like other Canadian women formed patriotic leagues and joined the Red Cross societies and other charity groups. Over the course of war, donations from Aboriginal Canadians in the various funds totalled $44 000.[12] Black Canadian women formed their own volunteer organizations as well, such as the Good Government Club in Windsor.

Expression of Culture
CANADIAN WAR ART

On January 4, 1919, Canadian war art was shown for the first time in a public exhibition at Burlington House in London England. Canadian Prime Minister Sir Robert Borden gathered with a large crowd of visitors to see how Canadian artists had depicted the horrors, the heroics, and the reality of the Great War. What they faced was an exhibition of works by both Canadian and British artists of varying subjects, from impressionistic landscapes to formal portraits, and large scale heroic battle scenes to emotionally charged, intimate canvases of battle-torn grounds.

The man of the hour, at the London War Art exhibition, was Lord Beaverbrook a Canadian-born businessman who oversaw the creation of the Canadian War Memorials Fund (CWMF). Born in New Brunswick, Max Aitken, later to be knighted and known as Lord Beaverbrook, made his first million by the age of twenty-eight. He moved to Britain and obtained a seat in British Parliament and acquired shares in the *Daily Express*. During the Great War, Beaverbrook found himself in charge of the Canadian War Records Office and at the centre of the devastating events which were unfolding in Europe. Spurred on by the travesty of the second battle of Ypres and the fact that it had not been photographed, Beaverbrook was inspired to capture the war on canvas.

The Canadian War Memorials Fund was created in November 1916 and managed by Lord Beaverbrook in Europe. Beaverbrook's initial idea was to commission well-known British artists to record Canadian efforts in large-scale works that would be displayed later in Canadian government buildings. Prominent British artists, including Richard Jack, Augustus John, and Gyrth Russell found themselves working for Beaverbrook on Canadian subjects. Richard Jack was granted the first commission—to depict the Canadians in the second battle of Ypres. The resulting work, *The Second Battle of Ypres, 22 April to 25 May, 1915* (1917, oil on canvas), measures twelve by twenty feet and depicts the Canadian soldiers heroically engaged in the throws of combat.

A.Y. Jackson, who had first enlisted in the 60th Battalion and was later wounded, was sent to France to draw Canadians on the front. He described a common problem for the war artist, "There was nothing to serve as a guide. War had gone underground, and there was little to see. The old heroics, the death and glory stuff, were gone for ever...." He also noted, "The impressionist technique I had adopted in painting was now ineffective, for visual impressions were not enough."

In response to growing criticism from Canadian art officials and artists, Beaverbrook set out to employ a number of Canadian war artists. William Beatty, Frederick Varley, Maurice Cullen, and Charles Simpson were among the first Canadians to become official war artists under the CWMF. They were given official rank and status of Captain and were paid for their work.

The Canadian war artists followed the Canadian contingent from Passchendaele to Cambrai and Vimy to Canada's last One Hundred Days. They completed small sketches first in the field and later worked these into larger canvases back in the studio

Some of the most compelling works created during the Great War for the CWMF, were not the large-scale battle scenes with soldiers in action or formal portraits, as one might expect, but were panoramas of land, ruins and barren battleground. Some artists depicted the land and ruins as strangely calm and beautiful in the wake of the destruction, such as William Beatty's *Ablain St-Nazaire* (1918, oil on canvas) and A.Y. Jackson's *Gas Attack, Liévin* (1918, oil on canvas). Other artists produced shockingly violent works of the war-torn ground filled with dead bodies and the tangled remnants of war, as in Canadian

(Continued)

artist, Fred Varley's *For What?* (1918, oil on canvas). These works are interesting not only for the scene that each depicts, but for the artist's emotional response that is expressed through colour, line, and rhythm.

Canadian women were also encouraged by Eric Brown to contribute to the Canadian War Memorials Fund. They were given the task of documenting the activity of the Canadian war effort on the home front. Canadian artist Mabel May painted *Women Making Shells* (1919, oil on canvas), a lively illustration of women hard at work in a crowded and bustling munitions factory. Florence Wyle and Frances Loring created sculptures of Canadian munitions workers.

Male artists also captured the activity of Canadians on the home front. Manly MacDonald depicted women working on a farm near Belleville, Ontario; while, Arthur Lismer, future member of the Group of Seven, captured the activity of the Halifax Harbour and recorded the devastation of the Halifax explosion.

The Canadian War Memorials Fund, made up paintings, sculptures and prints, remains a Canadian legacy of the Great War. The CWMF also brought Canadian artists, art officials and critics together, spurring much-needed discussion and debate over the state of the Canadian art scene.

Women Making Shells by Mabel May, CWM, 8409

Mabel May's *Women Making Shells* (1919)

Canadian women helped fuel the war effort on the home front by volunteering for the Red Cross and other women's clubs that raised money and sent supplies to soldiers overseas

Land Girls Hoeing by Manly MacDonald, CWM, 8390

Canadian artist Manly MacDonald captured women working on farms in Belleville, Ontario. *Land Girls Hoeing* (1919)

Canadian women also went to work and took over those occupations previously considered "men's work". In this way, the Great War offered an unprecedented opportunity for women to prove their abilities. Women worked on farms assisting with the harvest, and joined organizations like the Government of Ontario's Farm Service Corps.

Up to thirty thousand Canadian women found work as labourers in the new munitions factories. Elaine Nelson from Parry Sound moved to Toronto to work in one such factory. She remembers the experience, "There was everybody, every single class...I thought it was fascinating. You get in the canteen or up in the big restroom there and hear them talking. It was very, very interesting. And there's every kind: wonderful, brave women who were saving every nickel they could so they'd have enough money to buy a home when their husband came back."[13]

Although the opportunities were new and exciting, women would have a long battle ahead of them for equal rights. Morty Stein, an active member of unions in Toronto, Ontario, and Truro, Nova Scotia, recalls "People had two thoughts on it. Unions' thoughts were: these women are going to take our jobs. The ordinary man who had a brain to study it said, 'Well, what's the difference? They need money was well as we do. Nobody liked women working, they were afraid for their own job."[14] Women were often paid less for the same position previously held by men and often faced hostile

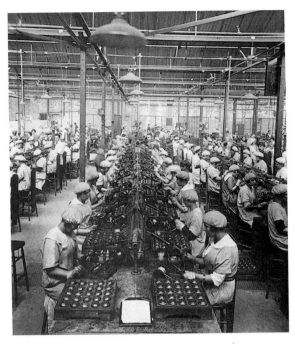

Thirty thousand women went to work in munitions factories in Canada. These women are soldering fuses.

This soldier is reading an election poster urging people to vote against the Government.

working conditions. When the wars ended in 1919, women were expected to leave their jobs and return to the home, and in many cases, they were actually fired to open up employment for the returning soldiers. Clearly, the fight for equality was far from over. Yet, the contribution of Canadian women during the war was a key component to Canada's growth during the Great War, and to Canada's role in the war itself.

Conscription Crisis

In the summer of 1915, Prime Minister Borden went overseas to visit the Canadian troops. He was appalled by the harsh realities of trench warfare and the growing casualty list. In his 1916 New Year's Eve speech Borden declared, "On this last day of the old year the authorized force will be 500 000.

This announcement is made in token of Canada's unflinchable resolve to crown the justice of our cause with victory and with an abiding peace."[15] In a country of barely eight million citizens, this was an incredible request.[16]

By mid-1916, voluntary enlistments had slowed down to a trickle. Horrifying stories of the brutality of modern warfare and life in the trenches had reached home and many able-bodied men had found good work in munitions factories. Widows and women whose husbands, sons, or sweethearts were off at war put pressure on the young, able-bodied men on the home front to also go overseas and fight for Britain. Recruiting drives were organized, where women sang patriotic songs and waved flags. Many women approached and taunted men on the street. Posters were everywhere and added pressure on men at home. A common image was of Lord Kitchener pointing at the viewer and saying "We need you".

By 1917, conscriptionóforcing men to join the serviceówas the only way to find additional troops for the war overseas. Conscription was meant to solve the problems of soldier shortages in Europe, but it would also create conflict at home. The relationship between Quebec and the rest of the country, between French and English Canadians, was already on uneven ground. The Manitoba School Act of 1890 and Ontario's Regulation 17, which restricted French instruction in school, were still open wounds in the eyes of Quebecois. Canada's role in the Boer War and its decision in the Naval Service Bill had also created conflict between French and English Canada. Conscription would only heighten the tension.

Sam Hughes' recruiting tactics did little to improve the French-English situation during the Great War. His disregard for the needs of French Canadians and poor recruiting efforts in Quebec only heightened resentment. Prime Minister Borden recalls in his memoirs,

> General Hughes' maladroit methods reached their highest point in his arrangements for recruiting among French-Canadians. He placed an English Protestant in charge of recruiting propaganda, and from time to time emphasized the foolishness of this action by more mischievous activities. He imagined that he was extremely popular in the Province of Quebec, but this was only one of many delusions from which I found him suffering on various occasions.[17]

The first division that had gone over to England had a single French-speaking brigade.

Once overseas, French-speaking brigades were broken up and distributed to other battalions where instructions and orders were only given in English. French Canadians became increasingly reluctant to sign-up as the war progressed. In turn, English-speaking Canadians criticized the Quebecois for not "doing their part."

In May 1917, Borden announced to Parliament his plan to introduce conscription. His statement divided Parliament along French and English lines and sent a ripple of anxiety across the country. Quebecois, who felt little allegiance to either France or Britain, were outraged. Referring to the lack of French instruction in Canadian schools, Henri Bourassa argued that Canada should not concern itself with a war overseas when injustices were occurring at home.

Conscription, however, was not simply a French-English issue. Farmers across the country, especially in the prairie provinces, resisted mandatory service, fearing that their livelihood would be lost if young men were forced to leave the family farm. On May 15, 1917, five hundred Ontario and Prairie farmers stormed Ottawa.[18]

Prime Minister Borden turned to his Minister Arthur Meighen to draft the Military Service Act, which became law on August 29. Borden then asked Laurier, the leader of the Opposition, to form a Union Coalition Government that would make way for the Military Service Act and eliminate two party politics. Laurier refused the offer fearing that the alliance of Liberals and Conservatives would abandon Quebec nationalists, such as Henri Bourassa, and push them to separate.

Conscription and the Vote for Women

An election was called in December of 1917. Conscription was the main issue, with Borden on one side, Bourassa on the other, and the compromising Laurier in the middle. Borden passed a series of controversial bills that would help him secure victory. The Military Voters Act gave the vote to men and women serving overseas. The message was clear; they could simply cast a vote for "government" or for "opposition." Even British subjects, serving with the Canadian forces were given the vote. Moreover, if a man or woman serving overseas could not identify his or herself with a specific district, a vote could be counted for any district he or she had resided in before the war.

The Wartime Elections Act was passed that gave Borden the means to pick and choose his voters. He gave the right to vote to women at home who had relatives serving in the military. This was the first time women were allowed to vote in a federal election. He also ensured that Canadian citizens who had emigrated from enemy nations were unable to vote.

The victory was Borden's. Laurier's Liberals secured 82 seats, 62 from Quebec, while Borden's Union Government triumphed with 153.[19] Borden's tactics during the 1917 election were then and have since been highly criticized. He effectively chose whom he wanted to vote, ensuring that pro-conscriptionists had the vote, and that anti-conscriptionists did not. He also manipulated votes overseas, creating a surplus of floating votes that could be applied where necessary.

Throughout the conscription crisis Borden held fast to his conviction that Canada owed it to Britain, to the troops overseas and to itself to maintain its commitment to the war. In 1917 he declared,

> All citizens are liable to military service for the defence of their country, and I conceive that the battle for Canadian liberty and autonomy is being fought today on the plains of France and Belgium. There are other places besides the soil of a country where the battle for its liberties and it institutions can be fought; and if this war should end in defeat, Canada, in all the years to come, would be under the shadow of German military domination.[20]

Borden believed that the Union Coalition Government was the only way to make conscription a reality and he did everything necessary to ensure his victory. He also believed that the Coalition would help smooth over tensions between French and English Canadians. He was wrong. Just over 400 000 men were called up to service under the Military Service Act. Of these 379 629 sought exemptions and only 241 32 draftees ever made it to France. On Good Friday, 1918, police seized a draft-resister in Quebec City and started a riot. On Easter Monday, cornered soldiers fired into an angry mob. In the end, the war was over before the Canadian draftees could make a difference and the conscription crisis had only fuelled the fire in Quebec.

Tragedy at Home: The Halifax Explosion

To Canadian civilians on the home front for the most part, the battles of the Great War were distant events that took place a world away. On December 6, 1917, however, disaster occurred in Canadian waters when the French ship, *Mont Blanc*, carrying twenty-four hundred tonnes of explosives collided with the Norwegian relief vessel *Imo* in Halifax Harbour. The ships caught fire and exploded, resulting in the largest non-atomic explosion in history. The noise broke windows in

The Halifax Explosion was one of the greatest tragedies in Canadian history, killing 1 600 people and injuring 9 000.

the town of Truro, one hundred kilometres away, and could be heard as far away as Prince Edward Island. Sixteen hundred Canadians were killed and nine thousand were injured. Homes and buildings in Halifax were completely destroyed.

Relief poured in almost immediately from the rest of Atlantic Canada, central Canada, and New England. The Halifax Relief Commission was established in December 1917, to administer the $30 million in funds raised. A significant amount of aid, $750 000 in cash and goods, came from the Massachusetts Relief Committee. Pressure to rebuild the city led to a number of innovations, including Canada's first public housing project, the Hydrostone Development, which was administered by the Commission. In 1948, the Halifax Relief Commission became a pension board to disburse the remaining funds to disabled dependants.

Halifax has not forgotten the generosity of others and sends an annual Christmas tree to the city of Boston. They have also not forgotten the loss of lives and damage to the city. Every December 6 at 9 a.m. there is a service by the Memorial Bells at Fort Needham, close to where the *Mont Blanc* exploded.

The Tides of War Turn

It was not until 1917 that significant changes in world politics and on the battlefield turned the tides of the Great War. Tensions were mounting in Russia, as Czar Nicholas was seen as a weak, corrupt leader. Troops deserted the Russian army and strikes broke out in St. Petersburg and Moscow. Lenin and his Bolshevik followers promised to remove Russia from the war and give food to the poor. Lenin overthrew the government in October 1917 and negotiated a peace treaty with Germany in November. At peace with Russia, Germany could now concentrate all its troops on the Western Front.

The United States had remained neutral during the first three years of the war. Many Americans were isolationists who believed that the United States should not be entangled in a distant conflict.

Isolationists saw the United States as an example for other countries, remaining peaceful while others resorted to war. As the conflict waged on, however, it became more difficult for such a large and powerful country to remain neutral. Spurred on by the sinking of the *Lusitania*, the United States declared war on Germany on April 6, 1917.

Canadian Victories Overseas

On April 9, 1917, Arthur Currie, commander of the First Division, was promoted to general. He was the first Canadian to earn this distinction. He led all four divisions of the Canadian Corps to capture a key ridge on the Western front—Vimy.

Currie believed in thorough training and meticulous preparation. He readied his troops by playing out the battle on a mock version of the ridge, so that his men would have a clear sense of the terrain and the distance they would need to travel. Scenarios

Arthur Currie was the first Canadian promoted to general, and after playing a lead role in the Canadians' victory at Vimy Ridge, he was promoted to commander of the entire Canadian Corps.

The Battle of Vimy Ridge is heralded as Canada's "coming of age."

Canadian Corps. The battle was known generally in the Great War as the Battle of Arras; however, most Canadians, out of pure enthusiasm for their role, referred to it simply as "Vimy."

Vimy remains one of our most important victories as a country. At Vimy, men from across Canada fought together as one Canadian corps, and the battle tactics were the vision of a Canadian general. It is most significant that this Allied victory was spearheaded by a young "dominion" of the Empire, with a small population. It was a conquest that British and French troops had failed at earlier in the war. The conquest of Vimy Ridge was the largest advance British forces had made since the war began. Vimy was a triumph for Canada.

The Battle of Vimy was followed by other victories for the Canadians. The Battle of Passchendaele

were played out again and again until every individual knew his role. Preparations began well in advance and involved engineers who dug tunnels and planted mines under "no man's land." Roads were built and signals and supplies orchestrated. Currie ordered the first troops to advance and create a curtain of shells to protect the second line of troops.

The German army was unprepared for the sudden and violent attack. The Canadian troops advanced with speed and brilliant accuracy. During the attack the Canadian Corps suffered 10 602 casualties, including 3598 dead, but Canada still succeeded in taking the ridge.

It was a great victory for Canada. Four Canadians won the Victoria Cross and Currie was promoted to replace Sir General Byng as the Commander of the entire

The battle of Passchendaele was the most controversial battle of the Great War. Canadians fought on wet, muddy, uneven ground.

was again a triumph for Arthur Currie and his Corps. However, it was also one of the most controversial battles in the Great War. Canadians fought in abominable conditions on what was considered the worst battlefield on the Western Front. Currie had warned the British, before the battle, that he had reservations. The conditions were too rough and the casualties would be too high. Despite Currie's protest, the battle began on October 26th, and ended in victory for the Allies on November 7th. The Canadians suffered a devastating 15 654 casualties.

On Borden's trip to England in 1917, Currie raised his frustrations over the Passchendaele tragedy with the prime minister. He was quick to paint a picture of the incompetence and disorganization of British officials. Borden then confronted Lloyd George directly and warned him that, "If there is a repetition of the Battle of Passchendaele, not a Canadian soldier will leave the shores of Canada so long as the Canadian people trust the government of their country to me." [21]

Also in November 1917, the Canadian Calvary Brigade and the Newfoundland Regiment took part in the Battle of Cambrai. It was the first successful tank assault. The Newfoundland Regiment was granted the title of "Royal" for its role in the battleóa unique distinction during the war.

Canada's One Hundred Days

In March 1918, the Germans led a full-scale attack on the Allies on the Western Front. In April 1918, 500 000 American troops joined the Allies on the battlefield and the German army rushed to capture Paris. On August 8, Arthur Currie led the Canadians, flanked by French and Australian troops, in the Battle of Amiens, where Canadians captured more than five thousand Germans on the first day. August 8 went down in history as the "black day" for the German army.

Rather than digging in, Currie and his troops switched fronts and were given the significant task of breaking the Hidenburg Line, Germany's main line of defence. The Canadians broke through on September 2, with French Canadians playing a particularly significant role. Every officer of the Canadian Vandoos was killed or wounded, including a young Georges Vanier who would later become Canada's governor general.

Through September and October the Allies launched attack after attack, utilizing aircraft, tanks, and infantry, making remarkable advances in a short period of time. Canadians made their way to the Belgian town of Mons, capturing over thirty thousand enemy soldiers.

By November 1918, Germany's surrender was inevitable. A cease-fire was declared at 11:00 a.m. on November 11, 1918.

The last three months of the Great War were significant for Canada, in that the Canadian army had once again proven that it was formidable and reliable. Canada had played a critical role in the final Allied victory that won the Great War. This last phase of the war has gone down in history as Canada's One Hundred Days.[22]

An Independent Nation

The Great War ended old-school imperialism. British Canadians who had hurried to enlist in 1914 to protect the "mother country" were no longer British Canadians but simply Canadians. Victories, such as Vimy, Passchendaele, and Amiens, had earned the Canadian troops an auspicious reputation and Canada a new self-image.

During the Great War, Borden's only means of obtaining information about the Allied effort was through Britain, as he was rarely consulted on military procedure or strategy. Borden had become increasingly impatient with the Britain's lack of respect for their contribution and fought for Canada to have a greater voice in international affairs.

Expression of Identity
VIMY RIDGE

Close by the town of Arras, France near the French-Belgium border, Vimy Ridges rises about sixty-one metres to overlook the plains of Douia. From April 9 to 14 in 1917, this was the site of one of the most hellish and important battles of World War I.

On April 9, 100 000 Canadian soldiers launched an offensive against German positions that for over two years had proved impossible for Allied forces to capture. Unsuccessful attempts had cost the French Army dearlyóover seven thousand, seven hundred casualties in December 1914, and a staggering 100 000 in May of 1915. A combined French-English attack in September 1915 had claimed almost forty thousand Allied lives.

Vimy Ridge was strategically important to the German defence system, since it protected an area of occupied France in which mines and factories provided crucial supplies for Germany's war effort. The gradual slopes of the Ridge greatly favoured defenders, because advancing troops had to cross open ground, where they would be easy targets for rifle fire. If anyone made it past this shooting range, they encountered a maze of trenches and concrete machine-gun nests protected by barbed wire.

From the crushing defeats of French and British forces, Canadian commanders had learned how costly frontal assaults could be. Over the winter of 1917, British Corps Commander Sir Julian Byng, and his chief assistant, Canadian Commander Major-General Arthur Currie, took particular care in planing so that Canadian casualties could be kept to an absolute minimum.

Continual reconnaissance raids carried out from mid-March cost nearly one thousand, four hundred Canadian casualties, but the intelligence gathered from these dangerous missions allowed Allied forces to eventually accomplish their military objectives. A full-scale replica of the battle area was laid out, marked with coloured tape and flags behind the Canadian lines. Here Canadian troop rehearsed exactly what they would do throughout the days of the attack. Maps were distributed to guide the smallest units.

Battle preparations also involved designing and building a maze of tunnels and caverns. The extensive underground network was intended to reduce casualties among the advancing infantry and returning wounded, and to allow supplies to be brought to the front more safely. As well, Canadian and British engineers repaired and constructed roads and tramways to transport armaments and reinforcements.

A massive artillery barrage, which began on March 20, preceded the infantry assault. By the time the infantry set out, a million artillery shells had battered the Germans. During the time leading up to the advance, one Canadian soldier to commented that shells poured over his head onto the enemy "like water from a hose." When the attack began on April 9, Lieutenant-General Sir Julian Byng's plan called for an assault by four Canadian divisions on a front about seven kilometres long. The fighting was intense and included hand-to-hand combat. However, the heaviest Canadian losses came from German machine-gun placements.

Overcoming fierce resistance, the Canadians captured their first Ridge objective by midday. Then, one of the greatest challenges was taking a prominent part of one hill known as "the Pimple" from which German fire inflicted heavy losses on advancing waves of Canadian soldiers. It was not until the afternoon of April 10 that a fresh assault by a brigade of fresh Canadian troops placed Vimy Ridge in Canadian hands. Two days later, units of the 10th Canadian Brigade successfully stormed the Pimple. By that time, the enemy had accepted the loss of Vimy Ridge and retreated more than three kilometres.

Canadians fought valiantly with four men earning the Victoria Cross for bravery, three of them did so on the first day. The cost in Canadian casualties was 10 602, of which 3598 were killed.

Significance of the Vimy Victory

Vimy Ridge was a significant moment in our countryís military history, as it marked the first time Canadians had attacked as one force. At Vimy Ridge, Canadian soldiers captured more ground, more prisoners, and more guns than any previous British offensive in two-and-a-half years of war. Indeed, it was one of the most complete and decisive victories of World War I.

As a tribute to those who served Canada, either risking or losing their lives, a memorial was erected at Vimy Ridge. Designed by Canadian sculptor and architect Walter Allward, the Vimy Memorial stands on Hill 145, overlooking the Douai Plain from the highest point of Vimy Ridge, where the fiercest fighting occurred. It took eleven years to complete the monu-ment, which was unveiled on July 26, 1936 by King Edward VIII before more than fifty thousand Canadian and French veterans and their families. In his address, the King noted, "It is a memorial to no man, but a memorial for a nation."

Some people argue that Vimy Ridge marked Canadaís emergence in world status from a colony to a nationóabout fifty years after Confederation. For example, Brigadier-General Alexander Ross, who had commanded a battalion at Vimy Ridge, said of the battle: "It was Canada from the Atlantic to the Pacific on parade. I thought then...that in those few minutes I witnessed the birth of a nation."

Canada's WWI contributions, of which Vimy Ridge was the pinacle, won for Canada a separate signature on the Versailles Peace Treaty, which ended the War.

The Vimy Ridge Memorial in France.

An important step to independence was taken in 1917. After Lloyd George was elected Prime Minister of Britain, he organized an Imperial War Cabinet and invited the Dominion leaders to participate. For Borden, the War Cabinet was the vehicle needed to move toward greater independence. Canada's participation in the Great War and its enormous sacrifice was the fuel. At the Imperial War Cabinet, Borden presented Resolution IX that was seconded by the South African Minister of Defence, Jan Smuts. Resolution IX gave the Dominions recognition as autonomous nations of an Imperial Commonwealth.

Following the November 11 cease-fire, the Treaty of Versailles was drafted and signed at the Paris Peace Conference in June 1919. The terms of the Treaty were harsh. Germany was forced to limit the size of its army, return Alsace and Lorraine to France, demilitarize the Rhineland, pay reparations to the Allies and give up colonies in Africa. Most humiliating for Germany was the clause that stipulated that it accept all guilt for causing the war.

Borden insisted that he have a seat at the Peace Conference. The United States was angered by the idea, arguing that a seat for Canada meant more power for Britain. Canada barely played a role in these negotiations, but Borden insisted that Canada sign the Treaty of Versailles independent of Britain. Canada also joined the newly formed League of Nations, dedicated to collective security and preservation of peace, and the International Labour Organization.

American President Woodrow Wilson played a very decisive role at the Peace Conference. However, the United States refused to join the League of Nations, partly in protest of the British colony's new voice, and partly due to public pressure from a growing group of American isolationists who wanted to avoid American involvement in European conflicts.

Review...Reflect...Respond

1. If in the beginning of World War I, Henri Bourassa supported the war effort in the hopes that it may unite the country, why did he vehemently oppose conscription and believe that Canadians should not be fighting Britain's war?

2. Was giving the right to vote to women a result of the women's suffrage movement, or was it merely a political lever used by Borden to pass the Military Service Act?

3. Why is the victory of Vimy Ridge often referred to as Canada's "coming of age?"

The Effects of War on a Nation

The Great War brought about significant change for Canada. Industry flourished and diversified, urban populations grew, women joined the workforce and took on duties previously considered men's work, and the country took on a large national debt. Most significantly Canada had earned a new reputation and had cultivated a distinct relationship with Britain. Canadian troops had triumphed on the battlefield and Prime Minister Borden had fought for, and won, a greater voice for Canada on the global stage.

Canada's independence, however, was not earned without bloodshed. Of the over 600 000 Canadians who served during the Great War, over sixty-one thousand died and another 172 000 were wounded. With a population of only eight million, Canada had made a major contribution and paid an enormous price.

In a field hospital, after the second battle of Ypres, a Canadian doctor, John McCrae, wrote a poem, entitled *In Flanders Fields*, in memory of a friend who died in battle. The poem was featured in the British magazine, *Punch*, in 1915 and quickly became well known in many countries. The words of the poem speak to the loss and sacrifice of the Canadian troops, but also to the duty of all Canadians to contribute to the war effort. Although John McRae died during the war, his poem, recited by crowds of school children across the country each November 11, and the poppy have lived on as symbols of remembrance throughout the world.

Conclusion

The Great War was not simply a unifying experience for the young Dominion of Canada. It also left the country divided. The Conscription Crisis had enraged Canadians from coast to coast and the War Measures Act saw Canadians turn on the country's immigrant populations, isolating groups who had emigrated from enemy nations. In the end, the First World War had both brought Canadians together and had torn them apart.

Notes

1. Speech given by Sir Robert Laird Borden, delivered in a special session of the Dominion Parliament, August 1914.
2. C.P. Stacey, *Canada and the Age of Conflict: Volume 1: 1867-1921*, (Toronto: Macmillan, 1984).
3. Read, *The Great War and Canadian Society*. (Toronto: New Hogtown Press, 1978) p. 96.
4. For first hand accounts on the reaction from the Canadian public to the outbreak of war read Daphne Read, *The Great War and Canadian Society*, (Toronto: New Hogtown Press, 1978).
5. William Rawling, *Surviving Trench Warfare: Technology and the Canadian Corps, 1914–1918* (Toronto: University of Toronto Press, 1922).
6. For a closer look at the political career of Sam Hughes and his role in WWI see Ronald Graham Haycock. *Sam Hughes: the Public Career of a Controversial Canadian 1885–1916*, (Waterloo, Ont.: Wilfrid Laurier University Press in collaboration with Canadian War Museum, Canadian Museum of Civilization, National Museums of Canada, 1986).
7. "Honour Before Glory" Veterans Week 2001, Veterans Affairs Canada Web site, <http:www.vac-acc.gc/general/sub.cfm?source=feature%2Fweek20011%2Fnatnews%2Fnov701>.
8. "Native Soldiers Foreign Battles" Veterans Affairs Canada Web site, <http://www.vac-acc.gc/general/sub.cfm?source=history/other/native response>.
9. Reginald H. Roy, *The Journal of Private Fraser, 1914-1918 : Canadian Expeditionary Force / Donald Fraser* ; edited and with an introduction by Reginald H. Roy, (Victoria, B.C.: Sono Nis Press, 1985) p. 36.
10. Letter from J. H. Rivers, Warden, Lethbridge Provincial Gaol to the Deputy Minister of Justice, July 6, 1918. National Archives of Canada, RG 13, series A-2, vol. 225, file 1918–1982.
11. For more information on the IMB and Joseph Flavelle see Michael Bliss, *A Canadian Millionaire* (Toronto: Macmillan, 1978).
12. "Native Soldiers Foreign Battles", Minister of Supply and Services Canada, 1993 Cat. No. V32-56/1993E ISBN 0-662-19850-6 Veterans Affairs Canada Web site <http://www.vac-acc.gc.ca/general/sub.cfm?source=history/other/native/sacrifices>.
13. Daphne Read, *The Great War and Canadian Society*, P. 156
14. Ibid., p. 163.
15. Henry Borden, *Robert Laird Borden: His Memoirs, Volume II* (Toronto: McClelland & Stewart, 1938) p. 523.
16. According to Stats Canada the estimated population of Canada in 1915 was 7 981 000.
17. Henry Borden, *Robert Laird Borden: His Memoirs, Volume II* p. 613.
18. Desmond Morton, *A Military History of Canada* (Toronto: McClelland & Stewart, 1992) pp. 151–158.
19. A critical exploration of the Conscription Crisis is found in Jack L. Granatstein and J. M. Hitsman, *Broken Promises: A History of Conscription in Canada* (Toronto: Oxford University Press, 1977).
20. Henry Borden, *Robert Laird Borden: His Memoirs, Volume II* p. 698.
21. Pierre Berton, *Marching as to War, Canada's Turbulent Years* (Toronto: Doubleday Canada, 2001) p. 207.
22. A detailed account of Canada's contribution to the end of the War is found in Shane B. Schreiber, *Shock Army of the British Empire: The Canadian Corps in the Last 100 Days of the Great War*. (Westport: 1997).

Chapter 15 Review

Knowledge & Understanding

1. Identify the following terms, people, and events and explain their historical significance to Canada's developing culture and identity:

   Valcartier
   Vimy
   Ross rifle
   Conscription Crisis
   Mabel May
   Athur Currie

2. Create a timeline to identify the key events in World War I that signified the growing independence of Canada on the world stage.

Thinking & Inquiry

3. It is often quoted that at the battle of Vimy Ridge, "we went up as soldiers, and came down as Canadians." In a well-written paragraph, explain what you think is meant by this statement.

4. In his 2001 book, *Marching As to War: Canada's Turbulent Years, 1899–1953*, Canadian author Pierre Berton wrote, "The mothers who so proudly sent their boys abroad to be sacrificed must never know how their sons really lived or died in the wastes of no man's land, nor must they be exposed to an even more dreadful truth: that the Men Whose Names Will Live Forever died for no good reason in a futile and foolish war that solved nothing." In at least two well-written paragraphs, disagree or agree with Pierre Berton's statement. Be sure to use historically correct facts to support your argument.

Application

5. Critically examine the painting *Women Making Shells* by Mabel May in the Expression of Culture feature. Now look at the photo of the trenches in this chapter. Which one has a deeper impact on you? Write a well-argued paragraph supporting your choice.

6. Imagine that you are a journalist working on a story entitled, "Canadian's Contributions to the Great War: Reflections After 75 Years." Prepare a list of at least ten interview questions for one of the following survivors (be sure to think about what information you would like to find out before writing the questions.)

   A Canadian soldier who survived the Battle of the Somme
   A Belgian farmer
   A sailor who served in the North Atlantic
   A former German air force commander

Unit Four Research Activity

Research

1. Many organizations, such as the Salvation Army, Children's Aid, and the Humane Society sprung up in Canada as part of the Social Gospel movement. Find at least three other organizations that came out of the Social Gospel movement. Choose one of these organizations for in-depth research. Research the following aspects:
   - the founder
   - the motivations behind those who joined the organization
   - the strengths and limitations of their work
   - important accomplishments of the organization
   - how the organization transformed into its present-day status, or what happened if the organization disappeared

Interpretation and Analysis

2. How does the organization you researched compare and contrast with the general principles of the Social Gospel movement as outlined in this unit?

3. What mark has this organization made on Canadian history? Does it still exist? Has it changed its focus? How has it worked to promote human or animal rights within Canada?

Applying and Communicating Your Skills

4. As a magazine writer, you have been asked to write about the 100th Anniversary of one of the Social Gospel organizations. Your story will be on the leading article of the magazine and will be featured on the cover. Write a four-page biography on the organization you have researched, and its importance to Canadians. Be sure to include a good title as it will appear on the cover. You will also want to select a photo that will appear on the cover and other photos that will be in your article. Be sure to include captions with your photos. You may also want to include highlights of a mock interview that you had with a key member of the organization.

5. Create a poster to attract new members to your organization. You may want to set it in the time period of the turn of the nineteenth century, or you may also set it in the present, and include historical visuals of your organization. You will need to show the purpose of the organization and some of its accomplishments, and why it is important to the lives of Canadians.

Maturing Culture and Identity, 1919–1945

In this unit you will:

- evaluate the evolution of Canada's role on the international stage

- describe Canada's transformation from a rural, agricultural nation to an urban industrial nation

- describe the role of literature, the arts, and popular culture in the development of a distinctive Canadian culture

- describe the development of Canada's social programs and their significance in terms of Canadian identity

- analyse how women's participation in Canadian society has changed over time

Between 1920 and 1945, Canadians experienced crucial changes in society, politics, the economy, and Canada's involvement in international affairs. After World War I, many Canadians enjoyed the prosperity of the "roaring twenties"— automobiles, jazz, telephones, radio, new Canadian art and literature, a booming economy— and Canada focused on itself rather than on world events. With the stock market crash of 1929, Canadians were jolted from the roaring twenties into the desperation of the dirty thirties and the worst economic depression in history. From the depths of the Depression, Canada once again found itself in a world embroiled in war.

As Canadians embraced the new radio programs and going to the movie theatres, there were also questions about how much American content was being absorbed by Canadian listeners and viewers. With the 1930s came the beginnings of efforts to protect and foster Canadian cultural programs and attempts to stop the growing influx of American influence.

In society, the years between 1920 and 1945 would see both shining moments and horrific failures of the Canadian people. Aboriginal Peoples suffered in residential schools, immigrants were the first to be blamed for loss of jobs during the Depression, and in World War II, Canada denied its own Japanese-Canadian citizens of the most basic human rights. On the other side, women were legally declared "persons" and in World War II, many found new freedoms in the employment opportunities that were opened to them.

Canada in 1930

Iceland

Kalaallit Nunaat
(Greenland)
(Denmark)

Alaska (U.S.A.)

Yukon
Territory

Newfoundland

British
Columbia

Alberta

Saskatchewan

Manitoba

Quebec

Ontario

P.E.I.

New
Brunswick

Nova
Scotia

U.S.A.

Canada 1919–1929: A Quest for Change and Stability in an Era of Ambiguity

The Great War is past; the war that tried through and through every quality and mystery of the human mind and the might of human spirit.

– ARTHUR MEIGHEN

F ollowing World War I, Canadians had to confront powerful and contradictory forces. There was a desire to suppress the trauma of war and an urge to build and secure the future. During the years from 1918 to 1930, powerful ideas and actions drove Canadian society. This was a period when conflicting or contradictory ideas were proposed. Leaders and participants in this drive for change were conflicted about the direction of change, the anticipated results of which were never entirely clear. During the 1920s, Canada experienced new political movements that attempted to reform regional grievances, new technologies that transformed society, and a growing sense that Canadian culture was something that had to be nurtured and protected.

In July of 1920, on the insistence of his doctor, Prime Minister Robert Borden resigned. He was replaced by Arthur Meighen, a gifted analytical debater and parliamentarian, but with a reserved personal style, who many viewed as an aloof "upright figure of ice." Opponents and voters often interpreted his manner as hard and arrogant. As minister of justice during the war, Meighen was viewed as the principal architect of the War Measures Act and the conscription crisis in Quebec. Many immigrants were resentful of their treatment as "enemy aliens" during the war, and workers viewed him as the force behind the violent suppression of the Winnipeg General Strike in 1919. Farmers were angry at his insistence on the maintenance of high tariffs protecting "eastern" industry and the high freight rates they were charged to transport their grain. Business interests in Montreal did not find his defence of the National Policy compelling, rather, they were alienated by his role in creating the government-controlled Canadian National Railways. For them, a government-owned railway posed a competitive threat to the privately owned Canadian Pacific Railway. Added to all of this was a post-war economic depression in 1921. Canadians were ready for change, and Meighen's unrepentant and uncompromising approach in the 1921 election led to his defeat.

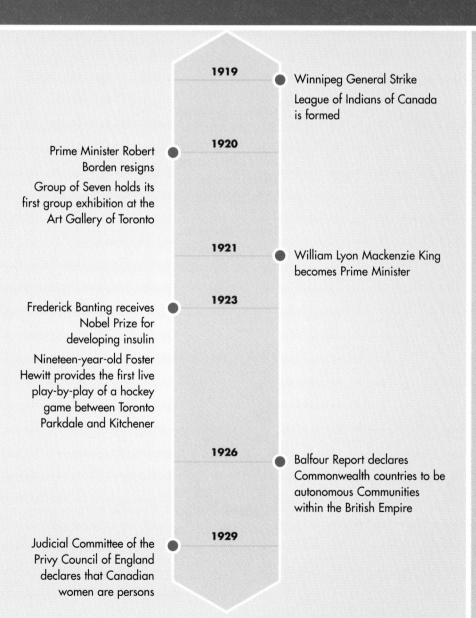

16

1919
Winnipeg General Strike
League of Indians of Canada is formed

Prime Minister Robert Borden resigns
Group of Seven holds its first group exhibition at the Art Gallery of Toronto
1920

1921
William Lyon Mackenzie King becomes Prime Minister

Frederick Banting receives Nobel Prize for developing insulin
Nineteen-year-old Foster Hewitt provides the first live play-by-play of a hockey game between Toronto Parkdale and Kitchener
1923

1926
Balfour Report declares Commonwealth countries to be autonomous Communities within the British Empire

Judicial Committee of the Privy Council of England declares that Canadian women are persons
1929

By the end of this chapter, you will be able to

- analyze Canada's development as an autonomous nation in the first half of the twentieth century

- assess the effectiveness of attempts to protect Canadian culture from American domination

- demonstrate an understanding of the development of citizenship in Canada

- analyze the evolution of the women's movement in Canada (the Persons case)

- analyze the evolutions of the Labour movement in Canada

- describe the contributions of selected prime ministers (Borden, King) to the evolution of Canadian identity

- assess the origins and results of Macdonald's National Policy

- analyze the reasons for Canada's close political and economic relationship with the United States

- analyze how Canadians have been portrayed by writers, artists, musicians, composers, television, and filmmakers

A Political Quest for Stability and Change

In the 1921 election, Arthur Meighen faced a Liberal rival who, in almost every respect, was a study in contrasts. William Lyon Mackenzie King had succeeded Laurier as Liberal leader in 1919. King's grandfather was William Lyon Mackenzie, the ill-fated leader of the Upper Canada Rebellion of 1837 and this association would always give King an aura of respectability in progressive circles. After graduating from the University of Toronto, King went on to study at the University of Chicago and there, was influenced by the University Settlement movement. This movement had sprung up in 1884 in Britain, and drew its members from the ranks of young university men who used their educational advantages to better the lot of the disadvantaged. As a member of this movement, King joined other university students, for a short while, living and working with slum dwellers to improve their lot in life. He left Chicago and completed his education at Harvard University, spending the next few years in reformist activities, resulting in a position in Canada as editor of the *Labour Gazette* in July of 1900. In August of the same year, King used his carefully cultivated contacts to procure the position of deputy minister of the Canadian Post Office, a position he would hold for the next eight years, frequently engaging in difficult labour negotiations. In 1908 King was elected as a member of the House of Commons and appointed as Minister of Labour in Laurier's government, however he soon lost his seat in the election of 1911 and returned to the civil service. Then, taking an abrupt turn he accepted a management position with the Rockefeller Foundation. King's reputation rocketed when he negotiated an end to labour strife in the Rockefeller's mines in Colorado. The Rockefellers and the Carnegies both tried to offer King advancement and financial security in their firms, but King wanted nothing more than to re-enter politics. Following the war, and Laurier's death, he returned to run for the leadership of his party and on August 17, 1919 he was elected leader of the federal Liberal party. King's virtually unblemished and rapid rise to power was remarkable.

King remained vague about his platform for the federal election campaign of 1921, offering some alternatives to the Conservative platform, but he was careful not to provide details of their implementation. All he had to do was to shine a spotlight on Meighen's stubborn adherence to an intensely unpopular record and set of policies. King and his Liberals took 117 seats to the Conservatives fifty and every seat in Quebec, Nova Scotia, and Prince Edward Island, but still failed to win a clear majority. Voters in rural Ontario and

I PREACH THE SAME POLICY IN THE WEST AS IN THE EAST. YOU NEED A HIGHER TARIFF ON EVERYTHING YOU BUY. OF COURSE IT WILL MAKE PRICES HIGHER — BUT THEN YOU CAN'T BUY SO MUCH AND YOU'LL SAVE MORE. THAT WILL MAKE YOU PROSPEROUS

Few Canadians found much appeal in Arthur Meighen, Robert Borden's replacement as prime minister.

William Lyon Mackenzie King becomes Prime Minister of Canada for the first time, in 1921.

the west had elected sixty-one Progressive Conservative members. This new party would put Mackenzie King's pragmatic skills to the test.

The Progressive Interlude

Farmers in Ontario and the west had long resented the perceived control of the economy and politics by central Canadian business interests and they were especially concerned about two components of the National Policy. First was the tariff protecting manufactured goods produced in central Canada. These tariffs forced farmers to buy Canadian manufactured goods, with the profits from these sales going to the central Canada industrialists. Second were the high freight rates that the railways charged for shipping grain to market, leaving the farmers with no control over prices.

In lean economic years, freight rates often jeopardized farmers' livelihood. In the early 1920s farmers comprised about thirty percent of the population in Canada. Nevertheless, migration to the cities was increasing and as farmers saw their economic and political influence declining they

searched for political remedies. In the post-war recession, grain prices fell from $2 to $1 per bushel and in combination with a drought in the southern prairies, farmers faced hard economic times trying to pay loans and mortgages that they had entered into during better times. They were open to political solutions not offered by traditional parties.

In 1920, at a political convention in Winnipeg, the National Progressive Party was formed. Led by T. A. Crerar, from Manitoba, the Progressives laid out a "New National Policy," demanding such things as lower tariffs, financial assistance for farmers facing difficult economic times, and public ownership of utilities.

The Progressive Party and its New National Policy appealed to voters in agricultural Ontario and the prairie provinces. In the 1921 federal election they won sixty-one seats compared to the Conservatives' fifty. The Liberals with only 116 seats needed Progressive support to maintain a voting majority in the House of Commons and King had to acknowledge the wishes of the Progressives to stay in power.

From the beginning, it was clear that the Progressive party was split on fundamental issues. The Manitoba wing, led by Crerar wanted to reform the existing parties, opening them to progressive policies that would erode the influence of the rich and powerful. The other wing of the Progressives was led by Henry Wise Wood from Calgary East, who identified the party system as the root of political problems. His solution was to ensure that elected officials were directly responsible to their constituents and not to the party, confounded by party doctrine, and vulnerable to the entrenched interests of the established and powerful. Crerar had no such reservations about parties, and attempted to make formal alliances with the Liberals. These attempts were blocked by Henry Wise Wood and other opponents in his own party and the frustrated Crerar, decided to resign in 1922, as others began to defect to the traditional parties.

As the decade passed relative prosperity returned for farmers, and better economic times began to diminish the force and conviction behind many of the Progressive demands. Moreover, Mackenzie King began making small concessions in response to some of their traditional demands. He restored the Crow's Nest Railway rate, a subsidy for grain shipments. He also constructed a railway line to Hudson Bay, a port closer to the grain belt that promised to reduce the cost of grain shipments. He re-established the Canadian Wheat Board to bring a small measure of stability to grain marketing for farmers.[1] King was able to introduce these reforms all the while ensuring that they were not substantial enough to upset the core of his business support. In his classic pragmatic style, King had managed to calm some of his critics without making too many concessions.

The accomplishments of the Progressive Party were mixed and relatively short-lived. The federal Progressives did hold the balance of power following the 1921 election and they also held provincial office in Ontario, Manitoba, and Alberta. To a degree the provincial governments met with success but at the national level the new party had little. Farmers in British Columbia, Quebec, and the Maritimes came to believe that the Progressives were essentially representing the interests of prairie farmers, and turned to the existing parties to express their discontent. Within the members of the federal Progressives, internal divisions and the populist wing's brand of "anti-partyism" combined with legislative ineffectiveness in better economic times, brought an end to the Progressives as a force to be reckoned with. In the 1925 election they retained only twenty-four of their seats. Many members migrated to the old-line parties. The National Progressive Party had run its course by 1930.

Maritime Rights Movement

After the 1925 election, Mackenzie King faced another minority government due to political discontent in the Maritimes. The early 1920s, were a time of drastic political and economic decline for the Maritimes. World War I had signalled an end to the shipbuilding and ship transportation boom and a lack of demand for wartime coal and steel hobbled Maritime mining and manufacturing. A series of corporate takeovers and mergers had reduced the number of companies in the region. Other major manufacturing companies had relocated to Quebec and Ontario in order to be closer to their markets. Railway costs were rising dramatically, and protective tariffs to assist in the transport of products were cut, making Maritime manufacturing much less competitive. The British Empire Steel Company (BESCO), an important company formed by a merger of steel, coal mining, and shipbuilding industries in Nova Scotia, was facing bankruptcy. Miners and steel workers responded to BESCO's attempts to cut wages by launching one of the most intense and violent strikes in Canadian history.[2] Between 1917 and 1921, Maritime production dropped by 40 percent. Historians estimate that over 100 000 people left the Maritimes to find a living elsewhere. Population decline was reflected in a loss of 25 percent of their seats in the House of Commons between 1882 and 1921. This desperate situation called for a political response.

The task was initiated by a group of business and professional men. They revived the Maritime Board of Trade to bring regional pressure on the federal government, becoming known as the Maritime Rights Movement. The movement demanded larger federal subsidies for rail transportation of goods to distant markets. They insisted upon tariffs to protect steel and coal. Finally, they asked for more trade through the ports of Halifax and St. John. Unlike the Progressives, the Maritime Rights Movement decided to lobby the traditional mainline parties rather than form their own. In the 1921 election the movement pressured Liberal candidates to pledge they would "advocate and stand by Maritime rights if elected". King's Liberals won all but six Maritime seats in the 1921 federal election.

After the election King was able to deflect the demands of his backbench Maritime members. He was unable to deliver on the pledge of protective tariffs, since the Progressives, upon whom he depended to maintain his majority, were against protective tariffs for industry.

In the 1925 election, Maritimers ready for revenge over the unfulfilled pledges, handed all but three of thirty-one seats to the Conservatives. King faced another minority government. In a House of Commons with 245 members, the standings were Conservatives, 116; the Progressives, twenty-four; and others six. The Liberals were left with ninety-nine. King moved to maintain his government with accommodations like a farm loan for the Progressives and the old age pension for J.S. Woodsworth and his socialist contingent. His minority government lasted until a scandal arose in the customs department.

Civil servants had taken bribes in return for allowing bootlegged liquor to enter the United States during Prohibition. The Progressives, offended by what they considered a lack of moral standards in the government, voted against the Liberals and the government was defeated. King realized he faced defeat in a no-confidence motion in parliament.

The King-Byng Affair

Rather than damaging his party any further, King went to Governor General Byng and asked him to call an election before the loss-of-confidence vote was taken. Byng refused on proper constitutional grounds, and asked Arthur Meighen, who had the most seats in parliament to form a government.[3] The Meighen government only lasted three days, the shortest term of office in Canadian history. His government won four crucial votes in the House of Commons, but lost a fifth. With the defeat of this crucial vote Meighen was forced to request the dissolution of parliament. This time Governor General Byng agreed and a general election was called.

In the 1926 election, King won a safe majority. In the campaign he exploited the threat to Canadian sovereignty, claiming that the representative of imperial Britain (the governor general) had no right to interfere in the affairs of a self-governing country. After the election, King established a Canadian high commissioner in London so that a representative of the Canadian government communicated directly with the British government, instead of the governor general.

After the election King turned his attention to the demands of the Maritime Rights Movement in order to recapture the support of voters in the region. He appointed Arthur Rae Duncan to head a Royal Commission on Maritime Claims in 1926. The Commission recommended a number of accommodations for the Maritimes, including: federal subsidies for industries in need, tariffs to protect manufacturing, and a reduction in rail shipping costs.

King appeared to endorse the recommendations, and although he did introduce slight reductions on Maritime freight rates, he did little more. The small concessions were enough to pacify the most vocal leaders of the Maritime Rights Movement and by 1927 they had disappeared from the political landscape. As with the Progressives, King was able to ease Maritime discontent with small ambiguous concessions and delay.

Aboriginal Peoples: The Beginnings of Political Mobilization

In 1919, Lt. Frederick O. Loft, a Mohawk who had served overseas as a lieutenant in the Canadian army in World War I, formed the League of Indians of Canada as Aboriginal Peoples began to politically mobilize. Meeting in various locations throughout Canada several times a year, the League discussed issues that were of increasing concern to Aboriginal Peoples. In 1923, the League sent a list of requests to the federal government including: provincial control of Aboriginal education (as opposed to residential schools);

Aboriginal representation on school boards; and returning the control of reserved lands to the Aboriginal Peoples. The League also sought freedom to practice religious ceremonies such as the Sun dance and the potlatch.[4]

Loft and the League of Indians of Canada faced opposition and suspicion from the Canadian government. Members who attended meetings were often charged by the police for violating the Pass Laws of the Indian Act that forbid Aboriginal Peoples, from leaving their reserves without a government pass. As Loft tried to gain support for his belief that the Department of Indian Affairs was responsible for the decaying conditions of the Aboriginal Peoples, the Canadian government tried to dismantle the organization. The League was now under police surveillance, and rumours that the League had communist undertones crippled its growth. By the mid-1930s, the League of Indians of Canada had collapsed, but the cornerstones for a political voice among the Aboriginal Peoples had been laid.

Searching for a Canadian Identity

Many historians argue that the foundations of Canadian nationalism began in the midst of World War I, since previously Britain had obscured Canadian identity on the world stage. At the end of the war, a separate Canadian delegation signed the Treaty of Versailles and although Canada's involvement was largely symbolic, it did represent independence to

many Canadians. At the Paris conference Canada gained entrance, as a separate country, to membership in the League of Nations and the International Labour Organization. However, for Borden and his successors, the war had taught them never to be drawn into foreign entanglements where the fate of Canadians relied so completely on the whims of another country.

Members of the League of Indians of Canada, with Fred Loft.

Expression of Identity
GREY OWL (1888-1938)

Side by side with modern Canada lies the last battleground in the long drawn out bitter contest between civilization and the forces of nature. It is a land of shadows and hidden trails, lost rivers and unknown lakes, a region of soft-footed creatures going their noiseless ways over the carpet of moss, and there is silence, intense, absolute and all embracing.[5]

Was he a visionary conservationist or a complete imposter? This question has shadowed the legacy of Grey Owl, who gained international recognition during the 1920s and 1930s for his writing and his lectures about the Canadian wilderness. Grey Owl's real name was Archibald Stansfield Belaney, and he was born in 1888, in Hastings, England. As a boy, Archie was fascinated with North American Aboriginal Peoples.

At seventeen, Belaney left England for Canada. Living with the Ojibwa of northern Ontario, he learned about the wilderness and soon began presenting himself as the son of a Scot and an Apache. He also acquired an Ojibwa name—Grey Owl.

Grey Owl excelled at canoeing and wilderness travel, but initially was a somewhat irresponsible trapper. A family with whom he lived taught him Aboriginal ways of trapping, always emphasizing that the number of animals taken must be sustainable. Once, Delaney used dynamite to blast a beaver dam and the family threw him out of their home.

Grey Owl was similarly irresponsible in his personal relationships, marrying four women, each time failing to divorce his previous wife, and sometimes fathering children he eventually abandoned. In 1925 he married an Iroquois woman, Anahareo, who travelled with him on his trap line. She detested the cruelty of trapping and instilled in Grey Owl a strong environmental ethic.

An amazing transformation occurred in Grey Owl's life when he rescued two beaver kits, "McGinnis" and "McGinty," and took them to his cabin, where he and Anahareo cared for them. Of the experience, he wrote:

Grey Owl: conservationist or imposter?

To kill such creatures seemed monstrous. I would do no more of it. Instead of persecuting them further I would study them, see just what there really was to them. I perhaps could start a colony of my own; these animals could not be permitted to pass completely from the face of this wilderness.

In the winter of 1928 and 1929 he started his first beaver colony. To make ends meet, Grey Owl began to write. The British magazine, *Country Life*, accepted one of his first nature articles. Other articles were soon commissioned.

The beaver-colony plan suffered a setback when McGinnis and McGinty returned to the wild, but they were replaced by a female, Jelly Roll, and a male, Rawhide.

Meanwhile, Grey Owl's reputation grew to such an extent that in the public's eyes he was becoming a

(continued)

symbol of conservation. Commissioner of National Parks, James Harkin saw the potential for making a documentary film about Grey Owl and his two new beavers. With the positive press generated by the film, Harkin persuaded the federal government to employ Grey Owl within the National Parks Service, which would, he argued, lure in valuable tourist dollars and secure "publicity for the National Parks and for wildlife conservation."

In 1931 Grey Owl boarded a westbound train with Jelly Roll and Rawhide—travelling to Manitoba's Riding Mountain National Park and a cabin that was built especially for him on the shore of Beaver Lodge Lake. He soon concluded that he could find a better habitat for his beavering plan, and only six months after arriving, took his beaver and their new kits and moved to Ajawaan Lake in Prince Albert National Park, Saskatchewan. Authorities at Riding Mountain National Park maintained Grey Owl's beaver reintroduction program, and the beaver population that had been decimated by years of trapping rebounded.

Grey Owl's transformation into a conservationist inspired him toward more writing. The magazine article from *Country Life* was expanded into his first book, *The Man of the Last Frontier* (1931). *Pilgrims of the Wild* (1934) recounted his flight with Anahareo through the slash and burn of ruined country. *The Adventures of Sajo and her Beaver People* (1935) is based on Grey Owl's early days in Temagami. His final book was *Tales of an Empty Cabin* (1936).

In 1935 his English publisher arranged a British tour. Grey Owl, ever the performer, played to his European audience's romantic idea of North American Aboriginal Peoples by wearing moccasins and his black hair braided in two braids. The tour was extended to four months and saw Grey Owl give two hundred lectures to more than a quarter million people. His second British tour in 1937 culminated with a presentation to the royal family, where he discussed threatened beaver populations with the king.

After Grey Owl's death in 1938, the press discovered his English birth and headlines appeared: "GREY OWL HAD COCKNEY ACCENT AND FOUR WIVES".

In fact, several people had known Grey Owl's true identity before his death. Two North Bay journalists, for example, learned of his English heritage, but kept the story quiet. And on his final trip to a northern community, Grey Owl ended the presentation with a war dance, but his "authentic" war song lacked rhythm and Aboriginal words. The Aboriginal people present appeared silently amused.

All who knew that Grey Owl was part imposter seemed to understand that it was his message about protecting Canada's precious wild spaces and wildlife that really mattered.

Grey Owl's messages about environmental protection are still quoted by Canadian conservationists today, but when his true identity was discovered at his death, his ideas about conservation lost credibility.

---

1. How does knowing the personal life of a leader or writer affect our interpretation of his or her ideas?

2. Can a person be both an imposter and a visionary?

Borden and Meighen wanted to place Canada in a more influential position in the British Empire. They hoped to use this influence to leave a Canadian imprint on all policies of the Commonwealth. In contrast, King's quest for autonomy was more defined and was fuelled by the conscription crisis of 1917. French Québécois were angry because they had been compelled to fight a war on behalf of Britain and its Empire. As always, King was mindful of the Quebec vote, so crucial for his party's survival. On the other hand, much of English Canada was loyal to the Empire. Although this allegiance was somewhat tempered by the war experience, King could not be seen entirely as anti-British. Beneath the politics, however, King wanted real autonomy for Canada.

The Chanak Affair

The first real indication of King's pursuit of autonomy came with the Chanak Affair in the autumn of 1922. A small group of British soldiers had been threatened by Turkish nationalist forces in Chanak, a small seaport in the Dardanelle's of Turkey. Britain responded by sending a telegram to the nations in its empire demanding they send soldiers to support the fight against the Turks should an open conflict begin. King responded that Canada would no longer automatically send troops to aid Britain in foreign conflicts. Any commitment of Canadian military assistance would have to be approved by a vote in the Canadian parliament. The British soon resolved their differences with Turkey. Nevertheless, King had sent a message that Canada was seeking a more independent path in the Empire and world affairs.

King's Continued Drive for Autonomy

A breakthrough came at the Imperial Conference of 1923. Imperial conferences traditionally had been a gathering of countries at the invitation of Britain to make decisions on economic, trade, and defence policies. Before World War I, especially, the nations of the Empire were obliged to follow British-sponsored policies formed at the conferences. Borden's strategy had been to ensure that Canada had more influence on the decisions made at the conferences. King insisted upon more autonomy. Largely upon King's insistence, and much to the chagrin of the British, the 1923 conference report concluded with the statement that any "views... are necessarily subject to the action of the Governments and Parliaments of the various portions of the Empire."[6]

Canada concluded its first independent treaty with a foreign nation in 1923 with the Halibut Treaty between Canada and United States. The British ambassador in Washington had wanted to add his signature to the treaty but King said no and insisted that the Canadian representative Ernest Lapointe sign the treaty.

Mackenzie King with King George V at the Imperial Conference, 1923

Shameful Isolationism

After World War I, the desire for Canada's autonomy became torn between those who felt Canada should play a leading role in world events, and those who believed it was time to concentrate on affairs at home. In this article, Vincent Massey proclaims that the idea of isolationism is shameful and that Canada has an international responsibility in its developing state as a Dominion.

...But for all our cloistered life, we have learned that an obscure Balkan quarrel can cost us thousands of lives and millions of money, and it would seem that the Great War should have shaken us out of our habitual provincialism, not only through the repercussion of world events in Canada, but also through the personal experience of hundreds of thousands of Canadians overseas...

But with the crisis over, we relapsed into our traditional indifference to events beyond our shores, and, instead of stemming the full current, we have slipped into a backwater of provincial aloofness. The other day, I was counting up the number of days that had been spent on the subject of external affairs in the Canadian House of Commons in the last five years. By "external affairs" I mean everything outside our own internal affairs—trade treaties, the estimates of the Department of External Affairs, Trade Commissioners, in fact every-

thing that is not "our own show." Out of the 548 days of the last 5 sessions, 13 days were devoted altogether to external affairs. I do not suppose that a smaller proportion of time has been spent on foreign business in the legislature of any country in the world.

There are, I suppose, three schools of thought in Canada on the subject of foreign affairs, or to be more accurate, two schools of thought and one given to mental inertia. In the first place there are persons with the "colonial mind", those fewer now than before the war, who still regard the Empire as being in conflict with the Dominion nationality, who sentimentalize over the one to the disparagent [sic] of the other. They give us not sentiment, which is a good thing, but sentimentality, which is not.

Then there are the "continentalists," men who believe that in North American life there is something inherently superior to the European, that the Almighty has established a larger reservoir of virtue for this continent, to preserve which we should keep entirely detached from Europe—"the plague spot of the world." They believe, too, that is the more profitable. I came across a letter in a Toronto paper, on the occasion of the Chanak incident, which represents this point of view. May I quote a sentence: "It is time to decide, once for all, that, hereafter,

European nations shall be left to settle their own quarrels and that America, all America, shall attend strictly to human business at home."

Then, thirdly, there are those of us whom, for lack of a better term, I shall call the "ostriches" who, metaphorically speaking, keep their heads in the sand and think that by so doing they will avoid a knowledge of what is going on in the world and so escape all worry over the matter. Someone must attend to these things, but they are content to "let George do it" [King George V]. This is the prevailing attitude of indifference to the issue of external affairs of which most of us our guilty. They seem too remote from us to attract attention...

This attitude of negation is, of course, inconsistent with the status which we achieved in 1919, and its persistence will not only threaten imperial unity but will be injurious to our nationality...

We in Canada, apparently, have a decision to make. It remain [for us] to make a conscious choice between two alternatives. Either we accept the implications of the status, which we have half-unconsciously received, or we reject the implications and the status too. We have for the last ten years quite rightly been insisting upon the rights of Dominions. Now that they have been fully granted our attention might appropriately be directed to our obligations...[8]

---

1. Why was Vincent Massey critical of Canada's foreign policy?
2. Who was the intended audience for this article? Would they have supported or opposed his criticisms? Why?
3. What biases are in this article? What are the frames of references?

At the 1926 Imperial Conference, King again led the drive for Canadian autonomy. The conference concluded with the Balfour Report in which Britain and its Commonwealth countries were declared to be, "autonomous Communities within the British Empire, equal in status, in no way subordinate to one another in any aspect of their domestic or external affairs, though united by a common allegiance to the Crown, and freely associated as members of the British Commonwealth of Nations."[7] In effect this meant that Canada was not automatically bound to decisions made by the British in matters such as declarations of war and the signing of treaties with other nations.

By 1929 Canada had set up diplomatic offices in Washington, London, and Paris. This readied the path for the Statute of Westminster in 1931, which explicitly declared the constitutions of the commonwealth countries on equal status with Britain.

King was proud of his new autonomous foreign policy. A more independent Canadian identity had been forged. He had no reservations about an independent Canada with close association with both Britain and the United States. In his view, Canada could act as a crucial mediator between the two, ensuring that Canada would emerge on the world stage as a vital and useful nation. Unfortunately, for King, the western world in the interwar years was isolationist and Britain and the United States were not eager to have the young nation play such a vital role. Nevertheless, the role of mediator between Britain and the United States would remain central to King's foreign policy for years to come.

Industrializaton and Americanization

In the twenties, Canada experienced unprecedented growth in industrial development. But it was unevenly distributed and did not entirely occur as Canadian economic nationalists would have wished.

As Canada's economic welfare depended largely on exports, when wartime demand for raw materials disappeared, the Canadian economy went into depression. The situation was made worse by the introduction of American tariffs in 1921 and 1922. In 1921 the Canadian gross national product slipped by 20.1 percent and the value of exports dropped 60 percent in the years from 1920 to 1922. Virtually every sector of the Canadian economy was affected. Businesses closed and unemployment rose. High inflation rates hampered business investment and consumer spending. The government refused to act saying that interfering with economic laws would only prolong hardship. Only in 1924 did it become apparent that economic growth had returned. U.S. loans to Britain and other European countries opened the markets for Canadian goods, such as grain and pulp and paper, once again.

Canada experienced unprecedented industrial growth in the 1920s. Above is a pulp and paper mill in eastern Canada, from that time.

Between 1926 and 1929, manufacturing output grew in Canada at a rate of 9.8 percent. The focus for much of this industrial growth came from the exploitation of Canada's natural resources such as hydro electricity, pulp and paper, oil, and mining. Major Canadian corporations such as Power Corporation, Dominion Steel, Canada Cement, and Alcan Aluminum were formed in this era. Many of these corporations grew as a result of mergers; 315 industrial mergers took place between 1924 and 1930 and often these new entities achieved virtual monopolies in their sectors.

These large corporations worked together with investment institutions to arrange financing for their mergers and growth and in turn, these financial interests grew, prospered, merged, and consolidated. By 1927, for example, The Royal Bank, the Bank of Montreal, and the Bank of Commerce held 70 percent of banking resources in the country.

This growth in the Canadian economy received assistance from government. Tariffs provided a protected and reliable market for central Canadian manufactured goods. Governments also provided subsidies to corporations to ensure their growth and survival. The creation of publicly owned corporations was endorsed by business. For example, prominent business people actively lobbied for the formation of the Hydro-Electric Power Commission of Ontario to ensure a reliable and reasonably priced supply of electricity for their industries. Similarly, the Canadian government had purchased two financially distressed railway companies to form the government owned Canadian National Railways. Despite the laissez-faire protests from its private competitor, the CPR, the railway provided transportation crucial for a growing industrial base.

Finally, a vital drive for industrial growth came from American investment. By 1926 the Americans held 53 percent of foreign investment in the Canadian economy. One of the most dramatic forms of investments came when Ford,

A Canadian automobile plant in the 1920s.

General Motors, and Chrysler set up manufacturing plants in Canada. They were drawn to Canada in order to avoid a 35 percent Canadian tariff on foreign-built cars and to take advantage of preferential Canadian international tariffs in order to sell cars to Britain and other Commonwealth countries. In 1929, GM and Ford made 250 000 cars in Canada. Of these 100 000 were exported to other countries.[9] Cities, especially in Ontario and Quebec, used tax breaks and other incentives to attract consumer goods manufacturers such as auto, household appliance, radio, and furniture manufacturers. Between 1918 and 1930, Americans had established 641 branch plants in Canada. Most of them were located in Ontario and Quebec, close to most of the consumers in the country. This was the beginning of the branch plant system that still flourishes today.

In Quebec, Henri Bourassa was troubled by the increasing amount of American money and ownership in the Canadian economy:

At this rate, American capital will soon run Canada and Canadians. We could and should be alarmed. It's not surprising. It's the direct result of the folly of our wartime spending spree. We wanted to play the part of a grand nation. We've gone bankrupt to save "civilization" and "democracy".[10]

By the 1930s Americans controlled almost one-quarter of Canadian manufacturing, easily outstripping British investment and this development would have both good and bad lasting implications. As King was gaining more political independence, Canada was becoming increasingly dependent on American economic interests. King's quest for political autonomy had to be reconciled with economic reality.

Review...Reflect...Respond

1. What steps did Mackenzie King take to further Canada's autonomy?

2. How did economic regionalism affect Mackenzie King's leadership abilities in the early 1920s?

3. Did Canada have a choice not to welcome American investment in its industries in the 1920s? Could Canada's economy have developed as well without it?

Return to Unrest: The Rise and Fall of Labour in the 1920s

After the end of World War I, the returning soldiers faced unemployment and inadequate resources when they arrived home. Many of these discontented young men found an ally in the union movement, which had been a militant and potent force during the war. Thousands of men had gone overseas to fight and as a result, Canada had experienced an acute labour shortage, providing an opportunity for labour organizers. Employers could not dismiss workers who organized or joined unions as easily as they had in times of labour surpluses. Union membership grew rapidly in numbers and in employment sectors never organized before. In order to attract prospective members, organizers and leaders had to promise protection, enhanced wages, and better working conditions for workers but employers did not readily comply. They were able to use a variety of legal measures to disrupt union organization drives and thwart strikes, resulting in even more militancy.

The main labour organization at the time was the Trades and Labour Congress (TLC). It was affiliated with the American Federation of Labour, which adhered to the trade union principles expounded by Samuel Gompers. Gompers, founder of the AFL, believed that unions should refrain from direct political action. Instead, he thought it best to organize a select group of highly skilled workers whose superior abilities would help gain concessions from employers; this was called the craft union approach. This craft union was opposed by more radical elements in the Canadian labour movement. Leaders of the group pressed for political action by as large a union membership as possible. This was known as the industrial union approach. Industrial unionism was prevalent in the west, especially in Vancouver, Calgary, and Winnipeg. In March of 1919 at the Western Labour Conference the radicals out manoeuvred the craft unionists, by calling for secession from the TLC to form a union on industrial lines. The new organization would be called "One Big Union." The rationale behind this move was that employers and the government would be more inclined to make concessions if they were confronted by a large, unified radical labour presence.

The proponents of "One Big Union" may have been inspired by a strike in Winnipeg in April of 1918. The strike was initiated by the civic unions striking for higher wages. The city refused to move on their demands. By May 24, thirteen trades and nearly seven thousand workers were on strike. City services of every description had been disrupted. On that day the city government caved in and the workers were granted their demands.

The Winnipeg General Strike

A year later in May of 1919, the organizers for the "One Big Union" had called its founding convention at Calgary and another general strike was brewing in

Winnipeg. The Winnipeg building trades wanted increased wages and the metal workers demanded recognition as a union. Ninety-four of ninety-six unions joined the strike, including city police, firefighters, and water workers. They were joined by a number of demobilized soldiers, disgruntled by the conditions they faced upon their return from Europe. The city came to a standstill. This time, unlike 1918 where the strikers confronted city officials, the strikers faced the coordinated resistance of the municipal, provincial, and federal of governments. Government officials were supported by the Committee of 1000, a group of anti-strike activists sponsored by leading businesses in Winnipeg.[11] Arthur Meighen, then Minister of the Interior and acting Minister of Justice was convinced that the strike was inspired by Bolsheviks bent on violent revolution of the sort that had occurred only two years before in Russia. Along with other government officials, Meighen believed the strike had to be terminated in Winnipeg before it spread to other Canadian cities where similar unrest had been noted.

After months of negotiations and sporadic violence the strike culminated on June 16. After disturbances, the Northwest Mounted Police were called to confront a large crowd. The skirmishes between strikers and the police escalated and mayor Gray read the "Riot Act". In Canadian law this meant that in response to a menace or threat posed by an unlawful assembly a government official could order the crowd to disperse and then take measures to end the disturbance. Following Mayor Gray's pronouncement the Northwest Mounted Police then began to fire shots into the crowd. One of the strikers was killed instantly and another man was wounded and later died in hospital. Many more strikers and police were injured. The gunshots scattered the crowd and the police then proceeded to arrest over eighty of the strikers. The day, to be remembered as "Bloody Saturday", brought an abrupt halt to the Winnipeg General Strike. The workers obtained none of their demands. The federal government moved quickly to put an end to the kind of radical organizations

Marchers in the Winnipeg General Strike of 1919.

they perceived were behind the strike. In July the federal government passed Section 98 of the criminal code that banned organizations that advocated governmental, industrial, or economic change by force. Belonging to a radical organization carried with it a possible twenty-year jail sentence.

Most historians agree that the Winnipeg General Strike was a turning point in the fortunes of organized labour in Canada. From that point on, and through the twenties, labour was in retreat. Employers gained the upper hand in most strikes. The percentage of labour wins in strikes declined from 35 percent in 1917 to a level of only 18 percent in 1920. Union membership declined from a level of 380 000 in 1919 to 240 000 in 1924, as many new companies were non-union.

Web Connection

www.mcgrawhill.ca/links/definingcanada

Go to the Web site above to read more about the Winnipeg General Strike and labour history in Canada.

Women Become Persons

Like the labour movement, women made some of their most notable gains during the First World War, only to face adversity and substantial setbacks in the twenties.[12] Beginning with Manitoba in 1916, seven provinces and the federal government had given women the vote before 1920.[13] No doubt, many of those who had played important roles in those victories expected to build on the success of the previous decade. This was not to be.

During the war women had taken jobs and responsibilities in the workplace to fill the place of men engaged in the war. When the men returned, most Canadians felt that the soldiers deserved to take their rightful place in positions temporarily filled by women. Historian Allison Prentice captured the sentiment:

It was taken for granted that when the hostilities ceased and men returned, women would cheerfully surrender their newly acquired positions in the workforce. To make certain that women understood this, the federal government bombarded them with a poster campaign. "Do you feel justified in holding a job which could be filled by a man who has not only himself to support, but a wife and family as well?" one such poster demanded. "Think it over." Women were urged to seek "feminine" areas of employment where they would not threaten the position of male workers.[14]

Women were urged to return to the home and become wives and mothers. Many of them complied. But even under these circumstances, the work of women was considerable and without direct financial reward. In many cases women were forced to engage in part-time work to make "ends meet" in the home. On farms, work was especially difficult. In addition to household work, women were expected to help in the physically demanding work of the farm.

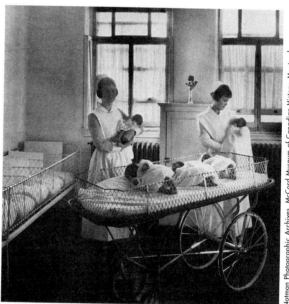

After World War I, women had been expected to return to their traditional occupations and roles in the family.

Notman Photographic Archives, McCord Museum of Canadian History, Montreal

If employment was necessary, women were encouraged to pursue training for careers such as secretaries, sales clerks, teachers, nurses, and librarians. Frequently women as young as fourteen were encouraged to leave school so they could to find work and help with finances in their homes. By 1921 approximately 17 percent of women over the age of seventeen were engaged in paid employment. Most of these were engaged in work such as garment making, house servants, waitresses, secretaries, teaching, and nursing. These jobs were low paying, low status, and in many cases, unsafe. Women were virtually excluded from skilled positions reserved mainly for men. When performing the same job as men they were usually paid much less. Even when governments introduced minimum wage laws for women they earned an average of 54 to 60 percent of men's earnings. There was no serious consideration of equal pay for work of equal value.

Historians have pointed to the marked differences between blue collar and pink-collar employment for women. Domestic servant work for women was the lowest paying, lowest status position. Nevertheless, domestic service was the largest sector of female employment in this period of Canadian history. The number of domestic servants grew from 78 118 in 1921 to 134 043 in 1931. From 1918 on, there was a growing trend for immigrant women to fill these positions. Those with little education and a strong constitution were considered best suited for long hours of physically demanding work with very little pay. Many worked from seven in the morning to seven in the evening with only a half-day off on Sundays.

Working conditions were even worse for women who worked in the textile industry. Regularly, the machinery was dangerous and serious injuries were common. Employers resisted purchasing safety equipment, insisting it was too expensive and it would make them less efficient in a competitive marketplace. Women often worked twelve hours or more, six days a week. Usually their only rest during was a half-hour lunch break. Bathroom breaks were

During World War I, women often performed jobs previously held by men.

discouraged or forbidden. Factories were often poorly lit, noisy, hot, the air was dusty, the sanitary conditions abysmal. Work related illness was rampant. Those who objected to conditions could easily be fired. The conditions for subcontracted workers were even more demanding. Under this system women produced garments in segregated factory spaces or their homes for piecework rates that rarely met minimum wage standards.[15] When demanding quotas were met, employers often responded by asking for even higher rates of production. When new technology was introduced the pace of work increased. Wages often fell below legislated minimums, only to be ignored by inadequate government inspection systems. Executives in prominent department stores like the T. Eaton Company and the Robert Simpson Company ignored the plight of the women who produced the fashionable clothes for their thriving new department stores.

Pink-collar work contained fewer of the physical hazards of blue-collar employment. Professions like secretaries, teachers, and nurses remained "ghettoized" from comparable male positions.

Women in secretarial positions rarely were promoted into middle management or senior positions. Although female teachers were successful in organizing into teachers associations, they were paid less than male teachers. In many jurisdictions the jobs of female educators were automatically terminated when they got married. Similarly, in the federal civil service women were made to resign following marriage. Between 1921 and 1931 the number of female civil servants declined by 13 percent while the ranks of male civil servants rose by 6 percent. The work of nurses rose to heroic levels as a result of their work in the first war. After the war, however, they struggled to regulate and control their own profession. They were successful in instituting nursing degree programs and lobbying for recognition as a legitimate profession. On the whole, however, nurses were unable to gain significant increases in wages, certainly when compared to male-dominated medical doctors.[16]

There were women who made it into the "male professions" in the 1920s and 1930s. These women often obtained these credentials and positions as a result of extraordinary toil and personal cost. Notable women doctors, lawyers, university professors, engineers, and scientists are often highlighted in historical treatments of this era. While no one can diminish the way in which these individuals pioneered entry into these professions, their actual rates of participation were miniscule.

Women continued to be strong advocates for their rights. Activists in such organizations as the National Council of Women of Canada, the Women's Christian Temperance Association, the women's institutes, the Associated Country Women of the World, the National Council of Jewish Women, the Pioneer Women's Association, the Young Women's Christian Association, as well as women's religious organizations, all vigorously worked to enhance the role of women in Canadian society. Women were active in union life and played an integral role during the Winnipeg General strike.[17] These efforts were to pay dividends in years to come.

Women became engaged on the political front as well. In 1921 Agnes McPhail was elected as the first female Member of Parliament, encountering great skepticism and resistance. However, McPhail ensured her voice was heard advocating for such things as prison reform, family allowances, old age pensions, and unemployment insurance. Other women soon followed and were successfully elected to provincial legislatures, often as members of third parties. In Alberta, which had elected a United Farmers of Alberta government, women like Irene Parlby lobbied for such issues as a minimum wage for women, women's property rights, and children's welfare. Many of Parlby's initiatives were legislated into law.

The Persons Case

Most historians of this decade point to the Persons Case as a landmark decision in women's rights. In 1919 the Federated Women's Institutes of Canada passed a resolution urging the prime minister to appoint a female senator. They believed that

Irene Parlby advocated for women and childrens' rights and welfare.

female senators could have an impact in the "second house of sober reflection." Both Meighen and King refused, saying that under the terms of the British North America Act, women were not considered as persons and therefore could not be appointed. Eight years passed, and after a series of refusals by the government, Emily Murphy, led a group of five prominent women activists—Nellie McClung, Irene Parlby, Louise McKinney, and Henrietta Muir Edwards—who petitioned the government to direct the Supreme Court to rule on whether the concept of "qualified persons" in Section 24 of the BNA Act could include women. If the Supreme Court ruled in their favour, women persons could be appointed to the Senate. In 1928 the Court ruled that women did not constitute as "qualified persons". The "famous five" then successfully appealed to the Judicial Committee of the Privy Council of England, the final court of appeal in the British Empire. The Judicial Committee reversed the Canadian Supreme Court decision ruling that women were indeed persons. In their decision the Judicial Committee commented that the archaic interpretation of the law by the Canadian Supreme Court was a "relic of days more barbarous than ours." The first woman senator, Cairine Wilson, was appointed in 1930.

The day had finally arrived when denying the personhood of women became unacceptable. On the other hand, the progress of women's rights during the interwar years demonstrated ambiguity. While developments following the first war set the stage for important progress in later years, progress by women leaders was slow during the twenties. This is perhaps best exemplified by the fact that only five women were elected to the Canadian parliament before 1950.

Web Connection

www.mcgrawhill.ca/links/definingcanada
Go to the Web site above to find out more about the Famous Five and highlights from the Person's Case.

The Famous Five statues on Parliament Hill, Ottawa. This is a monument to the women who fought for and won legal status for women in Canada — Emily Murphy, Nellie McClung, Louise McKinney, Henrietta Muir Edwards and Irene Parlby.

Roaring Cultural Contradictons in the 1920s

In an oft quoted statement, Canadian painter Arthur Lismer stated: "most creative people whether in painting, writing, or music began to have a guilty feeling that Canada was as yet unwritten, unpainted, unsung....In 1920 there was a job to be done."

Lismer was one of the Group of Seven, likely the most recognized visual artists in Canadian art history. Lismer was joined by Lawren Harris, A.Y. Jackson, Frank Carmichael, Frank Johnston, and James E.H. Macdonald. Their first exhibition was held in Toronto in 1920 but their collaboration had begun years earlier. In the twenties, the public began to respond to their body of work. One of the early reactionary critics called labelled the group "the Hot Mush School." He was referring to the non-representational bold brush strokes on their canvases. While the group and many of their admirers cultivated a revolutionary image it is likely they had been influenced by the postimpressionists like Van Gogh, Gauguin, and Matisse. However, it would be wrong to say that the Group's style was entirely derived from European painters. Their distinctive vivid colours and designs captured the essence of northern Canada, principally the Algoma region of Ontario. The Group's paintings received generally favourable international review. The most unreserved acclaim came from the Canadian public. In time the revolutionaries had become the most esteemed members of the Canadian art community. To this day, most surveys of the distinct nature of Canadian identity are obliged to feature the significant contributions of the Group of Seven.

Literature and poetry also came of age in the twenties. Mazo de la Roche's popular *Jalna* series fed a voracious Canadian appetite for romantic and sentimental novels. Charles Yale Harrison's *Generals Die in Bed*, R.J.C. Stead's *Grain*, and Morley Callaghan's *Strange Fugitive* followed American realism in their unvarnished portrayal of contemporary life. In poetry modernism began to appear.[18] In Montreal a group of poets led by F. R. Scott defied traditional forms in their embrace of modernist free verse and experimentation. Poets such as F. R. Scott continued writing for many years, and interestingly, he wrote a poem about Mackenzie King after King's death:

> W.L.M.K.
> *How shall we speak of Canada,*
> *Mackenzie King dead?*
> *The Mother's boy in the lonely room*
> *With his dog, his medium and his ruins?*
>
> *He blunted us.*
>
> *We had no shape*
> *Because he never took sides,*
> *And no sides*
> *Because he never allowed them to take shape*
>
> *He skillfully avoided what was wrong*
> *Without saying what was right,*
> *And never let his on the one hand*
> *Know what his on the other hand was doing.*
> ...
> *He seemed to be in the center*
> *Because we had no center,*
> *No vision*
> *To pierce the smoke-screen of his politics*
>
> *Truly he will be remembered*
> *Wherever men honour ingenuity,*
> *Ambiguity, inactivity, and political longevity.*
> ...[19]

The Social Elite and Canadian Culture

There seems to be little doubt among historians that Canada's cultural elite attempted to foster a sense of Canadian identity and nationalism. In her article "The Nationalist Network: English Canada's Intellectuals and Artists in the 1920s" historian Mary Vipond writes about the roles that intellectuals and the cultural elite saw themselves playing:

Canada was almost a nation in a political sense, but it still lacked the spiritual cement of a national will or purpose—or at least that was the intellectuals' diagnosis. And the cure? That, they assumed, lay in their hands. They believed it to be their responsibility to "mould public opinion" in the direction of a national consciousness. They were the "innovative minority"; it was their job to formulate social goals, to give direction to the national will, and thus to give cohesion to Canadian society. They were Canada's leaders, and as such their obligation was clear. J. W. Dafoe, for example, threw out the challenge to the Canadian Authors' Association: "National consciousness doesn't happen. It can be encouraged. It is a product of vision, imagination, and courage, and can be created and established by men and women who devote themselves to it."[20]

There was a growing feeling among the Canadian intellectual and cultural elite that the fostering of a Canadian identity was their business. Many historians argue that the majority of this cultural elite, were English Canadians, and that their views did not take into account the large groups of immigrants that were increasingly playing a part in the Canadian cultural identity.

American Influence on Canadian Culture

The "Roaring Twenties", sandwiched between the horrors of the Great War and the greyness of the Great Depression is often characterized as a carefree period of release from rigid social mores and conventions, in an effort to try forget the pain and troubles of the war generation. The twenties were an age of adventure. Charles Lindbergh made the first solo flight over the Atlantic in 1927 and Richard E. Byrd was the first to fly over the North Pole. Thousands were drawn to barnstorming exhibitions of acrobatic bi-planes, many of them flown by world war flying aces. This was an age of stunts and endurance contests. Dance marathons and flagpole sitting contests captured the escapist imagination of Americans and Canadians.

Doing the laundry and listening to the radio in 1920s Canada

In the twenties, America dominated the popular culture scene. One of the main paths for its entry into Canada was radio. The first radio broadcast in Canada was transmitted in 1920. By 1929 Canadians owned 297 000 radios. From the beginning American programs dominated the airwaves. Canadian nationalists were dismayed by the dominance of American commercial radio.[21] In 1929 the government commissioned the Aird Report recommending a government-supported noncommercial radio network.

The same applied to the movie industry. Canadians flocked to see Hollywood movies being produced in a feverish pace. With admission prices ranging from five to twenty-five cents the price was right for Canadian moviegoers. They were enthralled by the change from silent to talking pictures. As with radio, Canadians preferred American films to more artful ones produced in Europe and Canada. While Canadians did attempt to produce feature films they generally were not well received.

The vast majority of movie theatres in Canada during the '20s were owned by American corporations.

Moreover, Canadian film producers had difficulty distributing their films in cinemas owned by American movie theatre chains. By 1929, ninety percent of movies were being produced by American filmmakers.

American magazines owned the Canadian market. The circulation rates of *Maclean's* and *Chatelaine* were dwarfed by *McCall's* and *Saturday Evening Post* from south of the border.

It was only in subsequent decades that Canadians took measures to protect Canadian culture. The National Film Board of Canada (1939), and the Canadian Broadcasting Corporation (1936) were created to guarantee a place for Canadian film, radio, and later television programming. In 1936 the Board of Broadcast Governors (1936) and later the Canadian Radio-Television Commission (1967–69) were created to regulate all aspects of the Canadian broadcasting system. Tariffs to protect Canadian publications were all attempts to ensure Canadian culture was preserved. However, today, as in the twenties, Canadian regulators have always struggled with a public that is often more attracted to the lure of American popular culture.

There were some notable exceptions to the American dominance of Canadian entertainment and popular culture. Sport is one of these exceptions. For decades, hockey has been a national preoccupation of Canadians. The National Hockey League was formed in 1917 with four Canadian teams, the Ottawa Senators, Montreal Canadiens, Toronto Arenas, and the Montreal Wanderers. In the early years, the winners of the NHL would play for the Stanley Cup against teams from western Canadian leagues that included Vancouver, Calgary, Edmonton, Regina, and Saskatoon.[22] In 1924 the Boston Bruins was the first American team to join the NHL. By 1926 the NHL re-organized to include ten teams, six of which were from the United States. Gradually, many star members from western Canadian teams migrated to the NHL. Even though from that point on, American NHL teams outnumbered Canadian ones, the overwhelming majority of players were Canadian born. Players like Howie Morenz, Eddie Shore, Charlie Conacher, Bill Cook, and George Hainsworth were the "Canadian superstars" of their age.

In the 1920s, excellence in sports was not reserved for men. The Edmonton Grads, a women's basketball team had been formed in 1915 by Percy Page, a coach at McDougall Commercial High School in Edmonton. The Edmonton Grads won city, provincial, national North American, and international tournaments from 1915 to 1940. They represented Canada at four Olympic games (1924, 1928, 1932, 1936) winning all twenty-seven matches. Because women's basketball was not recognized as an Olympic sport at the time, they did not receive gold medals. Over their history the Grads compiled a record of 502 wins and 20 losses. The Edmonton Grads silenced the concerns of critics who warned that women were not physically able to sustain the physical hardship of tournament basketball. They became an inspiration for women who aspired to become successful in sports usually dominated by men.

Expression of Culture

Our geography has defined our country and affected our development since the first explorers arrived. Both our most distinctive treasure and our greatest obstacle, our vast countryside, from the Maritimes to the Pacific and from our Southern border to the far reaches of the Arctic, has challenged leaders and nation-builders for centuries. It is not surprising to find that our landscape also dominates the history of Canadian art.

No other artists or groups in Canada are more closely associated with the landscape as are the Group of Seven. A loose association of artists, who first made a name for themselves in the 1920s, the Group of Seven are considered by many to be the first truly Canadian art movement.

J.E.H. MacDonald, Lawren Harris, A.Y. Jackson, Arthur Lismer, Frank Carmichael, Fred Varley, Frank Johnston and Tom Thomson met in the early 1910s and spent their spare time sketching in small groups north of Toronto. Most of these men worked at the commercial art firm, Grip Ltd., and gathered after work at the Arts and Letters Club to discuss their sketching trips and their common concern for the lack of support for artists in Canada.

The first official Group of Seven exhibition was held in 1920 at the Art Museum of Toronto (now the Art Gallery of Ontario). Tom Thomson, who had died in Algonquin Park in 1917, was never officially a Group member. The first catalogue read, "an Art must grow and flower in the land before the country will be a real home for its people". Their shows, which were held across Canada in the twenties and thirties, stirred controversy and excitement among galleries, art critics and the general public.

The Group of Seven were not the first Canadians to paint landscape – artists had been doing this for centuries. It was the details they painted and the techniques they utilized that were revolutionary. The Group shared a common motivation to journey deep into the woods, and paint the areas of Canada that had been considered 'unpaintable' by the generations that preceded them. In canoe and on foot, the men traversed the landscape with paint box in hand looking for subject matter. Eventually, their sketching trips took them further north, from Algonquin Park to the shores of Lake Superior and on across Canada to the Rocky Mountains and the Arctic. To an audience familiar with the somber tones of English landscape paintings and the delicate colour of impressionist scenes, the Group's techniques seemed 'unschooled'. Their canvases revealed bright, shocking colours and, often, thick, sweeping strokes of paint.

There are many contemporaries of the Group of Seven, who were inspired by their unique style and grand vision, and made a name for themselves as landscape painters in their own right. Emily Carr, who lived in Victoria, British Columbia, is most notable among this group. Carr met the Group of Seven late in her career in 1927, at the age of fifty-six. She instantly recognized in their work a common goal to develop a vocabulary big enough to tackle the magnificence of the Canadian landscape. After viewing their work and sharing ideas with the Group, Carr returned home to find the appropriate artistic language to translate her beloved British Columbian forests. She was particularly motivated by her conversations with Lawren Harris who explored his theosophical philosophies through his art. Carr personally believed that, "the only thing worth striving for is to express God. Every living thing is God made manifest". She saw an energy in nature. "Feel this growth, the surging upwards, this expansion, the pulsing life, all working with the same idea, the same urge to express the God in themselves" Carr proclaims. This force is palpable in her paintings — large oil sketches and canvases of the forest underbrush, painted with bold, swirling strokes and lush blues and greens.

Expression of Culture

The 1930s saw the emergence of artists with more regional concerns than the Group of Seven. Artists like Carl Schaeffer, retreated to their homes during the Depression and painted what was most familiar. Schaeffer is renowned for a series of landscape paintings of the thirties and forties that depict the rural countryside of Hanover, Ontario. Unlike the Group of Seven, who were often criticized for omitting the human element in their landscapes, Schaeffer's scenes show the hand of man on the soft rolling countryside.

The Group of Seven disbanded in 1937. They were superceded by the Canadian Group of Painters, a larger more diverse association of artists who tackled a wide range of subject matter. Many of the members of this group abandoned landscape art altogether to paint social themes that preoccupied their generation: cityscapes haunted by the Depression, expressive portraits of working-class Canadians and images of the environment being swallowed by industry.

Silkscreen prints were made of the Group of Seven's paintings during the Second World War, and were distributed to schools and government buildings across the country. Both the paintings of the Group of Seven and those of Emily Carr continue to be mass-printed today to be sold in galleries and gift shops across Canada. These images – barren snow-filled spaces, the bent pine, the rugged Canadian Shield and the tangled underbrush of the forest — are etched in our minds and our culture.

Cathedral Peak and Lake O'Hara (1927) by J.E.H. MacDonald

The Automobile

No discussion of changing Canadian society in the 1920s can be complete without looking at the impact of the automobile. In 1904, there were fewer than one thousand automobiles in Canada, and these were largely located in urban centres. By 1930, there were over a million automobiles in Canada, changing the way Canadians travelled in both rural and city regions. By the end of the 1920s, Canada had over 128 000 kilometres of surfaced roads. The automobile revolution allowed people to live a greater distance from their work, and thus the sub-urbanization phenomenon that began as a trickle in the late 1800s started to grow. The automobile also allowed for decreased isolation of rural families, allowing them easier opportunities to visit friends and relatives in the city. The automobile also allowed city dwellers greater access to the country, and the 1920s experienced a great boom in the cottage and resort industries, especially in Ontario and Quebec.

The automobile revolution also gave birth to a large sector of industries that were dedicated to

Canadian Tire store in the 1920s — the first auto-supply service store.

servicing and manufacturing cars. Thousands of Canadians found work in industries producing rubber, steel, glass, nickel, and aluminum. The automobile also led to the creation of hundreds of "spin-off" industries such as road construction, auto-parts plants, and service stations. In 1922, the Billes brothers opened their first store dedicated to the auto-supply service—they called it Canadian Tire.

By 1930, there were more than one million automobiles in Canada.

Review...Reflect...Respond

1. Explain the events leading up to the Persons Case and why it was a landmark decision for women's rights in Canada.

2. After the Winnipeg General Strike , why did labour unrest go into decline in the 1920s?

3. Was Canada forging its own culture and identity in the 1920s or was it "borrowing" culture from the United States?

Conclusion

In some respects Canada in 1929 appeared to be very different country than the one that dealt with the issues of armistice and demobilization. In a fundamental way, however, Canada was confronting the same ambiguity as before. Complexity and uncertainty always accompanied the drive for change. New industries created unprecedented economic growth. For a select numbers of Canadians, growth in the new economy provided ample economic rewards but the vast majority of Canadians, struggled in modest circumstances. Social conventions were also challenged. The landmark Persons Case had to be reconciled with retrenched social attitudes and setbacks for women in the workplace.

Canada forged a new cultural identity, but American popular culture threatened to overwhelm it. On the political-economic front, Canada was freeing itself from Imperial constraints only to struggle with the attractions and perils of being drawn into an American orbit. Prime Minister Mackenzie King, who personified complexity and ambiguity, used cautious and pragmatic measures to answer the demands of reformers and satisfy his important base of support amongst financiers and industrialists.

This state of ambiguity would reside in Canada for many years to come. As Canadians faced the grey decade ahead, the forces of ambiguity would only be aggravated by declining resources to cope with them.

Notes

1. The Canadian Wheat Board had originally been set up to ensure a regular supply of grain during the war years of 1917 to 1918. King's new version had few of its original powers of market control. The positive financial effect of the new wheat board was not felt by restive farmers.
2. The provincial government brought in troops to put an end to the violence at New Waterford, Cape Breton Island.
3. The controversy that accompanied Byng's refusal to call an election at King's request became known as the King-Byng Affair.
4. Olive Dickason, *Canada's First Nations: A History of Founding Peoples from Earliest Times, 2nd Edition* (Toronto: Oxford University Press, 1996) p. 303.
5. The opening lines of Grey Owl's first published article, "The Passing of the Last Frontier," *Country Life* magazine, March 2, 1929, p. 302.
6. Thompson, 1985 p. 46.
7. Bothwell et.al., 1987 p. 238.
8. Vincent Massey, "Canada and External Affairs," *Journal of the Canadian Bankers' Association*, April 1925, pp. 381, 384–385, 388–390. Quoted in Jeffrey Keshen and Suzanne Morton, *Material Memory: Documents in Post-Confederation History.* (Toronto: Addison Wesley, 1998), pp. 198–199.
9. Mass produced American cars were priced right for many Canadians. In 1925 a Model T Ford for $595 and a Chevrolet for $625. By 1930 there were 1 235 000 automotive vehicles registered in Canada, an increase of 827 000 from ten years before.
10. Don Gillmor et al. *Canada: A People's History, Volume II* (Toronto: McClelland & Stewart, 2001) p. 135.
11. The Citizens' Committee of One Thousand was composed of anti-strike volunteers who offered to operate services no longer being provided by strikers. Leaders of the Committee were prominent business leaders and lawyers in Winnipeg who consulted with government officials wishing to put an end to the strike.

12. Historians of women and labour would acknowledge that both groups faced adversity in the twenties. Scholars of women's history challenge the assumption that the twenties was a decade of setbacks only. A great deal of research has demonstrated that the years of adversity of the twenties served to make many women more resolved to recapture and enhance the gains they had witnessed in earlier times.

13. Manitoba, Alberta, and Saskatchewan in 1916, British Columbia in 1916, Nova Scotia and the federal government in 1918, New Brunswick in 1919. Prince Edward Island followed in 1925. Women in the province of Quebec were not granted the vote until 1940.

14. Alison Prentice, Paula Bourne, Gail Cuthbert Brandt, Beth Light, Wendy Mitchinson, Naomi Black, *Canadian Women: A History* (Toronto: Harcourt Brace Jovanovich, 1988) p. 218.

15. Piecework refers to a system where a worker is paid by the amount of work done. In the case of garment workers, for example, a worker would be paid for the number of dresses sewn rather than by an hourly wage.

16. According to a 1929 study, 60 percent of private duty nurses said they were unable to save money for their retirement. (Prentice et al. 1988, p. 226)

17. Women telephone operators and confectionary workers were among the first to go on strike in Winnipeg. Helen Armstrong led the Women's Labour League that provided up to fifteen hundred meals a day for striking workers. (Prentice et. al., 1988, p. 219)

18. In poetry modernism was an early twentieth century movement that broke with sentimental images and replaced them with critical and vivid ideas. In many cases, a conventional rhyming structure was replaced with free verse.

19. F. R. Scott, "W.L.M.K." from *The Eye of the Needle: Satire, Sorties, Sundries* (Montreal: Contact Press, 1957). The entire poem can be read at:
http://www.library.utoronto.ca/canpoetry/scott_fr/poem5.htm

20. Mary Vipond, "The Nationalist Network: English Canada's Intellectuals and Artists in the 1920s" in J. M. Bumstead, *Interpreting Canada's Past: Volume Two–Post-Confederation, Second Edition* (Toronto: Oxford University Press, 1993) p. 457.

21. In the early days radio stations like CFRB Toronto were actually American affiliates. Canadian owned stations often bought "American content" to attract listeners.

22. Seattle Washington was a prominent American team that played in the western leagues.

Chapter 16 Review

Knowledge & Understanding

1. Identify these people, places, and events, and explain their historical significance to Canada's developing culture and identity:

   William Lyon Mackenzie King
   Chanak Affair
   Grey Owl
   Maritime Rights Movement
   King-Byng Affair
   League of Indians of Canada
   Balfour Report
   Winnipeg General Strike
   Person's Case
   Group of Seven
   Canadian Tire Corporation

2. How did economic regionalism grow in Canada during the 1920s? How effective was the federal government in handling regionalist concerns?

Thinking & Inquiry

3. Explain the cultural struggle waged in the 1920s between the emerging Canadian cultural and "the siren call" of the American culture? In what ways was it similar to the struggle being waged today? How was it different?

Application

4. You are a journalist interviewing one of the recently jailed leaders of the Winnipeg General Strike (for example J.S. Woodsworth). Compile a list of ten questions that you would ask him and the answers you might expect to receive.

5. Many new products for the home were introduced in the 1920s. Research one of these products and then record a 30-second radio advertisement for that product. Bring your recording to class and listen to each other's radio advertisements. What product would you have wanted to buy?

Communication

6. As the lawyer for the "famous five" you have to give the closing statement for the Person's Case to the Judicial Committee of the Privy Council of England. Write a one-page closing statement that must convince the Privy Council to see that women are persons in Canada. What evidence will you use to support your closing argument?

7. Vincent Massey argued that a policy of isolationism was a shameful role for Canada. What responsibilities did Canada have to world affairs as it increasingly fought for more autonomy, and for its own place on the world stage? Should Canada have focused on its own affairs and problems, or did it have a responsibility watch and be a part of international events? Write down at least five arguments to defend what position you believe Canada should take after World War I. Find a partner in your class who hold the opposite beliefs and conduct a five-minute debate. Be sure to record your opponent's strongest argument. After the debate, hold a class discussion on what major points were argued for each side. What are the overall beliefs for the class, or is it divided?

The Great Depression in Canada

A recession is when your neighbour has to tighten his belt. A depression is when you have to tighten your belt. And a panic is when you have no belt to tighten and your pants fall down.

—TOMMY DOUGLAS

For those who lived through the 1930s, the decade had an identity and importance all of its own. Those who bore the brunt of the hardships were changed forever and many were driven beyond the boundaries of human endurance. But it was in the midst of these hardships that strength of character and determination were forged.[1]

The thirties did leave a remarkable cultural, social and political legacy. Analysts from a variety of intellectual disciplines continue to draw insights and lessons from the thirties.

Economic analysts often refer to the Great Depression as the benchmark that measures and defines the magnitude of every subsequent correction, recession or depression in the economy.[2] If the Great Depression was *the* defining economic depression then understanding how and why it happened is vital. To this day historians and economists have intense disagreements over how and why the Depression occurred. This is largely because examining the causes and consequences means that we have to carefully examine and evaluate the very nature of our economic system.[3]

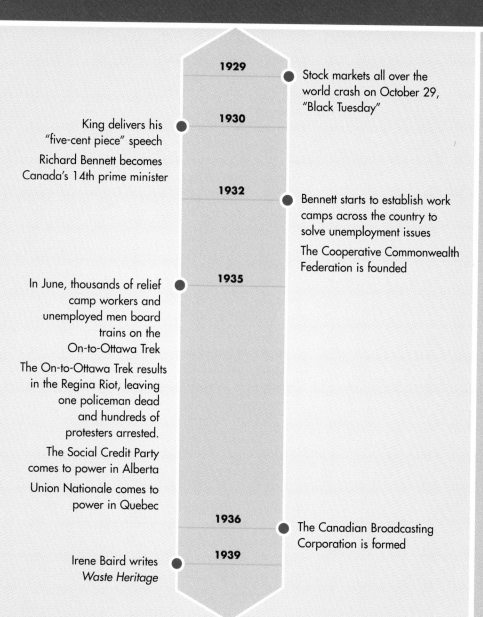

17

1929
Stock markets all over the world crash on October 29, "Black Tuesday"

1930
King delivers his "five-cent piece" speech

Richard Bennett becomes Canada's 14th prime minister

1932
Bennett starts to establish work camps across the country to solve unemployment issues

The Cooperative Commonwealth Federation is founded

1935
In June, thousands of relief camp workers and unemployed men board trains on the On-to-Ottawa Trek

The On-to-Ottawa Trek results in the Regina Riot, leaving one policeman dead and hundreds of protesters arrested.

The Social Credit Party comes to power in Alberta

Union Nationale comes to power in Quebec

1936
The Canadian Broadcasting Corporation is formed

1939
Irene Baird writes *Waste Heritage*

By the end of this chapter, you will be able to

• assess the origins and results of Macdonald's National Policy

• demonstrate an understanding of the causes and implications of Canadian regional differences

• analyze how obstacles that made it difficult for immigrants to participate fully in Canadian society

• describe the origins and various incidents of prejudice and discrimination in Canada's history

• identify how various provincial and federal statutes (e.g., British Columbia's Unemployment Relief Act, 1931) have sought to protect the human rights of Canadians

• demonstrate an understanding of the history, development, and extent of Canada's social programs

The Legacy of the Great Depression

Economic hardship and displacement often generate social and political protest movements. In the first decade of the twenty-first century, protesters have rallied against the policies of the World Trade Organization, The World Bank, the International Monetary Fund and other forces of globalization.[4] In the current domestic political scene, Canadians have been debating the role of the government in the lives of individuals. What role should the government have in assisting the less fortunate? Should social programs be curtailed? To what extent should individuals be responsible for themselves and their families? Should government programs like medicare, employment insurance, and the old age pension be universally extended to all Canadians? Those who want to debate these issues in an informed way have to first learn about the Great Depression, where many of these programs were forged.

Today Canadian agriculture is in crisis, with global warming and climatic change a source of concern for many Canadian farmers. Some experts are worried that the belt of arable land in the southern part of Canada may be replaced by semi-arid wasteland, too dry to grow crops. Discussions about drought often refer to the sustained drought on the Canadian prairies in the 1930s. Even without climate change, hundreds of farmers lose their farms every year to banks and multinational agribusiness operations. The response to drought and economic loss raises interesting questions. Are family farms simply small businesses or are they a way of living worth preserving? The most notable forerunner for these concerns and questions is found in the drought and crisis that challenged the agricultural base in Canada during the thirties.

The Great Depression

The Great Depression is aptly named—no depression before or since has been as severe. The Great Depression affected almost every economy in the world. Beginning in the autumn of 1929, most economies had to endure economic decline until the beginning of World War II.[5] The economic devastation resulting from the Depression was the gravest in the history of capitalism. Where did it begin?

The stock market crash in October of 1929 signalled the beginning of the Great Depression. While historians and economists agree that the crash of 1929 was a symptom of an underlying illness in the economy, the exact illness remains the subject of great debate. There are, however, some causal factors that most agree upon. Companies, spurred on by optimism in the 1920s, had produced too many products and there were not enough customers to buy them. While a minority of people had gained great wealth in the '20s, many consumers were poor and in debt.[6] This was especially true for farmers who went into debt assuming that prices for their produce would continue to rise as they had throughout most of the 1920s. Many European countries were still struggling with the debts they had incurred during the war and eventually were in no position to purchase large quantities of North American products. The resulting weaknesses in trade and purchasing power were not reflected in the stock market. Stock market speculation in the 1920s had driven up the prices of stocks such that they no longer reflected the true value of companies. The inevitable "correction" of stock prices exposed the underlying problems in the economy.

Financial markets had fluctuated earlier in 1929, but each downturn was accompanied by a strong rally. All this changed on Thursday, October 24, 1929. That day, the stock markets of the world began to drop at a sharper rate than analysts had seen in some time. In New York, 12 894 650 million shares were traded. In Montreal, nearly 400 000 shares were traded—a significant jump from the 25 000 that were normally traded each day. The slide levelled out on Friday and investors were given the weekend to contemplate their financial futures. The optimists amongst them may have found solace in the reassurances of leaders of large financial corporations who insisted that the correction was natural, and even necessary, but certainly only temporary. These assurances were forgotten the following Monday when the market began to slip again. True disaster came the following day.

October 29, 1929 became known as Black Tuesday. Stock prices plummeted. The *Toronto Star's* index of sixteen critical Canadian stocks lost $300 million. Analysts of that fateful day have observed that the Canadian Stock Exchanges were losing $1 million for every minute stock was being traded. In New York a record level of 16 410 030 shares traded. Investors, large and small, were trying to sell. The capitalist economy was gravely ill—it had been for some time.

The devastating losses of October 1929 had a great impact on the economy. While there were minor rallies in the market in the months immediately following the crash, it soon became apparent that the setback would not soon disappear. Investors, many of them heavily indebted because of losses in the crash, could not or would not risk further funds in the new economic climate. Even those who had survived the crash and wanted to buy stocks at greatly reduced prices had a difficult time borrowing investment money because governments and banks maintained tight money lending policies. Without the capital to back up production, industrial output began to fall.[7] This resulted in massive unemployment. Unemployed workers could no longer afford to buy anything. Lack of consumer demand produced further declines. So began a seemingly irreversible downward spiral.

The front page on Black Tuesday—could it happen again?

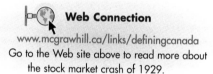

Web Connection

www.mcgrawhill.ca/links/definingcanada
Go to the Web site above to read more about the stock market crash of 1929.

By 1933 the annual Gross National Product, (the total value of goods and services produced by a nation in a year) had dropped 40 percent from its pre-crash levels. In the same period, Canada's exports had declined by half. The Canadian economy was especially vulnerable because it was heavily dependent upon the export of raw materials. In Canada, 33 percent of the Gross National Income was dependent on revenue from exports. As foreign economies shrank in the Depression, so did sales of Canadian goods. Sales of metals, coal, lumber, pulp and paper, oil, cereal grains, and livestock were all in sharp decline. Businesses, even prominent ones like Canada Power and Pulp went bankrupt. The ripple effect from the decline of exports and the general downturn in the economy were felt everywhere.

Unemployment Rates in Canada 1926–1939

What was the average unemployment rate for Canada throughout the 1930s?

While most Canadians had not lost money on the stock markets, they did feel the effects of the economic decline. Perhaps the most devastating evidence of the new depression was unemployment. In 1928 the annual unemployment rate in Canada was 2.6 percent. In 1930 it jumped to 12.6 percent. By 1933, the depth of the Depression, the rate had risen to 26.6 percent.

In some regions of Canada, the provincial unemployment rates rose from 30 to 50 percent. In addition, many who were not counted as officially unemployed faced underemployment. Many Canadians worked in part-time or very low paying jobs that barely provided the means to get by. Also, not counted in the unemployment rates were farmers, who faced hardships that in many cases exceeded that of the urban unemployed.

Early Impact and Initial Responses

By early 1930, evidence of the impact of the Depression was beginning to filter in. Reports of four or five thousand unemployed men in Vancouver, twenty-five to thirty thousand in Toronto, thousands laid off in Windsor. Four hundred families were reportedly being fed by the city in Edmonton. Popular historian Pierre Berton claims that the government did not have the means or even the inclination to verify these reports.[8]

"A Five-Cent Piece"

Prime Minister Mackenzie King barely acknowledged the crisis. The Conservative opposition called for aid to poverty stricken provinces, especially those in western Canada. In April 1930, rankled by Conservative calls for federal assistance to alleviate the crisis in the provinces, King declared that he would not give them a "five-cent piece." Why should he give assistance to provinces, often led by Conservative governments that were opposed to his policies? King's views on the role of government assistance might well have echoed those of U.S. President Calvin Coolidge who declared, "the business of government was business." King believed that any solution to the crisis would have to come in the form of a business-led recovery. In his "five-cent speech" King claimed that in drawing attention to the unemployment problem the opposition would only highlight the negative state of the economy and discourage foreign investors from

Canadian Prime Minister R. B. Bennett

investing in the Canadian economy. He concluded, "What is needed today if we are to solve any unemployment problem is to get more capital into the country to increase the investment of capital; and we will get it as people come to have confidence in conditions here."[9]

Even if King had wanted to help the provinces, he would have had great difficulty providing the funds. The government was constrained by debts incurred by loans to railway interests. Moreover, the ability to generate revenue for such assistance was hampered by the poor economy. In the 1920s only 130 000 Canadians in a population of ten million actually paid taxes. Most revenue came from tariffs and sales taxes, and in a time of economic inactivity these revenues were hard to come by. The response of King was clear—if government aid were forthcoming at all it would have to come from provincial and municipal governments.

The response of Canadians to King's lack of assistance was decisive. In the federal election campaign of 1930, King tried to distance himself from the "five-cent piece" remark—but it was no use. The Conservative leader, Richard Bedford Bennett promised his government would deal with the ailing economy and unemployment. He promised to blast his way into the world's economic markets and create trade for Canadian industries heavily dependent on foreign trade. The Conservatives swept to power with a clear majority of 137 seats to the Liberals' 91.

The Depths of the Depression

The optimism that accompanied Bennett's decisive win was short-lived. The Depression deepened and widened. There likely is no more compelling evidence of the hardship faced by Canadians than the personal letters sent by Canadians to Prime Minister Bennett.[10]

The hardest hit were the unemployed, the elderly, the sick, the handicapped, the indebted business people, and the farmers. For these people there was very little help to rely on. Programs like welfare, unemployment insurance, and medicare did not exist. Bennett was not inclined to provide for those who were not earning their way in society. He was steadfast in this widely shared principle even though it clearly did not apply to himself.[11] By the time he had taken office as Prime Minister, Bennett was one of wealthiest men in Canada. As the letters to his office from Canadian citizens described the plight of the unemployed and poor, it was obvious that the Depression had reached devastating levels that could not be ignored. There were also election promises to end the Depression. Something had to be done and Bennett was forced to set aside his views on self-reliance and accountability.

Just weeks into office, Bennett introduced the Unemployment Relief Act. The Act legislated $20 million to be used for relief in 1930 and 1931. In a total federal budget of less than $500 million per year this was a considerable sum. Having reluctantly put aside his laissez-faire dislike for relief, Bennett had then to decide how it would be distributed.

Hamilton, Ontario
April 6, 1934
To His Excellency The Rt. Hon. R.B.Bennett,
Parliament Buildings, Ottawa, Ontario.
Att: Mr. Bennett.

Dear Sir:

I am writing you as a last resource to see if I cannot, through your aid, obtain a position and at last, after a period of more than two years, support myself and enjoy again a little independence.

The fact is: this day I am faced with starvation and I see no possible means of counteracting or even averting it temporarily! ...

My father is a farmer at Pilot Mound, Manitoba and during the past years his income has been nil, so I cannot get any assistance from him. In fact, until I joined the list of unemployed I had been lending the folks at home my aid. To save my Mother from worries I have continually assured her that I am working and till the end I will save her from distress by sticking to this story.

When the Sanderson-Marwick Co., Ltd., went out of business I had saved a little money and there being no work there for me I came to Hamilton. Since then I have applied for every position that I heard about but there were always so many girls who applied that it was impossible to get work. So time went on and my clothing became very shabby. I was afraid to spend the little I had to replenish my wardrobe. Always the fear was before me that I would fail to get the position and then I would be without food and a roof over my head in a short time. Many prospective employers just glanced at my attire and shook their heads and more times than I care to mention I was turned away without a trial. I began to cut down on my food and I obtained a poor, but respectable, room at $1 per week.

First I ate three very light meals a day; then two and then one. During the past two weeks I have eaten only toast and drunk a cup of tea every other day. In the past fortnight I have lost twenty pounds and the result of this deprivation is that I am so very nervous that I could never stand a test along with one, two and three hundred girls. Through this very nervousness I was ruled out of a class yesterday. Today I went to an office for an examination and the examiner just looked me over and said; "I am afraid Miss, you are so awfully shabby I could never have you in my office." I was so worried and disappointed and frightened that I replied somewhat angrily: "Do you think clothes can be picked up in the streets?" "Well," he replied with aggravating insolence, "lots of girls find them there these days." ...

Day after day I pass a delicatessen and the food in the window looks oh, so good! So tempting and I'm so hungry!

Whiteway N.B.
Oct 7, 1935

> Right Hon. R.B. Bennett,
>
> Dear Sir:
>
> I am writing to ask you if you could or would help me. As I have a big family and all are going to school at present, but I will soon have to keep them home as they have no clothes and very little to eat. I have been working nearly all summer but my pay was so small that I barely got enough eat for them There are six children, ages from 15 to 7, four of which are boys, one boy 13, and in Grade Vlll. I would like for him to be in school till he get through. But with out help of some kind, I can't. I try every way to get work. There is no work and wages so small. All I can do is to get something to eat for my wife and children, and so many schoolbooks to buy, besides three of our children have one book between them. No way of getting any more The times have been so hard around here that everything one had is all worn out. This very night we haven't a baking of flour in our house. I have order some whether we will get it I can't tell. No work nor no money I think it is a terrible thing for a man that is able and willing to work he has to see his little children go to school hungry and half enough cloth on them to keep them warm. I always support the Consevative Goverment, and intend to do the same next Monday if nothing happen.
>
> I don't mind myself so bad. The children I am thinking most of now. I don't know how I am going to get clothes for them. If you help me I would be very thankful to you.
>
> I remain Yours Truly,
>
> Bruce Bass

For the most part, responsibility for distributing assistance was shifted to municipal governments. Bennett did not want the burden or the permanent federal responsibility of administering relief. Provincial governments were at first hesitant to ask for money for cities and municipalities because, under the constitution, they were obligated to share costs for relief. Municipalities did not have the human resources to administer the distribution. In this climate, relief distribution became a set of patchwork plans carried out by municipal governments, churches and private charitable organizations.

Most of the relief funds came in the form of public works projects. "Relief men" had to work for their assistance by working on municipal projects such as cutting grass and digging ditches. Waste, inefficiency, and general disorganization characterized many projects. Under the terms of the original Relief Act only $4 million of the $20 million was granted in the form of direct relief to Canadians. Direct relief was granted only in areas of the country where "make work" projects could not be organized.

Registering and qualifying for relief was often a difficult and humiliating process. To register for relief, men often had to join lines in public places where neighbours and acquaintances could see their desperation. To qualify for relief, men had to demonstrate destitution. In Ontario for example, men had to swear they did not own a radio or a telephone. Cars had to be sold, licence plates and driver's licences had to be turned in to confirm that no one on relief was driving a car. In some jurisdictions, Relief Inspectors would come to the recipient's home to ensure that relief was being obtained legitimately. Discoveries of liquor in the home, or surpluses of food or money meant the end of benefits. Citizens were encouraged to turn in cheats—and many complied. In some cities, a one to three year proof of residence was required as a measure to guard against the town becoming a

An emergency relief order for $10.00 worth of goods and fuel.

haven for the many transients flocking to major urban centres in search of work. In many instances these transients were deported from cities so they would not meet residence requirements.

Those who did qualify for relief hardly lived in luxury. In many places in Ontario, for example, relief came in the form of food vouchers, used clothes, food, heating fuel, and cash. These supplies usually fell well short of the minimal needs of recipients.

Depression on the Prairies

No region in Canada experienced greater hardship during the Depression than the prairies.[12] Residents in Alberta, Saskatchewan, and Manitoba faced the effects of record low prices for grain. To this was added a drought that was the most severe and prolonged in recorded history.

In the prairie provinces, the Depression became known as the "Dirty Thirties" with good reason. In the Paliser Triangle bounded by Melita, Manitoba; Lethbridge, Alberta; and North Battleford, Saskatchewan, the drought began in 1929 and lasted until mid-summer 1937. Especially in this region, sand and dust storms would blacken the sky for hours and sometimes days. The prolonged drought and wind often stripped the land of topsoil and made it non-arable. In regions of the prairies where drought was not as pronounced, rust (plant mold) or infestations of grasshoppers often destroyed the crops. Prairie grain production in the 1920s had averaged seventeen bushels per planted acre. In the 1930s the average dropped to 9.5 bushels per acre. In Saskatchewan, the most adversely affected province, the average yield dropped to 2.7 bushels per acre in 1937.

The onset of the drought came as the world price for grain fell in the Depression. Prices that had been set at $2 during the First World War fell to thrity-nine and three-eighths cents per bushel in 1932–33. This was the lowest price for grain in three hundred years. For the prairie economies that were largely based on grain production, the results were disastrous.

Even when prices began to recover in the later years of the Depression, crop failures ensured that farmers found no financial relief. Farmers were in dire financial straights. By the end of 1937, in Saskatchewan two out of three families on the farm were destitute.

Like their counterparts in urban centres, farmers had to appeal for relief. Farmers gathered in rural towns to collect food, clothes and fuel, animal feed, grain seed for

Losing the Farm: by 1937 two out of three farm families were destitute.

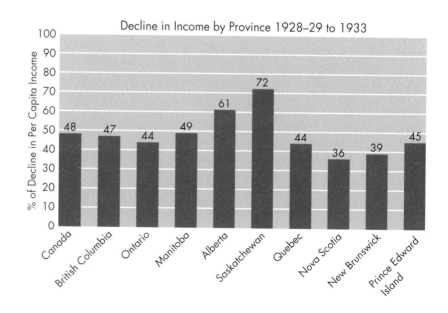

Decline in Income by Province 1928–29 to 1933

% of Decline in Per Capita Income

Canada	48
British Columbia	47
Ontario	44
Manitoba	49
Alberta	61
Saskatchewan	72
Quebec	44
Nova Scotia	36
New Brunswick	39
Prince Edward Island	45

planting, and farm supplies. Stories of children kept home from school because they had no shoes or clothes to wear were not exaggerations. Other children came to school in clothes fashioned out of material cut from cloth flour bags or burlap sacks. Often the plight of the rural teacher was no better. A letter from two teachers to the minister of education in Saskatchewan expressed anger and despair at the inadequacy of the government grant given to their local school board.

The hard fact was that the government didn't have money to send Mrs. Nickel and their employees. The federal government under both Bennett and King had largely let the provinces and municipalities deal with the financial crisis on their own. Prairie premiers made repeated requests of the federal government for increased money for relief and government fiscal help. Premier Jimmy Gardiner, the premier of Saskatchewan sent this telegram to R.B. Bennett in 1934. The pointed and repetitive nature of the telegram expresses his frustration with Bennett's unwillingness to take any substantial responsibility for the crisis in his drought stricken province.

Often, farmers could no longer afford the fuel and parts to maintain their automobiles.

Wymark Sask,
April 17, 1937
The Honourable J.W. Estey
Minister of Education,
Regina, Sask.

Dear Hon. Sir,

I am teaching in the Wymark S.D. 3265. This is my eighth year in this school. I am married and have a family. For some time I and the primary teacher, Miss Anna Gertzen, have received only the grant. As you know, that is not sufficient for family to live on and for a teacher to be well enough dressed to appear in a classroom. At the present time we have no money to buy meat and we are allowing our little boy one small cup of milk per day while we drink water. There is not a cent of money to purchase any clothes for summer. I had difficulty in managing to get a stamp for this letter. This not a hard luck story, but a statement of facts which will bear open investigation. I have been sick often but dared not go to a doctor on account of the expense.

Now, we have been told by our Board [of Education] that the grant together with a loan was to be paid every two months. This was to make a total of $30.00 per month for each teacher. At the end of Feb. we filled out a Departmental form, but this is all that has happened thus far. I wonder Hon. Sir, if action is as slow with regard to your own salary!

We were given reasons to hope that grants would be increased as from Jan. 1st, 1937. Now, however, it appears that this hope is shattered.

When the teachers' lot is considerably below the standard of living provided by the state to relief recipients, many of whom laugh at us because we are foolish enough to try make our own living and serve the state which shows by every action that it (the state) does not appreciate our services and sacrifices, then you cannot in all fairness blame teachers for becoming strike minded. When the social injustices are so glaring and when the stomach gets empty any human begin becomes desperate even though it may be against his principles. This is the case with us. I shall never favor a strike as long as I have a bare existence. I believe you know that this is the case with most teachers. That is why nothing is done.

If millions were needed to make powder to blow innocent beings to atoms, they [governments] would be immediately forthcoming. However, to relieve suffering and provide bread, there is no money. I am absolutely certain that if you were to live for one week under the conditions of the average teacher, you would become desperate and believe it impossible to endure. Oh God, what a world of injustice! Oh God, give us men and governments with a spirit of righteousness!

Yours sincerely,
V.E. Nickel

Miss A.M. Gertzen Primary Teacher[13]

Telegram copy - Canadian Pacific Telegraphs
Regina, Sask.
August 30, 1934

To Right Honourable R.B. Bennett
Prime Minister of Canada

Ottawa, Ont.

We think the Federal Government should assume fair share of cost of a problem national in its effects. We can and will handle provincial share but where it is possible for Federal Government which controls the financial policy of this country, to assist us in doing so by securing money for such purposes at lower rates of interest than we, we seek your cooperation. We ask you to loan us $5,000,000 to speed up the machinery pending an agreement as to respective obligations. Our Minister of Agriculture is already on his way to Ottawa under arrangement with Mr. Wier to negotiate this loan and adjust other matters. A personal audience might clarify the situation...

May we ask cooperation in meeting the needs of the drought area through prompt reply to the question. Will you loan us $5,000,000 at four and one-half percent to be used for this purpose?

(Sgd) James G. Gardiner

They had to resort to removing the engines from their cars and converting them to horse-drawn vehicles. These makeshift vehicles were nicknamed "Bennett Buggies" a sarcastic reference to the person many held responsible for their deprived circumstances. Two-wheeled versions of the new form of transportation were called "Anderson Carts" named after James Anderson, premier of Saskatchewan from 1929–34. In the end many farmers deeply in debt with no means to pay had to abandon their farms. Fifty thousand of them moved to less arid parkland and northern parts of the prairie provinces to start again. Two hundred fifty thousand left the region altogether.

By 1932 it was evident that the relief program was not working. More than 1.5 million Canadians were on some form of relief. Apart from the general concern about the hardship experienced by Canadians, a general alarm was raised about the young men who were unemployed and roaming the country looking for work.

A Bennett Buggy—a horse-drawn car.

An Anderson cart—the Saskatchewan model.

The Labour Camps

One of the most enduring images of the Depression is of young men hopping freight trains—"riding the rods"—across the country desperately searching for work. In most areas, priority for employment went to family men. Thwarted in their quest for employment these young men resorted to lining up for food in soup kitchens and relying on the charity of citizens. Especially in urban centres, unrest among the men began to grow.

Prime Minister Bennett watched the mounting social unrest with growing alarm. Unwilling to let this unrest fester any longer; Bennett began to search for solutions. Major General A.G.L. McNaughton, Chief of General Staff for the Department of National Defence, proposed the establishment of a number of work camps for young unemployed men. The camps, under the jurisdiction of The Department of National Defence, and in consultation with the minister of labour, would provide food, clothing, and supply a nominal wage of twenty cents a day. In return, the men would work as labourers on needed federal projects like land clearing, and building landing strips, airports, roads, military bases, and radio communications systems. On October 8, 1932, Bennett began to establish work camps around the country. To save money the work camps were often located in existing military camps. Most of the camps were located in isolated areas, far removed from urban centres where they feared the young men would cause unrest. MacNaughton and Bennett were hoping to obtain much more than building projects from the camps. MacNaughton hoped that in building "morale through work" the men would learn the habits of regular work and diligence that could be of use should this generation be called upon to fight in a conflict similar to the First World War. The more pressing goal of the camps was to relieve the congestion of the young and unemployed from the cities and stem the growing tide of radical unrest.

From the beginning, the labour camp organizers were plagued by a lack of funds. The Conservative government had promised taxpayers that costs for

Moving (a) house on the Prairies in the dirty thirties. Many families moved north to make a new start.

A 1930s work camp—an incubator for radicalism.

Camp Workers' Union (RCWU), associated with the Communist Party, organized active protests. The government responded by deducting wages of the protesters and expelling the ringleaders. It became apparent that rather than improving morale and diffusing unrest, the camps had become an incubator for radicalism. From 1934 onward, the RCWU began organizing protests for decent wages in the camps. The appeal was particularly successful in British Columbia, where discontent was very pronounced.[18] It was here that the On-to-Ottawa Trek began.

care of the men would be kept at $1.00 per person per day. But even as costs rose to $1.30 per day, it was hardly enough to sustain a reasonable working or living standard. The government economized by cutting back on machinery and tools for the work projects.[15] This meant that men worked long days at demanding physical labour. The foremen and the bosses on the job were often severe. In many cases the food budget was inadequate and the cooks were not well trained.[16] At a wage of twenty cents a day most men could not save any money and when they left the camps they were as poor as when they had entered. This raises the question: If conditions in the camp were so harsh, why were men inclined to enter the camps at all?[17] The government always insisted that the enrollment in the camps was voluntary, but the reality was that most of the men had no choice. Unemployed young men were often refused relief and expelled from cities. The camps were their last and only resort. As time passed, MacNaughton's and Bennett's hope for an improved sense of morale was never fulfilled.

Despair soon led to unrest in the camps. In the four-year term of the camps, 359 strikes, riots, and disturbances occurred. In many camps, the Relief

The On-to-Ottawa Trek

In April of 1935 over three thousand relief camp workers converged in Vancouver. For weeks they conducted protests and demonstrations, demanding work and fair wages. Following a riot and a standoff between the workers and security forces, over eighteen hundred men boarded trains and headed for Ottawa. Mayor McGeer, fearing more riots and threats to his city, ensured that the police and the Canadian Pacific Railway quickly helped the men board the trains. Led by Arthur Evans, the men, many of them used to riding the rods, headed east.[19] The goal of the On-to-Ottawa Trek was to take their protest to the seat of federal power in Canada. Few of the leaders actually thought they would be allowed to enter the capital. Nevertheless, they were confident their protest would not be ignored. As the trek moved east, men from towns, cities, and work camps joined the trek. On June 14, 1935 the trek, now comprised of two thousand men, converged upon Regina. Three hundred more men from the work camp in Dundurn, Saskatchewan joined the trek there. By now, Bennett had determined that the trek would go no further. After heated discussions with two federal ministers in

ON TO OTTAWA

The Relief Camp Strikers will leave Regina via C.P.R. Freight

Monday, June 17th
at approx. 10 p.m.

The Federal Government have declared an embargo on our leaving Regina by the same means by which we came.

Only the mass support of Regina Citizens will force the Authorities to keep their hands off us on our way to Ottawa.

We call upon every citizen who supports us in our fight against Forced Slave Labor to assemble at the C.P.R. freight yards between Albert and Broad Street

Monday, June 17th from 10 p.m. until we leave

We extend to Regina Citizens our heartiest thanks for their splendid support in this vital issue.

Publicity Committee,
Relief Camp Strikers.

How did an organized protest turn deadly?

3. That a democratically elected committee of relief workers be recognized by the authorities.
4. Relief camps be taken out of the control of the Department of National Defence.
5. A genuine system of social and unemployment insurance in accordance with the provisions of the Workers' Social and Unemployment Insurance Bill [be provided].
6. That all workers be guaranteed their democratic right to vote.

The prime minister responded by saying that the allotment of twenty cents a day was a gift from the government—any more could not be fiscally justified. He insisted that the conditions in the work camps were adequate and that Evans and his followers were communist inspired radicals ready to break down a system of law and order in the country. The acrimonious meeting ended in a stalemate, and no concessions were granted. Evans and his delegation returned to Regina.

The Regina Riots, July 1, 1935.

Regina, Evans and seven of his men agreed to a meeting with the prime minister in Ottawa.

Evans and his delegation received a cool reception from the prime minister as they presented their work camp demands.

The Six Demands of the Ottawa Trekkers

1. That work with wages be provided at a minimum rate of 50 cents an hour for unskilled labour; union rates for all skilled labour. Such work to be on the basis of a five-day week, six-hour working day, and minimum of twenty days' work per month.
2. All workers in relief camps and government projects be covered by the Compensation Act. Adequate first aid supplies on all relief jobs.

City of Regina---Police Department
PROVINCE OF SASKATCHEWAN
CANADA

WANTED FOR MURDER
$2000.00 REWARD

The Province of Saskatchewan and the City of Regina each offer a REWARD of $1000.00, making a total sum of $2000.00 for information leading to the conviction of any person or persons responsible for the murder of DETECTIVE CHARLES MILLAR of the Regina City Police Department, who was killed about 8.30 p.m. on July 1st, 1935, when assisting in suppressing a riot of Relief Camp Strikers in this City.

According to witnesses Detective Millar was attacked by three men with clubs, receiving a fractured skull, from the effects of which he died within a few minutes.

DESCRIPTION OF SUSPECTS

No. 1. About 5 ft. 10 inches; slender, with tapering shoulders; medium complexion; 165 or 170 lbs.; clean shaven; wore a dirty white or fawn colored shirt; no braces, vest or coat; peaked cap.

No. 2. Young man; fat face; mouse colored hair which was rather long; wore grey suit and khaki shirt.

No. 3. About 5 ft. 10 inches; 155 lbs.; clean shaven; dark red hair; fair complexion; wore a dark shirt and grey and black tweed trousers.

Referring to our CIRCULARS of AUGUST 9th and SEPTEMBER 1st, 1933, regarding the MURDER of CONSTABLE GEORGE A. LENHARD of this Department. The murderers of Constable Lenhard have not yet been brought to justice. The Province of Saskatchewan and the City of Regina are still prepared to pay the REWARDS of $1000.00 each (total of $2000.00) offered in this case.

In each of these cases the Board of Police Commissioners for the City of Regina reserves the right to apportion the reward should there be more than one claimant.

Any information obtained should be forwarded without delay to the undersigned.

Regina, Saskatchewan,
October 18th, 1935.

MARTIN BRUTON,
Chief Constable.

Had the authorities over reacted?

Upon their return to Regina, Evans and the trekkers faced a dilemma. They knew it would be difficult to make their way to Ottawa, yet they were determined not to give in and return to the camps. On July 1, 1935, Evans had organized a rally at Market Square in the city centre. As RCMP officers and city police began to move through the crowd to arrest the leaders of the trek, gunshots were heard, and a riot ensued. After hours of violence one policeman was dead, and approximately one hundred protesters were arrested. Eight, including Evans, were convicted and sent to jail. The men left Regina with some returning to the camps, and others going home or setting off for other destinations. Bennett and his authorities had successfully derailed the On-to-Ottawa Trek.

Bennett's apparent victory in Regina was a hollow one. Public opinion, already strained by the continuing hardship of the Depression, was dismayed at the violent suppression of the trek.

Confronting the Depression

When the world markets began to collapse after 1929, countries raised tariffs on imported goods in an attempt to protect their industries from foreign competition. Canada too placed tariffs on imports. The United States, Canada's main destination of exports, instituted the Smoot-Hawley Tariff on foreign goods in 1930, that placed tariffs and duties ranging from 30 percent to 60 percent on a wide range of foreign imports. For Canada, the Smoot-Hawley Tariff had devastating results.

In July 1932, Bennett hosted the Imperial Economic Conference in Ottawa. At the conference, Bennett proposed that Britain tax the products of non-commonwealth nations and allow the import of Canadian products without tariffs. In this way Canada could export its raw materials to commonwealth countries, (principally Britain) thus providing relief from the devastating consequences of American tariffs on the Canadian economy. Bennett, however, offered little to the commonwealth nations in return. He offered a list of products generated by the Canadian Manufacturing Association that would be exempt from Canadian tariffs. Upon examination, the British found few items of real trading value. Britain perceived that Canada wanted huge tariff concessions while retaining tariffs on most manufacturing items that would be of benefit for British manufacturing exporters. When combined with Bennett's abrasive and aggressive personal style, the British and the rest of the Commonwealth nations left without a significant agreement on tariffs.[20] Britain did grant preferential treatment of Canadian products like lumber, wheat, and apples as well as some meat and dairy products. For the most part, however, Canadian manufacturers continued to suffer under high tariffs. Bennett's half-hearted attempt at free trade came to an abrupt end, and Canadians were left without any significant improvement in trade and economic growth.

Bennett's New Deal

In the early years of the Depression, R.B. Bennett had insisted the economy would eventually recover on its own. He insisted that state intervention would only distort the free market economy and hamper economic recovery. But as the election year of 1935 approached Bennett knew he had to change course or face political ruin. In January 1935, Bennett addressed the nation in a series of radio broadcasts. Astonished Canadians listened as the Conservative prime minister announced that the old Toryism was dead, that the free competition in the market place they had known had lost its place and had to be replaced by government regulation and control. He proposed a "New Deal" fashioned after Franklin Delano Roosevelt's in the United States. In this excerpt from Bennett's "New Deal" speech that he delivered to the nation over the radio, Bennett endorsed a proposed a government program of unemployment insurance.

> I hold the view that if we are to have equality of social and political conditions throughout this land we must have equality in economic conditions as well. Labour in one part of Canada must not be at a disadvantage with labour in another part. That is wrong socially and it is foolish in a business sense, for it clearly creates a disequilibrium with the nation's industrial life...no man must be left to the uncertainties of private charity or to the humiliation of government gratuity. He must not be unemployed in the old, hateful sense of the word. As a member of economic society, he should have security—provided always that he is willing to work. That is a condition precedent. For our reformed economic system

is designed to encourage industry, not idleness.... This security [against unemployment] will be provided by means of unemployment insurance. For this reason, I believe in unemployment insurance, not as a means of bolstering up a faulty system, but as a means of bolstering up a sound modern one...[21]

Web Connection

www.mcgrawhill.ca/links/definingcanada
Go to the Web site above to read Prime Minister Bennett's 'New Deal' radio speech to the Canadian people.

Government money flowed into New Deal programs such as:

- The Prairie Farm Rehabilitation Act – to help restore and preserve farm land devastated by drought
- The Canadian Wheat Board – to administer the sale of grain and promote higher prices for wheat
- The Natural Products Marketing Board – to institute marketing boards ensuring that farmers received higher prices for their products than the free market could provide

While thwarted in the courts, Bennett also proposed legislation to pave the way for unemployment insurance and national health insurance. These were added to the Bank of Canada Act that created a central bank to regulate credit and currency in the best interests of the country.[22] This government agency, amongst other things, could ensure interest rates were not set at exorbitantly high levels for those in debt with little means to repay the principal let alone the interest. The central bank could increase the money supply thereby increasing the money flow and stimulating the economy. Former allies in conservative political and financial circles decried this move to government interference in the economy. But Bennett calculated that the support of the vast majority of Canadians was electorally more important than maintaining the good will of his former allies.

Canadians disillusioned with Bennett's handling of the Depression distrusted his newfound embrace of the New Deal. In papers across the country, citizens voiced their lack of trust in what appeared as Bennett's last minute attempts to save his political career. Just before the election, this editorial appeared in *The Globe and Mail*

NEED AND OPPORTUNITY
It is impossible not to feel profound sympathy for the Right Hon. R.B. Bennett, Prime Minister of Canada for the past five years. With eager – almost indefatigable – zeal he has labored ...at the task of national administration, only to see his projects fail dismally an meet the needs of the situation. Yet today, seeking another mandate from his fellow citizens, Mr. Bennett apparently nothing new to offer....

Early this year, toward the end of his term...in a series of radio addresses he stirred the public imagination by assurances that, at last, he proposed to do things that he believed would be effective – things that were radical, even revolutionary. He would introduce legislation providing for important social and economic reforms – in fact he was about to revise and reform the whole capitalist system. Again Mr. Bennett promised too much and performed too little.

Mr. Bennett is back on the radio again, In his first radio talk [of the 1935 election campaign] he promises the policies of the past five years – policies under which agriculture and industry have languished the burden of taxation and debt has grown and unemployment and distress have assumed tragic proportions. It will not do.[23]

In the election campaign of 1935 his opponent, Mackenzie King, made few promises. One exception was that he vowed to disband the work camps. On election day, October 14, 1930 the Conservatives lost three-fifths of the vote capturing only 40 seats as compared with Mackenzie King's Liberals who took 125 seats.

Mackenzie King's new government did adopt some of the New Deal policies proposed by Bennett. But as a general rule King's government was cautious and moved slowly. Canadians would have to wait

another five years before the effects of the Depression began to subside. Anyone looking for innovative ways to deal with the Depression had to look beyond the federal government to new parties and movements for inspiration.

Social and Political Responses

Federal politicians were not the only ones looking for solutions to the Depression crisis. A variety of new social movements and political parties emerged to confront this new and desperate era. Many of these movements were inspired by conditions in specific regions of the country.

The Social Credit Party

One of the most distinctive responses arose in Alberta with the formation of the Social Credit Party. At the heart of this new party was William Aberhart, a teacher and fundamentalist Christian preacher with a radio show. Aberhart's brand of Christianity emphasized a literal and careful reading of the Bible to interpret and predict world events. Aberhart showed no apparent interest in politics until the Depression.

For Aberhart, the heart of the problem facing Canadians in the 1930s was that there was poverty in the midst of plenty. Even though companies had the ability to produce a surplus of products, the poverty-stricken consumer had no money to buy them. Bankers refused to give loans or credit to common persons because they were a poor risk. Aberhart claimed that the government should extend "social credit" to consumers. In this way surplus products could be purchased by the people, the standard of living would improve, and manufacturing would be revived.

Aberhart soon incorporated Social Credit ideas into his religious radio broadcasts. His broadcasts were carried by a number of radio stations whose signals reached devoted listeners in Alberta, Saskatchewan, British Columbia, and the western United States. He organized sixteen hundred study groups around the province to help the people learn more about the Social Credit brand of economic salvation. He simplified the message of Social Credit so everyone could understand. After his ideas were rebuffed by the standing provincial government Aberhart decided to run for office. During a heated election campaign Aberhart refused to explain the details of his Social Credit proposals. He insisted that people had to have faith in Social Credit economic principles. The United Farmers of Alberta (U.F.A.) government was reeling after a scandal in which Premier Brownlee had been accused of having an extramarital affair. Aberhart railed against the immorality of his opponents. He appealed to longstanding grievances against central Canadian financial domination of the province insisting he would deal with the "fifty big shots" whose greed was ruining the economy of the province and the country.[24] He promised a $25 per month dividend to each Albertan to make up for their lack of purchasing power. Aberhart's religious-political message in the middle of the Depression had wide appeal. He was elected to office in a landslide. Aberhart and his party swept to power on August 22, 1935 capturing fifty-six of sixty-three seats. Two months later Albertans elected fifteen of seventeen Social Credit members to the House of Commons in the federal election.

The morning after the provincial election, eager supporters formed lines in front of City Hall in Calgary, expecting to receive the promised $25 dividend. It never came. Aberhart and his government became engaged in a long and largely unsuccessful struggle to implement their election promises. In 1936 the government issued "prosperity certificates" to be used by Albertans. This initiative was put into place to deliver on the election promise of the $25 dividend. The certificates, printed by the government of Alberta, could be used as a substitute for cash to compensate for the people's lack of purchasing power. The plan, however, failed as boards of trade and government agencies would not accept the certificates as a substitute for cash. The federal government did not even allow the certificates to be used in paying taxes. The scheme was shelved shortly after its introduction. Another form of the plan was revived in 1936 when Albertans were promised a dividend in return for their signing of a covenant in which they agreed to "cooperate most heartily" with the government. Seventy percent of Alberta's population signed the covenant. No dividends were issued.

Aberhart's more vital legislative plans also met with defeat. In August of 1937 the legislature passed the Credit of Alberta Regulation Act that shielded the government from any legal action by the banks or bankers and effectively put the banks under provincial control. The federal government intervened rendering the legislation null and void. Attempts at repealing the disallowance failed. In the end, eleven important pieces of legislation were disallowed by the federal government between 1937 and 1941. For the Social Credit and their followers, the disallowances and the federal hostility to their policies were just another example of the anti-western attitudes residing in central Canada. Albertan's resentment of central Canadian government and financial interests led to a "hands-off Alberta" sentiment.

Expression of Identity

WILLIAM "BIBLE BILL" ABERHART (1878-1943)

William "Bible Bill" Aberhart was a truly unique, western-Canadian, reform politician. Originally an educator and radio evangelist, Aberhart headed the world's first Social Credit government as premier of Alberta from 1935–43.

Born and educated in Ontario, Aberhart moved his family to Calgary in 1910, where he served as a school principal for twenty-five years. He spent each Sunday preaching sermons in a Baptist church, becoming popular with the congregation. Aberhart identified with fundamentalist movements, which embroiled him in controversy with the main church. As a result of the disagreement, in 1929 Aberhart founded his own sect, the Bible Institute Baptist Church. "Bible Bill" was one of the first preachers to realize the possibilities of radio and began broadcasting Sunday afternoon services in 1925.

The Great Depression was especially devastating for the farm-based Alberta economy. The inability of federal and provincial political parties to offer solutions for Depression hardships drove Aberhart to seek alternative remedies. He became interested in the "social credit" monetary theories of Major C.H. Douglas, a Scottish engineer. Douglas believed that conventional capitalism, because of the private control of credit, would lead to a chronic lack of mass purchasing power. For society to function properly, it had to obtain financial control by putting wealth into as many hands as possible.

When Bible Bill took to the airwaves, he used his fervor to preach social credit doctrine. His broadcasts provided a beacon of hope to many Depression-weary Albertans. Aberhart modified social credit doctrine into a proposal that each citizen receive a $25 per month basic dividend, which Aberhart was convinced would jump-start the ailing economy. At the time, for most Albertans, $25 was a phenomenal amount, and his ideas drew great popular interest.

Aberhart built a grassroots movement, the Alberta Social Credit League, to promote his ideas, and his own Prophetic Bible Institute in Calgary became headquarters for a new economic gospel.

Between 1932 and 1935, William Aberhart and the Social Credit League tried to persuade the governing United Farmers of Alberta party to adopt social credit policy.

When the party showed little interest, Aberhart took the League into the political arena. He organized Alberta's Social Credit Party, and its representatives contested the 1935 provincial election.

In September 1935, the Social Credit took fifty-six of the sixty-three seats in the Alberta legislature. Although Aberhart had not run as a candidate, he was appointed premier. On November 3, 1935, Aberhart was elected by acclamation in a by-election.

Once in office, Aberhart found there was not enough money in the Alberta treasury to meet the monthly payroll—never mind give $25 to every citizen. Aberhart's answer was that Alberta should have its own money. However, the Supreme Court declared that the certificates his government produced were not legal tender. Aberhart argued that the BNA Act did not give the provinces enough power, especially in times of emergency, an issue that is still argued about in federal-provincial debates today.

William Aberhat died in office in 1943 and was succeeded by Ernest C. Manning, the first graduate of the Calgary Prophetic Bible Institute and father of Preston, who later founded the Reform Party. Aberhart's Social Credit Party went on to govern Alberta for thirty-five years and eight months (1935–71), a record that has never been surpassed.

"Bible Bill" Aberhart– who were his successors?

Despite all of the federal-provincial disturbance caused by Aberhart's Social Credit, the party did go on to provide an attractive political alternative for Albertans. The Social Credit went on to win nine successive victories in Alberta until 1971. In later years, Ernest C. Manning, father of Preston Manning, succeeded Aberhart. He continued to promote a mix of fundamentalist Christianity and politics. Nevertheless, Ernest C. Manning's economic policies lacked the radicalism and were much more acceptable to the banks and the federal government. Social Credit went on to win provincial elections in British Columbia and continued to send members to the Canadian parliament from western Canada and Quebec for years to come.

The Cooperative Commonwealth Federation

Another political movement born of the Depression provided a distinctive alternative to Social Credit. While Social Credit criticized Canadian finance and credit policies, it retained its faith in the capitalist system. With the necessary adjustments, capitalism and consumerism would put an end to the hardships of the Depression. The Cooperative Commonwealth Federation (CCF), however, provided a different set of proposals for the symptoms of the Depression. The party was formed in 1932 at a political convention in Calgary. Representatives of farmers groups, labour unions, socialist party members, and socialist intellectuals were all present at the founding convention. In their first annual convention in Regina the party passed the Regina Manifesto. Crafted principally by Frank Underhill, an influential University of Toronto historian and political commentator, the Regina Manifesto espoused many of the principles of democratic socialism. Democratic Socialists rejected the non-democratic nature of communism, which supported revolution. Change had to be instituted in response to democratic will. The CCF did support the government takeover of key capitalist industries. In government hands, these industries would ensure that the interests of the people would be protected. The manifesto also promoted the welfare state and advocated state-sponsored medical care, unemployment insurance, and adequate levels of welfare. The first leader was J.S. Woodsworth, a labour M.P. who was a Christian socialist and pacifist.

The new party had limited success at first. In the 1935 federal election, they garnered 8.9 percent of the vote and seven seats. While not forming a government in the 30s, they did provide authentic opposition to government in many parts of the country. The party has never been a serious contender to form a government in federal politics. At this level, they have had more success pressuring governments to adopt policies like medicare, social housing, workplace protection, and other social programs. At the provincial party level they have met with more success. In Saskatchewan, in 1944 Tommy Douglas led the party to the first socialist electoral victory in North America. Subsequently, the CCF and its successor the New Democratic Party (NDP) have elected provincial governments in Ontario, Manitoba and British Columbia.

The Union Nationale

In Quebec, much of the early momentum for change in the Depression came from the church. The Ecole sociale populaire, a Jesuit-led organization, promoted social reforms in contradistinction to the establishment-oriented Liberal government. While remaining staunchly antisocialist they proposed programs to regulate monopolies and improve conditions for farmers, workers, and the destitute. Catholics within the Liberal government found the message of the church compelling. A breakaway group in the party formed the Action liberale nationale. Seizing an opportunity, Maurice Duplessis, the leader of the provincial Conservative Party, formed an alliance with the liberale nationale in 1935. The newly formed Union Nationale lost the next provincial election by a slim margin. But shortly thereafter

TOWARDS THE DAWN!

they forced the scandal-ridden Liberal Party to resign and call an election. The Union Nationale won decisively, garnering seventy-six of ninety seats.

Soon after gaining power, Duplessis displaced the liberale nationale members and dropped most of the reform platform on which they had campaigned. Duplessis soon became an ally of big business. Workers found little relief from the Union Nationale in the 1930s. Duplessis did maintain support for farmers, but his strongest base of support was to come from small town and rural Quebec. Duplessis adopted the anticommunist stance of the Church, instituting the Padlock Act (Act Respecting Communistic Propaganda) in 1937. The law allowed the Attorney General of Quebec to padlock or close for one year any building that had been used to propagate communism or Bolshevism. Any "red" propaganda materials could be seized and destroyed by the government. Those involved in the printing or distributing of the material could be arrested and held without appeal for a year. The Padlock Act had a chilling effect on civil liberties in

Quebec. It was also used to intimidate labour groups who were often treated as radical organizations by the Union Nationale and its supporters. It was not until 1957 that the Supreme Court of Canada finally ruled the Act unconstitutional.

Maurice Duplessis and the Union Nationale come to power.

Canadian Leaders

JAMES SHAVER WOODSWORTH: THE "CONSCIENCE OF CANADA"

J. S. Woodsworth was a clergyman, social worker, labour leader, Member of Parliament, and the first leader of the Cooperative Commonwealth Federation (CCF). His career was distinguished by concern for less-advantaged Canadians. During his time in Parliament, he was known as the "conscience of Canada."

Experiences during his time at Oxford University in England forged Woodsworth's strong socialist outlook. He worked helping the poor of East End London and witnessed the grim results of industrial capitalism.

After returning to Canada, Woodsworth worked with immigrant slum-dwellers in Winnipeg, running a mission where he witnessed the inequality of Canadian industrial society. Woodsworth saw that Winnipeg's social inequality problems were, to a significant extent, centred around the large number of immigrants who had integrated into a new country. He focused the mission's work on helping immigrants adjust to Canadian life. As a result of this perspective, he became the foremost expert on Canadian immigration and one of the country's leading sociologists. In such books as *Strangers Within Our Gates* (1909) and *My Neighbour* (1911), he wrote passionately about the desperate poverty faced by working-class immigrants. Woodsworth expanded his social research work as secretary of the Canadian Welfare League and later as director of the three prairie provinces' joint Bureau of Social Research.

When Canada entered World War I in 1914, Woodsworth faced a crisis of conscience. He was adamantly pacifist, seeing war as the result of capitalist and imperialist competition. As well, he strongly objected to churches becoming places to recruit soldiers. In 1916, he decided that he must document his opposition to conscription. In response to his protest writings, the federal government shut down the Bureau of Social Research, eliminating Woodsworth's

J. S. Woodsworth was known as the "conscience of Canada."

position, and in 1918 he resigned his ministry to protest church support of the war. Now jobless, he was forced to work as a longshoreman in Vancouver to feed his family.

Prior to the Winnipeg General Strike of 1919 Woodsworth came to the city to speak and write for a labour newspaper. During the strike he was arrested and charged with seditious libel for his editorials. Now viewed as a popular leader among labour groups, Woodworth organized the Manitoba Independent Labour Party and became increasingly committed to creating a fairer society. He was elected to the House of Commons in 1921, representing Winnipeg North Centre—a seat he held until his death in 1942.

Canadian Leaders

JAMES SHAVER WOODSWORTH: THE "CONSCIENCE OF CANADA"

When the Great Depression struck in the 1930s, Woodsworth joined forces with various labour and socialist groups to found a new federalist party, the Cooperative Commonwealth Federation. At Regina in 1933, this new party adopted democratic socialist policies outlined in the Regina Manifesto.

Woodsworth's uncompromising pacifism was again tested when Canada entered World War II. He wanted to withhold CCF support for Canada's entry into the conflict. A majority of CCF members, however, voted against their leader. Although Woodsworth's position was highly unpopular as Hitler invaded European countries, several colleagues admired his integrity. Prime Minister Mackenzie King interrupted a speech to address Woodsworth directly:

There are few men in this Parliament for whom, in some particulars, I have greater respect than the leader of the Co-operative Commonwealth Federation. I admire him in my heart, because time and again he has had the courage to say what lay on his conscience, regardless of what the world might think of him. A man of that calibre is an ornament to any Parliament.

Woodsworth paid a political price for steadfast commitment to his pacifist ideals. Though he won his Winnipeg seat for the last time in 1940, it was with a greatly reduced majority.

In the long term, J.S. Woodsworth is best remembered for the new ideas proposed by the party he led and helped found, which would go on to become the New Democratic Party, for bring focus to, and solving many of Canada's challenging social problems.

In all, Duplessis served as premier of Quebec for fifteen years. In historical terms, Duplessis' reputation as an authoritarian traditionalist is tempered by his advocacy of the rights of Quebec in Confederation, and the abundance of public works projects sponsored by his government. As for the Depression, little that he did had an ameliorating effect for Quebec's economy or its people.

The Maritimes and the Antigonish Movement

The Maritimes also generated their own remedy for the Depression. Before the Depression, two Catholic priests, James Tomkins and Moses Cody, at St. Francis Xavier University in Antigonish, Nova Scotia had begun to advocate for the needs of ordinary people. Their solution was to build organizations like credit unions and cooperatives to sell seafood or farm products. When farmers and fishers gained greater control over the marketing of their products or lending institutions, their standard of living was enhanced. Like other populist movements of the thirties, the Antigonish Movement resisted revolution and anti-capitalist ideology. Their goal was to alleviate the economic hardship for ordinary people. In this they achieved considerable success. In the '30s cooperative organizations would spring up all over the Maritime provinces of Canada.

The Communist Party

The small, but active Communist Party in Canada nurtured the seeds of discontent. While going effectively unheeded in Canada before and after the Depression, the Communist Party, under the leadership of Tim Buck, found a receptive audience of young men who, despite their concentrated efforts, could not find work or wages. In this desperate environment, it was not hard to convince young men that the capitalist system was not able to provide for even their most basic needs. Even though the federal government had officially outlawed the Communist Party in 1931, their numbers and activism began to take root and grow. Under growing fear from the Canadian government, Tim Buck and seven other leaders were jailed from 1932 until 1934. Resolute and well organized, the communists recruited members and organized protests, hunger marches and strikes that could not be ignored by the government of the day.

Aboriginal Peoples in the Depression

During the 1930s, the plight of Aboriginal Peoples throughout Canada reached distressing levels. Government did nothing or little more than the bare minimum of fulfilling duties outlined in the treaties. But as the Depression worsened, services such as public healthcare in the north, were cut back to almost non-existent levels. While the birth rate was almost twice as high as other Canadian rates, the death rate was four times as high among Aboriginals. Even before the worst years of the Depression in 1929, the Canadian mortality rate was ten per thousand. Among Aboriginal Peoples, however, it was 39.7 per thousand.[25]

Conditions for the Métis were even worse. No treaties had been signed between the Métis and the Canadian government, which meant that even the few provisions that the government made to other Aboriginal Peoples were not granted to the Métis. Conditions became so bad that in 1934, the Alberta government set up a provincial commission to look into the situation of the Métis, and their findings were shocking. Close to 90 percent of the Métis population was infected with tuberculosis, paralysis, blindness, or syphilis and the entire population was in danger of extinction. In response to the report, the government set up six Métis colonies and provided schools and healthcare, but did not give the reserves any means to survive economically.[26]

Residential Schools

The area in Aboriginal affairs where the government did remain active was in the continuation of residential schools. As historian J.M. Bumsted writes,

> Between the wars, apart from handouts guaranteed by treaty and legislation, government concerned itself with native peoples chiefly by encouraging the establishment of boarding schools off the reservations. The number of native children enrolled in such schools was the chief statistic proudly publicized by Indian Affairs...[27]

In 1930, the number of residential schools for First Nations people reached an all time high of eighty. Residential schools were located in every province and territory in Canada except New Brunswick and Prince Edward Island. Most were located in northern Ontario and Quebec, as well as in the western provinces and territories. The schools were run by federal and provincial governments in partnership with religious organizations such as the Catholic, Anglican, Presbyterian, and United Churches.

The explicit aim of the residential schools was to assimilate Aboriginal children into the civic-religious values and ways of "typical" Canadians. To accomplish this, residential schools were often located far removed from the reservations of the students. Students were not allowed to speak their own languages, and the curriculum in the schools ignored or discouraged the study of Aboriginal culture or history. Instead, the emphasis was on learning manual labour skills for males and home-making skills for females. Living conditions were challenging, with the clothing and food provided by the schools usually inadequate. Many students experienced physical and sexual abuse at the hands of school teachers and administrators. Students were uprooted from their families and their communities, and stripped of their cultures and religions. The short- and long-term effects that residential schools had on Aboriginal Peoples were devastating. It would take another sixty years before the last residential school in Canada was closed.

Confronting the Outsider

During the Depression, recently arrived immigrants to Canada often faced more difficulties than others. They were treated as outsiders who were draining already stretched resources away from "more established" Canadian citizens of British origin. These outsiders faced discrimination. In 1931, eighty-three of the 150 Chinese applicants who applied for relief in Calgary received $1.12 per week as compared to non-Chinese who received $2.50. After prolonged protests and demonstrations, the weekly amount for the Chinese rose to $2.12 per week in 1937.

Many immigrants faced an even greater threat in the 1930s. Sections 40 and 41 of the Immigration Act, provided for the deportation of unemployable recipients of relief. Especially in the west, government officials associated immigrants from central and

Residential schools have left a painful legacy, still being felt by Aboriginal people today.

COUNTRY ADMITTING JEWISH REFUGEES FROM NAZIS 1933–45	NUMBER OF REFUGEES
UNITED STATES	240 000
GREAT BRITAIN	85 000
CHINA	25 000
ARGENTINA	25 000
BRAZIL	25 000
COLOMBIA AND MEXICO (combined)	40 000
CANADA	5 000*

* THE ACTUAL NUMBER WAS BETWEEN FOUR AND FIVE THOUSAND.

southern Europe with radical activities. These were prime candidates for deportation. In Alberta, between 1930 and 1934, a total of 2547 immigrants were deported from the country. Between 1930 and 1933, twenty-three thousand immigrants on relief or those accused of radical political activities were deported. This had a terrible impact on those who were returned to their countries of origin in the midst of the Depression. Facing the prospect of potential deportation, many of the immigrants who remained in Canada were discouraged from applying for relief.

Even before the Depression, Canada was beginning to discourage immigration. Canadian officials believed that the once wide-open west was filled with enough settlers. By the mid-twenties immigration levels began to decline. This trend became even more pronounced in the 1930s when Canadian officials became convinced that the country could no longer "support" immigrants. Immigration levels dropped from a yearly average of 124 000 in the 1920s to 20 000 in the 1930s. In this time of reduced immigration, some immigrants were less welcome than others. This was especially true for prospective Jewish immigrants.

When Adolph Hitler assumed power in 1933, he soon embarked upon a systematic persecution of Jewish citizens in Germany. Thousands of Jewish

people became refugees, fleeing Germany to other countries in Europe.[28] The number of refugees increased as the threat of war drew nearer. Jews sought refuge in countries outside of Europe. The United States and Canada were natural destinations for Jewish refugees since prior to the mid-1920s, these countries had been prime destinations for thousands of immigrants from Europe.

Canada proved to be far from a welcoming land for Jewish refugees in the 1930s. Frederick Blair was a civil servant and director of the immigration branch of the Canadian government from 1936 to 1943. Blair held strong anti-Semitic views and acted upon them. Many in the government and the opposition shared his opinion. As far as Blair and many government officials were concerned, when it came to the issue of admitting Jewish refugees "none was too many."[29] In the end, Canada did admit some refugees, but its efforts were minute in comparison to other more accepting countries.

Canadian Culture in the Depression

In the 1920s, Canadian artists began to explore abstract and non-objective painting. While this continued into the 1930s, as the Depression became

Longshoremen by Miller Brittain (1923–1968) is a portrayal of unemployed longshoremen in his home town, Saint John NB.

more severe many artists began to bring realism back into their art. Artists such as Leonard Hutchinson, Miller Brittain, and Carl Schaefer began to draw upon the increasing plight of Canadians during the 1930s as inspiration. Images of the unemployed, foreclosed farms, and helplessness became the new subjects for many artists in Canada.[30]

To escape the trials of the Depression, reading became a more popular form of recreation. Romance and adventure stories allowed many Canadians the chance to escape the life of poverty and despair that surrounded them. As with art, however, realism began to penetrate Canadian novels as authors reflected on the world around them.

Irene Baird wrote *Waste Heritage* in 1939, which centred around the unemployed and labour unrest in Depression-era Vancouver.[31] Morley Callaghan, who would go on to be one of Canada's most prominent literary figures of the twentieth

century, wrote seven novels during the Depression: *It's Never Over* (1930), *No Man's Meat* (1931), *A Broken Journey* (1932), *Such is My Beloved*, (1934), *They Shall Inherit the Earth* (1935), *Now That April's Here and Other Stories* (1936), and *More Joy In Heaven* (1937).[32] In Quebec, realism also crept into literature when Philippe Panneton (under the pseudonym of Ringuet) wrote *Trente Arpents (Thirty Acres)*. Instead of glorifying the rural life of the Quebec habitant, *Trente Arpents* captured the reality of the growing numbers of Quebec farmers leaving the countryside for factory work in the city.[33]

Radio became the dominant player in Canadian culture during the 1930s. Foster Hewitt and "Hockey Night in Canada" continued to be a favourite for Canadians. The Canadian Broadcasting Corporation, formed in 1936, also provided popular radio programs such as "The Happy Gang" and

"Amos 'n' Andy," which helped Canadians escape the gloom of unemployment, failing crops, and poverty. Even the opening song for "The Happy Gang" acknowledged that the program was there to help people to temporarily forget their problems:

> *Here we are: the Happy Gang's here*
> *Here we are: How do you do?*
> *Here we are to chase away your troubles*
> *With a song, a melody or two*
> *So gather 'round, come on, let's get together*
> *And we'll start our program with a bang!*
> *For it's time to laugh and sing and shout out*
> *With the Hap- Hap-, Happy Gang!*

In Quebec, serial programs were written specifically for French Canadian radio, and shows such as "Le Curé de village" and "La pension Velder" enjoyed enormous success.[34]

During the Depression, Canadian culture continued to thrive and grow, as Canadians looked for both a means to escape and for comfort in the growing realism that reflectedthe pain and suffering so many were going through.

Review...Reflect...Respond

1. Why did the third parties that were formed in the 1930s have the majority of their support in the Prairie provinces?

2. How did the Depression mark a new stage in government intervention in the economy and in the lives of Canadians?

3. Why did many Canadian artists and writers turn to realism to express their ideas and works of art during the Depression?

Conclusion

In Canada, signs that the Depression was subsiding first appeared in 1939 when the GNP began to improve. Unemployment remained high until the turn of the decade. It was not until the beginning of World War II when the demand for materials used in manufacturing military goods finally pushed Canada out of the Great Depression. Some historians are tempted to conclude that Canadians, preoccupied with the war, soon put the Depression behind them. They may further argue that the recovery in the forties put a practical end to reservations about the free market economy. While it is true that the war and economic recovery did shift attention from economic peril and hardship, the legacy of the Depression did not diminish until decades later. The growth of the welfare state and the government supervision of vital aspects in the economy continued to flourish until at least the 1980s. In the political arena, many of the movements and parties created in the '30s still play important roles in Canadian society.

Notes

1. For one of the latest popular accounts of the impact of the Depression see Robert Collins, *You Had To Be There: An Intimate Portrait of the Generation that Survived the Depression, Won The War, And Re-Invented Canada* (Toronto: McClelland & Stewart, 1999).

2. Here are some examples "Understanding 1929" *Wall Street Journal*, March 7, 1997. A summary of the article reads: A better understanding of what caused the 1929 stock market crash would help Federal Reserve Chairman Alan Greenspan stop worrying so much about the current high price of stocks. Column, Wayne D. Angell.

3. "Too many goods, too few buyers—a repeat of 1929?" *The Christian Science Monitor*, Feb 2, 1996, v88 n47, p. 19. The summary reads, current conditions of a rise in productivity and concurrent drop in public buying power due to increase in unemployment resemble economic conditions that prevailed just before stock market crash of 1929 that set off the Great Depression, Column, Joseph C. Harsch.

4. See for example the introduction to John Kenneth Galbraith, *The Great Crash 1929* (London: Andre Deutsch, 1980). Galbraith recalls that his book, critical of some of the weaknesses and excesses of the stock market and written in the 1950s, came under heavy scrutiny and criticism. As he appeared before the Senate Committee and Banking and Currency he outlined the views contained in his book only to be accused of being a communist by some of the more staunch defenders of the stock market which was, ... indisputably an integral institution of capitalism and the American system."(1980: xvii) Other commentators in the media attributed a temporary downturn in the stock market to his critical analysis.

5. Large anti-globalization protests have taken place in Seattle, Washington, Genoa, Italy, and Quebec City.

6. In 1937 there was some hope of recovery in the world economy. These hopes were dashed by a sharp decline in 1938. From an overall point of view the economy remained "depressed" for the entire decade.

7. According to historians Alvin Finkel and Margaret Conrad, the wages of workers in the 1920s rose only by 8 percent, while company profits rose by 80 percent. Finkel and Conrad, *History of the Canadian Peoples: Volume II.* (Toronto: Addison Wesley, 1998) p. 263.

8. Pierre Berton, "Depression" in *The Great Depression, 1929–1939.* (Toronto: Penguin Books, 1991).

9. Michiel Horn ed., *The Dirty Thirties: Canadians in the Great Depresssion.* (Toronto: Copp Clark Publishing, 1972) p. 572.

10. Michael Bliss and L.M. Grayson *The Wretched of Canada: Letters to R.B. Bennett, 1930–1935.* (Toronto: University of Toronto Press, 1971).

11. In the 1920s Bennett had inherited a vast fortune from long-time friends Jennie Eddie and her brother Joseph Thompson Shirreff of the Eddy Match Company. This windfall dwarfed his existing personal assets accumulated from his activities as a politician, lawyer and businessman in Alberta.

12. Newfoundland, not yet part of Canada, also faced great hardship. Without markets for its raw materials, Newfoundland went deeply into debt and had to declare bankruptcy. In return for British aid Newfoundland was taken over by a British-appointed commissioner and democratic government was suspended.

13. Source: Saskatchewan Archives Board #R-B 2464 (1)-(3)

14. Source: Saskatchewan Archives Board

15. In comparison, the American Civilian Conservation Corps, spent 13 cents per day (MacDowell, (1995: 215) "Relief Workers in Ontario in the Great Depression," *Canadian Historical Review*, Vol. LXXVI, No. 2, June 1995.

16. According to one account, at a total cost ranging from 19 to 26 cents per day the food ration for each man was, "one pound each of bread, meat, and potatoes, 6 ounces of fresh vegetables, 3 ounces of bacon and sugar, 2 ounces of beans, jam and butter, 1 ounce of tea and one-third ounce of pepper. This was not a great deal of food for a full-grown man doing manual labour all day in cold weather." MacDowell (1995: 219)

17. Or, conversely, why didn't men leave once they found out what the camps were like? The simple reason is that if men left for any reason, they were likely to be denied relief on the outside. In other words, once in the camp men had little recourse but to stay.

18. British Columbia had long been a centre for radical political activity. Many of the men had experience as activists before they were sent to the camps.

19. Arthur Evans was a union organizer in Canada and the United States. After joining the Communist Party in 1926, Evans moved to British Columbia as an organizer for the National Unemployed Workers' Association and the Workers Unity League. In 1934–35 he was a leader in the Relief Camp Workers' Union. Evans coordinated the demonstrations in Vancouver and was the leader of the Trekkers as they entered Regina for their confrontation with the federal government.

20. A disgruntled would-be prime minister Stanley Baldwin commented on the style of R.B. Bennett, using a quote that had been applied to Bennett previously. Bennett he quipped, "has the manners of a Chicago policeman and the temperament of a Hollywood film star."

21. NAC, MG27 111 F18, Miss Muriel E. Black papers, "Text of the Radio Broadcast delivered by the Right Honourable R.B. Bennett," January, 4, 1935.

22. Interestingly, Bennett had also passed the Canadian Radio Broadcasting Act that founded the Canadian Radio Broadcasting Commission, the publicly owned radio network that was the predecessor to the Canadian Broadcasting Corporation.

23. Editorial, *The Globe*, Toronto, Monday, September 9, 1935 (Excerpted)

24. Aberhart did not have an exact list identifying the names of the "fifty big shots" he would deal with. The "fifty big shots" was symbolic and represented rich and powerful central Canadian bankers and industrialists who were controlling the economy at the expense of the common people of Alberta.

25. J.M. Bumsted, *The Peoples of Canada: A Post-Confederation History* (Toronto: Oxford University Press, 1992) p. 214.

26. Finkel and Conrad, *History of the Canadian Peoples: 1867 to the Present* (Toronto: Copp Clark, 1996), p. 300.

27. J. M. Bumsted, *The Peoples of Canada*, p. 213.

28. Between 1933 and 1945, 400 000 Jews fled to Switzerland.

29. Irving M. Abella and Harold Troper. *None Is Too Many: Canada and the Jews of Europe, 1933–1948*. (Toronto: Lester & Orpen Dennys, 1982).

30. Finkel and Conrad, *History of the Canadian Peoples*, p. 293.

31. R. Douglas Francis et al., *Destinies: Canadian History Since Confederation, Third Edition* (Toronto: Harcourt Brace, 1996) p. 280.

32. A complete listing of Morley Callaghan's works can be found at www.track0.com/ogwc/authors/callaghan_m.html

33. Francis, *Destinies: Canadian History Since Confederation, Third Edition*, p. 280.

34. Ibid., p. 278.

Chapter 17 Review

Knowledge & Understanding

1. Identify these people, places, and events, and explain their historical significance to Canada's developing culture and identity:

   "Black Tuesday"   *Happy Gang*
   On-to-Ottawa trek Bennett Buggies
   CCF   Unemployment Relief
   "five-cent piece"   Act
   work camps   New Deal
   Trente Arpents

2. In a chart, list the various solutions that King, Bennett, and the third parties devised to help Canadians survive the Depression. In a second column, describe the reasons for their success or failure. In your opinion, which solution had the best results? Give reasons for your answer.

3. How did the Great Depression affect gender, class, and race relations in Canada?

Thinking & Inquiry

4. In her book *Waste Heritage*, Canadian author Irene Baird opens with the character of Matt Striker, a young, single, transient in search of work,

   Sure, I'm a transient," he said quietly, "I was born back in the province of Saskatchewan but that province don't own me no more. Six years now I bummed around trying to rustle up some kind of steady job. I bummed around so long even the country don't own me no more.

   In three well-written paragraphs, support or refute the following statement: Single, young, men living in the cities suffered the most in Canada during the Great Depression.

On the blackboard, write the following statement: "Resolved: Work camps were a positive and constructive solution to the unemployment problem in Canada during the Depression." Conduct a class debate on the statement.

Application

5. Many photos in this chapter show the devastation of the Depression in Canada. Which photo affects you the most? Why? In response to the photo write a poem or short story based on who or what you see in the photo.

6. Imagine that you are a panelist selected to ask Mackenzie King and R.B. Bennett questions during a radio debate in the 1935 election campaign. Create 10 questions that you will ask the two leaders, and write down the responses that you might receive from the two men.

Communication

7. Angered by what you feel is the federal government's lack of response to the Depression, you turn to one of the new "third" parties that are increasing in popularity. Which party do you choose to join? Why? Write three well-developed paragraphs that explain your reasons for joining that party.

8. Choose one of the following characters and write a letter to Prime Minister Bennett as that character: a young, male transient, a farmer's wife in Saskatchewan, or a married man and father who has been put in a work camp. Describe what you see around you and what you are going through. What do you want the government to do?

CHAPTER 18

Canada and World War II

Out of the last war emerged their status, out of this one their stature.

–VINCENT MASSEY

It seemed unbelievable to Canadians that only two decades after their soldiers had returned from the muddy battlefields of the Great War, they would again be called to arms. The burden of war debt, the conscription crisis, and the memories of those who had not returned home from World War I were still all too vivid. By the mid-1930s Canadians were still pulling themselves out of the Great Depression, and pre-occupied with troubles at home, did not foresee that the events unfolding on the other side of the world would ultimately involve them. By 1939, the powers of Europe were involved in a struggle for dominance, and once again, Canadian men and women would be asked to do their part.

Canada would play a crucial role in the Allied victory of World War II—changing both the way Canada saw itself, and the way the international community viewed it. However, World War II would also expose a country still struggling to unite and denying the basic human rights of its own citizens.

The Treaty of Versailles and the League of Nations were created after World War I to resolve the issues that had led the world into the Great War. However, by the end of the 1930s both institutions began to unravel and old rivalries began to resurface. The harsh terms of the Treaty of Versailles divided existing German colonies among the Allied nations and dismantled the Austro-Hungarian Empire, thereby creating the smaller nations of Czechoslovakia, Yugoslavia, and Poland. Along with heavy monetary reparations and restrictions on its army, the War Guilt Clause ensured that Germany accepted all responsibility for the war, which played a major role in destroying the country's very foundations. The conditions of the Treaty of Versailles only served to enrage Germany and became a motive for revenge.

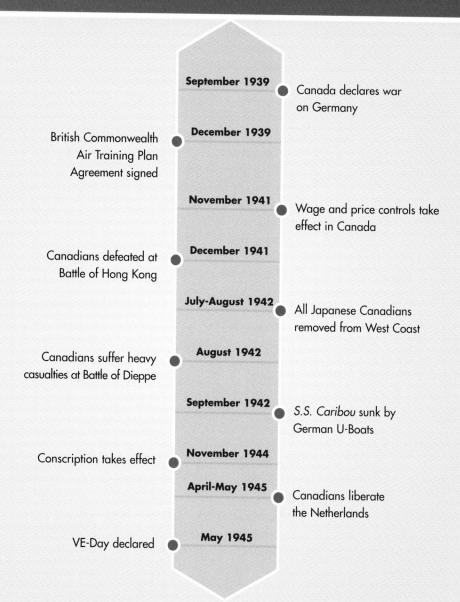

September 1939 — Canada declares war on Germany

British Commonwealth Air Training Plan Agreement signed — **December 1939**

November 1941 — Wage and price controls take effect in Canada

Canadians defeated at Battle of Hong Kong — **December 1941**

July-August 1942 — All Japanese Canadians removed from West Coast

Canadians suffer heavy casualties at Battle of Dieppe — **August 1942**

September 1942 — S.S. *Caribou* sunk by German U-Boats

Conscription takes effect — **November 1944**

April-May 1945 — Canadians liberate the Netherlands

VE-Day declared — **May 1945**

By the end of this chapter, you will be able to

- demonstrate an understanding of how Canada's participation in significant international conflicts changed the way the country was perceived by the international community

- describe the ways in which the world wars of the twentieth century altered Canadians' self-image

- describe the origins and various incidents of prejudice and discrimination in Canada's history

- analyze the individual and social costs of human rights violations in Canadian history

- analyze women's changing participation in the paid labour force

The World in Conflict

Following World War I, some countries adopted a policy of isolationism, preferring to distance themselves from world affairs. The United States, for example, refused to join the League of Nations, partly because they believed that Britain was using it for its own means, and partly because they wanted to avoid implication in distant conflicts in which they were not directly involved. It is Ironic that the U.S. did not join the League, even though the organization had been a vision of American President Woodrow Wilson, and was outlined is his "Fourteen Points."[1] In the years following the Great War, a series of events unfolded that tested the strength and influence of the League of Nations.

Tension in the Pacific

Japan was on the side of the Allies during the Great War and through the Treaty of Versailles was awarded German colonies on the Marianas, Marshalls, and Caroline Islands in the Pacific Ocean. As Japan's population grew, it put a strain on the country's resources, and the increasingly militaristic nation gazed hungrily beyond its borders for more land. In 1931, Japan invaded Manchuria, a Chinese province that Japan had sought to control since the turn of the century. Despite a plea made by China before the League of Nations, Britain, France, and other League members, fearing that this event might spark a larger conflict, refused to take action. Canadian Prime Minister R.B. Bennett remarked about himself, "What can one man do who represents only ten and a half millions of people?"

The Rise of Fascism

Fascism in Italy

Italy entered the First World War fighting with Germany in the Axis Alliance. Switching sides when the Allies promised to grant them land if victorious, Italy was disappointed with the terms of the Treaty of Versailles as it failed to give them the territory in the Austro-Hungarian Empire that they had wanted. In the years following the Great War, Italy, hampered by a series of failed coalition governments and national debt, entered a severe economic depression. The people of Italy turned to a new political leader, Benito Mussolini, who promised prosperity and a renewed powerful Roman Empire. Mussolini came to power in 1922, bringing an end to democracy in Italy. Referred to as "Il Duce" ("the leader"), Mussolini introduced fascism, a combination of potent militant nationalism and totalitarianism, that stressed the glorification of the state over the individual. Mussolini executed or imprisoned anyone who disobeyed him. He established a cooperative state, in which the government controlled the economy and clear distinctions were drawn between classes. In 1935, in an attempt to create a great Italian Empire, Mussolini invaded Ethiopia. Again, the League of Nations did nothing.

During League negotiations, the Canadian delegate in Geneva, W.R. Riddell, proposed that oil be added to a League embargo, an action that would have made invasion impossible for Mussolini. Prime Minister Mackenzie King, however, was not consulted on the matter. When he found out, he demanded that oil be removed from the embargo. Thus, Canada played a minor role in appeasing Italy.

The Rise of Nazi Germany

After World War I ended, Germany faced economic ruin from trying to meet the financial obligations of the Treaty of Versailles. A young soldier from World War I, Adolf Hitler, was determined to return Germany to its former glory. In Munich, Hitler took control of a right-wing political party and renamed it the Socialist German Worker Party—later known as the Nazis. Hitler promised a weary and battered country jobs, power, and a return to greatness. While in prison for a failed political revolt, Hitler outlined his mission and beliefs in his book *Mein Kampf (My Struggle)*. The book sold over

Hitler promised Germany a return to greatness.

five million copies and rallied a desperate nation.

In *Mein Kampf*, Hitler stated that the Aryan race (Caucasians of pure German descent) was superior and should rule over all other races, such as the Slavs and especially the Jews. The Nazis' hatred and blame of the Jews would create one of the most horrifying legacies of World War II—the Holocaust. Hitler's beliefs became so popular across Germany that in 1933, he was elected chancellor of Germany.

Calling himself *"der Führer"* (the leader), Hitler demanded loyalty from his people, and like Mussolini, punished those who resisted. With a flurry of powerful propaganda and public speeches, Hitler's popularity and influence over the German population escalated. Nazi ideals were taught in schools, children were enrolled in Nazis youth organizations, and men were forced into the Labour Service where they carried out manual work and prepared for the army. Hitler even controlled media such as books, newspapers, radio, and film. In 1933, Hitler withdrew Germany from the League of Nations. He then directly violated the Treaty of Versailles by introducing conscription in order to rebuild the German army and by sending troops into the Rhineland.

Policy of Appeasement

Britain's Prime Minister Neville Chamberlain and other world leaders adopted a policy of appeasement following the Great War. Chamberlain believed that Hitler had good reason to make demands on the League of Nations and felt that if the League agreed, Hitler would hold to his promises and the world could avoid going to war. The British public, who believed that Germany had been ill-treated at the end of the Great War, supported Chamberlain.

Mackenzie King and Appeasement: Abroad and at Home

Canadian Prime Minister Mackenzie King backed Chamberlain in his policy of appeasement.[2] King, like Chamberlain, believed that war could be avoided by giving in to Hitler and Mussolini's demands. For the most part, Canadians, were not ready to relive the Great War, and welcomed King's policies. Much to King's dismay, however, when the Spanish Civil war erupted in 1936—a war that pitted communism against fascism—sixteen hundred Canadians supported by the Communist Party in Canada, volunteered to fight. The Mackenzie-Papineau Battalion was formed and sent to Spain in 1937. Only half of the men returned.

Behind Prime Minister King's motives during these interwar years, was his desire to keep Canada united and to ensure that French Canadians supported his military policies. He had made it clear that it was up to parliament to decide if Canada would go to war. At an Imperial Conference in May 1937, he refused to make any military commitments to a Commonwealth war until it was absolutely necessary. When another world war seemed inevitable, Canadians wondered if the country would be prepared to contribute. Foremost on King's mind was to escape the mistakes of his predecessor Borden. He wanted to avoid the severe war debt, the high casualty list, and the civil strife of the First World War. King was determined to commit only a "limited effort" to Britain if the world went to war. After being reelected in 1935, King cautiously put funds behind the Canadian militia, distributing more money to the Royal Canadian Air Force (RCAF) and the Royal Canadian Navy (RCN) than to the army. King believed that Canadians would support the idea of "home defence," for which the RCAF and RCN could be used, and he wanted to avoid alarming the country with a major infantry expansion.

After the Imperial Conference in May of 1937, King visited Hitler in Germany. He reported that Hitler was a man of "deep sincerity and a genuine patriot" and that "there were conditions in Germany itself which accounted for much that had been done there." In his diary he wrote, "He [Hitler] smiled very pleasantly and indeed had a sort of appealing and affectionate look in his eyes. My sizing up of the man as I sat and talked with him was that he is really one who truly loves his fellow man...."[3] King remained confident that Canada would not have to be involved in another world war.

In 1938, the German army marched into Austria in a forced takeover, or what Hitler referred to as *Anschluss*—the union of the German people of Austria and Germany for a "Greater Germany". The League again stood idly by. Hitler then turned to Chamberlain and demanded the Sudetenland, in Czechoslovakia, promising that this would be his last request. At the Munich Conference, in 1938, in a move later known as the Munich Pact, Germany, Great Britain, France, and Italy relinquished the Sudetenland to Hitler without consulting Czechoslovakia or the Soviet Union. Britain and France pressured Czechoslovakia to release the land without a fight. At first news of the Munich Pact, King sent a message to Chamberlain thanking him on the behalf of the Canadian people for his

Mackenzie King in Nazi Germany.

"unremitting efforts for peace." Hitler had fooled everyone. In March 1939, he abandoned his promise and sent his army in to takeover the rest of Czechoslovakia. Hitler then made it clear that he had no intention of avoiding war and demanded that some of the territory of Poland be relinquished to Germany. Britain and France, finally realizing that Hitler could not be stopped through peace talks, promised to protect Poland if any militant action were taken against them.

That August, Hitler signed the Nazis-Soviet Pact—a secret agreement between Hitler and Stalin to expand their Empires and divide up Poland and the rest of Eastern Europe. The Soviet Union feared aggression from the east, and saw Germany as their only means of avoiding invasion on two borders. Germany saw the Nazi-Soviet Pact as a way to isolate Poland from Britain and France, as well to avoid having to fight on two fronts. Hitler's plan was to take Poland first, turn attention to France and Britain and, ultimately, return to take the Soviet Union.

The Nazi army invaded Poland on September 1, 1939, in what was known as a *blitzkrieg* or light-ening war. The world could no longer stand aside. Two days later Britain and France declared war on Germany, and once again, the world was at war. This time, however, Canada was not automatically at war through Britain's declaration.

Canada Off to War

In 1939 Canada had a much different relationship with Britain than it had had on the eve of the Great War. Because of the Statute of Westminster, Canada had control over its own foreign policy and could make an independent decision to support the war.[4] King knew that a majority of Canadians still felt a strong allegiance to Britain and were becoming increasingly concerned about the rise of Nazi Germany. He was also all too aware of the anti-war, anti-imperialist sentiments still alive in Quebec. The conscription crisis of the Great War was not easily forgotten. But Mackenzie King's skillful ability in the interwar years to evade military com-mitments and his parliamentary pledge of March 1939 to avoid conscription, brought a united Canada into the war. King's decision to contribute a Canadian division to the Allied war effort was backed by parliament and, although there was no enthusiasm for war in Quebec, there was also little resistance. For the most part, French Canada was against the war, but stood behind King. Despite this feeling of unity, the Canadian Prime Minister waited ten days to declare war on Germany to assert the country's new independence.

This state of harmony did not last long as on September 25, Maurice Duplessis, leader of the Union Nationale and premier of Quebec, dissolved his provincial parliament. King immediately saw this as a move by Duplessis to renew his party's mandate and run his election campaign on an anti-war platform. Quebec members of parliament, Ernest Lapointe, P. J. A. Cardin, and Charles Power, vowed to resign if Duplessis won. French Canadians feared that if they voted for Duplessis, Quebec would lose its anti-conscription contingent in Ottawa, and it would surely bring about conscription. Crisis was averted as the liberals were victorious and Adelard Godbout was made premier of Quebec. King was ecstatic and he praised Lapointe, Cardin, and Power for their work, declaring that Lapointe was on par with Laurier.

The first Canadian contigent departing from Halifax.

The Phony War

On September 17, the Nazis invaded Poland from the western border, and the Russians invaded eastern Poland as part of the secret pact between the two countries. Caught between two relentless forces, Poland surrendered and a strange calm fell over the Western Front. This quiet period, known as the *Phony War*, gave the Allies time to build up forces and sup-plies. In Canada, the unemployed flocked to enlist. In September 1939 alone, over fifty-eight thou-sand Canadian men and women

Understanding Cause and Effect

Historians spend a great deal of time analysing causes and effects. No historian gets very far without answering the question, "Why?" Historians gather, organize, and interpret information to explain the reasons why an event happened and what were the consequences of that event. They may investigate an event that has many causes or many effects, or an event that has many causes and many effects, or a chain of causes and effects where the first event caused the second, the second caused the third, and so on. Examples of historians' causal questions include,

- What imperial and historical factors caused the growth of the fur trade in the 1600s?
- What were the economic causes of the Great Depression?
- What were the political, social, and cultural effects of Canada's participation in World War II?
- What is the chain of causes and effects that has resulted in Aboriginal Peoples' land claims?

Causal Analysis

When you analyse, you try to explain "a subject by dividing it into its parts and showing how the parts relate to the whole."[1] In causal analysis, a writer tries to show how causes, effects, or causes and effects relate to an event or a situation. When you are planning a presentation on causes and effects, your research question and your thesis statement should guide you towards the most valid and pertinent evidence. When you are evaluating a cause-and-effect discussion in your research sources, you will want to ask yourself, Is this writer's causal analysis objective? Is it valid and logical? What is the writer or speaker's perspective on the subject? Is there evidence of bias or stereotyping? Is the chain of cause and effect logical?

Causal Evidence

Whether you are evaluating the discussions of cause and effect in your research sources or explaining cause and effect in your own essays, the evidence should be not only reliable but also[2]

- Pertinent: The facts and information should be relevant to the relationship between cause and effect under discussion; the evidence needs to clearly contribute to the conclusion reached.
- Sufficient: There should be enough reliable facts and information to justify the conclusion reached; within reason, all of the possible causes or effects should be considered.
- Representative: The evidence should represent a valid, objective, well-substantiated, and unbiased selection of causes and effects.
- Plausible: Two events that occur close to each other in time may not have a cause-and-effect link; causal relationships need to be substantiated with likely and reliable facts and arguments.

Interpretation

An historian's analysis of cause and effect is an interpretation of the evidence. The cause-and-effect relationship does not exist in the facts or in the data. The way that an historian interprets the facts and proposes a cause-and-effect relationship can often tell you a great deal about his or her perspective. In addition, historians usually establish some hierarchy of causes; they consider some to be more significant and carry more weight than others. The creation of this hierarchy can also show the historian's perspective or frame of reference. Indeed, one of the benefits of comparing different historians'

---

[1] Kay L. Stewart, Marian E. Allen, *Forms of Writing*, 2nd edition, Prentice Hall Canada Inc., 1997, page 43.
[2] Oliu, Walter E., et al, *Writing That Works*, 2nd Canadian edition, Nelson Canada, 1994, pages 163-165.

interpretations of causal relationships is that such comparisons can help you see bias or prejudice in the reasoning process. Finally, a useful analysis and interpretation of causes and effects will often not just tell the reader about past events, but also suggest the likely effects of current events on the future.

Using Cause-and-Effect Organizers

Graphic organizers can help you record, organize, and understand facts, relationships, and interpretations. They are especially useful when trying to see patterns and relationships in complex subjects, such as causal analysis.

Practice

Write a research question on the causes-and-effects of one event in World War II; for example, the battle of Vimy Ridge, the policy of Appeasement, the Battle of Britain, or the dropping of atomic bombs on Hiroshima and Nagasaki. Use one of the cause-and-effect organizers below to track the causes and effects of that event. Then write a paragraph summarizing your interpretation.

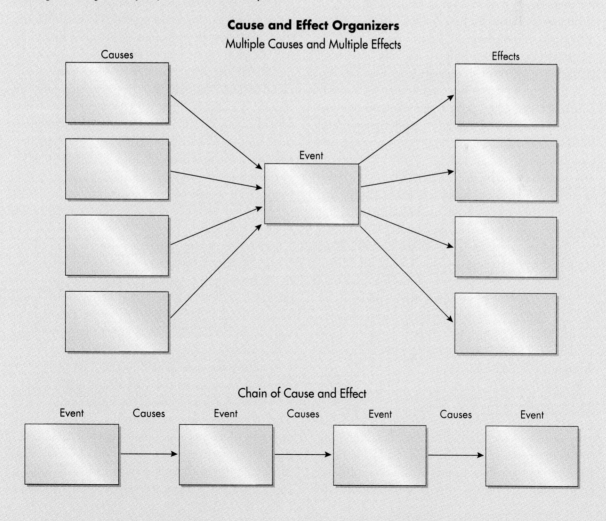

Cause and Effect Organizers

Multiple Causes and Multiple Effects

Chain of Cause and Effect

volunteered for service. On December 10, the 1st Canadian Division of seventy-four hundred men set sail for Britain.

The Phony War ended in April of 1940, when Germany invaded Denmark and Norway. By May, moving with great speed and force, the Germans swept around France's major fortifications along the border of Germany and France, known as the "Maginot Line", and invaded the Netherlands and Belgium. Overwhelmed by the German force and strategy, British officials ordered soldiers located in France, including some Canadian troops, to retreat to Dunkirk. In what became known as the Miracle of Dunkirk, 350 000 men were evacuated across the English Channel by over nine hundred boats of all shapes and sizes. By June 13, the Germans occupied Paris and, on June 22, France surrendered.

With the fall of France, Britain looked to Canada for additional support and Canada was pressured to increase its commitment to the war effort. In response, Mackenzie King sent four destroyers, an RCAF squadron, and a second and third infantry division. A single tank brigade was also assembled and would eventually make up the 4th and 5th Armoured Divisions. King also launched the National Resources Mobilization Act, allowing the government to conscript men for home defence. These men, nicknamed "Zombies", could not be forced to serve beyond Canada. King argued, that they could and he hoped, would volunteer for overseas service. With the National Resources Mobilization Act (NRMA), King tried to soothe public paranoia over conscription by relegating the troops to home defence. Sixteen thousand men were conscripted under the Act, sixty thousand volunteered.

Canada's BCATP

The British Commonwealth Air Training Plan (BCATP) was arguably one of Canada's greatest contributions to the Second World War. Britain knew, from the outset, that it was necessary to concentrate great resources and energy on building a powerful Allied air force; Britain also knew that it was much too small and too close to the war to undertake large-scale training. On the other hand, Canada was a perfect location for the training program, as it was far enough away from the enemy, but close enough to Britain to manoeuvre troops. Canada also had the capacity to support the production of new aircraft, easy access to American industry, and the space to build new schools and train crew.

Prime Minister Mackenzie King was initially reluctant to welcome Britain's idea of the BCATP. Canada had already made a commitment to the war and King made it clear that he wished the proposal had been suggested earlier. He was also less then enthused that Britain expected Canada to comply with its demands and that Lord Riverdale, the British delegate, announced Britain's commitment of $140 million as a "free contribution" to the effort. King wanted it to be clear that it was Canada who was making the generous contributions and it led him to snap "it was not Canada's war in the same sense it was Great Britain's". However, King accepted the offer, reasoning that the BCATP would commit Canadians to an effort on Canadian soil, keeping them far away from the fighting overseas.

The prime minister had a number of conditions. Britain would have to declare that the BCATP took priority over all other Canadian contributions to the war and that Canadians would administer the plan. The final hurdle was that of Canadian identity. King demanded that Canadians serve overseas in separate RCAF squadrons. Riverdale's response was that requests for RCAF squadrons would be met "in all circumstances in which it is feasible". The Canadians felt this was a weak response and it was merely a way for Britain to keep Canadians under their control. An alternative agreement was put forward on December 14, stipulating that if Canada could provide the ground crews, then independent RCAF squadrons would be

An artist painted the activities of the British Commonwealth Air Training Plan in Alberta. Peter Whyte, *Control Tower* (1944).

The Commonwealth Air Training Plan in 1939, with light craft, Cornells, used for preliminary training purposes.

formed. King and Riverdale argued for the next three days over the wording. In a race to announce the proposal on December 17, the Canadian prime minister's birthday, the question of the Canadianization of the BCATP was never truly resolved.

The British Commonwealth Air Training Plan Agreement was signed on December 17, 1939, by Canada, Britain, Australia, and New Zealand. The Agreement stipulated that Canada would bare the burden of the cost. After the fall of France, RAF crews were transferred to Canada and training began, and the first BCATP Aircrew graduated in late 1940.

The BCATP brought economic prosperity to the country as a whole and also to the small communities that welcomed the training camps. Many communities rallied to host a new aerodrome; construction created new jobs, and the influx of trainees meant business for local merchants. Communities across Canada, in every province, bustled with activity.

Canada's role in the BCATP was one of its greatest contributions to the Second World War.

By the end of the war, Canada had spent $1.6 billion on the BCATP, more than one third of the total cost. The BCATP established 151 schools across Canada and turned out 131 355 graduates, fifty percent of whom were Canadian

Battle of the Atlantic

By the end of the Second World War, Canada boasted the third largest navy in the world with 471 fighting vessels at its disposal and 99 688 men and 6500 women enlisted. During the war, Canadian navy ships were found as far away as the Mediterranean and the Pacific.

As in the First World War, Canada contributed greatly to the war effort by organizing convoys in its eastern harbours. Convoys provided protection for troops and supplies being shipped from Canada to Britain. From the outset of war, German U-Boats once again dominated the Atlantic and posed a major threat to the Allied convoys. In the spring of 1940, with control over Norway and France, Germany had unprecedented access to the Atlantic waters. By September, German U-Boats were attacking in "wolf packs," large groups of U-Boats organized to attack at night. The wolf packs were sinking Allied boats faster than the Allies could replace them. In March 1941, British Prime Minister Winston Churchill declared that "The Battle of the Atlantic" had begun.

In an attempt to counter the U-Boat attacks, Canada embarked on a massive shipbuilding program. Canada produced a number of new vessels, including the famous corvette, a small, swift boat that could outrun a German U-Boat. The living conditions on these vessels were deplorable, as the corvette was not designed for mid-ocean sailing and, therefore, the crew spent most of their time crowded and wet.

Although still not officially involved in the war, by September 1941, the United States was active in the Battle of the Atlantic. While preoccupied on other missions, the British put an American Commander in charge of the war effort in the Atlantic. Rear-Admiral L.W. Murray, the Commander of the Canadian Navy, was not even consulted. By December of that same year, however, when the U.S. officially joined the war, they withdrew many of their boats from the Atlantic and moved to the Pacific arena. Germany saw this as a point of weakness and redirected its efforts to the American coast. The Canadian navy, with two years of experience behind them, was sent to lead the protection of the U.S. coastline.

For the most part, the war remained a distant conflict, however, six enemy U-Boats did manage to enter the St. Lawrence River, coming within 300 kilometres of Quebec City. Bringing the war closer to home for Canadians, German U-Boats in Canadian waters sunk three Canadian warships and twenty convoy ships. Eventually, panic provoked the Canadian government to close the St. Lawrence waterways and troops were ushered in to the area. On October 14, 1942, in the worst inshore disaster during the Second World War, a German U-Boat destroyed the *S.S. Caribou* and 137 Canadians were killed, many of them women and children. The *Caribou* disaster made Canadians realize that the war was not just overseas.

Ship construction in Canada began to meet the demands of the war in the Atlantic by November 1942 and Canadians discovered that they could increase the number of merchant ships in a convoy without increasing the number of warships. Extra warships then had the freedom to help combat U-Boat attacks. The British also invented the Merchant Aircraft Carrier, a ship that had a landing strip for aircraft, increasing the potential of the air force. Special airborne radar was developed, helping the Allies locate German U-Boats.[5] In May 1943, Allied escorts sunk thirty-one enemy U-Boats, forcing Germany to surrender the Battle of the Atlantic. During the Battle of the Atlantic, Canada provided about half the naval escorts needed. The battle at sea involved the skill and Air Force. Canadians were given credit for sinking forty-seven U-Boats and two Italian submarines.

An Atlantic convoy in 1942 assembling at Halifax harbour.

The Battle of Britain

With the fall of France in July 1940, Britain was in a precarious position as the Germans were poised menacingly across the English Channel. Hitler then ordered the German Luftwaffe (German air force) to target British airfields and destroy the RAF. Superiority in the air, Hitler reasoned, would be the key to destroying the British Navy. When a German aircraft accidentally bombed London and prompted the RAF to retaliate and bomb Berlin, an outraged, Hitler ordered the Luftwaffe to concentrate all of its energy on destroying London. The RAF put up a considerable defence in the daily raids and the Germans were forced to attack by night. Hundreds of Canadians fought with the RAF in this crucial battle and by October 1940, the Luftwaffe was defeated.

Canadians in the Air

From the Battle of the Atlantic to the Battle of Britain and from Egypt to Asia, Canadian men with the Royal Air Force and Royal Canadian Air Force (RCAF) flew in almost every theatre of war.

By the end of 1940, the first BCATP graduates arrived in Europe. Most of these men served with the British RAF, but eventually enough graduates arrived overseas to form RCAF squadrons, although they were still under British control. Charles G. Power, Minister of National Defence (Air), fought British officials to have his senior Canadian officers serve overseas rather than simply be absorbed into running the BCATP. Eventually, there were more Canadian aircrew prepared then there were RCAF positions, and in January, 1941, Ottawa announced that another twenty-five RCAF squadrons would be formed overseas and those RCAF graduates serving in RAF squadrons would wear Canadian uniforms. Administrative problems continued, however, and Power had to fight for better lines of communication and control over Canadian airman serving in the RAF.

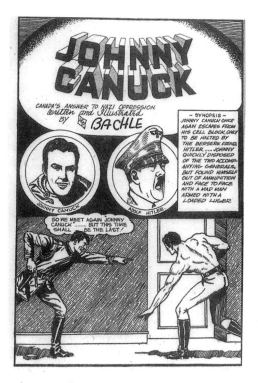

Johnny Canuck—"Canada's answer to Nazi oppression"

In total, forty-eight RCAF squadrons served overseas. No. 6 Bomber Group was formed under RAF Bomber Command in January 1943. Its main purpose was to perform night bombing raids over Germany, following the Battle of Britain. These night raids were particularly dangerous and resulted in the loss of over ten thousand Canadian lives.

King's plan to keep Canadians from battle by establishing the BCTAP was ill-fated. Aircraft were utilized extensively during the Second World War for bomb raids and for air support in battle, and casualties were numerous. Over seventeen thousand Canadians with the RCAF lost their lives.

Invasion of Russia

By 1942, the fate of the Allies seemed hopeless, as Germany had taken Norway, Denmark, Holland, Belgium, and France. On June 22, 1941, Hitler launched *Operation Barbarossa* and sent three million troops into Russia, betraying the Nazi-Soviet pact. In the first few months, the German blitzkrieg on Russia seemed to be working, and the German army approached Moscow. But, Russian soldiers refused to give up and as the brutal Russian winter set in, Germany could not win a quick victory and was locked into a long cold battle on the Eastern Front.

Pearl Harbor

Like Italy, Japan had also fought on the side of the Allies in World War I, but had joined the Germans in this war. At the end of 1940, Japan launched an ambitious plan to take control all economic development in the Pacific and to dominate Asia, and that same year, the U.S. stopped all exports of iron, steel, and military supplies to Japan. On December 7, Japan struck at the heart of the American Pacific fleet and bombed Pearl Harbor bringing the U.S. into the Second World War. Approximately six hours after the Japanese attack on Pearl Harbour, the Japanese bombed the Kai Tak Airport and the camp at Sham Shui Po, both situated on the Island of Hong Kong where the Royal Canadian Signals were positioned, fatally wounding two men. They were the first Canadians killed in the Second World War.

The attack on Pearl Harbor caused Canadians to fear a possible Japanese invasion on the Pacific coast. The U.S. pushed to have a road built to Alaska, something that had been discussed for years; but now as Canadians feared invasion, it seemed necessary. The Alaska Highway was constructed between 1942–43 from Dawson Creek, British Columbia to Fairbanks, Alaska, and by the end of 1942, over fifteen thousand Americans were in the north, as the Japanese occupied the Aleutian Islands just off the coast of Alaska. The creation of the Alaska Highway made King question the possible threat or influence that the U.S. might have over Canada. As a precaution, Brigadier W.W. Foster, an army officer, was assigned as a special commissioner to the project and was stationed in Edmonton.

Canadians in Hong Kong

Despite McNaughton's continuing effort to keep the Canadian troops together, in the fall of 1941, two battalions, the Royal Rifles of Canada and the Winnipeg Grenadiers, were sent to help protect Hong Kong, a British colony since the nineteenth

After Hong Kong—Canadian POWs in Japanese concentration camp.

century. The Canadians joined two British and two East Indian battalions, and endured a short period of intensive training. It was believed that the reinforcement of Hong Kong would be enough of a deterrent to convince Japan not to strike against the Allies and that the Canadian troops would not see action. The Canadian battalions arrived in Hong Kong on November 16 and were unprepared for battle, since both battalions had been on garrison duty previous to this post.

On December 11, the Winnipeg Grenadiers were sent as reinforcements to the mainland of Hong Kong and saw some action, but quickly retreated back to the Island. On December 18, Japanese troops arrived on the beach of the Island of Hong Kong where both Canadian battalions were positioned. In the ensuing battle, the Japanese had the advantage of heavy artillery, air coverage, and reinforcements. Nevertheless, both the Canadians and the Japanese suffered serious casualties and, despite their small force and lack of reinforcements, the Canadian, British, and Indian troops held on until December 25.

In the Battle of Hong Kong, 290 Canadians were killed and 493 were wounded. The soldiers captured by the Japanese lived out the remainder of the war in prisons, living in appalling conditions, suffering abuse, and near starvation. One hundred and twenty-five men died in Japanese prison camps and another 1184 men were sent to Japan to carry out hard labour, working in deplorable conditions; 135 of these men died while still in Japan.

The Disaster at Dieppe

In the spring of 1942, the Allies planned the first major amphibious assault (an attack by water) to reclaim France. The plan involved the Allies attacking the small coastal town of Dieppe from across the English Channel, in an attempt to penetrate Hitler's *Festung Europa* (Fortress Europe). Six thousand and one hundred men, five thousand of whom were Canadian, were to take part in what was termed *Operation Jubilee*, a complex battle that involved the army, navy and air force working together.

Operation Jubilee was launched in the early hours of August 19, 1942 and from the outset, the attack was a complete disaster; only a small party

Canadian troops in a landing craft alongside a British destroyer, waiting to take their Bren-gun carriers onto shore for the Dieppe Raid on the French Channel coast.

of British Commandos met with some success. The 2nd Canadian Infantry Division, under the command of Major-General J.G. Roberts, did not achieve any of its objectives. As the Allies approached the eastern sector, a German convoy opened fire, alerting German soldiers. The element of surprise was lost and those who made it up the beach met German infantry strategically placed in the high cliffs above the beach. The tanks of the Calgary Regiment arrived late on the beach and were stopped short by enemy fire and the steep rocky terrain. Those who made it to the streets of Dieppe were trapped by blockades. In the air, the RAF and RCAF were able to provide some protection for the ships off the coast, but the battle that ensued cost the Allies over one hundred aircraft, thirteen of which were Canadian planes.[6]

As is true in most battles, ordinary men emerged as the heroes on the beaches of Dieppe. Honourable Captain J.W. Foote, a padre with the Royal Hamilton Light Infantry, stayed on the beach to comfort the wounded, in spite of the barrage of enemy fire. Lieutenant-Colonel C.C. Merritt of the South Saskatchewan Regiment led his party across the bridge over the River Scie, walking calmly and bravely into enemy fire. Both men were recognized for their heroism with the Victoria Cross, the Commonwealth's highest military honour.

The Dieppe Raid lasted only nine hours, but in that time 907 Canadians were killed and 1946 were taken prisoner. Only 2211 Allied soldiers made it back to England.

Looking Back at Dieppe

The official historian of the Second World War, C.P. Stacey noted that in the immediate aftermath of the battle, "There is no doubt whatever that in the Army it produced a new sense of pride."[7] A report was released from Canadian headquarters within two weeks of the battle, attempting to justify the battle as a learning experience. Stacey also noted, however, that once the effects of the disaster sunk in, the public took a different stance, "At home in Canada....Canadian civilians, particularly those who had lost relatives, saw only the casualty

Noted Canadian war artist Charles Comfort reconstructs the action at Dieppe. Charles Comfort, *Dieppe Raid* (1946).

Dieppe Raid by Charles Comfort, CWM, 12276

lists and the failure."[8] On September 19, after reading the official account of the Dieppe Raid, Prime Minister Mackenzie King wrote with regret, "I question if the information gained could begin to equal the heavy losses.... It is a very serious blow to the Canadian forces."[9]

Today, Canadian historians still debate the value of Dieppe. Noted Canadian historian, Desmond Morton argues that loses at Dieppe were not in vain as the raid convinced officials of the resources needed for future amphibious attacks.[10] Pierre Berton, author of *Marching as to War* takes a different stance, "Few valuable lessons were learned that weren't already known or that couldn't have been learned more cheaply and more easily by other means."[11] According to Berton, Dieppe was, "A political excursion billed as a military attack," one in which both British and Canadian politicians and military leaders deserve some of the blame.[12] David J. Berguson in his detailed account of Canada's military role in WWII argues that Dieppe was the greatest disaster of the Second World War and that it should have been avoided.[13] Whether one believes Dieppe was needed for future reference or not, it was a battle fraught with tactical errors, and a great tragedy.

The Princess Patricia's Canadian Light Infantry in action against German vehicles, on fire in the background, during the invasion of Sicily, July 1943.

Web Connection

www.mcgrawhill.ca/links/definingCanada

Go to the Web site above to read first-hand accounts of World War II shared by Canadian women and men in the armed forces.

The Allies in Italy

It was a dilemma for Prime Minister Mackenzie King from the outset of war as to how much to contribute to the war effort. He wanted to avoid casualties, but he also wanted it to appear that the Canadians had done their part. At the same time, the public pressured him to send the troops into battle, while McNaughton fought to save the Canadians for a major assault across the Western Front.

On July 10, 1943, Canadian troops landed on the southern tip of the Sicily and had a fairly easy time of pushing inland. Short on ammunition and artillery, the Canadians were forced to outmanoeuvre the enemy rather than engage in battle: they perfected a strategy of travelling at night and taking German soldiers by surprise.[14] The Allies reached Messina, the gateway from Sicily to Italy, on August 16, but the German infantry had already escaped to the mainland. The Allies suffered twenty-nine thousand casualties in the Battle of Sicily; the Canadians lost 562 men, 1664 were wounded, and 84 taken prisoner. Praise given to the Canadians for their role in Sicily was well earned: they had outsmarted and outflanked German troops.

Canadians at Ortona

Moving to the southern tip of Italy in December, the Canadians took part in the Allied effort to take the village of Ortona. Locked in a month-long battle with German infantry, fighting on foot, from house to house, they used explosives to blow up the walls of the buildings and close in on German infantry.

Ortona took on mythic proportions as the press built up the battle. At home, Canadians heard about the dramatic events unfolding, through the familiar voice of Matthew Halton, senior war correspondent in Italy with CBC, "The Germans were demons; the Canadians were possessed by demons...."[15] The German commander stated that the English saw Ortona "as important as Rome" and, on Christmas Eve, Hitler himself declared that Ortona would be held at all costs. In the end, the battle at Ortona was an important victory for the Canadians, but came at a heavy cost: 502 dead and 1837 wounded.

The 5th Armoured Division united with the other Canadian troops in Italy in November 1943. Together, the two divisions stayed on in Italy until the summer of 1944 and with two divisions operating in Italy, the Canadians could rightfully set up a Corps headquarters. They joined the Allies in penetrating the Gustav Line, a German defence line running across Italy, and then the Hitler Line. They helped the American and British troops drive toward Rome, finally capturing the Eternal City on June 4, 1944.

While fighting in Italy that spring, the Canadian troops missed the first step in the Normandy Campaign, the D-Day landings, back on the Western Front. Canadians teasingly referred to the Italian campaign soldiers as "D-Day Dodgers". A poet for the 51 Highland Division wrote new lyrics to a popular song at the time:

The Moro and Ortona were taken in our stride,
We didn't really fight there, we went there for the ride.
Sleeping 'til noon and
playing games,
We live in Rome with lots of dames.
We are the D-Day Dodgers, in sunny Italy

On our way to Florence, we had a lovely time,
We drove a bus from Rimini, right through the Gothic Line
Then to Bologna we did go,
We all went swimming in the Po,
We are the D-Day Dodgers, in sunny Italy.[16]

Termed the "soft underbelly of Europe" by Winston Churchill earlier in the war, Italy had proved to be nothing of the sort. The Italian Campaign was long, arduous and costly. In total, 5764 Canadians lost their lives fighting in Italy.

Reinforcements Moving up on the Ortona Salient by Lawren P. Harris, CWM 12712

Lawren P. Harris, an official Canadian war artist, captures the drama of the Canadians at Ortona. Lawren P. Harris, *Reinforcements Moving up in the Ortona Salient* (1946).

Canadian tanks and troop carriers moving up the Liri Valley after overcoming German opposition, May 1944.

Web Connection

www.mcgrawhill.ca/links/definingCanada

Go to the Web site above to find more information on Canadian soldiers in Italy in World War II

Canadian troops entering a destroyed city of Caen, France, July 10, 1944.

Canadians in the Normandy Campaign

By 1943, the events of the Second World War had taken a turn for the better for the Allies. By winter, Russian forces, now fighting against Germany, had stopped the Nazi Army at Stalingrad and 330 000 German troops were killed or captured. In May, Germany and Italy were defeated in North Africa and another 300 000 troops surrendered. By July 10, British, Canadian, and American troops captured Sicily.

That same year, the Allies began to plan their second large-scale amphibious attack for the coast of France. On June 6, 1944, *Operation Overlord* was launched on the beaches of Normandy. Called the "greatest combined operation in history" by Canadian historian Desmond Morton, D-Day involved the collaboration of 130 000 British, American, and Canadian troops, 800 warships and 11 000 aircraft.[17] Hard-earned lessons of Dieppe were on their side and, this time, the Allies were well organized and had the advantage of surprise. Fourteen thousand Canadians from the 3rd Canadian Division and 2nd Canadian Armoured Brigade, assisted by ten thousand men from the Royal Canadian Navy, were committed to Juno Beach on D-Day. The Canadian infantry covered more ground in one day than all of their Allied counterparts. One thousand and seventy-four Canadians were dead, wounded, or missing in one day.[18]

Once established on the beaches, the Allies still had to reach their assigned targets and still faced the greater challenge of taking France. The Allies outnumbered the Germans in Normandy, but the German army was better equipped and put up a vigorous fight. A bitter stalemate followed. The Canadian army was pulled out of action from mid-June until July 4, but was back in time to take part in a number of important battles. They supported the British in taking the city of Caen on July 10 and, as a result, suffered over 1194 casualties, 334 of which were fatalities. A single Canadian battalion, the Black Watch was almost completely annihilated on July 25 in a battle at Verrières Ridge. On August 16, the Canadians played a strategic role in taking Falaise, an important line of retreat for the Germans. It took the Allies over two months from the D-Day landings to push the Germans out of France. On August 25, American and French troops liberated Paris.

On to Victory

In late March 1945, the 9th Canadian Infantry Brigade, the 1st Canadian Parachute Battalion, and later the 3rd Canadian Division joined the Allies in the assault across the Rhine. German collapse was imminent, with the Allies approaching on the Western Front and Soviet troops advancing on the Eastern Front. After the Battle of Rhineland, the remaining Canadian troops arrived on the Western Front and were given the task of driving the Germans out of western and northeastern Netherlands. In April, the Canadians liberated these areas of the Netherlands, where thousands of Dutch civilians had died from lack of food. By the time the Canadians arrived thousands more were near starvation, but several days after their liberation, food and supplies were moved into the cities. On May 7, Germany officially surrendered and Victory in Europe Day (VE-Day) was declared. Cheering crowds around the world celebrated the end of war in Europe.

Fighting continued in the Pacific and Japanese troops refused to admit defeat. Eighty thousand Canadians volunteered to aid in the Pacific, but the war ended before their help was needed. U.S. President Harry Truman gave Japan an ultimatum to surrender or be destroyed. Japan refused and on August 6, the U.S. dropped an atomic bomb on the city of Hiroshima. The effects were devastating; nearly half the city was destroyed and seventy thousand people were killed. A second bomb was dropped on Nagasaki three days later. On August 14, 1945, Japan surrendered and World War Two was officially over. Few people knew at the time that much of the research for the A-bomb had been carried out in Canada by British and French Scientists, and that Canadian uranium was used in its creation.

Present-day celebration in the Netherlands, thanking Canadians for their liberation.

Review...Reflect...Respond

1. What were the major battles that Canadian forces participated in during World War II?

2. Of these battles which do you believe was the most significant in shaping Canada's international identity?

3. If you had been Prime Minister Mackenzie King, how would you have reacted to the disaster at Dieppe?

The Changing Face of the Canadian Military
Aboriginal Canadians in the Service

At the outbreak of war, the Aboriginal community in Canada responded quickly. Indian Affairs recorded over three thousand Aboriginal Canadians who served in the Second World War, although Inuit and Métis were not included in this tally. As RCAF and RCN had entrance restrictions, including education restrictions and a preference for Canadians of British decent, the great majority of Aboriginal Canadians who did serve did so with the army. Aboriginal men joined for the same reasons as other men across the country, to gain employment, to fight Nazism, and to carry on the tradition of their fathers and uncles who served in the First World War.[19]

As in the Great War, Aboriginal Canadian heroes emerged from the battlefield. Thomas George Prince, the most decorated Canadian war hero, served with the Royal Canadian Engineers and later became part of an exclusive battalion, called the Devil's Brigade by the Germans, which took on specialized reconnaissance and raiding missions. He served in Italy and France spying on German positions. After finding an enemy reserve battalion in Southern France in the summer of 1944, Prince walked seventy kilometres across rugged terrain to report the location and led the brigade back to the German camp, joining in the ensuing battle. Prince was summoned to Buckingham Palace and decorated with the Military Medal by King George VI.

Women in the Service

As war waged on, Canadian women were recruited into the fighting corps for the first time in history. Over forty-five thousand women joined the newly created Women's Army Corps (CWAC); the Auxiliary Force of the RCAF, later renamed the Royal Canadian Air Force (Women's Division); and the Women's Royal Canadian Naval Service (Wrens). Another 4518 women served in the medical corps. The idea behind the creation of women's auxiliaries was for women to "back the attack" or free up men to take on the more difficult tasks. Known as "Jill Canucks", these women were not permitted to fight but were often close to the front lines and under enemy fire while performing duties. While in the service, women were reminded to act ladylike,

A new recruit receiving a blessing.

were not permitted to command other women, and were paid less then their male counterparts. As war waged on, women's pay increased from two thirds of men's pay to four fifths in some ranks.

The entry of women into the armed forces challenged the accepted role for women in Canadian society. The war gave women a new sense of equality. "Shoulder to Shoulder" was the motto adopted by the Canadian Women's Army Corps and the title of their official marching song. Many Canadians, men and women alike, feared that women's participation in the services would betray their femininity. Women were supposed to be nurturers not combatants. "They are still Women After all" was the title of L.S.B. Shapiro's article in *Saturday Night*, September 1942. Written by Canadian war correspondent and future novelist, Shapiro argued that women might cease to be "feminine individuals" if they took on male roles.[20]

Public opinion surveys conducted in 1943 indicated that few people believed joining the services was the best way that women could support the

The Canadian Women's Army Corps, stationed in a battered German town, during World War II.

war, that women were aware that their families would disapprove, and that women actually expected resistance from their families. The surveys were followed by an education campaign, including magazine advertisements, recruitment films, radio spots and posters, that tried to dispel the notion that enlisting would jeopardize femininity. Propaganda stressed that female recruitment was an emergency measure, that recruitment was temporary, and that women would return to their previous roles after the war. Efforts were also taken to make the uniform attractive. Enlistment ads boasted that the women of the CWAC were the "best dressed" in the war.[21]

Canadians on the Home Front

In 1939, the country was still emerging from the Great Depression, and was not prepared for a world war. Once again, however, the war eventually brought industrial growth to the country as factories turned out munitions, aircraft, and ships for the Allied effort. In total, during the Second World War, financial assistance from Canada to the Allies amounted to over $3 billion. Thousands of Canadians from coast to coast found employment in these factories.

Women on the Homefront

After the First World War, women had been forced or urged to leave their wartime jobs in factories across the country. During the Second World War, however, they were once again needed. Propaganda was used to encourage them to join or return to the work force. As a result, during the Second World War, one million Canadian women worked in jobs outside the home, driving trucks, running streetcars as "conductorettes," and working in construction and in munition factories. "Rosie the

Woman lathe-tender working on a gun barrel at Hamilton, Ontario, during World War II.

Riveter," "The Bren-Gun Girl," and other images of women donning their overalls and bandanas were strong role models for women and it became popular for women to wear pants.

In a national selective service broadcast, August 19, 1942, Prime Minister Mackenzie King attempted to ease Canadians fears, as women joined the work force:

> Concern has been expressed as to the effect of the employment of women on the welfare of the family. That concern is fully shared by the government. It must, however, not be forgotten that a total war effort is needed to protect everything we hold dear, including the family and family life, and that the employment of women is essential to a total war effort. We have only to think of what has happened to family life in enslaved Poland to realize what will happen to the Canadian family if this war is not won.

In the same speech, King explained that to "safeguard the welfare of the family, day nurseries for the care of children of working mothers are being established in co-operation with the provincial authorities in the two large industrial provinces." Although many exciting new steps were taken as women joined the paid labour force, as in the First World War, women were still paid less for the same work as men and would once again be encouraged to leave when the war was over. In a 1945 *Mayfair* magazine article, it was written:

> Look Ladies; it's reconversion time. Tanks and tail guns have vacated the priority list in favour of new refrigerators and nail scissors. We've written two V-Days in the record, and re-establishment, rather than re-armament, is the order.
>
> So how about coming out from behind those welder's masks and swapping your overalls for aprons? The menfolk are returning from overseas; they will take a very dim view of the situation if they find that you have permanently muscled in on their toiling territory... It will be

quite a shock to him to discover that instead of staying at home and crocheting borders for the hand towels, his better half is driving a streetcar... Refrain from any act which would even suggest your ability to lift anything heavier than a dry mop. Make like a lady, not like a lady wrestler...[22]

Nevertheless, important strides toward equality for women in the workforce were taken.

Financing the War

Victory Bonds were reintroduced in the Second World War to help pay for Canada's contribution to the war effort. Canadians bought Victory Bonds on the promise that the money would be repaid after the war at a slightly higher interest rate. The Victory Bond Campaign was well received by the Canadian public and raised twelve billion dollars.

As Canada turned its attention to the war effort, consumer goods became scarce and there were many more restrictions on civilians and businesses than during the First World War. By 1942, the government instituted rationing of goods, giving Canadians equal access to food and other consumer products. Taking steps to control prices, the government punished "Profiteers," those who tried to sell goods under the table. They also introduced wage controls, to avoid having skilled labourers demand unreasonable salaries, and a cost of living allowance to maintain a minimum standard of living. Government intervention extended to the creation of a Wartime Information Board controlling war propaganda and censored radio broadcasting. Civilians could not escape government wartime messaging, from posters to short news clips played in theatres.

A number of social services were introduced during the Second World War that still exist today. These social changes were introduced partly because King wanted to compete with the rise in popularity of the Cooperative Commonwealth Federation Party (CCF), which fought for the establishment of social services. King established Unemployment

World War II rationing sign in a store window, Ontario.

World War II poster appealing for help at the home front.

Insurance in 1940 and Family Allowance, monthly payments for families with children under sixteen, in July 1945.

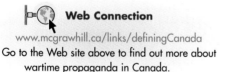

Web Connection

www.mcgrawhill.ca/links/definingCanada
Go to the Web site above to find out more about wartime propaganda in Canada.

The Conscription Crisis: "Not Necessarily Conscription, But Conscription if Necessary"

As the war raged overseas, Prime Minister Mackenzie King became increasingly concerned that there would not be enough volunteers to replace those already serving. Like Robert Borden before him, he had made a promise to the Canadian people, most significantly to French Canadians that he would not resort to conscription. But, once again, he was faced with the reality that the war was not soon coming to an end and that more troops would be needed. For King, this was perhaps his most critical moment. He had brought Canadians into the war united, but conscription would surely tear the country apart.

In 1942, King skillfully turned the conscription issue around and put the decision in the hands of the Canadian public, releasing himself from his earlier pledge. King planned a national plebiscite that would ask Canadians to vote on whether or not they would permit conscription. It would be worded such that it focused on the "possibility" rather than the implementation of conscription. On April 7 he pleaded:

> The restriction upon the power of the government was necessary at the outset to preserve national unity....You know full well that a foremost aim of my public life has been the preservation of the unity of Canada. I must say that under the changed conditions of today, and with Canada's record in war what has been over the past two and a half years, I see no reason why the removal of the restriction should weaken our unity. Instead, I believe firmly that its removal will help to overcome a source of irritation and disunity within our own country. It will, I believe, also help to remove a source of misunderstanding in the other countries united with Canada in the common effort to preserve freedom in the world.

La Ligue pour la défense du Canada emerged in Quebec, rallying citizens to vote against conscription in the plebiscite. *La Ligue* published a manifesto in January and circulated the leaflet throughout the province. Meetings were held, literature distributed, and memberships sold, and *la Ligue* gained momentum and popularity. For the most part, however, the press in Quebec criticized *la Ligue*. Only *Le Devoir* argued adamantly for its readers to vote against conscription.[23]

On April 27, 1942, a vote was taken. The majority of Canadians in every province said yes to the idea of conscription; seventy-three percent of French Canadians said no.[24] Once again *Canadiens* and Canadians were divided.

The results of the plebiscite released King from his earlier promises, but the heavy "no" vote in Quebec haunted him. King put the issue aside, and delayed introducing conscription as long as possible. His promise to parliament of "not necessarily conscription, but conscription if necessary" summed up his approach.

The draft was not introduced until November of 1944, after the Normandy Campaign, and when it seemed unavoidable to King. The men of the National Resources Mobilization Act serving for home defence were targeted for conscription. For the most part, the Canadian public supported King and felt that he had kept his promise as best he could. The men of the NRMA, however, put up a fight and many fled from their duties. Of the twelve thousand NRMA men sent overseas, only twenty-five hundred ever reached the battlefield. In the end, the Conscription Crisis of the Second World War could have been avoided.

A National Shame

Intense anxieties that result from war can lead to rash and ill-conceived decisions. The internment of Japanese Canadians as well as the rejection of Jewish immigrants during the Second World War represents a dark period of Canadian history.

Canada and the Holocaust

Hitler believed that other ethnic groups were weak and inferior to the Aryan Germans. Much of his unfounded hate and anger was focused on the Jewish people, who he claimed had caused Germany's problems, such as the failing economy. In the 1930s, German Jews fled Nazi Germany, seeking refuge in the western world. Frederick Blair, in charge of immigration during Mackenzie King's administration, effectively "shut the doors" on Jewish immigrants. Fewer than five thousand Jewish people were allowed into Canada during Hitler's reign, a significantly smaller number than allowed into the United States. Blair found support for his policy with individuals such as Abbé Grouix, a French priest, who wrote for *Le Devoir* and publicly aired his anti-Semitic feelings.

An Anti-Conscription rally—could the crisis have been avoided?

Address on the National Security Plebiscite

On April 7, 1942, Prime Minister Mackenzie King gave his "not necessarily conscription, but conscription if necessary, "speech to the Canadian public.

I wish to speak to you tonight, my fellow Canadians, on a matter which, at this time of war, is of first importance—of first importance to the present position of our country, and to its future security; and, therefore, of real concern to the homes and lives of all.

On Monday, the 27th of this month, you will be asked to give the government a free hand in the discharge of its duty in carrying on the war.

When those who hold representative and responsible positions have given a definite promise to the people, they have created an obligation to act in accordance with that promise, until the people are again consulted. Such an obligation may not be binding according to law, but as an obligation it is no less sacred.

The pledge from which the present government is asking to be freed is not related to any ordinary day-to-day matter of policy....The pledge to which I refer is, as you are all aware, that, as a method of raising men for military service overseas, resort would not be had to conscription...

That promise is a restriction upon the government today. It is, as I have said, not a legal restriction. It is a moral obligation and I need not add a moral obligation of the most solemn kind. It is equally the one and only restriction upon the exercise by the government of its full power.

You ask: why was the restriction ever imposed? Why was the promise given?...

The pledge not to impose conscription for service overseas was given in order to maintain the unity of Canada. Without this assurance, I do not believe that parliament would have given, as it did, prompt and wholehearted approval to Canada's entry into the war. It was the trust of the people in the pledged word of the government which then maintained our national unity.

...National unity is, I believe, more essential to the success of the war effort of any country than most other factors combined...

The restriction upon the power of the government was necessary at the outset to preserve national unity. It has helped until recently to maintain national unity. In the past few months it has, however, become a matter of controversy and a threat to unity....I must say that under the changed conditions of today... I see no reason why the removal of the restriction should weaken our unity. Instead, I believe firmly that its removal will help to overcome a source of irritation and disunity within our own country...

I come now to the question: why have the government and parliament not tackled this question on their own responsibility without resorting to a plebiscite?

The answer is very simple....Had the present government attempted to do such a thing, does anyone imagine it would have been able to retain the confidence of parliament? For the government to have disregarded its pledged word would, I believe, have helped to destroy faith, not merely in the government, but in democratic institutions....By such an arbitrary act, we might well have destroyed the national unity on which our war effort is founded.

...The truth, of course, is that our army today is just as large as it would have been if conscription for overseas service had been adopted. The absence of conscription for overseas service has not limited our war effort. The lack of power to impose such conscription has, however, placed our war effort in a wholly false light before our own citizens, and, what is worse, before our allies. In other words, conscription has been made the symbol of a total effort, regardless of all Canada is doing to help win the war.

The issue at present is not conscription; it is whether or not the government, subject to its responsibility to parliament, is to be free to decide that question itself in the light of all national considerations. The government is not asking you to say whether or not conscription should be adopted. That responsibility the government is asking you to leave to itself and to parliament, with entire freedom to decide the question on its merits.

The question of conscription, properly viewed, is a military question. The place to discuss it is in parliament....A part of our forces should be kept in Canada to protect us against attack; a part of our forces should be sent overseas to help defeat the enemy and thus prevent him from attacking Canada. Both tasks are equally essential to our safety. Anyone who tells you that only one of these tasks is necessary is deceiving you...

Address on the National Security Plebiscite *(continued)*

...To a nation, there is one thing even more important than the preservation of its unity. That is the preservation of its existence. To those who, beyond the events of today, are able to look into the future, it is no longer the unity, it is the very existence of our country as a free nation which they see is in danger today. We are no longer in a world where even the most powerful nation is able, by itself, to save itself from the ambition and greed of the aggressor nations....With our immense territory, great resources and small population, no country may come to need the help of the other countries more than our own. Unless we continue to do all we can to help others, we shall have no right to expect them to do all they can to help us...

In the British Commonwealth of Nations, Canada and South Africa are the only countries not immediately subject to attack....Is anyone so blind as to believe that already they have not cast their covetous eyes upon the vast territory and resources of our own Dominion? ... One thing is perfectly certain. If the enemy is not kept at bay on the oceans, and defeated beyond the waters of the Atlantic and the Pacific, the final battles of the world conflict will be fought in the waters and upon the soil of Canada and the United States.

...We cannot defend our country and save our homes and families by waiting at home for the enemy to attack us....But we must also take our full part in the combat, we must go out to meet the enemy before he reaches our shores; we must, if we can, defeat him before he attacks us, before our cities are laid waste and before the women and children of Canada are injured or killed in our streets and our homes.

Here is the strongest of reasons why no excuse should remain for anyone to say that because of a restriction upon the exercise by the government of its full powers, Canada's war effort is not all it might be. Should the day come-and it may come soon-when Canada is faced with attack, and we need help from the United States or Britain or any of the United Nations, how would we feel if we thought their governments were restricted in their power to aid Canada?...Danger threatens us from the east and from the west. It is in the face of this peril that for the defence of our freedom and of our country, the government asks you to give it a free hand.

Canadian War Museum, 1993-0002-002

Recruiting poster for the Royal Canadian Air Force in World War II.

In 1939, those Jewish people remaining in Germany were forced into ghettos and then into concentration camps. As Germany took over neighbouring countries, Hitler rounded up millions of Jews; some were shot en masse, others were killed in gas chambers, while many were tortured or died of starvation in concentration camps. Over the course of Hitler's rule, the Nazis killed over six million Jewish people.

The Internment of Japanese Canadians

Racism against Japanese Canadians ran deep on the west coast of Canada well before the Second World War. One of the major concerns was that Japanese Canadians were competitive in the labour market and were taking jobs from other Canadians for smaller wages. In 1907, in Vancouver's "little Tokyo", a riot broke out in which windows were smashed and Japanese civilians terrorized. Prime Minister Mackenzie King did little to diminish these racist attitudes, before the war. In fact, he restricted the number of Japanese allowed to enter Canada.

After the Japanese bombed Pearl Harbor in 1941, Canada declared war on Japan, and fear of the enemy escalated, as it had during the First World War. Pressured by the Canadian public and parliament, Mackenzie King again called up the War Measures Act and announced that Canadians of Japanese decent would be forcibly evacuated. By September 1942, over twenty-two thousand Japanese men, women, and children, were stripped of their possessions and herded to relocation camps, mostly in ghost towns in the B.C. interior. Many were only given twenty-four hours notice to vacate their homes before being forced to leave. Homes, businesses, and possessions, were left behind and auctioned off by the Canadian government, or liquidated for a fraction of their value. The money from these auctions was used to pay for the operating expenses of the internment camps. Able-bodied men were generally separated from their families and sent to work in road camps, and the families that managed

R.C.N. officer questioning and confiscating a Japanese-Canadian fishing boat off the British Columbia coast, December 9, 1941.

to stay together, were sent to harvest sugar beets in Manitoba and Alberta. The conditions of the internment camps were deplorable, and in many cases, the Red Cross had to bring in food.

This abuse did not end with the surrender of Japan at the end of the Second World War. King insisted that Japanese Canadians be questioned to determine their "loyalty" to the country and their potential to be a threat. As a result of this interrogation, over four thousand Japanese were forced to leave the country. Restrictions on Japanese Canadians lasted almost four years after the end of the Second World War, and their civil liberties were not returned until 1949.

Redressing the Japanese Internment

In the late 1970s, the opening of government documents to the public revealed that both the Department of National Defence and the Royal Canadian Mounted Police believed that Japanese

Canadians posed no threat to the security of Canada. It was not until 1988 that the Canadian government offered an official apology and some compensation for their losses. The landmark settlement included such restitution as:

- A formal apology to Japanese Canadians and acknowledgement of violation of human rights
- Symbolic redress of $21 000 for each Japanese Canadian who was interned
- The sum of $12 million to the Japanese Canadian community for educational, social, and cultural activities that promoted the well-being of the Japanese Canadian community and human rights
- The sum of $24 million to establish the Canadian Race Relations Foundation to help eliminate racism
- Canadian citizenship for people of Japanese descent who had been expelled from Canada or who had their citizenship revoked during this time

---

Review...Reflect...Respond

1. What benefits did World War II bring to the homefront in Canada?

2. What did Prime Minister King mean by "not necessarily conscription, but conscription if necessary."

3. Do you believe the Canadian government's restitution and apology to the Japanese Canadians who were interned during World War II was enough? Why or why not?

Conclusion

The Second World War left its mark on the Canadian people. At home, the country was pulled out of the depths of the Depression, and prospered in wartime productivity. The BCATP saw the creation of training camps and headquarters across the country and men from around the world trained on Canadian soil. Canadian women went to work in factories, proving their ability in skilled trades and even serving overseas "shoulder to shoulder" in the armed forces with Canadian men. At the end of the war, public opinion polling proved that Canadians were confident about the country's future.

William Lyon Mackenzie King, Canada's wartime prime minister, deserves much of the credit for Canada's success and productivity during the Second World War. He established the beginnings of the Canadian social welfare system and, most significantly, averted a full-blown conscription crisis with skill. Canada went in to the war united, thanks to King, and came out of the war optimistic about the future.

Overseas, the role of Canada in the Second World War was more diverse than it had been during the First World War, with Canadians serving in many theatres, from the Atlantic to the Pacific. The Canadian force was divided, with small units being dispersed between Hong Kong, Italy, and the Western Front. It was not until the end of the war, after the Normandy campaign that the balance was readdressed and the Canadians fought together to liberate Holland.

Undoubtedly, other Allied countries, such as Britain and the U.S., had fought in far greater numbers than Canada. But Canada had made a considerable contribution as a newly independent power with a comparatively small population. Moments such as the D-Day landings and the liberation of the Dutch people were triumphs for the young country. Today, Dutch civilians still celebrate the brave Canadian soldiers who secured their freedom.

Despite Prime Minister King's great efforts to limit the number of casualties, Canada had made a costly contribution: forty-five thousand men and women died in the Second World War. Out of a population of just ten million, one million Canadian men and women had served and thousands more were found in volunteer organizations, on farms and in factories from coast to coast.

Notes

1. At the Peace Conference in 1918, U.S. President Woodrow Wilson presented his Fourteen Points, a peace plan that included the creation of an international peace organization and stipulated that there be no revenge against the countries that lost the war. Not all of the Fourteen Points, including that about "no revenge", were incorporated into the final draft of the Treaty of Versailles.

2. Read more about Mackenzie King's policies during the Second World War in C.P. Stacey's *Canada and the Age of Conflict*. (Toronto: 1981.)

3. William Lyon Mackenzie King. *The Mackenzie King Diaries, 1893–1949*. (Toronto: University of Toronto Press, 1973–1980).

4. On December 11, 1931 the Statute of Westminister granted Canada full legislative authority domestically and in external affairs.

5. As described in W. A. B. Douglas and Brerton Greenhouse in *Out of the Shadows, Canada in the Second World War*, (Toronto: Oxford University Press, 1977) pp. 84–85.

6. For a detailed description of the Dieppe Raid see John Mellor, *Forgotten Heroes*: The Canadians at Dieppe. (Toronto: Methuen Publications, 1975).

7. C.P. Stacey "The Significance of Dieppe" in C.M Wallace and R.M. Bray, *Reappraisals in Canadian History: Post Confederation*. (Scarborough: Prentice Hall, 1999) p. 435.

8. C.P. Stacey "The Significance of Dieppe" in C.M Wallace and R.M. Bray, *Reappraisals in Canadian History*: Post Confederation. p. 436.

9. J.W. Pickersgill, The Mackenzie King Record. (Toronto: Unniversity of Toronto Press, 1960) p. 417.

10. Desmond, A, Morton, *Military History of Canada*. (Toronto: McClelland & Stewart, 1999) pp. 203–204.

11. Berton, Pierre. *Marching as to War*. (Toronto: Doubleday Canada, 2001) p. 378.

12. Ibid. p. 374

13. David J. Bercuson, *Maple Leaf Against the Axis*. (Toronto: Stoddart Publishing, 1995) p.73.

14. Ibid.

15. J.L. Granatstein and Desmond Morton, *A Nation Forged in Fire*. (Toronto: Lester & Orper Dennys, 1989).

16. Lyrics by Hamish Henderson, as quoted in Terry Copp and Richard Nielsen, *No Price Too High*: Canadians in the Second World War (Toronto: McGraw-Hill Ryerson, Ltd, 1996) p. 144.

17. Desmond Morton. A Military History of Canada. p. 213.

18. For a detailed description and analysis of the D-Day invasion see J.L. Granatstein and Desmond Morton's *Bloody Victory: Canadians and the D-Day Campaign*. (Toronto: Lester Publishing, 1994).
    ID #20941 Credit: H.G. Aikman / National Archives of Canada / PA-116510.

19. Based on article on Veteran Affairs Canada Web site "Native Soldiers Foreign Battlefields" found at site.

20. As referenced in Ruth Roach Pierson's "Wartime Jitters Over Femininity" in J.L. Granatstein's and Peter Neary's *The Good Fight, Canadians and World War II*. (Toronto: Copp Clark Ltd., 1995). p. 141.

21. Based on Ruth Roach Pierson's article "Wartime Jitters Over Femininity" in J.L. Granatstein's and Peter Neary's *The Good Fight, Canadians and World War II*.

22. Mayfair, December 1945, pp. 40–41 as quoted in Jeffrey Keshen and Suzanne Morton, eds., *Material Memory: Documents in Post-Confederation History* (Toronto: Addison Wesley, 1998) p. 239.

23. Jack Granatstein discusses *La Ligue pour la defense du Canada* and the reaction of the Quebec papers in his *Canada's War, The Politics of the Mackenzie King Government, 1939–45*. (Toronto: University of Toronto Press, 1975) pp. 222–228.

24. The results ranged from 69.1 percent to 82.4 percent "yes" in every province except Quebec where 27.1 percent voted "yes". Results taken from "The Dominion Plebiscite Act, 1942" in Dave De Brou and Bill Waiser's *Documenting Canada, A History of Modern Canada in Documents*. (Saskatoon: Fifth House Publishing, 1992) pp. 388–89.

Chapter 18 Review

Knowledge & Understanding

1. Identify these people, places, and events, and explain their historical significance to Canada's developing culture and identity:

   Zombies
   BCATP
   "Jill Canucks"
   Operation Jubilee
   Operation Overlord
   Dieppe
   Ortona

   Netherlands
   La Ligue pour la défense du Canada
   CWAC
   Thomas George Prince

2. World War II diversified Canada's economy, allowed women to take on greater roles in the workforce, and saw Canada's emergence as a strong military force. Yet it also divided the country along French-English lines, it took away civil rights of some of its own citizens, and it saw the massacre of thousands of young Canadian men and women. Was World War II more of a cost or a benefit to Canadians, Canada, and its position on the world stage? Create a cost-benefit chart of Canada's involvement in World War II.

Thinking & Inquiry

3. It is often believed that women's equality achieved great strides in World War II, but then took steps backward when the war ended. In her article "Women in the Labour Force in World War II" Ruth Pierson argues that,

   ...Canada's war effort, rather than any consideration of women's right to work, determined the recruitment of women into the labour force. The recruitment of women was part of a large-scale intervention by government in the labour market to control allocation of labour for effective prosecution of the war.

   If Pierson is correct, did women achieve any greater equality during World War II, or was it a false equality due to outside circumstances? Write a thesis statement agreeing with or opposing Pierson's opinion and support it with three well-written paragraphs using historical evidence. You may also want to conduct a mini debate with a partner in your class.

Application

4. As a 26-year-old single woman, you started working in a munitions factory in 1941 and have worked your way up to floor manager by 1945. When the war ends, you would like to keep working, but are feeling pressure from friends and the public to quit your job to free the position for returning soldiers. What would you do? Write a letter to the president of your company outlining your reasons to stay or leave your employment.

Communication

5. In both World War I and World War II, the issue of conscription divided the country between French and English Canadians. Who do you believe handled the conscription crisis better—Borden or King? In a clearly articulated essay, state your opinion in a thesis statement and support it with at least three arguments. Be sure to use historically correct evidence to support your arguments.

Unit Five Research Activity

Research

1. The internment of Japanese Canadians during World War II raises many questions for historians about identity, humanity, and the conduct of countries during wartime. Investigate closely this episode in Canadian history. History books, novels (such as Joy Kogawa's *Obasan*) and the Internet can all serve as good sources for your research. Look for information in at least these categories
   • the sequence of events
   • the different measures that were taken
   • the attitudes of people at the time
   • How did the internment of Japanese Canadians differ from the internment of Japanese Americans?
   • How was the internment of Japanese Canadians redressed?

Interpretation and Analysis

2. Was there any real threat from Japanese Canadians to the security of their country?

3. Why did many of those interned never return to their homes after the war?

4. How do the dark realities of history such as the Japanese internment shape the Canadian identity?

5. Why did it take over 40 years for the Canadian government to formally apologize to Japanese Canadians?

Applying and Communicating Your Skills

6. Construct a visual essay of the Japanese internment. Show the chronology of events and the impact on the people and on Canada as a whole. Use quotes, reproductions of photographs, and your own artwork to illustrate your project.

7. As Prime Minister Mulroney's Minister of Canadian Heritage, you are to write and deliver an apology to Japanese Canadians who were interned during World War II. Your speech must include what happened, why it happened, and an apology. Record your speech in front of a video camera, as if giving a news conference. Be sure to hand in both your speech and your research notes along with your video to your teacher.

Canada's Coming of Age, 1945–1970

In this unit you will:

- assess the significance of successive waves of immigration in the development of regional, provincial, and national identities in Canada

- evaluate the evolution of Canada's role on the international stage

- describe the relationship between major social and technological changes in Canada

- analyse the evolution of citizenship in Canada

- describe the development of Canada's social programs and their significance in terms of Canadian identity

- describe the role of literature, the arts, and popular culture in the development of a distinctive Canadian culture

Before World War II ended, the Allies had split into two camps — democratic states and their allies versus communist states and their allies. Canada occupied an uneasy middle position between the United States and the Soviet Union. Canada, which was slowly becoming a multicultural society, sought to develop an independent peacekeeping role in a nuclear-armed world. However, Canada was also challenged at home by Quebec's Quiet Revolution, workers rights, and the need for human rights policies to overcome past injustices.

Even though post-war politics was frightening, the postwar economy was very prosperous. Wartime industry adapted easily to producing consumer goods for well-paid and increasingly suburban workers. An enormous postwar birth rate created a steady demand. Also, the desire to avoid the horrors of the Great Depression created a need for social programs, especially health insurance, pensions, and unemployment insurance.

Throughout the first half of the twentieth century, most Canadian artists had to pursue professional careers abroad. Postwar prosperity enabled Canada to start developing artistic talent at home, which led to a postwar cultural renaissance within the country.

Canada in 1949

Iceland

Greenland
(Denmark)

District of Franklin

Alaska (U.S.A.)

Yukon
Territory

Northwest
Territories

District of
Keewatin

District of Mackenzie

Newfoundland

British
Columbia

Alberta

Saskatchewan

Manitoba

Quebec

Ontario

P.E.I.

New
Brunswick

Nova
Scotia

U.S.A.

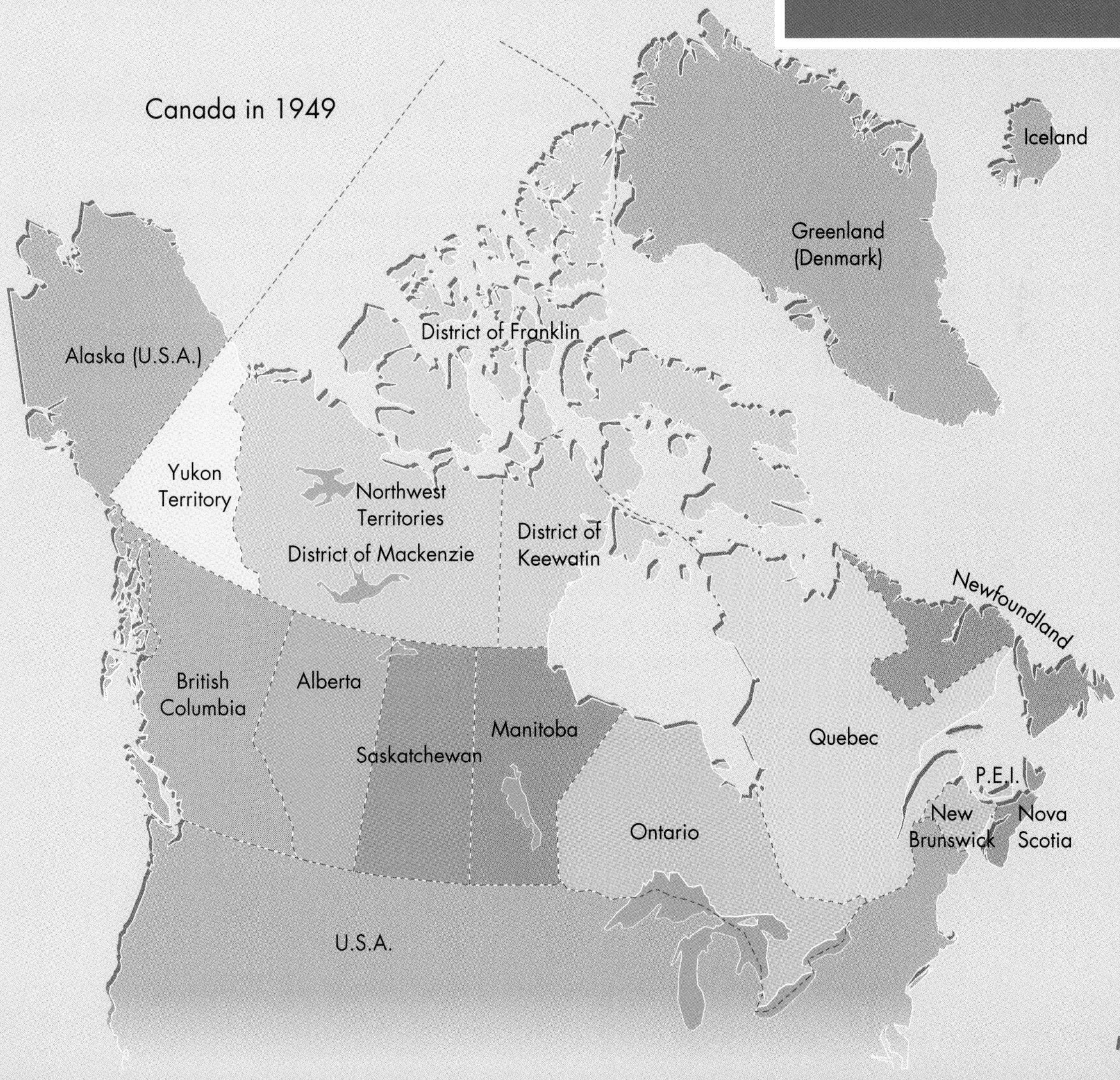

Crucible of a New Canadian Identity, 1945–1968

> Canadians can...make Canada a better and better country for all its citizens to live in, while...[helping] to heal the world of its grievous wounds.
>
> **– MARGARET MCWILLIAM, *THIS NEW CANADA, 1948***

After World War II, the world changed greatly—and so too did Canada's position in it. Even before the war ended, the Allies had split into two hostile camps: the liberal western democracies and the communist Soviet bloc. The hostilities between the United States (the dominant nation of the western world) and the Soviet Union (the dominant nation of the communist world) threatened to start World War III, a war that would be fought with nuclear weapons.

Canada was no longer seen as an inevitable ally of Britain. Britain was preoccupied with rebuilding after the devastation of World War II. As a result, Canada's relationships with Britain, France, and the United States underwent dramatic changes, as did its role in the Commonwealth.

Under these circumstances, Canada sought to develop an independent peacekeeping role, principally through the United Nations, of which it was a key founder. The peacekeeping role had major advantages for Canada: It enabled the country to avoid complete identification with the United States, and it offered a genuine opportunity to work for peace, perhaps even to help prevent a nuclear war.

At the same time, many social changes were reshaping Canada's identity from within. What did it mean to be a Canadian? In a world that increasingly focused on human rights, what rights should a Canadian have?

19

Timeline

Year	Event (left)	Event (right)
1945		Igor Gouzenko defects to Canada and provides evidence of a Soviet spy ring in Canada
1946	The Canadian Citizenship Act is passed	
1948		The Asbestos Strike in Quebec pits English business owners against French workers
1949	Canada is one of the twelve founding countries of NATO	
1950		Canada enters the Korean War; more than 300 Canadian soldiers are killed in three years
1956	Lester Pearson introduces the concept of peacekeeping to end the hostilities in the Suez Canal	
1958		Canada and the United States form NORAD
1959	Diefenbaker cancels the Avro Arrow	
1960		Jean Lesage becomes premier of Quebec. The Canadian Bill of Rights is passed
1962	The Canadian forces are put on high alert during the Cuban missile crisis	
1968		The National Indian Brotherhood is founded

By the end of this chapter, you will be able to

- describe how ethnocultural identities have been expressed in different provinces and regions at different times

- describe the nature of Canada's role in international organizations in the twentieth century

- demonstrate an understanding of how Canada's participation in significant international conflicts changed the way the country was perceived by the international community

- describe the ways in which the world wars and other conflicts of the twentieth century altered Canada's self-image

- analyze the evolution of the labour movement in Canada

- describe the role of significant Quebec-based political figures in the development of the French presence in Canada

The Cold War

For geographical reasons, Canada was an inevitable ally of the United States during the Cold War—but it was also a willing one. Most Canadians believed in liberal democracy rather than communism. However, the alliance with the United States created many complex political problems. The key problem was finding a way to benefit from U.S. protection while retaining an independent foreign policy. U.S. protection was itself equivocal: Canada was at risk during the Cold War principally because it lay between the United States and the Soviet Union. Canadian leaders tended to feel that the United States was overly aggressive in dealing with the Soviet bloc and that it created unnecessary confrontations. This view, when expressed, was a major source of tension between the two countries.

The Gouzenko Spy Case: Understanding Canada's New Status

Canadians saw the Soviet Union not only as a totalitarian state, but also as an aggressive threat to democracy, determined to spread communism as far as it could by any means. Whether that was true or not, the Gouzenko affair in 1945 demonstrated that Canada was not going to be able to just go home after the war and forget about world conflicts.

During World War II, Igor Gouzenko, a clerk at the Soviet Embassy in Ottawa, became disillusioned with communism and envious of the freedom enjoyed by Canadians. In 1945, he learned that he and his family were about to be sent home. He decided to defect, and on September 5, three days after the war had ended, he bundled up documents that proved that the Russians were spying on Canada. He walked out of the embassy—into the hands of Canadian authorities. At first, the Canadian government did not take Gouzenko seriously, mainly because officials doubted that the Soviet Union cared what Canada knew or did.

Then, on September 7, Gouzenko's apartment was ransacked in what may have been a failed Soviet attempt to recapture him. Alarmed, the authorities put Gouzenko and his family into protective custody and examined his documents closely.

After months of investigation, the government arrested more than twenty people, accusing them of espionage. One of those arrested was Canada's only communist Member of Parliament, Fred Rose, who was later sentenced to six years in prison. In July 1946, a Royal Commission confirmed that a spy ring had indeed been operating in Canada and that one of its objectives was to get hold of advanced Canadian nuclear technology.

The Gouzenko case helped persuade Canadians that there was a Soviet threat to Canada. Other disquieting international events included a communist coup in Czechoslovakia in 1948 and a Soviet blockade of western-controlled West Berlin in the same

Many historians mark the defection of Igor Gouzenko as the beginning of the Red Scare. His defection gave enormous momentum to anti-Communist sentiment in Canada. Investigations led to the arrest of eleven Canadians, who were convicted of spying or conspiracy.

year. (Berlin was inside communist East Germany, an ally of the Soviet Union.) Western governments airlifted supplies to Berlin and got the blockade lifted, but it was becoming increasingly clear that tensions between the western bloc and the Soviet bloc were the key fact of postwar international politics and that they would necessarily shape Canada's foreign policy.

North Atlantic Treaty Organization (NATO)

One of Canada's major strategies for postwar peace and self-defence was the promotion of a defensive alliance against the Soviet Union that would include Canada, the United States, Britain, and the nations of Western Europe. Although Canada's leaders might have preferred to rely on the United Nations to keep peace, they were worried that the UN would be paralyzed by the veto power of the USSR. An alliance of North American and Western European powers was first proposed by Canadian diplomat Escott Reid at the Couchiching Conference in August 1947. Under his proposal, each member would be required to

come to the defence of the others and to contribute personnel and equipment for defence strategies.

Canadian diplomats were especially worried that the United States would follow an established pattern of isolationism, that is, it would retreat into its own affairs after the war. However, at that point, Britain and France, which were devastated by the war, were in no position to lead the western world. Louis St. Laurent, then Canada's minister of external affairs, took the idea of a North Atlantic Treaty Organization (NATO) to the UN General Assembly in September 1947. He delivered a speech in which he talked of "an association of democratic and peace-loving states willing to accept more specific international obligations in return for a greater measure of national security."[1]

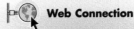

Web Connection

www.mcgrawhill.ca/links/definingcanada
Go to the Web site above to find out more about Canada and NATO.

How did Canada's involvement with NATO change its self-image and the way other countries viewed Canada?

On April 4, 1949, twelve countries signed the NATO agreement: Canada, Belgium, Denmark, France, Great Britain, Iceland, Italy, Luxembourg, the Netherlands, Norway, Portugal, and the United States. Canada succeeded in getting a few words into the treaty about cooperation on non-military issues to eliminate economic conflicts. Canada had grander plans for NATO than mutual self-defence: Canada was hoping that NATO would evolve into a general dispute-resolving mechanism for the western nations. However, nothing much came of this "Canadian article" as it came to be called.

Even though NATO was originally promoted by Canadian diplomats, membership in it was more controversial at home than was membership in the United Nations. NATO was a military alliance, specifically designed to facilitate war if necessary, not to find peaceful solutions to world problems. It was also the first military alliance Canada had joined in peacetime. The Korean War (1950–53), the first serious conflict that Canada entered after World War II, tested Canada's commitment to such alliances.

The Korean War

After World War II, Korea had been divided into two territories: North Korea, under the control of the Soviet Union, and South Korea, under the control of the United States. The Soviet Union established a well-armed communist regime in the north. The United States supported a weak democracy in the south. Once the Soviets were confident that the north was militarily superior, they withdrew their own troops. The Americans then had to do the same in the south.

On June 25, 1950, North Korea invaded South Korea. Led by the United States, the United Nations passed a resolution asking its members to "furnish such assistance to the Republic of Korea [South Korea] as may be necessary to repel the armed attack and to restore international peace and security in the area."[2] The Soviet Union would have vetoed this move at the Security Council level, but it was in a weak negotiating position at the time—it was boycotting the Council because the People's Republic of China had not been given a seat.

Canadian soldiers serving in Korea; more than 300 would be killed between 1950 and 1953

Most Canadians feared communist expansion. Even so, Lester Pearson, then Canada's secretary of state, was concerned that the Americans were getting both themselves and their allies too deeply embroiled in foreign conflicts. Canada's first response was to send only three destroyers and an air-transport squadron to South Korea. The Americans thought that contribution wholly inadequate and pressed for more assistance. In August, the Canadian government agreed to send ground troops. Though the United States was clearly in command of the war, Canada was careful to maintain the formal understanding that it was fighting under the direction of the United Nations.

By February 1951, Canadian troops were in Korea. In April, they fought valiantly at Kapyong, reinforcing once again the fierce reputation of the Canadian soldier. For the next two-and-a-half years, infantry, air, and naval forces from Canada played a key role. The war ended on July 27, 1953, when an armistice was signed. In all, 21 940 Canadians had served in the army, and 312 were killed.

The main effect of the Korean War on Canada was that it forced the Cabinet to reflect carefully on the "increasingly troubling" character of American leadership.[3] General MacArthur, for

example, had talked about expanding the war into China. Although MacArthur was dismissed by President Truman in 1951, concern persisted that American foreign policy was overly aggressive and that the Americans risked nuclear confrontation over situations that neither Americans nor Canadians fully understood.

Foreign defence commitments were costly. Even when there was no war, troops had to be stationed abroad, for example, in Germany and France, as part of the new NATO force. For fifteen years, the single largest expense in the Canadian federal budget was defence spending. In addition, critics of Cold War strategies became even more vocal when NATO forces were given nuclear weapons in 1963. In 1969, Prime Minister Pierre Trudeau cut Canada's support to NATO, despite ongoing criticism from NATO partners.

The Price of Security: Nuclear Weapons in Canada?

A possible nuclear attack by the Soviet Union on the United States was a major concern in postwar Canada. The shortest route for Soviet bombers to take to the United States was over the North Pole, and hence, over Canada. Canada formed unprecedented partnerships with the United States to build military outposts to detect Soviet bombers.

Distant Early Warning (DEW) Systems and Missiles

Canada had wanted to establish a chain of radar stations in the far north as early as 1946, to provide early warning of a possible Soviet attack. After the Soviet Union developed its own atomic bomb in 1949, the American government announced its intention to place radar stations on the American border with Canada. It made obvious sense for the two

Ovide Mercredi, Grand Chief of the Assembly of First Nations, lays a wreath in memory of Aboriginal soldiers killed in Korea.

nations to work together on a chain of radar stations placed for strategic geographical advantage, rather than worry about border issues. However, much negotiation was required. Many Canadians were very sensitive to the idea of an American military presence on Canadian soil. In 1954, the Pinetree Line was completed (thirty-three radar stations from Vancouver Island through to the Labrador coast). Of the $450 million, Canada paid $150 million. An all-Canadian project of ninety-eight unstaffed radar stations was also completed in 1957. The chief benefit of this Mid-Canada Line, as it was called, was that it had not required cooperation with the Americans. However, "going it alone" was not going to be realistic for Canada over the long term, because of the high costs of effective defence.

In the same year, the 1957 Distant Early Warning (DEW) Line, which stretched from Alaska to Baffin Island, was also completed, but the terms involved close work and tough negotiations with the United States. The U.S. government bore the entire cost and was required to use Canadian firms and employ Aboriginal Canadian workers. Canada also retained ownership of the sites, and major stations were commanded by Canadians. Still, national sovereignty issues persisted; access to DEW stations was controlled by American authorities, for example, even though the stations were on Canadian soil.

By the early 1960s, all these radar lines had become obsolete. The Soviets had developed intercontinental and submarine-launched missiles, against which radar stations were useless. The lasting effect of the construction of these lines was that they introduced and intensified defence cooperation with the United States even when Canada was not at war. That created a constant challenge to maintain Canadian sovereignty. This challenge became a hot issue when the American government

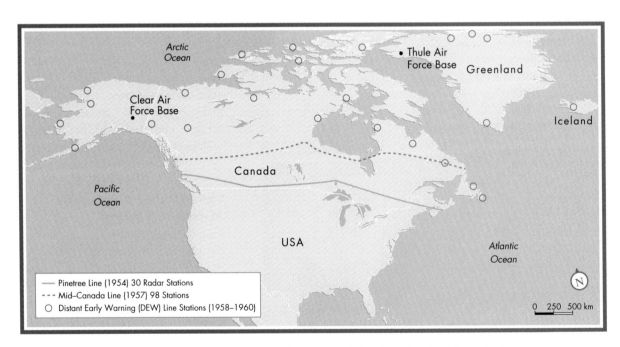

Fearing the threat of Soviet bombers, Canada and the United States created three lines of radar defence: the Pinetree Line, the Mid-Canada Line, and the Distant Early Warning Line. How did the establishment of these defence lines affect Canadians' anti-Communist sentiment?

started to pressure the Canadian government to accept nuclear weapons on Canadian soil, a policy that many Canadians strongly opposed.

NORAD

In 1958, Canada and the United States created the North American Air Defense Command (NORAD). It integrated the air-defence forces of the two countries, to intercept attacks instead of simply detecting them. The agreement stipulated that an American would always be the commander, and a Canadian would always be the deputy commander. The headquarters are buried beneath a mountain in Colorado. Prime Minister Diefenbaker's decision to go ahead with NORAD in 1957 was controversial, because it integrated Canada's national defence organizationally with that of the United States.

In 1981, NORAD changed its name to North American Aerospace Defense Command, to emphasize its role in detecting missiles. Its key roles today include detecting drug smugglers flying into North America and monitoring space for objects whose orbits may be decaying, resulting in their falling to Earth.

The Avro Arrow

Cold War defence strategies sparked the creation of an airplane that has become a legend in Canada. The Avro Arrow provokes debate today, more than half a century after it disappeared. To some it is a symbol of clear thinking by the Canadian government. To others, it symbolizes the heartbreaking collapse of Canadian willingness to pursue the best. In 1949, A.V. Roe Canada started building the Arrow (officially the CF-105), which was to be the world's most advanced jet fighter. It could fly faster and higher than any other. However, it also cost much more than the government had anticipated. The original estimate of $2 million per plane rose to $12.5 million during the project, and the government scaled back its order from six hundred to one hundred. Unless Canada could sell the Arrow to the United States Air Force, the project could not continue.

The Americans were not eager to purchase the Arrow; they were promoting Bomarc missiles instead. In any case, the

How would the establishment and then the closure of the Distant Early Warning stations affect the life of Canada's Aboriginal Peoples in the north?

The Avro Arrow has been called Canada's "national dream." Why?

Soviet Union had just launched its first intercontinental ballistic missile (ICBM). The value of a fighter jet declined dramatically because military threats now came from space, not from pilot-flown bombers.

On February 20, 1959, Prime Minister John Diefenbaker said, "The Arrow has been overtaken by events. There is no purpose in manufacturing horse collars when horses no longer exist."[4] And with that, he cancelled the Arrow program. A.V. Roe Canada promptly fired 14000 employees and ordered the destruction of all planes, parts, and design papers. Bob Johnson, an employee of A.V. Roe Canada, remembers the cancelling of the Avro Arrow:

> The thing that always bothered me was the way it was done; the cold, callous, deliberate way it was cancelled. Not *that* it was cancelled, but the way it was cancelled....We salvaged nothing. We scrapped everything. Five million dollars worth of parts—brand new instruments, equipment, laboratories, simulators—we're just cut up and scrapped with nothing salvaged. Even the drawings had to be burnt.... They should have saved those drawings. Even the information itself could have

been used by the British aviation industry and the States, because, let's face it, the Arrow was the most advanced aircraft of its day. Yet all that knowledge, all that development, years and years of study, was wiped out. Deliberately wiped out. No salvage.[5]

The employees included some of the best aerospace engineers in the world. Many went to the United States to continue to work on advanced technologies.

The decision to cancel the Arrow was bitterly controversial, and many Canadians worried that it signalled a willingness on Canada's part to settle into "branch plant" status, where Canadians would no longer participate in the development of innovative technologies. Dennis McDermott of the United Auto Workers Union, who represented the employees of A.V. Roe Canada, said, "We will now lose the cream of our skilled aircraft technicians to the United States. You just don't open and shut an industry like a workhouse. History will prove this to be one of the most colossal blunders made by a prime minister in the history of Canada."[6]

Years later in the House of Commons, Diefenbaker reflected on his decision to cancel the Avro Arrow:

> Some people talk about courage. Well, we took a stand in reference to the Arrow. No one wanted to take that stand.... As I look back on it, I think it was one of the decisions that was right. Here was an instrument beautiful in appearance, powerful, a tribute to Canadian production.... This instrument that contributed little, in the changing order of things, to our national defence.[7]

However, Canada did continue to play a key technological role in telecommunications satellites and space technology, such as the Canadarm of the space shuttles.

The Bomarc Missile Crisis

In 1958, the Canadian government decided to meet the threat of Soviet attack by installing the American-made Bomarc intercontinental missiles in Canada. At first, Diefenbaker was willing to accept the B-series Bomarcs that were to be fitted with nuclear warheads. However, he became increasingly reluctant as Canadian nuclear disarmament groups protested when they discovered that warheads were part of the deal. The Americans were completely baffled by Canada's mixed signals on this issue.

At a face-to-face meeting between Diefenbaker and U.S. President John F. Kennedy, the prime minister seemed to indicate that Canada was willing to take the missiles, because that was its duty under the NORAD agreement. However, Diefenbaker actually accepted the missiles *without* the warheads. The United States, furious at this outcome, released a statement that accused Canada of refusing to live up to its responsibilities. It stated that Canada was playing a dangerous game, saying one thing but doing another: "The Canadian government has not as yet proposed any arrangement sufficiently practical to contribute effectively to North American defence."[8] The

rebuke was so public, so extraordinary, that Canada's ambassador to the United States was recalled as a diplomatic protest, the first time that had ever occurred.

When Lester Pearson became prime minister in 1963, he accepted the warheads, because he believed that Canada had promised to take them. Then he immediately began negotiating for their removal. By 1969, under Pierre Trudeau, it became official Canadian policy that no nuclear weapons would be located in Canada and that the country's armed forces have no nuclear role in NATO. In 1971, the Bomarc missile was phased out.

The Cuban Missile Crisis

The Bomarc dispute had made the United States so mistrustful of Canada that the Canadian government was given just one-and-a-half hours' notice of President Kennedy's crucial speech on October 22, 1962, announcing that the Soviets were installing offensive missiles in Cuba and that the United States was blockading Cuba. The Americans and the Soviets seemed poised for nuclear war. The American government asked Canada to put its NORAD forces on high alert and send its Navy to sea on anti-submarine patrol. The Canadian Cabinet responded by debating the issue for two days, because the ministers were concerned that U.S. policy and behaviour provoked the Soviet Union unnecessarily and heightened the danger. In reality, the Canadian forces had already been quietly put on high alert while Cabinet debated. On October 24, the alert was made official. After a few days, the Soviet Union backed down and removed the missiles, and the crisis subsided.

Many Canadians blamed Diefenbaker for antagonizing the Americans by his delay over the Cuban missiles, which probably contributed to his 1963 election loss to Pearson. Diefenbaker himself blamed his loss on American interference in the election. However, if the Americans had hoped that Pearson would be easier to deal with on Cold War issues, they were probably disappointed. In 1965,

Canada did not give the United States the support it demanded for the Vietnam War, and by 1967, the Canadian government was openly expressing disagreement with American policy in Southeast Asia. Canadian cooperation with the United States for nuclear defence against the Soviet Union during the postwar period did not mean support for American policies and initiatives around the globe.

The Cold War Mentality

Although some historians have argued that Canada overreacted to the threat of enforced communism or nuclear attack by the USSR,[9] the fear was certainly genuine. The basic assumption of western governments was summed up in the political doctrine of "mutual assured destruction." Essentially, it was assumed that neither side would attack the other because retaliation would destroy both. The acronym for this doctrine was MAD, and it did not reassure most Canadians.

The Canadian government went so far as to construct an underground fortress at Carp, Ontario, in 1961, where top government officials were to be housed in case of nuclear war. It became known as the "Diefenbunker," after the prime minister. The shelter included a CBC radio studio so that the government could broadcast emergency messages, a hospital, a morgue, and a Bank of Canada vault.

Especially during tense times such as the Cuban Missile Crisis, ordinary Canadians also made survival plans. Some built their own fallout shelters, others made at least half-hearted attempts to construct a shelter in the basement and store canned goods. Schools taught children duck and cover drills (the art of hiding under a desk). Most people sensed, however, that these measures were futile. Survivors of the detonation and the fallout would probably perish in the aftermath, because of the collapse of all public services.

One outcome of pervasive public fear during the postwar period was the growth of the antinuclear movement in Canada. Groups such as the Campaign for Nuclear Disarmament and the Voice of Women not only reflected the desire of many Canadians to prevent nuclear war, but also provided them with experience in exerting pressure for social change. Many Canadians who first became involved with antinuclear activism went on to advocate other social reforms. Students who grew up during the period of nuclear terror and MAD had little confidence in the political and social establishment of their day, compared with previous generations. This was likely one of the drivers of the great social ferment of the late Sixties.

Nuclear anxiety began to decrease by the Eighties, when it became clear to most observers that the Soviet Union was in internal disarray. The "Diefenbunker" was decommissioned in 1994 when Canadian Forces Station (CFS) Carp closed. It remains a Cold War Museum and sponsors antiwar exhibits.

The Cold War, like World War II, was the source of many inventions. For example, in 1962, the U.S. Air Force asked a RAND Corporation employee to develop a way to maintain control of Air Force operations in the event of a nuclear attack. The employee suggested a computer telecommunications network in which each computer would communicate as an equal, sending a packet of data exactly as if it were a letter in an envelope. Such a system would be hard to destroy because it did not require a central computer, whose destruction would shut down the system. A network of this type was built for the U.S. Advanced Research Projects Agency (ARPA) in 1968 and was called the ARPANET. Because many people found this method of sending information very convenient, the network quickly grew beyond ARPA, at which point it became known as the Internet.

The Voice of Women organization was among those in Canada opposed to having nuclear weapons on Canadian soil.

Evolution of Canada's Peacekeeping Role

Canada's identity as a peacekeeping nation arose in large part from the Cold War. Being sprawled between two hostile powers and being much weaker than either, Canada could not afford to be hostile or neutral. Its interest lay in identifying with the United States and using the opportunity to promote peace and workable compromises in world affairs. One way of promoting peace was through the United Nations.

Canada's Role in the United Nations

The expression "United Nations" first referred to a group of twenty-six nations, including Canada, who pledged in 1942 to continue to fight the Axis powers. It was understood that once the enemy had been defeated, the world had to find a better way to settle disputes than world wars. In 1945, fifty countries, including Canada, drew up a UN Charter in San Francisco. Most Canadians subscribed to what the new organization stood for: cooperation among sovereign states to promote their common interest in international peace and security, friendly relations, and solutions for international economic, social, cultural, and humanitarian problems.

Canadian diplomats were very active in founding most of the constituent organizations of the UN because they believed that the UN provided the best opportunity for consensus building and diplomacy across many different fronts. Lester Pearson, a key Canadian diplomat who later became prime minister (1963–68), premised Canada's postwar foreign policy on positioning Canada as a mediator in key conflicts. He envisioned Canada as a "middle power," not only in size and in strength, but also in the positions it would adopt.

In 1946, Canadian law professor John Humphrey was the principal writer of the original draft of the UN's Universal Declaration of Human Rights, passed in 1948. Although the Declaration is often violated, its major achievement is the fact that it recognizes human rights as an international concern, not merely the concern of those nations that support the idea. Human rights have become part of "customary international law." That means that nations can act on violations by other nations of which they have evidence; the violations are not merely "an internal matter," as violators so often argue. Ironically, the Canadian delegation to the UN abstained from voting for the measure when it was first introduced—some said because of fear of federal–provincial conflict—but in the end, Canada supported it.[10]

The Development of a Peacekeeping Force

The United Nations has been the catalyst for the development of one of Canada's most recognized international roles—that of peacekeeper. The UN Charter of 1945 allowed for a peacekeeping force, but the Cold War made it impossible to develop an official force for most of the first decade after the UN's founding. Nonetheless, Canada had been engaged in unofficial peacekeeping missions with UN approval, such as in 1948 in Kashmir and in 1953 in Palestine. The Suez Crisis of 1956 showed the value of an official UN peacekeeping force.

The Suez Crisis

The Suez Canal is a vital waterway linking the Mediterranean Sea to the Red Sea, a shortcut for ships that must otherwise circumnavigate Africa. Constructed by the French in 1859–69, from 1869 onward it was operated by English and French interests. In July 1956, President Nasser of Egypt nationalized the Canal by taking over the company that ran it. Angered by this blow to western power and business interests, Britain and France attacked the Canal Zone in October. They

demanded that Egypt withdraw, but Egypt refused. The Soviet Union supported Egypt, and suddenly the world seemed on the brink of another major war, perhaps a nuclear war.

Most western nations found themselves facing a dilemma. They were unwilling to risk nuclear war to help Britain and France hang on to the Canal. There seemed no reason why Egypt should not control the Canal. However, it was important to keep NATO, of which Britain and France were members, intact. Here, Canadian diplomatic expertise proved to be critical.

Instead of backing Britain, which would have been the traditional Canadian course, Canada adopted the position of peacemaker. The Minister for External Affairs, Lester Pearson, proposed an international force to secure and supervise the cessation of hostilities. Seizing the opportunity, the United Nations organized a ten-nation Emergency Force, led by a Canadian, General E.L.M. Burns. Canada contributed the largest number of soldiers, about eight hundred. By the end of the year, all foreign troops had withdrawn, but the peacekeepers stayed in place for another decade.

In 1957, Lester Pearson was awarded the Nobel Peace Prize for his efforts. He is the only Canadian ever to win it. In accepting the prize, Pearson tried to point out the potential of the peacekeeping idea. "I do not exaggerate the significance of what has been done," he said. "But it may have prevented a brush fire becoming an all-consuming blaze...and it could do so again in similar circumstances in the future."[11] However, although Pearson's strategy may have promoted world peace, it proved costly at home. Perceived lack of support for Britain was a factor in the Liberal government's defeat in 1957, the same year in which Pearson won the Nobel Prize. The incident provided an important test of Canada's understanding of itself and of its own new position in the world. Not all Canadians found the new role easy to adjust to.

Canadian Peacekeepers in Action

Buoyed by the Suez diplomatic success, Canadians began to see themselves as a peacekeeping nation. With considerable public support, Canadian troops participated in peacekeeping efforts in the Congo, Irian Jaya, and Cyprus. Despite some concerns, Canadian troops have taken up the challenges of peacekeeping repeatedly. Indeed, it has become a part of our national identity. More than 100 000 Canadians have served in more than forty peacekeeping missions. More than one hundred peacekeepers have been killed while on duty. The end of the Cold War increased the number and importance of UN peacekeeping missions, chiefly because many ethnic and religious conflicts flared up only after the collapse of the Soviet Bloc.

Canada's Other International Roles

Not all of Canada's international roles in the post-war period related to the Cold War. Canada's identity and culture were slowly changing in other ways, and many new functions emerged.

The Commonwealth

The Commonwealth nations (nations that had formerly been British colonies but were in various stages of achieving independence) were uncertain about their relationship with Britain and with one another. Cooperation had its advantages, such as shared development, but it also had its disadvantages, such as the risk of being dragged into foreign disputes.

After World War II, many developing nations achieved independence and joined the Commonwealth. Many Canadians hoped that the Commonwealth would become an eloquent example of anti-racism and mutual assistance in a mistrustful world. However, both the Cold War and local economic benefit worked against this hope. Each time nations decided to support the United States, the USSR, both, or neither, they determined their friends and enemies, apart from the Commonwealth. Local trade advantages could not be ignored in favour of Commonwealth ties.

Canadian leaders continued to support the Commonwealth for the sake of the international ties for peace and development that it was able to maintain. For example, Prime Minister Diefenbaker forced out South Africa over apartheid in 1961. Although this action did not stop apartheid, it effectively communicated the disapproval of diverse nations across the world. South Africa was reinstated after its all-races election in 1994.

The Colombo Plan

In a 1950 meeting in Colombo, Ceylon (now Sri Lanka), Commonwealth foreign ministers established a development assistance program for impoverished countries in Southeast Asia. They were concerned that communism might take hold where impoverished people felt that no other hope existed. Later, the plan was extended to non-Commonwealth countries that wanted to participate. The United States became the largest donor to the plan, but Canada was also a generous contributor during the 1950s, especially to India, Pakistan, and Ceylon. The plan fit well into Canada's hopes for nonmilitary solutions to Cold War issues.

La Francophonie

The worldwide network of public and private organizations that encourages ties among francophones is called *la Francophonie*. Since the network's emergence after World War II, Canada has been an enthusiastic bilingual participant. Both Quebec and New Brunswick are ranked as participating governments. Although *la Francophonie* is not organized in the same way as the Commonwealth, it has provided Canada with an opportunity to cooperate with francophone governments in development projects in many parts of the world.

Peaceful Uses for Nuclear Technology

In 1942, a joint British–Canadian laboratory was set up in Montreal to design a nuclear reactor. In

September 1945, the lab achieved self-sustaining nuclear reactions. In 1947, the federal government opened the Chalk River, Ontario, facility as a "research" reactor. In 1951, the facility pioneered "cobalt bomb" (cobalt-60) cancer therapy, and today, 85 percent of the cobalt-60 used for cancer therapy around the world is produced in Canada. In 1952, Atomic Energy of Canada Limited (AECL) was formed as a Crown corporation to develop peaceful uses for nuclear energy. In 1963, a second AECL research laboratory was established in Pinawa, Manitoba: the Whiteshell Nuclear Research Establishment.

In the 1960s, Canada began to market its nuclear technology to energy-hungry countries such as Pakistan and India, but this has been a controversial strategy. On the one hand, nuclear energy provides power for development that does not produce air pollution or global warming. On the other hand, it can easily be converted to military uses. On May 18, 1974, India detonated a nuclear device, claiming that it was a "peaceful" explosion. Canadian policymakers and scientists continue to struggle with this question: Can the world's energy needs be satisfied without nuclear power? If not, how can nuclear power be kept from aggressive extremists?

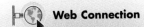

Web Connection

www.mcgrawhill.ca/links/definingcanada

Go to the Web site above to learn more about Canada's peacekeepers and their missions.

From Sea to Sea: Newfoundland as Canada's Tenth Province

Entry into Canada was bitterly controversial in Newfoundland and Labrador in 1949. That might surprise you. Studying the historical background will help you to understand why an issue that might not seem controversial today was once controversial.

In 1867, Newfoundland and Labrador sent observers to Confederation but decided not to participate. The province had become a self-governing colony in 1855; however, self-rule did not bring long-term prosperity. The decision to build a railway and to support a regiment in World War I had proven costly, especially when the Great Depression hit in 1929. In 1933, Newfoundland was short $97 million for loan payments, and its political system and economy collapsed. Britain agreed to bail out Newfoundland but imposed direct rule as a consequence.

During World War II, Newfoundland's fortunes changed. The economy recovered, because the colony was a source of natural resources and a site of key military bases. In 1949, Newfoundland had a surplus of $40 million after the debts of 1933 were paid.

In 1946, Britain asked the 325 000 people living in Newfoundland and Labrador to make a decision about their future. A national convention was elected to deliberate whether to continue under British rule or return to self-rule. At the convention, Joey Smallwood, a journalist, radio broadcaster, and union organizer, introduced a third option, the one that had been rejected nearly eighty years earlier: join Confederation with Canada. All the options were submitted to public referendum.

Review...Reflect...Respond

1. What was the "increasingly troubling" character of American leadership that concerned Canadians as a member of NATO? How did this affect Canada's foreign policy?

2. How did the Cold War affect Canadian sovereignty?

3. Why is peacekeeping so intertwined with the Canadian identity

The referendum results of June 1948 did not produce a clear majority. Forty-four percent voted for responsible self-government, 41 percent for Confederation, and 15 percent for British rule. Therefore, a second referendum was organized for the following month, with only the top two choices on the ballot.

Smallwood dominated the campaign by using radio to reach people in every part of the province. He promised Newfoundlanders that Confederation would bring immense improvement to their lives and predicted that continued independence would bring economic failure and lives of poverty and disease for their children. This argument was powerful, because living conditions in Newfoundland had been significantly worse than in Canada throughout the century. But anti-Confederation forces had powerful arguments as well. The Newfoundland economy had become much stronger in recent years; could Newfoundlanders not solve their own problems using their own money? Many resented the idea that independence could not produce sound government and prosperity.

These two opposing letters, printed in St. John's newspapers, reflect widespread sentiments:

> Let us not sell our country. The crime would be just as black as if we sold our mother. Let us elect our own people, to govern our own country, and let us see to it that those we elect do a faithful and honest job. We can do it. Let us make one last desperate effort to hold our country, our self-respect, and our honour.[12]

> I honestly believe that Confederation with Canada is the best solution to our problems. I believe in fair distribution of taxes, with the wealthy bearing the heavier burden. Also, our cost of living will come down, and our standard of living will rise, meaning a healthier population, less TB, a lower infant mortality, better care for our aged and blind. I believe in union with Canada, a powerful and progressive unit in our British Commonwealth of Nations. We have stood too long alone.[13]

The second referendum, held on July 22, 1948, was very close, 52 percent to 48 percent in favour of Confederation. At midnight on March 31, 1949, Newfoundland and Labrador became a province of Canada. Joey Smallwood became the province's first premier, and he held the job for twenty-two years.

Was Confederation the right thing for Newfoundland and Labrador? The province's inhabitants differ in their views even today. Modern industrial methods and a social safety net improved most people's lives. Richard Cashin, a former Member of Parliament from Newfoundland and a nephew of one of the important leaders of the anti-Confederation movement, says, "We could have lived on our own but not with the same standard of living. If it had gone the other way, people would not have been able to stay. Unquestionably, this was the right thing."[14]

However, one consequence of modernization for a resource-based economy like Newfoundland and Labrador's was high unemployment. Maura Hanrahan, a sociologist at Memorial University in St. John's, says Newfoundlanders suffer from a lack of self-esteem because they are seen as dependent on Canadian welfare.[15] New offshore oil developments offer some hope for an improved economy, but increasingly, Newfoundlanders support technical training for young people to reduce dependence on the fluctuations of their resource-based economy.

The Quiet Revolution in Quebec

During the postwar period, Canada began to experience serious national unity problems at home. Although French-Canadian nationalism had been a factor in Quebec for two centuries, it was usually linked to conservative causes and focused on preserving a traditional francophone society. As a rule, it did not threaten national unity. However, from about 1960 to 1966, Quebec underwent a social revolution, called by an anonymous *Globe and Mail* writer the "Quiet Revolution."[16] This revolution resulted in both the modernization of Quebec and the steady growth of a popular separatist movement.

Expression of Identity

Newfoundland and Labrador's entry into Confederation in 1949 was as controversial as when it was first proposed in 1867. Although the province did end up joining Canada in 1949, many Newfoundlanders fought hard to convince the population that Confederation would mean the end of life as they knew in Newfoundland and Labrador. Anti-Confederation songs became popular once again, just as they had in 1867.

Don't Vote Confederation

A fisher boy was leaving and going to Labrador,
Fishing the same old trap berth where his father fished before,
And as he was leaving his Mother, while standing on the quay,
He threw his arms around her neck and this to her did say.

Chorus
Don't vote Confederation, and that's my prayer to you.
We own the house we live in, likewise the schooner too.
But if ye heed Joe Smallwood's Canadian patois,
Ye'll always be paying taxes to the men up in Ottawa.

But if ye heed my warning, when we come sailing home,
We'll be loaded to the scuppers, and I'll have no need to roam,
I'll buy a new accordion, and we will dance all night
And the man who mentions Canada, he sure will have a fight!

Oh Mother, dearest Mother, God guard our fishing room.
It is the best one on the coast from Hebron to Quirpon.
But if Confederation should win on polling day,
The ghost of Uncle George will rise and this to you will say.

So Mother, dearest Mother, don't let them win you over.
On polling day just mark your X for good old Terra Nova.
Tell Sarah Jane, fish or no fish, I'll wed her in the Fall,
And Joey's Baby Bonus interests me not at all.

Our life has not been easy, and our fight was hard and long.
But if we have faith in ourselves, we'll carry right along.
We want no strangers in our crew, let us be on our way,
And mark your X Responsible on Referendum Day.

Now Mother, dearest Mother, we are Newfoundlanders true.
Our ship is sound from stem to stern and we can get the crew.
So keep the old flag flying, and keep her off the land.
As loved our Fathers so we love, God Guard Thee Newfoundland.

–ANONYMOUS

---

1. What does this anti-Confederation song warn will happen to Newfoundlanders if they join Confederation? What items does it refer to that Canada used to entice Newfoundland and Labrador to join Confederation?

2. Using the music to one of your favourite popular songs, rewrite the lyrics to create a pro-Confederation song that could be used to retaliate against this anti-Confederation song.

Maurice Duplessis, the leader of the Union Nationale party, had won his first term of office (1936–39) by exposing the corruption of the Quebec liberals, who had governed for thirty-six years. Duplessis was out of office during World War II but then returned in 1944 and continued to govern Quebec until 1959, the year he died. He made many changes that strengthened the power of Quebec against both the Catholic Church and the federal government in Ottawa. He also modernized Quebec through vast public works projects. However, his government became riddled by corruption and he himself became ruthless when dealing with unions, which were achieving an important place in Canadian life.

In any event, Quebec was changing around Duplessis. The society was becoming much more urban. His personal style of government (he was known as "le Chef") was out of keeping with

Liberal Quebec Premier Jean Lesage takes power in 1960.

modern aspirations for democracy and liberalism. In the 1960 election, his successor was defeated by the Liberals, led by Jean Lesage.

Lesage had ridden to power on the slogan "It's time for a change." The new style that he brought helped to launch the Quiet Revolution. As one historian writes, "Everything came under scrutiny, everything was discussed; a new age of open debate began."[17] Indeed, there was a great deal to discuss. Although Quebec had become modern, urban, and industrialized, in 1961 the average French-Canadian in Quebec earned about 40 percent less than the average English-Canadian in Quebec. Under Lesage, the Quebec government moved to tackle the problems that contributed to this situation. For example, Natural Resources Minister René Lévesque nationalized private electricity companies and folded them into a giant Hydro-Quebec, which stimulated industry across the province. The government also created the *Caisse de dépôt et placement du Québec* to invest the money placed in the Quebec Pension Plan, and the Caisse became one of the largest financial institutions on the continent. To help small businesses, the government set up the *Société générale de financement du Québec*. All these measures were intended to enable Quebec francophones to achieve economic equality in North America.

In addition, the government took control of education, which had previously been managed by the Roman Catholic Church. For the first time, Quebec established a department of education. Schools began preparing students not only for the traditional professions of medicine, the law, or the clergy, but also for careers in business management, engineering, economics, and science. Lesage also worked out a new financial relationship with Ottawa, under which Quebec could "opt out" of federal programs but still get federal money for similar programs run by the province.

All this led to a surge of pride in francophone Quebec. In fact, many people stopped thinking of themselves as "French-Canadians" and began to describe themselves as "Québécois." This change had consequences. Many Québécois, among them Lévesque, began to believe that the solution to Quebec's problems was separation from Canada. In 1966, Lévesque abandoned the Liberals, and in 1968, he founded the Parti Québécois, whose key political platform was (and is) separation from Canada. A few people, like Pierre Vallières, likened the Québécois' situation to that of Algeria, which was a French colony.[18] The *Front de libération de Québec* (FLQ), of which Vallières had been a member since 1965, advocated violent revolution as a solution. The FLQ was implicated in more than two hundred bomb incidents between 1963 and 1970, as it sought to "liberate" Quebec from Canada. In 1967, Charles de Gaulle, war hero and president of France, raised the stakes by shouting the separatist slogan *"Vive le Québec libre!"* from the balcony of Montreal's city hall. Quebec separatism had been seen in Canada as a regional matter, but now it appeared that it might receive the support of France.

Pierre Trudeau, a Quebec lawyer who was beginning to come to national prominence, had a completely different view from Lévesque, Vallières, or de Gaulle: "It's not the fault of the English that we're a backward province. We're responsible for our own mess."[19] Trudeau was firmly on the side of both bilingualism and national unity, and he was prompted to seek the Liberal Party leadership in 1968, because of the growing national unity issue that Quebec separatism represented.[20]

Aboriginal Peoples Challenge the System

Québécois were not the only Canadians who were dissatisfied with their status in postwar Canada. The Aboriginal Peoples, heartened by their effective participation in World War II, began to challenge the restrictions of the Indian Act and the problems created for their culture by the residential schools that aimed to assimilate them. However, Aboriginal Peoples had difficulty defining a relationship with Canada that effectively recognized the group rights that they sought. Canada was becoming much more oriented to individual rights, and a major clash on this issue occurred at the end of the postwar period.

The major difficulty for Aboriginal Peoples after World War II lay in the fact that the Indian Act prevented them from improving their lives while retaining their identity and culture. For example, the Act (1876) outlawed many of the cultural and religious ceremonies that bound Aboriginals together. The Act (1927) made it an offence to prosecute a land claim without the consent of the superintendent of Indian affairs. Aboriginal people did not have the right to vote. They could, of course, give up their Indian status, which many did. However, those who did not do so could not function effectively either in their own culture or in dealings with the majority culture outside the reserves.

ANTHONY JENKINS/*The Globe and Mail*

A political cartoon commenting on the plight of Aboriginal people on Ellesmere Island.

Canadian Leaders
JAMES GLADSTONE

James Gladstone was Canada's first Aboriginal senator, and he spent the greater part of his life fighting to improve conditions for Aboriginal Canadians. Although he was born at Mountain Hill in the Northwest Territories, Gladstone spent his childhood on the Blood Blackfoot Reservation in Alberta. A Blood band member of Cree and Scottish descent, Gladstone gained acceptance on Canada's largest Indian reserve through marriage and the study of the Blood language and culture. He attended St. Paul's Anglican Residential School and the Calgary Industrial School, and then apprenticed as a typesetter and worked briefly for the *Calgary Herald*. He also wrangled cattle on ranches in the Fort Macleod area and later worked for the RCMP as chief scout and interpreter in the west.

Gladstone farmed on the reserve and was particularly renowned for his progressive farming methods. He and his two sons built a prosperous 325-ha ranch-farm with about four hundred cattle. Early in the 1920s Gladstone introduced the first tractor to the reserve and encouraged fellow Aboriginals to apply modern farming methods and technology. His outstanding farming abilities were widely admired, and during World War I he helped fellow Blood farmers more effectively tend their cattle and increase crop yields.

The transition from agricultural to political leadership was smooth and natural for Gladstone. During the 1950s he served three times as president of the Indian Association of Alberta (IAA), one of the most effective Aboriginal political organizations in the country.

Often a consensus builder, Gladstone is widely credited with achieving harmony between Alberta's two main Aboriginal groups: the Cree and Blackfoot nations in southern Alberta. Through Gladstone's leadership, and that of a few others, the focus of the IAA became lobbying provincial and federal governments, and raising public support.

Native Voices Speak Together

Despite the fact that Aboriginal Canadians were not full citizens, during World War II they enlisted in disproportionately high numbers versus the general population and made significant contributions to Canada's war effort. It is estimated that six thousand Aboriginal Canadians enlisted. Yet, when they returned home, oppressive reserve restrictions appeared glaringly unjust. Because of changed public and political mood, the Joint Senate and House of Commons Committee on the Indian Act held hearings with a view to revising the Indian Act from 1946 to 1948. Many Aboriginal Canadians rejected the first draft of proposed revisions, claiming the changes removed the advantages of the original Act.

James Gladstone

Consequently, the federal government sought Aboriginal advice, which was a significant milestone, since it marked the first time this level of government had listened to Aboriginal Canadians' input.

As an IAA delegate to Ottawa, Gladstone fought against the original revisions to the Indian Act. Because he spoke effectively on behalf of a strong and unified organization, about three quarters of the IAA's objections to the original draft were remedied in the new Act. This included the granting of more powers to band councils.

Still, the revised Indian Act of 1951 contained measures that by today's standards are oppressive. It continued to prohibit Aboriginal people from drinking, subdividing their lands, and having the federal vote. Although the Act no longer endorsed forced assimilation, it contained no clauses specifically protecting Aboriginal Peoples unique cultures.

Gladstone's attitude toward the Act was ambivalent. On the one hand, he fought to improve it. On the other hand, he wanted it abolished completely, since he thought it impeded Aboriginal people's ability to govern themselves and undermined fundamental equality. Gladstone once said of the Act: "Indians are the only ethnic group in Canada with a special act."

Canada's First Aboriginal Senator

When John Diefenbaker campaigned during the 1957 election, one of his promises was to appoint a senator for the Aboriginal people. On February 1, 1958, Diefenbaker delivered on that promise by appointing Gladstone to the Canadian Senate, at the same time sending a signal that his government was willing to work on behalf of Aboriginal interests.

In a gesture that demonstrated Gladstone's commitment to preserving the traditions of his people, he delivered part of his first speech as a senator in the language of the Blackfoot nation "as a recognition of the first Canadians." In the speech, Gladstone said, "My work will be aimed at improving the position of Canada's Indians, obtaining for them better conditions as they want them and are ready for them. I'm particularly interested in seeing more encouragement given to Indians for individual, rather than collective, effort."

Senator James Gladstone was known as a fighter—his Indian name was *Akay-na-muka*, which means "Many Guns." Yet he was a soft-spoken fighter who continually battled for a better deal on behalf of his fellow Aboriginal people. Gladstone played a prominent role in the struggle for improved Aboriginal education, greater respect for treaty rights, participation of Aboriginals in their own administrations, and in 1960 the granting of treaty Indians the right to vote in Canada's national elections.

After the war, Aboriginal Peoples formed many regional, provincial, and traditional bodies, and they succeeded in getting the more oppressive prohibitions of the Indian Act removed. In 1949, non-status Indians (persons of Indian ancestry who do not have legal status) were permitted to vote. The Inuit gained the franchise in 1950. During the 1950s, bands gradually gained the right to administer their own funds. In 1960, status Indians (persons who have the legal status of Indians under the Indian Act) were permitted to vote in federal elections for the first time.

In 1961, the National Indian Advisory Council was formed, representing status and non-status Indians and the Métis. However, the goals of these groups were often different, and in 1968, the status Indians formed the National Indian Brotherhood, which became the Assembly of First Nations in 1980. The non-status Indians and Métis formed the Native Council of Canada, now called the Congress of Aboriginal Peoples.

A pressing issue for Aboriginal Peoples was education. In the 1880s, the federal government established boarding and day schools for Aboriginal children, with the express intention of assimilating them into white society. Generally, these schools were operated by mainstream churches. In 1920, attendance was made compulsory. However, the schools were underfunded and partly subsidized by the children's own labour. There were repeated complaints about the low quality of both education and boarding facilities, and the children were punished for speaking their traditional language or following traditional culture. By 1951, the Indian Act allowed Aboriginal children to attend provincial schools. By 1968, the federal government formally ended the partnership with religious organizations in Aboriginal education. During the 1990s, many persons of Aboriginal descent launched lawsuits against both the government and churches on charges of sexual abuse or loss of language and culture at residential schools.

In 1969, Pierre Trudeau responded to the aspirations of Aboriginal groups by putting forward a White Paper on Indian Policy. A White Paper both reports on a government committee's investigation and summarizes government policy with respect to it. Trudeau wanted to terminate the special rights and status of Indians, in return for a small financial settlement. He did not propose this because he was prejudiced against Aboriginal Peoples; rather, he strongly supported individual rights and believed that Aboriginal people would be better off without a special status that sometimes conflicted with individual rights. However, he was forced to retract his policy in the face of vehement denunciations by the Aboriginal Peoples. One form the opposition took was a contrary Red Paper, arguing for continued Aboriginal status. One beneficial outcome of the controversy was that, by the end of the postwar period, Aboriginal Peoples were beginning to work together to identify their own vision for the future.

Today, Canada has more than 630 First Nations. Approximately 488 000 Aboriginal people are registered under the Indian Act. More than 1 400 000 Canadians claim Aboriginal ancestry.

Immigration and the Beginnings of Multiculturalism

After World War II, Canada began to be reshaped by immigration from Europe. Many immigrants from Europe came to Canada during the first decade of the twentieth century, and they largely populated the Prairies with farms. From 1931 to 1941, more people actually emigrated *from* Canada than immigrated *to* Canada (241 000 out, 149 000 in). As a result, during the first half of the twentieth century, immigration did not have as much of an effect on shaping Canadian culture as the numbers of immigrants might suggest.

However, in the aftermath of World War II, new patterns of immigration emerged. Some immigrants were accepted for humanitarian reasons.

For example, at the close of the war, hundreds of thousands of Europeans were living in camps for "displaced persons." The term *displaced person*—or DP for short—was coined during this period to refer to the vast numbers of Europeans who could not return home, either because violence or oppression awaited them or because they no longer had a country to return to. Canada took in more than 165 000 DPs between 1947 and 1952.

Other large waves of immigration occurred as well. In 1956, for example, the people of Hungary revolted against domination by the Soviet Union, but the rebellion was crushed. In the aftermath, Canada admitted 40 000 Hungarian refugees. Similarly, in 1968, the "Prague Spring" liberalization of Czechoslovakia was squelched by an invasion from the Soviet Union, and Canada admitted 12 000 persons from Czechoslovakia.

Many people who were not displaced persons or refugees were also seeking to leave Europe after the war, primarily for economic reasons. From 1941 to 1961 immigration to Canada far outweighed emigration (more than 2 000 000 in, only

Canadian immigrants during the 1950s. How were they different from immigrants today?

850 000 out). The new immigrants who came to Canada after World War II moved mostly to the cities and took jobs in the expanding industrial economy. They did not necessarily expect to blend into "British" culture in Canada. They wanted to feel comfortable with their own culture in the context of a liberal democracy. British culture was losing its hold on Canada during this period anyway, because Canada no longer saw itself politically or economically as a British colony. Canada slowly began to develop a multicultural look.

Italian Immigration to Canada

The largest single group of immigrants to Canada during the postwar period was from Italy. Lured by the postwar economic boom (and consequent labour shortage), Italians represented about 70 percent of all immigrants. Because extended family groups typically immigrated to urban centres in Canada, they introduced to many cities an intact culture that was neither English nor French. One outcome was that they introduced significant cultural changes to Canada. For example, they greatly broadened Canadian eating habits by introducing pizza and pasta to the traditional bland diet. In fact, eating in an Italian restaurant was often the first foray that Canadians of British descent made into a multicultural environment. The successful blending of Italian immigrants in urban Canadian life, like that of Chinese and many other immigrants, started the idea of a multicultural, and eventually global, society.

The Beginnings of a Global Society

Before World War II Canada allowed little immigration from Asia, or from any country that was not white. New non-white immigrants experienced severe discrimination. Prime Minister Mackenzie King told the House of Commons in 1947 that the government was determined that the complexion of Canada would not change:

With regard to the selection of immigrants, much has been said about discrimination. I wish to make it quite clear that Canada is perfectly within her rights in selecting the persons whom we regard as desirable future citizens. It is not a fundamental human right of any alien to enter Canada. It is a privilege. There will, I am sure, be general agreement with the view that the people of Canada do not wish, as a result of mass immigration, to make a fundamental alteration in the character of our population. Large-scale immigration from the Orient would change the fundamental composition of the Canadian population.[21]

Because of these policies, immigration from non-white countries was less than a trickle. In 1951, for example, an agreement was worked out with India, Pakistan, and Ceylon, to allow three hundred people into Canada. In 1955, a deal was made with the British West Indies for one hundred people. They all had to be single women between twenty-one and thirty-five years old who would agree to work as domestic helpers for at least one year.

However, King, who died in 1950, was recommending a policy that, had it been followed, would have seriously undermined the role that Canada was beginning to play in the world. Canada was beginning to establish itself as a country that made serious efforts in the area of human rights. Throughout the 1960s, Canadians, of both British and non-British descent, were beginning to insist on non-racist immigration policies. In 1962, Minister of Citizenship and Immigration Ellen Fairclough eliminated racial criteria from the new Immigration Act. In 1967, the "points system" was introduced, in an attempt to provide an objective means for immigration officials to assess the suitability of applicants.

In 1971, for the first time, most new immigrants were of non-European ancestry. Part of the reason for this reversal was that Europe had begun to recover from World War II, so fewer Europeans were candidates for immigration. The new, non-racist immigration policy enabled Canada to continue to attract new immigrants when the flow from Europe tapered off.

The Developing Idea of Canadian Citizenship

Before 1947, the concept of a "Canadian" citizen was unknown; Canadian citizens were legally classed as British subjects. Paul Martin, Sr., a Liberal cabinet minister, first proposed the idea of a distinct Canadian citizenship. He introduced a bill in 1945, saying, "For the national unity of Canada and for the future and greatness of this country, it is felt to be of utmost importance that all of us are able to say with pride, and say with meaning: 'I am a Canadian citizen.'"[22] Parliament passed the Canadian Citizenship Act in June 1946, and the first Canadian citizenship certificate was presented in a ceremony in Ottawa on January 3, 1947. Certificate number 0001 was bestowed on Prime Minister King.

The new Act represented an advance in women's rights over the legislation before 1947, in that it did not link the citizenship status of a married woman to that of her husband. Under the new legislation, a woman neither gained nor lost Canadian citizenship when she married.

Where are today's new Canadians coming from?

Evolution of Human Rights

Struggles at Home

World War II, which claimed an estimated fifty million lives, brought home to the western world the high cost of ignoring human rights issues. Canada, like many countries, began gradually to confront issues of racism, sexism, and exclusion within its own society—issues that had been put on hold during the war. However, it was not easy. Canada had initially abstained from voting in favour of the United Nations' Universal Declaration of Human Rights because there were many human rights issues at home that it did not want to confront.

For example, because of Gouzenko's revelations, Canada was taking action against avowed communists that might not meet the standards of the Declaration. It was also feared that Jehovah's Witnesses, who were often persecuted, might consider themselves entitled to invoke freedom of religion, even in provinces such as Quebec where the government was hostile to their religion. And, in 1948, the same year as the Declaration, Canada had just renewed the measures that deprived Japanese Canadians of the right to vote.[23] However, in the end, urged on by Lester Pearson, Canada did end up voting for the Declaration—and then struggled to determine what putting it into practice at home might mean.

The war did not affect every group that was victimized by prejudice in a negative way. For example, black Canadians found that the shortage of workers during World War II meant that the systemic prejudice against them was somewhat lessened. They were able to get jobs in wartime industries that would have been closed to them before. However, it was not until the close of the postwar period that changes in immigration laws enabled large numbers of black people to immigrate to Canada, principally from the Caribbean. Black Canadians were active during the entire postwar period, challenging many instances of discrimination and removing them.

Although black Canadians were gaining new rights, the brutal realities of racism in Canada had yet to be faced. Chapters in history such as the story of Africville remain as permanent scars on who we are as Canadians today.

The Tragedy of Africville

Many former American slaves who had escaped to Canada after the War of 1812 established Africville, a small town on the edge of Halifax on the Bedford Basin. A tiny community that never had more than four hundred residents, it had the vibrancy of a close-knit family. Africville developed in an era of ignorance when black people did not have human or political rights in North America.

As Halifax grew and prospered, it did so often at the expense of the residents of Africville. Essential institutions that Halifax needed but that were deemed "unpleasant" were placed close to Africville. The Rockhead Prison (1853), Halifax's fertilizer disposal pits (1858), its Infectious Disease Hospital (1870s), and an open dump and incinerator (1955) were all built dangerously close to the residents of Africville.[24]

Halifax failed to install water service, sewage systems, street lights, or adequate fire and police services. Most homes were without plumbing or electricity. Because of their own racist decisions, the people and city councillors of Halifax looked at Africville as a slum.

In the 1950s and 1960s, Halifax began a number of postwar city development projects. Looking for new land, the city cast its eyes toward Africville. Without consulting the residents, the city removed and rehoused them, with little more than a token compensation, to various locations in Halifax, and bulldozed the entire community to the ground. More than 150 years of history and the homes of many Canadians were destroyed forever.

The mayor of Halifax tried to hide the outright discrimination by explaining that the decision was done for sanitary reasons and by saying that integrating the black residents throughout the city would help end racial segregation in Halifax. But in truth, it was nothing more than racism that destroyed the homes, the community, and the church.

In 2002, the federal government of Canada declared Africville a national historic site and apologized for the eviction of the black residents. At the ceremony, Heritage Minister Sheila Copps said, "As the fabric has been torn apart, so the fabric can be mended. And what we're doing today is the beginning of a process that I hope will place the name of Africville on the lips of every Canadian."[25]

Although former residents of Africville appreciated the apology and the declaration of their former community as an historic site, many still want compensation for the loss of their homes and community. Irvine Carvey, president of the Africville Genealogy Society, who was 13 years old when his home was destroyed, said,

> There's never been a more racist act committed in Canada than what happened to Africville. Canada wants to stand up in international forums and flaunt how great a country it is...until the question of Africville is settled, Canada can not hold its head up and say it is a fair and just country to live in.[26]

The Bill of Rights

When John Diefenbaker became the Conservative prime minister in 1958, he was proud to call himself an "unhyphenated Canadian." His view was popular with many Canadians who saw Canada as a land of opportunity. A defence lawyer in private life, Diefenbaker sought to change a culture in which Canadians were treated differently according to their ethnic ancestry. However, as you will have observed already in this chapter, during the postwar period, Canada had a patchwork legacy of many different discriminatory laws that covered many different situations. No single piece of legislation could hope to address all of them at once.

Meanwhile, the Jehovah's Witnesses, a religious sect that had been persecuted in Quebec after World War II, had been floating the idea of a bill of rights that would guarantee freedom of religion and other civil rights.[27] Drawing on his law experience, Diefenbaker proposed such a Bill of Rights for Canada. The Bill recognized the right of individuals to life, liberty, personal security, and enjoyment of property, as well as equality before the law, freedom of religion, speech, assembly, association, the press, and the right to legal counsel and to a fair hearing. Under the Bill, laws were not to be interpreted in such a way as to undermine these rights and freedoms.

Diefenbaker would have preferred a Bill of Rights that was part of Canada's Constitution, in the way that the U.S. Bill of Rights was part of the American Constitution. Such a bill is difficult to change, set aside, or undermine. However, in 1960, Canada's Constitution was still the British North America (BNA) Act and under the control of the British Parliament. Because of federal–provincial conflict, bringing the Constitution to Canada and changing it would be no simple matter, as Pierre Trudeau later discovered. Diefenbaker settled for what he knew he could get at the time—a Bill of Rights that was simply legislated by Parliament. The Bill was at least an important statement about the kind of country Canada wanted to be. It passed a unanimous vote in the House and was proclaimed law on August 10, 1960.

The Canadian Bill of Rights

The Parliament of Canada affirming that the Canadian Nation is founded upon principles that acknowledge the supremacy of God, the dignity and worth of the human person and the position of the family in a society of free men and free institutions;

Affirming also that men and institutions remain free only when freedom is founded upon respect for moral and spiritual values and the rule of the law;

And being desirous of enshrining these principles and the human rights and fundamental freedoms derived from them in a Bill of Rights which shall reflect the respect of Parliament for its constitutional authority and which shall ensure the protection of these rights and freedoms in Canada;

Therefore Her Majesty, by and with the advice and consent of the Senate and House of Commons of Canada, enacts as follows:

Part 1: Bill of Rights

1. It is hereby recognized and declared that in Canada there have existed and shall continue to exist without discrimination by reason of race, national origin, colour, religion or sex, the following human rights and fundamental freedoms, namely,
   a) the right of the individual to life, liberty, security of the person and enjoyment of property, and the right not to be deprived thereof except by due process of law;
   b) the right of the individual to equality before the law and the protection of the law;
   c) freedom of religion;
   d) freedom of speech;
   e) freedom of assembly and association; and
   f) freedom of the press.
2. Every law of Canada shall, unless it is expressly declared by an Act of the Parliament of Canada that it shall operate notwithstanding the *Canadian Bill of Rights*, be so construed and applied as not to abrogation, abridgment or infringement of any of the rights or freedoms herein recognized and declared, and in particular no law of Canada shall be construed or applied as to
   a) authorize or effect the arbitrary detention, imprisonment or exile of any person;
   b) impose or authorize the imposition of cruel and unusual treatment or punishment;
   c) deprive a person who has been arrested or detained
      i. of the right to be informed promptly of the reason for his arrest or detention,
      ii. of the right to retain and instruct council without delay, or
      iii. of the remedy by way of *habeas corpus* for the determination of the validity of his detention and for his release if the detention is not lawful;
   d) authorize a court, tribunal, commission, board or other authority to compel a person to give evidence if he is denied counsel, protection against self crimination or other constitutional safeguards;
   e) deprive a person of the right to a fair hearing in accordance with the principles of fundamental justice for the determination of his rights and obligations;
   f) deprive a person charged with a criminal offence of the right to presumed innocent until proven guilty according to law in a fair and public hearing by an independent and impartial tribunal, or of the right to reasonable bail without just cause; or
   g) deprive a person of the right to the assistance of an interpreter in any proceedings in which he is involved or in which he is a party or a witness before a court commission, board or other tribunal, if he does not understand or speak the language in which such proceedings are conducted.
3. The Minister of Justice shall in accordance with such regulations as may be prescribed by the Governor in Council examine every proposed regulation submitted in draft form to the Clerk of the Privy Council pursuant to the Regulations Act and every Bill introduced in or presented to the House of Commons, in order to ascertain whether any of the provisions thereof are inconsistent with the purposes and provisions of this Part and he shall report any such inconsistency to the House of Commons at the first convenient opportunity.
4. The provisions of this Part shall be known as the *Canadian Bill of Rights*.

---

1. How does the Canadian Bill of Rights differ from the Charter of Rights and Freedoms that was introduced in 1982?

Diefenbaker was fiercely proud of the Bill of Rights. "It will make Parliament freedom-conscious," he proclaimed, "It will make Parliament realize that rights are to be preserved. It will make Parliament more cautious in passing laws that would have the effect of interfering with freedom."[28] In practice, the Bill affected only federal legislation. It was not accepted at first by the provinces, and it was undermined by the tendency of judges to regard it only an as aid to their own interpretations. However, it was used, for example, in *R v. Drybones* in 1970, to invalidate a provision of the Indian Act that applied different liquor laws to status Indians than to other individuals. The Bill of Rights was widely posted in public places, and what it primarily did was create an assumption among Canadians that all laws should reflect Canadian beliefs about human rights. The concepts in the Bill of Rights are strikingly similar to those that would appear more than twenty years later in the Canadian Charter of Rights and Freedoms, which is part of the Canadian Constitution, 1982.

Unions: Labour Finds a Legitimate Voice

As increasing numbers of people came to live in urban areas and found industrial jobs working for large corporations, a key human rights issue in

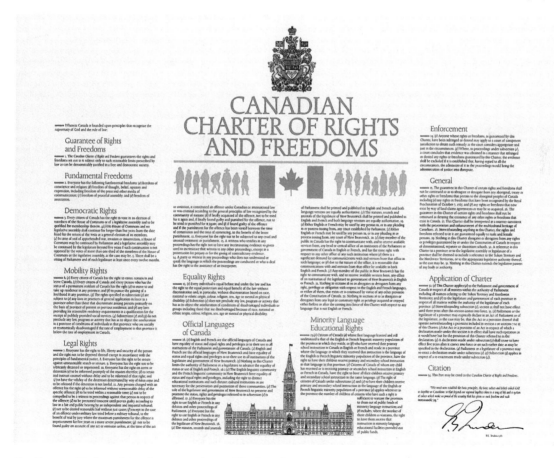

The Charter of Right and Freedoms. How does it differ from the Canadian Bill of Rights?

Canada became the rights of organized labour. During the first half of the twentieth century, labour had not really had the right to organize in Canada, and the constant influx of new, often desperate, immigrants typically undermined labour organization. Canadians endured violent strikes, radical unions, and ruthless strikebreakers. Although the Winnipeg General Strike of 1919 rallied workers and gave them a strong sense of class consciousness, it also frightened government. Only during World War II, faced with severe labour shortages, did government become willing to recognize the right to collective bargaining. About 30 percent of all workers, more than a million people, were members of unions by 1950.

Despite the large numbers of returning soldiers after the war, the unemployment rate was low, about 2.9 percent. This was partly because Canada was in the middle of a huge postwar economic boom and partly because many women who had held jobs during the war had left the labour force and were not seeking employment. ("Unemployed" refers only to those who are seeking work but cannot find it.)

Canadian culture adapted reasonably well to labour rights, in large part because employers recognized that their own interests were served by paying workers enough that they became consumers of mass-produced goods as well as producers of them. However, several key labour–management confrontations during the early postwar period helped to shape subsequent Canadian labour history.

The Windsor Strike and the Rand Formula

In September 1945, 17 000 workers walked off the job at the Ford plant in Windsor. For two years, Ford had refused to recognize the United Automobile Workers Union as the bargaining agent for the employees. Wildcat (illegal) strikes had taken place during the war, but no resolution was reached. With the end of the war in view, employees seized the opportunity to press the issue before the market was flooded with returning soldiers. The Ontario government tried to help Ford break the strike, but the workers responded by blocking key streets of downtown Windsor with their own parked and locked cars, paralyzing the city. The fact that the workers could afford to own so many of the cars that they made showed how much Canadian society was already changing.

In December, with no end to the strike in sight, both employees and management agreed to accept binding arbitration under Mr. Justice Ivan Rand of the Supreme Court of Canada. Binding arbitration meant that both parties had to agree to what Justice Rand decided, as if the strike were a court case. He criticized both union and management for their behaviour during the strike and ordered that the following formula be used: Employees could not be forced to become union members—as the union had wanted—*but* all employees had to pay dues to the union through their paycheques, because the union represented their interests. This procedure came to be called "compulsory dues checkoff." Rand also imposed financial penalties for employees, the union, or both if they engaged in strikes while the employer was complying with the collective agreement. The Rand Formula came to be widely adopted throughout Canada; it was a typical Canadian compromise in that it respected the interests of all three groups—unions, employees who did not believe in unions, and employers—without giving any one of them complete power over the others.

Stelco Strike in Hamilton, 1946

The strike at the Steel Company of Canada (Stelco), based in Hamilton, Ontario, showed just how far labour, management, and the government were prepared to go to win postwar economic battles. United Steelworkers of America (USWA) had asked for a forty-hour workweek (down from forty-eight hours) and other demands that mirrored settlements that were current in many other industries, including a pay raise of nineteen cents an hour and more vacation time. The company thought it could not make a profit under those conditions and refused to meet the demands.

In May 1946, the union voted overwhelmingly (3114 to 80) to strike. The federal government feared that a strike in such an important industry would undermine the country's postwar recovery. The Governor General appointed a government controller to oversee the three big steel companies, including Stelco, and threatened any worker who struck with a fine or jail. A strike was called anyway on July 15 and pickets were set up around the main entrance. Some workers chose not to participate in the strike. They continued to produce steel for the company for a raise of 10 cents an hour, courtesy of the Governor General. They had to be paid for twenty-four hours a day, because they could not leave the plant, which was blockaded by the strikers.

The House of Commons held public hearings but was not able to settle the strike. Meanwhile, management used rowboats on Lake Ontario to bring in supplies for the workers trapped inside. The union responded by buying a motorboat, *The Whisper,* to chase the supply boats. It also made use of a light plane to drop leaflets supporting the strike. Then the company built a private airstrip to fly in supplies. By late August, the RCMP had to be called in to maintain order.

Finally, on October 1, the company offered the union a pay increase of 13 cents an hour, which the union accepted. The episode was considered a huge victory for the union, because it signalled a willingness on the part of Canadian workers to dig in for the long haul when they considered the terms offered to them to be unfair. Steelworkers also won the right to represent an additional two thousand workers at Stelco, which helped it become one of the largest and most powerful unions in Canada.

The Asbestos Strike and the Quiet Revolution

During the postwar industrial boom, asbestos was highly valued for its ability to withstand heat.

Workers striking in Quebec, 1948.

Some of the oldest and most productive asbestos mines were located in Quebec. In February 1948, the workers at the mine at Asbestos, halfway between Montreal and Quebec City on the South Shore, struck illegally over a health issue. The owner company, John Manville Co., refused to agree to a clause in the union's proposed agreement on the asbestos dust that threatened the miners' health. The strike soon spread to other asbestos towns as well.

Maurice Duplessis's government decertified the union. The president of John Manville declared the strikers to be communists. The police, who were based in mining company offices, were thought to side more with the owners than to keep the peace. Then, in the spring, when a settlement appeared likely, the company demanded the right to punish those workers who were responsible for the strike. The talks collapsed and violence spread, especially when some workers decided to cross the picket line.

The Catholic Church, breaking publicly with Duplessis, took the strikers' side and ordered special collections for the asbestos workers. The Archbishop of Montreal, Joseph Charbonneau, said:

> The working class is the victim of a conspiracy which wishes to crush it, and when there is a conspiracy to crush the working class, it is the duty of the Church to intervene.
>
> We wish social peace, but we do not wish the crushing of the working class. We are more attached to man than to capital. This is why the clergy has decided to intervene. It wishes that justice and charity be respected, and it desires that more attention cease to be paid to financial interests than to the human factor.[29]

Other opinion leaders in the province thought the same. *Le Devoir*, probably the most influential newspaper in Quebec, took up the strikers' cause in its editorials. Then, twelve weeks into the strike, John Manville announced that its strikebreakers were producing the normal quota of asbestos. Fury erupted on the picket lines, and the next day, the Quebec government responded by reading the Riot Act, which banned protests and gave the police new powers of arrest and detention.

The terms of the settlement, which did not come until June, were not especially favourable to the union. Even so, the Asbestos Strike was seen as a great victory for the labour movement. For one thing, it brought together many people who were convinced of the need for major social changes in Quebec, including Jean Marchand, a key union figure during the strike. Marchand was lured to Ottawa by Lester Pearson to help defend federalism against the rising tide of Quebec separatism. Marchand insisted on bringing with him two friends, Gérard Pelletier and Pierre Trudeau. Trudeau had spent more than three weeks in and around Asbestos, urging the strikers to stand united and earning himself a reputation among the authorities as an "outside agitator."

The mine workers were right to be concerned about the health risks of asbestos. Although it was called a "miracle fibre" in the postwar period, it turned out be a source of fatal cancers that appear in the victims a decade or two after exposure. After 1975 it was no longer used much in consumer goods or industry. Those who work with it today are required to follow hazardous materials protocols.

Conclusion

After the war, Canada and Canadians underwent changes on almost every level. Internationally, Canada took on new roles as a member of NATO and NORAD and began to define itself in the position of peacekeeper. Geographically, Canada finally stretched from sea to sea, with Newfoundland and Labrador joining Confederation. Culturally, postwar immigration began to further the development of ethnocultural communities within Canada, and French Canadians underwent a new revival of pride and the desire to preserve their French Canadian identity. In postwar Canada, Canadians began to ponder and test the bounds of what it meant to be a Canadian in the world, and at home.

Notes

1. Louis St. Laurent, Minister of External Affairs, *Address to the United Nations General Assembly*, September 1947.
2. June 27, 1950.
3. John English, "Korean War," *The Canadian Encyclopedia 2000 World Edition* (Toronto: McClelland & Stewart, 1999).
4. *Hansard*, February 23, 1959.
5. Greig Stewart, *Shutting Down the National Dream: A.V. Roe and the Tragedy of the Avro Arrow* (Toronto: McGraw-Hill Ryerson, Limited, 1988), pp. 275–76.
6. Ibid., p. 267.
7. Ibid., p. 271.
8. From a press release from the United States Department of State, January 30, 1963, "United States and Canadian Negotiations Regarding Nuclear Weapons."
9. See, for example, Reginald Whitaker and Gary Marcuse, *Cold War Canada: The Making of a National Insecurity State, 1945–1957* (Toronto: University of Toronto Press, 1994).
10. CBC *This Morning* Sunday Edition for week of December 10, 1998, "John Humphrey and the Universal Declaration of Human Rights," by Bob Carty ex Montreal.
11. The entire text of Pearson's Nobel speech is available online at http://www.nobel.se/peace/laureates/1957/pearson-lecture.html.
12. *St. John's Daily News*, May 29, 1948.
13. *St. John's Evening Telegram*, July 20, 1948.
14. *National Post,* March 27, 1999.
15. Ibid.
16. René Durocher, "Quiet Revolution," *The Canadian Encyclopedia 2000 World Edition* (Toronto: McClelland & Stewart, 1999).
17. Ibid.

18. Marc Laurendeau, "Front de libération du Québec," *The Canadian Encyclopedia 2000 World Edition* (Toronto: McClelland & Stewart, 1999) references his book, *Nègres blancs d'Amérique,* which sets out this view.

19. Alan Edmonds, *The Years of Protest 1960/1970* (Toronto: Natural Science of Canada, 1979), p. 114.

20. A turning point was apparently a TV debate with Quebec Premier Daniel Johnson on February 6, 1968. (W.A. Wilson, *The Trudeau Question*, Toronto: General Publishing, 1972.)

21. *Hansard*, May 1, 1947.

22. *Hansard*, October 22, 1945.

23. CBC *This Morning* Sunday Edition for week of December 10, 1998, "John Humphrey and the Universal Declaration of Human Rights," esp. the comments of William Schabas, law professor at the University of Quebec at Montreal, on his own research.

24. Parks Canada, "Africville." Available online at <http://parkscanada.pch.ca/library/background/44_e.htm>.

25. CBC News, "Africville Named Historic Site in Halifax," July 5, 2002. Available online at <http://cbc.ca/cgi-bin/templates/view.cgi?category=canada&story-/news/2002/07/05/Africville?>.

26. Ibid.

27. M. James Penton, "Jehovah's Witnesses," *The Canadian Encyclopedia 2000 World Edition* (Toronto: McClelland & Stewart, 1999). For example, in a Supreme Court decision, *Roncarelli v. Duplessis,* 1959, Premier Maurice Duplessis was held to have wrongfully removed Frank Roncarelli's Montreal restaurant liquor licence in 1946, an act that ruined Roncarelli's business. Duplessis took this action because Roncarelli provided bail for Jehovah's Witnesses accused of attacking Roman Catholicism. In the meantime, the Witnesses had narrowly won the right, in a five to four decision by the Supreme Court in 1953, to distribute their literature. John Diefenbaker supported the Witnesses' subsequent petition for a Bill of Rights.

28. Interviewed on *The Nation's Business*, CBC, June 30, 1960.

29. *Le Devoir,* May 2, 1949.

Chapter 19 Review

Knowledge & Understanding

1. Identify these people, places, and events, and explain their historical significance to Canada's developing culture and identity:
   Canadian Citizenship Act
   Asbestos Strike
   Korean War
   Lester Pearson
   Canadian Bill of Rights
   NORAD
   Avro Arrow
   National Indian Brotherhood
   peacekeeping
   DEW line
   Africville

2. A number of social groups in postwar Canada made gains either in their legal rights or social position. Identify five such groups and provide a) at least one example of a gain, and b) at least one factor that helped the group make this gain. Use a three-column chart organization, with the headings Group, Gain, Factor.

3. Identify three factors that enabled labour organization (unions) to become much more powerful and successful during the early postwar period. Explain the specific effect of each factor.

Thinking & Inquiry

4. "[L]et's face it, the Arrow was the most advanced aircraft of its day. Yet all that knowledge, all that development, years and years of study, was wiped out. Deliberately wiped out. No salvage". In these poignant words, an Avro employee mourns the vanished fighter jet. Based on what you have learned about the Cold War and Canada's postwar position, explain in a paragraph why you think all material related to the Arrow was destroyed. Also, give your own view of the decision.

5. "Students who grew up during the period of nuclear terror and MAD had little confidence in the political and social establishment of their day, compared with previous generations". Do you agree that they had less reason for confidence than previous generations? Have a class debate on this issue.

Application

6. You are an American diplomat in Canada during the Cuban Missile Crisis. Write a confidential memo to President John Kennedy, explaining why you think that the Canadian government behaved in an ambivalent way. Use your knowledge of Canada's postwar position up to 1963.

Communication

7. Research the life of Georges-Henri Lévesque, one of the key architects of the Quiet Revolution. a) Write a few paragraphs explaining the contributions he made and the effect that they had. b) What difference did his position as a Dominican priest make?

8. Choose one of the following scenes and write a page of realistic dialogue for several characters. The dialogue should reveal what they think and why: a) Two Canadian security officials who have just learned of the raid on the Gouzenko family apartment. b) Strikers at the Ford plant in Windsor, blocking downtown streets overnight with their cars. c) A family in 1963, discussing at the dinner table whether to build a fallout shelter. d) A scene of your choice from this chapter that generates conflict or tension.

CHAPTER 20

Postwar Prosperity

I'm so excited about Canadians ruling the world.

—JOHN DIEFENBAKER

Immediately following World War II, Canada experienced a great economic boom. The well-organized industrial system Canada had developed to fight the war was easily adapted to the peacetime production of consumer goods, especially since unions found it easier to organize under the Rand Formula. The country undertook major public works projects such as the St. Lawrence Seaway and the TransCanada Highway, and the industrial and business opportunities that these projects provided greatly expanded the economy.

The economic boom led to increasing urbanization, and with it came a new suburban lifestyle. Despite regional disparities, standards of living in many parts of Canada began to rise dramatically after the war. Average Canadians gained access to central heating, indoor plumbing, labour-saving devices, a family car, and store-bought clothes. An enormous rise in the postwar birthrate created a steady demand for consumer products and an expansion of social programs. Increasingly, the government was asked to provide social benefits such as medical care, pensions, and unemployment insurance to ensure that the Canadian social system would keep people out of the poverty that many Canadians had heard about from their parents or had known themselves.

One outcome of these lifestyle improvements was that citizens, whose basic needs were satisfied, came to expect more from their governments and from society. Toward the end of the postwar period, many people who would not have voiced dissatisfaction with their economic and social position during a time of war or great poverty began to feel that they should speak up. The most significant postwar social force for change was the growth of the women's movement.

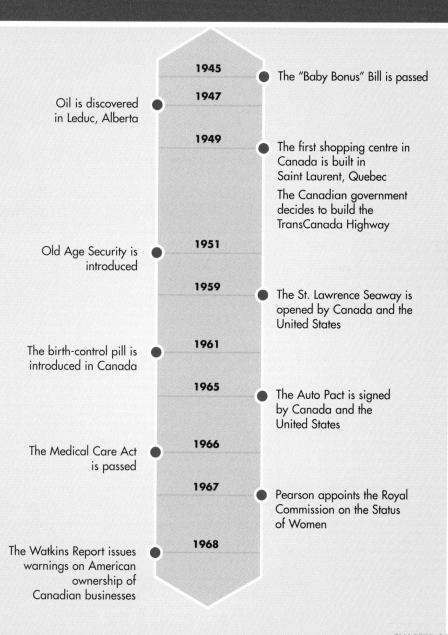

1945 The "Baby Bonus" Bill is passed

1947 Oil is discovered in Leduc, Alberta

1949 The first shopping centre in Canada is built in Saint Laurent, Quebec

The Canadian government decides to build the TransCanada Highway

1951 Old Age Security is introduced

1959 The St. Lawrence Seaway is opened by Canada and the United States

1961 The birth-control pill is introduced in Canada

1965 The Auto Pact is signed by Canada and the United States

1966 The Medical Care Act is passed

1967 Pearson appoints the Royal Commission on the Status of Women

1968 The Watkins Report issues warnings on American ownership of Canadian businesses

By the end of this chapter, you will be able to

- analyze the reasons for Canada's close political and economic relationship with the United States

- analyze the extent to which women's traditional roles as wives and mothers and their status in Canadian society have changed since Victorian times

- analyze women's changing participation in the paid labour force

- demonstrate an understanding of the history, development, and extent of Canada's social programs

The Postwar Transportation Boom

The history of Canada has been largely a history of transportation and communications. In the postwar period, developments in both industrial and consumer transportation reshaped Canada's economy.

St. Lawrence Seaway

Canals were built as early as 1783 along the St. Lawrence River to enable large vessels to reach ports along the river. By 1895, the Canadian and American governments had discussed constructing a deep waterway that would reach from the Atlantic Ocean to the Great Lakes. The waterway would allow large freight-carrying vessels to navigate to the heart of North America, saving untold dollars in ground transportation from the east coast. In 1927 U.S. President Herbert Hoover said, "I know of

Building the St. Lawrence Seaway.

nothing that should so appeal to the imagination of the people of North America as the final consummation of the struggle of generations to open these Great Lakes as part of the 'Seven Seas.'" But nothing came of the grand idea until 1951, when the Canadian government threatened to build a seaway entirely within Canadian territory if the United States did not want to participate.

In 1954, a final agreement was signed between the two countries. Canada agreed to pay three-quarters of the $470 million cost, and construction began that year on the section that stretched from Montreal to Lake Ontario. In 1959, the St. Lawrence Seaway, also called the Great Lakes Waterway, was officially opened by the Queen, Prime Minister Diefenbaker, and U.S. President Dwight Eisenhower.

The waterway stretches 3790 km from Anticosti Island to the head of Lake Superior, so that large commercial ships can travel from the Atlantic Ocean as far inland as Duluth, Minnesota, at the western end of Lake Superior and back again. In 1959, the icebreaker *D'Iberville* was the first ship to travel from Montreal to Duluth. The Seaway is a major engineering feat because the lift system raises ships measuring up to 225.5 m long (twice as long as a football field) more than 180 m above sea level (about twice as high as a sixty-storey building) entirely by the power of gravity.

The Seaway's economic impact has been immense. For example, it allowed the huge deposits of iron ore in Quebec and Labrador to be mined, and Canada became a net exporter rather than importer of iron ore. In 1986, 37.6 million tonnes of cargo travelled through the St. Lawrence seaway, versus 11 million tonnes in the 1960s. All this created many more jobs, consumer goods, and general development than would have been possible without the Seaway.

The project did meet some opposition, because the Canadian portion was publicly funded via a Crown corporation, the St. Lawrence Seaway

Authority. Railway companies and east coast ports that stood to lose freight protested that it was unfair for the government to subsidize the competition with their tax money. During the postwar period Canadians tended to accept government intervention in the market economy if economic benefits accrued, so these protests did not bring a halt to the project. The creation of Lake St. Lawrence (part of the project) also displaced 6500 people whose homes were flooded, but who received compensation and were relocated to other towns in the area.

⌁ Web Connection

www.mcgrawhill.ca/links/definingcanada

Go to the Web site above to find out more about the St. Lawrence Seaway system and its importance to the North American economy

The TransCanada Highway

The success of the Canadian Pacific Railway, despite difficult geographic conditions, encouraged Canadians to believe that they should be able to travel across the country unhindered. The first recorded automobile trip across Canada was accomplished in 1912 by Thomas Wilby and Jack Haney. It took them two months, from August 17 to October 17, to drive from Halifax to Victoria in a 1912 five-passenger REO, built in St. Catharines. Here are some excerpts from the diary that Haney kept:

Aug. 27 *Left Halifax at 4:30 PM. Arrived at Truro 8 PM. Bum roads most of the way. Mud got in carburetor, will fix protection for it in the morning....*

Sept. 2 *Had trouble getting up a hill about 20 miles [thirty-two kilometres] out of Quebec. It was too steep for gas to feed with full tank so I tried backing up, but when about 100 ft. [30.5 m] from top could not get traction. [Haney solved his traction problem by getting four local men to volunteer to sit in the car, and then backed over the hill.]*

Sept. 9 *[Scotia Junction, Ontario] Got stuck in sand hill north of town and had to be pulled out. Twisted trans. shaft so will have to stay here till a new one comes.... About everything that has tried that hill has had to be pulled out.*

Sept. 24 *Left Portage 8:15. Got stuck in slough for 2 hrs.*

Oct. 2 *Left Lethbridge 9:40 AM.... Got off road three times and come near going through break in bridge.*

Oct. 13 *[Hope, B.C.] Got stuck on hill for an hour on account of loose gravel.*

The TransCanada Highway under construction.

Haney's diary could be summed up with the phrase "[r]oads were bad." In the early twentieth century, Canada's roads were sufficient for draft wagons and buggies, but motor vehicle traffic required smooth, graded, mud-free roads. Not surprisingly, as early as 1910, governments began to hear rumblings in favour of a national highway, the TransCanada.

Between 1945 and 1955, Canadians bought 3.5 million cars. They soon discovered that in many parts of Canada, no substantial improvement had been made to the roads since Haney's day. Prodded by voters in 1949, the federal government and the provinces agreed to build a two-lane highway across Canada, with extra lanes for heavily populated areas. The provinces would do most of the construction work, and for every dollar they spent, the federal government would contribute a dollar.

Things did not go smoothly. Although the highway was scheduled to be completed by December 1956, it ran into serious technical difficulties and cost overruns. For example, snowsheds, earth mounds, and other control devices were needed to protect the highway from avalanches in the Rockies. It cost $75 million to build just the one kilometre of highway that runs beneath the St. Lawrence River at Boucherville, Quebec. The final cost of the highway was more than $1 billion, compared with its estimated $300 million. It was formally opened at Rogers Pass in British Columbia on July 30, 1962, but it was not actually finished until 1970. At 7821 km, the TransCanada is the longest national highway in the world. Like the railway before it, the highway helped to bring Canada together.

The Auto Pact

Postwar Canada was a very profitable market for automobile makers, but the Canadian government needed to think carefully about how to manage this market. Automobiles have always been very expensive compared with most goods, costing half a year's income for the average buyer. They also create significant public expenses in terms of roads, traffic lights, administration, policing, medical care, and so on. The only way Canada could afford to encourage the trend to private passenger automobiles was if Canadians got a large share of the jobs that went into producing them.

In 1965, the federal government negotiated the Canada–U.S. Automotive Products Agreement, usually called the Auto Pact. Under this agreement, if a U.S.

The Chrysler auto plant Windsor, Ontario in the mid 1960s.

car manufacturer wants to sell cars duty-free in Canada, it must also build cars in Canada. The value of vehicles produced must meet or exceed a specified proportion of the manufacturer's annual sales. The Auto Pact helped to make the Canadian auto industry one of the most powerful sectors in the country during the postwar period. It survived the Free Trade Agreement negotiated with the United States in 1989 but was struck down by the World Trade Organization in 2000.

Taking a Stand Against the Risk of the Branch Plant Economy

Throughout the twentieth century, Canada had a unique economic relationship with the United States. Besides Canada, no other country has ever allowed a foreign power to own so much of its economy. Allowing a large amount of foreign investment dated from the days when Canada was a British colony and British investors provided the capital for its development.

Far from protecting businesses from foreign ownership, Canadian governments often encouraged it. For example, when American firms wanted to buy timber from Canada, provincial governments refused to simply let them buy logs. They made them build branch plants in Canada to create local employment and tax opportunities.[1] Similarly, the development of the Canadian mining industry was largely financed by American capital.

This arrangement worked to the United States' advantage as well as Canada's. During the 1920s, American manufacturers realized that if they set up branch plants to serve the Canadian market, they could avoid both freight costs and import duties. Aside from the benefits they gained when marketing to Canadians, the American firms also profited from reduced tariff rates when they shipped from Canada to countries that were still part of the British Empire. To the extent that these arrangements created jobs and cheaper consumer goods, most Canadians were comfortable with them during the first part of the twentieth century.

After a standstill during the Great Depression and World War II, American investment in Canada increased rapidly during the postwar period. For example, between 1950 and 1995, American investment increased from $3.4 billion to more than thirty times that figure.[2] American firms began to buy established Canadian firms as well; Canadians preferred to sell to Americans because they tended to get the highest prices from them.

However, during the postwar period, Canadians began to recognize that there were real dangers to a branch plant economy:

- Unless the smaller power manages the relationship carefully, its economy will come to be operated in the interests of the nation that houses the head office.
- If foreign companies are large enough or united enough, they may be able to dictate to the government, even on domestic and foreign policy.
- Critical research and development that provides opportunities for national advancement does not take place in the branch plant economy. It usually takes place in the head-office economy.
- Talented young workers may be forced to emigrate to be part of cutting-edge projects. Quite apart from the fact that they may not want to emigrate, their ability to do so depends on the immigration laws of the head-office country.
- During a downturn, the foreign-owned firm will close the Canadian branch plant rather than the plant in the head-office country.[3]

Recognizing these dangers and dilemmas, many Canadians began to advocate government supervision of business transactions that increased foreign control of Canada's economy. They were especially concerned about foreign control of cultural industries.

Formulating Research Questions

Why do you need research questions?

Questioning lies at the heart of both research and learning. Developing good research questions helps you to explore topics with a greater depth of understanding. You increase your understanding by investigating, reflecting, developing and supporting alternative solutions to your questions. Good research questions can frame and guide your inquiry by providing structure and focus. The answer to your research question can become the thesis statement for your presentation, seminar, or essay.

What are some strategies for developing good research questions?

Finding the best research question to suit your subject, your purpose, and your audience may take several attempts. As you go through the research process, be ready to revise both your research question and the thesis statement that you develop in response to that question. The following strategies may be useful to you as you write your research questions:

- Begin with some general ideas and a broad topic that interests you.
- Search for books, articles, and online resources related to the topic.
- Think about what you already know about the topic, what you believe and what you would like to know or understand.
- Narrow the scope of your topic to fit the parameters of your essay, presentation or seminar.
- Brainstorm as many questions as you can on a sheet of paper. Try to think of questions that can help to clear up a controversy about your subject, shed light on an unresolved issue, or clarify different historical interpretations.
- Chose a question that focuses on an issue that has many possible answers or approaches.

What is a good research question?

Good research questions should

- act as a roadmap–they guide, shape, and focus your research
- be controversial–not everyone will accept the same answer to the question
- be debatable–there should be more than one possible answer
- allow for depth of research–such depth enables the answer to the question (your thesis) to shape and frame the presentation or essay
- focus both your topic and your research into a specific area of investigation.
  Some sample research questions are
- Did the social welfare policies of the 1960s reject or support capitalism?
- Who was really to blame for the cancellation of the Avro Arrow?
- Did Pierre Eliot Trudeau deliver his promise of a 'just society'?

How can you find information that best helps you answer your research question?

Finding information that best helps you answer your research question involves using all of the skills discussed in the Historical Skills features of *Defining Canada: History, Identity, and Culture*.

Using Historical Sources (p.168)

- Is this a primary source or a secondary source?
- Does the source reflect the historical conditions of the time period?
- How current is the information?
- Is the source detailed or does it provide an overview?
- What is the theme of the source?

Frame of Reference (p.14)

- Who wrote the book, article, or editorial? What are the author's credentials?
- What is the author's frame of reference?
- What is the author's thesis or main idea?
- What are the strengths and weaknesses of the supporting evidence that the author uses?
- What sources are used by the author? If this is an Internet page, is there a contact site where I can email the author with questions and comments?
- What was the author's main reason for writing t his document? Who is (or was) the author's main audience?

Analyzing Information (p.260)

- What are the main arguments and evidence in the research material?
- Is the supporting evidence accurate?
- Are there any flaws in the logic or reasoning of the argument?
- Does the information in this source help support my thesis?
- How will I use this information in my essay?

Understanding Cause and Effect (p.440)

- Does the author explain the causes for the event, situation, or issue I am interested in?
- What effects flow from the event, situation, or issue in the view of this author?
- Are the cause-and-effect relationships reasonable and accurate?
- Has the author dealt with the most important causes and effects?

Organizing and Classifying (p.302)

- Does the classification system used by this author fit into my classification scheme for this essay or presentation?
- Do I agree with the categories and subcategories that this author has used for classification?
- Has the author used narrative, descriptive, definition, expository, analysis, or comparison organizational structures in this document?
- Would any elements of the organizational structure of this document suit my purpose and fit my thesis statement?

Practice

Review the topics in this chapter. Look for a subject that you would be interested in researching further. Write three or four possible research questions you could use to get started investigating your subject. Then meet with three other students and peer review each other's questions. Decide which question each of you would like to begin with and draw up an outline of how you would research to find an answer to your questions.

In 1963, Finance Minister Walter Gordon proposed a tax on the takeovers of Canadian companies, but the idea was rejected. In 1967, Liberal Prime Minister Lester Pearson appointed a task force that included eight economists to study the question of foreign ownership. The resulting Watkins Report of 1968 recommended a more interventionist foreign policy. Pierre Trudeau, who succeeded Pearson, agreed with the need for controls and in later years established the Canada Development Corporation (1971), Foreign Investment Review Agency (1973), Petro-Canada (1974), and the National Energy Program (1980).

Several postwar incidents caused many Canadians to become concerned about American ownership. One of them involved natural gas pipelines, and two others involved Canada's complex relationship with two communist countries: China and Cuba.

The Natural Gas Pipeline Debate

Alberta had a surplus of natural gas, and the federal government decided that a pipeline should be built to supply fuel to Ontario and Quebec. The Liberal Minister of Trade and Commerce, C.D. Howe, wanted the pipeline to follow an all-Canadian route. Such a pipeline would be very expensive, especially because the stretch between Winnipeg and Sudbury would not serve many customers. In 1951, Howe put together a group of Canadian and American business investors to create TransCanada Pipelines and to raise money. Both the Cooperative Commonwealth Federation (predecessor to the New Democratic Party) and the Progressive Conservative Party opposed the idea of allowing this group to build the pipeline, because American interests were dominant.

The Pipeline Debate, which lasted from May 8 to June 6, 1956, is remembered as one of the most bitter in Canadian history. Howe, who was well known for getting things done quickly, openly supported American involvement, because he felt that it would take far too long to assemble the necessary resources within Canada; Howe needed to pass his pipeline law quickly, so that construction could begin before the ground froze. To ensure success, the Liberals used the parliamentary procedure of closure to end debate. In other words, they had enough seats to shut down the debate. Construction proceeded and by October 1958 the 3700-km pipeline was completed.

Over time, TransCanada Pipelines became primarily Canadian-owned, with foreign ownership representing about 30 percent by 1999. The federal Liberals had not counted on the anger many Canadians felt about the fact that closure had been imposed on the discussion. The incident

A photo showing the building of the TransCanada pipeline.

is widely believed to have contributed to their defeat by Diefenbaker's Conservatives in the 1957 election.

Selling Wheat to China

In 1954, the United States began subsidizing the production of wheat by American farmers. This practice allowed the grain farmers to export their crop at low prices. Canadian farmers, who were not receiving equivalent subsidies, could not compete with them. The Canadian farmers were growing more wheat than ever, but they were forced to store most of it instead of selling it.

Diefenbaker attempted to resolve the problem by marketing the wheat to the People's Republic of China, starting in 1958. He knew that because of strong opposition to communism, the Americans would not deal with the Chinese. Most Canadians opposed communism, but that did not necessarily mean that they would refuse to trade with any communist country. Nor did Canadian anti-communism necessarily imply support for American foreign policies with respect to communist nations. The Americans, however, expected Canada's support. When they learned that Canada was negotiating to sell wheat to the Chinese, the Americans made their opposition to trading with the "enemy communists" clear.[4]

Issues at home about the deal with China had to be sorted out as well. Domestic textile manufacturers did not like the plan, because they knew that the Chinese would want to market their competitively priced textiles in Canada. Commonwealth supporters were angry because China was hostile toward India. But Diefenbaker closed the deal anyway. Under a 1960 agreement, Canada shipped $422 million worth of wheat and barley over two and a half years. On the Prairies, income on an average farm tripled. For years after the sale, the Conservative Party did well in the west at election time. Grain sales to China continue to be worth hundreds of millions of dollars yearly to Canada.

Trade with Cuba

During the Suez Crisis, Canada was unable to support Britain on control of the Canal. Canada faced a similar problem with the United States over Cuba. In 1959, Fidel Castro overthrew the government of Cuba, which had been friendly to the United States. Castro's revolutionary government proceeded to expropriate many valuable American properties. In 1960, the United States imposed various trade sanctions on Cuba. In 1961, it severed diplomatic relations and launched the Bay of Pigs invasion, which failed. In 1962, the Soviet Union entered the conflict, precipitating the Cuban Missile Crisis.

To gain support for its continuing campaign, the United States tried to prevent Canada from trading with Cuba. For example, the U.S. government attempted to prevent American subsidiaries in Canada from trading with Cuba, because the American companies themselves were not allowed to do so. Many Canadians deeply resented these attempts, not because of great sympathy for Castro but because they did not feel that the United States had the right to impose its laws in Canada.

The Canadian government took the view that American trade sanctions and embargos were a policy mistake. They forced Cuba to become more dependent on the Soviet Union. For example, Cuba could not sell sugar to the United States, so it sold sugar to the Soviets.[5] One outcome of this situation was to entrench communism in Cuba, which encouraged the Soviet bloc to make further attempts to intervene in the Americas. Canada believed that trade with Cuba was beneficial, because it would erode Cuba's dependence on the Soviets and encourage democratic reforms and more individual freedom.

The disagreement between Canada and the United States over trade with Cuba survived the collapse of the Soviet bloc in the late 1980s. In 1992, for example, the United States passed a law that allowed criminal charges to be brought against foreign subsidiaries of U.S. companies that did business with Cuba. Again, the U.S. law was widely resented in Canada, but by that time it had little practical effect. The Soviet collapse crippled the Cuban economy, so humanitarian aid is a more pressing concern than trade policy.

Regionalism and National Unity

Because Canada is a very large country, its regions have different economic interests. Regional differences became quite important in national politics during the postwar period. A difference in the standard of living among regions always makes a big difference in politics, but during this period Canadians began to expect the government to manage the economy to reduce the regional differences. Even so, the differences sometimes led to major conflicts that shaped regional identities. Consider, for instance, the postwar fortunes of Alberta.

Alberta: Black Gold and the Pipeline Debate

Imperial Oil had been trying to find oil in Alberta since the early 1920s. It had drilled 133 dry wells and was ready to give up. But well No. 134, drilled in February 1947 just south of Edmonton in Leduc, was a gusher. By the end of the year, thirty wells were in production, pumping out 3500 barrels of oil every day. Ten years after the first strike, there were 7390 working wells in the province, and annual production reached 144 million barrels.

To understand the economic difference that oil made to Alberta, it is helpful to compare its population growth rate with that of Saskatchewan. Before the discovery of oil at Leduc, both provinces were agricultural societies with populations of roughly 830 000. By 1951, Alberta had 940 000 people, but Saskatchewan still had only 830 000. By 1961, Alberta had reached

The Leduc oil well in Alberta, a turning point in the province's economy.

1.3 million, and Saskatchewan had 925000. In 1981, Alberta's population was 2.2 million, while Saskatchewan's was still below 1 million. Calgary, which has been the headquarters of the petroleum industry from the outset, grew from a city of 104 000 people to a city of almost 800 000 people in fifty years.

One reason for the difference in fortunes was that the money that came from pumping the oil wells brought a huge amount of new business development: construction, trucking, insurance, surveying, research, housing, shopping, social services, arts, and much more. Significantly, the Royal Bank of Canada opened a branch in Leduc the very day after oil was struck.

Many people moved to Alberta to find work. Young Albertans who might have moved to Montreal or Toronto to pursue careers stayed home and worked in the oil industry or in one of the many businesses spun off from oil. Peter Lougheed, who was just finishing high school in

Canada's Economic Growth, 1945–1976			
Year	GNP*	GNP in 1971 dollars*	GNP per capita in 1971 dollars*
1945	11 863	29 071	2400.81
1951	21 640	35 450	2530.52
1956	32 058	47 599	2959.95
1961	39 646	54 741	3001.48
1966	61 828	74 844	3739.40
1971	94 450	94 450	4379.17
1976	191 031	119 249	5195.02

*millions of dollars

Source: F.H. Leacy, ed., Historical Statistics of Canada, 2nd ed. (Ottawa: Statistics Canada 1983), tables A1, F13, F15

1947 and who would one day be premier of Alberta, said, "My generation knows that if we didn't have Leduc and its consequences, we probably would be living elsewhere."[6] This boom hastened the growth of regional identity, because many promising careers were tied to the development of Alberta. Today, Alberta's economy is third only to Ontario's and Quebec's.

Equalization Payments

The economic fortunes of Canada's ten provinces have been far from equal. Since 1910, Ontario has usually provided 40 percent of Canada's income and production, and Quebec has provided about 23 percent. These two provinces have tended to dominate Canada's economy. B.C.'s share has increased since 1910, whereas the shares of Manitoba and Saskatchewan have decreased steadily since the Great Depression. The share of Atlantic Canada declined from 16 percent in 1890 to 5 percent in 1994. By contrast, Alberta's share rose dramatically after oil was

discovered and again when it later gained control of its oil resources in the 1970s.[7] Although economics does not rule everything, many political issues are easier to understand if economic issues are considered. For example, Alberta's improved economic position as a supplier of oil gave it a significant voice in national politics during the postwar period.

Many Canadians were concerned about how regional income differences would affect social justice and national unity. The federal government began to intervene to reduce these income disparities. In 1957, it introduced the first formal equalization payments program. Ottawa transferred tax money raised from the richer provinces to the poorer provinces. The program quickly became more comprehensive, and by 1967, the amount transferred had risen from 10 percent to 24 percent.[8] Over time, equalization has probably reduced the impact of regional disparity. For example, in 1956, average incomes of New Brunswickers were 65.9 percent of the Canadian average but by 1994, they were 81 percent.[9]

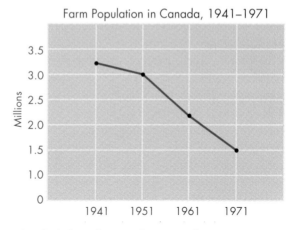

Farm Population in Canada, 1941–1971

What do declining farm populations say about a province's economy?

Key Postwar Social Changes

The Baby Boom (1947–1966)

After World War II, Canada experienced a huge increase in the annual birth rate, an increase that came to be called the Baby Boom. More than 400 000 babies were born each year, peaking at 479 000 in 1959.[10] In comparison, only 253 000 babies were born in 1940. In fact, Canada experienced the largest proportionate increase in births in the western world, nearly "half a baby" per person more than the United States.[11] This trend had a major effect on Canada's economy and social life throughout the postwar period and even today. As University of Toronto demographer (population scientist) David Foot writes, "changes in social and economic behaviour resulting from the aging process are more evident in Canada than in European countries that have not had such sharp fluctuations in birth rates."[12]

Demographers examine trends such as the Baby Boom with great interest for two reasons. First, a baby boom is not usually an accident; many social factors work together to produce a sudden, sustained increase in the birth rate. Second, the increase affects society for many decades. A demographer can successfully predict many future trends simply by identifying an increase in the number of people born in a given year—because age alone determines many social trends. For example, an increase in births eleven years ago might create a high demand for skateboards this year, but an increase in births fifty-one years ago would not have the same effect today.

According to Foot, several factors worked together to produce a postwar baby boom so large that, at its height, Canadian women were averaging four children each.

- Although many more soldiers took part, the number of Canadian soldiers killed and wounded in World War II was lower than in World War I. Thus, more soldiers returned to help start families.
- World War I was followed by an influenza epidemic that killed as many Canadians as the war. No such epidemic followed World War II. In fact, public health improved significantly during the decades following World War II.
- World War II followed the Great Depression, when many people had already postponed families. If they wanted to have families at all, they had to start right after the war.
- The war had been good for Canada economically, making it an industrial power whose people were enjoying high incomes.[13]
- The Canadian birth rate was further spiked by high immigration from Europe during the early postwar period. Because immigrants were usually young adults, they started families here.

A key outcome of the high birth rate was that the Boomers dominated the postwar period as babies, children, and then teenagers. The things that were important to them tended to receive a lot of attention from government, manufacturers, advertisers, and the media. This is still true today, because almost one-third of Canadians are Boomers.

Not all Boomers fared equally well following the postwar period. The group of Canadians born toward the end of the Baby Boom in the early

1960s are sometimes called Generation X, after the title of a novel by Canadian writer Douglas Coupland (who was born in 1961). Many Gen-Xers found that the huge numbers of Boomers ahead of them had driven up prices and taken the good jobs. As a result, Gen-Xers were often less successful in their careers, despite having similar talent to older Boomers. In the novel *Generation X*, Coupland's characters are much more unsure of what to do with their lives than would be typical of Boomers.

The Baby Bust

The period from 1967 to 1979 saw a great decline in births, the Baby Bust. The decline was partly due to more women joining the workforce full time and partly due to the introduction of the birth-control pill. However, from 1980 to 1995, the postwar Baby Boom generation started having children, which raised the birth rate once again. According to Foot, if you were born between 1985 and 1990, you are probably a little better off than your younger siblings, because your demographic position is more similar to the front end of the Baby Boom than it is to Gen-X.

Family Allowance

The federal Committee on Post-War Reconstruction published a major report in 1943 that advocated, among others things, a family allowance. This monthly allowance would be paid to a mother for each liveborn child. The purpose was to reduce the hardship of poor families by putting cash into their hands.

Prime Minister Mackenzie King was not happy with most of the social reforms that had been advocated by the committee, because he thought they were far too radical. However, he did see the family allowance as a sure vote-getter for the 1945 election. He could take votes away from the left wing, which was arguing for more radical reforms by promising every family a bit of cash now, with increases for each birth.

Critics argued that the allowance was a waste of money, especially because it was universal; tax-free cheques would be mailed to every family in the country, rich or poor. There were also rumblings about King buying the favour of Quebec voters who tended to have large families. The "Baby Bonus" Bill passed the House of Commons unanimously.

For every child under age five, the government sent $5 a month. Six- to nine-year-olds earned a family $6; for ten- to twelve-year-olds, it was $7; for thirteen- to fifteen-year-olds, $8 a month. When the program first started, a family's fifth child incurred reduced payments. This provision was eliminated in 1949, possibly because postwar parents did not think that five was an unreasonably large number of children.

Canadian families quickly became used to the cheque. The fact that the scheme was universal meant that it could not specifically target the poor and give them extra help; however, it still helped. Many poor people during the early postwar period had little access to cash, and more access to "in-kind" goods. They often scraped by on hand-me-downs, garden produce, canned goods drives, and toys collected and repaired by church groups. The family allowance made the low-income family a retail market for products aimed at children. One benefit of the fact that the cheque was universal was that there was no "welfare"-style humiliation attached to cashing it. After all, a poor woman's baby bonus cheque was the same as a rich woman's and very welcome in the children's departments of major stores such as Eaton's or Simpson's or at the checkout counters of the steadily growing number of supermarkets.

It is hard to say whether the family allowance helped to swell the Baby Boom. Ottawa never really incorporated family allowance into its major programs. From 1945, when the program was introduced, to 1973 when it became taxable, family allowance payments were raised just once. In the meantime, the payments were badly eroded by inflation. In 1989, Ottawa decided to target low-income families for the family allowance. In 1992, the Child Tax Benefit replaced the allowance altogether. Quebec, however, which had started its own family allowance plan in 1961, still has a universal family allowance.

The Decline in Contagious Disease

During the postwar period, several diseases that had killed and maimed many thousands of Canadians in the early part of the century were brought under control. Two key examples are tuberculosis and polio.

The Decline of Tuberculosis in Canada

Tuberculosis, a corrosive lung disease, is most frequently associated with poverty, overcrowding, and air pollution. It was quite common among impoverished Canadians in the early twentieth century. During the late nineteenth century, the practice had developed of sending patients to large sanatoriums ("sans") out in the country where, it was hoped, rest, fresh air, and good nutrition would help them. In any event, even if they themselves were doomed, they were less likely to spread the dreaded, highly contagious disease.

By 1938, Canada had sixty-one sanatoriums with close to nine thousand beds for tuberculosis patients. Although many more beds were needed, the lack of progress against the disease meant that the government was slow to invest in this area. However, antibiotics, introduced in World War II, made enormous advances against TB. By 1953, Canada had 19 000 beds, with the average length of stay at a "san" being one year. By 1963, only half as many beds were needed, because treatment was gaining ground and people were going home. Slowly, in later decades, the sanatoriums were converted to other uses.

Public attitudes to TB, and to contagious diseases in general, began to change in the 1950s, largely because of medical successes. One ex-sanatorium patient, known only as "Thankful," expressed surprise at not being ostracized on returning to the community in 1950 and wrote to the sanatorium to say so:

> Contrary to custom I usually tell my neighbors I had tuberculosis for years. Those, I figure, who tend to avoid me because of "my case history" are not worthy of my friendship. You would be surprised how FEW people treat me with less regard on account of this....[14]

Young TB patients at a Canadian sanitorium. What appears to be the average age of these children?

Today, TB is comparatively rare in Canada versus other countries, mainly due to improved living conditions during the postwar period. It is usually treated on an outpatient basis by a regimen of drugs.

Canada's Contribution to the Defeat of Polio

In 1947 and 1953, Canadians were struck by epidemics of polio, a contagious disease of the spinal cord, which left many of its victims paralyzed. Some died; others survived but never left their "iron lungs," large tubular structures that enabled paralyzed survivors to breathe. The American president during World War II, Franklin Roosevelt, was paralyzed in both legs because of the polio he contracted in 1921.

Epidemics actually worsened in the industrial democracies during the twentieth century, ironically because improved public health and cleanliness meant that most people did not get the disease in infancy (the historic name for polio was "infantile paralysis"). Getting it later in life usually meant a worse outcome. During the early postwar period, summer was considered "polio season," and Canadian newspapers featured frantic headlines when the disease struck. Many people feared polio more than death itself, because it might lead to a lifetime of confinement in an iron lung. Non-paralyzed survivors such as Paul Martin, former finance minister of Canada, came to be called "lucky polios."[15]

Canadian scientists played a key role in eradicating polio. American physician Jonas Salk had developed a vaccine against the disease, but there was no simple way of safely producing enough virus to manufacture sufficient quantities of vaccine. The "Toronto method," developed at the University of Toronto in 1953, used a synthetic medium to grow enough virus to start a vaccination program. The polio program that followed was the largest field trial in medical history, and the Toronto method proved its worth. In Canada, the number of polio cases shrank from 4755 in 1952 to 1886 in 1959. By 1962, thanks to vaccination, polio had all but disappeared.

Decline in Child Mortality

Overall, infant mortality declined very significantly in postwar Canada, compared with the rate in the 1930s, primarily because of improved health conditions. For example, in 1931–35, bronchitis and pneumonia killed 864 of every 100 000 infants. By 1956–60, these diseases killed only 447 of every 100 000 infants and by 1966–70, only 213 of every 100 000. Meanwhile, by the 1960s, surgical advances meant that many health conditions became operable for the first time. Popular media featured many stories about historic medical advances, including major surgery for babies and children.

Demand for Publicly Funded Health Care

The many significant medical advances against disease during the postwar period changed Canadian

A young polio victim learning to walk with braces in the mid-1950s.

society in an important way. Average Canadians began to feel that they had a *right* to medical care and that, as a matter of social justice, the government should ensure that every Canadian had access to it. Earlier generations had not felt as strongly about medical care, in part because the benefits were not as clearly established.

Suburbs

Urbanization, the process by which most people end up living in cities, continued to grow rapidly after World War II. In 1871, less than 20 percent of the Canadian population lived in cities. The urban percentage grew steadily, and by 1941, 54.5 percent of Canadians lived in cities. This proportion increased slowly to 76 percent by 1971.[16] It then started to level off and has not significantly increased since.

Several push and pull factors contributed to rapid urbanization during the postwar period. Mechanized farming, which replaced horses with tractors, meant that farms grew larger and fewer people were needed to operate them. Instead, the

new businesses, factories, government departments, stores, schools, and social programs produced by the economic boom needed employees. Immigrants no longer came to Canada to farm, as they had at the beginning of the twentieth century. Typically, they took jobs in the cities and stayed there.

The boom, combined with good wage settlements negotiated by unions, had a major impact on how cities developed. The parents of the Baby Boom expected a better life than their own parents had had. They did not want to raise their families in the crowded urban shacks that had been the lot of many Canadians before World War II. They wanted sturdy, standardized homes with running water, indoor plumbing, central heating, electricity, and front and back yards. They also wanted a family car and a wringer washing machine. The schools they intended to send their children to would have teachers trained in modern methods, teaching in separate classrooms for each grade. They would vote and pay taxes for libraries, community centres, parks, hospitals, and arenas. However, their wishes could only come true if communities were systematically planned and

Healthbridge Park, a typical suburb. A new lifestyle for postwar families

developed on the fringes of existing cities—in other words, the lifestyle that postwar parents wanted created the suburbs. The demand for bungalows in the suburbs sparked a home-building boom across the country.

Generally, the suburbs were created by developers (corporations that build housing), who laid them out according to a plan. The corporate developer had the resources to introduce new building styles as well, for example, high-rise apartment buildings for those who continued to rent, office towers downtown, industrial parks in the suburbs, and shopping centres.

The New Pastime: Shopping

Average Canadians had money during the postwar period, and retailers were glad to advise them on how to spend it. New types of shopping facilities grew up in the suburbs. The first shopping centre in Canada was Norgate Shopping Centre, built in 1949 in Saint-Laurent, Quebec, just outside Montreal. It was an L-shaped group of stores surrounding a large parking lot. The parking lot was the key feature; the postwar suburban consumer shopped with the aid of a car whenever possible. Typical shopping centres featured either a department store or a supermarket as an "anchor" store to draw in as wide a customer base as possible.

Later, in the 1950s, shopping centres began to be sheltered and landscaped. The more pleasant the environment, the longer the customer might stay, which usually meant buying more. The 1950s customer, typically a mother of several

Baby Boom children, usually had at least some money for "extras," for example, from the family allowance cheque. It was worth taking the time to introduce her to an ever-expanding array of new products and services.

However, these new customers were also learning to be skeptical. In 1947, the Canadian Association of Consumers was formally established; it grew out of the work of women's organizations that volunteered to monitor prices during the war. Over the years, the organization campaigned for many health and safety issues, such as safer school buses, lower speed limits, no smoking on public vehicles, and a ban on long-life pesticides. The organization had its own testing facilities and provided publications for consumers. In 1961, it permitted men to become members.

By 1960, the Yorkdale Shopping Centre was under construction in Toronto. Yorkdale was a regional shopping centre with two department stores, a supermarket, ninety shops, vast parking lots, and access to two superhighways. It soon had

Yorkdale Shopping Centre in the 1960s–how have such malls changed over the years?

many imitators and competitors. However, despite the intense pace of retail development during the postwar period, the shopping centre did not become the place for extensive recreation and social activity as many malls are today. Generally, the early shopping mall was a place where the customer shopped in pleasant surroundings, had a grilled cheese sandwich and fries at the lunch counter, and then went home.

More Shopping: The War Between Eaton's and Simpson's

Postwar prosperity sparked intense "store wars" between two of Canada's biggest retailers: Eaton's and Simpson's. The battle and its outcome pointed out the growing interdependence of the Canadian and American economies.

In the early 1950s, Eaton's had fifty department stores across Canada, as well as the biggest mail-order business in the Commonwealth. Simpson's had five stores and a mail-order business about half the size of Eaton's. (Mail order was a very important part of every store's business because nearly half the population still shopped by catalogue.) In 1952, however, Simpson's and Sears Roebuck each invested $20 million to launch Simpsons-Sears. Sears-Roebuck brought worldwide connections and buying power to the deal. Simpson's gave Simpsons-Sears its existing mail-order business. Then the new entity launched a big store-building program, which was tied into the newly established need for anchor stores at shopping plazas.

A war ensued, involving advertisements, aggressive price cutting, and Cold War–type spying—spies hired by one store regularly patrolled the "enemy's" store, disguised as shoppers. When they reported on bargains, their store would retaliate as quickly as the preparation of ads would permit.[17] Consumerism was serious business in the postwar era.

Simpsons-Sears raised the stakes by putting out a lavish new catalogue, promoting a consumer lifestyle in a way that the Eaton's catalogue had never done. It pitched the catalogue directly at the new suburban and small-town market. To those who did not want to wait for the modern lifestyle, it offered much easier credit terms ($10 down for anything in the store). Eaton's was soon forced to follow suit, and new, generous credit policies paved the way for acceptance of the credit card. Meanwhile, nationalism came to the fore. Eaton's attempted to cement customer loyalty by advertising its "all-Canadian" background. It called itself "Eaton's of Canada" now, sending a subtle message about Simpsons-Sears. It also drew attention to the fact that many of its goods were British-made. Simpsons-Sears downplayed the fact that its goods were U.S.-made. Both firms had their corporate headquarters in downtown Toronto, from which they were, in the words of *Maclean's* reporter Fred Bodsworth, "eyeing each other's movements like belligerent eagles on neighboring crags."[18] They tried hard for first place in representing Canada to shoppers, especially in connection with events that touched the public, such as Marilyn Bell's Great Lakes swim:

> The day Marilyn Bell swam across Lake Ontario last September [1954], Eaton's window-display staff worked late and secretly behind drawn curtains setting up a special window to honor the teenager who had suddenly become Toronto's sweetheart. Then they crossed the street hopefully to see if they had scooped "the other people." It was a draw. The Simpson's display staff was just putting the finishing touches on their Marilyn Bell window.[19]

As retailing became an ever larger and more global business, market forces dictated that both companies would eventually lose. The Hudson's Bay Company acquired Simpson's in 1978. In 1991, the two companies merged and the Simpson's name disappeared. Sears Canada remained. Eaton's declared bankruptcy in 1999, after a long decline in market share. Sears Canada bought many of the Eaton's stores and converted them to Sears' stores in 2002.

The Growth of Government Social Programs

During the postwar period, Canadians began to expect government to play an increasing role in promoting their health and well-being. They were comfortable with government intervention—as long as it worked. After all, governments had intervened heavily in wartime, and it *had* worked, in the sense that the Allies had won the war. By contrast, during the early part of the Great Depression, the federal government had trusted the economy to right itself, but it had not. Because of this historical experience, the Canadian public was ready to turn to the government for solutions to social problems—and government was ready to provide them.

In that respect, Canada differed significantly from the United States. The United States had ten times the population, a much stronger economy, and thus a much stronger tradition of free enterprise. Canada could seldom prevail in direct competition with much larger nations. Canadians turned to their government to forge a high standard of living so that they could market talents and resources effectively in a world where Canada was a middle power.

Before the end of the war, some key figures in Canadian social policy were ready to step into this new role of government participation in society. Social scientist Leonard Marsh, a research adviser on the federal Committee on Post-War Reconstruction, published the *Report on Social Security for Canada* in 1943, which eventually became the basis of the modern Canadian social security system. Most major elements of the report, including measures to alleviate unemployment, illness, and poverty, were not enacted in the immediate postwar period, because they were con-

sidered too radical, but all major portions had become law by 1966.

Unemployment Insurance

Unemployment insurance had been proposed as early as 1919. The idea received a boost from the Great Depression, when unemployment peaked at 20 percent, and from expanded government powers during World War II. In 1940, the federal government introduced the Unemployment Insurance Act. The government was motivated in part by wartime labour shortages. Wartime employment bureaus were used to administer unemployment insurance as needed. The program has continued ever since, with various adjustments to address regional differences. For example, significant differences exist between the problems associated with finding work in a seasonal industry in a resource-based province and finding work in a year-round industry in a major city. In 1996, the program's name was changed to Employment Insurance, to focus claimants' attention on the need to look for work.

Health Insurance

The Great Depression brought home to many Canadians a fact that was always well known to the poor: Sick people cannot work and cannot afford a doctor. In many cases, poverty conditions had made them sick in the first place. During the postwar period, medical advances and a concern for social justice hastened the belief that every Canadian should have access to medical care. In 1945 Saskatchewan introduced a province-wide hospital insurance program. In 1957, the federal government offered to share the cost of hospital insurance with any province that established it. A proposed expansion of Saskatchewan's program in 1959 produced the historic Saskatchewan Doctors' Strike, but by 1961, all ten provinces were providing some form of hospital insurance.

Ottawa was very cautious about following Saskatchewan's example. It set up a Royal Commission to examine whether a national medical insurance plan was feasible. In 1964, the Commission, chaired by Supreme Court Justice Emmett Hall, was unequivocal. Hall concluded, "The only thing more expensive than good health care is no health care."[20] He called for a universal and comprehensive national health insurance program with minimum standards set across the country. The federal Medical Care Act, passed in 1966, was a key piece of legislation, because it offered federal funding to provincial plans, if they met the minimum conditions.

From the time it began, the public health care system has probably been the most popular social program in Canada. Unlike programs such as unemployment insurance, it was rarely attacked for making problems worse. Controversies have usually swirled around the concern that it might be eroded. Even proposals to supplement public health care with private health care assume that the public care will continue. Comprehensive health care is regularly cited by Canadians as a way in which Canada differs favourably from the United States, which has not been able to enact such a system.

Pension Plans

Improved living conditions and medical care meant that life expectancy slowly increased through the twentieth century. In 1920, the average life expectancy for men was fifty-nine and for women, sixty-one. By 1950, it was sixty-six for men and seventy-one for women. Those who predicted that life expectancy would continue to increase were right. By 1990, it was seventy-five for men and eighty-one for women.[21] Often, however, during the postwar period, people were retiring in extreme poverty, especially elderly women who had never worked outside the home and who had never expected to live so long.

The first public pension legislation in Canada was the Old Age Pension Act (1927), but it did not become national until 1937, when all the provinces had compatible legislation. In 1951, it was replaced by Old Age Security (OAS). Every citizen who was at least seventy years old qualified for a monthly cheque. In 1965, the qualifying age was reduced to sixty-five. In 1966, the Guaranteed Income Supplement (GIS) was introduced to provide a 40 percent extra payment to seniors with little or no other income.

The OAS was supplied to every senior citizen, whether working or not. As the workforce grew during the postwar period, the government came under increasing pressure to provide an additional pension plan for workers. The Canada Pension Plan (CPP) came into force in January 1966. It deducts money from the payrolls of employers, the paycheques of employees, and the declared income of the self-employed, according to the amount earned. It provides disability, survivor, orphan, and death benefits, indexed to the cost of living. In 1957, the federal government also established the Registered Retirement Savings Plan (RRSP) program, by which people can save money tax free for their retirement.

Both the CPP and RRSP programs became controversial following the postwar period, though for different reasons. Many Canadians have worried about how the retirement of the Baby Boom will affect the CPP. RRSPs have also been criticized because they mainly provide benefits to Canadians with above-average incomes. However, the increase in the number of self-employed Canadians during the 1990s blunted the criticism of RRSPs somewhat, because they are the main retirement savings plan for self-employed people.

Canada Assistance Plan (CAP)

The Canada Assistance Plan (CAP), which became law in 1966, proposed that the federal government evenly share the cost of welfare with the provinces.

However, Ottawa required that national standards for the provision of welfare be met. These standards included assessments based on actual need, and they eliminated both work requirements and residency requirements. Provinces had difficulty meeting these standards because of changing circumstances, and many of these provisions were eroded in later years. For example, Ontario did impose a work requirement ("workfare") in the 1990s.

Web Connection

www.mcgrawhill.ca/links/definingcanada

Go to the Web site above to find out about the history of public health insurance in Canada.

Women: The 51 Percent Minority?

Because of wartime labour shortages, women were hired and trained to perform many jobs that had previously been closed to them. After the war, they were expected, or even required, to quit these jobs so that returning veterans could have them. Government-run daycare centres were closed, and women were expected to return to their traditional roles. However, despite the large Baby Boom families, women's traditional roles were disappearing and changing.

Not all women left the workforce. Huge numbers of new jobs were available, both blue collar and white collar. Many of these jobs were with the greatly expanded government sector that oversaw the new social programs. Others were jobs with the new factories, department stores, and businesses. In 1951, slightly less than one-quarter (24.4 percent) of women aged fifteen years and older were part of the labour force, representing 22.3 percent of the total labour force.[22]

However, in 1961 women employed full-time year-round earned 59 percent of what men did in the same job categories. If part-time workers were factored in, women's wages were only 54 percent of men's.[23] These women began to challenge the inequities between men's and women's incomes. In 1955, restrictions in the federal public service on the employment and advancement of married women were removed.[24]

Although most women still expected to stay home when their children were small, before or after this period, many wanted to—and often had to—work for pay. What started as a trickle of women who either continued to work or returned to work in the 1950s became a torrent by the 1970s. For example, as the auto industry continued to expand through the 1950s and 1960s, many women went to work in auto plants, even though considerable discrimination prevailed. By the 1960s, many women had worked in auto plants for more than twenty years. With newfound confidence, they challenged the auto industry, and by 1970, they had won equal pay for women.[25]

Economic and cultural issues played a key role in this transition. During the postwar economic boom, durable goods—washers, dryers, refrigerators, freezers—were marketed widely to Canadian women. These "big ticket items" greatly reduced the amount of time spent on traditional women's work, even for women who had several children. Supermarkets circumvented the need to spend the long hours preparing and preserving food that had characterized rural life early in the twentieth century. As labour at home became less necessary, many women began to resent the newly shrunken "housewife" role, especially when their children were in school full time. Ironically, the "happy housewife" advertising that sold the big ticket items became a special focus of resentment, even while the items themselves liberated the customers from traditional labour.

The advent of consumer credit during the postwar period was another example of the many economic changes that affected women's roles. Because the law required a husband to be responsible for his

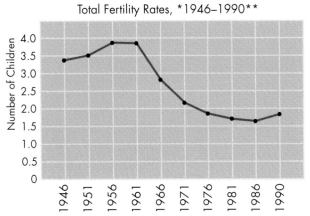

Total Fertility Rates, *1946–1990**

Number of Children (y-axis: 0, 0.5, 1.0, 1.5, 2.0, 2.5, 3.0, 3.5, 4.0)

Years (x-axis): 1946, 1951, 1956, 1961, 1966, 1971, 1976, 1981, 1986, 1990

* Total fertility rate measures the number of children the average Canadian woman will bear based on birth rates in a given year.
** Newfoundland, Yukon, and the Northwest Territories are excluded in the 1946 figure.

wife's debts, a married woman had to have her husband's permission to have a credit card. Women saw this as demeaning, especially when they were, in fact, working at least part time. The status of a woman separated from her husband was uncertain; should she be given credit or not? Women began to want more economic independence and political power.

A major factor that changed women's lives late in the postwar period was the advent of the birth-control pill in 1961. Even though disseminating information about birth control was illegal until 1969, contraceptives, mainly barrier methods, had been in wide use in Canada since World War II. The birth-control pill was better suited to long-term family planning, because it was a routine medication. Women could plan families, work, or go to school with much more confidence. After the pill's introduction, the birth rate began to decline significantly, as increasing numbers of women chose to spend more time in the workforce or to plan careers that required higher education.

The fact that more women sought higher education produced other important changes. Women had made up only a small proportion of each profession in Canada in 1961. For example, 0.25 percent of

engineers were women; and 2.64 percent of lawyers, 4.49 percent of dentists, and 7.33 percent of physicians were women.[26] This was in large part because women were less likely than men to go to university. At that time, 11.3 percent of male high-school graduates went to university, but only 4.6 percent of female graduates did so.[27] As more women pursued higher education and increased their representation in the professions, they put themselves in a better position to advocate women's rights. As a result, women's advancement in society grew even more quickly.

Women's Social Action Groups

Through Canadian history, many women's social action groups have promoted peace, temperance, and social justice issues. For example, Voice of Women, which started in 1960, promoted disarmament and peace and enabled many women to articulate concerns about the Cold War. However, agitation was growing about women's own roles and problems, and by the 1960s, a second wave of feminism was under way (the first wave at the turn of the twentieth century had won women the right to vote).

In 1967, Prime Minister Pearson appointed a Royal Commission on the Status of Women. The commission travelled across Canada for four years and listened to women's concerns. In 1970, it published a landmark report that established the first benchmarks of equality for Canadian women. The report made 167 recommendations to help eliminate inequality. These recommendations included paid maternity leave, fair employment practices, and changes to the Indian Act so that Aboriginal women did not lose their status when they married men who were not status Indians. The report united many women who subsequently developed several women's groups that worked to bring about major social changes, including the National Action Committee on the Status of Women.

Review...Reflect...Respond

1. What long-lasting effects would the baby boom have on Canada?

2. How would the new social programs of the 1950s and 1960s change the way Canadians felt about what it meant to be a Canadian?

3. Why did the image of the "happy housewife" cause resentment among Canadian women?

Conclusion

While Canada was forging new roads internationally during the postwar years, many of its citizens and governments were enjoying an economic boom. In stark contrast to the deprivation of the Depression years and rationing of World War II, many Canadians enjoyed new luxuries such as suburban homes, new automobiles, and shopping malls, creating images of the perfect family, with the perfect mother, in the perfect house. In the 1960s, however, these images of perfection began to be questioned. Many women were discontent with the "happy housewife" image.

Notes

1. Ruben C. Bellan, "Foreign Investment," *Canadian Encyclopedia 2000 World Edition* (Toronto: McClelland & Stewart, 1999).
2. Ibid.
3. Ibid.
4. Biography of Francis Alvin George Hamilton, Agriculture Minister 1960–1963, Agriculture and Agri-Food Canada. Available online at ⟨http://www.agr.gc.ca/bios/hamilton_e.phtml.⟩
5. See the historical analysis of the issue of trade with Cuba on the Department of Foreign Affairs and International Trade pages of the Government of Canada Web site at ⟨http://www.dfait-maeci.gc.ca, (accessed June 13, 2002).
6. *Calgary Herald,* Feb. 13, 1997.
7. Mario Polese, "Regional Economics," *Canadian Encyclopedia 2000 World Edition* (Toronto: McClelland & Stewart, 1999).
8. T. J. Courchene, "Equalization Payments," *Canadian Encyclopedia 2000 World Edition* (Toronto: McClelland & Stewart, 1999).
9. Polese, "Regional Economics."
10. David K. Foot, *Boom, Bust and Echo, 2000* (Toronto: Macfarlane Walter & Ross, 1998).
11. Ibid., p. 25.
12. Ibid., p. 15.
13. Ibid., p. 24.
14. An excerpt from a letter written by an ex-patient of a Saskatchewan Sanatorium, taken from the 1950 *Valley Echo* [vol. 31 (12), page 6], a sanatorium publication.
15. "Martin lends polio experience to charity." Available online at ⟨http://www.globeandmail.com⟩, (accessed May 27, 2002).
16. CANSIM data, quoted in *The Sustainability Report,* York Centre for Applied Sustainability, York University, June 15, 2002. Figures have been rounded here.

17. Fred Bodsworth, "Simpsons vs. Eatons: The Battle of the Big Stores," *Maclean's*, February 1, 1955, republished in *Canada in the Fifties: From the Archives of* Maclean's (Toronto: Viking, 1999). This article tells the whole story in considerable detail. The story recounted here is from that source.

18. Ibid., p. 68.

19. Ibid.

20. Supreme Court Justice Emmett Hall. Available online at the Canadian Heritage Web site *Path of Heroes* at ⟨http://www.pch.gc.ca/poh-sdh/english/routeseven/r7-hero6.html⟩.

21. Statistics Canada, Catalogue no. 82FOO75XCB.

22. Status of Women Canada. Available online at ⟨http://www.swc-cfc.gc.ca/whm/whm2000/whm2000-e.html#40-60⟩, posted July 12, 2001.

23. From Civilizations.ca, the Canadian Museum of Civilization Web site. Available at ⟨http://www.civilization.ca/hist/labour/labh35e.html⟩.

24. Status of Women Web site, July 12, 2001. Available online at http://www.swc-cfc.gc.ca/whm/whm2000/whm2000-e.html#40-60.

25. "Some Assembly Required: A History of Auto Work and Auto Workers in Windsor," Windsor Public Library. Available online at ⟨http://www.windsorpubliclibrary.com/digi/sar/part8.htm⟩, accessed June 17, 2002.

26. Women in Alberta and Saskatchewan History site. Available online at ⟨http://tdi.uregina.ca/~maguirec/chron.html⟩, accessed June 17, 2002.

27. Ibid.

Chapter 20 Review

Knowledge & Understanding

1. Identify these people, places, and events, and explain their historical significance to Canada's developing culture and identity:

   St. Lawrence Seaway   family allowance
   TransCanada highway   polio
   trade with Cuba   Old Age Security
   oil   the Pill
   equalization payments

2. Using a five-column chart with the headings Initiative, When, Why, Beneficiaries, Effect, briefly explain each of the following postwar government initiatives: the Auto Pact, foreign ownership review committees, equalization payments, Family Allowance, Unemployment Insurance, Old Age Security, Canada Pension Plan, Registered Retirement Savings Plan, Canada Assistance Plan, publicly funded health care, Royal Commission on the Status of Women.

3. Overall, how did each of the following regions fare economically during the 1950s and 1960s: British Columbia, Alberta, Saskatchewan, Manitoba, Ontario, Quebec, Atlantic provinces? Which government measures were specifically intended to address regional disparity?

Thinking & Inquiry

4. "Most Canadians opposed communism, but that did not necessarily mean that they would refuse to trade with any communist country. What economic and political factors might contribute to the difference between Canada's view on trade with China and Cuba and the United States' view? Explain in a well-written paragraph.

5. A 2002 Environics poll reported that 46 percent of Canadians viewed the creation of government health insurance (medicare) during the postwar period as the "most price-less" event in Canadian history. By comparison, only 29 percent chose the *Charter of Rights and Freedoms*. Drawing on what you have learned in this chapter, suggest reasons why so many Canadians feel so strongly about health insurance.

Application

6. Research some typical fads and fashions from 1945 through the late 1960s in one of the following areas: food, dress, hairstyles, jewellery, furnishings, automobiles, or housing styles. In a visual essay, explore any major changes that occurred during the period and suggest reasons for why these changes happened.

Communication

7. Prepare drafts of two advertisements for an automatic washing machine.

   (a) The first advertisement assumes that the primary customer is a woman who does all the housework for a family of seven and does not ever expect to be employed.

   (b) The second assumes that she works the evening shift at the auto plant while her husband, also an auto worker, keeps an eye on their two children and shares the chores.

   (c) Write a paragraph identifying key differences between the two advertising strategies.

8. "Resolved: The consumer society introduced after World War II has devastated Canada's ecology." Research and prepare an argument for the affirmative or the negative of this resolution. Be prepared to debate it, as your teacher directs.

CHAPTER 21

The Postwar Development of Canadian Culture

The work with which we have been entrusted is concerned with nothing less than the spiritual foundations of our national life. Canadian achievement in every field depends mainly on the quality of the Canadian mind and spirit. This quality is determined by what Canadians think, and think about; by the books they read, the pictures they see and the programmes they hear. These things, whether we call them arts and letters or use other words to describe them, we believe to lie at the roots of our life as a nation.

–REPORT OF THE ROYAL COMMISSION ON NATIONAL DEVELOPMENT IN THE ARTS, LETTERS, AND SCIENCES

Throughout the first half of the twentieth century, many Canadian artists either remained amateurs or migrated to more populous, wealthier countries to pursue their art. When Canada became a leading industrial nation after World War II, the economic boom created a large increase in the standard of living, letting Canadians develop talent at home. By the end of the postwar period, many Canadians could afford to make a living in the arts in Canada; their living was often precarious, but they did not differ in that respect from artists of other nations.

After World War II, government involvement in the promotion of Canadian culture became much more common. Royal commissions showed that there was an increasing danger of Canadian culture becoming dependent on American culture. Music, television, publishing, and radio were already dominated by American content. Unless something was done, a distinctive Canadian culture would cease to exist.

A key trend during this period of Canadian history was that an ever-increasing proportion of the population was finishing high school and attending university. The large Baby Boom generation, newly empowered by education, began to think that it could reshape society according to the patterns of social justice and equality that seemed right to them. Although most students simply began to vote for change, some rioted or went on strike, making university campuses scenes of much political activism.

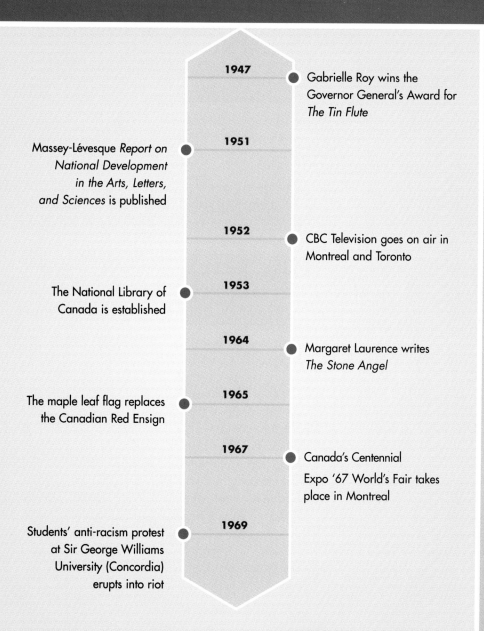

21

1947 — Gabrielle Roy wins the Governor General's Award for *The Tin Flute*

Massey-Lévesque *Report on National Development in the Arts, Letters, and Sciences* is published — 1951

1952 — CBC Television goes on air in Montreal and Toronto

The National Library of Canada is established — 1953

1964 — Margaret Laurence writes *The Stone Angel*

The maple leaf flag replaces the Canadian Red Ensign — 1965

1967 — Canada's Centennial

Expo '67 World's Fair takes place in Montreal

Students' anti-racism protest at Sir George Williams University (Concordia) erupts into riot — 1969

By the end of this chapter, you will be able to

- assess the effectiveness of attempts to protect Canadian culture from American domination

- evaluate the economic and cultural contributions of Canadian cities

- analyze how Canada and Canadians have been portrayed in television shows and by a representative sample of writers, visual artists, musicians, composers, and filmmakers

- analyze how American movies, television, music, advertising, professional sports, and other consumer products have posed challenges to the creation of a homegrown Canadian identity

- analyze how Canadian governments and leaders have used symbols and supported organizations to promote Canadian culture

- assess the influence of the anti-war sentiment in Canadian history

The Massey-Lévesque Report on Canadian Culture

Before World War II, Canadian cultural life had depended largely on amateur, volunteer community activities. For example, the young adult group of a church or the senior grades of a school would put many hours into creating a play, musical, or concert for the public. These performances were significant social events in towns across Canada, but few Canadians of that period could hope to make a living from arts activities. As society grew in numbers, urbanization, and complexity after WWII, it became clear to many observers that if the arts had a future in Canada, they would have to become more national, more urban, and more professional. Did these new requirements mean—given the difference in size and wealth between Canada and the United States—that they would become more American?

In 1949, the Privy Council (a council appointed by the Governor General to advise the government) established a Royal Commission on National Development in the Arts, Letters, and Sciences, chaired by Vincent Massey. His co-chair was Georges-Henri Lévesque, a Quebec priest and sociologist who was one of the architects of the Quiet Revolution. Their Massey–Lévesque Commission toured Canada over the next two years, finding out as much as they could about existing Canadian culture. In the process, they held 114 public hearings, with about 1200 witnesses and 462 formal submissions, as well as hundreds of letters.

Canadian Culture on the Brink of Extinction?

The commissioners' resulting 1951 report was a wake-up call to government. They reported, "No novelist, poet, short story writer, historian, biographer, or other writer of non-technical books can make even a modestly comfortable living by selling

Some people argue that the Massey Commission was a "top-down" solution for Canadian culture. What does this statement mean?

his work in Canada. No composer of music can live on what Canada pays him for his compositions. Apart from radio drama, no playwright, and only a few actors and producers, can live by working in the theatre in Canada."[1] In other words, Canadians either starved at home or went abroad. The commissioners also warned that unless Canada acted to enable Canadians to make a living in homegrown cultural industries, the country would soon be overwhelmed by American culture. A distinctive Canadian cultural or intellectual life would cease to exist.

Most Canadians wanted to protect their culture, according to the commissioners, but the government would need to develop structures and provide funding to enable them to do so: "If we in Canada are to have more plentiful and better cultural fare, we must pay for it. Good will alone can do little for a starving plant. If the cultural life of Canada is anemic, it must be nourished, and this will cost money."[2] The commission's report also revealed an embarrassing fact: Most support for the arts in Canada actually came from American foundations such as Carnegie and Rockefeller.

Report on the Royal Commission on National Development in the Arts, Letters, and Sciences

In the Royal Commission on National Development in the Arts, Letters, and Sciences, the introduction deals with the growing dependence of Canada on the United States for its money and culture. In these excerpts, the Commission discusses the infusion of American money into the development of Canada's cultural institutions, which was needed for a country that is so vast and has a sparse population. But as the report states, "We have gained much. In this preliminary stock-taking of Canadian cultural life it may be fair to inquire whether we have gained a little too much."

9. We are thus deeply indebted to American generosity. Money has flowed across the border from such groups as the Carnegie Corporation, which has spent $7,346,188 in Canada since 1911 and the Rockefeller Foundation, to which we are indebted for the sum of $11,817,707 since 1914. ... Applied with wisdom and imagination, these gifts have helped Canadians to live their own life and to develop a better Canadianism.... Many institutions in Canada essential to the equipment of a modern nation could not have been established or maintained without money provided from the United States....

11. Finally, we benefit from vast importations of what might be familiarly called the American cultural output. We import newspapers, periodicals, books, maps and endless educational equipment. We also import artistic talent, either personally in the travelling artist or company, or on the screen, in recordings and over the air. Every Sunday, tens of thousands tacitly acknowledge their cultural indebtedness as they turn off the radio at the close of the Sunday symphony from New York and settle down to the latest American Book of the Month.

12. Granted that most of these American donations are good in themselves, it does not follow that they have always been good for Canadians. We have not much right to be proud of our record as patrons of the arts. Is it possible that, beside the munificence of a Carnegie or a Rockefeller, Canadian contributions look so small that it seems hardly worth while making them? Or have we learned, wrongly, from our neighbour an unnecessary dependence on the contributions of the rich? A similar unworthy reliance on others appears in another field. Canada sends a number of students abroad, many of them on fellowships provided by other countries; Canada offers very few of her own fellowships to non-Canadians, none at all until very recently. Perhaps we have been tempted by a too easy benevolence, but this leaves us in an undignified position, unworthy of our real power and prestige.

13. Canada has, moreover, paid a heavy price for this easy dependence on charity and especially on American charity. First, many of our best students, on completing their studies at American institutions, accept positions there and do not return. The United States wisely relaxes its rigid immigration laws for all members of "learned professions" and profits accordingly....

18. It may be added that we should also have been forced to produce our own educational materials— books, maps, pictures and so forth. As it is, the dependence of English-speaking Canada on the United States for these publications is excessive. In the elementary schools and high schools the actual texts may be produced in Canada, but teachers complain that far too much of the supplementary material is American with an emphasis and direction appropriate for American children but unsuitable for Canadian. As an illustration of the unsuitability of even the best American material, the statement was made in one of our briefs that out of thirty-four children in a Grade VIII class in a Canadian school, nineteen knew all about the significance of July 4 and only seven could explain that of July 1...

25. The American invasion by film, radio and periodical is formidable. Much of what comes to us is good and of this we shall be speaking presently. It has, however, been represented to us that many of the radio programmes have in fact no particular application to Canada or to Canadian conditions and that some of them, including certain children's programmes of the "crime" and "horror" type, are positively harmful. News commentaries too, and even live broadcasts from American sources, are designed for American ears and are almost certain to have an American slant and emphasis by reason of what they include or omit, as well as because of the opinions expressed. We think it permissible to record these comments on American radio since we observe that in the United States many radio programmes and American broadcasting in general have recently been severely criticized. It will, we think, be readily agreed that we in Canada should take measures to avoid in our radio, and in our television, at least those aspects of American broadcasting which have provoked in the United States the most out-spoken and the sharpest opposition....

26. American influences on Canadian life to say the least are impressive. There should be no thought of interfering with the liberty of all Canadians to enjoy them. Cultural exchanges are excellent in themselves. .... It cannot be denied, however, that a vast and disproportionate amount of material coming from a single alien source may stifle rather than stimulate our own creative effort; and, passively accepted without any standard of comparison, this may weaken critical faculties. We are now spending millions to maintain a national independence which would be nothing but an empty shell without a vigorous and distinctive cultural life. We have seen that we have its elements in our traditions and in our history; we have made important progress, often aided by American generosity. We must not be blind, however, to the very present danger of permanent dependence.

FROM: ROYAL COMMISSION ON
NATIONAL DEVELOPMENT IN THE ARTS,
LETTERS, AND SCIENCES. REPORT.
OTTAWA : KING'S PRINTER, 1951.

A typical Carnegie Library. Steel magnate and philanthropist Andrew Carnegie donated funds to build a number of libraries like this in Southern Ontario, and around the world, during the early twentieth century.

Strategies for Change

The Massey-Lévesque Report, which was considered a masterpiece of clarity and usefulness, fitted in with the postwar expectation that government should intervene to deal with identified social and economic problems. However, there was a difficulty associated with government support of the arts: The idea reminded many Canadians too much of the way in which Communist and Fascist governments used culture to support their propaganda. Authentic cultural voices were stifled in favour of whatever ideology the government wanted to portray to the world. That kind of government support for Canadian culture might be worse than no support at all. To avoid this problem, the commission proposed that an independent body award the grants.

This advice was taken; the Canada Council, established in Ottawa in 1957, provides federal and private grants and services to professional Canadian artists and arts organizations. It must account for the management of its funds to the auditor general, but it has full responsibility for its decisions on the funding of programs and the award of grants. Although the Council chair and director are appointed by the government, the Council's staff relies on the advice of Canadian artists and their chosen representatives.

The National Library of Canada was another outcome of the Massey-Lévesque Report. Established in 1953, it accumulates and provides information on all types of publishing in Canada. By 1998, its collection comprised about 16 million items, and more than 600 000 items are added each year.

During the postwar period, successive Canadian governments tabled a number of additional reports (Royal Commission on Broadcasting, 1957; Royal Commission on Publications, 1961; Special Senate Committee on Mass Media, 1970; Royal Commission on Book Publishing, Ontario, 1972; Royal Commission on Newspapers, 1981; and Federal Cultural Policy Review Committee, 1982, for example) and created a number of institutions, laws, and instruments to assist with cultural development. These moves have had varying levels of success. The advent of North American free trade in the 1990s and of globalization in general required major changes in cultural strategy. A development that typified the way in which culture was developing in Canada during the postwar period was that Vincent Massey later became the first Canadian-born Governor General.

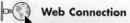 **Web Connection**

www.mcgrawhill.ca/links/definingcanada

To read the entire *Report on the Royal Commission on National Development in the Arts, Letters, and Sciences*, go to the Web site above

The Maturing of the Canadian Publishing Industry

World War II greatly bolstered publishing in French Canada. Many writers who had fled Nazi-occupied France to preserve their freedom of expression turned to publishers in Montreal to keep publishing their works. Between 1940 and 1946, twenty-one million books were printed in Montreal, and French Canada was able to sell its products in fifty-two countries abroad.[3] But when world trade with France resumed, writers returned home, and business fell off sharply.

Since books in English were available from several unoccupied countries, English Canadian book publishers didn't enjoy a similar boom during WWII, but they did benefit from the upbeat war economy. This stabilized in the 1950s at a level somewhat higher than before WWII. However, in the late 1950s, English Canadian publishers found that their customers still read three American or British books for every one Canadian.[4] And Canadians did not read much anyway. Only twenty-five bookshops across Canada didn't have to sell other merchandise to stay in business.[5] Then, as today, most of the Canadian book publishing industry—which includes the academic, educational, fiction, and nonfiction markets—was centred in Ontario and Quebec, notably Toronto.

Expression of Culture

In 1951 it seemed inconceivable that the small, south-western Ontario city of Stratford would one day become a North American centre for theatre with an internationally acclaimed drama festival.

During the Depression and World War II, the energy of many Canadians was focused on survival. But the affluence of the 1950s brought more time for cultural pursuits. Still, ambitious cultural undertakings were generally greeted with indifference and insufficient funding.

A Drama Festival Is Born

Enter Tom Patterson, a Stratford businessperson and visionary. Patterson served in WWII, and on his return to Canada, he became convinced that a large-scale annual Shakespeare festival was viable in his hometown. He formed a local committee to explore the possibility of such an event and persuaded Stratford City Council to give him $125 for a trip to New York City. Patterson planned to ask famed British actor Laurence Olivier to mount a Shakespearean festival. Patterson never did see Olivier, but in 1952 he contacted respected British director Tyrone Guthrie, who agreed (for a $500 fee) to fly from England to investigate Patterson's proposition.

Guthrie liked what he saw and agreed to become the artistic director of the Stratford Festival, a position he held until 1955. For the first season, Guthrie mounted two Shakespearean works, *Richard III* and *All's Well That Ends Well*. The productions were performed in a converted circus tent beside the Avon River before an audience of about fifteen hundred.

Guthrie recruited renowned stage designer Tanya Moiseiwitsch, who created a revolutionary stage based on Elizabethan design, which allowed the audience to be extremely close to the performance. Guthrie also added star power. He persuaded noted British actor Alec Guinness to play the lead role in *Richard III*, thus increasing chances of box-office success.

Even during the earliest Festival planning, Guthrie sensed that he was part of a grander, Canadian theatre adventure, as he communicated in a letter to Alec Guinness, "We must not try to annex the project and use it for our own private advancement. It should be a Canadian scheme carried through by Canadians."

When Alec Guinness walked on stage July 13, 1953, as Richard III, a new era in Canadian cultural life was born. Both the audience and the critics responded enthusiastically to the performance. A *Globe and Mail* drama critic prophetically hailed the event as "the most exciting night in the history of Canadian theatre."

The Stratford Festival soon captured the imagination of Canadian and international theatre lovers. In the second season, it expanded from six to nine weeks, and in 1955 music programs were added. By 1957 the modified circus tent was replaced by the Festival Theatre, which was designed by Canadian architect Robert Fairfield in consultation with Tyrone Guthrie. Increased demand for quality theatre required more venues, so in 1963 the Avon Theatre was opened and in 1971 the Tom Patterson Theatre.

Over the years, the Stratford Festival has also broadened its artistic scope. In 1980 with the presentation of *Titus Andronicus*, the Festival had produced all the plays of the standard Shakespearean canon. In addition to Shakespearean plays, it has also presented works by other great playwrights, including Beckett, Brecht, Chekhov, and Ibsen, as well as highly popular works by Gilbert and Sullivan and musicals such as *My Fair Lady*. Most important, the Festival has showcased plays by Canadian writers such as Roch Carrier, Henry Beissel, Sharon Pollock, Michel Tremblay, and Elliott Hayes.

Nurturing Canadian Talent

In the early years it was difficult to maintain Guthrie's vision of a "Canadian scheme carried through by Canadians." As late as 1958, more than half the cast were British-trained actors, as were the majority of back-stage personnel. Such imbalances emphasized the need for Canadian theatre training facilities and funding, both at Stratford and through institutions such as the National Theatre School.

Throughout its more than fifty-year history the Stratford Festival has played a vital role in nurturing and sustaining Canadian theatrical designers, technicians, directors, and actors, such as Brent Carver, Cynthia Dale, Colm Feore, Paul Gross, Lorne Greene, Christopher Plummer, William Shatner, and Al Waxman.

Culture and Cash

With such phenomenal success, it is easy to forget that during the 1950s, this prestigious Festival struggled economically. Fortunately, a key recommendation of the 1951 Royal Commission on National Development in the Arts, Letters, and Sciences had been the creation of the Canada Council to fund Canadian culture. Although the Canada Council was not established until 1957, it is doubtful that cultural institutions such as the Stratford Festival and many regional theatres would have survived the 1950s without its financial support.

Today, the economic health of the Festival is robust. The Stratford Festival directly employs more than 800 people, features more than 650 performances over a twenty-nine-week season in four theatres, and annually brings about $170 million into the regional economy. Less than 5 percent of the Festival's revenue now comes from government funding. Not bad for one man's seemingly impossible dream that began in a modified circus tent. The Stratford Festival's amazing success story has proven—and continues to prove—that first-rate culture is economically viable in Canada.

The Massey–Lévesque Commission reported a major criticism of Canadian publishers. They let Canadian best-sellers slip through their fingers, into the hands of foreign competitors. Examples cited include the following: "An American publisher...undertook to translate and publish in English *Bonheur d'occasion* by Canadian Gabrielle Roy," which turned out to be a huge best-seller, and "Canadian publishers also missed their chance with Canadian Edward Mead's novel, *Remember Me*. It was published by a British firm in London where ten thousand copies were sold in a few months in Great Britain alone."[6] However, the commissioners' suggested remedy, the Canada Council, helped to address this issue. Authors who received grants in 1968–69 included Margaret Atwood, Timothy Findley, and Michael Ondaatje. These Canadian writers, who went on to become household names, were able to launch their careers in Canada.

The Role of Small Presses

Starting in the 1960s, numerous small presses, bolstered by high hopes and nationalism, sprang up across the country. The Council's grants were a boon to these concerns, usually dedicated to experimental or low-profit publishing ventures and typically run by writers and their friends. Some, like First Statement Press (Montreal) and Contact Press (Toronto), had already begun publishing without the Council's funding, but Council funds ensured that many more Canadian works went to press. As a result, there was a great upsurge in the number of Canadian works available.

Hawkeshead Press of Toronto published Margaret Atwood's first book, *Double Persephone,* in 1961. Between 1965 and 1975, 107 books were published at Coach House Press in Toronto. In 1967, Coach House published Michael Ondaatje's *The Dainty Monsters*. Having gained a foothold, published writers could approach—and be approached by—the bigger publishing houses, such as Toronto's McClelland & Stewart.

Jack McClelland

Son of the founder of McClelland & Stewart and head of the company until 1986, Jack McClelland was not one of the people criticized for letting Canadian talent slip away. He is generally considered to have launched the careers of Margaret Laurence, W.O. Mitchell, Margaret Atwood, Leonard Cohen, Mordecai Richler, Irving Layton, and many others who went on to become well known outside Canada. In 1958, he also introduced quality softcover books to Canada. Paperbacks brought Canadian literature within the reach of many more people, both in Canada and abroad. Overall, trade publishers such as McClelland built on the foundation provided by the Council and small presses to continue developing the Canadian publishing industry.

University Presses

A university press publishes books and periodicals that interest university professors and other academics. Some university presses have existed since the turn of the century, but many more sprang up after 1960, as graduate and undergraduate enrollment climbed steadily. Because of liberal government funding, university libraries increased their stock, and professors at Canadian universities were encouraged to publish their ideas.

These ideas had an impact on Canadian postwar society, because the results of research often forced Canadians to take a second look at themselves. For example, in 1965, University of Toronto Press published John Porter's *The Vertical Mosaic: An Analysis of Social Class and Power in Canada*. Porter showed that, contrary to what most Canadians supposed, Canada was not an equal opportunity society; power was still firmly in the hands of the traditional British elite. His work was followed by many others from many presses, studying issues and calling for change. Without an academic (university) publishing industry, few people would do research on many problems in Canada, however serious those problems might be. Foreign publishers would not be interested in publishing books on Canadian issues, because they could not sell them in world markets; Canadian trade publishers might not have the funds to invest in books with small press runs, which is typical in academic publishing.

Often, a university press will also print exams, textbooks, reference works, and even popular books. Some university presses have signature publications. The University of Toronto Press, for example, publishes *Who's Who* in Canada, featuring more than fifteen thousand biographical sketches.

Growth of Publishing in Canada

Canadian publishers continued to encounter traditional problems throughout the postwar period: the relatively small size of the Canadian population, competition from the United States and Britain, competition from other media, and the expenses of

marketing to a widely distributed and diverse population. Nonetheless, during the 1960s, Canadians began to read more books. Between 1969 and 1985 the size of the domestic Canadian market for books rose from \$222 million to \$1.4 billion.[7]

Key Canadian Writers of the Postwar Period

Canadian literature of the postwar period reflected the issues that Canadians had grown up with and were still struggling with, but it began to reach an increasingly larger international audience. This section attempts to identify some key postwar figures. Because of the sheer number of Canadians who had an impact, inevitably, many more figures are left out than are listed.

Morley Callaghan (1903–90)

Callaghan, who worked as a journalist in Toronto and Montreal, published novels from 1928 to 1983. He received the Governor General's Award for *The Loved and the Lost* in 1951, which is thought by many to be his masterpiece. He was probably better known abroad than in Canada, in part because his novels explore universal themes such as time and eternity, the physical versus the spiritual, and the plight of the common people. During the postwar era, many expected a Canadian writer to deal with "Canadian" issues. When the leading American critic Edmund Wilson called him "unjustly neglected" in 1960, many of his earlier works were reprinted.[8]

Leonard Cohen (1934–)

Cohen was one of the best known and most influential writers in Canada in the 1960s, partly because he was a poet, novelist, and songwriter. He gained international fame for his songs, some of which were recorded by folk singer Judy Collins (*Suzanne* and *Dress Rehearsal Rag* in 1966). His

Jack McClelland, Canadian publisher extraordinaire.

poetry collection *The Spice Box of Earth* (1961) launched his career. His novel *Beautiful Losers* (1966) is considered by many to be the most radical experimental novel of literary worth ever published in Canada. In 1967, the first of his own albums was released, *The Songs of Leonard Cohen*. Cohen was widely praised for his beautiful lyrics, which have become internationally known.

Robertson Davies (1913–95)

As editor and then publisher of the *Peterborough Examiner* from 1940 till 1965, Davies encountered a vast array of characters and abundant material for the novels he would later write. Davies, who taught literature at Trinity College at the University of Toronto, believed that a spiritual life is more important than worldly concerns.[9] He used key psychological theories such as Jungian psychology in his novels, which were often quite funny despite the fact that they had a serious intent. For his work, he received many honours, including several firsts for a Canadian. Some of his best-known works are *Fifth Business* (1970), *The Manticore* (1972), and *What's Bred in the Bone* (1985).

Northrop Frye (1912–91)

With the publication of *Anatomy of Criticism* in 1957, Northrop Frye came to be seen as a major international literary critic. Frye, who taught at Victoria College at the University of Toronto through most of his career, showed that literature is not simply thousands of individual stories that do not relate to each other; it is a whole worldview in which the reader learns to recognize key types of characters, situations, and language. A later work, *The Great Code: The Bible and Literature* (1982), showed how much western literature depends on the stories and situations found in the Bible. Frye was not especially optimistic about Canadian literature, because he feared that it was the product of a "garrison mentality"—the point of view of people who always see themselves as under some sort of threat.[10]

Margaret Laurence (1926–87)

Margaret Laurence, born in tiny Neepawa, Manitoba, explored the theme of women rebelling against a defeatist small-town heritage in four novels: *The Stone Angel* (1964), *A Jest of God* (1966), *The Fire Dwellers* (1969), and *The Diviners* (1974). The novels are all set in the fictional town of Manawaka on the Prairies. Laurence's fictional town translated well into international literature. *The Stone Angel* became the first Canadian novel to be required reading in France's prestigious *agrégation* examination.[11]

Hugh MacLennan (1907–90)

MacLennan, who was born in Nova Scotia but taught at McGill University in Montreal (1951–81), is remembered as the first significant English-speaking writer to deal with Canada's "national character." His writings explored the Halifax Explosion (*Barometer Rising*, 1941), which he survived when he was ten years old, English–French conflict in Quebec (*Two Solitudes*, 1945), and the differences between Canada and the United States. *Two Solitudes* is probably his best-known novel, and its title has been widely used to describe the conflict between English and French identities in Quebec. However, because he was able to give his works universal significance, he is one of the most widely translated Canadian novelists.[12]

Marshall McLuhan (1911–80)

McLuhan, a professor of English at the University of Toronto, was one of the best-known critics of the communications media in the western world in the 1960s. He studied and tried to explain how society was changing as a result of TV replacing radio. In *The Gutenberg Galaxy* (1962), he argued that the western world had been shaped by the advent of printing in the late Middle Ages but was shaped by electronic media from the 1950s onward. He is best known in popular culture for his distinction between hot media (newspapers, radio) and cool media (TV). His ideas were controversial and difficult to understand, especially because he refused to confirm the hope that the new global world would necessarily be a peaceful place. Although he died before the Internet became widely used, he predicted something similar to it in 1964.[13]

Mordecai Richler (1931–2001)

Richler was born in Montreal, and his writing brought his native city to life. Although he moved to London, England, as a young man and did most of his early writing there, Richer remained close to his Canadian, Jewish, and working-class roots. "No matter how long I live abroad," he wrote, "I do feel forever rooted in St. Urbain Street. That was my time, my place, and I have elected myself to get it right."[14] In 1959, he published *The Apprenticeship of Duddy Kravitz,* the story of a young Jewish man determined to gain wealth no matter what the cost to the people he considered friends. It was his signature novel, at times hysterically funny, at times poignantly sad.

Richler wrote many more novels, including *St Urbain's Horseman* (1971), *Joshua Then and Now* (1980), and *Barney's Version* (1997). He also wrote children's books (*Jacob Two-Two Meets the Hooded Fang,* 1975). He was a literate and caustic critic of Quebec nationalism, never more wittily than in his 1992 work of nonfiction, *Oh Canada! Oh Quebec!,* in which he dissected what he considered "the western world's goofiest and most unnecessary political crisis."[15]

Gabrielle Roy (1909–83)

The best-known francophone writer of the postwar period was Gabrielle Roy, who was born in St. Boniface, Manitoba, the youngest of eleven children. Her impoverished childhood became part of her writing. Her first novel, *Bonheur d'occasion,* published in 1945, was an immediate success and became a classic of French-Canadian literature. The story depicted a mother and daughter living in a Montreal slum, trying desperately to deal with a world that was passing them by. Roy captured the *joual* spoken by average Québécois, but the novel translated well into English as *The Tin Flute,* and it won the 1947 Governor General's Award for fiction.

Roy wrote nine more novels and won two more Governor General's Awards (*Rue Deschambault,* translated as *Street of Riches,* 1957; and *Ces Enfants de ma vie,* 1977). Her work showed remarkable range as she moved beyond her own experience to write with deep feeling about Ukrainian and Chinese immigrants, the slums of Winnipeg, and the clash of cultures between Inuit and whites.

Maclean's magazine said of Roy, "[o]nly a few modern writers could match her gift of portraying warmth without sentimentality, joy without delusion. Even when her work described alienation and loneliness, it also reached out in hope."[16]

Josef Skvorecky (1924–)

The Soviet invasion of Czechoslovakia in 1968 forced Josef Skvorecky and his wife Zdena Salivarova to flee to Canada. He had already been fired and had his works banned during communist purges of intellectuals in the 1950s. He and Salivarova founded Sixty Eight Publishers in Toronto to publish the works of Czech exiles. The translations of works such as *The Bass Saxophone* (1963) into English added to his growing reputation, and he has received a number of national and international literary prizes for his gentle, comic portrayals of life.

Michel Tremblay (1942–)

Born in Montreal, Tremblay wrote both plays and novels, but he became better known as a playwright. In 1968, he wrote the play *Les Belles-soeurs (The Sisters-in-law), h*is story of working-class women playing bingo and talking about life, sex, and even abortion in their natural *joual.* He has introduced many creative devices into his work, including antirealism and realism.

Canadian Magazines

World War II greatly increased the circulation of magazines that provided information and opinion. *Maclean's* circulation was 275 000 in 1940.[17] *Time Canada,* a Canadian edition of the American magazine *Time,* was introduced in 1943. After the war, the sheer number of American magazines in English Canada was seen as eroding the circulation of Canadian magazines. The advent of television advertising in 1952 also cut seriously into Canadian magazine revenues. French Canada was not affected in the same way. Francophone magazines actually improved their position during the postwar period, chiefly because Quebec society became better educated and more urbanized, which meant large numbers of new readers for French magazines. By 1984, Canada had 270 francophone magazines.[18]

Magazines became a significant political issue in Canada. In 1956, the Liberals put a tax on advertising in Canadian editions of U.S. magazines, but the Conservatives, who came to power the following year under Diefenbaker, repealed it. However, the Conservatives also appointed Grattan O'Leary, editor of the *Ottawa Journal,* to study the issue. The O'Leary Commission reported in 1961 that 75 percent of the general-interest magazines sold in Canada were American. Worse, the American publications *Time* and *Reader's Digest* received 40 percent of the money from magazine advertising. There were only five Canadian general-interest magazines, and two of them were in bad shape financially. O'Leary recommended tax measures to encourage advertisers to use Canadian publications; advertising in U.S. publications would not be deductible.

Nothing much was done, however, until 1974, when *Saturday Night,* Canada's oldest magazine, stopped publishing. *Saturday Night* was rescued, and the same year, the Canadian Periodical Publishers' Association was formed to represent the Canadian magazine industry more effectively to the government. Overall, the key problem for Canadian magazines during the postwar period was the fact that Canadian consumers preferred American magazines—and that Canadians were spending increasing amounts of time watching television for news and entertainment.

The Development of a Canadian Music Industry

In music, as in literature, there was a huge explosion of activity after World War II. One reason was a new emphasis on professionalism. For example, the Quebec government founded the *Conservatoire de musique du Quebec* in 1942, and the University of Toronto developed similar courses for professional performers in the late 1940s. *Jeunesses Musicales du Canada* was founded in 1949 and the National Youth Orchestra in 1960. University music faculties became common and so did summer music camps and annual folk music festivals, such as the famous Mariposa Festival, first held at Orillia in 1961.

The composition of original music increased as well, in part because Canada was no longer cut off from contemporary and avant-garde influences. For example, Toronto's Glenn Gould was one of the most remarkable musicians of the postwar era. His interpretations of classical music for the piano were controversial, as was his preference for recording over giving concerts; however, his interpretations became famous during his lifetime, and long after his death in 1982, he continues to attract a huge international following.

Popular Music in Postwar Canada

Popular music benefited from the new vitality as well. Paul Anka and groups such as The Crew Cuts and the Diamonds had cracked the profitable American market in the 1950s. In 1957, when he was sixteen, Ottawa-born Anka topped the charts, with *Diana,* a tune celebrating a woman four years

Paul Anka beside a poster of his younger self.

older than he was. Meanwhile, in Toronto's Yorkville, Ian and Sylvia Tyson, Gordon Lightfoot, Ronnie Hawkins, Neil Young, and Bruce Cockburn, among others, were trying out their music in murky cafes. Many other young Canadians such as Buffy Saint-Marie were performing new music in similar "scenes" in cities across Canada. More and more young Canadians thought that these scenes were the only place to be on Friday or Saturday night, but the commercial entertainment media were very slow to catch on.

Oscar Peterson

The most accomplished jazz pianist in Canadian history began his performing career during the war. Oscar Peterson, born in Montreal, played his piano first on a local radio station, then on CBC radio, and then with small orchestras at clubs. He made a stunning impression at New York's Carnegie Hall in 1949, which launched his international reputation. His own compositions include *I Got Rhythm*, *Hymn to Freedom*, and the *Canadiana Suite* in 1963. He made more than 130 albums and won many recording awards. Montreal's Concordia University named its concert hall after him.

The Canadian Content Dilemma

Even as Canadian composers and performers were increasingly sought after by American and European recording companies, Canadian radio stations during the postwar period were playing the top American or British music. Canadians still had to go to the United States to be recognized in Canada. The stations argued that the public only wanted to hear music that was already big in the United States or Britain. Performers, however, argued that the stations were suffering from a "colonial" mentality. They meant that the stations wanted to import a culture from a dominant country rather than invest in the increasingly vibrant culture at home. The reality was that the station owners could make an adequate living in the music business in Canada by relying on imports alone. They did not need to participate in the troubles and expenses of developing the Canadian music culture, and most did not choose to do so. This reality spurred the Canadian government to create content rules that would create an explosion in Canadian music.

Oscar Peterson, a well-known Canadian jazz pianist.

In 1965, a Winnipeg band named Chad Allen and the Expressions released their single *Shakin' All Over*. They left their name off the record label and disc jockeys, judging only the music and not the nationality of its creators, began to play it. Not knowing the band's name, they began to call the musicians "The Guess Who." The name stuck, and the acclaim became universal. *These Eyes* (1968), *American Woman* (1970), and *Share the Land* (1970) were all hits.

The Birth of Television in Canada

In 1936, the year in which the Canadian Broadcasting Corporation (CBC) was founded, one million Canadian homes had a radio. However, when the eight CBC radio stations and their sixteen privately owned affiliates started broadcasting, they were only reaching 49 percent of the country. In urban areas, the signal suffered constant interference from American stations with more powerful signals. In 1937, the CBC did two things: it built new transmitters in Montreal and Toronto that increased coverage to 76 percent of the population, and it organized a North American conference in Havana on radio channels. At that conference, Canada was allocated a number of both clear and shared channels to aid in cross-country radio development. By 1952, the CBC provided radio coverage across Canada. By that time, nine out of ten Canadian homes had a radio, and audiences numbered in the millions. As a result, Canadians were prepared for the CBC to offer national television broadcasting.

At 4 p.m., on Saturday, September 6, 1952, CBC Television went on the air in Montreal. A bilingual station, CBFT, first played an English-language children's film, then an English cartoon, a French film, some news, a variety show, an inauguration ceremony for the network, and then a French-language play. Two days later, CBC television went on the air in Toronto. Things did not go as smoothly, however; the first thing that viewers saw was a slide identifying the station as CBLT. The slide was upside down.

Gradually, the box in the corner with the flickering black and white images became a cultural focus of more and more households. Families rearranged the parlour or living-room furniture around it and bought a new type of furniture—the foldup TV table—as well as a new type of TV cushion, a floor cushion designed for children to sit in front of a TV. Supermarkets began to sell tinfoil TV dinners that people could heat up in the oven and eat in front of the TV. These were a boon to the slowly growing number of women who were going back to work after their children were in school full time. Children in middle years were considered responsible enough to heat up their own dinners if both Mom and Dad were delayed at work.

The Struggle for Canadian Content

By 1954, there were one million TV sets in Canada, and 60 percent of all Canadians were watching CBC. But what they were seeing, largely, was American programming. The issue of American content was controversial, because the CBC was largely publicly funded by the federal government. Critics argued that the taxpayer was funding a program to carry advertising for large American corporations across Canada.

The reason for the American programming was not the CBC's preference but economics. The CBC could buy an American program for $2000 or $3000. Producing a Canadian program from scratch might cost $10 000. Getting the CBC signal across the huge country was also costly. In Great Britain, BBC Television was able to reach its viewers by laying about 1500 km of cable lines. It took the CBC 24 000 km of lines to reach across Canada. When the network finally reached from Halifax to Victoria, CBC became the most extended television network in the world. For the first time, a Canadian could actually see every part of the country on television, but the question was,

In the 1950s, families began re-arranging the living room furniture around the TV.

La Famille Plouffe premiered on French CBC Television in 1953 and then on English CBC a year later. *La Famille Plouffe* was the saga of a multigenerational family in the 1950s

could the CBC afford to represent Canadians to each other? If not, what was the point?

Despite these limitations, the CBC produced many highly regarded shows during the 1950s, such as *La Famille Plouffe, Front Page Challenge, Don Messer's Jubilee,* and *Cross Canada Hit Parade,* and during the 1960s, such as *Wojeck, Quentin Durgens, MP, Man Alive, The Nature of Things,* and the controversial *This Hour Has Seven Days.*

Front Page Challenge, which first aired in 1957, had an interesting format: panellists, who were usually top Canadian journalists, were asked to identify a mystery guest based on a series of questions about a major news story. Mystery guests included Indira Gandhi, Eleanor Roosevelt, Martin Luther King, Gordie Howe, and Igor Gouzenko. The show, which offered a distinctly Canadian take on world and national events, ran until 1995.

Generally, during the postwar period, the CBC's efforts to provide all-Canadian programs were hampered by the fact that carrying popular American TV programs was the only way to generate the advertising money needed to produce Canadian programs. When the private CTV network

was licensed in 1961, the pressure increased. By 1967, the CBC was coming under even heavier criticism than usual for having far too much American programming. In response, it increased Canadian content from about 52 percent to about 68 percent by 1974. New Canadian shows included *The Beachcombers, Performance,* and *the fifth estate.*

The Growth of the Canadian Film Industry

The first Canadian films were produced in 1897, depicting life on the Prairies. Most filmmaking in and around Canada before World War I focused on landscape and legends (rolling prairies, noble Mounties, villainous lumberjacks, etc.). A boom in independent production during World War I was snuffed out by the quick assertion of financial control by Hollywood. Unlike European governments, the Canadian government took no action to protect its domestic industry, and the Canadian industry had nearly died out by the end of the Great Depression.

The establishment of the National Film Board in 1939 provided an opportunity for the Canadian film industry to rebound, because its documentaries provided training opportunities for filmmakers. Some discussion ensued again after WWII about limiting the Hollywood monopoly on the distribution of films in Canada, but no action was taken. The Canadian industry remained small until the mid-1960s, and most talented Canadians emigrated to pursue their craft.

In the early 1960s, a number of developments signalled change, including the film *Nobody Waved Good-bye* (National Film Board, 1964), which featured two teens in contemporary Toronto. Shown in high-school auditoriums, it was a revelation to many young Canadians. They became aware, for the first time, of the possibilities of film as a medium for representing real life in Canada, as opposed to the popular fantasy usually depicted in big budget Hollywood films. The inexpensive mobile 16 mm camera pioneered in the 1960s facilitated low-budget feature productions, with the result that young film-makers could consider raising funds for filmmaking in Canada. The francophone film industry in Quebec also began to thrive during this period, focusing on the issues raised by the Quiet Revolution.

At the close of the postwar period, Telefilm Canada, a Crown corporation (originally the Canadian Film Development Corporation or CFDC), was established in 1967 to "foster and promote the development of a feature film industry in Canada." It began by investing in many low-budget English and French films, which enabled a film industry to develop even if the films themselves were not great art. However, many fine films were also produced, including *Goin' Down the Road* (Don Shebib, 1970), a film about two Maritime men pushed toward the western provinces by economic and social issues. Not only was *Road* an artistic success, but it was also a commercial success that portrayed Canadian life in an authentic way.

Front Page Challenge aired on CBC Television from 1957 to 1995. The quiz show and current affairs panel was a landmark in Canadian broadcasting. In this episode, panellists are interviewing their guest, Malcolm X.

The Canadian comedy duo *Wayne and Shuster* were favourites of Ed Sullivan, whose show from New York reached millions of Canadians and Americans every Sunday night for decades.

Postwar Art, Architecture, and Galleries

During the postwar era, the variety of media and the number of artists in the visual arts expanded throughout Canada, principally because many Canadians were able to stay in their own country and practise their art full time. The support of the Canada Council and provincial arts councils assisted many individual artists, but another factor was the growth of alternative spaces, artist-run co-ops, galleries, museums, craft fairs, and university and college art departments. Artists themselves often expressed conflicting and controversial views about the direction in which art should go, but the dialogue was a major source of creativity.

Because artistic movements were gaining significant depth in Canada, regional movements developed as well. For example, Quebec artists who were hostile to the traditional values of Quebec signed the *Refus global* (*Total refusal*) in 1948, attacking these values. Their advocacy of cultural change had a major influence on Canadian art. In Toronto, a group called Painters Eleven, which included Harold Town, exhibited abstract paintings from 1954 through 1960. London, Ontario, was home to an active group of artists in the 1960s that included Jack Chambers. In the Atlantic region, Alex Colville forged new paths for realist art and influenced many other artists. Similarly, the Emma Lake Artists' Workshops had a major effect on artists in Saskatchewan, as did the Banff Centre for Continuing Education in Alberta. Another key artistic development during the postwar period was the revitalization of Aboriginal art, as both First Nations and Inuit artists struggled to define and express the Aboriginal vision of life.

Canadians began to invest more heavily in their past. Many galleries and museums were founded or upgraded, including, for example, the Art Galleries of Windsor, Hamilton, and Ontario, the Glenbow Museum in Calgary (1954), and a host of others. The Centennial year in 1967, and other anniversaries of provinces and cities, provided additional incentive for a host of museum and art gallery projects during the 1960s. In the same way, many cities began to invest in modernist public buildings. These included the Vancouver Public Library and the BC Electric Building. The new Toronto City Hall by architect Viljo Revell, completed in 1965, expressed, perhaps best of all, the "utopian optimism of the era."[19]

Mary Pratt, *Two Pomegranates in a Glass Bowl*, Art Gallery of Ontario, Toronto

Two Pomegranates in a Glass Bowl, (1984), by Mary Pratt. Like Alex Colville, Mary Pratt is one of a number of renowned realist painters from the Atlantic region. Many of Pratt's paintings depict regular household items such as fish, kitchen utensils, and fruits and vegetables.

Expression of Identity

Throughout its more than sixty-year history, the National Film Board of Canada (NFB) has been a pioneer in such areas as documentary and animation production. As well, it has served the important cultural role of explaining Canada to Canadians.

Birth of the NFB

In 1938 the Canadian government invited British documentary filmmaker John Grierson to come to Canada to survey and report on the use of film and to identify possibilities for the medium. Grierson submitted his report, which recommended that a coordinating body be established for Canadian film production. In response to that report, the National Film Act was passed on May 2, 1939, by Mackenzie King's government, creating a National Film Commission (soon to be known as the National Film Board). The NFB's initial mandate was to make and distribute films designed to help Canadians in all parts of Canada understand each other's lives and problems.

However, when Canada entered World War II in September 1939, the NFB's priorities shifted dramatically. In October 1939, John Grierson became the first government film commissioner, heading the NFB. He quickly applied his expertise as a specialist in the psychology of propaganda, using film to instil pride and confidence in Canadians through such documentary series as *Canada Carries On* and *The World in Action,* which reached an audience of millions of Canadian and American moviegoers.

During the 1940s Grierson also laid a foundation for the creativity and technical excellence that have long characterized the NFB. In 1941 he recruited talented Scottish animator Norm McLaren to organize an animation division. That same year, the NFB production *Churchhill's Island* became the first Canadian film to win an Oscar—many other NFB Oscar nominations and awards have followed.

Grierson resigned from the NFB in 1945. His administration had many significant accomplishments: more than five hundred films (including wartime series) were released, distribution circuits were established, and, perhaps most important, nearly eight hundred Canadian filmmakers were trained. The NFB grew into one of the world's largest film production studios and served as a model for similar institutions around the world.

Changes and Challenges

In the postwar period the NFB acquired increasing administrative and creative freedom. A new National Film Act in 1950 established that the NFB was responsible to a single minister. In 1959 the minister in charge affirmed the NFB's arm's-length status, meaning that the minister neither supervised the agency nor interfered with its production process.

The introduction of television during the 1950s drastically altered NFB productions. By 1955, approximately half its films were made for television. During the early 1960s, the government approved funding to encourage development of a Canadian feature-film industry, and the first of several NFB feature-length films were made. Many people who created privately funded feature films questioned the appropriateness of such production within a state institution.

An important NFB cultural contribution has been encouraging film expression from a broad range of Canadian linguistic and cultural groups. In 1941 the NFB hired Vincent Paquette, its first French-Canadian filmmaker. He was the first francophone to make a film in French, *La Cité de Notre-Dame,* which celebrated Montreal's three hundredth anniversary. Initially, some Quebec artists viewed the NFB suspiciously, believing it to be a federalist agency that denied Quebec's cultural aspirations; the NFB hired

Expression of Identity

THE NATIONAL FILM BOARD OF CANADA (continued)

and trained a generation of young Quebec filmmakers who were responsible for the growth of a vibrant Quebec cinema.

The NFB has implemented many initiatives to give Canadians from different parts of Canada access to the means of film production. In the 1960s it made the first steps toward regionalization of English production. The NFB appointed producers in Vancouver, Toronto, and later in the Prairie provinces and the Atlantic provinces.

For many years women were largely ignored as makers and subjects of film. But this changed in 1974, with the creation of Studio D, a unit of the NFB that focuses on the production of films by and for women. Its leader, Kathleen Shannon, served as mentor for a generation of women filmmakers. During her remarkable twelve years at the helm of Studio D, she oversaw production of such noteworthy, award-winning, and controversial films as *Not a Love Story: A Film About Pornography, I'll Find a Way, To a Safer Place, Behind the Veil: Nuns*, and *If You Love This Planet*.

In the same way, Aboriginal and Inuit people were for many years underrepresented or misrepresented in Canadian film. First Nations people often objected to condescending images of them portrayed in cinema. To counter such distortions, the 1960s NFB program *Challenge for Change* offered a truer picture of Aboriginal Peoples' lives. Recently, the NFB has empowered Aboriginal and Inuit people by giving them access to training and equipment so they can tell their own stories through film.

In recent years, budget cuts have forced NFB to greatly curtail regional and feature film production. The NFB now places emphasis on co-productions with commercial producers, especially documentaries for television. Still, the National Film Board performs a vital cultural function and continues to fulfill its mandate of interpreting Canada for Canadians and other nations.

 Web Connection

www.mcgrawhill.ca/links/definingcanada

Go to the Web site above to learn more about the history and work of the National Film Board of Canada.

The Growth of Modern Nationalism: The Flag Debate and Expo '67

By the 1960s, Canadians were beginning to feel as if they were succeeding with the difficult problem of defining a national identity separate from Britain and the United States. Two public events that testified to this new awareness were the Great Flag Debate and the Centennial Year, whose centrepiece was Expo '67.

The Great Flag Debate

Until 1965, Canada's official flag was the Union Jack, the flag of Britain. Canadians had argued about the issue of a new flag for more than a century, with no resolution. In 1925, for example, a committee of the Privy Council began researching designs, but nothing happened. In 1946, a parliamentary committee was given a similar mandate and received more than 2600 designs. Once again, nothing happened, because no one could agree on a common symbolic identity.

By the 1960s, continued controversy over a proposed new flag had produced at least three distinct camps. French-Canadian interests, and later the New Democratic Party, wanted a flag with no allusions to a British past. Some, for example, John Diefenbaker, put forward compromise ideas, such as a flag that featured both a Union Jack and a fleur-de-lis. A third camp, comprising war veterans and others, wanted no change.

Who are the figures playing in the sand? What point is the artist trying to make about Canada's flag debate?

Origin of the Red Ensign

During World War I, Canadian soldiers had served under the Union Jack. After the war, when King George V granted Canada a coat of arms with red and white as official Canadian colours, the official coat of arms was put on a red ensign to produce a distinctive Canadian flag.

An *ensign* is a type of British maritime flag created in 1707. Ensigns can also be white or blue.

On the day the new flag was raised, the Honourable Maurice Bourget, Speaker of the Senate, said, "The Flag is a symbol of the nation's unity, for it, beyond any doubt, represents all the citizens of Canada without distinction of race, language, belief, or opinion." Do you believe this statement is true? Explain your answer.

Most members of the British Commonwealth still use the ensign (red, white, or blue) as their national flag, with the addition of their coat of arms or a significant country symbol to the right (on the "fly"). Australia has a blue ensign with stars on the fly, as does New Zealand. Ontario and Manitoba have red ensigns with their coats of arms on the fly. The armed forces history of the red ensign was the chief reason for the emotional attachment that many veterans felt to it. Occasionally, you still see a Canadian Red Ensign waving in the wind at a veterans' residence.

The New Flag Design

Prime Minister Pearson had promised the electorate a new flag during the campaign of 1963, and by 1964 there was no time to lose—the Centennial year was fast approaching. If there was going to be a controversy, it was best to get it out of the way. Pearson set up a committee to look at proposed designs. Again, thousands of Canadians responded with designs depicting everything from beavers nibbling on birch trees, through maple trees, to moose rearing up on their hind legs (a common heraldic symbol). It soon became clear that the debate was going to be as emotional as ever.

The beavers were considered passé. They symbolized a bygone economic era, the fur-trading days, and therefore did not create an effective symbolic identity. A maple leaf was considered; it seemed relatively harmless, and it had a long history of association with Canada. According to many historians, the maple leaf began to serve as a Canadian symbol as early as 1700.[21]

Pearson's favourite design featured three red maple leafs on a white background with a blue bar on each side, representing the concept "from sea to sea," which was Canada's motto. However, when he introduced it at a Canadian Legion in Winnipeg on May 17, 1963, the veterans were not pleased. A huge uproar ensued in Parliament and across the country.

Expression of Culture

PAUL-ÉMILE BORDUAS AND *LES AUTOMATISTES*: MONTREAL IN THE 1940S AND 1950S

During World War II, a group of artists living and painting in Montreal came together to create a new kind of art for Canadians. Like the Group of Seven before them, *Les Automatistes* saw themselves as revolutionaries, reacting against conservatism in Quebec and turning their back on the figurative tradition of their contemporaries.

Paul-Émile Borduas, who became the leader of *Les Automatistes*, joined the faculty of École du Meuble in Montreal in 1937. In the early 1940s, he met several young students, among them Pierre Gauvreau, Fernand Leduc, Jean-Paul Mousseau, Marcel Barbeau, and Jean-Paul Riopelle. In their studios, the men discussed art and philosophies and shared a common conviction that the Church in Quebec controlled art and culture. In the early 1940s, Paul-Émile Borduas completed a series of guache on paper (a type of watercolour painting) that were heavily influenced by surrealism, an approach to creating art, written, drawn or painted, that he had encountered in the poetry of André Breton, the leader of the French surrealist movement. A surrealist artist lets his or her unconscious and imagination guide the work, painting, or drawing spontaneously, ultimately creating a work free of associations.

The first exhibitions of *Les Automatistes* were held in New York and Montreal in 1946. The group displayed works that demonstrated their newly developed surrealist-abstract style. The Montreal show was the first public exhibition by a group of Canadian abstract artists. In 1947, a critic referring to the title of one of Borduas's paintings coined the term "automatistes," a title that the group welcomed since they had honed a distinct "automatic" approach to painting. Their exhibitions attracted attention both in Canada and abroad. More than once, the group was invited to make an official alliance with the International Surrealist Movement; however, they refused these invitations and maintained their distinctive identity as a Canadian art movement.

In 1948, Paul-Émile Borduas published *Refus global*, the manifesto of *Les Automatistes* and arguably one of the most important social documents in Quebec history. In this radical artistic statement, Borduas and the other members of the group not only discussed their surrealist philosophies, but they also argued that the Church had a stranglehold on Quebec culture. Borduas concluded that the time was ripe for revolt, for individuals to embrace spiritual and intellectual freedom. He boldly declared:

> We must break with the conventions of society once and for all and reject its utilitarian spirit. We must refuse to function knowingly at less than our physical and mental potential; refuse to close our eyes to vice and fraud perpetrated in the name of knowledge or favours or due respect. We refuse to be confined to the barracks of plastic arts—it's a fortress, but easy enough to avoid. We refuse to keep silent....We reject all forms of INTENTION, the two-edged, perilous sword of REASON. Down with both of them, back they go![20]

Refus global outraged educational authorities, who believed that Borduas was abusing his power and corrupting his students. Within a month of the appearance of *Refus global*, Quebec Minister of Social Welfare and Youth Paul Sauvé had Borduas discharged from his position at the École du Meuble. The document itself and Borduas's dismissal from his post stirred a media frenzy in Quebec.

By the early 1950s, the members of *Les Automatistes* had disbanded, but the artists continued to work and push the limits of abstraction. In 1953, Borduas departed for New York and spent a good part

Expression of Culture

of the remainder of his career in the United States and Paris. In his mature work, Borduas reduces spatial depth and limits his colour palette. *L'Étoile noire* (oil on canvas, 1957, Montreal Museum of Fine Arts) is a work of great energy and tension. On close study, you can see the complexity of the relationship between the black and the white paint.

Paul-Émile Borduas and *Les Automatistes* opened the doors to an art free of association, awakening in Canadians the revelation that the creative process of painting was as important as the subject itself. Their explorations of surrealism led them to an abstract art that had not been attempted in Canada before and placed them on an international stage. Their radical approach to painting and their revolutionary social statements, as expressed in *Refus global,* influenced artists in Quebec and across Canada for years to come.

Paul-Émile Bordaus, L'etoile noire, The Montreal Museum of fine Arts, MMFA, Brian Merrett

L'Etoile noire (1957) by Paul-Émile Bordaus.

The New Flag Almost Doesn't Fly

Pearson dodged the criticism by appointing Liberal MP John Matheson to chair a special parliamentary committee to bring a flag proposal to Parliament. Matheson eventually proposed the current flag, a red maple leaf on a white background with two red borders—a much simplified version of Pearson's choice. Matheson's proposed flag disappointed both the supporters of the Red Ensign and the supporters of Pearson's flag. After an apparently endless parliamentary debate that occupied the government for nearly six months, Pearson invoked closure to force a vote. In the end, the 163 Liberals voted for the current flag; the 73 Conservatives in the house were opposed.[22]

On February 15, 1965, at the stroke of noon, the Canadian red ensign was lowered on Parliament Hill, and the maple leaf flag was raised. At that exact moment, Canadian ships at sea, and Canadian embassies and high commissions around the world did the same. Pearson ended his address at the Ottawa ceremony by saying, "Under this flag may our youth find new inspiration for loyalty to Canada; for a patriotism based not on any mean or narrow nationalism, but on the deep and equal pride that all Canadians will feel for every part of this good land. God bless our flag. And God bless Canada."[23]

The Centennial Year

December 31, 1966, was a very cold night in Ottawa. Bundled up, Prime Minister Lester Pearson waited with thousands of others for the clock to strike midnight. When it did, everyone shouted, "Happy Birthday!" because Canada's Centennial year, the hundredth anniversary of Confederation, had started. The Centennial Flame has been kept burning ever since on Parliament Hill.

Generally, postwar Canadians felt good about their country. Canada in the late 1960s was characterized by low unemployment, high wages, low inflation, low interest rates, abundant consumer opportunities, and optimism. The Baby Boom was just beginning; the country felt young. Most Québécois had not really given up on federalism. It was a good time to have a yearlong party. Provincial, territorial, and municipal governments were eager to provide Centennial events and projects.

The federal Centennial Commission, formed in 1963, spent liberally. Many artworks, designs, songs, monuments, and buildings were produced all over the country. For example, the National Arts Centre in Ottawa, the Arts and Cultural Centre in St. John's, *Le Grand Théâtre de Québec* in Quebec City, the Centennial Concert Hall in Winnipeg, and the Performing Arts Centre in Regina were all Centennial

In 1967, Canada's Centennial year, people felt good about their country and were optimistic about the future.

projects. Chances are, there is a Centennial arena, park, school, or other project in your community.

Most major organizations made a point of doing something for Centennial year. For example, the Royal Mint produced special coins, and the first Canada Games were held in Quebec City. There was also a Centennial Train, among other projects. The Canadian Folk Arts Council, founded in 1964, received assistance to present folk festivals across Canada during 1967. Some 35 000 Canadians performed in provincial and regional festivals.[24]

Some projects were a bit more outlandish than others, but a major part of the Centennial celebrations was a spirit of fun. For example, in St. Paul, Alberta, organizers built a landing pad for Martians. St. Paul was not rebuked for silliness; in fact, the landing pad was declared officially open by the Minister of National Defence. A time capsule buried there is to be opened in 2067, with or without Martians.

Expo '67

The biggest event of the Centennial year was the World's Fair called Expo '67. It was only awarded to Canada because of an unexpected decision on the part of the Soviet Union. The country was to celebrate its fiftieth anniversary in 1967 and had applied to the *Bureau Internationale des Expositions* (BIE) in Paris to hold the world fair. Canada applied too, but the Soviets won by a vote of sixteen to fourteen. Later, Moscow officials, who were worried about insurmountable costs, changed their minds. Some suspected that the Soviets were also too secretive at that time to let foreigners walk around Moscow.

Montreal mayor Jean Drapeau, hearing that the Soviets had dropped out, was determined to win the fair for his city. Drapeau persuaded Diefenbaker, then prime minister, to

submit a new application, and in 1962 the fair was awarded to Canada. The World's Fair would begin on April 28, 1967, and run until October 27, 1967. The theme chosen was Man and His World, and the location was Île Ste-Hélène, a park in the middle of the St. Lawrence River linked to Montreal by the Jacques Cartier Bridge.

The project was huge; organizers needed to enlarge Île Ste-Hélène and build a whole new island, Île Notre-Dame. For months, dump trucks brought landfill twenty-four hours a day. The cost rose from the original estimate of $10 million to $40 million.[25] Many exercises in creative thinking resulted. For example, when Drapeau was told that the Habitat complex could not be ready in time, he announced that it would be left unfinished on purpose so that visitors to Expo could see the building process. It was completed later and became a landmark building in its own right.

Habitat 67 was designed by Canadian architect Moshe Safdie. An experiment not only in housing, but also in community life in the city, it put a great many people in a small space, while providing them with pleasant views and privacy. Safdie had originally wanted one thousand housing units and shops, and a school, but the cost was prohibitive.[26] It was scaled down to just 158

In Canada's Centennial year, 1967, it hosted the World's Fair in Montreal, Expo '67.

houses. It featured eighteen different types of urban house, ranging from one to four bedrooms, all constructed from boxes manufactured off-site. The top of one apartment box functioned as the outdoor deck of another.

Many of Expo's 113 foreign, provincial, industrial, and theme pavilions were also architectural achievements. Inside, they provided visitors with state-of-the-art movies, first-of-their-kind products, art, delicacies, and ideas. Many people waited more than five hours to get into the most popular pavilions, such as the United States' stunning geodesic dome, through which the Expo monorail ran. In addition to Habitat, Canada erected an upside-down pyramid called *Katimavik* (Inuit for "meeting place"). The Soviet Union provided a giant, glass-sided structure that showcased the benefits of communism and featured a huge bust of Lenin. However, the communist display produced some unexpected results; one visitor wrote in the guest book, "If slaves could do this, imagine what free people could do."[27]

The fair finished deeply in debt. The ever-inventive Drapeau came up with a plan to eliminate the Expo deficit. He started Canada's first government lottery, except that he did not call it that because lotteries were illegal at the time. He called it a "voluntary tax." Tax volunteers paid $2, and one lucky volunteer would win $100 000. The scheme raised so much money that the provincial government quickly shut it down and then stole the idea for itself. The new entity, Loto Quebec, was the first provincial lottery in the country.

Overall, Expo '67's six-month run drew more than 50 million visitors and established Canadians as a people who could put on a world-class event.[28] Shortly after it finished, Drapeau became one of the first Companions of the Order of Canada "for his efforts in making Montreal the host of Expo '67 and hence contributing to the growth of the city."[29] The Order of Canada itself was created during the Centennial year, on July 1, 1967, to honour outstanding Canadians.

The Growth of Universities

World War II had created a high demand for specialist skills, especially scientific knowledge. After the war, the Canadian government offered veterans financial help to attend university, and 53 000 enrolled between 1944 and 1951.[30] Ottawa supposed that after what the veterans had gone through, enrollments would drop, but they continued to swell instead. In fact, by 1963, twice as many people were going to university as had attended in the early 1950s. There were several reasons for this.

Higher wages and the increasing tendency of women with children to work at least part time meant that the labour of teenagers was not as highly valued as it had been earlier in the century. Postwar parents were less likely than prewar parents to encourage their teenagers to quit high school and get a job, to help with family expenses. In fact, many families began to think that perhaps their sons or daughters should be the first persons in their families to have higher degrees. In any event, postwar parents sensed that their children would do much better if they stayed in school longer. Eventually, a social and economic stigma became attached to not finishing high school. This reflected one of the most strongly held values of the postwar period—a belief that many social problems would be alleviated by more education.

The Baby Boom was *not* one of the original reasons for the increase in university enrollments during the 1950s and early 1960s, because the oldest Boomers were only sixteen in 1963. Rather, postwar society placed a much greater emphasis on education than prewar society had. This was partly because of the decline in the need for unskilled labour. Increasingly, workers needed literacy and math skills just to protect their jobs, as well as the ability to continue to learn new skills as the workplace evolved. Those who wanted to become management increasingly needed a university or college degree.

Because of the huge demand that the Baby Boom was expected to put (and did put) on universities, many new universities were built—for example, Carleton University (Ottawa, 1957), York University (Toronto, 1959), University of Waterloo (1959), and Trent University (Peterborough, 1963). Many colleges became universities, for example, Memorial University (Newfoundland, 1949), University of Victoria (1963), University of Calgary (1966), Mount Saint Vincent (Nova Scotia, 1966), University of Winnipeg (1967), and University of Regina (1974).

Of course, not every student wanted to go to university. Many were looking for "paraprofessional" training, for example, in rapidly growing new medical fields. Quebec opened a number of junior colleges called CEGEPs *(Collège d'enseignement général et professionnel).* Other provinces built community colleges. In 1960 there were twenty-nine community colleges in Canada, but thirty years later there were two hundred. By the end of the postwar period, the population of full-time undergraduates had tripled, and it became necessary to hire 23 261 new full-time university teachers.

A major social change occurred when governments began to make student loans and bursaries widely available. Students who were not socially privileged could now afford to attend university; indeed, they were encouraged to. Women, who made up about 25 percent of full-time undergraduates in 1960, made up almost 37 percent by 1970. Governments had two reasons for financially supporting those who wanted higher education: (1) higher education was thought to lead to a more productive economy, and (2) it was thought to lead to greater social justice.

Today, Canada has the highest participation rate in higher education of any western society.[31] This does not mean, of course, that all social justice goals proposed for higher education were met. Starting in the postwar period, many students complained that university curricula were not relevant to "the real world." Also, as many more

young people attended university, their degrees no longer assured access to high-status jobs. However, job seekers who had a university degree were more likely to get a job of some kind than those who lacked a degree. That feature of the postwar job market survives to the present day.

Activism at the Universities

One consequence of the fact that many young people from a variety of backgrounds were able to attend university was that they began to see themselves as people who could change the traditional values that they had begun to question. For example, traditional Canadian society permitted alcohol, and even alcoholism, and was relatively lenient with drunk driving, but the use of marijuana was a criminal offence. As far as sexual values were concerned, women were expected to be very moral and men were expected to want to experiment. Many students began to question and reject these values.

Many of the issues the students protested or went on strike over were quite complex. For example, students questioned the value of tenure, the practice by which a professor cannot be fired by the university, even if he or she is an incompetent or indifferent teacher. There were a number of student strikes at Canadian universities in the late 1960s over this issue. The university teachers, however, saw tenure very differently. They viewed it as a system that protects a professor who honestly holds unpopular views. Therefore, they saw tenure as essential to academic freedom, even if it was sometimes abused. Some recalled that in 1941, the University of Toronto had tried to dismiss historian Frank Underhill for predicting that after the war, Canada would have closer ties to the United States than to Britain. That is precisely what happened, but Underhill shocked many people by expressing such a view at the time, and some people wanted to punish him. Few Canadian academics wanted to return to a culture of that kind. In 1958, the Canadian Association of University

Teachers, founded in 1951, struck a permanent committee to deal with issues of academic freedom.

Sir George Williams University Riot

Sometimes, student unrest resulted in serious confrontations. In early 1969, at Montreal's Sir George Williams University (which in 1974 changed its name to Concordia University), six black students from the Caribbean accused an assistant biology professor of racism. The University set up a committee to hear the complaints, but the university students did not approve of the representatives. About two hundred students protested by occupying the university's computer centre on the ninth floor of a building in the heart of downtown Montreal.

Negotiations to end the occupation went on for eleven days, and then talks collapsed. The University asked the police to end the occupation. The students shut down the elevators, barricaded the staircases, and pulled out the telephones. Someone started a fire, computer data cards began flying out the windows, and the computers were smashed. The police arrested ninety-seven people, of whom sixty-nine were students at the university. Fifty-five of the students were white. Twelve minors were among those charged.

The assistant professor, who was suspended during the crisis, was reinstated because the committee hearing the case was not able to substantiate the charges. However, the incident showed how out of touch with student concerns the university system had become. Both at Sir George Williams and at other universities, administrators took note and began inviting students to sit on decision-making bodies.

The leader of the protest was identified as Roosevelt Douglas. He was sentenced to two years in jail, served eighteen months, and was then deported to his native country, the Dominican Republic. Thirty-one years after the riot, in February 2000, Douglas was elected prime minister of his country.

Canadians protesting the Vietnam War: A demonstration on Parliament Hill in Ottawa against the war in Vietnam. Fighting broke out between Ottawa Police and the protesters.

> ## Review...Reflect...Respond
>
> 1. Why was Expo '67 so important to Canada? Was it more important for Canada's self-image, or for Canada's international image?
>
> 2. The 1960s saw increasing numbers of Canadian youth becoming activists for political and social issues. Why is youth involvement in such issues so crucial to Canadian society?
>
> 3. Do you think the maple leaf flag is representative of all Canadians? Why or why not?

American Draft Dodgers

Thousands of young Americans who did not want to fight in the Vietnam War had significant influence on Canadian campuses in the late 1960s. At least twenty thousand draft dodgers and twelve thousand deserters from the U.S. army came to Canada for refuge. Many attended university here and encouraged other students to consider radical or anti-establishment ideas that were popular in the United States.

Canada's relationship to the Vietnam War was complex; although Canada was not at war with Vietnam, it helped the Americans in many covert ways. Approximately ten thousand young Canadians did fight in the war with the U.S. forces. The herbicide Agent Orange was tested at CFB Gagetown in New Brunswick and American bombers practised carpet-bombing over Suffield, Alberta, and North Battleford, Saskatchewan.[32] After U.S. President Jimmy Carter pardoned the draft dodgers in 1977 (the war had ended in 1973), many went home, but others stayed in Canada permanently.

Conclusion

In the past decade, many Canadian cultural institutions have celebrated their fiftieth birthdays: the Stratford Festival, *Hockey Night in Canada,* the CBC, the National Ballet of Canada, the National Library of Canada, and the *Théâtre du Nouveau Monde.* Fifty years ago, Canadians began to realize that their culture was being starved, as increasing numbers of American musicians, television shows, movies, books, and magazines fed the Canadian appetite for entertainment. Although realizing that economic ties to the United States helped put food on the table, Canadians also began sensing the dangers of relying on their southern neighbour to provide food for their souls.

As Timothy Findley wrote, "What people said was it's time to declare ourselves, our territory.... There was a turning point when a whole mass of people said who cares what others think, we're doing this for us."[33] This time to "declare ourselves" coincided with a time when youth became supreme in society, and young Canadians began to openly protest for what they believed was right. Often labelled the decades of Canada's Renaissance, the 1950s and 1960s saw a renewed and revived spirit in Canadian culture that is still strong today.

Notes

1. Jocelyn Harvey, "Canada Council," *The Canadian Encyclopedia 2000 World Edition* (Toronto: McClelland & Stewart, 1999).
2. *Royal Commission on National Development in the Arts, Letters, and Sciences, 1949–1951,* p. 272.
3. Maurice Lemire, "Book Publishing, French-Language," *The Canadian Encyclopedia* (Toronto: McClelland & Stewart, 2001).
4. Point 9, Section XV, *Book Publishing in Canada,* Royal Commission on National Development in the Arts, Letters, and Sciences, 1949–1951 (Attributed to Professor E.A. McCourt, Special Study, *Canadian Letters,* p. 22).
5. Point 6, Section XV, *Book Publishing in Canada,* Royal Commission on National Development in the Arts, Letters, and Sciences, 1949–1951.

6. Point 5, Section XV [228], *Book Publishing in Canada*, Royal Commission on National Development in the Arts, Letters, and Sciences, 1949–1951.
7. James March, "Book Publishing, English-Language," *The Canadian Encyclopedia* (Toronto: McClelland & Stewart, 2001).
8. Hugo MacPherson, "Callaghan, Morley Edward," *The Canadian Encyclopedia 2000 World Edition* (Toronto: McClelland & Stewart, 1999).
9. Elspeth Cameron, "Davies, Robertson William," *The Canadian Encyclopedia 2000 World Edition* (Toronto: McClelland & Stewart, 1999).
10. John Ayre, "Frye, Herman Northrop," by *The Canadian Encyclopedia 2000 World Edition* (Toronto: McClelland & Stewart, 1999).
11. Clara Thomas, "Laurence, Margaret," *The Canadian Encyclopedia 2000 World Edition* (Toronto: McClelland & Stewart, 1999).
12. Elspeth Cameron, "MacLennan, Hugh," *The Canadian Encyclopedia 2000 World Edition* (Toronto: McClelland & Stewart, 1999).
13. Frank D. Zingrone, "McLuhan, Herbert Marshall," *The Canadian Encyclopedia 2000 World Edition* (Toronto: McClelland & Stewart, 1999).
14. Quoted in *National Post,* July 5, 2001.
15. Mordecai Richler, *Oh Canada! Oh Quebec!* (Toronto: Penguin, 1992).
16. Elaine Kalman Naves, *The Writers of Montreal (*Montreal: Véhicule Press, 1993).
17. Sandra Martin, "Magazines," *The Canadian Encyclopedia 2000 World Edition* (Toronto: McClelland & Stewart, 1999).
18. Ibid.
19. Kelly Crossman, "Architecture, 1914–1967," *The Canadian Encyclopedia 2000 World Edition* (Toronto: McClelland & Stewart, 1999).
20. Translation of *Rufus global* by Ray Ellenwood, *Total Refusal* (Toronto: University of 1985), p. 37
21. National Library of Canada Web site, *The Canadian Flag,* Department of Canadian Heritage, 1995, *The Maple Leaf.* Available online at
22. Mount Allison University Web site, Canadian Studies, *The Flag Debate.* Available online at
23. Canada's Digital Collections Web site, *Address on the Inauguration of the National Flag of Canada, February 15, 1965,* speech by the Right Honourable Lester Bowles Pearson. Available online at
24. National Library of Canada Web site, *Centennial Celebrations 1967.* Available online at
25. "Expo '67," *The Canadian Encyclopedia* (Toronto: McClelland & Stewart, 2001).
26. The North American Integration and Development Centre Web site, University of California, *Expo '67.* Available online at
27. "Expo '67," *The Canadian Encyclopedia* (Toronto: McClelland & Stewart, 2001).
28. J.L. Granatstein, *Canada 1957–1967: The Years of Uncertainty and Innovation* (Toronto, McClelland and Stewart, 1986), p. 303.
29. Harry Palmer Gallery, *Documentary Art Photography of Canadian Places and People,* Jean Drapeau. Available online at
30. P. Anisef and J. Lennards, "Universities," *The Canadian Encyclopedia* (Toronto: McClelland & Stewart, 1999).
31. Ibid.
32. Victor Levant, "Vietnam War," *The Canadian Encyclopedia* (Toronto: McClelland & Stewart, 1999).
33. "The Weekend Review," *The Globe and Mail,* R1, April 6, 2002.

Knowledge & Understanding

1. Identify these people, places, and events, and explain their historical significance to Canada's developing culture and identity:

Massey-Lévesque Commission	*Les Automatistes*
	Centennial Commission
Jack McClelland	Expo '67
CBC Television	Sir George Williams
O'Leary	University Riot
Commission	Oscar Peterson
Stratford Festival	

2. Many types of cultural expression gained new strength in postwar Canada. a) Identify six types of cultural expression, b) provide the name of an institution or informal group that assisted development, and c) name a key individual. Use a three-column chart organization, with the headings Cultural Expression, Institution/Group, Key Individual.

3. How did changes in postwar culture affect a) university enrollment and b) student outlook? Identify both the changes and their effects, giving reasons.

Thinking & Inquiry

4. During the mid-60s, editorials routinely attacked the Great Flag Debate, the Centennial Year, and Expo '67 as irresponsible spending.
   a) Using material from this unit, write three paragraphs supporting that viewpoint. Identify i) major issues for Canada and ii) better uses for public money.
   b) Now write three paragraphs justifying the expense.
   c) Do you agree that these expenditures contributed to Canadian identity over the long term? Explain.

5. "Higher wages and the increasing tendency of women with children to work at least part-time meant that the labour of teenagers was not as highly valued as it had been earlier in the century". In what ways does this tightened labour market affect the life choices and chances of teenagers today? Overall, do you see it as a positive or negative change? Explain.

Application

6. Study the photograph in this chapter of Canadian comedians Wayne and Schuster with American variety show host Ed Sullivan in 1959. a) What impression of Canadians do the comedians convey to American viewers? b) Do you think that the American government had the same impression at that time? Explain. c) In what ways did Canada gain or lose during the Cold War from the impression the comedians conveyed?

7. Identify a building or other public work in your region that was a Centennial project. Does this project reflect the values of the postwar period? Explain.

Communication

8. Write an e-mail to Marshall McLuhan.
   a) Explain briefly how the Internet works.
   b) Tell him whether, in your view, it is a hot medium like newspapers or a cool medium like TV. Or is it something else altogether?
   c) Will the Internet help bring about world peace? Explain.

9. Assume you are a promising but penniless young Canadian musician in the mid-1960s. When you play, it is standing room only at the new downtown club. Write a folk song to perform at Mariposa about the prosperous local radio station that will only play American or British music, instead of your music.

Unit Six Research Activity

Research

Most Canadians who were adults in 1959 remember the cancellation of the Avro Arrow (CF-105) project as one of the key news events of the time. The jet, developed by the A.V. Roe Canada company in Malton, Ontario, was a twin-engine, all-weather jet that was reputed to be the fastest interceptor jet in the world. The life of the Avro Arrow and its ultimate destruction are shrouded in mystery, rumours of corruption, and confusion. Research the circumstances surrounding the planning, building, testing, and then abrupt cancellation of this important stage in Canadian aviation and aerospace history.

Interpretation and Analysis

1. What was the timeline of events for the Avro Arrow?

2. What reasons did the Diefenbaker government give for its decision to cancel the Avro Arrow project?

3. What other reasons have been suggested as to why the Arrow was cancelled and destroyed? How valid are these other suggestions?

4. Was the demise of this important airplane the fault of the Canadian government or American pressure, or was it truly obsolete in a new era of ballistic missiles?

5. Having researched the Avro Arrow project, should it, in your opinion, have been cancelled?

6. What consequences did the cancellation of the Avro Arrow have on Canada, Canadians, the Canadian aerospace industry, and Canada's reliance on the United States for military technology?

7. Why does the legend of the Avro Arrow continue to be a sore spot with some Canadians?

Applying and Communicating Your Skills

8. Write a short research paper (one thousand words) about the Avro Arrow, structured around the themes of Canadian–American relations, and Canadian identity. How did the Avro Arrow incident fit or not fit each theme? Your teacher might want to establish steps for the development of this short essay, including the following:
   a) an annotated bibliography of sources, including Internet sites
   b) a paragraph outline of your paper, including the Canadian–American, and Canadian identity themes that you have chosen
   c) a peer-reviewed draft that will give you a second opinion before you hand it in

   Be sure to use footnotes and endnotes for ideas and information that are not your own, and for quotations.

9. Draw a political cartoon on the fiftieth anniversary of the cancellation of the Avro Arrow. You will have to supply your research notes to your teacher to show how you created the idea for your cartoon.

Challenging Times: Shifting Identities, Many Cultures, 1970–2002

In this unit you will:

- assess the significance of successive waves of immigration on the development of regional, provincial, and national identities in Canada

- evaluate the evolution of Canada's role on the international stage

- demonstrate an understanding of the conflict between east and west and north and south linkages and their impact on the maintenance of Canadian identity

- evaluate the extent to which Canada has been transformed into a pluralistic society

- evaluate Canada's evolving identity as a just society by analyzing changes in Canadian perspectives, policies, and documents on human rights

- assess the impact of Canada's major economic relationships on Canadian sovereignty

Canadians have continued their fascination with and search for a definition of the Canadian identity. Although some argue that Canada will be a stronger and more united country once that identity is found, others believe that it is this lack of an identity that makes Canada's multicultural population so successful.

As the Cold War continued, Canada tried to steer its own course in foreign policy. International conflicts involved both Canadian peacekeepers and troops in the new millennium. At home, Canada's population continued to change its cultural makeup, and the nation still needed to face unresolved issues. Aboriginal Peoples struggle for self-government and for land claim settlements. Many Québécois fight for their cultural survival by arguing for the one option they believe will work—separation from Canada.

The three decades before the turn of the twenty-first century saw a growing number of Canadian artists, scientists, actors, and businesspeople reach international success. Yet Canada remains cautious about the enormous cultural influence of the United States.

As Canadians celebrated the new millennium—praising successes and acknowledging failures—the question remained: What is a Canadian?

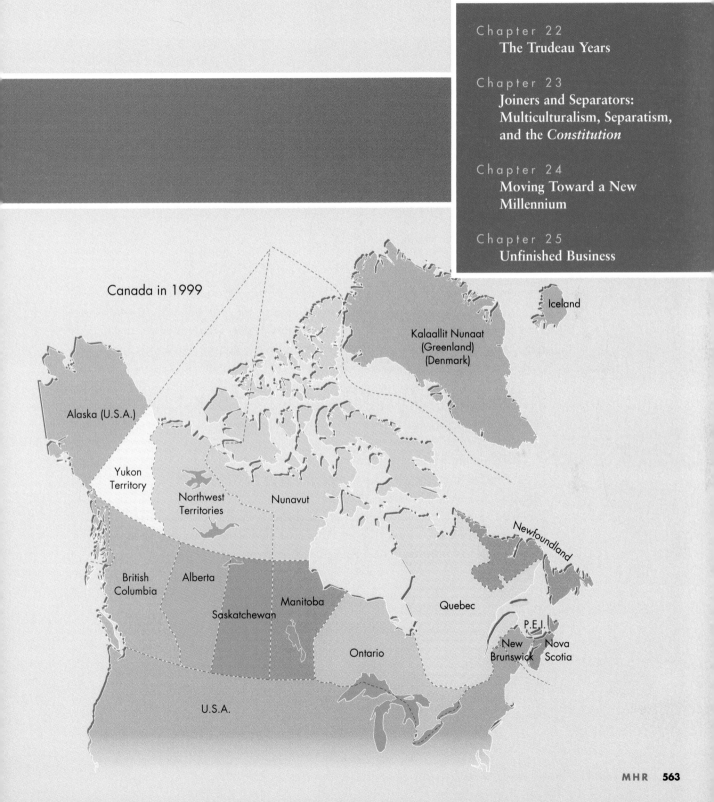

Canada in 1999

Iceland

Kalaallit Nunaat
(Greenland)
(Denmark)

Alaska (U.S.A.)

Yukon
Territory

Northwest
Territories

Nunavut

Newfoundland

British
Columbia

Alberta

Saskatchewan

Manitoba

Quebec

P.E.I.

New
Brunswick

Nova
Scotia

Ontario

U.S.A.

The Trudeau Years

Government is fun, isn't it?
   – PIERRE TRUDEAU

It is tempting to tell the story of a country's history through its political leaders. Kings, emperors, presidents, and prime ministers are certainly at the centre of significant events, such as wars and revolutions. Their decisions affect a country's financial well-being, because these leaders want to control the economy. Can political leaders also be a part of smaller events? Can they influence the books people read, the music they hear, the television shows they watch, the movies they see, the languages they speak? Do political leaders in different countries make their citizens feel differently about themselves, either as individuals or collectively as a country? Are they a presence in the daily lives of citizens?

Pierre Elliott Trudeau was one political leader who dominated Canada during his years as prime minister. He was a force in politics, leaving a body of legislative and constitutional accomplishments that forever changed the country's course. His policies affected the way Canadians thought about themselves and how Canadians related to each other. Trudeau's vision of how Canada should work, politically, economically, and socially, had profound consequences.

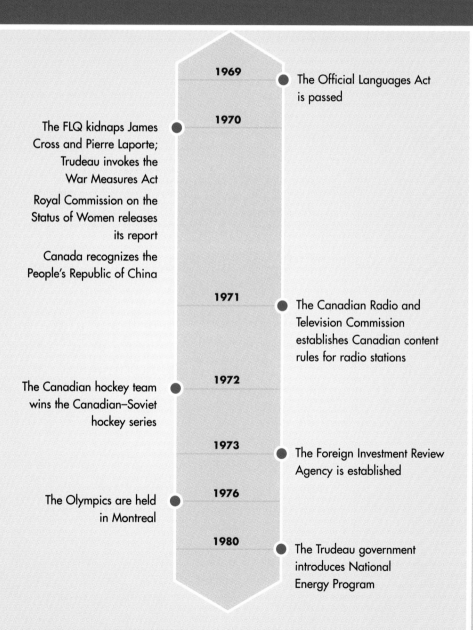

1969 The Official Languages Act is passed

1970

The FLQ kidnaps James Cross and Pierre Laporte; Trudeau invokes the War Measures Act

Royal Commission on the Status of Women releases its report

Canada recognizes the People's Republic of China

1971 The Canadian Radio and Television Commission establishes Canadian content rules for radio stations

1972

The Canadian hockey team wins the Canadian–Soviet hockey series

1973 The Foreign Investment Review Agency is established

1976

The Olympics are held in Montreal

1980 The Trudeau government introduces National Energy Program

By the end of this chapter, you will be able to

- analyze how conflicts and compromises between Canada and the United States have helped to shape Canadian identity

- assess the effectiveness of attempts to protect Canadian culture from American domination

- assess the relationship between modern economic and humanitarian practices in Canada

- describe the contributions of Pierre Trudeau to the evolution of a Canadian identity

- assess the effectiveness of post-Confederation govern- ment economic policies designed to promote Canadian sovereignty

- demonstrate an under- standing of the causes and implications of Canadian regional differences

A Just Society

Pierre Trudeau coined a phrase to describe the fundamental principle of his government: he wanted to create a "just society." He used the phrase in a few important speeches in 1968: "Canada must be unified. Canada must be one. Canada must be progressive. And Canada must be a just society." He later added, "I will use all my strength to bring about a just society to a nation living in a tough world." Trudeau believed that all Canadians should feel that they matter. He believed that no one should be too poor, too sick, or too limited to enjoy Canada's opportunities; and that no one should feel as if they speak the wrong language, have the wrong ethnic background, or live in the wrong part of the country. In other words, he wanted all Canadians to lead vibrant lives, feel good about their place in society, and enjoy all the benefits of living in one of the world's great democracies. Trudeau believed that "[t]he aim of life in society is the greatest happiness of everyone, and this happiness is attained only by rendering justice to each person."

Trudeau was elected in 1968, and by 1971, 64 percent of Canadians were under the age of thirty (compare that with 2001, when just 39 percent of Canadians were under thirty). The exuberant enthusiasm of youth was almost tangible. Pierre Trudeau, at age forty-nine was such a striking contrast to the older men who had been prime ministers before him that he captured the imagination of the country. But not everyone was an admirer; Trudeau inspired enmity and even loathing in some Canadians, but no one ever doubted that Trudeau was in charge of this country.

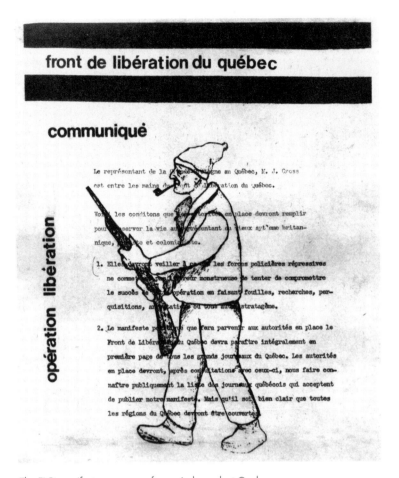

The FLQ manifesto—program for an independent Quebec.

The October Crisis

The 1960s had been marked around the world by violent revolution. From Cuba to Southeast Asia, armed liberation movements were active. In Quebec, the Quiet Revolution, though changing society dramatically, was progressing too slowly for some francophones, who claimed they were still subservient to anglophones. In 1963, a radical

The War Measures Act, troops in our streets.

group called the *Front de libération du Québec* (FLQ) started a campaign of violent terror by blowing up mailboxes and attacking armouries. Its mission was to separate Quebec from the rest of Canada and make it an independent country. The FLQ's manifesto expressed complete hatred for English Canada. One line from that manifesto stated, "We have had our fill of the Canadian federalism which penalizes the dairy producers of Quebec to satisfy the needs of the Anglo-Saxons of the Commonwealth."

On October 5, 1970, the FLQ introduced a new tactic in its terror campaign. Two armed men kidnapped British Trade Commissioner James Cross from his home in Montreal. Because Cross was a foreign diplomat, the federal government became involved immediately. The FLQ made seven demands for Cross's freedom, the most important of which was for the release from prison of twenty-three FLQ members. Ottawa refused the

demand. The government did offer safe conduct to another country for the kidnappers if Cross was released, and it did agree to one of the FLQ's minor demands—the public broadcast of the FLQ manifesto—but nothing more. In a national broadcast, Trudeau stated,

> To bow to the pressures of these kidnappers who demand that the prisoners be released would be not only an abdication of responsibility, it would lead to an increase in terrorist activities in Quebec. It would be as well an invitation to terrorism and kidnapping across the country. We might well find ourselves facing an endless series of demands for the release of criminals from jails, from coast to coast; and we would find that the hostages could be innocent members of your family or mine.[1]

On October 10, the FLQ escalated their hostilities by abducting Pierre Laporte, Quebec's Labour Minister. Two days later, the Quebec government and Ottawa decided to take action. Prime Minister Trudeau ordered the army to protect public buildings and senior government officials in Quebec.

The next day, Trudeau arrived on Parliament Hill and stopped to answer questions from reporters. His conversation with Tim Ralfe of CBC News stands as perhaps the most memorable exchange between a politician and a journalist in Canadian history.[2] Ralfe began by asking Trudeau why so many armed soldiers were in the streets, "Doesn't it worry you ... that you've got to resort to this kind of thing?" The Prime Minister responded, "It doesn't worry me. I think it's natural that if people are being abducted that they be protected against such abductions." Ralfe pushed back, saying that his own choice would be to live in a free society, where people did not run around with guns even if "one of the things I have to give up for that choice is the fact that people like you may be kidnapped." Trudeau considered Ralfe's comment briefly, and then stated,

> This isn't my choice obviously. You know I think it's more important to get rid of those who are committing violence against the total

society and those who are trying to run the government through a parallel power by establishing their authority by kidnapping and blackmail.... There are a lot of bleeding hearts around that just don't like to see people with helmets and guns. All I can say is go on and bleed. But it's more important to keep law and order in society than to be worried about weak-kneed people who don't like the looks of an army.[3]

Ralfe replied, "At any cost? How far would you go with that? How far would you extend that?" Trudeau retorted with four words that became his signature phrase, not just for this crisis, but also for his entire career: "Well just watch me."[4]

On October 16, after a plea for help from Quebec Premier Robert Bourassa, Trudeau invoked the War Measures Act. The Act suspended all civil liberties in the entire country and gave the police extraordinary powers to arrest anyone whom they suspected of being involved in any type of conspiratorial group or of holding conspiratorial beliefs. of search and arrest. It was the first time that the government had invoked the Act during peacetime. In the first twenty-four hours, 250 people were arrested and held without charge. The number would eventually reach 497. Some of those arrested were not known criminals—they were labour leaders, entertainers, students, and writers. Only sixty-two people were eventually charged with a crime.

The government acknowledged that it was using a crude weapon, but it said an insurrection was taking place, a rebellion against the government of Canada. Cabinet Minister Jean Marchand warned that dangerous people were equipped with "thousands of guns, rifles, machine-guns, bombs, and about two-thousand pounds [about 910 kg] of dynamite, more than enough to blow up the core of downtown Montreal." During the crisis, most Canadians accepted the necessity of the War Measures Act. A Gallup poll published December 12, 1970, showed that 89 percent of English-speaking Canadians and 86 percent of French-speaking Canadians approved of the government's action. Montreal's *Sunday Express* newspaper published an editorial that said, in part, "Nobody likes the government to act in a way that deprives Canadians of many of their civil rights. In the circumstances, what else could the government do? What would anyone in his right mind want the government to do?" The few people who publicly disagreed were sometimes physically attacked because their disagreement was seen by some as disloyal to the country. The parliamentary opposition was led by the New Democratic Party (NDP), whose leader, Tommy Douglas, said that the government had "used a sledgehammer to crack a peanut."

In today's political climate, would the government of Canada react in the same way?

 **Web Connection**

www.mcgrawhill.ca/links/definingcanada
Go to the Web site above to read Pierre Trudeau's national speech on October 16, 1970.

The War Measures Act did not prevent the FLQ from carrying out their threats. On October 17, the body of Pierre Laporte was found in the trunk of a car left just outside a Canadian Forces army base. He had been strangled with the chain of the religious medallion he wore around his neck. Trudeau angrily reacted to the murder: "Savagery is alien to Canadians," he said. "It always will be, for collectively we will not tolerate it."

On December 3, the police finally found James Cross. They surrounded a house in Montreal's north end, and after a day of negotiations, Cross was released. In return, the five kidnappers were flown to Cuba. Eventually, they moved to Paris, and though they had been banned from Canada for life, they were allowed to return years later to face trial. They were all convicted of kidnapping and were sentenced to prison for less than two years. Four members of the FLQ were arrested and tried in the Laporte case. Paul Rose and Francis Simard were given life sentences for murder in 1971. Bernard Lortie was sentenced to twenty years for kidnapping, and Jacques Rose was sentenced to eight years for being an accessory after the fact. All of them have since been released from prison.

The October Crisis was said to have made Canada less innocent and more aware that domestic tranquility was not something to be taken for granted. The country has never again experienced anything to rival the level of tension and anxiety created by this 1970 confrontation with terror, kidnapping, and murder.

A Second Look at the Crisis

Today, we know that the Trudeau government had no evidence of an insurrection. Cabinet documents that have since been released show that the government did not have reliable information that the terrorist had guns or dynamite. Cabinet Minister Jean Marchand's information was based on rumours. It was never proven to the government that the guns and dynamite existed. Some say this fact is proof that

the government panicked and overreacted. In his 1971 book *Bleeding Hearts...Bleeding Country*, Denis Smith, a professor at Trent University wrote, "What seems to have happened was that ten days of confusion, federal-provincial consultation, and playing for time put the governments into a psychological condition in which they felt their authority to be slipping away beneath them."[5] In effect, Smith says that the government just wanted to do something, anything, even if it was wrong.

Historian Jack L. Granatstein, one of the few academics who voiced opposition to the War Measures Act in 1970, now says, "The imposition of the War Measures Act, the awareness that the state would use its full powers, was precisely the boost the forces of order and public confidence required."

Bilingualism

Prime Minister Trudeau was determined to prove that Quebec could find itself comfortably at home in the Canadian Confederation, and he believed that language was the key. "It is essential," he said, "that both French- and English-speaking Canadians should be able to feel at home in all parts of the country and that their rights as members of our major language groups should be respected by the federal government." Although few disagreed with that goal, they did not agree on how to get there.

The Royal Commission on Bilingualism and Biculturalism

The debate over bilingualism predated Pierre Trudeau's time as prime minister. The Royal Commission on Bilingualism and Biculturalism was established in 1963 by Prime Minister Pearson as a response to the dissatisfaction in Quebec about the treatment of the French language and the lack of protection of the French culture. The commission's two chairs, Davidson Dunton and Andre Laurendeau, produced one of the most influential reports in Canadian history—a report that fundamentally changed the Canadian government's language policy forever. The commission found that francophones, indeed, were not treated fairly in Canada. They were underrepresented at the higher levels of the federal government, their children could not be educated adequately outside Quebec, they could not find employment in the federal public service, and they could not be served in their language by most of that public service.

Official Languages Act

In 1969, as a direct result of the Royal Commission on Bilingualism and Biculturalism, Ottawa passed an act that declared Canada an officially bilingual country. The federal courts were told to deliver all their rulings in both languages. The English and French versions of any parliamentary bill were given equal status. Government agencies and Crown corporations were ordered to provide services in both languages wherever "sufficient numbers" of citizens spoke the minority language. In a statement to the House of Commons to introduce the Official Languages Bill, Trudeau stated,

The Official Languages Bill is a reflection of the nature of this country as a whole, and of a conscious choice we are making about our future.... The great differences of geography, history, and economics within our country have produced a rich diversity of temperament, viewpoint and culture.... The most important example of this diversity is undoubtedly the existence of the two major language groups, both of which are strong enough in numbers and in material and intellectual resources to resist the forces of assimilation.... We believe in two official languages and in a pluralist society not merely as a political necessity but as an enrichment. We want to live in a country in which French Canadians can choose to live among English Canadians and English Canadians can choose to live among French Canadians without abandoning their cultural heritage.[6]

The bill met with strong opposition. One Conservative member of Parliament argued that "the cold hard fact is that Canadians of French origin should be learning English as fast as they can instead of the English learning French." He also said that "English is the easier and more reasonable language to learn."[7]

Some greeted the bill with more enthusiasm. Cabinet Minister Gerard Pelletier said, "I believe that Canadians, over and above constitutional or political considerations, recognize that a man loses nothing by granting justice to his neighbour, and that stretching out one's hand to another is one of the few noble gestures this life affords." The key elements of the 1969 Official Languages Act were enshrined in the *Constitution* in 1982.

French Immersion

Despite some opposition, Pierre Trudeau's vision of a bilingual Canada appealed to millions. Each of the nine English-speaking provinces worked to improve French

Many Canadians vehemently opposed the Official Languages Act.

schools for their French-speaking minorities. They also responded to a groundswell of support for schools in which English children would learn French. The first French immersion school program had been launched in 1965 in a suburb of Montreal. Now, French immersion became very popular, not just in Quebec, but everywhere. Parents lined up for hours outside schools to register their five-year-olds for immersion kindergarten. It was not a passing fad; in 2000, 318 000 students were enrolled in French immersion programs—that is about 8 percent of Canadian children.

Statistics indicate that more Canadians are bilingual today than ever before. In 1971, 2.9 million Canadians, or 13 percent of the population, were bilingual. By 1996, the number of bilingual Canadians had increased to 4.8 million, or 17 percent of the population. Some argue that the number is inflated by the inclusion of people who think they are bilingual but cannot manage anything but the most rudimentary conversation in the other official language.

Royal Commission on the Status of Women

In the late 1960s, many Canadian women became politically active. They were frustrated by their inability to make headway on several issues that they saw as fundamental. They wanted, among other things,

- equal pay for work of equal value
- paid maternity leave
- laws to protect them from sexual harassment
- control of their own reproductive rights

Even though women had been in Parliament since 1921 (Agnes Macphail was the first female MP) and in the federal cabinet since 1957 (Ellen Fairclough was the first female cabinet minister), women's groups considered the government at best neutral on women's issues and at worst obstructionist, unable or unwilling to pass laws ensuring

Canadian women demanded full participation in the political, economic, social, and cultural life of their country.

equal opportunities for women. In the mid-1960s, thirty-two organizations representing more than two million women pressed the federal government to establish a Royal Commission to examine the problems facing Canadian women and to propose solutions.

The idea met with great resistance, but Prime Minister Pearson did establish the Royal Commission on the Status of Women in 1967. It was the first in Canadian history chaired by a woman (Florence Bird) and to have a majority of female commissioners. The commissioners were to inquire into and report on the status of women in Canada and to recommend what steps the federal government should take to ensure that women had the same opportunities as men did in all aspects of Canadian society. The commissioners were also asked to consider the distribution of legislative powers under the *Constitution* of Canada, particularly with reference to federal statutes, regulations, and policies that concerned or affected the rights and activities of women.[8]

The commission was greeted with hostility by a society that had become accustomed to the status quo. Newspapers typically referred to the female commissioners as "girls." Charlotte Whitton, the mayor of Ottawa (and the first female mayor in Canada), said a Royal Commission would be unnecessary if women would simply stop being "sissy-prissies."

Three years, 890 witnesses, 468 briefs, and 1000 letters later, the commission delivered a report with 167 recommendations. It based them all on the principle that equality of opportunity for both men and women was not only possible, but also desirable. The commission reported that increasing numbers of women were staying in the workforce after marriage and were keeping their jobs after having children. One third of the workforce was female in 1971, but women were crowded into the lower paying jobs.

By the time the recommendations were tabled, the Trudeau government was in power. Trudeau reacted by creating a Status of Women portfolio in cabinet, although, ironically, the first minister was a man, Robert Andras. The department was mandated to promote gender equality and to ensure the full participation of women in economic, social, cultural, and political life. It could accomplish this by suggesting new laws, ensuring that the federal government treated its female employees fairly, and by providing money to women's groups and women's causes. That did not make equality an immediate reality, of course. It would take time.

Looking Back at the Royal Commission— How Far Have We Come?

The women's movement still exists because full equality has not yet been achieved. In 2000, Pamela Cross wrote in the *Report of the Royal Commission on the Status of Women: Where Are We After Thirty Years?*

What is left to do? Sadly, a great deal. While women in Canada are situated very well in comparison to women in many parts of the world, we are not situated well in comparison with women in parts of the world with similar economic privileges. Indeed, although Canada is consistently ranked in UN studies as the best place in the world to live based on the economy, political climate, physical environment and a number of other factors, in the same studies it is ranked as only the 8th best place in the world for women to live.[9]

 Web Connection

www.mcgrawhill.ca/links/definingcanada

Go to the Web site above to read the complete text of Pamela Cross's *Report of the Royal Commission on the Status of Women: Where Are We After Thirty Years?*

But women have won many victories and achieved notable milestones in Canadian women's history since the Royal Commission on the Status of Women:

- 1973: Air Canada withdraws its policy prohibiting married women from being flight attendants.
- 1974: The RCMP hires its first female officer.
- 1974: The National Film Board of Canada establishes Studio D to produce and promote films about and by women.
- 1980: The Supreme Court rules that when a common-law relationship ends, a woman is entitled to a share of the assets acquired during the relationship, just as if the couple had been legally married.
- 1980: Jeanne Sauvé becomes the first woman Speaker of the House of Commons.
- 1982: Bertha Wilson is appointed as the first female Justice on the Supreme Court of Canada.
- 1984: Jeanne Sauvé becomes Canada's first female Governor General.
- 1985: Part of the Indian Act is repealed, allowing Indian women to marry non-Indian men without losing their Indian status.

Do you recognize these prominent Canadian women?

- 1986: The federal government passes employment equity legislation.
- 1989: Audrey McLaughlin becomes the first woman to lead a federal party, the New Democratic Party.
- 1989: Heather Erxleben becomes Canada's first woman combat soldier when she graduates from Canadian Forces Base Wainwright in Alberta.
- 1991: Rita Johnson becomes the first woman in Canadian history to become premier of a province (British Columbia).
- 1992: Roberta Bondar becomes the first Canadian woman in space.
- 1993: Kim Campbell becomes Canada's first female prime minister.
- 1999: The Public Service Alliance, representing federal employees, wins a fifteen-year battle to obtain pay equity for its female members. It is estimated that Ottawa owes up to $5 billion to 200 000 female workers.
- 2001: Adrienne Clarkson is sworn in as the Governor General of Canada, and seven of the ten provinces have a lieutenant-governor who is a woman.

The Struggle for Equitable Treatment: Canada's Gay Community

During the Trudeau years, the fight for equal rights for gay Canadians began. In 1965, Everett Klippert was sent to prison indefinitely because he was, in the eyes of the law, a "dangerous sex offender." He had admitted to police that he had been having sexual relations with men for twenty-four years. The Supreme Court of Canada reviewed the sentence and let it stand.

Homosexuality was illegal in Canada until 1969. When the government decriminalized it, the Minister of Justice Pierre Trudeau, said "I think that what's done in private between adults doesn't concern The Criminal Code." Klippert was released from prison two years later. That was the beginning of the struggle for homosexual (the word *gay* in this context was not yet used) rights. The cause has greatly advanced, but full equality in Canada has not yet been achieved. Since 1969, a number of milestones in the fight for gay rights in Canada have been achieved:

- 1977: Quebec is the first province in Canada to pass a gay civil rights law when it includes sexual orientation in its Human Rights Code.
- 1978: A new Canadian Immigration Act removes homosexuals from the list of inadmissibles.
- 1980: Bill (C-242) is introduced in the House of Commons to add sexual orientation to the Canadian Human Rights Act, but it is defeated. It is defeated again in 1983, 1985, 1986, 1989, and 1992.
- 1988: Svend Robinson, an NDP Member of Parliament from British Columbia, becomes the first MP to announce that he is gay.
- 1996: Parliament finally passes Bill C-33, adding sexual orientation to the Canadian Human Rights Act.
- 2000: Parliament passes Bill C-23, which gives same-sex couples the same social and tax benefits as common-law heterosexual couples.
- 2002: The Ontario Superior Court rules for a court injunction to allow gay student Marc Hall the right to take his partner to the prom. The Durham Catholic School Board in Ontario had declared that he could not bring his partner, as it would send a message that the Catholic Church supports homosexual lifestyles.
- 2002: The Ontario Superior Court gives Ontario two years to extend marriage rights to same-sex couples.

Western Alienation

If some groups in society sometimes felt like outsiders looking in, so too did many western Canadians. The people of western Canada have had a love-hate relationship with the federal government since the early nineteenth century. In his first election campaign, at the height of Trudeaumania in 1968, Pierre Trudeau won just eleven of the forty-five seats on the Prairies. The feelings of alienation in the west were acute for many reasons. Trudeau's language policies had stirred up discontent, but that was not the worst of it.

Wheat Sales

Just months after Trudeau's first election victory, he flew to Winnipeg for what should have been a friendly dinner meeting with Liberal party members. The prime minister was agitated because earlier in the day he had been met by protesters carrying signs that were viciously anti-French. At the dinner, someone asked him, "How and when are you going to sell the western Canadian farmers' wheat?" Trudeau replied with an answer that would come back to haunt him, "Well, why should I sell the Canadian farmers' wheat?"

It sounded as if the prime minister were telling western farmers, important contributors to the Canadian economy, that he was not interested in their concerns. Although Trudeau went on to explain that Canadian farmers were "very productive, very progressive, and very aggressive," and that the Canadian government was fighting just as hard for its farmers as foreign governments fought for theirs, no one remembered anything but his first comment.

On a trip to Saskatchewan a few months later, Trudeau was again met with offensive anti-French signs, and some farmers threw spoiled wheat and manure at Trudeau. The prime minister counter-attacked the next day. "Yesterday, I saw signs that are not arguments. They are insults. This is not conducive to civil dialogue. If you want to meet me again, don't bring signs saying 'Trudeau is a pig' or that I hustle women, because I won't talk to you. And don't throw wheat at me either. I didn't get into politics to be insulted and I won't be insulted by people I want to talk to." Most of the crowd then cheered the prime minister, but the anger in the west never vanished—in fact, it was about to rise.

The National Energy Program

In 1973, the Organization of Petroleum Exporting Countries (OPEC), led by the rich Arab countries of the Middle East, decided to punish industrialized countries for their support of Israel by reducing the flow of crude oil. The price of a barrel of oil tripled. A recession resulted in most of the developed world, including Canada, causing high inflation and high unemployment. Even when the embargo ended, oil prices remained high. They soared again in 1979, when a revolution in Iran, one of the world's major oil producers, brought an anti-western regime to power.

What is the status of Petro-Canada as a company today?

Canada has oil, and most of it is in Alberta. According to the *Constitution,* the provinces have full control of their own natural resources. But in 1980, the Trudeau government created the National Energy Program (NEP). It was the most significant act of government intervention since World War II. Westerners believed that the NEP was an attempt by the federal government to get its hands on a good portion of Alberta's revenue; Ottawa maintained that the goal of the NEP was to protect consumers from large price increases, to protect the country from further foreign disruptions of supply, to achieve greater Canadian ownership of the oil industry, and to use the riches of oil to boost the rest of the country's economy.

Alberta was incensed. Ottawa was instituting new taxes, giving Petro-Canada (the new federal oil company) part ownership of every new oil well, and controlling prices for consumers by paying less for oil from established sources and more for oil from newly developed sources. Alberta retaliated by reducing its shipments of oil to other provinces by 180 000 barrels a day. Slogans began

appearing everywhere that said, "Let the East have Trudeau. Let the West have Freedom." It took a year for Ottawa and Alberta to work out a compromise, but almost as soon as the deal was in place, world oil prices began to fall. The creation of the NEP had been predicated on prices continuing to rise. The federal government had been counting on the tax windfall it would reap from inflated oil prices to subsidize Canadian exploration and consumer prices. Now the money was not there.

The NEP was ended by the Conservative government in 1984. The federal Liberals are still held in contempt by a large majority in the province and blamed for throttling the boom times. More than twenty years later, in 2001, Prime Minister Jean Chrétien made a speech in Edmonton in which he said, "We have to keep in mind that this country has been built because we have been able to share in this nation.... We have to make sure that every person in every part of Canada benefits from the potential and the wealth that belongs to the people of Canada. They have the right to have

How much foreign investment in Canada is too much?

Review...Reflect...Respond

1. List the powers that the War Measures Act grants the Canadian government. Should the power to invoke this act lie solely with the government?

2. Does the Official Languages Act truly reflect "...the nature of this country as a whole?" Explain.

3. Has Canada achieved Trudeau's vision of a just society? Why or why not?

their share of these opportunities. It's what building a nation is all about."

The prime minister did not say anything about the NEP, but the mayor of Edmonton said the speech sent shivers up his spine because it reminded him of the program. The deputy premier of Alberta also reacted by remembering the NEP: "We saw hundreds of billions of dollars leave this province in what was a very unfair program. We're just not prepared to accept that." A group called One Ten West, devoted to independence for British Columbia and Alberta, posted newspaper stories about the prime minister's speech on its Web site under the headline, "NEP II, Chrétien and Gang of Looters at It Again."

Keeping Canada in Canadian Hands

Money is often a contentious issue in Canada, and no subject is touchier than foreign investment. From a purely economic standpoint, foreign investment can be a good thing, as money from outside the country can fund ventures that might otherwise be unaffordable. By allowing foreign investment, Canada's standard of living rises. However, if foreigners control too much of corporate Canada, they might also demand effective control of government policies. In the early 1970s, Canada took steps to limit foreign control. In 1971, it created the Canada Development Corporation to invest in companies operating in Canada, a step toward a long-held vision by Canadian nationalists of "buying Canada back"— putting government money into companies so they did not have to look to foreign owners for capital.

The Foreign Investment Review Agency (FIRA) was established in 1973. FIRA had to approve the foreign takeover of a Canadian company if the deal was worth more than $5 million. The agency determined whether a proposed takeover would actually benefit Canada. The United States government (most foreign investment in Canada since the end of World War II has been from the United States) protested that FIRA was a hindrance to good business, and Canada suddenly had a reputation for being unfriendly to capitalism. In fact, although FIRA reviews often delayed takeovers, more than 90 percent of the deals it examined were allowed to go through.

FIRA was dismantled when the Liberals lost power in the early 1980s. Today, foreign takeovers are subject to the Investment Canada Act (ICA), and the Canadian government must be advised of all foreign takeovers.

Creating a New Foreign Policy

The NEP and FIRA were points of contention in Canada's relationship with the United States—our most important international partner—but there were many other irritants. Generally, sharing a border with a country as friendly as the United States is a blessing for Canada, and that was certainly acknowledged throughout the Trudeau years. In a speech to a joint session of the American Congress in 1977, Trudeau said, "The friendship between our two countries is so basic, so non-negotiable, that it has long since been regarded as the standard for enlightened international relations. No Canadian leader would be permitted by his electorate consciously to weaken it. Indeed, no Canadian leader would wish to, and certainly not this one." But the American president from 1969 to 1976, Richard Nixon, did not return the sentiment, saying that he found the Canadian prime minister too much of a pacifist, too much of a "small-l" liberal.

In 1970, Canada startled the world by recognizing the People's Republic of China as the legitimate government of China, rather than the Taiwan regime. It had been twenty years since communist Mao Zedong had seized power in Mainland China, but most of the world, and particularly western democracies such as the United States, still recognized Taiwan as the legitimate government. Canada's recognition of the People's Republic of China signalled that Trudeau was steering a foreign policy course independent from the United States. Trudeau was also the first NATO leader to visit and establish trade with Cuba since Fidel Castro had taken control in 1959. The Americans considered Canada's trade ties to communist Cuba an affront to the Western Hemisphere.[10]

Trudeau further infuriated Americans with his attitude toward NATO. He actually considered pulling Canada out of the alliance and thought about declaring Canada a neutral country, supporting neither the communists nor the west. In the end, the government did not go so far as to leave NATO, but it did reorder its defence commitments, listing NATO third in priority after national sovereignty and peacekeeping. Ottawa cut the number of Canadian troops in Europe in half, to about five thousand. Canada was then contributing less per capita to NATO than any other member.

Canada recognizes the People's Republic of China as the legitimate government of China. Chairman Mao and Prime Minister Trudeau greet each other.

Canada-U.S. relations—like sleeping with an elephant? Pierre Trudeau and Richard Nixon meet in Canada.

ious to defend French-language rights, wanted its own place at the *La Francophonie* table. A compromise was reached when the organization decided to extend membership to "governments" instead of "nations." A year and a half after Canada became a member, Quebec was allowed to join, but with conditions attached. Ottawa insisted that Quebec be allowed to speak only on subjects of provincial responsibility, such as education. (Canada's only officially bilingual province, New Brunswick, is also a member. In 1986, at the first summit of *La Francophonie* in Paris, there was the rather embarrassing spectacle of the province's premier, Richard Hatfield, trying to represent his citizens, though he neither spoke nor understood French.)

Cultural Sovereignty

Pierre Trudeau went to Washington in 1969 and made a speech in which he said, "Living next to you is like sleeping with an elephant. No matter how friendly and even-tempered is the beast, one is affected by every twitch and grunt."[11] That was his humorous way of describing a serious dilemma. Canada is affected by everything the United States does. In terms of culture, Canada has decided to fight the American influence. Since the movies at our theatres, the songs on our radios, the magazines on our newsstands, and the programs on our televisions are overwhelmingly American, the conclusion may be that Canada is losing the fight. Since the 1930s, however, Canada has tried to protect and nurture the development of its own culture, and in the second half of the twentieth century, that protection became even stronger.

Canadian Content

In 1968, Ottawa established the Canadian Radio and Television Commission (CRTC) to regulate two of the most important communications media in the country.[12] A democratic government does not

In 1971, during a visit to the Soviet Union, Trudeau stated that the American giant next door posed, "a danger to our national identity from a cultural, economic and perhaps even military point of view." President Nixon, in Ottawa in 1972, was just as blunt: "It is time for us to recognize that we have very separate identities; that we have significant differences; and that nobody's interests are furthered when these realities are obscured." The United States would not provide Canada with special treatment as long as Canada was willing to go against U.S. foreign policies.

As it tried to distance itself economically and culturally from the United States, Canada looked to relationships with other countries. It maintained its membership in the Commonwealth, and it joined a new organization, *La Francophonie*, a group of countries that use French either as a first or second language. Canada began a careful diplomatic dance with *La Francophonie*. The federal government had sole responsibility for foreign affairs, but the Quebec government, always anx-

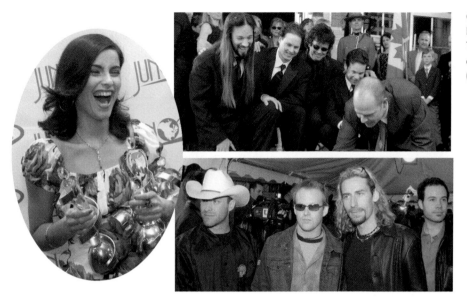

Canadian content—
Nelly Furtado (left),
Tragically Hip (top),
and Nickelback
(bottom).

try to regulate newspapers because that would be seen as an infringement of the freedom of the press. Regulation of radio and television is accepted because the airwaves are considered public property. The government therefore has a role in deciding who is allowed to broadcast on that property.

In 1971, the CRTC introduced the first requirement for Canadian content on radio stations. The CRTC ruled that 30 percent of the music played on Canadian radio stations between 6 a.m. and midnight had to be Canadian. Radio station owners were convinced that the new CRTC regulations would ruin them as they were making tidy profits by playing American music. Occasionally, they would play a song by Paul Anka *(Diana, Puppy Love)* or The Four Lads *(Moments to Remember, Standing on the Corner)*, but most of the time, they played anything but Canadian music. The station owners said that there was not enough Canadian music and that under the new rules, they would be forced to play the same few songs repeatedly. They were right—until Canadians recorded songs, there was nothing for the stations to play. But until radio stations played the music, artists had no reason to make it.

Once radio stations implemented the CRTC's mandate, the demand for Canadian music significantly boosted the Canadian music industry. Today, popular Canadian music is recognized around the world. The huge success of artists such as Céline Dion, Alanis Morissette, Nelly Furtado, Jann Arden, Shania Twain, Barenaked Ladies, Tea Party, Nickelback, The Tragically Hip, and other Canadians would not have been possible without the Canadian content rules. The CRTC still enforces Canadian content regulations, and radio stations are now required to play Canadian music 35 percent of the time. The chair of the CRTC in 1971, the man who faced ridicule because of the content requirement, was Pierre Juneau. It is in his honour that Canada's most prized music award is named—the Juno.

 **Web Connection**

www.mcgrawhill.ca/links/definingcanada
Go to the Web site above to read more about the CRTC's
Canadian content regulations.

Music

Rock and roll arrived in Canada with Ronnie Hawkins. He came to Canada from Arkansas in 1958 and he had enormous influence with Canadian musicians. An early version of his group The Hawks later became The Band. In 1966, they left Hawkins to tour with Bob Dylan. They released two albums (*Music from Big Pink*, 1968, and *The Band,* 1969) that were a mix of rock, folk, gospel, soul, and country.

During the 1960s, another Canadian folk legend became well known. Gordon Lightfoot was only thirteen years old when he made his first appearance at Massey Hall in Toronto. He went on to write songs for folk groups Ian and Sylvia, and Peter, Paul and Mary, among others. His breakthrough song was *If You Could Read My Mind* (1970).[13] Since then Lightfoot has written and recorded some of the most memorable songs in Canada's music history—many of them actually based on Canadian history, including *The Wreck of the Edmund Fitzgerald* (1986) and *Canadian Railroad Trilogy* (1976). In the rock and roll category, The Guess Who, a band of musicians from Manitoba, including future solo artist Burton Cummings, had great success internationally with hits such as *These Eyes* (1968), *American Woman* (1970), and "*Share the Land*" (1970).[14]

Anne Murray was Canada's first music star to owe her career to the CRTC regulations. She became a Canadian icon, not just because of her talent, but also because Canada's radio regulator forced the change in the demand for Canadian music. Anne Murray came to public attention on the CBC TV program *Singalong Jubilee*. In 1970, she recorded *Snowbird,* and with Canadian radio stations looking for Canadian music, Murray never looked back. Her Christmas specials on CBC Television are still among the highest rated programs every year. She has won twenty-five Juno Awards, four Grammys, three American Music Awards, three Canadian Music Association Awards, and in 1989, her hometown of Springhill, Nova Scotia, opened a museum in her honour. Among her long list of hits are *Cotton Jenny* (1972), *What About Me* (1973), and *You Needed Me* (1976).

Anne Murray—no help needed now.

Television

Canadian television has had Canadian content rules since 1958. They were refined in 1972 by the CRTC, and just as radio station owners complained about the new rules, most television networks complained about their new regulations. Making Canadian programs is more expensive than rebroadcasting American programs, but Canadian networks were given a big break. Cable companies, which retransmitted the signals of American networks (and did not pay for them), were forced to replace the U.S. signal with a Canadian signal if a Canadian network was broadcasting the same program at the same time. This change meant that someone in Canada watching a popular program such as *M*A*S*H* would see Canadian commercials even if the television set seemed to be tuned to CBS in the United States. Canadian networks owe a considerable proportion of their profits to simulcasting.

Today, Canadian television networks are required to devote 60 percent of their day to Canadian material. They are supposed to deliver 50 percent Canadian content between 6 p.m. and midnight. Most Canadian networks still overwhelmingly show American content during the peak evening viewing time. They achieve their Canadian content quota mostly during the fringe hours (between 6 p.m. and 7 p.m., and then after 11 p.m.).

Some argue that the government has no role to play in broadcasting. They believe the free market alone should decide what gets to air. To that argument the CRTC replies,

> The relationship between broadcasting and the development of a shared or common Canadian identity lies essentially in the quantity, quality, and diversity of the programming, more particularly in programming that is made in Canada by Canadians about Canadians. It is this programming that can directly influence and shape the listening and viewing public's collective sense as a distinctive Canadian society. It can enlighten Canadians about our history, our shared attitudes and values as a society and, in doing so, give us both individual and collective pride and a stronger national consciousness.[15]

Literature

By the 1970s, Canadian universities were beginning to add courses in Canadian literature. Playwrights were becoming more daring as experimental theatres multiplied. *Fortune and Men's Eyes* by John Herbert was about homosexuality in prison; George Ryga's *The Ecstasy of Rita Joe* was one of the first serious stage plays about Aboriginal Canadians. Rick Salutin's plays *1837* and *Les Canadiens* showed a strong sense of Quebec. Realism was the essence of *On the Job* by David Fennario.

Robertson Davies wrote three of his finest novels in the 1970s. The Deptford Trilogy (*Fifth Business* (1970), *The Manticore* (1972), and *World of Wonders* (1975) was Canadian to its core, the narrative catalyst of the series being a snowball thrown by a child.

Timothy Findley never went past Grade 10 in school, but his writing earned him several honorary doctorates. *The Wars* (1977) was his third novel, but it was the first one that Canadians noticed. It was based partly on letters written by his uncle during World War I and explored how a person can survive in a world gone mad.

Alice Munro is perhaps Canada's best-known writer. *Lives of Girls and Women* (1971) is a collection of short fiction that deals with the dilemmas of an adolescent girl coming to terms with her family and her town. It rings so true that some critics say it is autobiographical, not fictional, a claim that Munro denies.

Many Canadians only know about Canadian history through the works of Pierre Berton. He is the country's most populist historian. He was a newspaper reporter, columnist, television personality, and author of controversial books that attacked the Anglican Church and Canadian business. Then he turned to history. *The National Dream* (1970) and *The Last Spike* (1971) tell the story of the building of the CPR with colour and rich detail. Berton wove Canadian history into a story, and people began to enjoy learning about the past.

Berton churns out book after book (at least twenty-nine in all), best seller after best seller, on subjects that acquaint Canadians with their past. A few of these best-sellers include *The Dionne Years* (1977), *The Invasion of Canada* (1980), *Vimy* (1986), *The Great Depression* (1990), *1967 The Last Good Year* (1997), and *Marching as to War* (2001).

Robertson Davies   Pierre Berton

Expression of Identity
CANADA'S HISTORY IN SONG

What kind of popular music are you familiar with? How much of that music is made by Canadian musicians? Do you hear references to Canadian places, issues, events or personalities in their lyrics? Do you think you should? What happens to a country or region if the people living there only hear songs about other places?

Every culture in the world has its traditions of songs that describe that region's particular characteristics and natural wonders, as well as the celebrations, challenges, work and shared dreams of its people. Canada is no exception. However, it is often difficult in the multi-channelled, commercially-hyped modern media for these songs of local relevance to find an airing. Even so, bubbling just under the surface, the tradition thrives. From Aboriginal drum-circle chants to the latest Urban Hip-Hop track, songs have been an integral (if sometimes marginalized) reflection of the diverse cultures and identities of Canada.

The *voyageurs* of New France composed or adapted countless musical tales–songs that were as necessary to their work as their very paddles. Songs of migration, settlement, and working of the land echo down to us through the years, imparting some of the emotional information not found in annotated maps or statistics–information important to us as we try to imagine their lives in contrast to our own.

"A bustle-confusion a wonderful hustle, they're all jiggin' squid on the squid-jiggin' ground." Work songs of every kind sprung up from the saw-mills, fishing harbours and log-booms of the 19th century, often as locally unique variations of commonly-known melodies. In each case, they were songs that helped inspire a sense of community, of belonging, and of pride in labour.

All through the latter colonial days and through Confederation, the world of politics was peppered with satirical songs, tuneful editorials, electioneering marches and heroic ballads. Popular melodies from the rebellion of 1837 included the pro-Mackenzie satire *I'll Be A Tory*—"I'll drown Mackenzie's types, I'll cut'em into tripes, I'll be a Tory in Upper Canada!" In Lower Canada, there was the mournful exile's air, *Un Canadien Errant*—"Si tu vois mon pays, mon pays malheureaux, vas dis à mes amis que je me souviens d'eux"

The British sound and content of the many marches and heroic ballads connected to Canada's World War experiences provide a telling insight into the nation's new self-image in the first half of the twentieth century. But songs were also used all through that century as a vehicle of expression for participants in numerous social movements. Songs sung by Canadians seeking greater rights for women (*Bread & Roses*), workers and minorities (*The Estevan Strike*), movements concerned about nuclear weapons, environmental degradation (*If a Tree Falls*) and over-commercialization of Canadian society (*American Woman*) show how the popular song tradition has been mined to communicate urgent messages.

Some of Canada's greatest examples of song reflecting or influencing popular identity are from Quebec's Quiet Revolution. The incredible changes that occurred in Quebec society between the late fifties and mid-seventies were constantly being chronicled, celebrated and inspired by creative artists, playwrights, painters, film-makers, poets, and above all, singer-songwriters—Les Chansoniers. Felix Leclerc (for whom the modern-day Québécois music awards are named), Robert Charlebois, and Gilles Vigneault were the most famous of that era. Vigneault's *Mon Pays*, *Gens du Pays* and *Il Me Reste Un Pays* most graphically demonstrate the connection between singer and society. These artists drew on and expanded French Canada's immense folk-song tradition, and they, in turn, are followed today by groups and singers who have brought the concept of locally-relevant lyrics into the contemporary scene, such as Richard Desjardins, Les Colocs, Paul Piche.

The greater presence of American and British music on Canada's English airwaves has left less room for songs of the above-mentioned traditions, but that has perhaps made those who sing about us stand out even more. From the 1960s on, huge audiences have been reached by the likes of Stompin' Tom Connors (*The Good Old Hockey Game, The Blue Berets, Sudbury Saturday Night*), The Guess Who (*Runnin Back To Saskatoon*), Gordon Lightfoot (*Canadian Railroad Trilogy, The Wreck of the Edmond Fitzgerald*), Stan Rogers (*Barrett's Privateers*), Bruce Cockburn (*If I Had A Rocket Launcher*), The Tragically Hip (*Bobcaygeon*) and more recently Maestro (*416-905*), Choclair (*T.Dot Anthem*) and Great Big Sea (*Rant & Roar*). If one looks a little further, a huge wealth of modern material is waiting to be discovered. There are hundreds of established and newer acts writing lyrics about who they are, what they see, and what needs changing in 21st century Canadian society.

Perhaps the greatest reflection and influence music can present in this multicultural nation is not in the lyrical content at all—it is in the countless Canadian artists who create music based on styles hailing from every corner of the globe— often sung in languages other than our two official ones.

When working with people in the creation of relevant and socially-directed music, I always keep in mind an answer given to me by a Grade 5 student one day. I was teaching a young class the Stompin' Tom song *Bud The Spud*, a rollicking tune about a guy who delivers truckloads of red P.E.I. potatoes to Toronto week after week. I asked the class to imagine that at that very moment there was a truck driver on the 401 doing exactly the same job described in the song. "Imagine this driver turning on the radio as he drove and hearing *Bud The Spud* played on the radio. How would that driver feel?" A bashful 9-year-old stood up, cleared his throat, and after a short pause said, "He felt needed."

Imagine that. Songs that make us feel needed. Songs that reflect our lives, communities, landscape, jobs, diverse heritages and dreams. Who will sing your generation's Canada into existence? What would you celebrate in song? What would you scream in anger about? An eager nation awaits.

MIKE FORD IS A ROLLICKING CANADIAN MUSICIAN WHO BRINGS CANADIAN HISTORY TO LIFE IN CLASSROOMS WITH HIS PROGRAM, *CANADA IN SONG.*

Stompin' Tom Connors

Hockey Showdown

In the early Olympic Winter Games, Canada sent amateur hockey teams (among other athletes) to compete, and the hockey teams usually won easily. But starting in the 1960s, our amateur teams began losing to the Soviet Union. As Canada continued to lose, controversy grew over who had the better hockey team. Quite apart from sports, it was as if communism were beating democracy. At the height of the Cold War, these hockey games almost became a proxy war.

In 1972, the hockey showdown was organized—the best players in the National Hockey League (NHL) against the Soviet team. The teams would play eight games, the first four in Canada, and the final four in Moscow. Most people believed that Team Canada would probably win all eight games.

The country was crackling with excitement as the first game approached in Montreal. To the shock of the nation, the Soviet Union won 7–3. The coach of Team Canada, Harry Sinden, said, "A little piece of all of us died today. I never thought I could feel as badly about losing a single game as I did about this one."

After seven games, Canada had won three, the Soviet Union had won three, and one game had been tied. Game eight would decide the series winner. On the afternoon of September 28, 1972, televisions everywhere were tuned to the final game of the Canada–Soviet hockey summit. Canada was down 5–3 going into the third period, but they managed to tie it up with seven minutes left to play. Then, with only thirty-four seconds left in the period, Paul Henderson from Team Canada scored the winning goal. Canada celebrated from St. John's to Victoria, its citizens feeling a euphoria rarely experienced before or since. When victory came so dramatically, it was not just exciting, it made people proud to be Canadian.

Flash Forward to 2002

At the Olympic Winter Games of 2002, a younger generation experienced a similar jolt of hockey excitement when both the Canadian men's and women's teams won gold medals against teams from the United States. The final game for the men was seen on television by more than 8.6 million Canadians and almost 38 million Americans. In Canada, the game was the most-watched TV program—sports or otherwise—in our history.

But since that game was against the Americans, there was no hint of the ideological battle so central to the 1972 series—this one was NHL player against NHL player. The victory sparked celebrations from coast to coast, and Canada's identity once again became intertwined with hockey. Prime Minister Jean Chrétien remarked:

> I have just returned from a Team Canada trade mission to Russia, where, in the company of team members from both sides, we marked the 30th anniversary of the Summit Series of 1972—a series that transfixed Canadians from sea to sea to sea. In the past two weeks, in homes and schools, at work and at play, Canadians have once again been united in a way that only hockey can bring us together. And their victories have triggered a nationwide party of celebration.[16]

Calgary-born and Juno-award winning country singer Paul Brandt rewrote the lyrics to his hit *Canadian Man* and called it *Ode to Team Canada*. It was played on radio stations across the country for weeks after the victory:

> *Team Canada*
> *At your service from the land of the chill*
> *If they can't thrill you baby, nobody will*
> *Make way, here comes*
> *Team Canada*
> *Strong and free,*
> *Lead by our fearless hero, Gretzky*
> *He should be the prime minister if you ask me*
> *Oh, thank you*
> *Team Canada*

Well it's hush hush
Three man rush rush
Iginla, Sakic and Lemieux
He shoots, he scores
And all of Canada roars
From the warmth of our igloos
Sorry, eh,
We put the hurt on you, Team USA
And showed the whole world that it's still our game
Three cheers for Team Canada
We'll slide and glide
Skate over any line
Red or white or blue
What makes it nice
Is that we did it twice
'Cause our women beat you too
Gold at last
50 years sure took a long time to pass
So tip your hat or raise your glass
For the heroes of Team Canada
What a great game, Team Canada
You did us proud, Team Canada[17]

The 1976 Olympics

Four years after the hockey showdown in 1972, Canada was again in the world's sports spotlight. The 1976 Summer Olympic Games were in Montreal, and it was another chance for the city and the country to shine, just as it had during Expo '67, the World's Fair in Montreal in 1967, Canada's centennial.

The games were awarded to Montreal in 1970. Mayor Jean Drapeau had promised "humble" games, but he could not resist the urge to build monuments. The architect Drapeau had hired to build the facilities was from France and he did not understand Montreal's cold weather. Construction schedules fell far behind.

The pressure to get everything ready was crushing. When a reporter chased Drapeau through City Hall asking him if things would be ready, Drapeau replied "Would you please shut up. You need my permission to ask questions like that here." The mayor was under a lot of pressure. These were the games, after all, that Drapeau said, "could no more lose money than a man could have a baby."

The Games did start on time. The stadium wasn't finished, but it did not need a roof for the games. The 1976 Games were the first where the host country failed to win a gold medal and some African countries boycotted the Games because South Africa (still under apartheid) had been allowed to compete. In the end, many Canadians were outraged that the Olympics had a $1 billion deficit they had to pay for.

Canada's hockey teams, women's and men's, win gold in the 2002 Olympics.

Expression of Identity
FIFTY YEARS OF *HOCKEY NIGHT IN CANADA*

Hockey Night in Canada is the longest-running show in Canadian television history, having started broadcasting in 1952. The origins of *HNIC*, however, precede television—a radio version of the show first aired in 1932. The first coast-to-coast radio broadcast of a professional hockey game was in 1933, a contest between the Detroit Red Wings and Toronto Maple Leafs. Soon, every Saturday night, thousands of people from across Canada would huddle around the radio, listening to legendary play-by-play announcer Foster Hewitt call games from Maple Leaf Gardens.

A telephone survey conducted during the early 1930s estimated the combined per-game audience at just fewer than one million listeners. This was an amazing figure in a country that at the time had a population of about ten million, many of whom did not yet own radios.

Corporate sponsors came on board, but not all saw the potential. Imperial Oil replaced General Motors in 1936 when the new president of GM Canada, freshly transferred from the United States, declared that he "did not believe hockey would sell cars."

A significant milestone in *HNIC* history occurred on January 1, 1937, when the Canadian Broadcasting Corporation (CBC) was launched as a public network and assumed responsibility for carrying the program. The first televised hockey game in Canada was a Memorial Cup contest held at the Gardens in Toronto in the spring of 1952. Foster Hewitt handled the play by play, and the game was viewed on close-circuit TV by a group of hockey and broadcasting officials. The test run allowed Hewitt to demonstrate that the play-by-play style he so successfully developed for radio would translate to television.

Early broadcasts were technically crude by modern standards. There were few commercials and coverage began at 9 p.m. local time, or halfway through the game, because team owners feared arenas would not be full if the game were on television. Viewer perspectives of the game were extremely limited, since *HNIC* originally used only three overhead camera angles to capture the action.

The first-year television fees were small but quickly grew. Imperial Oil purchased the TV rights for the first season at just $100 per Maple Leafs game. The following season, Imperial bought games for $150 000 a year in a three-year contract. By the early 1960s, the rights sold for $9 million over six years, or about $21 000 per game. The *Hockey Night in Canada* post-game ritual of picking three stars began as a promotion for Imperial Oil's Three Star brand of gas.

With increased revenue came improved production and technical quality. *HNIC* pioneered the use of ice-level cameras around the net and instant replay technology in the 1950s. Beginning in the1960s, it used dramatic scripted openings, teasers, and directional microphones to capture the sound of thunderous body-checks, slap shots, and ricocheting pucks.

Although early television coverage focused on Toronto and Montreal, the CBC began covering other Canadian teams as they joined the league, beginning with the Vancouver Canucks in 1970, and later Edmonton, Calgary, Winnipeg, and Quebec City.

HNIC has consistently been CBC's most-watched program. At times, such as during playoffs, the show has commanded audiences of more than three million people—in a nation or around 31 million people. Analysis has shown that the viewing audience has risen between 1 percent and 5 percent a year over the past few years, which is an amazing statistic considering the fragmentation of the modern media marketplace by competing cable and digital channels.

It is not an exaggeration to say that CBC's *Hockey Night In Canada* is a Canadian institution. Through the years, the show's hosts, commentators, and play-by-play announcers have become as popular as many of the players themselves.

Will hockey always be part of our national identity?

Review...Reflect...Respond

1. What events marked Trudeau's new path for Canada's foreign policy?

2. How effective were the Canadian government's efforts to protect Canada's cultural sovereignty?

3. It is often said that the theme to *Hockey Night in Canada* is as well-known to Canadians as the national anthem. Why has hockey remained an integral part of Canadian culture?

Conclusion

During the years that Trudeau was prime minister, Canada underwent dramatic transformations. The country weathered a crisis as the FLQ brought Canadians face to face with terrorism. Canada tried to protect its economic sovereignty with policies such as FIRA and the NEP, which in turn caused regionalism and strife within Canada. At the same time, the Canadian government's protection of its cultural sovereignty provided a much-need boost to Canadian artists that helped launch many to national and international fame. It was a time when the Canadian government played an increasing role in the political, economic, and cultural protection of its country. In the words of Trudeau,

> One way of offsetting the appeal of separatism is by investing tremendous amounts of time, energy, and money in nationalism, at the federal level. A national image must be created that will have such an appeal as to make any image of a separatist group unattractive.

Resources must be diverted into such things as national flags, anthems, education, art councils, broadcasting corporations, film boards; the territory must be bound together by a network of railways, highways, airlines; the national culture and national economy must be protected by taxes and tariffs; ownership of resources and industry by nationals must be made a matter of policy. In short, the whole of the citizenry must be made to feel that it is only within the framework of the federal state that their language, culture, institutions, sacred traditions, and standard of living can be protected from external attack and international strife.[18]

Notes

1. Pierre Elliot Trudeau, *Notes for a national broadcast, October 16, 1970.* (Ottawa: Office of the Prime Minister, 1970) p. 10.
2. Some would say it was a debate rather than an exchange of words. Ralfe later said he thought he might be fired for being so aggressive with the prime minister.
3. In John Saywell, *Quebec 70: A Documentary Narrative* (Toronto: University of Toronto Press, 1971) pp. 71–74 (Originally published in the *Canadian Annual Review, 1970*).
4. *CBC News,* October 11, 1970.
5. Denis Smith, *Bleeding Hearts...Bleeding Country* (Toronto: M.G. Hurtig Limited 1971). p. 51.
6. Pierre Elliot Trudeau, *Statement by the Prime Minister in the House of Commons on the Resolution Preliminary to Introduction of the Official Languages Bill* (Ottawa: Office of the Prime Minister, 1968), p. 6.
7. Later, when the law required bilingual labels on all grocery products, corn flakes boxes angered some western Canadians who complained that French was being "rammed down our throats."
8. Royal Commission on the Status of Women (February 16, 1967).
9. Pamela Cross, *Report on the Royal Commission on the Status of Women: Where Are We After Thirty Years?* (Toronto: Ontario Women's Justice Network 1970) p. 46.
10. Those ties were so important to Cuba that when Trudeau died in 2000, Cuba declared three days of official mourning, and Castro travelled to Montreal for the funeral.
11. Pierre Trudeau, *Speech to the National Press Club,* 1969.
12. Today, the CRTC has a slightly broader mandate and its name is the Canadian Radio-Television and Telecommunications Commission.
13. Studio 54 remade *If You Could Read My Mind* into a successful dance hit in 2000.
14. United States rock star Lenny Kravitz remade *American Woman* in 1999, and the song became a hit again.
15. CRTC presentation to House of Commons committee (CRTC, 1991b), p. 6.
16. "Canadian fans erupt in celebration after Olympic hockey gold medal win," by James McCarten, February 24, 2002. Available online at <http://ca.sports.yahoo.com/020226/6/KOav.htm>.
17. *Ode to Team Canada,* by Paul Brandt, copyright 2002.
18. Pierre Trudeau, *"Federalism, Nationalism, and Reason,"* address, Canadian Political Science Association and the Association of Law Teachers, June 1964, as quoted in *The Essential Trudeau,* ed. Ron Graham (Toronto: McClelland & Stewart, 1998), p. 120.

Chapter 22 Review

Knowledge & Understanding

1. Identify these people, terms, and events, and explain their historical significance to Canadian history and the development of its culture and identity:
   - just society
   - October Crisis
   - Official Languages Act
   - Royal Commission on the Status of Women
   - National Energy Program
   - Foreign Investment Review Agency
   - Canadian content
   - hockey
   - Pierre Trudeau
   - Junos

2. Under the direction of Pierre Trudeau, the Canadian government began to map out its own path for foreign policy rather than simply following the United States' policies. Write a well-written paragraph that describes how this different path helped to shape the Canadian identity.

3. The Royal Commission on the Status of Women in 1970 is considered a major step in the evolution of the women's movement in Canada. Create a graphic organizer that shows the main recommendations of the commission and the impact each recommendation had on opportunities for women in Canada.

Thinking & Inquiry

4. Trudeau's final response, "Well just watch me," to CBC reporter Tim Ralphe's question about how far the government would go to control the October crisis became one of Trudeau's most famous quotes. In a well-written paragraph, describe how this quote mirrored Trudeau's position and actions in other events.

5. How effective is the CRTC's Canadian content rule in protecting Canadian culture from American domination? Be sure to use examples from both music and television to support your answer.

Application

6. As a French-Canadian citizen living in Montreal in 1970, you are intensely aware of the FLQ crisis as it unwinds. You read the newspaper on October 16 and discover the Canadian government has invoked the War Measures Act. Write a 300-word editorial to the *Montreal Gazette* explaining your support for or your disagreement with the government's decision. Be sure to support your opinion with historical facts.

7. As premier of Alberta in 1980, you are outraged at the Canadian government's National Energy Program. You arrange for an emergency meeting with Prime Minister Trudeau in which you argue against the program. Research and prepare three main arguments that you will use in your meeting, and be sure they are supported with historical evidence.

Communication

8. Before he was assassinated in 1980, famous Beatles member John Lennon met Prime Minister Trudeau. Lennon stated, "If there were more leaders like Mr. Trudeau, there would be world peace." Do you agree with this statement? Why or why not? Write three to four well-written paragraphs to support your opinion on whether John Lennon's statement was true or false. Be sure to provide historical evidence to support your decision.

Joiners and Separators:

Multiculturalism, Separatism, and the Constitution

The tragedy of Canada today is that just when we need a country that's pulling together in common cause, we have one that keeps finding new ways to pull itself apart.

–ANGUS REID POLL, 1996

Two powerful "isms" both became part of Canadian life starting in the late 1960s and early 1970s: multiculturalism and separatism. Each thrives in Canada today, and each identifies Canada as distinctly different from every other nation. Multiculturalism endeavours to bind Canada together by welcoming immigrants without erecting cultural barriers for them to cross. Separatism threatens to tear Canada apart.

Canada's policy of multiculturalism encourages new immigrants to maintain the traditions of their original culture. It is a radical departure not only from what other countries do, but also from what Canada did during its first century. The central tenet of multiculturalism is that as the definition of a Canadian becomes more flexible, more people will feel comfortable being Canadian.

Separatism is a movement that seeks to remove a province, especially Quebec, from Confederation. Its strength in Quebec springs from the belief that French-Canadians have never been, and can never be, equal partners in Canada. Separatism asserts that the only way that Quebec can fulfill its potential, protect its language, promote its culture, and live with dignity is by becoming a sovereign nation. What differentiates Canada's internal independence movement from others around the world is its dedication to achieving its goal only through the democratic process. It is no small irony that the presence and persistence of the separatists led directly to patriation of Canada's *Constitution*, the document that more than any other expresses our nation's fundamental aspirations.

Much of our national psyche is bound up in these two "isms." Both have fervent defenders. Both have passionate detractors. Very few Canadians remain neutral.

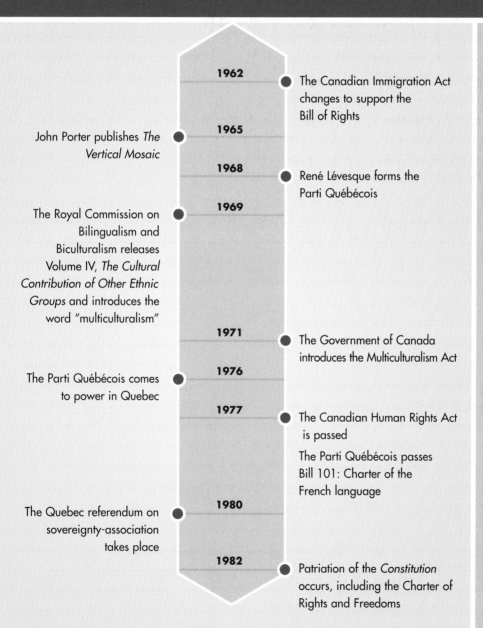

1962 The Canadian Immigration Act changes to support the Bill of Rights

John Porter publishes *The Vertical Mosaic* **1965**

1968 René Lévesque forms the Parti Québécois

The Royal Commission on Bilingualism and Biculturalism releases Volume IV, *The Cultural Contribution of Other Ethnic Groups* and introduces the word "multiculturalism" **1969**

1971 The Government of Canada introduces the Multiculturalism Act

The Parti Québécois comes to power in Quebec **1976**

1977 The Canadian Human Rights Act is passed

The Parti Québécois passes Bill 101: Charter of the French language

The Quebec referendum on sovereignty-association takes place **1980**

1982 Patriation of the *Constitution* occurs, including the Charter of Rights and Freedoms

By the end of this chapter, you will be able to

- explain the basic objectives of Canada's official policy of multiculturalism, and its relationship to bilingualism and biculturalism, and explain how support for and opposition to the policy have changed over time

- assess the difficulties in maintaining a united country while promoting diversity through multiculturalism

- analyze why and how the people of Quebec have acted to preserve their political identity

- describe the strategies that French Canada has used to preserve francophone culture

- describe the role of selected significant events and legislation in the development of the current Canadian political system

The Roots of Multiculturalism

Multiculturalism was anything but inevitable; a long series of events occurred that made it possible. Changes to Canada's immigration policies and the appointment of the Royal Commission on Biculturalism and Bilingualism were but two factors that led to the Canadian government's policy on multiculturalism.

Immigration Changes

The 1960 Bill of Rights made it illegal for federal agencies to discriminate on the basis of race, national origin, colour, religion, or sex. In 1962, the Canadian Immigration Act emulated the Bill, stating, "any suitably qualified person from any part of the world could be considered for immigration to Canada without regard to his [or her] race, colour, national origin, or the country from which he [or she] comes." In 1967, the federal government adopted a new immigration policy based on a points system. People who applied to come to Canada were ranked on a number of objective criteria, such as education, work skills, and financial resources. In this points system, none of the criteria was based on ethnicity, gender, or religion.

This system was a profound shift in how Canada chose its immigrants, and it resulted in a profound shift in who immigrated. The numbers tell a clear story. First, the number of immigrants who came to Canada increased. From the end of World War II to the beginning of the 1970s, about 125 000 immigrants arrived in this country each year. The number began rising steadily in the 1970s, and since 1990, the number of new immigrants each year has been about 200 000. Second, for the first time, Canada was attracting immigrants from diverse ethnic groups. Ninety-four percent of the immigrants who came to Canada before 1961 were

Definitions and notes	Total – Immigrant Population	Period of immigration				
		Before 1961	1961–1970	1971–1980	1981–1990	1991–1996
		Number				
Total – Place of birth	**4 971 070**	1 054 930	788 580	996 160	1 092 400	1 038 990
United States	244 695	45 050	50 200	74 015	46 405	29 025
Central and South America	273 820	6 370	17 410	67 470	106 230	76 335
Caribbean and Bermuda	279 405	8 390	45 270	96 025	72 405	57 315
United Kingdom	655 540	265 580	168 140	132 950	63 445	25 420
Other Northern and Western Europe	514 310	284 205	90 465	59 850	48 095	31 705
Eastern Europe	447 830	175 430	40 855	32 280	111 370	87 900
Southern Europe	714 380	288 145	244 380	131 620	57 785	52 455
Africa	229 300	4 945	25 685	58 150	64 265	76 260
West-central Asia and the Middle East	210 850	4 975	15 165	30 980	77 685	82 050
Eastern Asia	589 420	20 555	38 865	104 940	172 715	252 340
South-east Asia	408 985	2 485	14 040	111 700	162 490	118 265
Southern Asia	353 515	4 565	28 875	80 755	99 270	140 055
Oceania and Other	49 025	4 250	9 240	15 420	10 240	9 875

Source: Statistics Canada, 1996 Census *Nation* Tables.

Number of immigrants entering Canada by place of origin and time period.

European. Of those who came between 1981 and 1991, only 34 percent were European; 66 percent were of other ethnic origins. In 1954, fewer than 5 percent of immigrants to Canada came from the Caribbean, Africa, or Asia. By the mid-1990s, more than 60 percent of immigrants came from Asia alone, especially Hong Kong, India, Pakistan, China, Taiwan, the Philippines, and Sri Lanka. In 2000, the top eight countries sending immigrants to Canada were all in Asia.

A new expression became part of the Canadian vocabulary: visible minority. The 1996 census found that 11.2 percent of Canada's population fell into that category, defined as "persons, other than Aboriginal Peoples, who are non-Caucasian in race or non-white in colour." Population projections say that by 2016, visible minorities will make up more than 22 percent of the population; among children, the proportion is expected to be 25 percent of the population.

As a direct result of its immigration policies, Canada is now home to people from more than one hundred different ethnic groups who speak more than one hundred different languages. After English and French, the most common languages used at home are Chinese, Italian, Punjabi, Spanish, and Portuguese. Canada's largest city, Toronto, is on its way to becoming the most multicultural city in the world. Vancouver, the city with the fastest growing immigrant population, will soon be one of the world's most integrated cities.

Many countries derive national unity from a common heritage among their people and from common traditions. Canada has chosen a different route, opening its doors to people with a multitude of backgrounds, but some debate remains about how best to convert that diversity into national strength. It is a debate that goes back to at least the early 1960s.

The Royal Commission on Bilingualism and Biculturalism

In 1963, Prime Minister Lester Pearson established the Royal Commission on Bilingualism and Biculturalism. It was initiated to address the growing tension between English-speaking and French-speaking Canadians. Throughout its hearings, however, the "Bi and Bi" commissioners heard from ethnic minority groups (such as the Canadian Hungarian Federation, the National Japanese Canadian Citizenship Association, the Association of United Ukrainian Canadians, and the Trans-Canada Alliance of German Canadians) who were worried about their place in Canada. These people were concerned that, in an effort to satisfy the two major ethnic groups in Canada, the government would relegate other ethnic groups to the status of second-class citizens.

The 1990s saw more people from Asia enter Canada than from any other region.

The commission released Volume IV of its report in 1969. It was titled *The Cultural Contribution of Other Ethnic Groups*, and for the first time, "multiculturalism" was used in the context in which Canadians now understand it. Because of this, many people point to Volume IV as the foundation for the government policy that was eventually put into place. However, the Royal Commission raised multiculturalism only to reject it:

> There are many reasons, the first moral, against considering ethnic differences, either by group or by origin, as a basic principle for shaping society. This would tend to create closed membership groups with newcomers condemned to remain outsiders; accidents of history would be emphasized and rigid barriers would divide people. Legislation based on ethnic group or ethnic origin would be a direct denial of the principle that all are created equal before the law. In a multi-ethnic country, where inter-ethnic marriages are frequent and accepted, what could possibly justify legislation confining people within their so-called ethnic origin?[1]

The commissioners left no doubt that they had heard what ethnic groups had told them, but that they disagreed with the message:

> Among those of non-British, non-French origin, some accept official bilingualism without hesitation but categorically reject biculturalism. They consider Canada to be a country that is officially bilingual but fundamentally multicultural. In reply to this objection we wish to repeat that in our view biculturalism covers two main realities. The first is the state of each of the two cultures [of the founders of Confederation] and the opportunity to exist and flourish. The second is the coexistence and collaboration of those two cultures: the basically bicultural nature of our country and the subsequent contributions made by other cultures. It is thus clear that we must not overlook Canadian cultural diversity keeping in mind that there are two dominant cultures, the French and the British.[2]

The commissioners even created a metaphor for what they intended, saying that immigrants "continue to flourish and benefit through their integration with one of the two societies. Thus streams enter a river and their waters mix and swell the river's flow. Nothing should prevent those of other than British and French origin from keeping their attachment to their original culture once they have integrated into Canadian life." Volume IV concluded that in a multi-ethnic society such as Canada's, only an ongoing process of integration could ensure respect for "both the spirit of democracy and the most deep-seated human values [and]...engender healthy diversity within a harmonious and dynamic whole."

The commission did recognize that Canada's Aboriginal people were left dangling by biculturalism. It noted that integration was not working for the Aboriginal Peoples and that assimilation would be even worse. But the report resolved nothing, saying simply that the matter was beyond its mandate. The commission was willing to deal with English-speaking Canadians, French-speaking Canadians, and Canadians who had arrived just a few years before, but it was not prepared to deal with Canada's First Peoples.

The Vertical Mosaic

In 1965, John Porter, a University of Toronto sociologist, wrote *The Vertical Mosaic*. Porter analyzed the ethnic backgrounds of the elites in Canadian society and found that those with a British background were overrepresented. He also found that in Quebec, French-speaking people were rapidly gaining similar power. The idea of Canadian society as a "mosaic" was already popular. Unlike the American "melting pot," where immigrants were encouraged to adopt the habits and traditions of people already in the country, the mosaic described people with cultural differences coming together to make a country. What Porter said was that the mosaic was inherently unfair to most ethnic groups. It was not horizontal, with everyone equal. Instead, it was vertical, with some groups at the top and others below. He concluded that it was a dangerous model: "It seems inescapable that the strong emphasis on ethnic differentiation can result only in those continuing dual loyalties which prevent the emergence of any clear Canadian identity." Porter's book was the first important study of Canadian society that revealed it to be a society based on class. Though that notion is a common one today, it was a revelation in the mid-1960s.

The Government Chooses Multiculturalism

Ottawa had two sources, the Royal Commission and *The Vertical Mosaic,* that described Canadian society's ethnic diversity, and both agreed that the diversity was unhealthy. But the government was also hearing from ethnic communities that they were very unhappy about being overlooked in the battle between English and French.

In 1971, the federal government developed a policy of "multiculturalism within a bilingual framework." Prime Minister Pierre Trudeau told the House of Commons that Canada had two official languages, but no official culture:

> National Unity, if it is to mean anything in the deeply personal sense, must be founded on confidence in one's own individual identity; out of this can grow respect for that of others and a willingness to share ideas, attitudes, and assumptions. A vigorous policy of multiculturalism will help create this initial confidence. It can form the base of a society which is based on fair play for all.[3]

Canada became the first country in the world to adopt an official multiculturalism policy. In its policy, the government stated it would

- support ethnic groups in their efforts to preserve their cultures
- help members of all ethnic groups to overcome cultural barriers to full participation in Canadian society
- promote interchange among ethnic groups to encourage cultures to share their heritage

- help immigrants learn at least one of Canada's official languages so that they can participate fully in the country's economic and social life

At first, there was little controversy over multiculturalism. Some ethnic minorities complained that language and culture were inseparable and therefore multiculturalism without multilingualism was meaningless. Critics of multiculturalism were blunt in their views, saying that Canada would be reduced to "some kind of ethnic zoo where the function of the zookeeper is to collect as many varieties as possible and exhibit them once a year in some carnival where one can go from booth to booth sampling pizza, wonton soup, and kosher pastries."[4] The government was quick to argue against such ideas by saying that Canada's identity would not be undermined by multiculturalism. It stated that cultural pluralism was the "very essence" of Canadian identity. In a speech to the Ukrainian-Canadian Congress in 1971, Prime Minister Trudeau said:

> The fabric of Canadian society is as resilient as it is colourful. It is a multicultural society; it offers to every Canadian the opportunity to fulfil his or her cultural instincts and to share those from other sources. The mosaic pattern, and the moderation which it includes and encourages, makes Canada a very special place.[5]

When he was Governor General many years later, Romeo LeBlanc emphasized how firmly the policy was entrenched by quoting Phil Fontaine, Grand Chief of the Assembly of First Nations: "Canada can have no greater strength than to be seen as a society that respects the differences that exist among its people, in its languages, cultures, values, and histories, and that thrives and builds on that diversity. We are one people, one country."[6]

Canada's Aboriginal people had been entirely ignored by the multiculturalism policy. In Quebec, the policy was seen as another threat to the preservation of the French culture. Quebec believed that instead of consolidating their position as one of two major cultures in Canada, the policy of multiculturalism had reduced them to just another culture of many.

Human Rights

The first concrete programs of the multiculturalism policy stressed support for teaching "heritage" languages and providing money to establish cultural centres and such learning opportunities as folk dancing classes. But then the government (not just the Liberal government of the early 1970s, but also every subsequent government as well) moved to give practical meaning to the notion that all Canadians should have equal opportunities in life. The government put in place a framework to fight discrimination against newly arrived immigrants and their offspring. The Canadian Human Rights Act of 1977 prohibited discrimination in federal departments and federally regulated industries (airlines, banks, etc.) on grounds that included race, colour, and ethnic origin. A year later, the Canadian Human Rights Commission was established to enforce the law. Its mandate is to

- provide effective and timely means for resolving individual complaints
- promote knowledge of human rights in Canada and encourage people to follow principles of equality
- help reduce barriers to equality in employment and access to services

Canadians who feel they have been victims of discrimination can file a complaint with the Commission, and if it finds discrimination has occurred, it can order that it be ended.

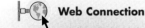 **Web Connection**

www.mcgrawhill.ca/links/definingcanada
Go to the Web site above to find out more about the Canadian Human Rights Commission.

Entrenchment of Multiculturalism in the *Constitution*

In 1982, the Canadian *Constitution* formally recognized Canada as a multicultural society. Going even further, it told the courts to interpret the *Charter of Rights and Freedoms* "in a manner consistent with the preservation and enhancement of the multicultural heritage of Canada."

In 1988, Parliament approved the Canadian Multiculturalism Act, which said that Canada understands that "multiculturalism is a fundamental characteristic of the Canadian heritage and identity and that it provides an invaluable resource in the shaping of Canada's future." The Act was updated in 1997, and federal institutions were ordered to carry out their activities in a manner that is "sensitive and responsive" to the multicultural reality. For example, those institutions should ensure that Canadians of all ethnic backgrounds have equal opportunity to obtain employment and secure promotions.

Employment Equity

In 1984, a Royal Commission chaired by Rosalie Abella tried to find ways to promote equality in employment for four designated groups: women, Aboriginal people, people with disabilities, and visible minorities. She concluded that equality does not always mean treating people equally, but rather "treating them as equals by accommodating their differences."

In the United States, the concepts of "affirmative action" (ensuring that you make minority candidates successful) and "quotas" (ensuring that minorities win a certain percentage of positions) were perceived negatively. Any attempt to change the rules so that minorities emerged with a greater percentage of jobs or places in universities was seen as reverse discrimination. Abella, however, said her solution was different and she came up with a Canadian term: "employment equity." In 1986, the Employment Equity Act was passed. Companies with more than one hundred employees were ordered to count women, Aboriginal people, people with disabilities, and visible minorities and report which groups were underrepresented as compared with their percentage of the overall population. The Act was amended in

1995 to include not just federal departments, but also agencies under federal control. If companies and departments see that minorities are underrepresented, they should take measures to improve the percentage, but they are not legally bound to do so.

This was a fundamental change in government intervention. It involved the government not just guaranteeing equal opportunity for all Canadians, but also trying to guarantee equal outcomes. The government said it would rather rely on a voluntary approach to employment equity, but it stated that "voluntary compliance has not been successful to any great degree."

Adopting Multiculturalism in the Provinces

In 1974, Saskatchewan was the first province to adopt legislation on multiculturalism. Today, every province has its own version of a multiculturalism policy, and they are very similar in their stated purposes. In Ontario, the Ministry of Citizenship and Culture is responsible for the promotion of multiculturalism, and it is mandated to "stress full participation of all Ontarians as equal members of the community." British Columbia's Multiculturalism Act says its goals are to recognize the diversity of the province and ensure the "free and full participation of all individuals in British Columbia society." The Manitoba Multiculturalism Act seeks to achieve "equal opportunity for all" in the province. Quebec calls its policy "interculturalism" and is concerned with accepting and respecting culturally diverse groups, but only within a framework that has established the unquestioned supremacy of French in the province's language and culture. Its policy is to help integrate ethnic communities into Quebec society. (The sensitivity of this area and the frustration of French-speaking Quebec with its inability to fold new immigrants into the majority culture were never more apparent than on the night of the 1995 Quebec referendum. When it was clear he had lost, Premier Jacques Parizeau bitterly blamed the result on "money and the ethnic vote.")

The Critics of Multiculturalism

At the federal level, every political party except the Canadian Alliance supports government assistance of ethnic communities that seek to preserve their heritage. The Canadian Alliance says it recognizes the country as a place "where people of different races and cultural backgrounds live and work together as Canadians, and we welcome the resulting cultural enrichment and enhanced economic prosperity." But it also states that "[w]hile cherishing our diversity, we believe that multiculturalism is a personal choice and should not be publicly funded." This position is not particularly radical; in 1991, the Citizens' Forum on Canada's Future (also known as the Spicer Commission), established by the government to help it find solutions to its constitutional conundrums, consulted more than 400 000 Canadians reporting that "[o]verwhelmingly, participants told us that reminding us of our different origins is less useful in building a united country than emphasizing the things we have in common."[7]

The Forum found widespread opposition to multiculturalism, even in ethnic communities. The Muslim Women's Study Circle told the Forum, "Ethnic Canadians find it hard to identify themselves as Canadians because they're always asked about their roots." And another participant said, "The effect of your multiculturalism is that nobody is Canadian. Instead everyone remains what he was before he came here, and 'Canadian' merely means the monetary unit and the passport."[8]

In 1994 Neil Bissoondath, a Canadian novelist born in Trinidad, wrote a book called *The Cult of Multiculturalism in Canada*. He states that multiculturalism has led immigrants to adopt a "psychology of separation" from the mainstream culture and that it encourages them to cling to their ancestral culture to the point where "there" is more important than "here." Bissoondath suggests that governments channel their energies into fighting racism and sensitizing people to other cultures, but leave the preservation of other cultures to individuals.

Prime Minister Chrétien has made it clear that the federal government still believes in its policy of multiculturalism. In October 1999, in a House of Commons speech looking ahead to Canada in the twenty-first century, Chrétien said, "We have established a distinct Canadian way, a distinct Canadian model: Accommodation of cultures. Recognition of diversity. A partnership between citizens and state. A balance that promotes individual freedom and economic prosperity while at the same time sharing risks and benefits."[9]

Review...Reflect...Respond

1. What factors led the Canadian government to adopt its policy of multiculturalism?

2. Why do some people believe that the policy of multiculturalism is a negative factor in Canadian unity?

3. The Spicer Commission noted that many Canadians felt that multiculturalism should not be funded by the government. Do you agree or disagree? Why?

The Roots of Modern Separatism

Tension has existed between French and English Canada almost since the first European settlements were founded here. Many French Quebeckers did not want to enter Confederation in 1867, and that feeling has remained in Quebec ever since. In the 1960s and early 1970s, there were violent reminders of Quebec's desire to separate. The FLQ bombings and attacks on federal symbols such as mailboxes and armouries, and the kidnapping of a foreign diplomat and murder of a provincial cabinet minister created a climate of mistrust and to the denunciation of the separatist movement.

The first time separatists organized themselves into political parties was for the 1966 Quebec election. The *Rassemblement pour l'independence*

nationale (RIN) and the *Ralliement Nationale* (RN) won 8.8 percent of the vote between them but no seats. These were hard-line separatists, who seemed to have as their primary motivation revenge against the English. Their goal was the separation of Quebec from the rest of Canada, but there was no serious, meticulous, carefully explored plan for how to make Quebec a nation, probably because they never expected to win an election.

René Lévesque

The personification of Quebec separatism came to be embodied by René Lévesque. He was perhaps the best-known journalist in Quebec, a star on the French network of the CBC. He then became an energetic member of the provincial Liberal Party

René Lévesque was a popular journalist before he turned to a career in politics.

cabinet from 1960 until the Liberals lost power in 1966. Reduced to the role of backbencher, Lévesque began to explore his options for the future. He tried to push the provincial liberals to adopt what he called an "Option for Quebec." It was Lévesque's vision for a new homeland: "We are Québécois. We are attached to this one corner of the earth where we can be completely ourselves." He wrote that Canada as "two nations in a single country has had its day." He went on to say that Quebec needed control over its own citizenship, immigration, employment, welfare, industry, and certain aspects of foreign policy. His conclusion was that "Quebec must become sovereign as soon as possible." He was open to an association with Canada for such things as the postal system, currency, and defence, but negotiations would be between equal countries. The Liberals rejected Lévesque's proposal and he quit the party. In October 1968, he founded a party of his own—the *Parti Québécois* (PQ). The PQ would become the prime instrument of the democratic movement to make Quebec independent from Canada.

Charles de Gaulle: *"Vive le Québec Libre!"*

One of the many visitors to Canada during its centennial year 1967 was the president of France, Charles de Gaulle. De Gaulle's arrival in Quebec City was greeted by huge crowds. The next day, he rode in a long convoy of limousines from Quebec City to Montreal, with people lining most of the roadway, waving and cheering enthusiastically. When de Gaulle arrived at Montreal's city hall, about seven thousand people were waiting for him, and he stepped onto a balcony to address the crowd: "Here tonight and all along the route I found myself in an atmosphere like that of the Liberation." He was referring to the liberation of France from Nazi occupation in 1945. De Gaulle continued. "I take with me an imperishable memory of this extraordinary meeting. France knows, sees, and hears what is going on here. *Vive Montréal! Vive le Québec! Vive le Québec libre!*" The crowd exploded. De Gaulle was puzzled. He turned to ask the Quebec premier what had set off the tremendous uproar. When told he had repeated the slogan of a separatist party, he was oblivious to the impact his remark would have.

The rest of Canada was outraged. Prime Minister Pearson convened a cabinet meeting to decide on a response to de Gaulle's statements. Telegrams and phone calls from ordinary citizens demanded that de Gaulle be reprimanded. Pearson's statement was forceful: "The people of Canada are free. Every province of Canada is free. Canadians do not need to be liberated." De Gaulle was supposed to come to Ottawa from Montreal, but the French president cancelled the trip. Although the cause of separatism probably was not advanced by de Gaulle, it was an electrifying moment and exposed how sensitive all of Canada was to the issue of Quebec separation.

In 1967, Charles de Gaulle, President of France made Québécois cheer—but the rest of Canada was outraged.

Canadian Leaders

PETER GZOWSKI — "MR. CANADA"

"Good morning... I'm Peter Gzowski... this is *Morningside.*" Every weekday morning for fifteen years, Canadians reached for their radio dials to hear this popular host of CBC's three-hour morning show. The reassuring, familiar voice drifted on the airways into thousands of homes across the nation. Peter Gzowski (pronounced zaw – ski) cared deeply about Canada, its people, its places and possibilities, and he invited listeners to join him on an unhurried journey to explore the majesty of their great country.

Peter Gzowski was born in Toronto and raised in the southwestern Ontario town of Galt. His high school years were spent at Galt Collegiate Institute and Ridley College in St. Catharines. After graduation from Ridley, he attended the University of Toronto, where he became editor of the student newspaper, *The Varsity.* Following university, he pursued a career in journalism, including assignments as editor at the *Moose Jaw Times Herald* and editor/writer at *Maclean's.* Although his early years were spent as a reporter, an editor and a writer, he became a prominent Canadian figure when he turned to radio.

As host of *Morningside,* Peter Gzowski became one of the best-loved radio voices in Canada. His wit, warmth, and gentle humour enriched the daily broadcast of personal essays, interviews, debate, drama, and music. He interviewed, not only dignitaries and celebrities, but also ordinary people from every corner of the country. He discussed a wide range of topics, from the Meech Lake Accord and the GST, to cross-country skiing and homemade raspberry jam. The engaging conversations kept Canadians connected, and gave them a sense of pride in their nation. "What was hugely important," Gzowski has said, "was we kept people in touch."

Although he earned fame as a broadcaster, Gzowski admitted that he "still thought of himself, if anyone asked, as a writer who was working in radio for a while." He wrote monthly magazine columns, national newspaper columns, and several successful books. His patriotism was as evident in his writing as it was in his discussions on the radio. In an essay written at Sioux Lookout, Ontario, Gzowski reports, "It's stunning country and very Canadian: lakes, rivers, hardrock, spruce."

Because reading and writing were so important to his life, Gzowski had a sincere concern for non-readers. This interest led him to organize golf tournaments called the Peter Gzowski Invitationals, which have raised millions of dollars to fund programmes to encourage adults to learn to read. The tournaments, which have been held in every province and all three territories, are cultural events with poetry readings and live music, raising money to promote, not only English and French, but also Aboriginal language and literacy.

Gzowski's passion for the North is reflected in his description of a golf tournament held at Pond Inlet, a hamlet four hundred miles inside the Arctic Circle,

We had journeyed there in late spring when the sea ice was still solid. On the ice, the people of the North had built us a golf course, scraping away the snow to make fairways and "greens" (whites, really, with brightly coloured flags planted in frozen holes). Our clubhouse would be an igluvigaq of snow. Dog teams would drive us out to the tees. Pale icebergs the size of triplexes towered in the background, and behind them, across the glistening white of Eclipse sound, loomed the majestic Bylot mountains.

Gzowski's success as a broadcaster and a writer earned him many distinguished awards including the Governor General's Arts Award for Lifetime Achievement in Broadcasting. He won seven Alliance of Canadian Television and Radio Artists awards. He was named a Companion of the Order of Canada and was a member of the Canadian News Hall of Fame. In 1997, he was presented with a Peabody Award for Outstanding Contribution to Broadcasting – the only Canadian ever to have received the award for work as an individual.

Both as a celebrated Canadian radio personality and as a talented writer, Peter Gzowski touched the lives of millions of people. Through his curiosity and candor, Canadians learned who they were. He was the voice of Canada, defining what it means to be Canadian.

Peter Gzowski 1934–2002.

Quebec Elections

The Quebec liberals, with their new leader, Robert Bourassa, won the 1970 Quebec election easily. But in its first election campaign, René Lévesque's *Parti Québécois* of won 23 percent of the vote. It was a phenomenal performance for the separatists. They won only seven seats because the province's electoral system still represented rural voters disproportionately. Lévesque lost his own seat (the seat he had held as a Liberal since 1960), but at his election night rally, he asked supporters, "Don't you find that this defeat has the smell of victory?"

In 1973, the PQ increased its share of the vote to 30 percent but won just six seats. However, the other opposition parties collapsed, leaving the PQ as the official opposition.

Étapisme

At this point, the *Parti Québécois* adopted a strategy that turned out to be its path to power. Claude Morin, who would become Lévesque's first intergovernmental affairs minister, said it was clear that some Quebeckers would never vote for the PQ as long as they felt they were simultaneously voting for Quebec independence. Morin suggested that the PQ run the next election campaign by promising nothing more than good government and stating that a vote for the PQ was not a vote for separation. The strategy was called *étapisme* (gradualism or sovereignty in stages).

In the Quebec provincial election campaign of 1976, Lévesque told voters that it was safe to vote for the PQ even if they were opposed to Quebec independence. He said that his party would not take victory as a mandate to separate but as a mandate to govern well. He said the issue of independence would be left to a referendum. It was an appeal to the so-called soft nationalists, people who liked the idea of a stronger Quebec but who were not ready for independence.

That strategy, along with a Liberal government that had become corrupt, pushed the PQ to victory. November 15, 1976, was a turning point in Canadian

The 1976 election in Quebec—a turning point in Canada's history.

history. Even though opinion polls had indicated that a PQ victory was possible, the result was nonetheless stunning. On television, one CBC reporter summed it up by saying: "The PQ is in power and Canada is in trouble."

The Federalists and Separatism

In English Canada, reaction to separatist sentiment in Quebec fell within a broad range. At one end were those who simply said that Quebec could leave if it did no want to be a part of Canada. At the other end were those willing to make any concession that Quebec demanded in exchange for the province remaining part of Canada. The majority were anxious to find a way to earn the province's enduring attachment to Canada.

Every major effort to make Quebec feel like a full partner in Confederation focused on the *Constitution*. The British North America (BNA) Act defined Canada as a country, but it had been drawn up for a colony of Great Britain. There was no provision to amend it, other than through another act of the British Parliament. When Canada became independent after the Statute of Westminster, several formulas were proposed for amendments, but no agreement was reached at federal-provincial conferences in 1927, 1935, and 1950.

The Fulton-Favreau Formula

In 1964 and 1965 two successive federal ministers of justice, Davey Fulton and Guy Favreau, worked to devise a new formula for amending the *Constitution*. Quebec had rejected earlier proposals because it believed that a majority of English provinces would impose a system that would not be favourable to Quebec and French Canadians.

Fulton and Favreau contemplated unanimous consent by all the provinces and the federal government to make important changes. This approach would give Quebec a veto. But the formula also proposed that two thirds of the provinces had to agree to any new powers for Quebec. The English provinces agreed, but Quebec rejected the notion that a majority of provinces could block its efforts to procure additional powers.

The Victoria Charter

Seven federal-provincial conferences took place between 1968 and 1971. The last was held in Victoria in June 1971, and it came close to being a successful conference. There seemed to be agreement on every issue among Ottawa, Quebec, and the other provinces: Quebec would have its veto over constitutional change, language rights would be promoted across the country, three justices of the Supreme Court would come from Quebec, a charter of rights would exist, and the *Constitution* would be patriated (brought home as a Canadian document rather than a British one). But when Quebec asked for more control over social policy, Prime Minister Trudeau decided the demand would leave the federal government as nothing more than a tax collector for the provinces, and so he rejected the demand. In response, Quebec Premier Robert Bourassa then rejected all the other changes, and the Victoria Charter failed to pass.

Language Laws

Quebec's place in Canada has always been tangled in the issue of language. By the early 1960s, it became an accepted opinion among francophone Quebeckers that the French language would gradually disappear from North America unless measures were taken to protect it.

Bill 63

In 1969, the Quebec government passed the first of its language laws, Bill 63. To resolve a suburban Montreal school board's clash with some parents over the language of instruction for children whose mother tongue was neither French nor English, the

Riots erupted, caused by the Common Front for a French Quebec, outside the National Assembly during the debate on Bill 63.

government decided that the teaching of French in English schools would be improved. But it guaranteed the right of immigrant parents to choose either English or French schools for their children. Most French-speaking Quebeckers were aghast. A group calling itself "The Common Front for a French Quebec" said, "Giving parents a choice [of language instruction] is the equivalent of giving the English language a legal status equal to the French language." Riots erupted outside the Quebec National Assembly as the bill was debated.

Bill 22

The passing of Bill 22 in 1974 was an attempt to promote and protect French in Quebec while protecting minority rights as well. Bill 22 declared that French was the only official language in the province. It also ordered all businesses to deal with the public, the government, and its employees in French. It forced businesses to use a French name and to advertise primarily in French. (The most famous example was the name change of Eaton's department stores. They removed the "apostrophe s" and became "Eaton." Steinberg's supermarkets became Steinberg.)

Unlike Bill 63, Bill 22 sharply limited parents' rights to choose the language in which their children would be educated. Although the bill guaranteed English Quebeckers access to English schools, it also stated that children who did not already speak English must attend French schools. To determine

A French-only sign?

whether children spoke English, the government set up a testing system for four- and five-year-olds. Only the children of parents who had gone to English schools were exempt from taking the tests.

English Quebec was so unhappy that it abandoned the Liberal Party in the 1976 election, contributing to the election of the *Parti Québécois*. Canadians outside Quebec saw Bill 22 as a slap in the face. It seemed to them that just as they were beginning to accept French as an official language, Quebec was turning its back on the English language.

Bill 101

The PQ government's Charter of the French Language in 1977 was a signature piece of legislation. It proclaimed French as the only language that could be used in every important facet of official life. The government, the judiciary, schools, advertising, and businesses were all subject to the law. English education was restricted to the children of Quebeckers who had been educated in English in Quebec.[10] Outdoor signs on commercial establishments were to be in French only.

Bill 101 became a symbol of division between Quebec and the rest of Canada. Francophones believed that Bill 101 was necessary for the protection of their threatened language and culture. Anglophones saw it as an undisguised attempt to eradicate English from Quebec. In the twenty years following the passage of Bill 22, as many as 400000 anglophone Quebeckers moved out of the province. Many businesses left as well, most notably the head office of the giant insurance company Sun Life, which had been located in Montreal since 1871.

The exodus changed the nature of Anglo-Quebec. Those who remain have accepted the fact that they must do much of their living and working in French. Today, two out of three English-speaking Quebeckers also speak French. In the rest of Canada, the figure is one in eleven.

Protesting Bill 101.

The First Referendum

In 1979, the PQ government was ready for its next step in *étapisme*. It had promised Quebec voters a referendum on independence, and the time had come. Recent polls, however, showed that a minority of Quebeckers wanted true independence from Canada, so the wording of the question on the referendum was crucial. René Lévesque knew he could not win if the referendum asked "Do you support Quebec becoming an independent country?"

Lévesque proposed the idea of limited independence, which he called "sovereignty-association." Quebec would be sovereign, but it would keep close economic ties to Canada. The question to the voters became

The government of Quebec has made public its proposal to negotiate a new agreement with

A house divided—Quebec votes Yes or No.

the rest of Canada, based on the equality of nations; This agreement would enable Quebec to acquire the exclusive power to make its laws, levy its taxes and establish relations abroad—in other words, sovereignty—and, at the same time, to maintain with Canada an economic association including a common currency; No change in political status resulting from these negotiations will be effected without approval by the people through another referendum; On these terms, do you give the government of Quebec the mandate to negotiate the proposed agreement between Quebec and Canada?[11]

Lévesque called it a "transparent" question. Pierre Trudeau called it a "trick" question.

Lévesque made the mistake at one referendum campaign rally of mocking Prime Minister Trudeau's name: "His name is Pierre Elliott Trudeau and this is the Elliott side taking over, and that's the English side, so we French Canadians in Quebec can't expect any sympathy from him." In Montreal at a NO-rally against the referendum, Trudeau responded to Lévesque's name-calling:

> Of course my name is Pierre Elliott Trudeau. Elliott was my mother's name. It was the name borne by the Elliotts who came to Canada more than two hundred years ago. It was the name of the Elliotts who, more than one hundred years ago, settled in Saint-Gabriel-de-Brandon, where you can still see their names on the tombstones in the cemetery. That is who the Elliotts are. My name is a Quebec name. But my name is a Canadian name also. And that's my name.[12]

At the same rally, Trudeau made a crucial promise,

> Following a NO vote, we will immediately take action to renew the Constitution and we will not stop until we have done that. And I make a solemn declaration to Canadians in the other provinces: we, the Quebec MPs, are laying ourselves on the line, because we are telling Quebeckers to vote NO and telling you in the other provinces that we will not agree to you interpreting a NO vote as an indication that everything is fine and can remain as it was before.[13]

On May 20, 1980, Quebec voters went to the poll. The NO vote was 59.6 percent. The YES vote was 40.4 percent. It was a major setback for Lévesque and the *Parti Québécois*.

Patriation of the *Constitution*

Trudeau went to work to fulfill his referendum promise within three weeks. He invited all the premiers to Ottawa for an informal discussion on the *Constitution*. Trudeau was determined that this round of talks would succeed. A few weeks later, as another federal-provincial conference was set to begin, the provinces presented Trudeau with a new set of demands. In response, Trudeau dropped a bombshell and announced that he was prepared to take unilateral action and to go to Britain without the provinces to demand patriation of the *Constitution*. Sterling Lyon, the premier of Manitoba said, "If you do that, you're going to tear the country apart." Trudeau responded, "If the country is going to be torn apart because we bring back from Britain our own *Constitution* after 115 years of Confederation, and because we have asked for a Canadian charter of rights, then the country deserves to be torn up."

Trudeau's vision of a Canadian charter of rights would fundamentally change how Canada worked. Under the British system, Parliament had the final say on everything. With a charter, certain basic rights are guaranteed no matter what

Parliament subsequently believes. The courts are empowered to uphold charter rights over and above the will of Parliament. That inevitably means that individual rights become more important than collective rights. A legislature might decide to pass a law that benefits most people even if some people are harmed. But a court upholding a charter of rights is forced to ensure that no one is denied their rights. Trudeau wanted to guarantee that protection.

The Gang of Eight

Only Ontario and New Brunswick supported Trudeau's plan to go it alone. The other provinces, the so-called Gang of Eight, took Ottawa to court, arguing that it was illegal for the federal government to pursue constitutional patriation unilaterally. The Supreme Court disagreed and said it was legal, though it was unconventional. The Gang of Eight also came up with their own proposal for constitutional change. It did not include the *Charter of Rights and Freedoms* and was unacceptable to Trudeau. One last round of bargaining was set for November 1981. That round had almost collapsed when a compromise deal was struck late one night among federal cabinet minister Jean Chrétien and ministers from Saskatchewan (Roy Romanow) and Ontario (Roy McMurtry).

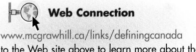

Web Connection

www.mcgrawhill.ca/links/definingcanada

Go to the Web site above to learn more about the *Charter of Rights and Freedoms*.

The point in argument was a "notwithstanding" clause the provinces were insisting on. They wanted the *Constitution* to say that a provincial legislature could override the *Charter of Rights* by inserting a paragraph into any bill acknowledging that it was contravening the *Charter*, but "notwithstanding" that contravention, the law was valid.

The 20th Anniversary of the Constitution: Something to Celebrate?

April 17, 2002 marked the twentieth anniversary of the patriation of Canada's constitution. While many celebrated the date and spoke about the importance of the Charter of Rights and Freedoms, others chose to use the date to focus on Canadians who still do not feel a part of Canada. In this article, Quebec sovereigntist Guy Bouthillier, believes that there is nothing to celebrate about a constitution that excludes a quarter of Canadians.

English Canada is celebrating today, but should it be?... For 10 years after Pierre Trudeau's 1982 coup, leaders tried to right the wrong and bring Quebec on board in a spirit of "honour and enthusiasm." Any dreams of honour and enthusiasm, however, were doused when Meech Lake and Charlottetown were rejected by English Canada, and then eliminated as the unilateral politics of the Liberals prevailed once again....

In 1982, instead of drafting a new Constitution and having it approved by the people, the Trudeau government chose to take the British document and add two new sets of provisions, a Charter and an amending formula whose net effect was to make power even more elusive for our elected representatives. For instance, the Charter specifically reduced the power of the Quebec National Assembly in matters of education and language.

Many people are trying to give the 1982 Charter of Rights and Freedoms an enhanced role in forging a Canadian national identity, especially in light of Canada's perceived loss of influence and sovereignty since September 11 [2001]....

Any discussion of the national identity, however, requires that we talk about the other national identity, the one that, according to Mr. Trudeau and Jean Chrétien, should be quietly disappearing. Well, surprise! It's not. Self-identification of Quebeckers as Quebeckers has grown steadily since the 1960s, and even faster since 1982....

Quebec has also developed in ways that many Canadians, due to a kind of historical prejudice, would have thought impossible. The key to success has been the innovative decisions made largely by Quebec's nationalist leaders, often despite Ottawa and the Constitution....

On the question of aboriginal nations and territorial integrity, often seen as our Achilles' heel, our sovereigntist government recently reached ground-breaking agreements and has been described by aboriginal leaders as "a model for Canada and the world."

And while there's been little talk of sovereignty for the past seven years, support for it remains at about 42 per cent, higher than it was just months before the 1995 referendum.

Time has therefore not brought Quebec and Canada closer together. All the cheering about the 1982 Charter cannot drown out the thundering facts that Quebec has not signed the fundamental law of this country and is not about to, that no political formation in English-speaking Canada is making any effort to correct the situation, and that Quebec's national identity has flourished even though the Constitution refuses to recognize it.

During a visit to Canada in 1943, Franklin Roosevelt declared in French: "Canada is a nation founded on the union of two races. The harmony of their association as equals can be an example to all of humanity—an example that holds throughout the world."

Since 1982, no visiting president could honestly make such a statement. As English Canadians wring their hands about their loss of influence and sovereignty in the world, perhaps they should start looking for answers in the fundamental law of their country, which is more like the fundamental flaw.

GUY BOUTHILLIER, "A DARK DAY IN HISTORY" IN
***THE GLOBE AND MAIL* (WEDNESDAY, APRIL 17, 2002).**

1. Who does Bouthillier blame for what he refers to as Canada's "fundamental flaw"?
2. Find two primary sources that you could use to read alternative views of the 20th anniversary of the patriation of the Constitution. Did they alter your views of what Bouthillier had to say?

Trudeau did not agree with the "notwithstanding" clause. He later wrote,

I saw the charter as an expression of my long-held view that the subject of law must be the individual human being; the law must permit the individual to fulfil himself or herself to the utmost. Therefore the individual has certain basic rights that cannot be taken away by any government. So maintaining an unweakened charter was important to me in this basic philosophical sense.[14]

But the deal was now too tempting for Trudeau to turn away. The federal government and nine provinces had agreed to bring home Canada's *Constitution*. The *Constitution* would have its *Charter*, but it would also have a "notwithstanding" clause.

René Lévesque felt that he had been betrayed by the seven other premiers in the gang of eight. He had not been consulted about the compromise, nor would he ever have agreed to it. He said, "I have been stabbed in the back during the night." It became known in Quebec as "The Night of the Long Knives."[15] Lévesque held an angry news conference where he warned that the consequences of the betrayal were "incalculable."

The *Constitution* Comes Home

The Queen came to Canada in April 1982, and on the seventeenth day of the month, at a ceremony on Parliament Hill, she affixed her signature to the Constitution Act. It was a singular moment for Canada—an act of nationhood achieved without revolution, rebellion, or bloodshed. The separatists had provided the impetus and Canada now had control of its *Constitution*. Quebec was bound by its terms, but the fact that it was not a willing partner would create further problems for the province and Canada.

Western Separatism

The issue of separatism in Quebec has long held centre stage in the country. But for as long as there has been a Canada, there has also been unhappiness in the west about its role in Confederation. From John A. Macdonald's National Policy, through Louis Riel and freight rates, to much more modern irritants such as bilingualism, metrication, and the NEP, the west has felt that it is alienated from central Canada. Westerners often say that federal politicians serve the interests of Ontario and Quebec. In federal elections since 1968, the Liberals have often formed huge majority governments even though they have won just a handful of seats west of Ontario.

Over the years, political parties have begun to try to better represent the west, with the Progressive Party, the United Farmers, and the Western Canada Concept among them. The Canadian Alliance was born from the Reform Party in the 1990s. It has tried to broaden its appeal across Canada, but it has so far failed to gain significant strength outside the west.

Queen Elizabeth II signs the Constitution Act in 1982.

We have come a long way in terms of cartoon portrayals of our national identity and our comic book super heroes. During the nineteenth century, political cartoonists created symbols for nations. The domineering John Bull represented the colonizing power of Great Britain, while the towering Uncle Sam stood for the United States. The young and impressionable Canada, on the other hand, was frequently personified as a young woman courted by John Bull or Uncle Sam.

From about 1860, editorial cartoonists began depicting Canada as Johnny, or Jack, Canuck. Johnny was a wholesome, simple-minded young fellow, who might wear habitant's, farmer's, logger's, rancher's, or

sodier's clothes. As Canada expanded westward, Johnny Canuck's clothing became more Western, and was frequently accessorized by knee-high leather boots and a Stetson.

ZAP!... BOOM!.... WHAM!...POW! Flash forward to the Second World War, when a foreign exchange crisis led to a Canadian ban on American comic books such as the highly popular Superman (co-created by Canadian native Joe Shuster), Flash Gordon, Captain Marvel, and Batman. The need to fill the super-hero vacuum ignited an explosion in Canadian comic book publishing. As a result, 1940 to 1947 is sometimes called the "Canadian Golden Age of Comics." The first super hero on the scene was Iron Man, who debuted in March, 1941. However, Iron Man lacked a distinct Canadian identity.

Other Canadian super heroes quickly followed, among them Freelance and, in April of 1941, Nelvana of the Northern Lights. Nelvana was the daughter of the King of the Northern Lights. A powerful heroine, Nelvana symbolized Canada's North, as she battled Axis enemies from real life, and assorted science fiction villains. She had the distinction of preceding the first US super heroine, Wonder Woman, by three months. Later, Nelvana was joined by other Canadian super heroines such as Elaine Kenyon, The Polka-Dot Pirate, and Trixie Rogers. Soon after the ban on American comics was lifted in 1947, however, most Canadian comic book publishing ended.

In the early 1970s Canadian alternative and underground publishers emerged, and with them a second generation of national super heroes. The first national super hero to appear in Canadian comics after the Golden Age was Captain Canada, who debuted in 1972 in the Ottawa-based satirical magazine *Fuddle Duddle*. Captain Canada's adventures spoofed US super heroes and Canadian attitudes. For example, one story pitted him against the treacherous Media-Master, who was bent on world domination.

In July 1975 Captain Canuck sprang into action as the first, full-colour Canadian super hero comic to appear since 1947. Captain Canuck wrapped himself in the national flag, wore red tights and "electro-thermic underwear" for warmth, and on his forehead sported a red maple leaf. Captain Canuck was an agent of the Canadian International Security Organization. His adventures were set in the future — the1990s! — when Canada would be a world superpower.

In French Canada, until the 1970s, comic books were largely dominated by religious content. However, in 1973 a group of young comic creators known as L'Hydrocephale entete created Quebec's first national superhero comic, *Les Aventures du Capitaine Kebec*.

The1980s saw the emergence of two very different types of Canadian comic super heroes. One was a new incarnation of Captain Canada. This version starred in a colour graphic novel *Atlantis*. In one novel page, Captain Canada flew past the Peace Tower after waging a fierce battle with a giant robot that had wrecked part of downtown Ottawa. A more sophisticated Canadian hero is seen in the comic *Northguard*. In one adventure, the young protagonist, Phillip Wise, thwarts an attempt to assassinate P.Q. leader René Lévesque at a rally in the Montreal Forum.

The frustration felt by some has led to the creation of groups promoting the idea of western separation from the rest of Canada. These groups maintain that the four western provinces (Manitoba, Saskatchewan, Alberta, and British Columbia) would be economically strong if they separated from Canada, and they would not have to endure that strength being siphoned off by central and eastern Canadians. They also say that a western government would be more attuned to western attitudes, and policies such as gun control would not be adopted.

Though support for western alienation does exist, it is clear that western separation is not popular.

Most polls put support for western separation at about 7 percent of the population. Only one separatist Member of Legislative Assembly has ever been elected in the west. That was in Alberta in the early 1980s—and he was not reelected. But as supporters of western separation are keen to point out, Quebec separatism started small, and they warn that it would be foolish for the people of central Canada to ignore western grievances. Despite the fact that current support for western separatism is not high, the fact that it exists at all demonstrates that regionalism remains a concern for Canada.

Conclusion

Multiculturalism and separatism remain important parts of Canada's political and cultural identity. But their place in that identity is not settled—far from it. As we will see in the last chapter, the issues of multiculturalism and separatism continue to be debated across Canada. Together they remain one of Canada's continuing challenges—how to promote diversity through multiculturalism and yet keep the country united.

Notes

1. Government of Canada, *Royal Commission on Biculturalism and Bilingualism,* 1969.
2. Ibid.
3. Pierre Trudeau, *The House of Commons,* October 8, 1971.
4. Evelyn Kallen. 1982. "Multiculturalism: Ideology, Policy and Reality." *Journal of Canadian Studies 17,* no. 1 (spring):51–63.
5. Pierre Trudeau, *Remarks, Ukrainian-Canadian Congress,* Winnipeg, October 9, 1971.
6. Speech on the occasion of the Order of Canada Investiture, Rideau Hall, Thursday, May 7, 1998.
7. From the Uni.ca Web site, "The Spicer Commission: The 1991 Citizen's Forum on Canadian Unity."
8. Ibid.
9. Jean Chrétien, House of Commons, October 1999.
10. This was later changed by a Supreme Court decision, opening English schools to children of parents educated in English anywhere in Canada.
11. From the Uni.ca Web site, "Parti Québécois." Available online at <http://www.uni.ca/pq.html>.
12. "Pierre Trudeau Is Dead at 80; Dashing Fighter for Canada," by Michael T. Kaufman, September 29, 2000, The New York Times Company. Available online at <http://www.nytimes.com/learning/general/onthisday/bday/1018.html>.
13. Pierre Trudeau, Speech at the Paul Sauvé Arena, Montreal, Quebec, May 14, 1980. From the National Library of Canada and National Archives of Canada Web site. Available online at <http://www.nlc-bnc.ca2/4/h4-4083-e.html>.
14. Pierre Trudeau, *Memoirs* (Toronto: McClelland & Stewart, 1993).
15. The original "Night of Long Knives" was in Germany in 1934. Adolph Hitler ordered the execution nearly 400 people for allegedly trying to overthrow him. The executions came about without any formal charges being laid and without any trials.

Chapter 23 Review

Knowledge & Understanding

1. Identify these people, places, and events, and explain their historical significance to Canada's developing culture and identity.

   Multiculturalism
   Bilingualism
   'visible-minority'
   sovereignty-association
   Vertical Mosaic
   Etapisme
   Bilingualism-Biculturalism Commission
   Charter of Rights and Freedoms
   Gang of eight
   Bills 63/22/101

2. What are the basic objectives of Canada's official policy of multiculturalism? How does it relate to bilingualism and biculturalism?

Thinking & Inquiry

3. What are the difficulties in maintaining a united country while promoting diversity through muliticulturalism?

4. On CTV's program W5, Pierre Trudeau said,

   Every man has his own reasons, I suppose, as driving forces, but mine were twofold: One, to make sure Quebec wouldn't leave Canada through separatism, and the other was to make sure Canada wouldn't shove Quebec out through narrowmindedness.

   Having read this chapter, do you believe that Trudeau succeeded in meeting his goals? Write two to three well-written paragraphs that explain your opinion.

Application

5. Imagine you are a journalist from the Ottawa Citizen, and have been assigned to interview Rene Levesque on the evening of November 15, 1976. Create a list of ten interview questions that you feel the rest of Canada would like to ask Levesque about his future plans for the Parti Quebecois and Quebec. Also write down what you anticipate Levesque's answers will be.

6. As a French-Canadian living in Montreal, your family business is a restaurant that is located in the heart of the financial district. Half of your customers are English-speaking business people who are in Montreal on business. When Bill 101 is introduced you are told that all signs and menus must be in French only. What is your reaction? Write an editorial to the Montreal Gazette.

Communication

7. You have been hired by the Ministry of Multiculturalism to develop a new marketing campaign that will be used across the country. Your first task is to create a symbol or logo for the Ministry of Multiculturalism. On an regular piece of paper, design the symbol or logo that you will present to the board of managers at the Ministry of Multiculturalism. Write a two-paragraph synopsis of what your symbol is, why you chose the images, and why it will appeal to Canada's citizens.

CHAPTER 24

Moving Toward a New Millennium

Our national condition is still flexible enough that we can make almost anything we wish our nation, No other country is in a better position that Canada to go ahead with the evolution of a national purpose devoted to all that's good and noble and excellent in the human spirit.

–LESTER B. PEARSON

Canadian Marshall McLuhan, one of the foremost intellectuals of the twentieth century, coined the term "global village" to describe the growing inter-connectedness among nations. Delicately balanced with its role in the global village is Canada's continuing struggle to protect both its political and its cultural sovereignty. This chapter examines the fast pace of change in Canada since the 1980s—its leaders, economy, and culture, and its role in international conflict.

Since 1980, Canadians have seen prime ministers come and go with incredible speed. In 1979, Joe Clark of the progressive conservatives, Canada's youngest prime minister at age thirty-nine, was in office just 272 days. Leading a minority government, he made the mistake of trying to pass a budget that raised the price of gasoline eighteen cents per gallon (about four cents per litre), believing that to reduce the deficit, Canadians had to endure "short-term pain for long-term gain." He believed that the House of Commons would approve the budget. When the House voted against the price increase, Clark was forced to call a new election, and he lost. Trudeau, who had retired, was convinced to return to politics and was elected prime minister once again.

In 1984, Liberal Prime Minister John Turner stayed only 78 days in office. Taking over from Pierre Trudeau, he outraged the country by not rescinding more than seventy patronage appointments made by Trudeau on his last day in office. At election time, voters turned against the Liberal Party and voted the Conservative Party to power.

1985

Canada's political sovereignty in the Arctic is tested in the Polar Sea affair

Free Trade Agreement is passed

1989

1990

Canada sends troops to Gulf War

1992

Federal government announces a moratorium on cod fishing in response to reports that cod stocks were rapidly depleting

Roberta Bondar is first Canadian woman to go into space

1993

Somalia Affair damages honourable image of Canadian peacekeepers

The North America Free Trade Act is passed

1994

1995

Premier Mike Harris' "Common Sense Revolution" results in a backlash of labour strikes in Ontario

Turbot War erupts between Canada and Spain

Terrorist attacks on the United States launch the War on Terrorism, in which Canadian troops are involved

2001

2002

Farm incomes on the Prairies return to Depression-era levels

By the end of this chapter, you will be able to:

- describe the evolution of economic relations among North American nations, and the impact on the Canadian economy

- describe the way in which conflicts in the twentieth century altered Canadians' self-image

- demonstrate an understanding of how Canada's participation in significant international conflicts changed the way the country was perceived by the international community

- demonstrate and understanding of the causes and implications of Canadian regional differences

- analyze how Canada and Canadians have been portrayed by a writers, visual artists, musicians, composers, and filmmakers

Changing Prime Ministers

Brian Mulroney

Brian Mulroney broke the chain of short commands, holding office as prime minister from 1984 to 1993; he used that time to change some fundamental aspects of Canadian life. Mulroney had inherited huge deficits from the former Liberal government and he tried to bring the debt under control by cutting spending and reducing or eliminating many services. Canadians became used to receiving fewer government services, with funding cuts to health care and education, and the end of family allowance payments and old-age pensions to the wealthy. But each government cut made the prime minister more unpopular. Mulroney then instituted the Goods and Services Tax (GST), and though no one has come up with a better method to raise taxes, the tax has become an irritant for Canadians.

Mulroney has been accused of destroying some vital Canadian institutions. He slashed the budget of the CBC. He privatized fifteen Crown corporations including Air Canada, Petro-Canada, and Canadian National Railways. He also reduced the funding available for passenger trains such as VIA Rail. Frustrated by his critics who waxed poetic about trains and their importance to the history and identity of Canada but ignored the financial arguments, Mulroney pointed out that Canadians would do anything for their beloved trains, except take one. Nothing Brian Mulroney did created more debate than the Free Trade Agreement and the North American Free Trade Agreement.

In 1993, Canada's first female prime minister, Kim Campbell, revived the losing streak, staying in office 131 days. She had the misfortune of succeeding Brian Mulroney as the Conservative prime minister when he resigned. Mulroney had managed two consecutive majority governments, but by the time he left office, he was perhaps the most unpopular man in the country. In the election that followed, the Conservatives won just two seats. Campbell's was not one of them. When Jean Chrétien was elected, Canada had five living former prime ministers for the first time in its history.[1]

A Brian Mulroney mask. By the time Mulroney resigned he was the most unpopular person in Canada.

Jean Chrétien

As Canada's twentieth prime minister, Jean Chrétien has enjoyed three terms leading the Liberal Party and the country. During his tenure, Chrétien has had to lead Canada through the 1995 referendum on Quebec separatism, direct Canada's role in several international conflicts, and forge new economic ties using a foreign policy based on trade. Chrétien has led numerous trade missions—nicknamed "Team

Prime Minister Chrétien at his 2000 election victory celebration.

Canada"—to Asia, Latin America, and the European Union.

As the 2000 election approached, the Liberals focused on what the Canadian public was concerned about: health care, education, and the Canadian economy. The Liberals' election platform, *Opportunity for All* (nicknamed "Red Book III"), promised increased funding for health care and education, tax cuts, and a new emphasis on funding for research and development in Canada.

The increasing popularity of the Canadian Alliance Party (formerly the Reform Party) under Stockwell Day made them the Liberal Party's main competitor in the 2000 election. When voters went to the polls, however, the Liberals won a landslide majority government. Despite nearly a dozen RCMP investigations focused on suspicious federal grants, the mismanagement of more than $3 billion in grants handed out by Human Resources Development Canada, and increasing pressure from provincial premiers for greater control of spending at the federal level, Chrétien remains popular according to Canadian polls.

The Canadian Economy

As Canada moved toward the twenty-first century, it found itself dealing with issues that have been a part of Canadian history for more than one-hundred years. Closer economic ties with the United States had fostered fears that the elephant next door would slowly trample Canada's cultural and political sovereignty—an argument that had been at the forefront of the 1911 election. Within Canada's borders, the disparity between provincial economies has continued to promote regionalism within the country—an issue as old as Sir John A. Macdonald's National Policy.

Canada's Participation in a North American Economy

Free Trade

Almost as soon as Brian Mulroney took office, he announced to an audience of more than fifteen-hundred Wall Street magnates at the prestigious Economic Club of New York that "Canada is open for business."[2] When he said he would pursue free trade with the United States, he set off a firestorm of protest that echoed from Canada's post. Mel Hurtig, a nationalist publisher, wrote a book called *The Betrayal of Canada* in which he stated that the result of free trade would be "as certain as the fact that you are now reading these words—the destruction and disappearance of our country."[3] Opponents of free trade argued that once Canada negotiated its economic sovereignty away, its political sovereignty would follow. They raised fears that the government would no longer support Canadian cultural industries, and they predicted that medicare could not survive. They also argued that Canadian jobs would be lost because companies would find it cheaper to open factories in places where unions were weaker than in Canada.

Supporters of the policy believed that free trade with the United States was a wise move. Since the United States has the largest consumer market in the world, businesses were anxious to reduce any barriers that restricted access to that market. They said our exports would grow, increasing the number of jobs in Canada and improving the general health of our economy. The country was so divided on the issue of free trade that Mulroney called an election to settle the matter. Just as it was in the 1911 election, free trade was the central issue in the 1988 election. Mulroney emerged with a majority government. Although most Canadians voted for political parties such as the Liberals and the NDP that were opposed to free trade, the Conservatives' 42.9 percent of the vote gave them 169 seats versus the combined 126 for the opposition parties. The Free Trade Agreement (FTA) was signed on January 1, 1989. Between 1989 and 1992, Canada's exports to the United States increased by 62 percent.

NAFTA

In 1994, Mexico was added to the free trade zone. The North American Free Trade Agreement (NAFTA) pushed Canadian exports even higher. In the first five years after the agreement, exports to Mexico increased by 65 percent and to the United States by another 80 percent. Supporters of free trade say NAFTA has protected Canada from economic hardship and that we have not experienced any loss of sovereignty.

The critics of NAFTA disagree. A group called the Council of Canadians points out that the Canadian dollar was worth 86 cents US in 1990, and now it is worth only

62 cents US It reports that American takeovers of Canadian businesses have increased, and that the real disposable income of Canadians has decreased by 5 percent since the FTA was signed; in the United States, disposable income has increased by 12 percent.

Economic Regionalism

Atlantic Canada: The Fish Disappear

The newest of Canada's provinces is also its poorest, and in the early 1990s, Newfoundland and Labrador became even poorer. The cod fishery was the most important industry in the province, providing employment for tens of thousands of fishers and fish plant workers. In about a thousand tiny communities, people were mainly or wholly dependent on fishing, and fishing was all most of these people knew—83 percent had not graduated from high school. But fishing is seasonal employment, and many fishers depended on unemployment insurance (the name was later changed to employment insurance) to get them through the winter.

An Anti-NAFTA demonstration on Parliament Hill.

In 1992, scientists reported that cod stocks were being depleted at such an alarming rate that soon none would be left. The federal government reacted by announcing a two-year moratorium on northern cod fishing. A Newfoundland and Labrador industry that had produced 1.6 million tonnes of fish a year in the 1960s was reduced to nothing overnight. Ottawa tried to retrain people for other employment and bought fishing licences from others to encourage retirement, spending almost $2 billion in the process.

The two-year moratorium was stretched to five years. In 1997, the fishery was reopened but only 10 000 tonnes of fish were allowed to be taken. It grew to 30 000 tonnes in 1999, but then scientists again reported that stocks were falling and the quota was cut by one third.

Some fishers found work catching shellfish such as crab, shrimp, and scallops. But even though that was worth about $900 million in exports in 2000, catching and packaging shellfish is not as labour intensive as the ground fish industry, because it does not require as much production work. Thousands of people were still without work. The fishers blamed the government for mismanaging the fishery and were bitterly unhappy with their treatment. They felt as if they had to beg or grovel for the money, rather than entitled to it. They were made to feel that they had destroyed the fishery even though they had no direct hand in its management.

Although the collapse of the fishing industry has hurt all the Atlantic provinces, new developments such as the Hibernia oil field, nickel mining in Voisey's Bay, and the new exploration of the Laurentian sub-basin (an offshore prospective oil and gas area between Newfoundland and Labrador and Nova Scotia), along with the traditional benefits of tourism, are helping to boost the Atlantic economy.[4]

The overpowering economic dominance of southern Ontario, has continued to breed feelings of economic alienation in the Atlantic provinces. A 1997 document entitled "Atlantic Canada and the Future: Trends, Challenges and Opportunities" states:

[T]he increasing integration of Ontario into the US market and the immigrant stream into Toronto and environs are eroding the psychological links to the East in the same fashion that they are contributing to the erosion of interest in Quebec's problems. Atlantic Canada more and more resembles what Alaska and Hawaii or Iceland and Norway are in American and European maps.[5]

Newfoundland fishers protesting the moratorium on northern cod fishing.

Central Canada

Central Canada, especially southern Ontario, is the economic powerhouse of Canada. With the heaviest concentrations of population, industries, and wealth, Ontario and Quebec dominate the Canadian economy. Despite its economic advantage Ontario has also seen major labour strife throughout the 1990s and into the 2000s. The Ontario government was run by the Progressive Conservatives under Mike Harris from 1995 to 2002. Harris's "Common Sense Revolution" platform reduced funding for health care, education, and welfare; decreased income taxes for middle and upper classes; drastically reduced social programs for people with

Protesting cuts to education spending in Ontario.

mental illnesses and abused women; closed dozens of hospitals; and sent the education system into a fury over teacher testing, reduced preparation time, and increased classroom sizes.

The cuts were felt across the province as hospitals became overcrowded and, in some cases, had to turn away emergency patients. Overcrowding in schools caused large student-to-teacher ratios. Frustrated by the Harris government, heath care workers, educators, and government employees went on numerous strikes to protest the spending cutbacks. Over a two-year period, unions organized one-day strikes in rotating cities to try to bring about change. Called "Days of Action," the strikes raised awareness but failed to bring about a significant change of plans by the Harris government.

After Harris's retirement in 2002, Ernie Eves, also a Conservative Premier, attempted to ease some tension by adopting a "pilot-project" approach to teacher testing and injecting millions of additional dollars for school expenditures. However, plans such as the privatization of hydroelectric power and ongoing strikes such as the one lodged by the Ontario Public Service Employees Union (OPSEU) that lasted for nearly eight weeks, continue to plague Ontario.

The close result of the 1995 Quebec referendum led many corporations to either reduce their workforce in Quebec or move out of the province. Businesses such as Canadian Pacific and aircraft engine producer Pratt and Whitney left Quebec.[6] Fears that separation from Canada would economically cripple Quebec caused many other businesses to move their head offices to Toronto or Vancouver. This led to limited economic growth for Quebec in the 1990s.

Quebec's growth rate decelerated from 3.5 percent between 1991 and 1996 to 1.4 percent between 1996 and 2001 because of declines in both its birth rate and the number of immigrants that it received.[7] Despite the fact that Quebec's gross domestic product is the second highest in Canada, it remains half of that of Ontario's. This difference in GDP has led

Expenditure—based Gross Domestic Product of the Provinces and Territories in Canada.

	1997	1998	1999	2000	2001
	$ millions				
Newfoundland and Labrador	10 575	11 242	12 369	14 081	13 916
Prince Edward Island	2 808	2 979	3 115	3 344	3 423
Nova Scotia	20 399	21 343	22 982	24 061	24 917
New Brunswick	16 888	17 578	18 688	19 709	20 211
Quebec	189 524	197 705	209 490	223 481	228 516
Ontario	359 953	378 124	405 625	429 530	440 051
Manitoba	29 810	30 913	31 760	33 780	35 084
Saskatchewan	29 218	29 112	30 103	33 512	33 059
Alberta	107 170	107 267	116 801	143 034	150 284
British Colombia	114 601	115 604	120 608	127 564	130 396
Yukon	1 109	1 077	1 106	1 124	1 131
Northwest Territories and Nunavut	2 528	2 694	2 637	–	–
Northwest Territories	–	–	–	2 476	2 920
Nunavut	–	–	–	895	912

– Nil or zero.

to antagonistic feelings toward Ontario beyond French–English issues. Quebec's economy, however, is an integral part of Canada's economy, with its diversity in industry and manufacturing.

The Prairie Provinces

From the 1880s to 1945, the Prairie provinces of Manitoba, Saskatchewan, and Alberta earned their nickname as "the breadbasket of the world." Transportation, cities, and government all grew and revolved around the needs of an economy based on grain exports. To this day, the popular image of the Prairies is one of wheat fields and farms. This image is in stark contrast to the reality of the changing Prairie economy. Farms and grain exports are in

decline as the provinces move toward diversifying their economies.

In 1951, fifty-five percent of the Prairie population was still rural.[8] By 1981, the rural population was reduced to 29 percent of the total Prairie population.[9] Between 1976 and 1996, the number of wheat farms on the Prairies declined by more than 50 percent, from 59 724 to 28 842.[10] What happened to the Prairie farm? Changes in the global market, including demand for different products such as oilseed, shifted many farmers away from wheat. But the overwhelming factor in the decrease in the number of farms was that the high subsidies paid by the European Union and the United States to their own grain producers made it impossible for most Canadian farmers to

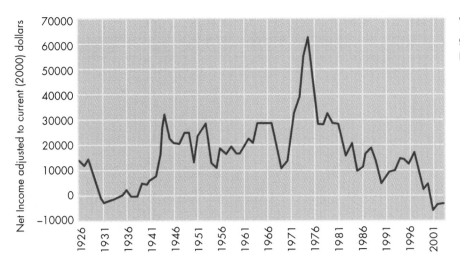

What explains the pattern of this graph showing Net incomes of Prairie farmers?

profitably compete in the global economy. Today, Prairie farm incomes have returned to Depression-era levels, and farmers can barely afford to keep up with the rising operating costs of the massive farms. Many family farms have been lost to rising debt, and for many Prairie farmers, the outlook is dim:

> Huge machines are necessary. They are a kind of grim poetry roaring down a field during swathing and harvest, but the romance stops at the bank. They are a king's ransom to own, take forever to pay off, expensive to run, hard to maintain. And for now, for many, impossible to buy.... Since 1980, the cost of combines has tripled while the price of grain has shrunk. The real menace is cost structure. The invisible machine that's devouring the family farm has three components: grain prices which are miserable; U.S. and European competition which is greatly subsidized; and the Canadian government policy of "Let our farmers do it on their own."[11]

Lack of federal help is a major sticking point for Prairie farmers, especially when they are faced with the drought conditions they have endured since the late 1990s. Federal bungling of an offer to subsidize NHL franchises in Canada while ignoring the plight of farmers enraged the Prairie community and forced the federal government to retract its offer to the NHL.

Although wheat exports have declined for the Prairie provinces, their diversification into broadly based natural resource economies has been successful. Oil, gas, mining, and forest products have all come to play a far more important role in overall sales than has agriculture. The image of the breadbasket of the world has dramatically changed, yet it is an image that many Canadians continue to hold.

HOW FARMERS SHOULD DRESS WHEN SEEKING AID FROM OTTAWA...

What is the message here?

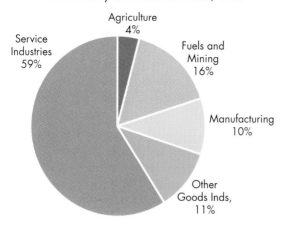

Total Economy of Prairie Provinces, 1997

- Agriculture 4%
- Service Industries 59%
- Fuels and Mining 16%
- Manufacturing 10%
- Other Goods Inds, 11%

The North

Yukon, the Northwest Territories, and Nunavut are often largely ignored or forgotten when discussing Canada's economy or regionalist issues—yet their combined territory makes up more than one third of Canada. The traditional economy of fur harvesting, resource mining, and tourism in the north has lately

Diamond mining in the Northwest Territories.

been enhanced by exciting discoveries. In the Northwest Territories, two of the fastest growing sectors are the diamond and natural gas industries. Diamond company Diavik opened two diamond mines at Lac de Gras, and in 2002, diamond giant DeBeers Canada was reviewing proposals for a diamond mine at Snap Lake.[12] The construction of the diamond mines has poured hundreds of millions of dollars into the northern economy while also providing hundreds of new jobs. Oil and natural gas exploration has also poured millions into the economy, and the possibility of building the Mackenzie Delta pipeline will only increase production and jobs. Along with a growing tourism sector, by 2001, the Northwest Territories enjoyed the highest employment rate in Canada.[13]

Nunavut's economy faces many challenges: the average income is low, unemployment is high, there is a need for more educational opportunities for its citizens, and high transportation costs mean a high cost of living. However, the wide expanse of Nunavut's territory holds prospects of wealth. Like the Northwest Territories, Nunavut also has plans for gold and diamond mines, along with mines for rare metals such as platinum and palladium, which have high market value. Currently, government is the biggest sector of the economy, followed by the traditional sectors of hunting, trapping, and fishing.[14]

British Columbia

As Canada's third wealthiest province, British Columbia has enjoyed the benefits of a healthy economy. Being on the other side of the Rocky Mountains, British Columbia is geographically (and among its citizens sometimes mentally) separated from the rest of Canada. This has led to increased tensions between British Columbia and Ottawa and has spurred the growth of small political groups such as the British Columbia Separatist Movement.

During the 1980s and early 1990s, many citizens from Hong Kong, fearful of being handed from Britain back over to Communist China in 1997, placed many of their investments in British Columbia and soon moved there. The infusion of people and money made the cost of living in British Columbia (especially Vancouver) very expensive, and the economy was bustling. After 1997, many investors moved their assets back to Hong Kong, and the economy slowed considerably.

By the late 1990s, British Columbia's economic slowdown, coupled with poor fiscal management by the NDP government, had caused British Columbia, of all the Canadian provinces, to have

- the lowest productivity growth
- the lowest growth in private-sector investment
- the lowest growth rate in per capita GDP
- one of the least competitive tax regimes in the country[15]

Since 1998, more than 50 000 people have left British Columbia for Alberta and Ontario. Between 2000 and 2002, British Columbia's economy was also crippled by the softwood lumber trade dispute between the United States and Canada. Arguing that the Canadian softwood lumber industry is heavily subsidized and is undercutting American wood, the United States government placed a 19.3 percent tax on softwood imports from Canada and added a "dumping duty" of 12.57 percent in 2001.[16] In 2002, the dispute was still going strong, and the American Trade Ambassador stated that the trade war would continue unless the Canadian government taxed its softwood exports. Since it affects one of British Columbia's biggest economic sectors, the softwood lumber trade war has cost thousands of jobs and created disagreements between the province and central Canada. The B.C. Lumber Trade Council believes that the Canadian government should accommodate the export tax, while the Free Trade Lumber Councils in Ontario and Quebec want to fight it out with the United States. Not only has the trade war further alienated British Columbia from central Canada, it has also greatly hampered British Columbia's economic recovery.

Canada's Political Sovereignty

As Canada's economy was becoming more intertwined with those of other countries around the world, it faced several situations in which it had to protect its territorial rights. In the 1980s and 1990s, Canada faced several disputes with nations when they failed to recognize Canadian sovereignty in its surrounding waters.

Arctic Sovereignty

Protecting Canada's waters was at issue in the summer of 1985, when the United States sent a Coast Guard cutter, *Polar Sea*, through the Northwest Passage from Greenland to Alaska. Canada has always claimed the Northwest Passage as internal waters, which means that any other country that wants to sail a vessel through them needs Canada's permission. The *Polar Sea* did not have that permission.

The United States considers the Passage an international waterway, free to use. Canada argues

The US ship *Polar Sea* traversing the Northwest Passage

in 1988, the United States, without accepting Canada's claim of sovereignty, signed the Agreement on Arctic Co-operation, in which it agreed to ask for Canadian permission for U.S. government-owned or government-operated ships to use the Northwest Passage.

Canada's sovereignty over Arctic waters has never been tested in an international court, and it is unlikely that Canada would want it to be tested. The Canadian government, though capable of monitoring surface vessels in northern waters, is incapable of detecting any submarine traffic. Therefore, it is not exercising authority and control over the area, the usual benchmarks of a country's sovereignty. It is interesting to note that due to global warming, the Northwest Passage is predicted to be open in a few decades, as ice in the Arctic Ocean is melting. Once the ice in the Passage melts, it is doubtful that Canada's claim to sovereignty would be upheld in the International Court of Justice, and the Passage will attract commercial ships travelling from Tokyo to London. Such a loss of sovereignty would mean Canada would not be able to protect its northern environment.[17]

that the area is unique in that the water is frozen much of the year and used as land, and the Indigenous peoples of the area are economically dependent on the water. That being the case, says Canada, it is justified in claiming sovereignty.

Canada has always seen itself as an Arctic nation. Though our national motto is "*A mari usque ad mare*," which means "from sea to sea," politicians are careful now to speak of Canada as stretching from "sea to sea to sea," to include the Arctic. Controlling the land and water in the far north is an important part of the Canadian identity. That land allows us to be the second largest country in the world—and it allows us to think of ourselves as a hearty nation, able to withstand the brutal cold of nature, even if few of us actually do face it. But for a country to claim sovereignty, it has to be prepared to defend it.

Canada told the United States it considered the *Polar Sea* incident an "unfriendly act." It promised to build the world's most powerful icebreaker to patrol the surface of the Arctic Ocean and buy nuclear submarines to patrol beneath it, but it did neither. Still,

The Turbot War

As discussed earlier, Newfoundland and Labrador's economy faced a catastrophe with the decline in cod stocks. No one is certain why the cod disappeared, but many fingers were pointed at foreign trawlers fishing in parts of the Grand Banks just off Canada's territorial waters, which extend 320 kilometres from shore. They were huge ships using a method called "deep sea dragging," towing huge nets along the ocean floor, scooping up more fish than had previously been possible. One commentator called it the equivalent of "underwater strip-mining."[18] These areas constitute only 5 percent of the Grand Banks, but 100 percent of the cod travel through them.

In 1995, Canada's fisheries minister, Brian Tobin, believed that a Spanish freighter, *Estai*, was using an illegal method to catch turbot and was taking fish that were smaller than allowed by law. Even though the freighter was outside of Canada's territorial waters, Ottawa ordered the Coast Guard to fire warning shots across the bow of the ship. When the *Estai* tried to escape the Coast Guard, they seized the ship. The European Union called it piracy (technically an act of war). But Tobin went on the offensive, inviting the international press to a barge in New York Harbor, where he displayed the netting that the *Estai* had cut while trying to escape. Tobin pointed to it, declaring that no young fish could escape that "ecological monstrosity," that "weapon of destruction."[19]

Negotiations finally produced an agreement from the Europeans to set a quota on their catch. Five years later, the Department of Fisheries and Oceans said turbot stocks were showing strong growth. Brian Tobin was tagged with the nickname "Captain Canada."

Cultural Sovereignty

Cultural sovereignty refers to Canada's ability to make laws and policies that can effectively protect and promote its culture and cultural industries.[20] Protecting Canada's cultural sovereignty has been an issue for more than one-hundred years, and as Canada moved toward the twenty-first century, efforts continued to ensure that cultural industries were not overwhelmed by foreign influences. Government initiatives such as the Federal Book Publishing Policy (1972), the Book Publishing Industry Development Program (1986; renewed in 1993), and the Cultural Industries Development Fund (1990) were just three of many policies dedicated to promoting and protecting Canadian culture

The Arts Thrive

By the 1980s, Canadian excellence in writing fiction and poetry was well recognized. Increasingly, literature has become reflective of the multicultural nature of the country. The stories being told were about the experiences of European, Asian, Caribbean, African, and Aboriginal Canadians.

Lee Maracle, a Métis woman, infused her work with opposition to racism and sexism. *I Am Woman* (1988) is a book of essays about what it is like to be an Aboriginal woman. *Ravensong* (1993) is a novel about a young woman trying to reconcile what she is learning from traditional Aboriginal sources with what she is learning from modern society in a small village near Vancouver in the 1950s. Joy Kogawa, a second-generation Japanese-Canadian, was moved by the government from British Columbia to Alberta during World War II. Her novel *Obasan* (1981) is a fictional account of internment. Rohinton Mistry, born in India, came to Canada at the age of twenty-three. His novels *Tales from Firozsha Baag* (1987), *Such a Long Journey* (1991), and *A Fine Balance* (1995) are all set in India. Nino Ricci was born in Canada to Italian immigrants. His first novels, *Lives of Saints* (1990), *In a Glass House* (1993), and *Where She Has Gone* (1998), explore the immigrant experience through the eyes of the fictional Vittorio Innocente. Michael Ondaatje came to Canada at the age of nineteen from Sri Lanka. *Running in the Family* (1982) tells the story of his parents and grandparents. *The English Patient* (1992), his novel about a World War II romance, won him a share of the Booker Prize, the first time it was awarded to a Canadian.

Lorna Crozier writes poetry about southwestern Saskatchewan (*The Garden Going on Without Us*, 1985), Phyllis Webb has a feminist sensibility (*Wilson's Bowl*, 1980), and Roo Borson's poems describe landscapes, townscapes, and interpersonal issues (*Rain*, 1980).

The increase in the number of Canadian writers has spawned an increase in the number of awards that are given in Canada. The Giller Prize has been considered the premier literary prize for fiction since 1994, but it is now one of many. The Marian Engel Award (founded in 1986) goes to a female writer in mid-career. The W.O. Mitchell Literary

Prize (1998) is for a body of work and for mentoring. The Stephen Leacock Medal for Humour (1985) and the Books in Canada First Novel Award (1983) are given for the best book of humour and the best first novel in English, respectively.

In music, there has been an explosion of talent in every genre. The Much Music TV channel and its French equivalent, *Musique Plus*, arrived in 1985 and allowed new artists to shine. Grapes of Wrath and Sons of Freedom were early discoveries. Many Canadian artists have achieved worldwide fame, including Nickelback, 54-40, Diane Krall, and Skinny Puppy from the west coast; k.d. Lang, Jann Arden, and The Watchmen from the Prairies; Jane Siberry, Kim Mitchell, Glass Tiger, The Tragically Hip, Treble Charger, Barenaked Ladies, Shania Twain, The Tea Party, Sum 41, and Alanis Morissette from Ontario; Gino Vanelli, Céline Dion, Roch Voisine, and Corey Hart from Quebec; and Great Big Sea, Stan Rogers, Lennie Gallant, the Rankin Family, Ashley MacIsaac, Sarah McLachlan, and Rita MacNeil from Atlantic Canada.

Canada had no film industry to speak of until the last two decades of the twentieth century. With the help of Telefilm Canada (originally the Canadian Film Development Corporation), the movie industry suddenly had some money to jumpstart projects. It is true that most Canadian feature films are still not attracting mass audiences (about 2 percent of the total Canadian market), but some have done well both domestically and internationally, including *The Decline of the American Empire* (1987), *Exotica* (1994), *Crash* (1996), and *The Sweet Hereafter* (1997).

Saving Canadian Football

The Canadian Football League (CFL) is dear to many Canadian hearts. It has become special to the country because the three-down game is played nowhere else. (The United States plays a four-down game. That means a team has four chances to move the ball ten yards before it has to give up the ball to the other team.) Teams in the CFL are required to employ a fixed number of Canadian players.

Just how important the league is as a symbol was made clear in 1974. The World Football League (WFL) was established with all its teams in the United States, except one—Toronto had a team called the Northmen. The federal government saw this as a threat to the CFL and forced them out. The team moved back to the United Stated and became the Memphis Southmen.

Even with government help, the CFL has had a shaky history. The league has never had a team in Atlantic Canada, reasoning that the market is too small. But in 1993, the CFL expanded into the United States, adding a team in Sacramento, California. It later moved into Las Vegas, Shreveport, Baltimore, San Antonio, Memphis, and Birmingham.

The foray into the United States was a failure, and it certainly did not seem like much of a Canadian league when Baltimore won the Grey Cup in 1995. (The Cup was donated to the Canadian Rugby Union in 1909 by Governor General Earl Grey. It has been the CFL's trophy since 1954.) In 1996, all the American teams folded and the CFL was all-Canadian again. The league still teeters periodically on the verge of collapse. Still, the Grey Cup telecast is usually the highest rated sports program of the year on television in Canada.

Out of This World: Research and Development

If the Canadian North seems a barren frontier, it pales beside what the television series *Star Trek* popularized as "the final frontier"—space. The first Canadian travelled into space in 1984, twenty-three years after the first human ventured up, and fifteen years after the first human walked on the moon. Still, when Marc Garneau flew on a U.S. space shuttle, it marked an important milestone for the country, making it part of the most "glamorous" aspect of space exploration.

Canada was much more aggressive in its pursuit of space than it is usually given credit for. It did not compete with the Russians or the Americans in the "space race" to the moon in the 1960s, but it quietly built a record of achievement. In 1962, Canada launched a research satellite, *Alouette 1*. Canada was the third country after the Soviet Union and the United States to design and build its own satellite. (No launches happened in Canada; the American space agency, NASA, provided those facilities.) In 1972, compelled by its large landmass to find better ways of communicating from one end of the country to the other, Canada launched the world's first commercial geostationary communications satellite, *Anik A1*.

Canada and Canadian astronauts have also played important roles in the Space Shuttle flights; Canadian technology is used on almost every mission. Perhaps the most well known Canadian contribution is the Canadarm. In 1981, a robotic manipulating arm, built in Canada, made its first successful flight on a U.S. shuttle. The Canadarm (officially the Shuttle Remote Manipulator System) became the symbol of Canada in space, instrumental in helping the shuttle perform crucial missions such as delivering satellites into space. Canadarm 2 (the Mobile Servicing System), a more flexible and manoeuvrable arm, was put into space in 2001. The Canadarm has gone on every Space Shuttle mission since 1981 and has recently been used to make major repairs to the Hubble Space Telescope.

Canada is one of sixteen countries building the International Space Station, which will be a base in low Earth orbit where research in microgravity will be conducted. It is a project of mammoth proportions. The International Space Station will be about 100 m long, have a wing span of about 120 m, and weigh about 377 000 kg. Though it is not scheduled for completion until 2006, it is already permanently crewed. It is likely that there will never again be a day when a human being is not in space.

Canada's astronaut program was initiated in 1983, when the United States invited Canada to send Canadian astronauts on some of its missions. The Canadian government established the Canadian Space Agency and has since sent eight Canadian astronauts into space. Marc Garneau became the first Canadian to go into space in 1984. In 1992, Dr. Roberta Bondar became the first Canadian woman to go into space. In 1999, Julie Payette became the first Canadian astronaut to participate in an International Space Station assembly mission and to board the Station when she went up in the Space Shuttle *Discovery*. In 2001, Chris Hadfield became the first Canadian astronaut to walk in space.

The Canadarm, Canada's best-known contribution to space research and development.

1. After Pierre Trudeau, why did so many Prime Ministers have problems staying in power?

2. How is economic regionalism affecting the unity of Canada?

3. In what area do you take the most pride in Canada's recent accomplishments—film, music, science, or sports? Why?

In 2001, astronaut Chris Hadfield became the first Canadian to walk in space. Why do you think Canadian astronauts are not trained to be Space Shuttle pilots and only U.S./NASA pilots actually fly the Shuttle on each mission?

Web Connection

www.mcgrawhill.ca/links/definingcanada
Go to the Web site above to find out more about the Canadian Space Agency.

Immigration and Demographic Changes: Shifting Identities

As discussed in Chapter 23, since 1980, Canada has experienced a profound shift in the make up of its immigrants. Before 1980, most immigrants to Canada were European, but today, the top eight countries of origin for immigrants to Canada are all in Asia. Nonetheless, Canada is facing a different kind of demographic challenge. Historically, Canada has a very low birth rate compared with the rest of the world, and our largest age cohort— the baby boomers—is aging. These factors combined mean that our population level is declining, making immigration an important ingredient for the continued prosperity of Canada. It is estimated that by 2011, immigrants will account for all net labour force growth, and by 2031, immigration will account for all population growth in Canada.[21] Given the importance of immigrants to Canada's growth and prosperity, it will be increasingly important for Canada to help new arrivals manage the transition into Canada's labour market and to place more emphasis on recognizing their education, skills, and language ability or helping them to acquire those skills.

Canada also faces the challenge of trying to redirect the flow of immigrants to regions outside its large metropolitan areas. In 2000, 90 percent of immigrants chose to live in Ontario, Quebec, and British Columbia, with 75 percent of that number settling in Toronto, Montreal, and Vancouver. The Atlantic region has only 8 percent of the Canada's population, and it receives less than 2 percent of the immigrants arriving in Canada; within that small number, more than 75 percent settle in areas such as Halifax.[22] For regions outside the three wealthiest provinces to fuel their economic growth and to allow for population and labour force growth across the country, the government must implement incentives and other programs to attract immigrants.

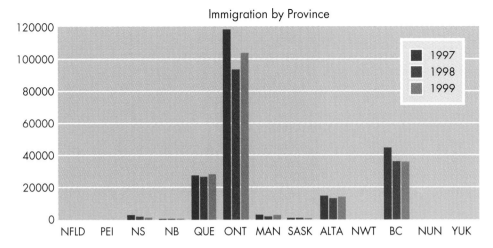

Immigration by Province

Legend:
- 1997
- 1998
- 1999

Considering the importance of immigration to the growth of Canada's labour force and population, what does this graph tell us about how immigration to certain parts of Canada will promote economic regionalism?

Refugees

Canada has become one of the world's havens for refugees. As a signatory to the United Nations Convention Relating to the Status of Refugees (1951), Canada agreed to refrain from returning anyone who came here from another country if that return would put that person's life or freedom in danger because of race, religion, nationality, membership in a particular social group, or political opinion.

In the early 1980s, the government put a system in place to judge whether people were genuine refugees. Word soon spread that the system was cumbersome and that refugee-claimants could stay in Canada for a long time before their cases were resolved. The number of claims jumped from 3450 in 1981 to 6100 in 1983. In 1985, the Supreme Court ruled that refugees, even though not citizens of Canada, had rights under the *Charter of Rights and Freedoms* and that slowed down the process again. There were 25 000 refugee claims in 1987. A feeling developed in Canada that many of the claimants were simply unwilling to go through proper channels to apply to immigrate. This was especially true in some highly publicized cases of refugees from Asia paying unscrupulous "immigration services" to smuggle them into the country in unsanitary conditions on barely seaworthy vessels.

Canada has one of the highest acceptance rates for refugees, many of which are children.

The Canadian Alliance Party took a hard line in its official policy on refugees:

> To ensure fairness and end queue-jumping, we will immediately deport bogus refugees and other illegal entrants, and will severely penalize those who organize abuse of the system. We will ensure that refugee status is arbitrated expeditiously, consistently and professionally. We will end the abuse of refugee claims as a fast track to gain the benefits of landed immigrant status.[23]

The government says it is trying to balance the refugees' right to fair hearings on their claims against the need to control the borders of the country. The Immigration and Refugee Board (IRB) hears every application for refugee status. It is not an adversarial process (though the claimant is entitled to a lawyer paid for by the government); it is instead supposed to be a chance for the claimant to make his or her case.

If the IRB rejects the application, the refugee can appeal to the federal courts for judicial review. While waiting for the appeal to be heard and decided, some refugee claimants are allowed to seek employment, their children can attend school, and their medical needs are looked after.

The number of refugee claims peaked in 1993 at 35 700; it has stayed at fewer than 30 000 since then. The IRB accepts most of the claims it hears. In 1989, its acceptance rate was 86 percent, and its lowest acceptance rate was 53 percent in 1997. Some believe that Canada has the highest acceptance rate of refugees in the Western world. Although that claim is difficult to verify (because every country calculates the number of refugees differently and each may have several categories of refugees), it is clear that Canada's acceptance rate is among the highest in the world.

Defining Canada's International Role: Going to War

The Gulf War

During the Cold War between communism and democracy, Canada was part of a world that seemed on the brink of nuclear annihilation. After the Cold War threat eased, Canada found itself involved in two wars in the 1990s. On August 2, 1990, troops from Iraq invaded neighbouring Kuwait. The United States organized a United Nations coalition that delivered several ultimatums to Iraq's president, Saddam Hussein. When Saddam refused to withdraw, the coalition moved ahead with a military campaign to force him out.

Canada was part of that coalition, which included the United States (the biggest force in the coalition), Afghanistan, Argentina, Australia, Bahrain, Bangladesh, Belgium, Czechoslovakia, Denmark, Egypt, France, Germany, Greece, Hungary, Honduras, Italy, Kuwait, Morocco, the Netherlands, New Zealand, Niger, Norway, Oman, Pakistan, Poland, Portugal, Korea, Spain, Syria, Turkey, the United Arab Emirates, and the United Kingdom. Prime Minister Mulroney called Saddam a criminal of historic significance and said Canada was ready to do its part to liberate Kuwait.

Canada sent air, land, and sea components to the Middle East. Two destroyers and one supply ship went to the Persian Gulf. Twenty-four CF-18 fighter planes were used to defend coalition ships and took part in bombing missions. The army set up a field hospital. In all 4500 Canadians served in the Gulf.

There was some opposition in Canada to its involvement in the war. Protesters said the west was interested in Kuwait only because it had oil. Canada's minister of defence, Bill McKnight, said that Canada "had to take a stand with the world community against Iraq's flagrant violation of international law and civilized values. We and our allies have learned the lessons of history; that we must not turn our backs on aggression, but unite our strength to maintain world peace and security."[24]

War in Yugoslavia

Yugoslavia had been held together after 1945 by Marshall Tito. Running a Socialist regime, he had managed to keep the peace among six nominally equal republics: Croatia, Montenegro, Serbia, Slovenia, Macedonia and Bosnia-Herzegovina. When Tito died in 1980, many expected the federation to fall apart almost immediately. It actually took a little longer for that to happen.

In 1992, Slovenia and Croatia broke away, but only after war with Serbia. The war in Croatia was particularly brutal, resulting in hundreds of thousands of refugees. Bosnia then went to war to gain independence. The Serbs in Bosnia preferred to remain within Yugoslavia. Muslims were driven from their homes in carefully planned operations that came to be known as "ethnic cleansing." Before long, the Serbs controlled about 70 percent of Bosnia. A peace accord in 1995 divided Bosnia between Serbs in one republic and Muslims and Croatians in another. Meanwhile, in Croatia, about 200 000 Serbs were forced into exile.

Kosovo was a province within Serbia that had once enjoyed autonomous status. In 1998, the Kosovo Liberation Army, supported by the majority ethnic Albanians, began a rebellion aimed at independence. Serbian President Slobodan Milosevic struck back ruthlessly, and despite warnings and pleas from the west to negotiate, things got worse. The campaign of ethnic cleansing against Kosovo's Albanians included summary executions, massacres, arbitrary detentions, rapes, and beatings. About 860 000 refugees poured out of Kosovo. Hundreds of thousands more were internally displaced.

In March 1999, NATO, an alliance created to defend against the threat of the Soviet Union, began its first offensive military campaign. It was an air war against Serbia. Canada sent eighteen CF-18s into action (part of 829 aircraft from fourteen countries), and they flew bombing missions throughout the seventy-eight days it took until Yugoslavia surrendered. They flew 678 combat sorties (about 10 percent of all missions) and delivered 532 bombs. No Canadian aircraft were lost, and no Canadian airmen were hurt.

As it was during the Gulf War, public opinion seemed to be behind the government in what it framed as a humanitarian effort. Prime Minister Chrétien said,

> Kosovo is about standing up against oppression and the systematic destruction of a people. These are a reflection of our values. The values that have built this country. The values that have made us a land of peace and opportunity. A land where we have made diversity not a tool for conflict but a means for a stronger, healthier way of life...it is these three elements: our values as Canadians, our national interest in a stable and secure Europe and our obligations as a founding member of NATO, that led Canada to take arms with its NATO partners. And it is because of our values, our national interest and our obligations that we must see the job through....To be a bystander on Kosovo today would be to betray our basic values, our national interests and our international obligations.[25]

But in Parliament, the NDP withdrew its support for the bombing after about a month. It said the bombing had not saved Kosovars and had made the Serbian president act with increased brutality toward them. The Serb community was vocal in its condemnation from the very beginning. The Ottawa Serbian Heritage Society, for example, said the bombings were responsible for the "wanton killing of thousands of innocent Serbians, old and young alike."[26] Canada took in about seven thousand refugees from Kosovo. Most of them chose to stay after the war.

A Stain on Canadian Honour: The Somalia Affair

Canada's participation in the war in Somalia has come to be associated with shame for the Canadian military, and by extension, for the entire country. In 1992, Somalia was suffering in anarchy. There was no government. Gangs with guns roamed the country, fighting each other for supremacy. International aid meant for starving people was being intercepted by so-called warlords. In August, the United Nations decided to use force to make humanitarian aid available. Canada agreed to take part in the mission, peacemaking instead of peacekeeping.

As the Canadian troops left for Somalia in December, the United States was sending 30 000 marines into the country to get food moving and deal with any gangs that tried to stop it. The Canadians took charge of the town of Belet Huen. They spent a good deal of their time keeping warring factions apart and stopping break-ins at their compound. On March 4, 1993, two Somalis were shot by soldiers on patrol at the compound. One was killed, the other wounded. According to a military surgeon, the man who was killed did live for a while but was then executed.

On March 16, Canadian soldiers caught sixteen-year-old Shidane Arone in the compound. He was tortured and murdered. One of the Canadian soldiers even took photos while Shidane was beaten. There was revulsion across Canada when the news came out and genuine shock when the pictures were released.

Master Corporal Clayton Matchee was arrested, tried to hang himself, and was eventually found unfit to stand trial. Private Kyle Brown was found guilty of manslaughter and torture and sentenced to five years in prison. No one else was convicted of anything more serious than negligent performance of duty. Senior officers were acquitted of all charges, though the chief of defence staff, Major-General Jean Boyle, resigned.

If it had stopped there, the damage to Canada's honour might not have been so deep. But videotapes surfaced that revealed the Canadian Airborne Regiment was home to racists and neo-Nazis, and other tapes showed the men taking part in repugnant hazing rituals. The Airborne, a regiment that had served with distinction since World War II, was disbanded.

The Somalia Commission Inquiry

The government established a commission of inquiry to find out what had gone wrong. After two years, the government shut the commission down, saying it had gone on long enough. But the inquiry report was still a searing indictment of the Canadian military. It said military leaders had no idea that the Airborne Regiment was full of racists, that discipline in the Canadian Forces seemed nonexistent, and that soldiers sent to Somalia were poorly trained and had no understanding of how they were to accomplish their mission.

The report underlined why the military's failure was so devastating: "Soldiers wear the official uniform of Canada. They display the Canadian flag on those uniforms when on missions out of the country. Society's expectations of the nation's flag-bearers are indeed higher than for the average citizen. Those expectations include the notion that soldiers serve as a symbol of the national character."[27]

Most Canadians seemed satisfied that the problems in Canada's military had been handled. Polls done as recently as 2002 show overwhelming support for idea of Canadian peacekeeping (only 8 percent strongly opposed it in a poll by Compas).[28] The Canadian Forces still have considerable support. In a Leger Marketing survey released in 2002, 76.8 percent said they were proud of the military.[29]

Web Connection

www.mcgrawhill.ca/links/definingcanada
To read the Report of the Somalia Commission of Inquiry, go the Web site above.

September 11

Most Canadians know the significance of the date September 11, 2001—it will forever be known simply as 9-11.

The sequence of events is now familiar through extended media coverage during and after the attacks on the World Trade Center and the Pentagon. In the immediate aftermath the United States closed its airspace and airliners en route to the United States were diverted to Canada. About 240 diverted flights with about 30 000 people on board landed in Canada. Three days later, a service of remembrance on Parliament Hill attracted more than 100 000 people. Prime Minister Chrétien said Canadians could not stop their tears. And he told Americans, "Do not despair. You are not alone. We are with you."[30]

American President George W. Bush said there were now only two groups of people in the world: those who supported American efforts to root out terrorists and those who did not.

NATO quickly invoked article 5 of its charter, which states that an attack on one NATO country is an attack on all. As a NATO member, Canada began to prepare to join the war against terrorism. It sent patrol frigates, a supply ship, and a destroyer to the Arabia Sea. It sent air surveillance planes and supply planes to Afghanistan. It also sent members of its highly secretive commando force, JTF-2. And it sent a battalion of the Princess Patricia's Canadian Light Infantry (PPCLI). About three thousand members of the Canadian Forces became part of the war, the largest commitment of Canadian troops to any operation since the Korean War.

An Ipsos-Reid poll in January 2002 found that two-thirds of Canadians supported the idea of Canadian troops in combat.[31] Of those opposed, some said it was better for Canada to continue to play its traditional peacekeeping role. But some were opposed more strongly. A group called "Lawyers Against the War" said the war was illegal because the United Nations prohibits the use of force to overthrow a sovereign government.

The September Eleventh Peace Coalition was formed with the support of the Canadian Labour Congress, the Council of Canadians, Science for Peace, the Canadian Peace Alliance, and the Canadian Federation of Students, among others.

After the World Trade Towers collapsed, thousands of people ran for cover from falling debris.

A Remembrance service for victims of September 11, on Parliament Hill, in Ottawa.

The Coalition's "Statement of Unity" reads, in part, "We utterly abhor the acts of terror of September 11. The perpetrators must be brought to justice through the rules of national and international law. We likewise abhor indiscriminate military assaults that inflict injuries and cause suffering, death, and the displacement of people."[32]

Jean Chrétien told the House of Commons that there is no more solemn decision that a prime minister must make than to send Canadians into a military campaign. He said he had made his decision because he believed Canada had to show "a firm resolve to stand up and be counted. To stand up for our people, for our values, for our way of life. To send a clear message to the cowards in the shadows who planned this crime against humanity that their days of being able to run and hide are coming to an end."[33]

Though the government of Afghanistan fell very quickly, it was impossible to root every Al-Qaeda fighter immediately from the thousands of caves in the country. Canadians stayed in the country to continue the search. In April 2002, four members of the PPCLI were killed. They were on a training exercise when they were killed by "friendly fire"—an American pilot mistakenly dropped a bomb on them. They were the first Canadian soldiers to die during a combat mission in almost fifty years.

Beyond the war, September 11 also meant changes in Canadian life. The federal budget, introduced three months after the terror attacks, directed $7.7 billion to security measures. Security at airports is much tighter, new immigrants are being screened more carefully, and Canadian passports were made more difficult to forge.

Prime Minister Jean Chrétien speaking at a Memorial service for the members of the PPCLI who died in Afghanistan.

In its determination to fight terrorism, the government passed a law giving the police much more power. There was an unprecedented provision for "preventive arrest," which allowed the police to detain a person not for committing a crime (the usual standard), but to prevent them from committing a crime. The law also forced people to give testimony about terrorism before a judge even without a formal trial. Civil libertarians said the law went too far. Alan Gold of the Ontario Criminal Lawyers Association said, "We don't want to turn into a police state.... To do so in the name of liberty is bizarre."[34] But Minister of Justice Anne McLellan said the law did not conflict with the *Charter of Rights*, which allows for limitations on freedom as long as those limitations are justified in a free and democratic society. In her view, "People who live in daily fear of their personal security cannot live in a free and democratic society."[35]

The government was careful to try to dispel the perception of some Canadians that immigrants, especially Muslims, were dangerous. Some Muslims felt they had to curtail their activities to avoid confrontations. Mosques in Montreal, St. Catharines, and Oshawa were firebombed. A Hindu temple was attacked in Hamilton because, the police said, it was probably mistaken for a Mosque. Prime Minister Chrétien went to a Mosque in Ottawa to say that he knew Islam was a religion of peace. He said,

> I want to stand by your side to condemn the acts of intolerance and hatred that have been committed against your community since the attack [in New York]. Let me say that I turn my back on the people who have done this. I have no time for them. Many of your faith have felt constrained when expressing your sympathy and solidarity with the victims. This despite the fact that many Muslims also perished in the

attacks... Some have been singled out for denunciation and violence. Acts that have no place in Canada or any civilized nation. And which have made me feel shame as Prime Minister.[36]

Review...Reflect...Respond

1. Why is immigration to Canada, and the placement of immigrants so crucial to Canada's future?

2. How does Canada's participation in international conflicts change Canada's self-image and how the international community views Canada?

3. Do you agree with Canada's involvement in international conflicts such as the war on terrorism? Why or why not?

Conclusion

As it faced the twenty-first century, Canada also faced many of the same challenges as it had in previous years. It also took on new challenges as well. The Canadian economy, while prosperous, suffered from regional differences that have only increased the disparity among provinces. On a national front, the Canadian government continued to take a more active role in protecting its territorial and cultural sovereignty. Internationally, the Canadian military brought both pride and shame through its actions in international conflicts. During these years, the world, and Canada, changed at a fast, and sometimes frightening, pace.

Notes

1. Only one Prime Minister in Canadian history has had a shorter term than Clark, Turner, or Campbell. That was Charles Tupper in 1896; he lasted just 68 days.

2. Ricardo Grinspun and Maxwell A. Cameron, eds. *The Political Economy of North American Free Trade* (New York: St. Martin Press, 1993), p. 324.

3. Mel Hurtig, *The Betrayal of Canada* (Toronto: Stoddart, 1991).

4. The Laurentian sub-basin became a major issue of contention between Newfoundland and Labrador and Nova Scotia as both provinces claimed the area to be in their territorial waters. In April 2002, a tribunal established a compromise boundary along the basin to equally divide the oil and gas prospects.

5. North American Policy Group, "Atlantic Canada and the Future: Trends, Challenges and Opportunities," submitted to the Atlantic Canada Opportunities Agency, September 1997, p. 30.

6. Alvin Finkel and Margaret Conrad, *History of the Canadian Peoples,* vol. II, 2nd ed. (Toronto: Addison-Wesley, 1998), p. 477.

7. Statistics Canada, 2001 Census.

8. Peter Arcus and Graham Parsons, "Changes in the Prairie Economy, 1980–2000," SIPP Public Policy Paper No. 8, p. 1.

9. Ibid, p. 2.

10. Ibid., p. 6.

11. Rex Murphy, "Down on the Farm," *CBC News Indepth*.

12. GNWT Department of Finance, *2002 Budget Address,* pp. 2–3.

13. Ibid., p. 3.

14. Department of Indian Affairs and Northern Development, Government of Canada. *The Nunavut Economy: Challenge and Potential,* 2002.

15. Honourable Gary Collins, Minister of Finance, *British Columbia Budget Speech 2002,* p. 5.

16. Amina Ali and Sabrina Saccoccio, *CBC News Online,* "Backgrounder: Softwood Lumber,"

17. Dennis Bueckert, Canadian Press. "Canada's sovereignty over Northwest Passage threatened: expert." January 25, 2002.

18. Rex Murphy, *Unpeopled Shores: The Unmaking of a Province.* Canadian Broadcasting Corp. (CBC). Documentary, 1993.

19. Raymond B. Blake. "Water Buoys the Nation. Fish and the Re-emergence of Canadian Nationalism." In Ahornblätter: Marburger Beiträge zur Kanada-Forschung. 12 Marburg, 1998 (Schriften der Universitätsbibliothek Marburg; 90). March 12, 1998.

20. The Standing Committee on Culture and Communications, *The Ties That Bind,* p. 6.

21. Citizenship and Immigration Canada. "Pursuing Canada's Commitment to Immigration: The Immigration Plan for 2002." (Ottawa: The Government of Canada).

22. "Immigration and Economic Development in Atlantic Canada" in *Atlantic Report,* Summer 2001 (Halifax: The Atlantic Provinces Economic Council), p. 2.

23. "CFIRC Praises Immigration Stand of Canadian Alliance," by The Canada First Immigration Reform Committee.

24. *The Wednesday Report: Canada's Aerospace & Defence Weekly,* vol. 4, no. 43, October 24, 1990.

25. Special House of Commons Debate (Kosovo), April 12, 1999.

26. Radmila Swann, President, Ottawa Serbian Heritage Society, "Every Life Counts." Presentation at the Coalition to Oppose the Arms Trade's Vigil for Nonviolence, Oct. 6, 2001, in Ottawa.

27. *The Military In Canadian Society, Report of the Somalia Commission of Inquiry.*

28. *Peacekeeping Survey: A COMPAS Report for the University of Calgary*, September 25, 2001. Compas Inc.

29. *Canadians and the Military,* a report by Leger Marketing and Canadian Press, January 2002.

30. *Speech* by Prime Minister Chrétien, National Day of Mourning, September 14, 2001, Parliament Hill.

31. A summary of the results of the Ipsos-Reid/Globe and Mail/CTV poll, January 2002.

32. The Canadian Peace Alliance, *Statement of Unity*, 2001.

33. Notes for an Address by Prime Minister Jean Chrétien on the occasion of a Special House of Commons "Take Note" Debate on the International Campaign Against Terror, October 15, 2001.

34. Daniel Leblanc and Campbell Clark, with a file from the Canadian Press, "Police to get sweeping powers under Ottawa's terrorism bill." From *The Globe and Mail*, Wednesday, October 16, 2001.

35. Ibid.

36. Address by Prime Minister Jean Chrétien on the Occasion of a Visit to the Ottawa Central Mosque, September 21, 2001, Ottawa, Ontario.

Chapter 24 Review

Knowledge and Understanding

1. Identify these people, places, and events, and explain their historical significance to Canada's developing culture and identity:
   - Free Trade Agreement
   - North American Free Trade Agreement
   - Brian Mulroney
   - Jean Chrétien
   - *Estai*
   - Somalia Inquiry
   - September 11
   - Canadarm
   - global village
   - Telefilm Canada

2. Why is controlling the law and the water in the far North an important part of the Canadian identity?

Thinking & Inquiry

3. Why is Brian Mulroney one of the most disliked prime ministers in Canadian history? What aspects of Canadian culture did he change that Canadians identify with strongly?

4. A document is quoted as saying, "Atlantic Canada more and more resembles what Alaska and Hawaii or Iceland and Norway are in American and European maps." What does this statement mean? Do you think this kind of feeling only applies to Atlantic Canada? What other geographic areas in Canada may have residents who feel the same way? How does this affect regionalism within Canada?

Application

5. The federal government is holding a National Round Table on the economy. You are the minister of economic development for one of the following provinces or territories:
   - Nunavut
   - Newfoundland and Labrador
   - British Columbia
   - Quebec

   Write a brief synopsis of the current economic situation in your province or territory. Then write a one-page proposal on what needs to take place to stimulate economic growth and stability in your province or territory. What areas will you focus on (tourism, resource development, and so on)?

Communication

6. In the Report of the Somalia Commission of Inquiry, it states,

   From its earliest moments the operation went awry. The soldiers, with some notable exceptions, did their best. But ill-prepared and rudderless, they fell inevitably into the mire that became the Somalia debacle. As a result, a proud legacy was dishonoured ...We can only hope that Somalia represents the nadir of the fortunes of the Canadian Forces. There seems to be little room to slide lower. One thing is certain, however: left uncorrected, the problems that surfaced in the desert in Somalia and in the boardrooms at National Defence Headquarters will continue to spawn military ignominy. The victim will be Canada and its international reputation.

   Why is Somalia a "stain on Canadian honour"? Write four well-written paragraphs that explain why the events in Somalia had such a profound impact on Canadian citizens.

Unfinished Business

We try—we must try to forgive what is past. The punishing society never forgets the wrongs of the past. The forgiving society works toward the actions of the future. The forgiving society enables people to behave well toward one another, to being again, to build a society in hope and with love.

–GOVERNOR GENERAL ADRIENNE CLARKSON

In the first years of the twenty-first century, Canadians have become embroiled in several debates, and how these are resolved will have a significant impact on the lives Canadians lead. One of the most important debates concerns our country's treatment of its Aboriginal Peoples.

Aboriginal Canadians, who make up less than 6 percent of the population, are burdened with a far greater percentage of Canada's hardships than are other groups. They are on the unhappy end of virtually every statistical measure of well-being. They are poorer than the average Canadian and are less educated. The Aboriginal unemployment rate is higher, and the incidence of divorce is higher, as is welfare dependence, infant mortality, child abuse, wife abuse, and alcohol and drug dependence. A report at the end of 2000 found that up to 90 percent of child and teen prostitutes in Canada are Aboriginal.[1] The suicide rate among Aboriginals is not just higher, it is frighteningly higher. Although the problems are clear, the solutions are elusive. Or perhaps more creative answers have to be found for ending the disparities. In a speech to the Canadian Bar Association in August 2001, Minister of Justice Ann McLellan said:

> Why is it that Aboriginal people continue to be imprisoned at a rate greater than the overall population? Why are Aboriginal accused more likely to be denied bail and spend more time in a pre-trial detention? Why are Aboriginal people more likely to be incarcerated? These are not easy questions. In fact, they should make all of us feel uncomfortable if we truly value fairness and justice."[2]

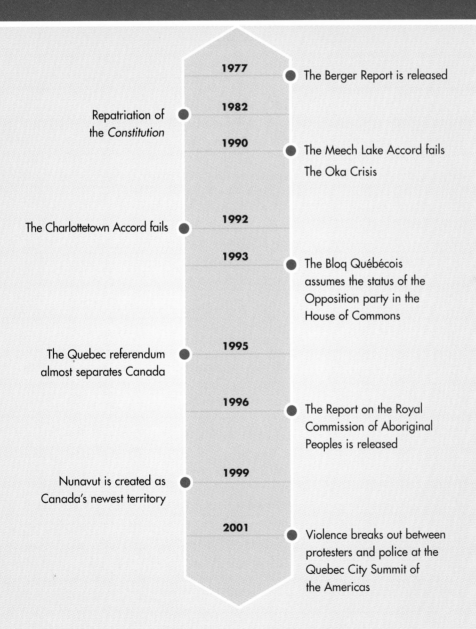

1977	The Berger Report is released
1982	Repatriation of the *Constitution*
1990	The Meech Lake Accord fails / The Oka Crisis
1992	The Charlottetown Accord fails
1993	The Bloq Québécois assumes the status of the Opposition party in the House of Commons
1995	The Quebec referendum almost separates Canada
1996	The Report on the Royal Commission of Aboriginal Peoples is released
1999	Nunavut is created as Canada's newest territory
2001	Violence breaks out between protesters and police at the Quebec City Summit of the Americas

By the end of this chapter, you will be able to

- describe the contributions of Aboriginal peoples to the development of Canadian identity and culture

- evaluate current developments within Canada that address the equitable treatment of individuals and groups

- describe past and present Aboriginal political organizations

- analyze why and how the people of Quebec have acted to preserve their political identity

- evaluate how the process of economic globalization has challenged Canadian economic and cultural autonomy

- analyze the growth of environmentalism and its influence on how Canadians live

Aboriginal Canadians

Residential Schools

For most of its history, Canada has tried to assimilate Aboriginal people into the larger non-Aboriginal society. Beginning in 1883, a government policy was enforced that took Aboriginal children from their homes on reserves and placed them in residential schools, usually run by the Church (Roman Catholic, Anglican, Methodist, Presbyterian, and United). The schools usually forbade the use of Aboriginal languages and discouraged Aboriginal traditions. Children were rarely sent home, even on holidays, so contact with their parents was rare.

The schools began to be phased out in the 1960s, though the last was not closed until 1996. But the consequences of the residential schools have remained an issue that Canada must deal with. Stories emerged of physical and sexual abuse at some schools. Aboriginal groups have described what had happened to Aboriginal children as kidnapping. In a report submitted to the Royal Commission on Aboriginal Peoples in 1994, the testimony of several victims of the schools was recorded:[3]

- "I stayed in that Residential School for 10 years. I hurt there. There was no love there. There was no caring there, nobody to hug you when you cried; all they did was slap you over."
- "I was molested when I was in the Residential School. I was sexually molested by a nun and I was abused."
- "I was seriously injured down there. I ended up in a hospital for I don't know how long, with my legs broken in three places."
- "I entered school when I was 6. It took me some 40 years before I could talk about my experience in Residential School, and that was just the first step. And I have a number of steps to take before I can consider myself a whole person, I don't know how to describe it without shame, without any sense of embarrassment."

In 1998 the federal government offered a formal apology for the residential school system, set up a $350 million healing fund, and offered counselling for victims. More than 11 000 lawsuits were filed against churches and governments (it is estimated that 105 000 children had attended the schools since 1900), not just for abuse, but also for loss of language, loss of family ties, forced religious indoctrination, and mental suffering. Millions of dollars have already been paid in damages. The final figure could reach $1 billion.

The White Paper on Indian Policy

In 1969, a government White Paper on Indians was a major milestone. Its most important proposal was to consider Aboriginal Peoples as no different from other Canadians. Prime Minister Trudeau said, "We can go on treating the Indians as having special status, adding bricks of discrimination around the ghetto in which they now live. Or we can say you're at a crossroads; the time is now to decide whether the Indians will be a race apart in Canada or whether they will be Canadians of full status."[4] The report called for

- the end of the Department of Indian Affairs
- the repeal of the Indian Act
- the elimination of reserves

But Aboriginal Peoples believed that implementing the White Paper would bring about the demise of Aboriginal Peoples in Canada and the cultural genocide of their people. A book by Cree tribal leader Harold Cardinal, *The Unjust Society: The Tragedy of Canada's Indians,* called the White Paper, "a thinly-disguised programme of extermination through assimilation." Cardinal wrote that the government believed "[t]he only good Indian is a non-Indian." Cardinal said he wanted to remain a "red tile" in the Canadian mosaic:

As a matter of fundamental principle, Canadians should recognize and accept the fact that First Nations and First Nation families possess and

Demonstrators demand compensation for victims of Residential Schools.

Indian and Northern Affairs Minister Jean Chrétien presenting the White Paper on Aboriginal Peoples, 1969.

are entitled to possess the primary and sole authority to decide what is in the best interests of their children. The principle should...recognize that First Nation children possess the God-given birthright to grow up as First Nation persons, to be raised in their own languages and in their own cultures and in their own traditions.... [L]egal recognition of this birthright is the only way to stop importing into the present the problems which occurred in the past. [5]

Cardinal's book was part of an Aboriginal reaction to the White Paper that was so hostile, the government was forced to abandon it. The most important legacy the White Paper left was a spark that ignited political awareness among Aboriginals. Four groups emerged to fight for Aboriginal rights: The National Indian Brotherhood (which became the Assembly of First Nations in 1982), the Canadian Métis Society (which became the Métis National Council), the Indian Brotherhood of the Northwest Territories (which became the Dene Nation), and the Inuit Tapitisat of Canada.

Despite overwhelming opposition by Aboriginals to the White Paper, many other Canadians agreed with its approach. A Compas poll in December 2001 found that only 45 percent of Canadians agreed

with the principle that "Aboriginal people have a special right as Canada's first inhabitants to continuing economic and social support." Sixty-nine percent agreed that "our longstanding policy of financially supporting bands and encouraging them to keep their traditions has not worked and we should try something new."[6]

The James Bay Agreement

Aboriginal groups often insist that they own any land that has not been ceded by treaty or through negotiations. The first test of this assertion came in 1972. In 1971, the Quebec government announced its plan to harness the hydroelectric power of the rivers draining into James Bay, and the government created the James Bay Development Corporation to develop the territory. The blocking and diverting of these rivers and tributaries, however, would have flooded traditional Cree hunting grounds. In 1972, the Quebec Association of Indians fought to save their territory. When the Quebec Superior Court ruled that the province did have an unfulfilled obligation regarding Aboriginal title to the land, three years of negotiations began between Quebec and the Cree.

When the James Bay and Northern Quebec Agreement was finally signed on November 11, 1975, Quebec was given title to 981 610 km² of land, and the Cree and Inuit were given $225 million, exclusive settlement rights for 13 000 km² of land, and another 150 000 km² of territory in which they would have exclusive hunting rights. The James Bay and Northern Quebec Agreement was Canada's first modern-day land settlement agreement. It significantly changed federal involvement in northern Quebec, and many of the services that the federal government used to provide, such as health and social services, were now only subsidized by the government. The agreement also led to such new steps as the establishment of Cree and Inuit school boards, the creation of programs of income support for hunters, and the sharing of wildlife management. Overall, the agreement left Inuit and Cree communities with more control over their social, economic, and political affairs.[7]

The Berger Report

In the early 1970s, the federal government began developing plans to build a pipeline that would carry American oil and gas from the Prudhoe Bay field in Alaska, through the Mackenzie River Valley, and into the United States. Under increasing pressure from the Dene to examine the effects of the pipeline on the local people and the environment, the Trudeau government appointed Justice Thomas Berger to head an inquiry into the potential impact of a pipeline.

Throughout 1976, Berger held hearings in thirty-five northern communities, in which more than one thousand people participated. Berger encouraged widespread media coverage of the hearings, which allowed Aboriginals a platform to air their grievances. The media coverage swayed public opinion in favour of the Aboriginals. In 1977, Berger submitted his final report.

Justice Thomas Berger stated that there were two distinct views of the North: one as a homeland, one as a frontier. Do you believe these two views still exist in Canada today?

Expression of Culture

CONTEMPORARY ABORIGINAL ART

Until the 1960s Aboriginal Canadian art was collected, but viewed as little more than souvenirs or ethnological artefacts. In the 1960s, however, the Ojibwa artist Norval Morrisseau found a market for his colourful paintings of the stories and legends of his people. A group of artists, known as the Woodland School, which included Carl Ray, Daphne Odjig, Jackson Beardy, and Alex Janvier, gathered around Morrisseau and imitated his style, painting bright, solid panes of colour, outlined by a thick black flowing line. Morrisseau and his followers made a name for themselves, using contemporary techniques, but exploring the traditions of their ancestors.

It was not until the 1980s that Aboriginal artists also found a place for their work in exhibitions and collections in Canadian museums and galleries across the country. This second generation of Aboriginal artists graduated from Canadian art programmes and were schooled in Western approach and techniques. While some Aboriginal Canadian artists revived the practice of their ancestors, others worked with diverse contemporary media, from paint to sculpture and mixed media to film. Many of these artists share a common concern—that of exploring and redefining their own role and that of Aboriginal Peoples in Canadian society.

The purchase of Carl Beam's *The North American Iceberg* by the National Gallery of Canada, Ottawa, in 1986 was certainly a watershed event for Aboriginal artists in Canada. Beam's *Iceberg* was the first Aboriginal work purchased by the National Gallery since 1927. In this powerful montage, Beam, an Ojibwa artist from Manitoulin Island in Ontario positions a sequence of native faces, old and new, himself and others, and diverse images, to explore the Westernization of Aboriginal Canadians and the role that technology has had in that process.

Jane Ash Poitras, a Chipewyan Aboriginal from Fort Chipewyan in northern Alberta, adapted a similar montage or collage technique in her art. She combines paint with a variety of materials, including photographs and newspaper clippings to juxtapose traditional images of Aboriginal peoples and Cree iconography with images of Western culture. In Poitras' *Indian Blackboard Series* she delves into the effect of assimilation of Aboriginal peoples through the education system and residential schools. In this series, Poitras takes over the role of educator, using the powerful medium of the blackboard and chalk to teach her audience something of her experience, history, and language.

Artist, writer and curator, Gerald McMaster, a Plains Cree Aboriginal from Red Pheasant Saskatchewan, is one of the more important figures in this second wave of Aboriginal artists. In his drawings, paintings, sculptures and assemblage, McMaster deals with critical issues, such as racism, Canadian and Aboriginal history and stereotypes, but uses humour, satire and visual puns as a means of relaying his message.

In 1991, the McMichael Canadian Art Collection launched an exhibition entitled, *The Cowboy/Indian Show*. Here McMaster put a comic, pop-culture spin on critical questions and concerns. Who are cowboys and Indians? Can we compare a job (the cowboy) with an entire race of people (the Indians)? What stereotypes are perpetuated through written history and commercial culture? The overt humour makes McMaster's art approachable, but he leaves us questioning and discussing stereotypes and injustices faced by Aboriginal Peoples in everyday life.

Aboriginal artists Shelley Niro and Mike MacDonald have exploited the more recent field of multi-media art. Shelley Niro, a Mohawk originally from New York, is one of the most prominent Aboriginal photographers exhibiting in Canada.

She is known for her self-portraits and studies of female family members that challenge Aboriginal stereotypes and offer alternative, strong roles of Aboriginal women. Her series, *This Land is Mime Land* (1992) is a sequence of sets of photographs that juxtapose images of her family, images of herself dressed as popular icons and self-portraits. Niro makes a statement on how her own Aboriginal identity is a blend of mainstream pop-culture icons, such as Marilyn Monroe, and members of her family.

A self-taught artist, Mike MacDonald of Mi'kmaq, Beothuk, Scottish, Irish and Portuguese decent, originally from Sydney, Nova Scotia, uses film to deliver his environmental message. Commenting on his video, *Seven Sisters* (1989), MacDonald questions who has control over natural resources, "the people who are living in a geography" or those that are sitting in "boardrooms of multi-national corporations".

Oka-boy/Oh!Kowboy (1990) by Gerald McMaster. This piece of artwork was displayed at the McMichael Canadian Art Collection in the exhibit entitled, *The Cowboy/Indian Show*. What does McMaster's artwork say about the stereotypes and injustices faced by Aboriginal Peoples?

Many Aboriginal Canadian artists, like those mentioned above, make a personal yet political statement in their art, helping their audience understand the world of a colonized people. The Aboriginal artist plays an important role in the education of the Canadian public in the twenty-first century as we move toward a deeper understanding and better appreciation of the diversity and rights of Aboriginal Peoples. In 1992, at the opening of *Indigena Perspectives of Indigenous Peoples on Five Hundred Years*, at the Museum of Civilization in Hull, Quebec, artist, curator and activist, Doreen Jenson concluded, "First Nations Artists have something vitally important to offer – a new (or ancient) aesthetic, a way of understanding art and the world that can heal this country, and help us all to find a place in it."

Berger concluded that there should be a ten-year delay in building the pipeline to allow for land claims to be settled. He was forceful and eloquent in framing his reasons:

> There are two distinct views of the North: one as a frontier, the other as a homeland. We [non-Aboriginals] look upon the North as our last frontier. It is natural for us to think of developing it, of subduing the land and extracting its resources to fuel Canada's industry and heat our homes. But the native people say the North is their homeland. They have lived there for thousands of years. They claim it is their land, and they believe they have a right to say what its future ought to be.[8]

Berger also reported on non-Aboriginal views of Aboriginal culture:

> We possess a terrible self-centredness, even arrogance, as a people.... History is what happened to us. We dismiss as curiosity what has gone before. The culture, values, and traditions of native people amount to more than crafts and carvings. Their respect for the wisdom of their elders, their concept of family responsibilities extending beyond the nuclear family to embrace a whole village, their respect for the environment, their willingness to share—all of these values persist within their own culture even though they have been under unremitting pressure to abandon them.[9]

The Berger Inquiry has been called a watershed event in the history of Aboriginal Canadians, as it examines the lives and living conditions of Aboriginals and the impact that Canadians and their development is having on them.

The Constitution

Although the focus of the negotiations to patriate the *Constitution* was on Ottawa and the provinces, the Constitution Act of 1982 held a vital victory for Aboriginal people. Section 25 says that none of the guarantees in the *Charter of Rights and Freedoms* was to be interpreted "so as to abrogate or derogate from any Aboriginal, treaty, or other rights or freedoms that pertain to the aboriginal peoples of Canada."

In section 35, Canada "recognized and affirmed" existing Aboriginal and treaty rights, including any that were already in place through existing land claim agreements and those to be determined by agreements still to be negotiated. It also guaranteed Aboriginal representation at any future conference that would amend parts of the *Constitution* that affected First Peoples.

In April 2002, the Assembly of First Nations National Chief Matthew Coon Come acknowledged the twentieth anniversary of the Canadian *Constitution* that recognized Aboriginal Peoples and their rights, but he expressed frustration about the government's delay in implementing those constitutional rights:

> The Constitution Act of 1982 was meant to be a landmark in Canada's dealings with the original peoples of this land.... Our leaders at the time fought for and won a place at the Constitutional table. The result of their hard work and diligence is a document that, in Section 35, explicitly recognizes the special status and rights of Aboriginal peoples.
>
> Unfortunately, since 1982, nowhere near enough has been accomplished with respect to these fundamental constitutional rights. We are too often set aside on issues that concern us, with the result that we continue to be comparably marginalized, landless, and poor. Governments rarely consult us, and when they do our major concerns do not make their agendas.... The challenge ahead of us is to give life to those words on paper. The twentieth anniversary means we have been pushing for two decades to work with Canada to implement our rights. When women were given the right to vote, they did not have to wait, nor should they have had to wait, twenty years before they could exercise their rights.... We now have to work on a real political relationship between First Nations and Canada. A Nation-to-Nation relationship that will bring about fundamental changes for First Nations in the same way the Charter of Rights has done for non-aboriginal Canadians.[10]

The Oka Crisis

The summer of 1990 was another turning point in relations between Aboriginal Canadians and the rest of Canadian society. A disagreement between two small communities became a conflict that captivated the nation. The town of Oka, Quebec, wanted to expand a nine-hole golf course to eighteen holes, but that required cutting into a forest that Mohawks from neighbouring Kanesatake declared was a sacred burial ground. When the Mohawks set up a dirt and log barricade to stop any construction, Oka secured a court order to have the roadblock removed. Women and children stayed behind the barricade, while the well-armed Mohawk men lined the sides of the woods. On July 11, the Quebec Police Force (*Sûreté du Quebec* or SQ) sent its riot squad to regain control of the road, where they were later joined by the RCMP. A violent clash broke out, and one police officer, Corporal Marcel Lemay, was killed.

A seventy-eight-day standoff ensued that was now about much more than a golf course. From the Mohawks' point of view, it was about standing up for their rights. To show support for the Kanesatake Mohawks, the Mohawks in Kahnawake near Montreal blocked highways leading to the Mercier Bridge, threatening to blow it up if there was a second assault on Oka. This led to occasional violent clashes between commuters, who were frustrated by the inconvenience of not being able to use the bridge, and the Aboriginal people. One morning, non-Aboriginal residents even pelted the vehicles of Aboriginal people with rocks.

At Oka, the Mohawks at the barricades were joined by Aboriginal people from nearby reserves. The Canadian Armed Forces (CAF) were sent in to replace the SQ and the RCMP on August 17. The tension was heightened by shots that rang out periodically. By early September, negotiations were underway to end the crisis, and from the front line, a striking scene was shown on television: a Mohawk warrior face to face with a Canadian soldier.

A Mohawk warrior during the Oka crisis.

The barricades were finally removed peacefully, but some Mohawk warriors retreated to the Oka Drug and Alcohol Rehabilitation Treatment Centre, where they continued the standoff. On September 27, the last warriors turned themselves over to CAF custody. The crisis was over, and the Mohawks believed they had won. They said they had succeeded in drawing attention to their position. In July 1992, thirty-four Mohawks were found not guilty of various riot and weapons charges for their roles at the Oka standoff. The golf course was never built. In 1997, the federal government bought the land from Oka and the Mohawks were allowed to expand their cemetery.

The crisis left a scar, and it set a precedent. Aboriginal people have been willing to use confrontational tactics ever since to pursue what they see as their legitimate rights. In 1995, for example, about thirty Chippewa Indians occupied Ipperwash Park in Ontario to protest what they said was the destruction of their burial ground. One protester, Dudley George, was killed. An Ontario provincial police officer was found guilty of criminal negligence causing death.

In Burnt Church, New Brunswick, in 2000, Aboriginal people tried to assert what they said was their right to trap lobster without restrictions by the Canadian government. Non-native fishers said that was unfair, and they vandalized boats owned by Aboriginal people and destroyed many of their traps. In April 2002, a federally appointed committee made recommendations that Aboriginal fishers should have the same fishing season as non-Aboriginal fishers and that Aboriginal fishers should fish under a Fisheries Department Licence that would be distributed by the band. Although many non-Aboriginal people welcomed the recommendations, Burnt Church band elder Lloyd Augustine stated, "They know what is ours but are just using the reconciliation process to take away more of what belongs to the Mi'kmaq people."[11]

Aboriginal fishers at Burnt Church, New Brunswick.

The Royal Commission on Aboriginal Peoples

One of the actions Ottawa took in the wake of Oka was to establish a Royal Commission on Aboriginal Peoples. Four of the seven commissioners were Aboriginal. In 1996, they produced one of the most extensive and thoroughly researched reports in Canadian history. It included 440 recommendations, among them

- the implementation of new legislation, including a new Royal Proclamation stating Canada's commitment to a new relationship with Aboriginal people and recognition of Aboriginal nations and governments
- the replacement of the federal Department of Indian Affairs with two departments, one to implement the new relationship with Aboriginal nations and one to provide services for non-self-governing communities
- the expansion of the Aboriginal land and resource base
- the increase of efforts to address social, education, health, and housing needs, including the training of 10 000 health professionals over ten years
- the establishment of an Aboriginal Peoples' university and the recognition of Aboriginal nations' authority over child welfare

The heart of the report dealt with how Aboriginal people should be governed. It recommended recognition of Aboriginal governments as a third order of government in Canada (only two are recognized in the *Constitution*: federal and provincial). It stated that an Aboriginal Parliament should be established that would evolve into a House of First Peoples and become part of Parliament. The report's recommendations were the polar opposite of what the 1969 White Paper had recommended. In contrast to the White Paper, the Royal Commission called for Aboriginal Peoples to be treated differently from other Canadians.

No serious consideration has been made of the notion of a third order of government. It is highly unlikely that the constitutional amendments required would ever attract enough support. Instead, Ottawa has embarked on two tracks of important negotiations: self-government and the settlement of land claims.

Self-Government

Aboriginal people believe self-government is their inherent right, a right that exists because they occupied and governed the land for thousands of years before Europeans arrived. Ottawa says it recognizes that inherent right under section 35 of the *Constitution,* but it says that the right must be exercised within the existing *Constitution* (thus rejecting the Royal Commission's recommendation of a third order of government) and that self-government should enhance the participation of Aboriginal people in Canadian society. Ottawa also insists that the *Charter of Rights and Freedoms* applies to any Aboriginal government; that federal, provincial, territorial, and Aboriginal laws must work in harmony; and that no new federal money will be used to pay for Aboriginal self-government. The range of matters Ottawa is willing to consider for self-government include marriage, language, culture and religion, education, health, social services, and policing. It is also willing to negotiate shared jurisdiction on areas such as fisheries management and gaming laws. It is not willing to negotiate about powers related to Canadian sovereignty or foreign affairs.

The process of implementing self-government is expected to take quite some time. In the interim, Ottawa decided in 2001 to press ahead with a law on what it calls "First Nations governance," designed to make reserves more democratic and Aboriginal leaders more accountable. For example, it wants to make clear the rules for how bandleaders are selected and how they answer to the people. Ottawa started consulting directly with Aboriginal people about what they wanted to see in such a law, and that infuriated most Aboriginal leaders. They accused the government of trying to impose white law on Aboriginal reserves. The Assembly of First Nations said, "We reject the process [the government] is currently pursuing, and instead we, as First Nations, will draw up our own laws based on traditional customs and practices at the local, community, regional, and national levels."[12]

Land Claims

Just as the Cree in Quebec asserted that they had never surrendered their land in any treaty, so do numerous other bands across Canada. Ottawa says it is committed to settling land claims, and negotiations have been underway with many bands for years. In many cases, land claims and self-government go hand in hand. Once an agreement is reached on how much land will be recognized as Aboriginal, it stands to reason that an agreement is needed on how that land will be governed.

The Nisga'a Treaty

Signed in 1998 and ratified by the governments of British Columbia and Canada by the end of 1999, the Nisga'a Final Agreement represented a huge step forward for Aboriginal Canadians. It settled the land claim of the Nisga'a Nation, located in British Columbia's Nass Valley. The Nisga'a quest for a treaty began more than one hundred years ago, in 1890, and the agreement stands as the first modern-day treaty in British Columbia. The Nisga'a received control over almost 2000 km^2 of land and more than $500 million in cash, grants, program funds, and area improvements. On top of that, they were given self-government over culture, language,

The Nisga'a Final Agreement

Nisga'a Chief Gosnell after signing the Nisga'a Treaty, 1998.

public works, and regulation of traffic, land use, and marriages. They can also choose to make laws in the areas of health, child welfare, and education.

Following the ratification of the Nisga'a Treaty in Ottawa, Nisga'a Chief Joseph Gosnell said,

> The Royal Assent of our treaty signifies the end of the colonial era for the Nisga'a people. It is a great and historic day for all Canadians, and this achievement is a beacon of hope for colonized people in our own country and throughout the world. Today, the Nisga'a people become full-fledged Canadians as we step out from under the Indian Act—forever. Finally, after a struggle of more than 130 years, the government of this country clearly recognizes that the Nisga'a were a self-governing people since well before European contact. We remain self-governing today, and we are proud to say that this inherent right is now clearly recognized and protected in the Constitution of Canada."[13]

Smaller land claim settlements happen quite regularly. In 2001, for example, the Fishing Lake First Nation in Saskatchewan agreed to settle a claim that went back to 1907. It accepted about $35 million from the federal government. But some claims are very difficult to settle. In 1997, Ottawa and British Columbia began negotiating with the Nuu-chah-nulth Tribal Council, which represents about 6500 Aboriginal people on the west coast of Vancouver Island. After five years of negotiations, and the largest offer ever made in the treaty-making process, Canada, British Columbia, and the Nuu-chah-nulth Tribal Council initialled an agreement in March 2001 that provides 550 km² of land on the west coast of Vancouver Island and $243 million. The agreement also allows for a central Nuu-chah-nulth government that will have its own law-making authority over treaty land.[14]

Nunavut

A happy northern development occurred in 1999. For the first time in fifty years (since Newfoundland

Raising the flag of Nunavut.

capital of Nunavut, is as far from the old capital, Yellowknife, as Vancouver, British Columbia, is from Thunder Bay, Ontario.

Nunavut (it means "Our land" in Inuktitut) covers about one fifth of Canada (1 994 000 km²) but has only 25 000 people. Eighty-five percent of the inhabitants are Inuit. They won not just a territory, but also a land claim settlement. It called for $1.1 billion in compensation, title to 355 842 km² of land, mineral rights to 35 257 km², a share of federal government royalties from oil, gas, and mineral development on Crown lands, and a guarantee that 85 percent of the government's employees will be Inuit. For the Inuit, the creation of Nunavut meant control over their own affairs.

The Future

As negotiations over Aboriginal land claims continue, the economic and social reality of most Aboriginal Canadians does not improve. Even though exploration continues in the north and new natural resources are being discovered, Aboriginal Peoples are not receiving a fair share of the new wealth. In northern Quebec, where the majority of the population is Cree, fewer than 3 percent of the Cree population hold jobs. For example, of more than 1800 forestry jobs, Crees hold only 3 percent, and at Hydro-Quebec, only seven Crees have jobs (1 percent of the employees).[15] Although governments are moving toward land claim and self-government agreements, most Canadians do not support the process. One opinion poll taken after the Nisga'a treaty was signed showed that only 25 percent of Canadians feel Aboriginal Peoples have an inherent right to self-government.[16]

Fuelled by the frustratingly slow pace of progress, Aboriginal leaders are expressing their views on the mistreatment of Aboriginal Peoples in

and Labrador joined Confederation), the political map of Canada changed. The third Canadian territory was created: Nunavut. The idea of splitting the Northwest Territories had been discussed since 1965, but it took years of negotiation and two referendums in the north to approve the division and agree on the new boundary.

Nunavut was created to bring the people of the eastern Arctic closer to their government. Iqaluit, the biggest community in the east and now the

Canada. In July 2001, Assembly of First Nations National Chief Matthew Coon Come said,

> It has been federal policy to not provide for adequate sanitation, drinking water, housing, health care, infrastructure, and services to our people. What is happening is the continuing implementation of policies of assimilation and extinguishment through infliction of conditions of social despair. These conditions are tolerated because of racism.... Our social problems, our day-to-day community needs are at crisis levels. They have been for many years, since the days the present prime minister [Jean Chrétien] was Minister of Indian Affairs. We are told that the gap between First Nations' life expectancy and that of [other] Canadians has narrowed. However, as a result of the gross social disparities facing our peoples, perhaps 500 and perhaps more excess deaths occur among our people each year. In addition, there is a terrible cost in lost human potential and other misery. These are enormous numbers. Canada's social policies are killing and stunting large numbers of our people.[17]

Although Coon Come has attracted criticism from the Canadian government for his outspoken condemnation of Canada's treatment of its Aboriginal Peoples, he does remain hopeful that the tides will turn:

> During the next year I will be undertaking bold new strategic steps, built on the strong foundation of the last year's work, to persuade the federal Crown and the Canadian people that the time is now for fundamental change. We will need to mobilize as never before in the history of this land. We will have to become a political force to be reckoned with. Our prescriptions for our inclusion into Canada must become irresistible.
>
> We are already experiencing resistance. It is no secret that Minister [of Indian and Northern Affairs Robert] Nault has attacked the AFN [Assembly of First Nations] at its core through

funding. This came as no surprise, I knew it would happen the day I was elected. We can survive this easily.... The government of South Africa never funded Nelson Mandela's African National Congress; it actually made it illegal for it to exist. It never stopped existing, and it prevailed. We will prevail.[18]

Review...Reflect...Respond

1. Describe the key events in the struggle for Aboriginal rights in Canada since 1970.

2. Why have the day-to-day community needs of Aboriginal people remained at crisis levels in Canada?

3. What strategic steps do you believe Aboriginal Peoples need to take to gain equality, or is it the Canadian government's responsibility to ensure this equality?

The Quebec Question

When Canada succeeded in patriating its *Constitution* in 1982, it looked to many Canadians as if the long-time skirmishing between Ottawa and the provinces was over. Though nothing says more about a country's core values than its constitution, it is also true that the Canadian *Constitution* is not generally a concern for most people.

Although Quebec was not a partner in the patriation deal, it is legally bound by the *Constitution*. Many politicians wanted to have Quebec join as a willing partner. Most had concluded that Quebec would never agree to any new deal as long as it had a separatist government in power. But when the Quebec Liberals took power under Robert Bourassa in 1985, hope was renewed.

Essays, Presentations, and Seminars

In a history course the historyical inquiry skills you have developed often culminate in a research essay, presentation or seminar.

The History Essay

A history essay is usually organized with an introductory paragraph, supporting evidence or body paragraphs, and a concluding paragraph.

Introductory Paragraph

Your introduction should catch the interest of the reader, frame the topic, define the scope and focus of your essay, and clearly state your thesis or point of view. Your introductory paragraph is very important because it provides a "roadmap" or "blueprint" for the rest of your paper. A strong thesis is integral to your introduction. Your thesis will be the answer to your research question. (See Methods of Historical Inquiry: Formulating Research Questions.)

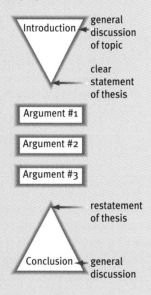

For example, for the research question "Did the social welfare policies of the 1960s reject or support capitalism?" a possible thesis answer may be,

The social welfare policies of the 1960s curtailed Canada's capitalist system by making both business and consumers dependent on government intervention and assistance.

The social welfare policies of the 1960s supported and sustained Canada's capitalist system by ensuring that no one sector of the production and consumption cycle gained an economic monopoly.

Supporting Evidence or Body Paragraphs

The supporting evidence paragraphs should always refer to the thesis and provide evidence and arguments that support the thesis. Include evidence, statistics, logic and reasoning that support your point of view. You could use the following strategy for your support paragraphs:

- Use a minimum of three supporting points in each of your paragraphs.
- Consider placing your second strongest evidence first, your weakest evidence second, and your strongest evidence last.
- Also try to explain the weaknesses in arguments that oppose your thesis. This shows that you are aware of the opposing arguments and that you have deliberately selected the stronger arguments.
  (See Methods of Historical Inquiry: Analyzing Information.)

Within each paragraph it is important to support your arguments with evidence from experts in the topic you have chosen. Integrate your quotations carefully to provide a flow between your style of writing and the expert you are quoting. The linking sentence before the quote should introduce and briefly explain the purpose of the quote while the sentence following the quote should show how it supports your reasoning.

Linking sentences: [Judge Thomas]Berger concluded that nothing should be built until land claims were settled. He was forceful and eloquent in his framing reasons.

Quotation: "There are two distinct views of the north: one as a frontier, the other as a homeland. We {non-aboriginals} look upon the North as our last frontier. It is natural for us to think of developing it, of subduing the land and extracting resources to fuel Canada's industry and heat our homes. But the native people say the North is their homeland. They have lived there for thousands of years. They claim it is their land, and they believe they have a right to say what its future ought to be"

Linking Sentence: Nonetheless, the Government built part of the pipeline anyway, but only part of it.

The paragraphs in the body of your essay can be organized in a fashion similar to that of your evidence within each paragraph. That is, you can place your second strongest argument first, your weakest argument second, and your strongest argument last. You may, of course, have more than three supporting arguments for your thesis, or you may have more than one paragraph dedicated to each of your arguments.

Concluding Paragraph

Your concluding paragraph should forcefully restate your thesis or main idea and should sum up your most important arguments and evidence. However, don't just repeat the same sentences that you used earlier in your essay. In addition, although you won't want to raise completely new issues in your conclusion, you could show how your essay fits into a wider context. For example, you could connect your thesis and your arguments to a larger issue or you could compare your subject with another one with which your reader may be more familiar.

Referencing

You must reference the information, ideas and reasoning that you obtain from other sources. Always reference
- factual information
- another author's ideas or opinions
- direct quotations
- an explanation of an idea or concept relevant to the essay topic

This can be done with citations in the essay body or in the form of footnotes or endnotes.

Bibliography

All history essays must have a bibliography that lists all of the research sources. References in a bibliography are always listed alphabetically according to the author's surname. If there is no author, the title appears in the appropriate alphabetical spot.

Sample Bibliography

Gillmor, Don., and Pierre Turgeon. *Canada: A People's History*. (Toronto: McClelland & Stewart Ltd., 2000), p. 4.

Lipset, S.M. "Agrarian Socialism." In Paul W. Bennett and Cornelius Jaenen, eds., *Emerging Identities*. (Scarborough: Prentice-Hall, 1986.), p. 245–256.

Newman, Garfield. *Legacy: The West and the World*. (Whitby: McGraw-Hill Ryerson Limited, 2002.), p. 456.

Annotated Bibliography

An annotated bibliography includes the same information as a regular bibliography but is extended to explain the main idea or premise of the book or article. An annotated bibliography can also indicate how the source was used for developing the essay.

Zolf, Larry, "1970–The October Crisis." Retrieved August 14, 2002, from <http://cbc.ca/millennium/timelines/feature_octobercrisis.html>.

In this article, Larry Zolf, a veteran CBC broadcaster, remembers the words and actions of Trudeau and other House of Commons' members during the hours leading up to the proclamation of the War Measures Act. Zolf also offers a personal analysis of the aftermath of Trudeau's decision.

Presentations and Seminars

Presentations and seminars should follow the same format as the history essay. In fact, presentations are often called "oral essays." State your thesis or point of view at the beginning and then use a variety of evidence, logic and reasoning to support your claims. Often, seminar presentations will require the development of a history essay. You can augment your presentations and seminars with visual material, audio visuals, and multimedia software.

The Meech Lake Accord

Bourassa came up with five principles that he said would have to be included in any new constitutional arrangement so that Quebec could sign with "dignity and honour":

1. a veto for Quebec on any constitutional amendments
2. Input for the province on the naming of justices to the Supreme Court of Canada
3. Limits on federal spending power in Quebec
4. Increased power for Quebec on matters of immigration
5. Recognition of Quebec as a "distinct society"

Much to the surprise of a country that had become used to constitutional impasse, Prime Minister Brian Mulroney and the ten provincial premiers signed the Meech Lake Accord in June 1987. Quebec had everything it wanted, and it appeared as if the long pursuit of constitutional harmony was finally over. Prime Minister Mulroney said, "This agreement enhances the Confederation bargain and strengthens the federal nature of Canada."[19]

The Canadian Parliament and each of the ten provincial legislatures had to approve the Accord, but that seemed a formality. In fact, Quebec's National Assembly ratified the deal almost immediately. As long as all the legislatures approved the Accord within three years, the deal would be sealed.

In Manitoba, New Brunswick, and Newfoundland and Labrador, however, the governments had changed hands and the new premiers had reservations about the Meech Lake Accord. In Newfoundland and Labrador, the Accord had been ratified, but the new government under Clyde Wells rescinded its approval. The longer the Accord remained open for discussion, the more it became a target for criticism. There were many complaints about what had been left out, especially Senate reform, Aboriginal rights, devolution of power to the territories, multiculturalism, the extension and protection of linguistic rights, and the improvement and further protection of individual rights within the *Charter*.

There was also an enormous uproar over the two words "distinct society." What did they mean? Were they simply a phrase that recognized the obvious (Quebec was mostly French-speaking, used civil law instead of common law, etc.)? Or were they the key to giving Quebec far more power to protect its "distinct society"? Those two words became the crucible for all the opposition. Some of the opposition was simply anti-French sentiment disguised as constitutional concern.

Then Pierre Trudeau, who was by then a legal consultant, stepped into the fray, because he thought the Meech Lake Accord presented a vision of Canada that he could not abide. He tore the Accord apart as a betrayal of everything Canada stood for. In front of a Senate committee in 1988, he spoke for five and a half hours and warned that if the Meech Lake Accord were approved, "the Canada we know and love will be gone for ever."[20] Trudeau said that the distinct society clause either meant nothing, in which case Quebeckers would ultimately feel double-crossed, or it did have meaning. In that case, he said, Quebec would legislate a distinct society leading to

> two constitutions, two charters [of rights] promoting two distinct sets of values, and eventually two Canadas.... For unscrupulous politicians, there is no surer way of rousing feelings than to trumpet a call to pride of race. French Canadians will be rid of this kind of politician if the blackmail ceases, and the blackmail will cease only if Canada refuses to dance to that tune.[21]

The premier of Alberta, Don Getty, said the distinct society clause was "window dressing." Prime Minister Mulroney said it was "nothing to worry about." A group of legal experts concluded that the clause did not confer any special powers on the Quebec National Assembly, and those opinions were made part of the record. But Robert Bourassa, trying to defend the interests of his province, told the National Assembly, "It cannot be stressed too strongly that the entire *Constitution*, including the

Canadian Leaders

NATIONAL CHIEF MATTHEW COON COME

Matthew Coon Come became National Chief of the Assembly of First Nations (AFN), the political organization representing First Nations, in 2000. Throughout his career as an Aboriginal leader, he has effectively championed Aboriginal Peoples' rights of self-determination.

Coon Come was born in a hut along the trap line his parents worked in northern Quebec, near the community of Mistissini. He did not see a white man until he was six, and that man was an Indian Affairs agent, who took the young boy away to a series of southern residential schools in Moose Factory, La Tuque, and Hull. Coon Come then enrolled at Trent and McGill Universities studying political science, economics, Native Studies, and Law.

A natural leader, Coon Come was only 21 when a delegation of Cree elders asked him to run for election as the band's deputy chief. He won and eventually became Chief of the Mistissini Cree, serving two terms, from 1981 to 1986. By the time Coon Come left this office to work on his father's trapline, the community had a new arena, an adult education centre, a bank, new administrative offices, new health facilities, and major improvements to its housing.

In 1987 Coon Come became Grand Chief of the Grand Council of the Crees, leading 12 000 Crees of northern Quebec. He was re-elected to serve four successive terms. One of his most significant achievements during that time was co-ordinating negotiations with Canada that enabled James Bay Crees to escape the *Indian Act* and gain the first ever Aboriginal self-government legislation in Canada, the Cree-Naskapi Act.

As Grand Chief, he successfully articulated the concerns of the James Bay Crees nationally and internationally. In the early 1990s, Hydro Quebec wanted to build the Great Whale hydroelectric project. It would have consisted of more than 30 dams and 600 dikes, blocking nine major rivers and irreversibly damaging the vast James Bay and Hudson Bay ecosystem.

The area supports large populations of caribou and waterfowl, and is home to the Cree, who have a led a subsistence lifestyle in the area for 5,000 years. Coon Come led Cree efforts to oppose the massive power project.

During this opposition campaign, Coon Come displayed a commanding grasp of both politics and public relations. In 1990 he masterminded a canoe trip by Cree elders from James Bay, down the Hudson River to a press conference in New York. The publicity helped generate public opposition to the project. As a result, New York State cancelled contracts to purchase electricity from Hydro Quebec. In 1992 the Cree succeeded in forcing Hydro Quebec to conduct an environmental assessment on Great Whale. The Cree won the environmental battle in November 1994 when the Quebec premier announced the suspension of the Great Whale project. For this important environmental achievement, in 1994 Coon Come was awarded the international Goldman Prize, which is considered the Nobel Prize of environmental awards.

Later, Coon Come played a pivotal role in opposing the Quebec secessionist movement, which threatened to trample Aboriginal rights. Traditional Cree, Naskapi, Innu, and Inuit territories made up two-thirds of the overall territory being claimed by Quebec. Although there are only 12 000 Crees in Quebec, Coon Come made sure the historical, moral, and legal credibility of their unified voice was heard. Under his leadership Quebec Crees boycotted the 1995 referendum and held their own referendum to decide *their* political fate. In this vote, 96 percent of Crees voted "No" to being included in any arrangement that would separate them from Canada. Then the Grand Council of Crees intervened during the Supreme Court Reference on Quebec Secession and successfully argued that rights of the Aboriginal Peoples should not be ignored.

(continued)

Canadian Leaders

NATIONAL CHIEF MATTHEW COON COME *(continued)*

Now National Chief of the Assembly of First Nations, an organization consisting of over 630 First Nations in Canada, Coon Come continues to articulate Aboriginal grievances nationally and internationally.

His position on Aboriginal rights in Canada is clearly outlined in the speech he delivered to Assembly delegates the night before the leadership vote, "If the government of Canada wishes to continue to stand tall as a member of the community of nations, (it) will have to recognize our right to share in the wealth of the land."

Matthew Coon Come, National Chief of the Assembly of First Nations.

Charter, will be interpreted and applied in light of the section proclaiming our distinctiveness as a society. We will be able to consolidate what has already been achieved and gain new ground."[22]

The Meech Lake Accord died a very public death. In Manitoba, an Aboriginal member of the legislature, Elijah Harper, single-handedly shut down the province's last-minute attempt to pass Meech. Angered by the absence of any effort to address Aboriginal concerns, he refused to give the unanimous consent necessary for the legislature to change its rules to deal with Meech.

When the deadline passed, Manitoba and Newfoundland and Labrador had not signed. There were desperate efforts to try to extend the deadline, and *CBC Newsworld* broadcast the speeches and news conferences of all the major players trying to salvage the agreement. But so much had already unravelled that their efforts were futile.

Proponents of the Meech Lake Accord had so often said that Canada's unity depended on the Accord, that its failure aroused fears about what might happen next. In Quebec, the separatists were overjoyed. They had opposed the Accord since they believed it gave Quebec too little power. Now they could emphasize that the rest of Canada would not accede to even "weak demands." Robert Bourassa said that he believed that Quebec was not understood by the rest of Canada.

The Bloc Québécois

A group of federal politicians from Quebec was so distraught at what they saw as English Canada's rejection of their province, and at what they perceived as the federal government's last minute attempts to appease English Canada, that they broke away from their parties. The highest profile among them was Lucien Bouchard, who had been a cabinet minister under Brian Mulroney.

Bouchard became the leader of what at first glance seemed to be a paradox, a federal party committed to the separation of Quebec from Canada. It

Lucien Bouchard, leader of The Bloc Québécois.

was called the Bloc Québécois (BQ). The party argued that as long as Quebec separatists paid federal taxes, they were entitled to representation in Ottawa. In their first election campaign in 1993, the BQ took 49 percent of the vote in Quebec and fifty-four of the seventy-five seats. The party had the second highest number of seats in the House of Commons, which meant that a party devoted to the breakup of Canada assumed the status of Her Majesty's Loyal Opposition.

The Charlottetown Accord

Although severely bruised by the failure of the Meech Lake Accord, Prime Minister Mulroney decided to try to get Quebec's agreement on the *Constitution* again. In 1992, he again came out of a federal–provincial conference (this time in Charlottetown, Prince Edward Island) with an agreement between the federal government and all ten provinces on how to amend the *Constitution* and allow Quebec to come on board.

The prime minister and the premiers reasoned that there had been too much concentration on Quebec's demands in the Meech Lake Accord, so they set out to address a wider audience. Virtually everything in Meech reappeared in the Charlottetown Accord, including the description of Quebec as a distinct society. But there was also a "Canada clause," which included a commitment to the health of English- and French-language minority communities; a statement on the principle of the equality of the provinces; and commitments to gender equality, individual and collective human rights and freedoms, parliamentary democracy, and racial and ethnic equality. The Charlottetown Accord included a commitment to negotiate the right of self-government with First Nations; a fundamental reform of the Senate (making it "triple-e": equal, elected, and effective), which was a major demand of all the provinces outside Quebec and Ontario; and a social charter guaranteeing the future of health, education, and welfare programs.

The prime minister and the ten premiers had been stung by accusations that they had tried to sneak Meech past the Canadian people. For example, Deborah Coyne, a professor at the University of Toronto, said, "Eleven men sat around a table trading legislative, judicial and executive powers as engaged in a gentlemanly game of poker."[23] To refute that charge, they decided to put the Charlottetown Accord to a referendum. They agreed that the Accord had to have majority approval not only in the country as a whole, but also in every province as well.

All the premiers stayed onside this time, but once again, Pierre Trudeau was opposed. And this time his critique was even stronger:

> Every time a new demand is announced, the self-appointed elites snap to attention, ready to feel humiliated if the ransom is not paid at once. Most incredible of all, there are still good souls in English Canada who are ready to take these temper tantrums seriously and urge their compatriots to pay each new ransom for fear of losing each "last chance" to save Canada. Poor things, they have not yet realized that the nationalists' thirst will never be satisfied, and that each new ransom paid to stave off the threat of schism will simply encourage the master blackmailers to renew the threat and double the ransom.[24]

On October 26, 1992, the Charlottetown Accord won approval in only four provinces (Newfoundland and Labrador, PEI, New Brunswick, and Ontario). Across Canada the vote was 45.7 percent in favour, 54.3 percent opposed. Quebec rejected it by a margin of 55.4 percent to 42.4 percent. Under those circumstances, it was difficult for Quebeckers to say that English Canada had turned its back on them. But some in Quebec had voted No because the Accord had not given enough to the province.

Mike Harcourt, the premier of British Columbia reflected on the mood of the country after the latest failure at constitutional politics, saying, "We should put the *Constitution* on the back burner for a while, and turn off the burner."[25]

What commentary was this cartoonist making about Brian Mulroney?

Quebec Referendum 1995

In 1995, the Parti Québécois was once more in power in Quebec, and once again it was prepared to ask the population to approve independence in a referendum. The question was: "Do you agree that Quebec should become sovereign, after having made a formal offer to Canada for a new Economic and Political Partnership, within the scope of the Bill respecting the future of Quebec and of the agreement signed on June 12, 1995?"[26] The bill referred to in the question allowed for one year of negotiations with Canada before sovereignty was declared. The agreement was a reference to a deal among three parties supporting separation: the Parti Québécois, the Bloc Québécois, and the Action Democratique. Again, the wording of the question was hotly contested. The Yes campaign

The Quebec referendum caused great debate in Canada. Canadians voting Yes or No went to rallies to show support for their position.

said the question could not be more direct and to look at the first eight words. The No side said if the question was meant to be direct, then why were the other thirty-five words there?

The campaign was emotional, and opinion polls indicated the result would be close. The vote was set for Monday, October 30, 1995. On Friday, October 28, a rare scene of unabashed patriotism was on display. Canadians from across the country descended on Montreal by car, train, bus, and plane. Several premiers were there, but mostly it was ordinary citizens who wanted to tell Quebeckers they were wanted. The Yes side was fairly cynical about the demonstration and complained that Quebec's referendum law had been violated because transportation costs for some people had been paid for by groups outside Quebec (meaning outside interests were interfering in Quebec politics). But by most accounts, the pro-Canada rally seemed to be a genuine outpouring of goodwill. No one can say for sure how many people took part (estimates ranged from 35 000 to 150 000) or whether it made any difference.

On election night, the vote could not have been much closer. With 4 757 509 votes cast, 50.58 percent voted no, 49.42 percent voted yes. Lucien Bouchard, who had been the most sparkling of the Yes side's leaders (and who would become premier of Quebec in just a few months), told supporters, "Let's keep the faith, because the next time will be the right time. And the next time could come quicker than you think."[27]

Prime Minister Jean Chrétien told Canadians that it was time to put aside any differences. But the government of Quebec was not willing to put aside its differences. It continues to support separation.

Questions for the Court

When the Parti Québécois was reelected in 1998, Ottawa decided it had to do more than react to moves toward separation. In 1999, Ottawa went to the Supreme Court of Canada, trying to set the legal rules for any Quebec declaration of independence.

Elijah Harper and the Meech Lake Accord

The following excerpt is MLA Elijah Harper's speech in which he voted against the Meech Lake Accord, and in so doing, defeated the Accord.

Mr. Speaker, we are united to meet our objectives. The fight that we are fighting is not with Quebec. We support their aspirations. We support the distinct society. We support the right for them to protect their culture, to be self-determining, a self-government. Those are the very same goals that we as Aboriginal people are trying to achieve....

As I mentioned before, the federal Government has determined what our rights, what our participation should be in Canada. We have an Act, an Indian Act, that has shackled Indian people. This human bondage must be done away with. I believe that Aboriginal people will some day obtain self-government, but that is with the co-operation from other governments....

Elijah Harper (arm raised) refused to consent to the Meech Lake Accord because it failed to address Aboriginal concerns.

We have been told that because we do not support Meech Lake that there will be economic consequences, that there will be a backlash, and that Quebec will separate. I do not believe that for a moment, because Quebec's goals are the same goals for Aboriginal people...

As I mentioned, our fight is not with Quebec, if Quebec is to separate, it is not because English Canada rejected Meech Lake Accord, but rather the Aboriginal people want to have a rightful place in Canadian society. I do not think Quebec has that moral authority to separate from Canada. We have never denied Quebec their rightful place in the Canadian society.

...I know the Prime Minister sent a letter to us, to the chiefs, a few days ago, hoping that we will support Meech Lake. The chiefs indicated that they were willing to hear the Prime Minister himself or his delegates to see what they had to offer. Of course, the Prime Minister's office sent a delegation to offer us some things that were unacceptable to the Manitoba chiefs, because we have heard it all before....

I hope the Canadian people will listen seriously to the greatest contributions we made to this country, the positive contributions we made to this country. There is no one group in Canada that can claim that they have made the greatest contribution except the Aboriginal people, for the land and resources so the other people may live within Canada. We are a rich country, a wealthy country, but we have not received these benefits....

We are prepared to live with the consequences of our actions, but I do not believe the Canadian people will support the actions of governments, a backlash of governments against aboriginal people. The disastrous situation in those communities [aboriginal reserves] is just horrendous. As one reporter asked me, what disastrous consequences would there be if we do not support Meech Lake? I mentioned, what more disastrous conditions can there exist on reserves as they are now? It cannot get any worse.

We are prepared to live for the rights that we are fighting for...We are not interested in short-term solutions. What we are fighting for is for our people, for our children, for the future of our children, for our culture, for our heritage and what we believe in. Most of all we are fighting for our rightful place in Canadian society and also fighting for democracy for aboriginal people and indeed all Canadians. Thank you.

SECOND SESSION, THIRTY-FOURTH LEGISLATURE OF THE LEGISLATIVE ASSEMBLY OF MANITOBA, DEBATES AND PROCEEDINGS, 38–39 ELIZABETH II, 21 JUNE 1990: 6017–6019.

---

1. If Elijah Harper sees the goals of Quebec as similar to those of Aboriginal Peoples in Canada, why did he vote against the Meech Lake Accord?

It asked the court, "Under the Constitution of Canada, can the National Assembly, legislature, or government of Quebec effect the secession of Quebec from Canada unilaterally?"[28] The court said it could not. It said that even with a clear yes vote on a clear referendum question, Quebec was legally bound to negotiate with Canada on the terms of any separation. Ottawa also asked the court whether Quebec had a right to declare independence unilaterally under international law. Again, the court said no, international law did not allow it.

The federal government then turned to the Quebec government and asked it to respect the Court's ruling. The minister of intergovernmental affairs, Stéphane Dion, said any unilateral declaration of independence by Quebec would be "impractical as well as illegal.... There are few things more dangerous in a democracy than a government that places itself above the law."[29]

The Quebec government had refused to take part in the Supreme Court case. Its minister of intergovernmental affairs, Joseph Facal, chose to see support for the independence cause in the Supreme Court's ruling. He said that for the first time the Court "imposes on Canada the obligation to negotiate in good faith should there be a vote favourable for sovereignty."[30]

The Clarity Bill

Ottawa decided it was time to try to end the uncertainty about how Quebec could separate from the rest of Canada. In 2000, it drafted and passed a bill detailing the circumstances under which the federal government would agree to negotiate secession with a province. The bill said that the House of Commons would examine the question of any referendum on independence to determine whether it was clearly stated. It would look for "a clear expression of the will of the population of a province that the province cease to be part of Canada." The bill expressly defines as unclear any question that focuses on a mandate to negotiate sovereignty or any question that envisages other possibilities in addition to the secession of the province, such as economic or political arrangements with Canada.

The bill also demands a "clear majority" on any referendum question. It does not define what a clear majority means, except to say that the House of Commons would consider the size of the majority, the percentage of eligible voters who voted, and "any other matters or circumstances it considers to be relevant." That has been widely interpreted as meaning Ottawa would never accept a yes vote of 50 percent plus one, the classic formula for deciding almost everything else in the Canadian democracy and the threshold the separatists have long insisted on.

Should there ever be a third Quebec referendum on sovereignty, the rules will be dramatically different from the first two. The federal government believes it has taken away the Quebec government's advantages: the ability to ask any question it likes and to decide on the definition of victory.

The Future

When he was premier of Quebec, Jacques Parizeau, warned the rest of Canada that the separatists were never going to go away. He promised English Canada that dealing with Quebec's demands while it remained in the country would be like "a never-ending trip to the dentist."[31] One of Quebec's most distinguished scholars, Leon Dion, respected by both nationalists and federalists in Quebec, once advised that if Quebec was serious about getting constitutional concessions from the rest of Canada, it must negotiate "with a knife at the throat."[32] The throat would be Canada's and the knife would be the threat of separation.

There is increasing evidence that although most Canadians outside Quebec want Quebec to be part of the country, there is less appetite for going to the dentist or dealing with people holding knives. The Clarity Bill is generally popular (one opinion poll put support for it at 70 percent outside Quebec and at 51 percent inside the province), probably because it pushes for finality.[33]

Particularly in western Canada, there is a sense that the country has wasted too much time, money, and energy dealing with Quebec while ignoring western concerns. The rise of the Reform Party beginning in the early 1990s was due in part to so many westerners looking for a political voice more attuned to them.

The urgency of the Quebec question rises and falls, but it rarely disappears completely from the National agenda and very few people believe we are close to resolving it. What René Lévesque said in 1963 could be spoken by any number of Quebec nationalists today: "To us, the basic thing is to have a homeland called Quebec. If we are not recognized in this sick Confederation, then we'll move out—and nobody is going to stop us."[34]

Globalization

The new century brought with it a concept that has created a new line of confrontation in Canadian society; globalization refers to the degree to which cultural, political, economic, and environmental activities are no longer restricted to one or two or a handful of countries at a time but instead stretch across continents, hemispheres, or around the world. The process is driven by technology, and as it becomes better, smarter, and faster, national borders become less important. Since technological improvement is unstoppable, one school of thought declares that globalization is inevitable, and very few people quarrel with that declaration. The issue that divides people is how globalization will be implemented, who will be making the important decisions, and how the negative consequences of globalization will be handled. Canada has become embroiled in the globalization debate from two perspectives. Because it is one of the wealthiest countries in the world, Canada has been criticized because of what some say globalization means for poorer countries. Canadian

nationalists are also concerned that Canada's sovereignty will be lost if globalization is allowed to spread without safeguards.

The Good It Can Do

U.S. President George W. Bush says that for those around the world who live in poverty, globalization is "their best hope for escaping."[35] Prime Minister Jean Chrétien says Canada looks at globalization as an opportunity to make the world better by "strengthening democracy, creating prosperity, and realizing human potential."[36]

These leaders' opinions are based on the following theory of globalization: global free trade promotes global economic growth. It creates jobs, makes companies more competitive, and lowers prices for consumers. It also provides poor countries with foreign investment, not only monetary investment, but also technological investment. That gives poor countries the chance to develop economically. And when a country is materially better off, it is fostering an environment in which democracy and respect for human rights can flourish.

The Harm It Can Do

Maude Barlow, the national chair of the Council of Canadians, is at the forefront of the fight against globalization. She summarizes her opposition by saying,

> Everything is now for sale. Even those areas of life that we once considered sacred like health and education, food and water and air and seeds and genes and a heritage. It is all now for sale. Economic freedom—not democracy, and not ecological stewardship—is the defining metaphor.[37]

The fear of globalization is rooted in the belief that multinational corporations are interested only in making money and that they have no interest in improving the lives of people in poor countries. So even if companies have statistics that show that economic growth is enhanced by foreign investment in poor nations, opponents of globalization argue that the extra money is going to the people who are already rich. They say average people are deprived of access to the technological, medical, and scientific advancements.

Critics of globalization say the pursuit of profit will destroy jobs, incomes, and the environment. They point out that corporations such as General Motors, Ford, and Wal-Mart are already richer than most countries, and although their profits grow more rapidly when trade barriers fall, there is no guaranteed benefit to the employees of those companies or to the people who buy their products.

Web Connection

www.mcgrawhill.ca/links/definingcanada
To find out more about the Council of Canadians, go to the Web site above.

Who Speaks for the People?

The concern of anti-globalization forces is that governments are listening only to the corporations as they plan to implement free trade zones. For example, globalization's opponents say that poor countries should be forgiven their debts without any conditions attached. They say when debts are forgiven only in exchange for certain concessions, the concessions are not necessarily in the best long-term interests of the country, simply in the interests of making it easier for businesses to operate.

Governments say that they are the true representatives of the people and that they can be trusted to work for everyone. At the summit of the Organization of American States in Quebec City in April 2001, Canada was responsible for inserting a clause into the final communiqué that insisted the benefits of free trade would go only to democratic countries. Prime Minister Chrétien said that clause "clearly and eloquently illustrates our intention to ensure the protection of human rights and to move ahead together in freedom and stability."[38]

Beginning with a meeting of the World Trade Organization (WTO) in Seattle in 1999, protesters have taken to the streets to make their position heard at every international gathering. They have gone far beyond the point of carrying signs and chanting; they have tried to shut down the meetings. Clashes with the police have become routine.

At the Quebec City Summit of the Americas, protesters turned their attention to the goal of the conference, the Free Trade of the Americas Act (FTAA), which would allow for free trade between North and South America and the Caribbean. Those in favour of the FTAA argued that it would allow for more competitive industries, better access to international markets for Canadian companies, and cheaper goods and services. Opponents argued that it would lead to lower wages, higher unemployment, lower environmental protection standards, fewer social programs, and less protection for developing industries and countries.

Unwilling to allow the same events to occur as did during an outbreak of violence at a meeting in Seattle, the Canadian government erected a three-metre-high cement and chain-link fence (nicknamed "the wall of shame") and put into place the biggest security operation in peacetime Canadian history. Sixty-seven-hundred specially trained police officers, thousands of soldiers, armoured tanks, plastic bullets, and more than two thousand canisters of tear gas were on hand to subdue the protesters. A jail was emptied in anticipation of arresting the protesters.[39] When protesters tried to scale the barrier, violent clashes with the police ensued. Hundreds of protesters were arrested and thrown into jail, many squeezed into tiny cells without toilet facilities or food. Many protesters were hurt, as well as several police officers. Against this backdrop of violence, it is interesting to read Minister for International Cooperation Maria Minna's comments to Parliament about the 2001 summit:

Canada's vision of the future springs from a broad, open conception of our national interests.

Thousands of protesters clashed with thousands of police and soldiers at the Quebec City Summit of the Americas in April 2001. What balance must a host country, such as Canada, seek between protecting the members of the Summit and recognizing the democratic rights of protesters? Was a balance achieved in Quebec City?

Our interests are not just commercial. They are democratic and human. Our future as a stable, democratic state is dependent on the presence of stable, prosperous democratic neighbours. After all, it's the right thing to do.... That is why Canada has worked hard to place development issues at the centre of the Quebec City Summit. Our goal is a proper balance of economic and social issues. Hence the Summit's three themes: human potential, prosperity, and democracy.[40]

Prime Minister Chrétien received harsh criticism for what was termed the "overly aggressive" behaviour of the security forces. The clashes between protesters and police received news coverage around the world.

In Genoa, Italy, at a meeting of the top seven industrialized countries and Russia (the G8) in 2001, an anti-globalization protester was killed.

A conflict between two competing fundamental principles is taking shape. On the one hand, elected leaders have the right to meet. On the other hand, people have the right to civil protest. In a democracy it is the duty of government to protect both rights.

Summits are increasingly being arranged in remote locations (for example, the 2002 G8 meeting took place in Kananaskis, Alberta), where access can be easily controlled. The protesters maintain that leaders should be able to see and hear their demonstrations or their right to protest is meaningless.

Saving the Environment

Just as the concern over globalization and Canada's role in it has drawn much attention, so too has another issue that is of global concern—the environment. The industrialization of the world's economies not only triggered massive changes in societies, but also started the decay of the world's environment. Since the late 1960s, Canada and Canadians have played an important part in trying to save the Earth's resources—a difficult task when Canada itself must take a fair share of the blame for creating environmental hazards.

Some movements in history can be traced to an exact time and an exact place. But that really cannot be done with the popularization of the environmental movement. Concern for the environment in the last years of the twentieth century, and the first years of the twenty-first, may have started in 1962 when Rachel Carson, an American biologist, wrote *Silent Spring*. The book told of the dangers of chemicals polluting the Earth's air and water, killing plants and marine life, and affecting the health of humans. The book was an eye-opener, awakening a realization in many people that abusing the planet would have-term consequences.

The Rise of Environmental Watchdogs

In 1969, two major groups were established in Canada to fight for environmental protection, and they are both still active today. The Sierra Club, founded in 1892 in the United States, came to Canada and began working on five areas: the protection of wildlife and plant species, the protection of oceans and air quality, the protection of wilderness lands, fighting the proliferation of toxic chemicals, and fighting population growth and over-consumption. In 2002 it had about 3000 members in Canada.

Pollution Probe began at the University of Toronto, and has grown right across the country and in 2002 had about 25 000 members. Pollution Probe tries to work with governments, businesses, and the general public to bring attention to environmental problems and find solutions. Over the years it has set up a used motor oil recycling program (1987), run a media awareness campaign about the harmful effects of smog (1993), and persuaded the government to remove lead from gasoline (1988), ban the pesticide DDT (1989), and cut the sulphur content of gasoline (1999).

Greenpeace

Perhaps the best-known environmental group in the world is Greenpeace. It is well-known because it attracts media attention by engaging in highly visible actions. The group was born in Vancouver in 1971. A small group of people rented a boat and set course for Amchitka, Alaska. That was where the United States was planning to test nuclear weapons. The testing went ahead, but before too long the United States shut down the site. Since then Greenpeace has become a world-wide organization with about 2.5 million members. Its stated goals are to protect biodiversity, prevent pollution, end all nuclear threats, and promote global disarmament. It still engages in what it calls, "peaceful acts of civil disobedience," to confront what it sees as threats to the environment. Its members have taken a small boat to the open sea to harass whaling ships, chained themselves to trees to stop clearcut logging, and been arrested in China for protesting against nuclear weapons. In 1985, the

Greenpeace ship *Rainbow Warrior* was docked in Auckland New Zealand, ready to protest against nuclear testing by France. French secret service agents bombed the ship, killing a crewmember.

Government, Citizens, and the Environment

The Canadian government had caught on to the importance of environmental protection by the early 1970s. In 1971, it created a federal cabinet department to look after our part of the planet. The first Minister of the environment was Jack Davis.

The Canadian people caught on as well. They began looking for ways they could contribute to a cleaner world. In the early 1970s, the first curbside recycling programs began. In 1985, Ontario began the blue box program, one of the most comprehensive recycling programs in North America. It won a United Nations award in 1989. Canadians now recycle tonnes of paper, glass, plastics, and soft-drink cans, conserving precious natural resources.

The Kyoto Agreement

In 1997, an international meeting in Kyoto, Japan, agreed to a series of measures to reduce greenhouse gases. Industrialized nations committed themselves to reducing emissions from 1990 levels by about 5.2 percent by 2012. The Kyoto protocol was signed by 84 countries, including Canada. The United States, which is by far the largest producer of greenhouse gases in the world, signed as well, but in 2002 President George W. Bush decided his country would not ratify Kyoto. Bush claimed it would be too harmful to the US economy.

There was a similar debate in Canada. We are the world's ninth largest producer of greenhouse gases, the third largest per-capita. The province of Alberta was especially opposed to ratification of the Kyoto protocol. Its economy, based on energy, would be especially hard-hit by reducing emissions. A poll taken while the debate raged found that 67 percent of Canadians (including 54 percent

of Albertans) supported ratifying the protocol. The country will not have an easy time making its targets. Since 1990, emission of greenhouse gases in Canada has increased by at least 13 percent.

Even if the world succeeds in stopping global warming, there is no danger that the environmental movement will stop. A United Nations report in May 2002, prepared by more than 1000 scientists, said that if we continue to exploit the Earth at the same pace as we are now, then by 2032, 55 percent of the world will face severe water shortages, and more than 11 000 plant and animal species will be extinct or in danger of extinction.

Conclusion

Canada is moving increasingly deeper into multi-national agreements. After all the angst that swirled through the 1980s when free trade with the United States was contemplated and then accomplished, it has become easier for the government to sign new deals, first with Mexico, then Chile, and fairly soon it seems with all of Central and South America. There is talk of making the border with the United States more of a meeting place than a barrier and of Canada accepting the American dollar as its unit of currency.

It is a sign of just how fast change has developed and just how far along globalization is in Canada that these notions are even raised. Less than a generation ago, they would have appeared treasonous. David Zussman, the head of a group called the Public Policy Forum, says,

> Canadians in all parts of civil society should actively encourage a growing debate over new ideas that, until a few years ago were completely taboo....I recognize, of course, that to many Canadians some of these ideas might seem a bit threatening, that even thinking about them might seem unpatriotic. But I see it as a discussion we cannot avoid.[41]

It is difficult to imagine how any of these changes could occur without vigorous debate.

Notes

1. Assembly of First Nations fact sheets, "Disability," September 2000.
2. Department of Justice Canada, "Notes for an Address by The Honourable Anne McLellan, Minister of Justice, Attorney General for Canada to the Canadian Bar Association," August 13, 2001.
3. Royal Commission on Aboriginal Peoples. *Report of the Royal Commission on Aboriginal Peoples.* Ottawa, Canada: Royal Commission on Aboriginal Peoples, 1996.
4. Prime Minister Trudeau, "Remarks on Indian Aboriginal and Treaty Rights, part of a speech given August 8, 1969, in Vancouver, British Columbia. From Indian-Eskimo Association of Canada, *Native Rights in Canada,* n.d., n.p.
5. Harold Cardinal, *The Unjust Society: The Tragedy of Canada's Indians* (Edmonton: New Press Publishers, 1969).
6. Compas Inc., *Big Heart, Big Impatience: Public Opinion on Aboriginal Policy,* A National Post/COMPAS Poll, December 5, 2001.
7. Olive Dickason, *Canada's First Nations: A History of Founding Peoples from the Earliest Times* (Toronto: Oxford University Press, 1977), p. 382.
8. Thomas R. Berger, *Northern Frontier: Northern Homeland, The Report of the MacKenzie Valley Pipeline Inquiry: Volume One.* (Ottawa: Minister of Supply and Services Canada, 1977).
9. Berger, *Northern Frontier.*
10. National Chief Matthew Coon Come, "AFN National Chief Acknowledges Twentieth Anniversary of Canadian Constitution that Recognized Aboriginal Peoples and Aboriginal Rights" (Assembly of First Nations, National Indian Brotherhood), April 17, 2002.
11. CBC News, "Panel Aims For Peace In Burnt Church Dispute" (April 9, 2002).
12. Assembly of First Nations, "Response to Proposed First Nations Governance Act" (May 21, 2002).
13. Press Release, "Historic Nisga'a Treaty Ratified; Receives Royal Assent" (April 13, 2000).
14. British Columbia Treaty Commission, "Nuu-chah-nulth and Sliammon initial agreements in principle," Treaty Commission Update, March 2001.
15. AFN, "Remarks of National Chief Matthew Coon Come to the Canadian Bar Association," 2000.
16. Compas Inc., *Big Heart, Big Impatience: Public Opinion on Aboriginal Policy,* A National Post/COMPAS Poll, December 5, 2001.
17. Ibid.
18. Ibid.
19. The Right Honourable Martin Brian Mulroney, Report on the First Ministers' Meeting at Meech Lake, May 1, 1987.
20. Pierre Trudeau, *Maclean's* (September 28, 1992) as quoted in Pierre Elliot Trudeau, *The Essential Trudeau* (Toronto: McClelland & Stewart, 1998), p. 167.
21. Ibid.
22. Translated speech by Quebec Premier Robert Bourassa, June 18, 1987, to the Quebec Legislative Assembly, as quoted by the Equality Party in their position on the issue of a distinct society.
23. Professor Deborah Coyne the University of Toronto, as quoted in Hon. Arthur Tremblay, Senator, and Chris Speyer, M.P., The 1987 Constitutional Accord: The Report of the Special Joint Committee of the Senate and the House of Commons, Chapter XIV, "The Process of Constitutional Change, First Ministers' Conferences." Available online at The Solon Law Archive.
24. *Maclean's,* September 28, 1992, as quoted in Pierre Elliott Trudeau, *The Essential Trudeau,* pp. 165–66.

25. As quoted in Garfield Newman, *Canada: A Nation Unfolding, Ontario Edition* (Toronto: McGraw-Hill Ryerson Ltd, 2001) p. 382.
26. Uni.ca, "The Parti Québécois."
27. "Canada Stays United but...Quebec Vote Is 'a Wake-up Call,'" CNN World News, October 31, 1995.
28. Department of Justice, "Government of Canada Files Reply to Arguments in the Quebec Secession Reference," Ottawa, January 15, 1998.
29. Department of Justice, "Statement by the Honourable Stéphane Dion in Response to the Ruling of the Supreme Court."
30. Joseph Facal, Quebec Minister of Intergovernmental Affairs, Answers Comments Made By Stéphane Dion, November 19, 1999. The full text of the answers is available online at
31. Bob Rae, "In Defence of Politics," Inaugural Allan J. MacEachen Lecture. St. Francis Xavier University, April 17, 1997.
32. "Political Scientist Leon Dion Dies," CBC-TV, *The National,* August 20, 1997.
33. Compas Inc., *Clarity Bill: Canada-Wide Majorities Even in Quebec,* Report to the *National Post,* February 17, 2000.
34. Ibid.
35. "Radio Address by the President to the Nation to the Nation," (July 21, 2001). Office of the Press Secretary, the White House.
36. "Chrétien Sketches Canada's Goals for OAS Meeting," *People's Daily Online* (February 6, 2001).
37. Maude Barlow, "Who's In Charge of the Global Economy?" Message from the Chair, Council of Canadians. 1998.
38. AmericasCanada.org, "Address by Prime Minister Jean Chrétien to the Closing Ceremony of the Summit of the Americas 2001" (April 22, 2001).
39. Maude Barlow, "Summing Up the Summit," Council of Canadians, April 25, 2001.
40. Maria Minna, Minister for International Cooperation, "Parliamentarians Can Shape an Inclusive Future for the Americas," March 8, 2001.
41. David Zussman, "What's After Nafta?" Notes for a Presentation by David Zussman, President of Public Policy at the Industry Canada Conference on Policy Challenges of North American Linkages (Calgary, June 21, 2001).

Chapter 25 Review

Knowledge & Understanding

1. Identify these people, places, and events, and explain their historical significance to Canada's developing culture and identity:
   - Royal Commission on Aboriginal Peoples
   - Oka
   - Meech Lake Accord
   - Charlottetown Accord
   - Nunavut
   - Elijah Harper
   - 1995 Referendum
   - globalization
   - Kyoto Agreement
   - 2001 Summit of the Americas

2. Since 1970, what have been the major events in discussing Aboriginal peoples in Canada? How did each event affect Aboriginal peoples in Canada, and how did it help or hinder their fight for self-government and recognition of their rights from the federal government?

Thinking & Inquiry

3. Has the growth of environmentalism in Canada affected the way Canadians live? If so, how? What environmental issues in Canada are currently in the news? If you were a Greenpeace activist, what actions would you take to bring media attention to the issue?

4. Why do you believe that the issues discussed in this chapter were listed under the title "unfinished business"?

Application

5. As a quiet protester at the 2001 Summit of the Americas in Quebec City, you are caught in a clash with police and are injured and thrown in jail. When you are released two days later, you write an editorial to the Ottawa Citizen. What are your feelings toward the Canadian government? Did they have a right or a duty to protect the Summit's participants? Were your rights violated?

6. The Council of Canadians "...lobbies Members of Parliament, conducts research, and runs national campaigns aimed at putting some of the country's most important issues into the spotlight: safeguarding our social programs, promoting economic justice, renewing our democracy, asserting Canadian sovereignty, advancing alternatives to corporate-style free trade, and preserving our environment." Go to their web site to see what campaigns they are currently pursuing. Which one would you choose to join? Why? Once you have decided, write a letter to a friend, and try to convince him or her to join the campaign.

Communication

7. What issues are discussed in this chapter? How different are they from issues discussed earlier in the book? In a country that is so ethnically and culturally diverse, why do these issues still dominate Canadian discussions? In five well-developed paragraphs, explain why you believe, or you do not believe, that these issues are of central importance to Canada, Canadians, and our national culture and identity.

Unit Seven Research Activity

Research

1. In the last thirty years of the twentieth century, Canada increasingly tried to map out its own path in international affairs, protect and nourish its own culture, and fight to keep its diverse population together. There was increasing concern over our national identity, or lack thereof, and what it meant to be a Canadian. In a series on Canada in the new millennium in *The Globe and Mail*, Arthur Erickson, a prominent Canadian architect wrote,

> Where should we be at the beginning of this millennium? I hope above all that we will have thrown off our inbred negativity about who we are as Canadians, our obsession with being the little brother tagging along after the big one...I hope we will realize that we are probably the only nation in the world prepared for the next millennium—that is, because we are almost a non-nation.

> What we have always thought to be our weakness—our lack of national identity—will prove to be our strength. Nationhood will be a hindrance to the progress of the pervasive humanity-wide consciousness of the next century....

> The next millennium will be one of acceptance in the most profound cultural and philosophical sense. It has to be if we denizens of this planet are to survive....And we in Canada are best prepared, having less to shake off and more to give the new age than anyone else. It will be our century — whatever "our" will imply!

What does Erickson mean when he states that "our lack of national identity will prove to be our strength" in the new millennium. Do you agree that Canadians do not have a national identity? Conduct a poll, first within your classroom, and then with other classmates and your family or relatives, on what people believe is Canada's national identity.

Interpretation and Analysis

2. In the polls that you conduct, do you find any similar responses, or is there a complete lack of a collective response? Can you group answers into any themes or sub-themes?

3. What evidence in this unit supports or opposes Erickson's statement about a lack of national identity?

4. If the next millennium is to "be one of acceptance in the most profound cultural and philosophical sense" how are Canada and Canadians best prepared for this task?

Applying and Communicating Your Skills

5. Using proper essay format, respond to Erickson's statement, "..our lack of national identity will prove to be our strength in the new millennium." Is a national identity a help or a hindrance to Canada in a global village? Create a thesis statement that either agrees or disagrees with Erickson's view, and support it with at least four arguments that use historical evidence to support your thesis.

Being a Canadian in the Twenty-First Century

That past is still, for us, a place that is not safely settled.

– MICHAEL ONDAATJE

Defining Canadian culture and identity in the twenty-first century is a daunting, if not impossible, task. As discussed in the Unit Seven activity, perhaps coming up with a specific definition of the Canadian identity is not necessarily a good idea. As Canada entered the millennium, questions about a Canadian identity were in many peoples' thoughts. Books were published that tried to capture the essence of Canada in the twentieth century. In one such book, Margaret Atwood's *Story of a Nation: Defining Moments in Our History*, the author of the preface, Rudyard Griffiths says,

> What defines a country? Is it the values a people share or the physical possession of some specific space or territory? Is it the memory of a common heritage or allegiance to a set of present-day institutions and ideals? These questions of identity are universal to all societies at all times.[1]

When applied to Canada and Canadians, none of these questions leads to a common answer. So where does that leave the question of what it means to be a Canadian? Some believe that it is what attracts immigrants to Canada, yesterday and today, and what unites Canadians. The CBC's Mark Starowitz, producer of the popular *Canada: A People's History* television series, said in *The Globe and Mail*,

> On the foundation of the Aboriginal people and two defeated peoples—Les Canadiens of New France and the American Loyalists—layers were built; peoples who were politically or economically disenfranchised, and came to seek a better life for their children. From the abandoned *filles de Roy*...to the last jetliner to land at Toronto's Pearson International Airport, we are all boat people. We just got here at different times....[T]here is a unifying idea of Canadian experience. We are the debris of history. We are the children of the expelled, the persecuted, the abandoned, and the marginalized. We are the remnants of empires and the refugees of lost causes. It's not blood that unites us, it's the experience of refuge.[2]

Looking at this textbook, is it the experience of refuge—the hopes for freedom, relief from persecution, the belief in a better life, the belief in compromise and cooperation—that unites Canadians in the past and today?

In the last chapter, three major contemporary issues—Aboriginal rights, the Quebec question, and Canada's role on the world stage—show that Canada's present problems are issues that have always been around. Since European contact, Aboriginal rights have been smothered and largely ignored. French-Canadians remain steadfast in their struggle to ensure the survival of their culture. And in a global village, Canada continues to fight for its own place and voice alongside the dominant world powers.

Interwoven with these issues are the tragedies and triumphs of Canadians and Canadian society. Despite its small population, Canada entered two world wars and changed both its image of itself and its image in the eyes of the rest of the world. Canada's peacekeepers have become a respected world police force. As the proverbial mouse keeps the elephant at bay, undaunted by the elephant's size, so too has Canada kept at bay U.S. cultural dominance. Our artists, singers, songwriters, actors, authors, comedians, and athletes are world renowned and respected for their talents. Canadian scientists have saved millions of lives, their technology exists around the world and in the frontiers of space, and Canada's healthcare system became the envy of most other countries. And all the while, we were becoming the most multicultural nation in the world.

Canada's past is scarred by many tragedies: the expulsion of the Acadians, the cruel treatment of Chinese labourers on the Canadian Pacific Railroad, the *Komagata Maru* incident, the internment of Ukrainians during World War I and of Japanese-Canadians in World War II, our refusal to admit Jewish refugees from Nazi Germany, the demolishing of Africville, the Somalia incident, our treatment of minorities, the government's failure to acknowledge Aboriginal rights. All these are in our past. To ignore them could lead to the unthinkable—they might happen again.

How do these triumphs and tragedies affect what it means to be a Canadian? Shame, forgiveness, and humility about our mistakes must become as necessary to us as the pride and passion that we feel in celebrating our victories.

The history of Canada is often looked on as unexciting and bland. Granted, Canada is a relatively young country, with no civil wars, no dictators, and no assassinated leaders to add dramatic highlights to its story. Yet, in what Governor General Adrienne Clarkson called a "450-year-old experiment,"[3] Canada has developed a reputation as one of the best countries in which to live. It is this experiment, this blend of cultures that exists nowhere else in the world, that makes Canada fascinating. In *The Globe and Mail*, Starowitz continues his idea of what unifies Canadians,

> Our streets are sparse in statues not because we have no history, but because we honour no dictators, we had no great conquering armies, we did not annihilate for religion or ideology. But the absence of such things is not evidence of the absence of history. We had every ingredient in Canada for the toxic stew that created Sarajevo: clashing religions, languages, races and contested land. By some alchemy, we took these same ingredients and became the kind of country that can't even imagine Kosovo; we mixed them into a

complex, multipart quest for equilibrium. That is Canadian history. We have to understand how this unprecedented accommodation was achieved, because we are its trustees, and it is our duty to the next generation to preserve the civility. Canadian history is not boring, or marginal to the world. In fact, how we didn't become Yugoslavia or Northern Ireland is a far more intriguing historical mystery than Napoleon, and far more pertinent to the modern world. The children of the defeated and the marginalized possess one of the most relevant histories in the global era.[4]

Canada's history, and the ability and desire of so many different peoples to come together and live peacefully, is a balance that war-torn countries can only dream about. And Canada's history may hold the keys to a more peaceful future for the world. To ignore the past or to be indifferent to it will jeopardize the future. We must acknowledge the great and the small, the weak and the powerful, the famous and the everyday heroes, the politicians and the poets, the men and the women, and the people of all lifestyles that have created Canada.

As Canada goes forward in the twenty-first century, its citizens face many challenges. Although we may be the envy of the world in many ways, we still have much to achieve. Although it is true that Canada is consistently ranked in United Nations studies as the best place in the world to live based on factors such as the economy, political climate, and physical environment, it is rarely acknowledged that in the same studies, it is ranked eighth in the world as the best place for women to live, and even lower as a place for Aboriginal Peoples to live. In looking to the past, Canadians can see the wrongs, as well as the rights, and build a stronger, more peaceful tomorrow.

We need to understand Canada's history. Who we are today and, perhaps more importantly, who we might become in the future, is determined by our people and our history. If we understand Canada's history, we can use it to create the culture, identity, and country that we want. The future of Canada belongs to those who use the past to point the way. This is your Canada.

Notes

1. Margaret Atwood, *Story of a Nation: Defining Moments in Our History* (Toronto: Doubleday, 2001) Preface.
2. Mark Starowitz, "Ignore the Past at Your Peril," *The Globe and Mail*, September 20, 2000, p. A15.
3. Ibid.
4. Ibid.

Credits

t=top, b=bottom, l=left, c=center, r=right, CMC=Canadian Museum of Civilization, CP=CP Picture Archive, NAC=National Archives of Canada, NLC=National Library of Canada, SAB=Saskatchewan Archives Board

Photo Credits

xvi t CP/Alex Kalnins, b *Noblesse Oblige - Queen on Moose* by Charles Pachter, acrylic and pastel, 1972, Private Collection Toronto; 11 Winston Fraser/Ivy Images; 16 CMC, image number: S2001-3141; 19 Victor Last/Geographical Visual Aids; 20 CMC, image number: S91-923; 21 Ivy Images; 22 t Glenbow Archives/NA-1093-2, b NAC/C-000403; 24 NAC/ C-030189; 25 Victor Last/Geographical Visual Aids; 33 The Newberry Library, Chicago; 36 NLC/C-099218; 40 t The Newberry Library, Chicago, b CMC, image number: 594; 41 Norval Morrisseau 1931 - / *Shaman and Disciples* 1979 / acrylic on canvas / 180.5 x 211.5 cm / McMichael Canadian Art Collection / Purchase 1979 / 1979.34.7; 42 CMC, image number: 73462; 45 912.1.33, With permission of the Royal Ontario Museum © ROM; 46 CMC, image number: 71124; 50 Royal British Columbia Museum/CPN 2797; 53 NAC/C-020845; 55 CMC, image number: 59642; 58 t CMC, image number: 20283, b CMC, image number: 36989; 60 t CMC, image number: 37092; b CMC, image number: 20288; 66 John DeVisser/Ivy Images; 68 CMC, image number: S97-5198; 69 © Bettmann/CORBIS/MAGMA; 70 Museum Mayer van den Bergh, Antwerp, Belgium/© Erich Lessing/Art Resource, NY; 73 NAC/C-028544; 80 NAC/ C-001994; 83 © Gunter Marx Photography/CORBIS/MAGMA; 84 CMC, image number: S88-1642; 96 NAC/C-007033; 97 NAC/C-009711; 98 NAC/C-106968; 100 NAC/C-005750; 102 l NAC/C-003202, r Ivy Images; 103 NAC/C-017338; 107 NAC/C-005855; 108 Ivy Images; 109 NAC/ C-010520; 115 © Réunion des Musées Nationaux/Art Resource, NY; 116 l Inventaire des œuvres d'art/Musée du Québec/Hotel Dieu/M-7; 116 r Archivo Iconografico, S.A./CORBIS/MAGMA; 118 National Gallery of Canada, Ottawa/Purchased 1954; 121 Joslyn Art Museum, Omaha, Nebraska; 122 NAC/C-006017; 123 NAC/C-007300; 124 Remington Museum, Ogdensburg, New York; 125 l Provincial Archives of Manitoba/Hudson's Bay Archives/1987/363/V-100, c Glenbow Archives/ NA-1406-21, r Ivy Images; 127 Victor Last/Geographical Visual Aids; 129 NAC/C-029486; 133 NAC/C-113193; 141 NAC/C-073429; 145 Toronto Library Board/T-16040; 146 t © Barrett & MacKay Photography Inc., bl NAC/C-021112, br NAC/C-070665; 149-152 Photographs courtesy of The History Section, Halifax, Nova Scotia; 153 NAC/C-003686; 155 NAC/ C-073709; 157 © Philip Gould/CORBIS/MAGMA; 158 The Granger Collection, New York; 166 l NAC/C-010612, r NAC/C-027665; 170 NAC/C-005907; 172 NAC/C-025662; 174 NAC/C-001078; 175 l NAC/ C-040741, r National Gallery of Canada, Ottawa/Transfer from the Canadian War Memorials, 1921/Gift of the 2nd Duke of Westminster, Eaton Hall, Cheshire, 1918; 178 NAC/C-011043; 179 t NAC/C-011250, b The Granger Collection, New York; 190 NAC/C-002833; 193 The Gilder Lehrman Collection on deposit at the Pierpont Morgan Library. GLC 4961.01/© Pierpont Morgan Library/Art Resource, NY; 197 National Gallery of Canada, Ottawa/Transfer from the Canadian War Memorials, 1921; 199 top NAC/C-010548, b NAC/C-002001; 209 NAC/C-000276; 211 NAC/C-000319; 212 NAC/C-005434; 215 *Burning of the Parliament Building, Montreal* by Joseph Légaré, McCord Museum of Canadian History, Montréal; 217 912.1.8, With permission of the Royal Ontario Museum © ROM; 220 NLC/C000261; 228 NAC/C-011811; 231 © J.A. Wilkinson/VALAN PHOTOS; 232 CP/Windsor Star/Scott Webster; 233 NAC/C-029977; 234 Toronto Library Board/JRR 745; 235 955.218.4, With permission of the Royal Ontario Museum © ROM; 236 Archives of Ontario/I0002217; 242 National Gallery of Canada, Ottawa / Purchased 1957; 245 NAC/C-012649; 250 NAC/C-011228; 253 tl National Museum of Science and Technology, Ottawa, br NAC/C-003284; 256 l NAC/ C-005962, r NAC/C-005961; 257 l NAC/C-008007, r Archives of Ontario/S15071; 264 NAC/C-000733; 265 NAC/C-016588; 267 NAC/C-095148; 276 Public Archives of Nova Scotia/N-9476; 277 NAC/C-022002; 278 NAC/C-033982; 281 912.1.26, With permission of the Royal Ontario Museum © ROM; 282 NAC/C-002775; 284 NAC/C-002424; 285 l NAC/C-001879, r NAC/C-022249; 288 NAC/C-10978; 289 NAC/ C-008200; 290 Glenbow Archives/NA-614-1; 292 Western Canada Pictorial Index/1424-43130; 298 Glenbow Archives/NA-3055-25; 301 tl Archives of Ontario/F229-1-0-26 Container #2; br Canadian Pacific Archives/1429; 304 Toronto Library Board/T10914; 305 Provincial Archives of Alberta, E.

Brown, B273; 307 W. Farmer/NAC/PA-103086; 308 NAC/C-38620; 311 Nova Scotia Archives and Records Management/N-0405; 312 City of Toronto Archives/RG-8-32-187; 314 NLC/C-062719; 316 Glenbow Archives/NA-748-41; 318 tr National Gallery of Canada, Ottawa/Gift of G. Blair Lang, Toronto, 1989, bl National Gallery of Canada, Ottawa/Purchased 1967; 319 BC Archives/F-04207; 320 CP/Toronto Star/David Cooper; 321 NAC/C-081683; 328 Glenbow Archives/PA-3409-2; 329 t NAC/C-6648, b Glenbow Archives/NA-789-161; 330 NAC/C-30620; 331 Glenbow Archives/NA-1687-37; 332 Glenbow Archives/NA-1687-38; 333 Glenbow Archives/NA-1255-22; 334 BC Archives/D-9118; 335 The Montreal Daily Star; 336 NAC/C-006097; 337 NAC/C-023354; 339 bl City of Toronto Archives/RG 8-32-246; br City of Toronto Archives/SC 244-343; 345 DS Reid/NAC/C-067075; 346 NAC/ PA-022705; 348 NAC/PA-66815; 349 t William Rider-Rider/DND/NAC/ PA-002279, b Prince Edward Island Public Archives and Records Office/ 2767-175; 350 l NAC/PA-2195, r NAC/PA-002792; 352 NAC/PA-000832; 353 The Whyte Museum/V295/LC-71; 354 NAC/C-034022; 358 *Women Making Shells* by Mabel May, Canadian War Museum, 8409; 359 t William James Topley/NAC/PA-800006, b *Land Girls Hoeing* by Manly MacDonald, Canadian War Museum, 8390; 360 l NAC/C-018734, r NAC/ PA-008158; 362 WG MacLaughlan/NAC/C-019953; 363 DND/NAC/ PA-001370; 364 tl NAC/PA-001123, br William Rider-Rider/DND/NAC/ PA-002084; 367 CP/Jonathan Hayward; 376 Glenbow Archives/ NA-3055-31; 377 Archives of Ontario/3117#2; 380 Manitoba Archives/ Foote Collection; 381 Archives of Ontario/S.12935; 383 NAC/C-024727; 385 Pulp mill, Laurentide Company, Grand'Mere? QC?, 1919-20, VIEW-18152.0, Notman Photographic Archives, McCord Museum of Canadian History, Montréal; 387 NAC/PA-052954; 388 NAC/C-034022; 389 Nurses, cribs, and baby trolley, Montréal Maternity Hospital, Montréal, QC, 1925-26, Notman Photographic Archives, McCord Museum of Canadian History, Montréal; 390 E.M. Finn/NAC/C-053850; 391 Glenbow Archives/NA-2204-12; 392 © John Fowler/VALAN PHOTOS; 394 Glenbow Archives/NA-1319-1; 395 BC Archives/H-06830; 397 J.E.H. MacDonald 1873 - 1932 / *Cathedral Peak and Lake O'Hara* 1927 / oil on panel / 21.4 x 26.6 x 0.2 cm / Gift of Mr. R.A. Laidlaw / McMichael Canadian Art Collection / 1966.15.9; 398 tr Canadian Tire Corp., bl Toronto Transit Commission/NAC/PA-054394; 405 The Toronto Star Syndicate; 407 Glenbow Archives/NA-751-21; 410 SAB/R-B2465-1; 411 SAB/R-B9057; 413 l SAB/R-A19945, r Glenbow Archives/NA-2118-9; 414 SAB/R-A4287; 415 Glenbow Archives/NA-2279-3; 416 tl SAB/R-A7866; br SAB/R-B171-1; 417 SAB/R-B8336; 421 Glenbow Archives/NA-2771-2; 423 t SAB/R-A27294, br NAC/C-024344; 424 NAC/C-055449; 427 Glenbow Archives/NA-5546-2; 429 *Longshoremen* by Miller Brittain, 1940, National Gallery of Canada, Ottawa, Purchased 1970; 437 Hulton-Deutsch Collection/CORBIS/MAGMA; 438 NAC/PA-119008; 439 NAC/C-024717; 443 l *Control Tower* by Peter Whyte, Canadian War Museum, 14304, r Glenbow Archives/PD-324-210; 444 NAC/PA-112993; 445 NAC/C-099610; 446 NAC/PA-137745; 447 NAC/C-014160; 448 *Dieppe Raid* by Charles Comfort, Canadian War Museum, 12276; 449 Frank Royal/NAC/ PA-163670; 450 l *Reinforcements Moving Up on the Ortona Salient* by Lawren P. Harris, Canadian War Museum, 12712, r Strathy Smith/NAC/ PA-140208; 451 Harold G. Aikman/NAC/PA-116510; 452 CP/Bas Czernwinski; 453 NAC/PA-129070; 454 Karen M. Hermiston/NAC/ PA-128229; 455 Nicholas Morant/NAC/PA-116928; 456 NAC/PA-108300; 457 NAC/C-033442; 458 Montreal Gazette/NAC/PA-107910; 460 Canadian War Museum, Accession number 19930002-002; 461 NAC/ PA-037468; 470 NAC/Montreal Gazette/PA-129625; 471 Hulton Archive/ Getty Images; 472 Bill Olson/NAC/PA-115564; 473 CP/Jim Young; 475 CP/Ray Giguere; 476 CP/Toronto Star; 478 The Toronto Star Syndicate; 479 NAC/PA-209888; 485 CP/La Presse; 486 Anthony Jenkins/The Globe and Mail; 487 Glenbow Archives/NA-1524-1; 490 NAC/PA-129829; 491 CP/Aaron Harris; 497 CP; 504 CP/Montreal Star; 505 NAC/C151721; 506 NAC/PA-112635; 510 NAC/C-047009; 512 Glenbow Archives/NA-5470-5; 516 Glenbow Archives/ND-3-5868b; 517 NAC/PA-116675; 518 City of Toronto Archives/Fonds 1266 item 107031; 519 Ivy Images; 530 CP/Wide World Photos; 535 © Barrett & MacKay Photography Inc.; 537 CP/Toronto Star/Boris Spremo; 541 tl CP/Ottawa Citizen/Dave Chan, br CP/AP/Joe Tabacca; 543 l © Inc. Lambert 03RLAM Archive Holdings/Getty Images/The Image Bank, r NAC/PA-200369; 544 l Canadian Broadcasting Corporation; r NAC/PA-195684; 545 © Lake County

Museum/CORBIS/MAGMA; 547 NAC/PA-169536; 548 Toronto Star Syndicate; 549 CP; 551 Paul-Émile Borduas / L'étoile noire / The Montreal Museum of Fine arts, Photo: The Montreal Museum of Fine Arts, Brian Merrett; 552 CP/Doug Ball; 553 Victor Last/Geographical Visual Aids; 556 © Bettmann/CORBIS/MAGMA; 566 CP/La Presse; 567 CP; 568 CP/Peter Bregg; 570 CP; 571 CP/The Globe & Mail/Dennis Robinson; 573 l and c CP/Fred Chartrand, r CP/Bill Becker; 575 Petro-Canada Library; 576 CP/Phil Snel; 577 CP; 578 CP/Peter Bregg; 579 l CP/Kevin Frayer, tr CP/ Toronto Star/Tannis Toohey, br CP/St. John's Telegram/Gary Hebbard; 580 CP/Andrew Vaughan; 581 l CP/Maclean's/Phil Snel, r CP/Jonathan Hayward; 583 CP/Sarnia Observer/Nora Penhale; 585 l CP/Tom Hanson, r CP/Winnipeg Free Press/Joe Bryksa; 587 CP/Winnipeg Free Press/Wayne Glowacki; 593 CP/Boris Spremo; 598 Canadian Broadcasting Corporation; 599 Montreal Gazette/NAC/PA-117531; 601 CP/The Globe & Mail/Peter Tym; 602 CP; 604 t CP/Peter Bregg, br © Deborah Vanslet/VALAN PHOTOS; 605 CP/Bill Grimshaw; 606 CP/Journal de Quebec; 609 CP/Ron Poling; 610 © Richard Comely, Comely Communications. Reproduced from the National Library of Canada's website www.nlc-bnc.ca); 611 © Pierre Fournier. Reproduced from the National Library of Canada's website (www.nlc-bnc.ca); 616 CP/Frank Gunn; 617 CP/Jonathan Hayward; 618 Reuters/John Hryniuk/Getty Images/Archive Photos; 619 CP/The Evening Telegram/Jonathan Hayward; 622 CP/Bob Weber; 624 Tim Doligan/Doligan Cartoons; 625 © CORBIS/MAGMA; 628-629 © AFP/CORBIS/MAGMA; 630 CP/Kingston Whig Standard/Michael Lea; 634 CP/AP/Diane Bondareff; 635 t CP/Tom Hanson, b CP/Adrian Wyld; 643 l CP/Tom Hanson, r Duncan Cameron/NAC/PA-170161; 646 CP/Ottawa Citizen/Lynn Ball; 646 Gerald McMaster / Oka-boy/Oh! Kowboy 1990 / 94.0 x 114.0 cm / McMichael Canadian Art Collection / 1991.10.2; 648 CP/Tom Hanson; 649 CP/Jacques Boissinot; 651 CP/Fred Chartrand; 652 CP/Tom Hanson; 658 CP/Fred Chartrand; 659 CP/Clement Allard; 660 Gable/The Globe and Mail; 661 Dick Hemingway; 662 CP/Wayne Glowacki; 666 CP/AP/Ricardo Mazala

Text and Illustration Credits

6 both Adapted from Robert McGee, *Ancient Canada*, (Hull, Quebec: Canadian Museum of Civilization, 1989), p. 14; 8 From Elaine Dewar, *Bones: Discovering the First Americans* (Toronto: Random House Canada, 2001), pp. 210-212; 9 Adapted from J.V. Wright, *Six Chapters of Canada's Prehistory*, (Ottawa: National Museum of Man, 1976), p. 32, adapted from J.V. Wright, *Six Chapters of Canada's Prehistory*, (Ottawa: National Museum of Man, 1976), p. 32; 11 Adapted from Olive Patricia Dickason, *Canada's First Nations, 2/e*, (Toronto: Oxford University Press, 1996), p. 4; 12 From J.V. Wright, *A History of the Native Peoples of Canada, Volume I*, (Hull, Quebec: Canadian Museum of Civilization, 1995), p. 84; 12 From Robert McGee, *Ancient Canada*, (Vancouver: Douglas & McIntyre, 1989), p. 51 and p. 54; 13 From David Morrison, *Arctic Hunters*, (Hull, Quebec: Canadian Museum of Civilization, 1992), p. 62; 17 Adapted from Robert McGhee, *Ancient Canada*, (Hull, Quebec: Canadian Museum of Civilization, 1989), p. 37, 17 From David Morrison, *Arctic Hunters*, (Hull, Quebec: Canadian Museum of Civilization, 1992), p. 63; 20 From Michael J. Caduto and Joseph Bruchac, *The Native Stories From Keepers of the Earth* (Saskatoon: Fifth House Publishers, 1991); 23-24 From *www.civilisations.ca/aborig/haida/happr01e.html*; 30 Adapted from Mary Beacock Fryer, *Brockville: A Pictorial History*, edited by Adrian Ten Cate, (Brockville, Ontario: Besancourt, 1986), p. 9; 32 Adapted from Robert McGhee, *Ancient Canada*, (Vancouver: Douglas & McIntyre), p. 61; 32-33 From Michael J. Caduto and Joseph Bruchac, *The Native Stories From Keepers of the Earth* (Saskatoon: Fifth House Publishers, 1991); 35 Adapted from Bruce G. Trigger, *Children of Aataentisc, Volume 1*, (Montreal and Kingston: McGill-Queen's University Press, 1976); 37 Adapted from the *Report of the Royal Commission on Aboriginal Peoples*, Vol 1, pp. 48-49; 43 Adapted from R. Bruce Morrison and C. Roderick Wilson, eds, *Native Peoples: The Canadian Experience, 2/e*, (Toronto: Oxford University Press, 1995), p. 576; 44 Adapted from Verna Kirkness, *Indians of the Plains*, (Toronto: Grolier Ltd, 1984); 47 Adapted from R. Bruce Morrison and C. Roderick Wilson, eds, *Native Peoples: The Canadian Experience, 2/e*, (Toronto: Oxford University Press, 1995), p. 472; 48 Adapted from Knut B. Fladmark, *British Columbia Prehistory*, (Ottawa: National Museums of Canada, 1986), p. 125 and pp. 66-67; 51-52 Adapted from R. Bruce Morrison and C. Roderick Wilson, eds, *Native Peoples: The Canadian Experience, 2/e*, (Toronto: Oxford University Press, 1995); 57 t From *Report on the Royal Commission on Aboriginal Peoples, Volume 1*, (Government of Canada, 1996), p. 83,

b adapted from R. Bruce Morrison and C. Roderick Wilson, eds, *Native Peoples: The Canadian Experience, 2/e*, (Toronto: Oxford University Press, 1995), p. 548; 69 Adapted from Waldman, *Atlas of the North American Indian* and Geoffrey Barroclough, ed., *The Times Atlas of World History*, (Toronto: Fitzhenry & Whiteside, 1978), p. 161; 70-72, 75 Quoted in Don Gilmour and Pierre Turgeon, *Canada: A People's History, Volume I* (Toronto: McClelland & Stewart Inc., 2000), p. 14 and pp. 10-11; 76 Quoted in Arthur J. Ray, *I Have Lived Here Since the World Began* (Toronto: Key Porter Books, 1996) pp. 38-40; 76 Quoted in Daniel N. Paul, *We Were Not the Savages* (Halifax: Nimbus Publishing, 1993) pp. 2-3; 78-79 Quoted in Robert McGhee, *Canada Rediscovered* (Hull, Quebec: Canadian Museum of Civilization, 1991), pp. 125-126; 79 Adapted from Don Gilmour and Pierre Turgeon, *Canada: A People's History, Volume I* (Toronto: McClelland & Stewart Inc., 2000), p. 22; 81-82 Quoted in Arthur J. Ray, *I Have Lived Here Since the World Began* (Toronto: Key Porter Books, 1996) p. 40; 94 © CORBIS/MAGMA; 114 From Paul W. Bennett, *Canada: A North American Nation, 2/e*, (Whitby: McGraw-Hill Ryerson Limited, 1995), p. 103; 130 From R. Cole Harris and Geoffrey J. Matthews, *Historical Atlas of Canada, Volume I*, (Toronto: University of Toronto Press, 1988), plate 45; 143 Adapted from William J. Eccles, *France in America*, (Markham, Ontario: Fitzhenry & Whiteside Ltd, 1990); 150 both Acadian Museum and Archives; 164 Adapted from J.L. Finlay, Pre-Confederation Canada: *The Structure of Canadian History, 3/e*, (Scarborough: Prentice-Hall, 1989), p. 68. Reprinted with permission by Pearson Education Canada.; 165 Adapted from Arthur J. Ray, *I Have Lived Here Since the World Began* (Toronto: Key Porter Books, 1996), p. 128; 171 National Archives of Canada, MG1, Series E11A, Recettes et dépenses Vol. 113, fols. 286-305; Vol. 115, fols. 119-133, 316-327; Vol. 116, fols, 134-135, 214-217; Vol. 119, fols. 333, 406-408; 173 Bibliothèque Nationale du Québec/TRBA0145; 180 Adapted from *Historical Atlas of Canada, Volume 1* (Toronto: University of Toronto Press, 1987); 191 Adapted from Paul W. Bennett, *Canada: A North American Nation, 2/e*, (Whitby: McGraw-Hill Ryerson Limited, 1995), p. 146; 202-203 Adapted from *Canada: The Story of Our Heritage*, (Whitby: McGraw-Hill Ryerson Limited, 2000), p. 162 and p. 172; 254 From Paul W. Bennett, *Canada: A North American Nation, 2/e*, (Whitby: McGraw-Hill Ryerson Limited, 1995), p. 248; 258 From "Series A 2-14. Population of Canada by province, census dates, 1851 to 1876," F.H. Leacy, *Historical Statistics of Canada, 2/e*, (Ottawa: Minister of Supply and Services, 1983) and James Hiller and Peter Neary, eds., *Newfoundland in the Nineteenth and Twentieth Centuries: Essays in Interpretation*, (Toronto: University of Toronto Press, 1980); 328 From *The Best of Robert Service*, (Whitby: McGraw-Hill Ryerson Limited, 2001), Copyright 1940 Robert Service; 339 tr Adapted from Garfield Newman, *Canada: A Nationa Unfolding, Ontario Edition*, (Whitby: McGraw-Hill Ryerson Limited, 2000), p. 65; 344 Adapted from Garfield Newman and Diane Eaton, *Canada: A Nation Unfolding, 1/e* (Whitby: McGraw-Hill Ryerson Limited, 1996); 347 Adapted from Bill Freeman and Richard Nielson, *Far From Home: Canadians in the First World War*, (Whitby: McGraw-Hill Ryerson Limited); 350 CBC interview with Gregory Clark, 4th Canadian Mounted Rifles, 1964; 352-353 CBC interview with Ken Goodyear, Royal Newfoundland Regiment, 1964; 353 CBC interview with Howard Morry, Royal Newfoundland Regiment, 1964; 354 Letter from J.H. Rivers, Warden, Lethbridge Provincial Jail to the Deputy Minister of Justice, 6 July 1918. National Archives of Canada, RG 13, series A-2, vol. 225, file 1918-1982; 406 National Bureau of Economic Research, Princeton University, 1957; 411 Rowell, Sirois Report, Book 1, Canada: 1868-1939; 474 Adapted from Graham Jarvis, *War and Peace: Canada's Global Role (Canada21)*, (Toronto: Pearson Education Canada, 1996), p. 66. Reprinted with permission by Pearson Education Canada Inc.; 513 tl F.H. Leacy, ed., *Historical Statistics of Canada, 2/e*, (Ottawa: Statistics Canada, 1938), tables A1, F13, F15, br F.H. Leacy, ed., *Historical Statistics of Canada, 2/e*, (Ottawa: Statistics Canada, 1938), series M1-11; 524 F.H. Leacy, ed., *Historical Statistics of Canada, 2/e*, (Ottawa: Statistics Canada, 1938), series B1-14, Canada Year Book, various years; 584-585 Paul Brandt; 592 Statistics Canada, 1996 Census tables; 621 Statistics Canada, CANSIM II, table 384-0002 and Catalogue No. 13-213-PPB; 622 National Farmers Union, *http://www.nfu.ca/feb17-brief.htm*; 623 From Peter Arcus and Graham Parson, *Changes in the Prairie Economy, 1980 to 2000*, SIPP Public Policy Pater No. 8, February 2002; 630 *Facts and Figures 1999: Immigration Overview*, Statistics Canada, © Minister of Public Works and Government Services Canada, 2000, Cat. No. MP43-333/2000E

Index